McGraw-Hill Publications in Industrial Education   Chris H. Groneman, Consulting Editor

DRAWING AND BLUEPRINT READING   Coover

GENERAL DRAFTING: A COMPREHENSIVE EXAMINATION   Blum

GENERAL INDUSTRIAL EDUCATION   Groneman and Feirer

GENERAL METALS   Feirer

GENERAL POWER MECHANICS   Crouse, Worthington, and Margules

GENERAL WOODWORKING   Groneman

TECHNICAL ELECTRICITY AND ELECTRONICS   Buban and Schmitt

TECHNICAL WOODWORKING   Groneman and Glazener

UNDERSTANDING ELECTRICITY AND ELECTRONICS   Buban and Schmitt

second edition

Technical Woodworking

Chris H. Groneman
Everett R. Glazener

McGraw-Hill Book Company

New York   St. Louis   San Francisco   Dallas   Düsseldorf   Johannesburg   Kuala Lumpur   London
Mexico   Montreal   New Delhi   Panama   Paris   São Paulo   Singapore   Sydney   Tokyo   Toronto

Editor:
Hal Lindquist

Production Supervisor:
John A. Sabella

Editing Supervisor:
Barbara Tannenbaum

Design Supervisor:
Cathy Gallagher

Cover Design:
Aspen Hollow Artservice

Library of Congress Cataloging in Publication Data
Groneman, Chris Harold, date
  Technical woodworking.

  McGraw-Hill publications in industrial education
  1. Woodwork (Manual training) I. Glazener, Everett Ruthven, date   joint author.   II. Title.
  TT180.G75 1976   684'.08   75-1071
  ISBN 0-07-024964-4

About the authors

Chris H. Groneman received B.S. and M.S. degrees from Kansas State College and a D.Ed. degree from Pennsylvania State University. His teaching experiences include several years in public high schools, East Texas State University, and Texas A&M University, where he served as head of the industrial education department for many years. He has also been associated with the technical and industrial education program at the University of Hawaii. At present he is a member of the department of industrial arts and technology at California State University at Fresno.

He is an active member of numerous professional organizations. He is consulting editor of the McGraw-Hill Publications in Industrial Education, of which *Technical Woodworking* is a part. He is also the author of *General Woodworking* and a coauthor of *General Industrial Education,* titles in 'this series. Dr. Groneman has done research for and contributed to *Encyclopedia Americana.* He was honored by his alma mater with the Meritorious Achievement Citation, the highest recognition that Kansas State College can confer upon one of its graduates.

Everett R. Glazener received B.S. and M.Ed. degrees from Texas A&M University. He was awarded the D.Ed. degree by Pennsylvania State University. He has had varied experiences as a teacher in public schools and colleges in Mississippi, Arkansas, Colorado, and Texas. He is presently head of the department of engineering technology at Texas A&M University, after having been a member, and later, head of the department of industrial education at that institution.

He has written numerous magazine articles for professional publications, authored or coauthored five textbooks and workbooks in the industrial education field, and is active as a member of numerous local, state, and national professional organizations and associations.

Preface

The second edition of *Technical Woodworking* is prompted by the enthusiastic response to the first one. The general content includes new and up-to-date materials and has been reorganized, based on new trends in manufacturing, construction, and the service industries.

Included in the new materials are a comprehensive treatment of career development, the metric as well as the U.S. customary system of measurement, and ecology and forest conservation. New wood products and the utilization of wood by-products, the building of plywood, and the application of veneers are discussed and illustrated. Numerical control and automation in the woods-products industries give insight into expanding technological developments.

Information and instruction are provided for some of the newer portable power and stationary machine tools, such as the motorized miter-box saw, the narrow-belt sander/grinder, the overhead router/shaper, and the rotary jointer/surfacer. An important unit discusses pneumatic (air power) tools and their operation.

The metric system of measurement is applied throughout the text to acquaint the student with the relationship between the U.S. customary and the metric systems. Some project suggestions are dimensioned in metric only; in these cases, the method of finding U.S. customary dimensions is included on each page.

This edition is the product of an exhaustive survey of city and state educational courses of study and teaching plans. Research has been conducted into technical and industrial methods, and conferences with technical personnel in the woods-producing industries have been held.

The contents are designed for use in high school industrial arts and vocational-industrial classes, post high school technical courses, and community college and university courses pertaining to wood processes and technology. Home craftsmen will make extensive use of the informational material and process presentations.

Technical Woodworking, second edition, is written in a vocabulary based on the reading level of high school students. Sentence and paragraph structure is designed to increase understanding of the material and to stimulate interest. New terms are explained, defined, and illustrated when first used.

A second color accents illustrations to indicate direction and action and to emphasize significant points. Approximately 1500 photographs and line drawings give realism to the vital activities and materials of the woods industries.

Chris H. Groneman
Everett R. Glazener

A word about metrication

At the time of publication of this text, the United States government has not yet committed the nation to a national policy of metric measure conversion. However, many states, as well as many industries, have made such a commitment, and so the United States is truly becoming a metric country. This edition of *Technical Woodworking* is taking a first step in keeping up with state legislation and industrial practice.

It is intended that the metric equivalents used in this book be practical. Therefore, the metric equivalents used are not always exact. When measures involving human judgment are given, they are rounded to the nearest millimeter, since decimal divisions of a millimeter are difficult to achieve and woodworking tolerances do not usually call for such accuracy. Conversion of hardware sizes is more precise, since the customary dimension is a fact and determining the equivalent involves only an exercise in mathematics. The exercise is valid because it familiarizes the student with the metric change. In some cases, the metric conversion is of no practical value, and these portions are clearly indicated.

Note that we have adopted the metric practice of leaving a space instead of using a comma to separate groups of three digits in a large number. This practice is being established because the comma is used as a decimal marker in many European countries.

There is current controversy over the spelling of meter (metre) and liter (litre). The *er* ending has been chosen by the editor for clarity of language; students usually expect to see the *er* spelling for words ending in the "er" sound.

Regardless of spelling preference, the symbols used throughout are SI metric.

Although some United States industries have committed themselves to metric measure, others are still waiting for some official governmental action before making the change. Therefore, standards may change slowly or rapidly in various areas of the woodworking field. As standards change, we will attempt to reflect those changes promptly.

The Editor

Acknowledgments

Sincere thanks is extended to the many companies, corporations, associations, and governmental agencies that have provided information, illustrations, and other pertinent data for this revision. Acknowledgment is given throughout the text whenever such materials are used. For purposes of unity, continuity, and clarity, individual line courtesies have not been cited in the sections dealing with hand and machine tools, finishing, and upholstery.

Special appreciation is due the following individuals, who assisted directly in producing this volume: E. J. Auer, Clark Foam Products Company, for information on special upholstery products and processes; Betty Fisk Baily, Drexel Furniture Company; J. H. Bramley, Esq., Managing Director, Educational Productions Limited, Yorkshire, England, for material adapted from the Paxton Lumber Company; Richard Campbell, Millers Falls Company, for hand-tool photographs; Robert Campbell, Educational Director, Stanley Tools Division, The Stanley Works, for hand-tool photographs and building-construction information; Franklyn E. Doan, the Seng Company, for special upholstery photographs, diagrams, and charts; J. Helsel, California State College, California, Pennsylvania, for project designs and illustrations; Dan Irvin, Director of Education, Power Tool Division, Rockwell International, for many machine and portable power tool photographs and process illustrations; W. H. Liggon, Ozan Lumber Company, for automated lumbering photographs; Dean F. Sherman, Editor, Ford Industries, for special information on automated lumbering; Dr. Ray Loyd, California State University at Fresno, for illustrations on metrics; Edward H. Daves, Industrial Arts Instructor, and Genevieve Ramos, Lynnis Bailey, and Rod Mitchell, students with the Fresno Unified School District. Sincere thanks are extended to Mrs. Jeane Glazener and Mrs. Virginia Groneman for their assistance in manuscript preparation.

Contents

section 1
TECHNICAL INDUSTRIAL INFORMATION

section 2
DESIGNING AND PLANNING

section 3
MEASUREMENT, LAYOUT, AND HAND TOOL PROCESSES

section 4
STATIONARY MACHINE TOOLS AND PROCESSES

section 10
THE BUILDING CONSTRUCTION INDUSTRY

section 11
PATTERNMAKING

section 12
CONDITIONING AND SHARPENING TOOLS

section 13
PROJECT IDEAS

section **1**

Technical
Industrial Information

unit 1

Careers in woods-related industries

Fig. 1–2 Carpenters attaching the subfloor to floor joists of a building. *National Forest Products Association.*

Woodworking as a hobby or leisure time activity is one of the most popular creative activities in America; however, millions of people earn their livelihoods by working in hundreds of woodworking occupations and related industries. Opportunities are unlimited for entering one of the skilled or semiskilled woodworking craft trade occupations. Other opportunities are possible for those who prepare for one of the related professions that can contribute to or be directly associated with the various wood-products industries. Almost every section of this text contains photographs of skilled, semiskilled, and professional personnel at work.

For example, a house or a building such as in Fig. 1-1 is often de-

signed by an architect. The skill of carpenters (Fig. 1-2 and as shown in SECTION 10) is needed to erect these structures. The cabinetmaker or finish-work carpenter does the special cabinetwork for a finished interior. Other occupations require only limited skills. Literally thousands of people have been involved in growing, harvesting, processing hundreds of different wood materials, selling the products, and eventually producing the house or other finished product for the consumer.

Only a few of the skilled, semi-skilled, limited-skill, professional, and semiprofessional occupations can be discussed in this unit. Incomes in these occupations range from very high to minimal, depending upon the knowledge, skill, education, training, and experience necessary to do the job.

In the wood-processing occupations, the untrained worker will probably begin at an unskilled job. Higher income jobs are often filled by the worker who has received on-the-job training. The worker progresses to jobs requiring greater knowledge and skill as training, skill, and experience are acquired. Most employers prefer workers to have at least a high school education. Those without this basic background who desire additional education can frequently attend classes offered to workers by the company, or they may attend night school or off-duty programs in public and technical schools and colleges.

Skilled, semiskilled, and limited-skill occupations in the woods industries

The skilled and semiskilled craftsman in the woodworking trades must be capable of safely using hand and power tools to produce and finish products made of wood or related materials. As a general rule, the man or woman progresses from limited-skill work as a helper or apprentice through a semiskilled occupation to reach the master craftsman, or skilled occupational, level.

Besides experience, the person must first secure appropriate educational training. Special educational background received in the public schools is a good base for learning. Technical schools and apprenticeship training offer more specific advanced

Fig. 1–1 A multiple-living chalet designed by an architectural firm. *California Redwood Association.*

1

training. Some abilities of the craftsman include reading detailed drawings, reading and interpreting specific descriptions and plans, and applying mathematical principles. Knowledge about the various parts of the occupation and the ability to perform are needed for carrying out the construction or manipulative phases of the work.

A **cabinetmaker** (see Fig. 149-14) can be both a skilled all-around wood craftsman and a specialist. Cabinetmakers construct and repair articles, such as store fixtures, office equipment, cabinets, and furniture, using woodworking machines and tools. They most often work from drawings or blueprints. The cabinetmaker must often choose and match materials for color, grain, or texture and set up and operate the various woodwork machines to cut and shape parts. A cabinetmaker foreman would supervise and coordinate the activities of other cabinetmakers.

Skilled carpenters (Fig. 1-3), a large group of the building trades workers, are capable of doing almost all jobs related to wood-building construction. Carpenters are employed to install heavy timbers where such work is needed, to do maintenance work, and to work in shipbuilding and mining. The carpenter can read and interpret plans, lay out foundations, construct framework, and do finished trim

Fig. 1–3 Carpenters at work placing roof decking on a building. *National Forest Products Association.*

Fig. 1–4 A skilled patternmaker at times must use hand tools even on large patterns. *American Foundrymen's Society.*

work on both the outside and the inside of a building. One person may desire to specialize in frame construction and become especially proficient in cutting rafters of all kinds. A finish-work carpenter may prefer to install interior trim, doors, paneling, or kitchen cabinets. Other carpenters (shown in Figs. 165-6 and 165-8) raise walls. Accurate measurements must be made in preparing the parts so that they will fit when placed on the subfloor deck. In this occupation, carpenters advance to carpenter supervisors or general construction supervisors. They frequently have a greater opportunity than most building craftsmen to become general supervisors because carpenters are familiar with the entire construction process. Self-employment is higher than in most other skilled building trades, and some carpenters become contractors who employ other workers.

The **patternmaker** (Figs. 1-4, 169-2, and 169-3) is one of the most important and most skilled craftsmen in the woodworking occupations. The ability to interpret pattern drawings for making patterns, to design patterns, and to use both regular and special hand tools and machines is a must. This craftsman must have a knowledge of the shrinkage of metals and metal alloys and must be familiar with foundry work because terminology is directly related to both areas of work. An exact pattern must be made before a mold and the resulting casting can be made. (See units in SECTION 11, "Patternmaking.")

The **millman** occupation can involve a wide range of activities. Some of them are to repair furniture, to set up and adjust equipment and fixtures, and to work as a maintenance cabinetmaker. This work can include being a machine operator; trimming parts for snug fits; assembling, repairing, and refashioning high-grade furniture; installing hardware; or preparing surfaces and applying stains and other finishes.

A **millwright** (see Fig. 176-1) is an important person in factories in which various saws and machine knives are used, as in lumber mills and cabinet and furniture plants. Basically this person repairs, conditions, and sharpens the saws and knives used on the numerous machines. Extensive knowledge about the various specialized machines is required, and reasonable mathematical ability is also required to understand such items as angles, pitch, and set as they relate to cutting numerous materials. The work must be very accurate for plant operation to be most efficient.

A **model maker** is an important woodworking craftsman. This artisan must have exacting skills and knowledge of the woodworking trades. Wood and clay models of such things as automobiles, aircraft, and architectural structures may be made full size or to scale. Models of scenes and settings are important to television, moviemaking, and the theater; thus the modelmaker may be employed in one of the communications industries.

Various amounts of training, knowledge, and manipulative skills are necessary for employment in some additional skilled, semiskilled, and limited-skill occupations. Some of these require only a limited knowledge of the activity, minimum skill, and brief training before a person begins to earn on the job. Others of these occupations may require one or more of these abilities: skill, physical stamina, knowledge, and training. Only a few of the numerous occupations involving inside or outside work are listed below.

Those who prepare timber in the forest for use in the many woods industries are the **lumberjacks** (Fig. 1-5), who require many abilities in topping a tall tree; the **fallers** (Figs. 1-6, 143-7,

Fig. 1–5 Topping a tree to prepare a spar tree for high-lead logging. The next task will be to fasten a cable network to the tree in order to haul logs from where they have been felled to a central location for loading onto trucks. *Weyerhaeuser Company.*

and 143-8), who fell the trees; the **swampers** or **limbers**, who trim the branches from the tree trunks; and the **log bucker** (see Fig. 143-10), who cuts trunks into standard lengths. A special type of felling operation is shown in Fig. 1-7.

Heavy-equipment operators (Fig. 1-8) manipulate their machines in the forest, at the plant (Fig. 1-9), and at the building site. They drive various forms of tractors and equipment for skidding and loading logs for delivery (Fig. 1-10) to the lumber or plywood mill. They are also shown in most photographs of Figs. 143-11 through 143-16. Figure

Fig. 1–6 A good faller can drop a 220-foot (67-meter) fir tree exactly to a spot where it will not break or damage other trees. Here the logger's chain saw bites out an undercut wedge that will direct the tree's fall. *Weyerhaeuser Company*

Fig. 1–7 A tractor-mounted shear-cutter harvests trees during a thinning operation on a tree farm. The tractor is also equipped with a hydraulic grapple. *Weyerhaeuser Company.*

Fig. 1–8 A rubber-tired skidder moves logs to the loading area. The skidder is one of a number of pieces of equipment designed to efficiently harvest timber. *Weyerhaeuser Company.*

Fig. 1–9 A front-end loader for loading and unloading trucks, sorting logs, and laying logs on decks to feed the mill. *Caterpillar Tractor Co.*

Fig. 1–10 On a large truck headed for the mill, a load of timber rolls out of a tree farm. *Weyerhaeuser Company.*

Fig. 1–11 Forklift truck loading lumber onto a railroad car. The lift capacity of the machine is 22 500 pounds (10 205.8 kilograms, kg). *Caterpillar Tractor Co.*

Fig. 1–12 Smaller lift trucks, which have a capacity of 4000 pounds (1814.4 kg), remove studs from roll case at planing mill. *Forest Industries.*

144-6 shows some preliminary debarking by using a heavy machine in the forest. A heavy-crane operator (see Fig. 144-3) handles logs after they arrive at the mill. Lumber is handled and transported at the mill by large fork-lift trucks (Fig. 1-11) and overhead carriers. Figure 1-12 shows a banded package of studs being handled with a smaller lift machine.

An important occupation is that of **scaler** (see Fig. 143-17). After logs reach the mill, this person measures the logs to determine the board-foot volume that may be sawed from them. In some areas, truckloads of logs are weighed, and workers must be able to read charts and tables to determine the accurate volume. Logs are separated by specie; debarked; moved into the mill, where they may be scaled again as a second check for board-foot volume; and then placed on the headrig for sawing. The **machine operator** (see Fig. 144-9) is an important semiskilled worker who must operate the controls to saw the log into slabs, **cants**, which will produce the greatest amount of lumber. The operator in Fig. 1-13 is operating a new "Chip-N-Saw" headrig in a log-processing center. Incorrect sawing can cause a loss to the employer. Other machine operators (see Fig. 144-11) are important but require less operational skill and knowledge.

Lumber may be graded before drying, but more often it is graded after it is dried. **Graders** (Fig. 1-14)

must have complete knowledge of lumber grades of various species and must make quick decisions to mark the grade, thickness, and width of the material when it passes on the conveyer.

Only limited skills and abilities are necessary to perform the work in such plywood-processing operations as shown and explained in most of the figures from 143-12 through 143-20. Similar abilities are needed in most other repetitive processing of products. However, many varied opportunities exist in related wood-products occupations.

Fig. 1–13 A relatively new chipping-and-sawing headrig operation in a log-processing center. *Forest Industries.*

The **upholsterer** occupations (Figs. 1-15 and 1-16) can range from the minimum laborer classification to the upper skill levels. Basic tools, materials, and processes for doing this work are discussed in SECTION 8. The laborers, supervisors, managers, and plant superintendent can do their jobs better and appreciate their work more if they have some background and knowledge about woods, hardware, tools and machines, fabrics, and all other materials needed.

A similar range of opportunities exists in the wood preparation and

Fig. 1–14 Lumber is given a preliminary grading before going on to kilns or yards for drying. *American Forest Institute.*

Fig. 1–15 Using an air-driven tacker to speed up chair-upholstering operations. *Fastener Corp.*

Fig. 1–16 Neat tailoring of upholstered dining room chair seats is made easier by tacker's one-hand operation, which frees the other hand to help adjust the material. *Fastener Corp.*

wood finisher occupations. The basic knowledge and skill needed in this work is discussed in SECTION 7. Most of this work is performed in industries as a part of producing their total product, such as furniture and cabinets. Many individuals and small groups establish their own businesses to do both custom upholstering and refinishing, especially on antique furniture.

Professional and semi-professional careers associated with the woods industries

The professional and semiprofessional personnel who are associated with the woods industries in production, manufacturing, and construction may or may not actually work with wood materials in their occupations. Many of these people are employed in creative activities in which products are designed but then are produced by others. Other people own, manage, teach, sell, and do research related directly and indirectly to the woods industry.

Owners and managers in building construction companies, lumber and related wood-products distributing businesses, and furniture manufactur-

ing and all those in occupations listed above can do their work better if they have a knowledge of wood products from raw materials in the forests to the finished product. A knowledge of the various occupations between these two ends will give them greater appreciation of the people involved and the finished item they produce. Ability to use the tools and machines for producing products from wood will help these career people to become more successful and to have a better understanding of the work to be done.

Most of the careers in the professional and semiprofessional categories are entered after completing the college degrees. The degree, its equivalent, or advanced training is not always necessary but offers the individual some fundamental abilities for the best opportunity to enter the profession, activity, or occupation. Some of these are explained below.

The **architect** and various **designer** careers require some common abilities and training and additional specialized attributes and knowledge. All these people should have creative abilities, some drafting skills, and knowledge of the numerous materials specified in their designs. The architect may design many kinds of houses, buildings, or other structures that involve hundreds of different materials made of wood or from wood. The architect must have a knowledge of materials for structural framing, inside and outside wall covering, roofing, hardwood cabinets covered with plastic laminates, floor covering, finishes, hardware, and other numerous materials.

The **interior decorator** or designer may select appropriate styles, materials, and colors of finishes and coverings for floors, walls, furniture, drapes, and other furnishings for a home or office interior. This professional could be a furniture designer and draft plans and specifications for special furniture. Drafting skills and knowledge of general construction, furniture, and cabinetmaking are some of the abilities needed. This person should also know the best sources to purchase quality products at reasonable costs to clients.

The **professional salesperson** must have a thorough knowledge of the products presented for sale. Knowledge of the raw materials and of the manufacturing processes are needed to present the quality of the products to customers. Basic knowledge of materials, machines, and processes used in production can be gained through training in colleges and universities offering industrial distribution, engineering sales, and management training in sales and marketing techniques. The professional sales representative must develop many personal abilities and attributes. Practical training and experience are excellent, but formal education often speeds the basic learning needed to enter this kind of occupation.

If you are using this textbook in a class, it is probable that the person directing your instruction and learning is a **professional teacher** of industrial arts, vocational trades, or technical education in a public school, post-high school vocational, or technical education program or in a college or university. Most teachers have one or more college degrees, are interested in teaching and directing others, and generally enjoy associating with different young people on a regular schedule. Practical experience in a trade or industrial work is quite common. These teachers have rewarding careers in teaching students the efficient, safe, fundamental use of tools, machines, processes, and operations related to various materials and products in our modern technical and industrial society. Other teachers instruct in product distribution, sales, marketing, labor relations, business law, graphic communications, technical writing, accounting, and many other subjects of special value to all students.

Fig. 1–17 Radioactive isotopes are used by forest scientists as they seek to discover ways to grow better trees faster. Seedlings grown in chemical solutions containing radioactive materials are tested with a radiation counter as part of advance research on the movement of nutritional elements within the tree. *Weyerhaeuser Company.*

Some teachers, experienced in forestry, teach students about this career. The graduate **forester** (see Figs. 3-2 and 3-10) and **forest scientist** (Fig. 1-17) help in development, conservation, and perpetuation of the forests. A **cruiser** (see Fig. 143-4) is a forester who surveys a tract of timber, draws a topographic map to show predominant species, estimates timber stand volume, and marks trees for selective cutting. The forester may use aerial photography to help in performing this cruising operation. A person can also work in parks and recreational activities as a forester and receive college training and a degree in this area.

The **engineer, geneticist** (Figs. 1-18 and 1-19), **special technologist** or **technician** (Fig. 1-20), and many other kinds of professional personnel may be involved with wood products. **R&D** is the common abbreviation for research and development activities in which the above people can be particularly active. Research can increase forest yields, help develop new products and improve old ones, reduce waste, and generally increase value and usefulness of forests and forest products for the benefit of all. The engineer may design a machine to perform work or produce a product better and more efficiently or may test and experiment (Fig. 1-21) to determine the strength and quality of a product. The chemist may perform chemical analyses of wood substances to improve a particular product (Fig. 1-22) or may extract materials from sawdust, slabs, and tree stumps (Fig. 1-23). From these substances can come benefits in the form of medicines, plastics, cattle and chicken feed, baking yeast, wood finishes, and hundreds of other products we do not commonly associate with the forests. In assisting the other personnel, the special technologist learns to perform many of their functions.

Fig. 1–18 A scion from a superior tree is grafted onto root stock at a seed orchard in the Northwest. *Weyerhaeuser Company.*

An occupation not generally associated with forest-products industries is that of the **pilot**. Planes may be used to dust forests to eradicate insects or to seed and replant barren areas. Figure 1-24 shows the use of a helicopter for fertilizing a forest area. By use of the same conveyance, logs may be removed from inaccessible areas of the forest to a loading area to await further transportation to a lumber mill.

The person desiring a more complete explanation about careers and occupational opportunities should study the descriptions of jobs of interest in the *Dictionary of Occupational Titles*. He or she should also discuss vocational ideas with the school vocational counselor. A visit to various companies to talk with people on the job and to visit company employment offices will provide knowledge about careers. Students may want to write letters to companies or to the U.S. Department of Labor for information about career opportunities.

Fig. 1–20 Fire-retardant-treated wood shingles are given a burning brand test by a technologist and a technician at the U.S. Forest Products Laboratory. *U.S. Forest Products Laboratory.*

Fig. 1–22 Pulp sheets made of stored hardwood chips are prepared by a technician for analysis of the storage effects on pulp brightness and other properties. *U.S. Forest Products Laboratory.*

Fig. 1–23 Loading a pallet with stumps from which turpentine and other materials can be extracted. *Caterpillar Tractor Co.*

Fig. 1–19 Up to 15 years of research may be needed to see if a seedling from superior stock will exhibit superior traits. *Weyerhaeuser Company.*

Fig. 1–21 A new foundation of wood and plywood treated with preservative is assembled for another experimental house on the grounds of the U.S. Forest Products Laboratory in Madison, Wisconsin. An earlier installation of a treated wood foundation was inspected and found to be in good condition after 29 years of service. *U.S. Forest Products Laboratory.*

Fig. 1–24 Broad-scale fertilization and other components of this high-yield forest program are aimed at improving wood fiber production by one-third. *Weyerhaeuser Company.*

unit 2

The importance of wood

Wood has always been one of the world's most important resources. Early people used wood to make fires, to make tools such as clubs, and to shelter themselves, either by stretching skins over poles or by weaving tree branches together.

Thousands of years later wood was still being used not only for shelter (houses) and for tools (handles), but also for early machines, such as the lever and the wheel. Wood became important to transportation when it was the main material for carts, wagons, canoes, and ships.

Throughout history people have used wood by changing its size, shape, and appearance to suit their needs.

Forests as an economic necessity

Forests are the only natural resource capable of renewing themselves in a relatively short time. They prevent soil erosion and they furnish shelter and protection for wildlife. In addition, forests provide recreation areas and beautify our country.

Forests give the raw material for thousands of products. Forest-products industries account for at least 10 percent of all manufacturing employment in the United States.

Lumbering, a part of the forest-products industries, is one of the

Fig. 2–2 Lumber and wood constitute the principal materials for modern homes. *National Homes.*

Fig. 2–1 Wood is a principal export item. *American Forest Institute.*

Fig. 2–3 Redwood is one of the most serviceable and durable home-construction lumbers. *California Redwood Association.*

largest contributors to our nation's economy (Fig. 2-1). Millions of board feet of lumber are produced annually. Lumber is used for modern homes (Figs. 2-2 and 2-3), for other construction (Figs. 2-4 and 2-5), and for pulpwood to make paper, which in turn makes life more comfortable and interesting.

Sawmills were in operation in America as early as 1610. Until 1892 the center of the lumber industry was in the eastern regions. Then, until 1909 the industry was most active in the Michigan—Wisconsin area. By 1920 the center of lumbering was found in an area from eastern Texas to the Atlantic Ocean. Since 1920 the center has been in the northwestern states.

Forest products in colonial America

The early explorers of North America harvested and sent timber to Europe to be used for fuel, ships, furniture, and buildings. The best white pine logs were selected and sent to be used as ship masts. Colonists were sent to America to harvest forest products and to ship these cargoes to England.

Tar, pitch, and turpentine were produced from pines for shipbuilding and ship repair. Clapboard lumber and wainscoting were sent for outside walls and inside paneling of homes. Wood was burned to yield potash, used in making soap and glass.

Figure 2-6 shows some typical hand tools used by the colonists. The Pilgrims at Plymouth, during the bitterly cold winters, used many layers of bark to make their huts or homes. Wooden boats were used for transpor-

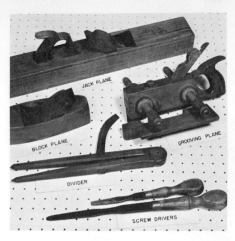

Fig. 2–6 Eighteenth- and nineteenth-century wooden hand tools. *The L. V. Hawkins collection.*

tation and exploration. Indians taught the Pilgrims how to make sugar and syrup from maple sap. They told them which nuts, fruit, berries, and greens were edible and how to make medicine from certain trees and shrubs.

Hemlock bark was used in tanning animal hides into leather. Spruce and pine gum were gathered to chew. Some bark and leaves provided dye for homemade clothing, food seasoning, ink (from galls on oak leaves), and a form of tobacco.

Until the twentieth century, most forest products were those from either the wood itself or its natural by-products.

Wood in the twentieth century

In the twentieth century, people have used wood without considering its value and potential for forms other than its natural ones.

The chemical industry is now supplementing the coal and petroleum industry by using forests as sources of supply for nitrocellulose, which is used in making such products as dynamite, rayon, and phonograph records. Typical by-products of experimentation are

Fig. 2–4 This double A-frame vacation home has a redwood deck which provides leisure space for family and friends. *California Redwood Association.*

Fig. 2–5 Laminated timber arches spanning 250 feet and rising 70 feet are used in an arena. *American Institute of Lumber Construction.*

9

Fig. 2–7 Imitation-leather products and decorative laminates are chemical creations from wood substances. *Rayonier, Inc.*

Fig. 2–8 Wood beams, paneling, millwork, and structural members form a beautiful home interior. *California Redwood Association.*

Fig. 2–9 Laminated fir runners accentuate the curved stairway in a modern motel. *National Lumber Manufacturers Association.*

Fig. 2–10 The Florentine Renaissance period influenced the design of this home-crafted grandfather clock made by coauthor Chris Groneman.

imitation-leather and plastic goods (Fig. 2-7), food packaging materials, food flavoring, and cosmetics.

Research and technology are developing numerous fabrication techniques (Figs. 2-8 and 2-9), treatments, and means of breaking down the wood structure, revealing new uses for wood and its substances.

At least half of the wood harvested today goes into construction. Home-building, paneling, furniture, shipping crates, newsprint paper, and other paper products are familiar uses.

Wood is also the basic material for many hobbies. Furniture construction (Fig. 2-10) done in the home workshop is useful and provides many leisure hours of pleasure. Physical recreation includes the use of boats, baseball bats (Fig. 2-11), bows and arrows, and rifles (Fig. 2-12).

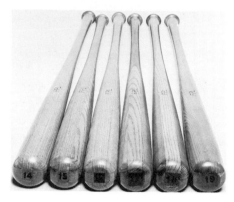

Fig. 2–11 These laminated baseball bats are made of a hickory core faced with ash. *American Forest Institute.*

Fig. 2–12 The evolution of a three-ply, fancy-grained, laminated walnut gun-stock. Left to right: the original thin laminations (as sawn from a wild-grained cull log) ready for treatment with polyethylene glycol to improve dimensional stability and prevent drying damage; the blank made of three laminations glued together; a machined stock ready for mounting; a completely finished stock fitted to a rifle. *U.S. Forest Products Laboratory.*

unit 3

Ecology and forest conservation

Forests are growing from one-fourth to one-third more wood than is cut for use or lost to destructive forces. Both private and national forests bring the most security to wildlife and prosperity to all humanity when they are kept in good condition.

Millions of acres of timberland are destroyed each year by insects (Fig. 3-1), disease (Fig. 3-2), severe weather (Fig. 3-3), improper grazing (Fig. 3-4), and fires. Most fires are caused by careless campers, smokers, and hunters. Nine out of every ten forest fires are caused by human beings and are therefore preventable.

Types of forest fires

There are three types of forest fires, surface, ground, and crown. The **surface fire** burns young trees and seeds. The **ground fire** may smolder for long periods, burning deeply into the humus and soil. A **crown** (treetop) **fire** is the most destructive. It occurs especially among cone-bearing trees. The gums, resins, and highly flammable branches permit the fire to burn rapidly in the crowns of trees during high winds. Total destruction (Fig. 3-5) can result.

Timber losses

Fires destroy millions of acres of forest yearly. Insects or disease are not as destructive as fire, but together they kill more timber than fire and do ten times the amount of damage. Most

Fig. 3–1 **Insects have ruined this once-proud ponderosa pine forest. The western pine beetle destroys millions of board feet annually.** *American Forest Institute.*

Fig. 3–2 **Galleries created by beetles under the bark of a ponderosa pine tree are examined by foresters. Infested trees will be yarded in tree length to a central landing area, salvaging the beetle-killed timber.** *American Forest Institute.*

Fig. 3–3 **Cyclonic winds have virtually destroyed this once-magnificent stand of timber.** *Weyerhaeuser Company.*

Fig. 3–4 **If kept under careful control, domestic cattle and sheep may profitably graze pine forests, but they can cause heavy damage to farm woodlots in hardwood forests.** *American Forest Institute.*

Fig. 3–5 **This photograph shows the aftermath of a fire that completely destroyed a 1600-acre (647.5-hectare) tree farm.** *American Forest Institute.*

Fig. 3–6   A forester marks a mature ponderosa pine for harvesting while two children are told about timber management for a continuous yield. The small trees in time will replace the large old ones. *Western Wood Products Association.*

Fig. 3–7   This stand of Douglas fir is being seeded from the air. Much aerial seeding is being done to start new timber growth. *Georgia-Pacific Corporation.*

losses occur in virgin timber stands. Cutting is the only cure for overmature trees (Fig. 3-6).

As diseased timber is cut, aerial seeding (Fig. 3-7) may start new growth. New seedlings are also planted by hand (Fig. 3-8) or with mechanical planters (Fig. 3-9). From these seedlings comes the great growth—more wood growing than is harvested yearly.

Education in forestry

Scientifically managed forests require personnel with special training in forestry education. Forestry deals with the development, conservation, and perpetuation of the forests. The first school of forestry was founded in 1898. Since that time, graduates of these schools have helped to manage forest lands, increase timber production, and find new uses and markets for wood (Fig. 3-10). Foresters are interested in preventing soil erosion, regulating the water supply for irrigation, and controlling the flow of streams for power and other uses. They also create outdoor recreational facilities (Fig. 3-11) and havens for wildlife.

Tree farming

One of the most dynamic developments in forest conservation is tree farming (Fig. 3-12). This scientific management system is organized and supervised by representatives of forest industries, government associations, and state forestry associations. Tree farms range in size from about 3 acres to nearly 1 million acres each. The products of these farms must meet high standards. Foresters inspect them often to advise the owner of profitable practices and to see that the high standards are met.

Fig. 3–8   Using a dibble to plant southern pine. In dibble planting, a slit is made and the seedling is inserted. The dibble is inserted again a few inches from the seedling and is rocked to pack dirt against the roots. *American Forest Institute.*

Fig. 3–9   A Rocky Mountain planter plants seed trees on contoured hillsides. *Weyerhaeuser Company.*

Fig. 3-10 A professionally trained forester taking a boring in a mature poplar tree. This tree proved to be 51 years old. *American Forest Institute.*

Fig. 3-11 Scientifically managed forest areas provide outdoor recreational sites. *Weyerhaeuser Company.*

Fig. 3-12 A timber stand in a certified tree farm. *American Forest Institute.*

unit 4

Discussion topics on technical industrial information

1. Name several different occupations of persons who would be employed in building a house or an apartment building.
2. Identify and discuss the methods by which an unskilled worker in a wood-construction occupation can progress toward better and more highly skilled jobs.
3. What are some of the duties of, and the differences between, the **cabinetmaker** and the **skilled carpenter?**
4. Discuss the duties of the **millwright.**
5. What are some duties of the **millman?**
6. Discuss the differences between the occupations of **model maker** and **patternmaker.**
7. What kind of relationship does the patternmaker who works with wood have with the person in the metalworking foundry?
8. Name three occupations of forest workers who prepare trees to be sent to the sawmill.
9. Name several occupations of those who work with the incoming logs at the mill and with the lumber produced in the mill.
10. Persons filling the occupations listed in the first nine questions are known as skilled, semiskilled, or limited-skill workers. In what category do we classify the **architect, designer, interior decorator, teacher, engineer, forester,** or **pilot?**
11. Discuss the work of the **forester** and especially how he or she helps our ecology.
12. In what way has the **chemist** contributed to the national welfare by working with wood?
13. What were some of the early American methods of transportation which depended on wood?
14. Discuss the major functions of a forest other than supplying lumber and wood products.
15. Discuss the importance of helping to prevent forest fires.
16. What are the major types of forest fires?
17. Name and discuss five destroyers of forests.
18. In what ways are forests directly and indirectly related to water supply, irrigation, and electric energy generation?
19. What does **tree farming** have to do with conservation?
20. What percentage of forest fires are caused by humans?

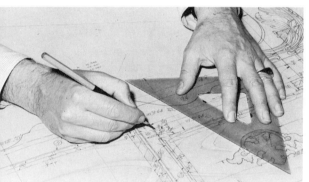

section **2**

Designing
and Planning

unit 5

Basic design principles

Designing is planning a direct and simple solution to the problems involved in creating a product. Although ancient people did not have the word **design** in their vocabularies, they were able to measure, cut, drill, bore, scrape, chop, saw, and burnish.

People's needs became wider as civilization developed. Craft guilds and specialization began to flourish. The guilds produced people known as craftsmen who took pride in the things they designed and produced.

Special-purpose tools and power machines were designed and constructed as the need arose and knowledge permitted. Tools and machines have helped produce items created through imagination, design, and proper planning.

Originality in changing an old design or in creating a new idea is an individual challenge. Two people are not likely to have the same ideas, likes, or dislikes for a particular design. Experimentation with different ideas and numerous wood products also helps to develop the talent for good design in woodworking.

Furniture styles

The word **style** in furniture design refers to, and identifies, work done by a famous designer or a group of designers. Leg and chair shapes (Fig. 5-1) are the easiest to recognize in style designs. Distinctive furniture is divided into three overall categories: (1) traditional, (2) provincial, and (3) contemporary.

Traditional (formal) styles were usually named after either the designer or reigning monarchs. The figures illustrate with line drawings, and some representative photographs, modern adaptations of famous styles. Listed in chronological order, they are Louis XIV (Fig. 5-2), Queen Anne (Figs. 5-3 and 5-4), Louis XV (Figs. 5-5 and 5-6), Chippendale (Fig. 5-7), Adam Brothers (Fig. 5-8), Hepplewhite (Fig. 5-9), Sheraton (Fig. 5-10), and Victorian (Fig. 5-11).

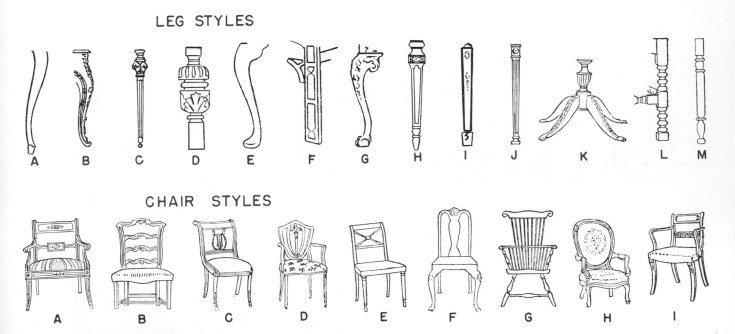

Fig. 5–1 Leg and chair shapes of furniture styles. *Legs:* (A) French Provincial, (B) Louis XIV, (C) Louis XV, (D) Tudor, (E) Queen Anne, (F) Chinese Chippendale, (G) Chippendale, (H) Sheraton, (I) Hepplewhite, (J) Adam Brothers, (K) Duncan Phyfe, (L) Jacobean, and (M) Colonial. *Chairs:* (A) Adam Brothers, (B) Chippendale, (C) Duncan Phyfe, (D) Hepplewhite, (E) Sheraton, (F) Queen Anne, (G) Colonial, (H) Victorian, and (I) Regency. *The Seng Company.*

Fig. 5–2 Modern use of Louis XIV style, 1643–1715. *Mount Airy Furniture Company.*

Fig. 5–4 Twentieth-century adaptation of Queen Anne furniture. *National Association of Furniture Manufacturers.*

Fig. 5–3 Queen Anne style characteristics, 1702–1714. (A) Lower edge of seat frame often shaped; (B) chair splat (center back); (C) highboys and tall cabinets have ''broken'' parts with shaped finials at outer edges and center; (D, E, and F) cabriole leg; (G) vase-shaped splat; (H) plain brass ball handles or pierced handles; (I) flat tops in early models; (J) escalloped shell decoration; and (K) fiddle-shaped splat. *The Seng Company.*

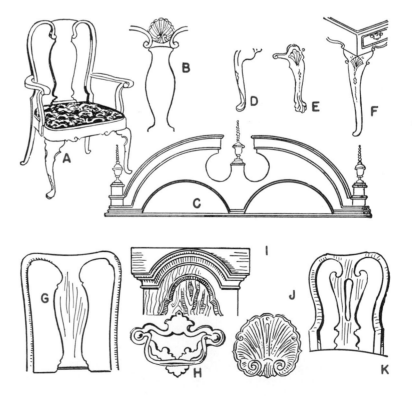

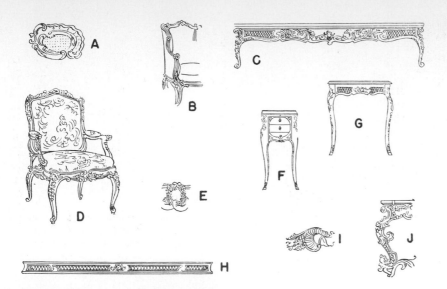

Fig. 5–5 Louis XV furniture features, 1723–1774. (A, E, H, and I) Carved decoration; (B) carved knees; (C) carved rails; (D) scroll feet; (F and G) curved legs; and (J) elaborate carving for ornamentation. *The Seng Company.*

Fig. 5–6 Modern Louis XV furniture. *Drexel Furniture Company.*

Fig. 5–7 Chippendale styles, 1740–1779. (A) Claw-and-ball foot; (B) curves on legs more pronounced than in Louis XV style (later pieces had straight legs); (C) ladder back; (D) legs more slender in form than in Queen Anne chairs; (E and G) extensively carved splats in backs; (F) carved cabriole leg; (H and J) "broken" pediments on large pieces; (I, K, and N) ribband (ribbon) back legs and straight front legs; (L) carved decorations; (M) carved leaf design; (O) scroll design; and (P) Chippendale settee. *The Seng Company.*

17

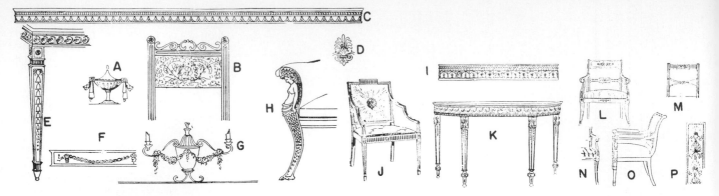

Fig. 5–8 Adam Brothers designs, 1760–1792. (A) Classic urn was most commonly used feature; (B) backs frequently were solid panels or caned; (F, C, I, and P) daintily carved moldings; (D and G) floral swags and pendants; (E, N, and O) slim, tapered round or square legs; (H) use of human figures; (J) upholstered seat and back; (K) decorative moldings on tables; (L) arms supported by extension of front legs; and (M) square or curved open splats. *The Seng Company.*

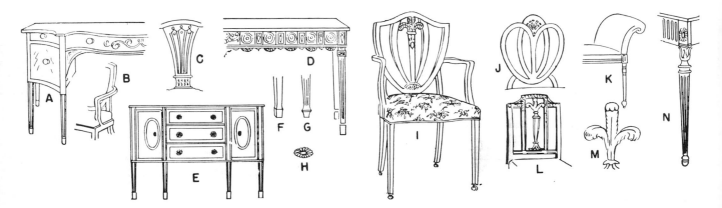

Fig. 5–9 Hepplewhite identification, 1770–1786. (A) Concave corner construction; (B) arms short or concave; (C) hoop-design splat; (D, G, and N) slender fluted legs; (E and F) tapered feet; (H) rosette decoration; (I) shield splat; (J) heart-shaped splat; (K) curved wings on arms; (L) vase-shaped splat; and (M) Prince of Wales feather decoration. *The Seng Company.*

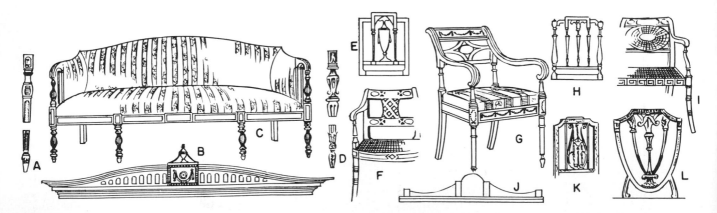

Fig. 5–10 Distinctive Sheraton patterns, 1780–1806. (A and D) Tapered reeded legs; (B and J) shaped pediments on bookcases or doors; (C) light, slender legs on sofas; (E) urn-shaped splat; (F and I) rounded legs splay outward; (G) fretwork panels; (H) turned posts for splats; (K) central panel rises above top; and (L) shield splat. *The Seng Company.*

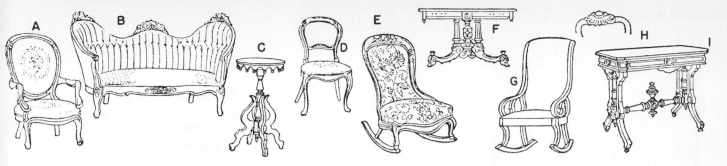

Fig. 5–11 Victorian furniture, 1830–1890. (A) Oval back and rounded seat; (B) carved ornaments on top rail of curved sofa backs; (C) round or oval occasional table; (D) horseshoe-shaped back; (E) low, rounded seat and high back on rockers; (F) turned columns for central pedestals for early tables; (G) arms low and curved, joining seat rail near back; (H) carved flower motif; and (I) oblong marble table tops. *The Seng Company.*

Provincial (informal styles were influenced by the traditional. Different skills, cruder tools, and application of personal, plain ornamentation helped to make provincial furniture different from previous basic designs. Names for these styles came either from the people who produced them or from the geographical area of their origin. Some examples of this group are the Early American Colonial (Fig. 5-12), French Provincial (Figs. 5-13 and 5-14), Pennsylvania Dutch (Fig. 5-15), Late American Colonial (Fig. 5-16), Italian Provincial (Fig. 5-17), Duncan Phyfe (Fig. 5-18), and American Frontier, or Primitive (Fig. 5-19).

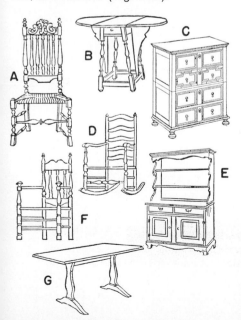

Fig. 5–12 Early American Colonial identifications, 1620–1670. (A) Composite furniture with woven rush seats; (B) drop-leaf table imported from England by colonists; (C) high chest; (D) ladder-back rocker; (E) cupboard; (F) New England version of Jacobean and Puritan styles; and (G) trestle tables. *The Seng Company.*

Fig. 5–13 French Provincial, 1650–1900. (A) Shaped tops and aprons; (B, C, D, G, and H) cabriole legs on later pieces; (E) upholstered chair with turned straight legs; (F and J) curved and turned stretchers; (I) curved-front chests and buffets; (K) straight legs on early pieces; and (L) high posts and canopies on beds. *The Seng Company.*

Fig. 5–14 French Provincial furniture of modern design. *National Association of Furniture Manufacturers.*

Fig. 5–15 Pennsylvania Dutch furniture, 1680–1850. (A) Cupboard; (B and G) round legs; (C) bride's dower chest; (D) chest-on-chest cupboard; (E) chest; and (F) square legs. *The Seng Company.*

Fig. 5–16 Late American Colonial styles, 1700–1790. (A through G) Late Colonial copies of Queen Anne, Chippendale, French, and English styles; (H) hoop-back chair; (I) barrel-back chair; (J) braced-back chair; (K) comb-back chair; (L) bow-back rocker; and (M) fan-back chair. *The Seng Company.*

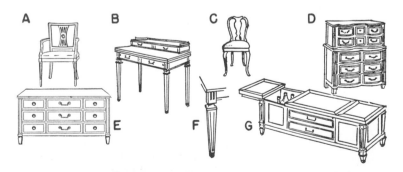

Fig. 5–17 Italian Provincial lines, 1700–1850. (A) Smooth curves on dining chairs; (B) desk; (C) occasional chair; (D) molding following outline of drawer or door; (E) sideboard; (F) straight, square tapered legs; and (G) a chest. *The Seng Company.*

Fig. 5–18 Duncan Phyfe design, 1790–1830. (A) Lion's-head drawer pull; (B, I, and M) column pedestals and three or four curled feet; (C) plain splayed legs; (D) rolled-over top rails; (E) dressing table; (F) carved molding on side rails; (G) distinct Duncan Phyfe lyre; (H) lyreback and carved splayed legs; (J) "sleigh-front" arms; (K) wheat motif; and (L) carved feet. *The Seng Company.*

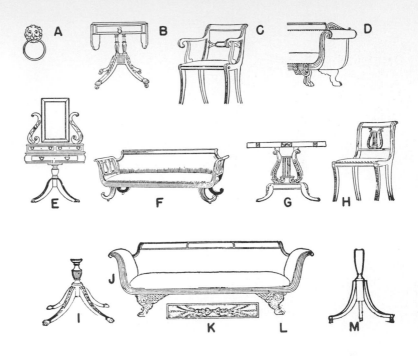

Fig. 5–19 American Frontier (Primitive), 1790–1890. Wagon-seat twin chairs are characteristic of those used by early Midwest settlers. *The Seng Company.*

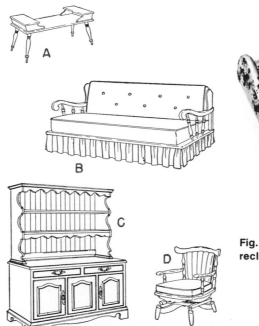

Fig. 5–20 Early American Contemporary pieces (current). (A) Ornately turned legs; (B) sofa bed; (C) scrolled hutch; and (D) revolving chair. *The Seng Company.*

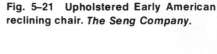

Fig. 5–21 Upholstered Early American reclining chair. *The Seng Company.*

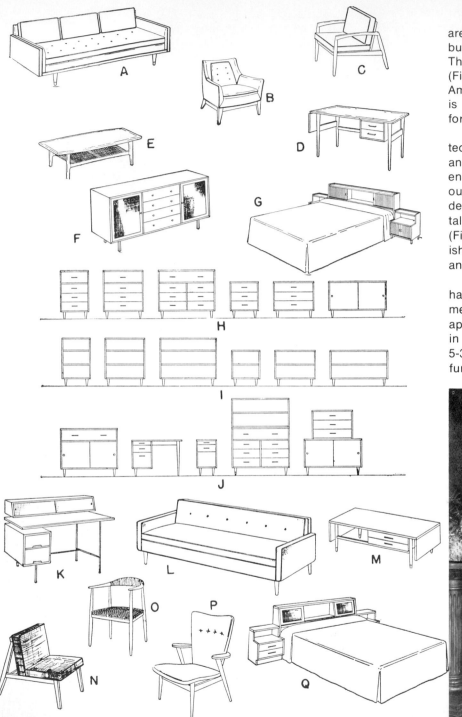

Contemporary (modern) styles are products of the twentieth century, but designs may reflect earlier tastes. The current Early American design (Figs. 5-20 and 5-21) is a revision of the American Colonial. Swedish Modern is an adaptation of classic period forms.

Mass-production methods, new techniques and materials, comfort, and American likes and dislikes influence selections and uses of the various patterns. Some of these functional designs are Modern (Fig. 5-22), Oriental (Figs. 5-23 and 5-24), Ranch Style (Fig. 5-25), and Scandinavian (Swedish and Danish) Modern (Figs. 5-26 and 5-27).

Dual-purpose furniture (Fig. 5-28) has been much in demand, and it meets a real need in small homes and apartments. Special molded designs in plywood and plastic (Figs. 5-29 and 5-30) are changes from the solid wood furniture of the past.

Fig. 5–22 Modern: a period still in transition. (A through D) Square and round tapered legs; (E) coffee table; (F) cabinet; (G and Q) bookcase and cabinet headboard; (H through J) modern sectional-assembly designs; (K) desk; (L) sofa bed; (M) dropleaf coffee table; and (N through P) upholstered and woven-seat chairs. *The Seng Company.*

Fig. 5–23 Modern Oriental lingerie chest. *Drexel.*

Fig. 5–24 Oriental influences (current). (A and D) Ends of legs; the geometric treatment of upholstery and frames (B and C) still shows the influence of early Chinese and Japanese styles. *The Seng Company.*

Fig. 5–25 Ranch-style details (current American). (A) Rope drawer pulls; (B, C, E, and K) no attempt to hide juncture of joined pieces; (D and F) cushions often used on wood seats; (G and I) legs usually square cornered and tapered; (D, F, H, and J) use of interlaced leather, plastic, or rawhide cords to maintain ranch, or western, atmosphere. *The Seng Company.*

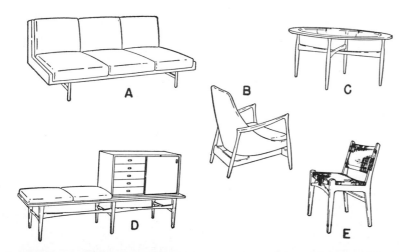

Fig. 5–26 Scandinavian Modern influence (Swedish and Danish Modern). (A and B) Modern plastics or fabrics evident in upholstery treatment; (C and D) legs square and round tapered; and (E) woven fiber widely used in chair seats. *The Seng Company.*

Fig. 5–27 A typical Scandinavian chair. *Georg Jensen, Inc.*

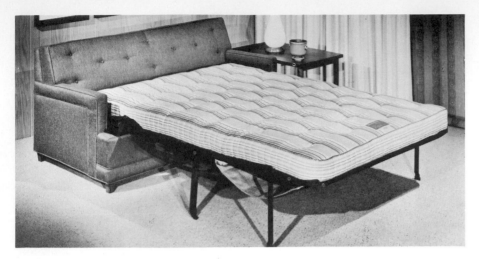

Fig. 5–28 A multiple- or dual-purpose upholstered sofa sleeper. Some are available with a raised headrest. *The Seng Company.*

Fig. 5–29 Wood and plastic utility chair. *Burke Division, Brunswick Corporation.*

Fig. 5–30 Plastic and wood chairside table. *Burke Division, Brunswick Corporation.*

Furniture periods

The word **period** refers to a particular time in history, a cultural era, when different peoples preferred furniture of similar design. It is almost impossible to determine when one period ends and another begins. Styles overlap periods: (1) Gothic, (2) Sixteenth-century Renaissance, (3) Seventeenth and Eighteenth Century, (4) Nineteenth Century, and (5) Modern.

Study of the chronology in Table 5–1 gives a quick reference to the relationships between styles and periods.

Design principles

Design is either **formal** or **informal**. When someone plans, sketches ideas, makes necessary detailed drawings, determines materials and processes to be used, and constructs a product, it is called **complete formal design**. Construction without the aid of all or part of these steps is **informal**.

Whether formally or informally designed, a functional product created for the modern era should reflect certain principles. These include simplicity of line, economy of materials, usefulness, strength, durability, and originality. Replicas (copies) of past eras should still reflect many of

these principles when placed in modern settings.

There are three major aspects of design: (1) the creative aspect; (2) the construction, or technical, aspect; and (3) the beauty, or aesthetic, aspect. The three are equally important.

The **creative** aspect of design involves the application of ideas to the form and shape of an object. Some of the problems are those of simplicity, balance, and proportion.

Simple designs are usually more pleasing to the eye. They are easier to construct, more functional, and more economical.

The two kinds of balance are **axial** and **radial**. Axial balance can be either formal or informal. In formal axial (symmetrical) balance, all shapes and parts on each side of a balance point, or center line, are equal. Examples are turned fruit bowls, tidbit trays (Fig. 5-31), candle holders, bud vases,

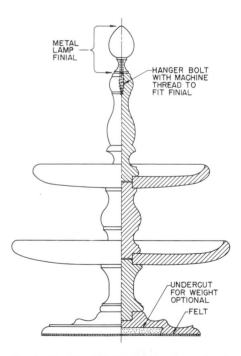

Fig. 5–31 The tidbit tray is an example of formal axial (symmetrical) balance. *Power Tool Division, Rockwell International.*

Table 5-1 CHRONOLOGICAL TABLE OF FURNITURE PERIODS AND STYLES*

Time	England	France	America	Other countries
Early styles	Gothic (1100–1500)	Gothic (1100–1500)		Gothic (1100–1500) in Spain, Germany, Italy, etc.
Sixteenth century	Renaissance Tudor (1509–1558) Elizabethan (1558–1603)	Renaissance (1500–1610)		Early Renaissance (1500–1600) in Italy, Spain, Holland, Germany
Seventeenth century	Jacobean (1603–1649) Commonwealth (1649–1660) Carolean (1660–1688) William & Mary (1689–1702)	Louis XIII (1610–1643) Louis XIV (1643–1715) Early French Provincial (1650–1700)	Early Colonial (1620–1700)	Late Renaissance (1600–1700) in Italy, Spain, Holland, Germany
Eighteenth century	Queen Anne (1702–1714) Early Georgian (1714–1754) Late Georgian (1754–1795), including: Chippendale (1740–1779) Hepplewhite (1770–1786) Sheraton (1780–1806) Adam Bros. (1760–1792)	French Regency (1715–1723) Louis XV (1723–1774) Louis XVI (1774–1893) Directoire (1795–1804) Darly French Provincial (1700–1800)	Late Colonial (1700–1790) Copies of English French Dutch styles Duncan Phyfe (1790–1830)	European furniture of this time greatly influenced by French, Dutch, English craftsmen
Nineteenth century	English Regency (1793–1830) Victorian (1830–1890) Eastlake (1879–1895)	French Empire (1804–1815) Late French Provincial (1800–1900)	Federal (1795–1830) (also Duncan Phyfe) Victorian (1830–1900)	Biedermeier (1800–1850) in Germany
Twentieth century	Arts & Crafts (1900–1920) Modern Utility (1939–1947)	L'Art Nouveau (1890–1905) Arte Moderne (1926) Modern	Mission (1895–1910) Modern	Swedish Modern in Sweden Modern in other countries

*It is virtually impossible to determine the exact date when one period ends and another begins, since furniture styles have a tendency to overlap. The above dates, however, are approximately correct, and they delineate the years of maximum popularity for each style. This table will serve as a quick reference to determine the leading styles in each century. It also shows the interrelation of styles in the various countries given.

lamps, and posts of beds. In informal axial (asymmetrical, or not symmetrical) balance, areas of shapes and parts are not the same on both sides of the balance point. To achieve this balance, a large area near the center line is balanced with a small area at a greater distance from the center line. Radial balance is best characterized by a central point of rotation. The face of a modern electric clock (Fig. 5-32) best illustrates this kind of balance.

Proportion is the ratio of one part to another. The ratio of lines, different areas of color, and different areas of space must be balanced to secure an appealing and useful product. Common ratios of size are 2 to 3, 3 to 5, and 5 to 8. The ancient Greeks developed what they called the **Golden Mean,** or **Golden Rectangle.** It was considered the ideal proportion. If the short side of the rectangle measures 2 units, the long side should measure approximately $3\frac{1}{4}$ units. This Golden Mean is a proportion which is still used by designers today.

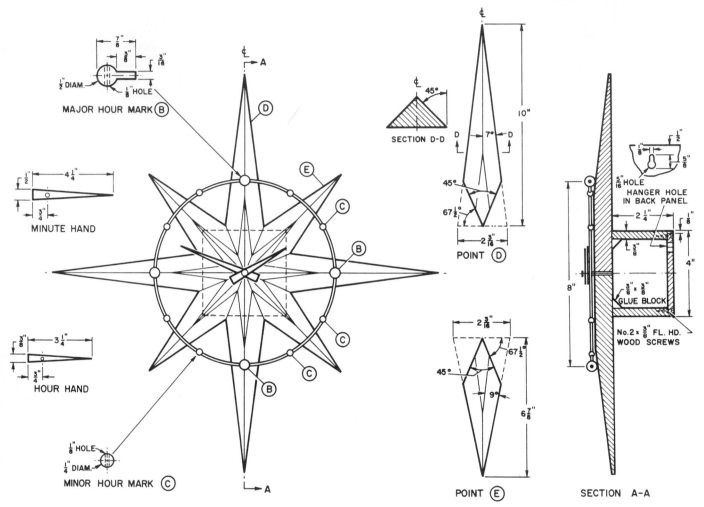

Fig. 5–32 Radial balance is illustrated by a modern clock face. *Power Tool Division, Rockwell International.*

mm	3.18	4.76	6.35	7.94	9.53	12.70	15.88	19.05	22.22
IN.	$\frac{1}{8}$	$\frac{3}{16}$	$\frac{1}{4}$	$\frac{5}{16}$	$\frac{3}{8}$	$\frac{1}{2}$	$\frac{5}{8}$	$\frac{3}{4}$	$\frac{7}{8}$
mm	55.56	57.15	82.55	101.60	114.30	174.62	203.20	254.00	
IN.	$2\frac{3}{16}$	$2\frac{1}{4}$	$3\frac{1}{4}$	4	$4\frac{1}{2}$	$6\frac{7}{8}$	8	10	

Round off metric dimensions to nearest mm except for hardware, such as 1/8 inch drill.

The **construction,** or **technical,** aspect of design involves (1) making detailed drawings of the object and its parts so that craftsmen can read and follow the notes and measurements for construction, and (2) studying and planning the orderly procedure of the processes and operations. These include planing, jointing, sawing, turning, drilling, assembling, and finishing. Knowledge of this part of design is absolutely necessary before a person can read, plan, or make drawings or follow directions for doing the work.

Beauty, or the **aesthetic** aspect, requires answers to these questions: Are the lines pleasing to the eye? Does the project look the way it is supposed to look? Is it graceful? Will the color harmonize with the setting in which it will be placed? At least three problems are encountered in developing beauty: (1) rhythm, (2) harmony, and (3) color and texture.

Rhythm is orderly repetition and symmetry of straight lines, curves, angles, spaces, and color. It is often seen in modern architectural structures, and it is almost always present in early masterpieces. Architecture has been called "frozen music" because of this quality.

Harmony groups similar spaces, shapes, and colors to achieve a feeling of complete agreement. A circular object, for example, should be decorated with a similarly shaped design, if decoration is used.

Color and texture are brought together in colors of woods, grain, structure, and patterns. A beautiful surface texture and finish and a pleasing color contribute to the beauty of the final product.

Color harmony in design

Proper color combinations make a home, office, or any other area more beautiful and more enjoyable. The colors used in furniture should harmonize with those in the room where the furniture is to be used. Scientists have discovered that colors influence and affect people. They can inspire, stimulate, soothe, or relax an individual. When improperly used, color can bring about nervousness, restlessness, or fatigue.

Color makes an object or area seem larger or smaller than it really is. Light colors enlarge; dark ones diminish. Yellow can usually be seen at a greater distance than many other colors; it has a longer wavelength than darker colors and therefore pro-

jects. An unbroken length of color (color dimension) makes an object appear taller than it does if the color dimension is broken (Fig. 5-33).

The color wheel (Fig. 5-34) is a guide to the selection of harmonious color combinations. The color sequence of the chart is based on the three primary colors: **red, yellow,** and **blue.** When these are mixed, secondary colors are obtained. These are **orange, green,** and **violet** (purple). All other color mixtures are called **tertiary** (third order). Four basic harmonies are used to derive many pleasing color plans from the primary ones: analogous, triadic, and complementary.

Analogous, or **related,** color harmony is obtained by using any three adjoining colors on the color wheel (Fig. 5-35). For example, orange, yellow-orange, and yellow give a north room sunny brightness.

Triadic color harmony (Fig. 5-36) results when the three colors used are spaced equal distances from each other on the color wheel. The three primary colors illustrate this principle.

Complementary, or **opposite,** color harmony (Fig. 5-37) uses two colors which are opposite each other on the color wheel. This gives dramatic effects: for example, red-orange and blue-green.

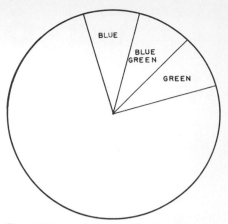

Fig. 5–35 Analogous color harmony is obtained by using three adjoining colors on the color wheel.

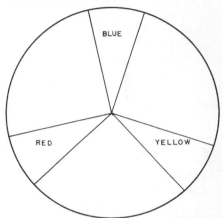

Fig. 5–36 Triadic color harmony is obtained by using three colors equally spaced on the color wheel.

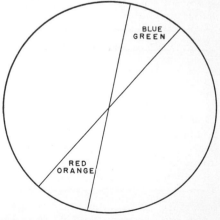

Fig. 5–33 Unbroken color dimension makes an object seem taller.

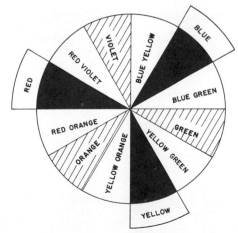

Fig. 5–34 The color wheel is a guide for selecting color combinations.

Fig. 5–37 Complementary color harmony is formed by using two colors opposite each other on the wheel.

unit 6

Understanding working drawings

Drafting is a universal language with a special alphabet of lines, letters, and symbols. Working drawings and plans are often made and read in planning, experimentation, and construction activities.

A drawing is a pictorial description. It shows the sizes of all the parts of an object and how they are fitted and joined together. Words alone cannot be used to describe the construction of aircraft, automobiles, or interplanetary space vehicles. A drawing is needed even for much simpler objects, such as chairs, chests, and cabinets, which do not have as many parts.

A neat sketch or drawing should be made of each project before construction is started. The material needed, the procedure of operations, and the tools and machines necessary

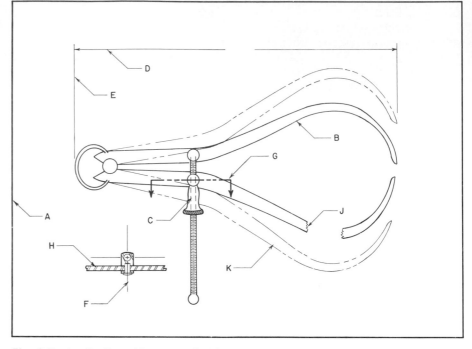

Fig. 6–2 Application of lines on a drawing.

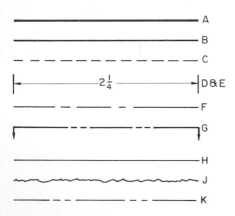

Fig. 6–1 An alphabet of drafting lines.

for completing the project can be determined by reading the basic drawing. One must learn to read and interpret the language of drawings quickly.

Alphabet of drafting lines

Lines are the alphabet of the language of drafting. Each different kind of line has a different use. They should be recognized quickly and used properly when drawing an object (Figs. 6-1 and 6-2). Ten different kinds of lines are shown in Fig. 6-1: (A) border, (B) object, (C) hidden, (D) extension, (E) dimension, (F) center, (G) cutting plane, (H) section, (J) short break, and (K) phantom.

A **border line** (Fig. 6-2A) is usually drawn as a wide or heavy line on student drawings. This line, which is thicker than an object line, is used to frame or border the drawing sheet.

An **object line** (Fig. 6-2B) is a solid heavy line and one of the most important. It outlines the visible edges and surfaces of the object being drawn.

Hidden lines (Fig. 6-2C) are used to show the invisible edges and surfaces of an object. They are made of thin dashes about $1/8$ inch long with about $1/16$ inch space between.

Extension lines (Fig. 6-2D) are used in connection with dimension lines. They are thin and dark and begin about $1/16$ inch away from an object line and extend about $1/8$ inch beyond the last dimension-line arrowhead.

The **dimension line** (Fig. 6-2E) shows the size of an object or of some part of it. This line is usually placed between two extension lines. It should be as narrow as extension and center lines and broken near the middle for the insertion of the measurement. Arrowheads should be on each end touching the extension lines. In small spaces, the number may be placed between extension lines with the dimension lines outside. Dimension lines should not cross main lines on a drawing.

A **center line** (Fig. 6-2F) shows the center of any arc, circle, or cylindrical object. It is as narrow as an extension line and is made of alternately long and short dashes. Short dashes should cross at the centers of arcs and circles.

The **cutting-plane line** (Fig. 6-2G) suggests that an object has been cut to remove a part to show its internal construction. It is made by one dash about $3/4$ inch long and two short dashes, each about $1/8$ inch long. About $1/16$ inch of space is left between dashes.

Section lines (Fig. 6-2H) are narrow lines similar to extension lines. Solid and dashed lines are used to indicate the part of the object "cut" by the cutting plane. Various lines designate the type of material (Fig. 6-3).

A **break line** (Fig. 6-2J) is frequently used to eliminate the repetition of, or to shorten, a long part and to draw it in less space. It is also used when sectioning a solid part. This line is made freehand. It is about the width of an object line.

The **phantom line** (Fig. 6-2K) is used to show that some parts move to other positions. Even dashes about $1/2$ to $3/4$ inch in length are used with a slight break between them.

The **construction guideline** is not shown. It is a trial line drawn so light that it should not have to be erased. It is used to outline the shape of parts and to act as a guide in making proper letters and numerals.

Letters

Well-made letters improve the appearance of a drawing and make it easy to read. Guide- (construction) lines help to make uniform sizes of letters for notes and other information. These include the kind of material, part names, and numerical sizes of parts. The ability to letter is of special value if a person chooses a profession such as engineering, architecture, technology, industrial education, or related technical activities.

The single-stroke Gothic capital letter is most widely used. Some draftsmen use special lettering devices to form letters. Practice making letters and numbers (Fig. 6-4).

Practice spacing letters properly. Since letters do not take up the same space, they look odd if equally spaced (Fig. 6-5). Letters for notes (special directions) and whole numbers should be about $1/8$ inch high on most drawings. The accurate metric conversion for $1/8$ inch is 3.175 millimeters (mm). A practical metric conversion for the height of letters and numbers is 3 mm.

Numbers

Dimension numerals (whole numbers and fractions) show the exact size of a space, hole, curve, or other part of the object. The total height of a fractional dimension should be a little more than twice as high as that of a whole number (Fig. 6-6). Whole numbers are to be made the same height as letters. Numbers for the numerator and the denominator of a fraction are each $1/8$ inch high also. The division line is drawn in the space between them. It is always aligned with the dimension line unless unidirectional dimensioning is used (see Fig. 6-11). An arrowhead is drawn at one or both ends of the dimension line, as needed.

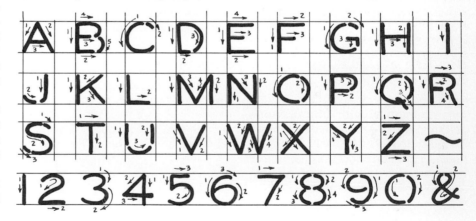

Fig. 6–4 Single-stroke vertical Gothic letters and numbers.

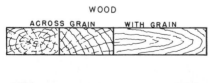

WOOD

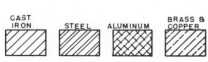

Fig. 6–3 Section lines for building materials.

Fig. 6–5 Properly spaced letters.

Arrowheads

Arrowheads are made freehand on the ends of dimension lines. The head is about $1/8$ inch (3 mm) long, or three times as long as it is wide (Fig. 6-7). Arrowheads, numbers, and letters assist the worker in locating measurements.

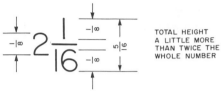

Fig. 6–6 Proportions of fractions and whole numbers.

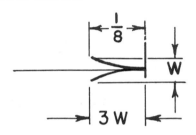

Fig. 6–7 Proportion of arrowheads.

Reading and making measurements

Reading a rule, or scale, and making measurements with the various squares and measuring devices are discussed in SECTION 3. Accurate measuring in drawing or constructing a project is one of the first requirements of good craftsmanship.

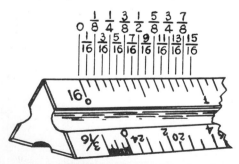

Fig. 6–8 Measurements given in sixteenths of an inch.

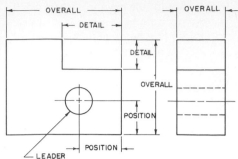

Fig. 6–9 Overall, position, and detail dimensions.

Measurements in woodworking are usually expressed in sixteenths ($1/16$) of an inch (see Fig. 6-8). The scales, squares, and rules used are divided into these units. When working with metric measurements, the millimeter (mm) is the unit to be used. Measurements to be converted should be rounded to the nearest millimeter. To do this, drop the decimal if it is less than $1/2$. If the decimal is more than $1/2$, add 1 to the whole millimeter. If the decimal is exactly $1/2$, drop it if the whole number is even; add 1 if the whole number is odd.

Dimensions

Well-placed dimensions on a drawing give the exact sizes of various parts of a project. Size and location dimensions are of three types: (1) position, (2) detail, and (3) overall (Fig. 6-9).

Position dimension shows where a hole or other detail is located. A **detail dimension** gives the correct length, width, height, or depth of some specific detailed part. **Overall dimension** shows the total length, width, and height of an object.

The following rules and procedures for dimensioning are helpful:

1. Dimensions should be outside, between, and to the right of the views whenever possible. Other dimensions are placed on and around the views as needed (see Fig. 6-10).

2. The first line of dimensions around views should begin about $1/4$ to $3/8$ inch (6 to 8 mm) away from the nearest object line. Overall dimensions are farthest from the object.

3. Some drawings have dimensions which all read from the bottom of the sheet. This is called **unidirectional** dimensioning. In woodworking, most dimensions are placed to read from both the bottom and the right of the sheet. This is **aligned** dimensioning. Both methods are shown in Fig. 6-11.

4. The dimension of a particular part is usually given only on the one view where the part is most clearly shown.

5. Sizes of very small spaces are usually placed outside the area dimensioned (Fig. 6-12).

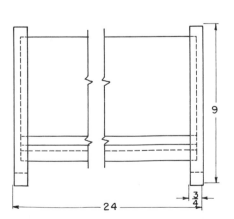
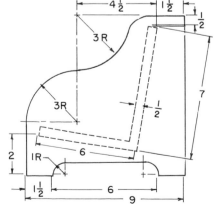

Fig. 6–10 The correct placement of dimensions on the views of an object.

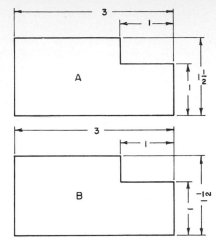

Fig. 6–11   Unidirectional (A) and aligned (B) dimensions.

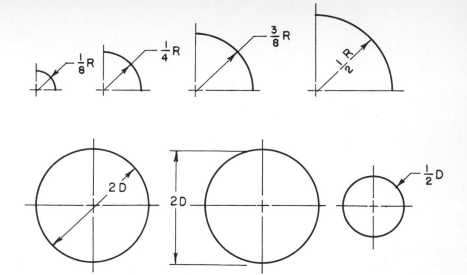

Fig. 6–13   Dimensioning large and small arcs and circles.

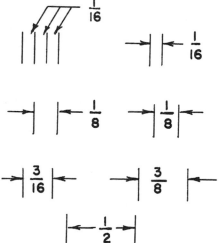

Fig. 6–12   Dimensioning small spaces.

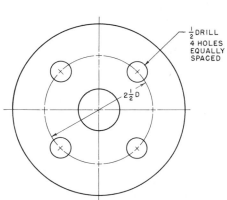

Fig. 6–14   Dimensioning equally spaced holes of the same size.

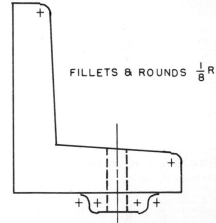

Fig. 6–15   Fillets and rounds on patternmaking drawings.

6. Large arcs and circles, or holes, are usually dimensioned on the view where they appear in true form (Fig. 6-13). The letter **R** follows the size numeral to indicate **radius.** The abbreviation **DIA** is used if it is *not* clear that the dimension is a diameter.

7. One leader, dimension, and note are sometimes used to dimension several holes. This is done when the holes are equally spaced on the same center line and are the same size (Fig. 6-14).

8. Precision measurements are shown as whole numbers and decimals.

9. Very small arcs and internal and external corners of a project are called **fillets** and **rounds.** Their size is designated by a note and a dimension (Fig. 6-15). This is common practice on patternmaking drawings.

10. Angles are dimensioned either in degrees or linear measurements or in a combination of both (Fig. 6-16).

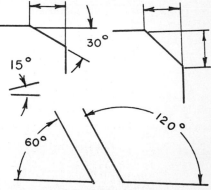

Fig. 6–16   Dimensioning angles.

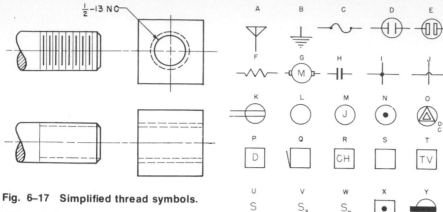

Fig. 6-17 Simplified thread symbols.

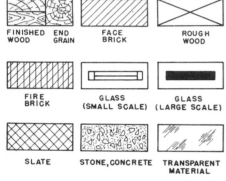

Fig. 6-18 Construction material symbols.

FINISHED WOOD — END GRAIN — FACE BRICK — ROUGH WOOD
FIRE BRICK — GLASS (SMALL SCALE) — GLASS (LARGE SCALE)
SLATE — STONE, CONCRETE — TRANSPARENT MATERIAL

Fig. 6-19 Some common electrical symbols. (A) Antenna, (B) ground, (C) fuse, (D) power plug, (E) power receptacle, (F) resistor, (G) motor, (H) condenser, (I) wires connected, (J) wires not connected, (K) duplex convenience outlet, (L) lighting outlet, (M) junction box, (N) floor outlet, (O) dishwasher and clothes dryer, (P) electric door opener, (Q) buzzer, (R) chime, (S) interconnection box, (T) television outlet, (U) switch, (V) three-way switch, (W) automatic door switch, (X) push button, and (Y) stove or range outlet.

Symbols

A system of conventional standard symbols is accepted for general use on all types of drawings. Those that follow are of value in reading or making drawings:

1. Threads on bolts and screws (Fig. 6-17).
2. Construction symbols used in cabinet and architectural drawings (Fig. 6-18).
3. Electrical drawings are called **schematics** and are made by using lines and symbols. They are seen on electrical circuit diagrams for products such as radios, meters, and television sets. Electrical plans for architectural construction contain some of these same symbols, as well as many others (Fig. 6-19).

Pictorial drawings

When people look at an object, they receive a picture impression. A photograph presents a similar picture. When drawings are made to resemble these impressions, the results are called **pic-**

Fig. 6-20 Common pictorial drawings and their relation to a photograph.

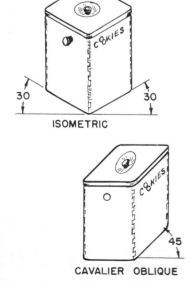

ISOMETRIC

CAVALIER OBLIQUE

PHOTOGRAPH ALL WOOD COOKIE JAR

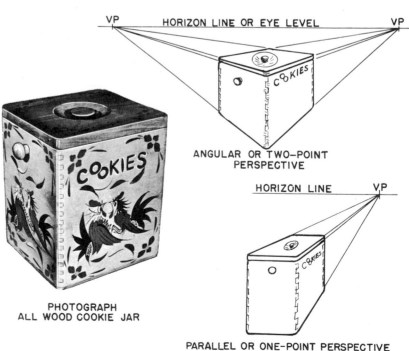

ANGULAR OR TWO-POINT PERSPECTIVE

PARALLEL OR ONE-POINT PERSPECTIVE

torial drawings. These are valuable to give general ideas of how an object will appear when it is completed.

There are three major kinds of pictorial drawings: (1) isometric, (2) oblique, and (3) perspective (Fig. 6-20).

Isometric drawing is similar to perspective drawing. Several sides of an object are shown in one view. It is most valuable in sketching the view of a rectangular object.

Three axes are used in isometric rendering. They may be placed in different positions to show an object (Fig. 6-21). One axis is vertical and represents the corner of the object nearest the viewer. The other two axes recede at 30 degrees from the horizontal, making the axes 120 degrees apart. In drawing the object, measurements for total height, width, and length of an object are made along these axes. Hidden lines are shown on pictorial drawings only when they are absolutely necessary.

Several basic steps are used in laying out and making a simple straight-line isometric sketch or drawing (Fig. 6-22). A different procedure is followed when constructing circles which appear as ellipses (Fig. 6-23).

There are two kinds of **oblique drawing:** (1) cavalier and (2) cabinet (Fig. 6-24). Oblique drawing is sometimes the best drawing method because the front side (the one nearest the viewer) is drawn in true shape. The axes representing the top and the side surfaces recede at 30-, 45-, or 60-degree angles (Fig. 6-25). Axes usually recede at 45 degrees. If measurements along the receding (slant) lines are made full scale (size), the drawing is called **cavalier oblique** (Fig. 6-24A). The object appears out of proportion and distorted. To eliminate this appearance, the depth measurements are made one-half their true length (Fig. 6-24B). The resulting drawing is **cabinet oblique.** Although these slant lines are drawn half size, measurements on the drawing give full size.

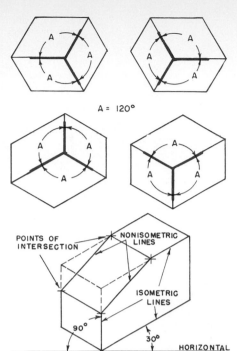

Fig. 6–21 Different positions of isometric axes and nonisometric lines.

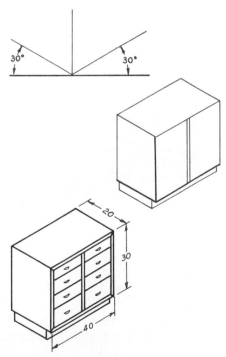

Fig. 6–22 Basic steps in making an isometric drawing.

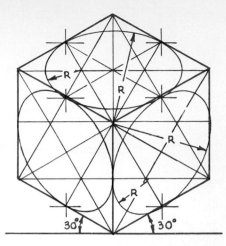

Fig. 6–23 Circles appear as ellipses in isometric rendering.

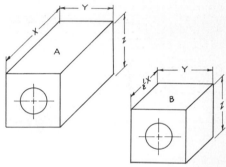

Fig. 6–24 Cavalier (A) and cabinet (B) oblique drawings.

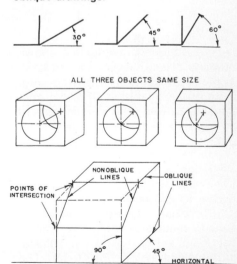

Fig. 6–25 Oblique axes recede at 30, 45, and 60 degrees.

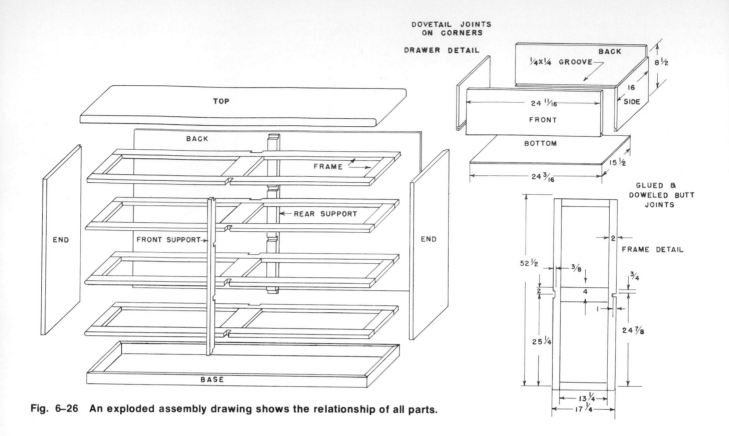

Fig. 6–26 An exploded assembly drawing shows the relationship of all parts.

An oblique drawing that shows all parts of an object separated is an **exploded assembly drawing** (Fig. 6-26). It is valuable to show the relationship between the various parts of an entire object and how they fit together.

In oblique drawing, circles on the front side of an object appear in their true shape. On the top and sides, they appear as ellipses.

Pictorial drawings occasionally include dimensions (Fig. 6-27). Intricate parts are best shown in detailed, multiview drawing (Fig. 6-28). The multiview drawing is the one used most in actual construction; it is known as a **working drawing**.

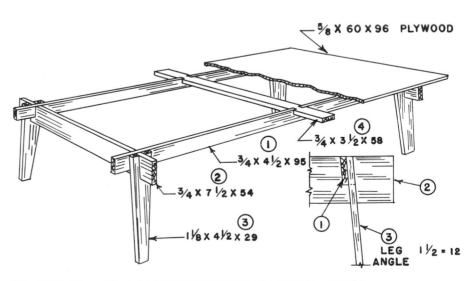

Fig. 6–27 Dimensions on a pictorial drawing of a table-tennis table.

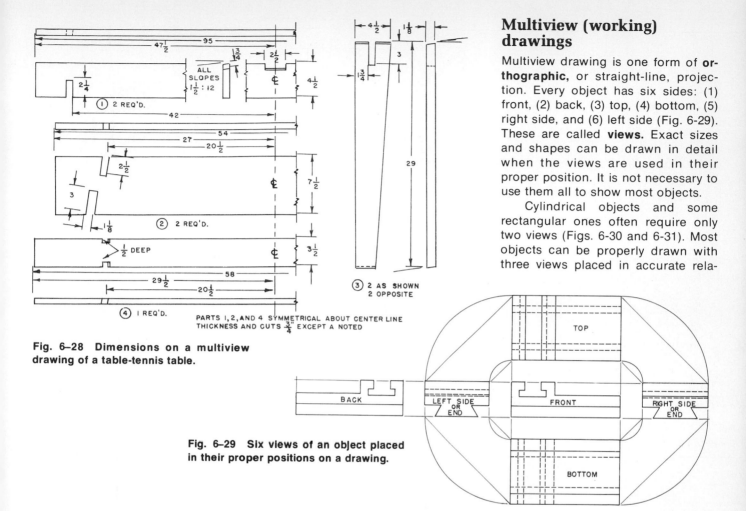

Fig. 6–28 Dimensions on a multiview drawing of a table-tennis table.

PARTS 1,2,AND 4 SYMMETRICAL ABOUT CENTER LINE
THICKNESS AND CUTS $\frac{3}{4}$" EXCEPT A NOTED

Fig. 6–29 Six views of an object placed in their proper positions on a drawing.

Multiview (working) drawings

Multiview drawing is one form of **orthographic**, or straight-line, projection. Every object has six sides: (1) front, (2) back, (3) top, (4) bottom, (5) right side, and (6) left side (Fig. 6-29). These are called **views.** Exact sizes and shapes can be drawn in detail when the views are used in their proper position. It is not necessary to use them all to show most objects.

Cylindrical objects and some rectangular ones often require only two views (Figs. 6-30 and 6-31). Most objects can be properly drawn with three views placed in accurate rela-

Fig. 6–30 Two views describe some large objects.

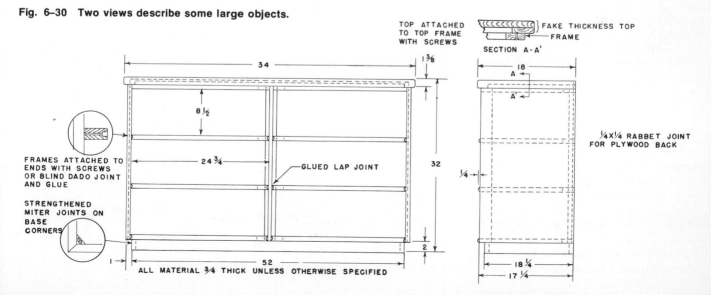

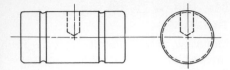

Fig. 6–31 Two views are required on some cylindrical objects.

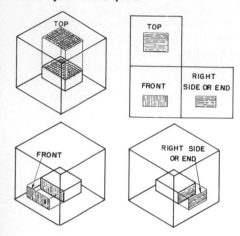

Fig. 6–32 Three views placed in proper position show most objects.

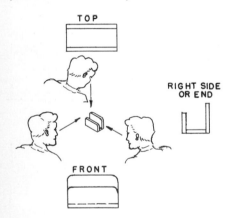

Fig. 6–33 Observing an object from the proper positions.

tionship (Fig. 6-32). The views are drawn as they are seen from the position of viewing (Fig. 6-33). In multiview drawing, all details are shown. These include all parts, notes, symbols, dimensions, and hidden lines.

The front view shows the most important details of the object. It usu-

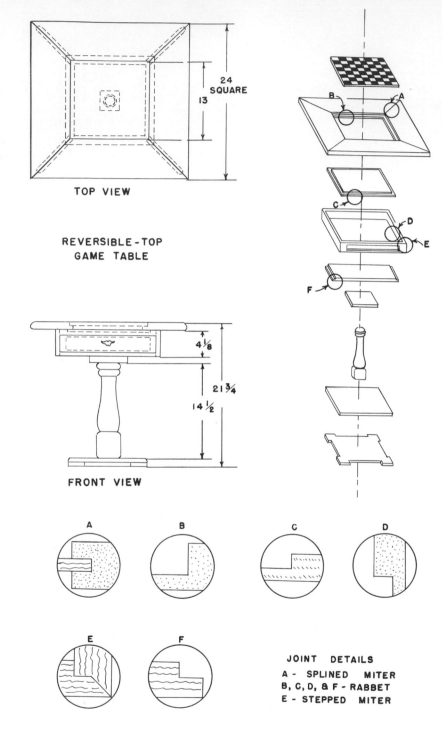

TOP VIEW

REVERSIBLE-TOP
GAME TABLE

FRONT VIEW

JOINT DETAILS
A - SPLINED MITER
B, C, D, & F - RABBET
E - STEPPED MITER

Fig. 6–34 Sectioning parts and enlarging details.

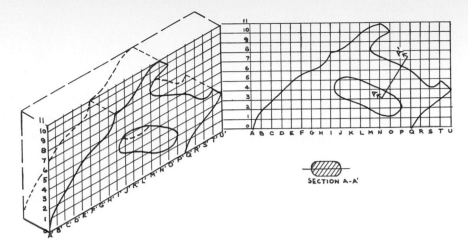

Fig. 6–35 Making a pattern of an irregular object drawn in isometric rendering by the coordinate method.

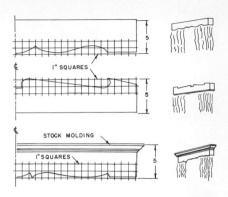

Fig. 6–36 Valance patterns drawn in parallel-line rendering.

ally depicts the greatest length or width and height of the subject. The right-side view is immediately to the right of the front view. The top view is drawn directly above the front one. The correct location of lines and parts on these views is projected from one view to another. Adequate space for dimensions and notes is allowed between views.

Only the views necessary to describe the object completely are used. Complicated objects must have three or more views, and sometimes a section as well, to show detailed parts.

Sections

Part, full, or **half sections** are used to show the inside of an object, especially irregular and complicated shapes. Drawings of these sections are made directly on the part of the object to be shown. They can be offset and enlarged to show the part in detail (Fig. 6-34). On some drawings, section lines show what part is cut by the cutting plane.

Enlarging or reducing designs

Patterns, or templates, for irregular parts of an object are enlarged or re-

duced from drawings. One method is to use a machine or piece of equipment called a **pantograph.** The method used most in woodworking is called the **coordinate** method. It is effective for either isometric or parallel line drawing (Figs. 6-35 and 6-36).

The following procedure will assist you: steps 1, 2, and 3 can be eliminated if the design already has crosshatch lines on it (Fig. 6-37).

1. Tape or otherwise fasten a piece of transparent paper over the scaled drawing.

2. Draw vertical and horizontal lines to form squares over the entire area of the irregular design. The squares should be small ($\frac{1}{8}$ to $\frac{1}{4}$ inch, or 3 to 6 mm) on small designs and larger ($\frac{1}{2}$ to 1 inch, or 13 to 25 mm) on large ones.

3. Trace lightly the shape of the object or design.

4. Lay out lightly the *same* number of *larger* squares on another piece of paper.

5. Where each line of the irregular shape crosses a vertical or horizontal line in the tracing, place a point (dot) on the corresponding line of the larger (or smaller) squares drawn in step 4.

6. Connect the points with a light line.

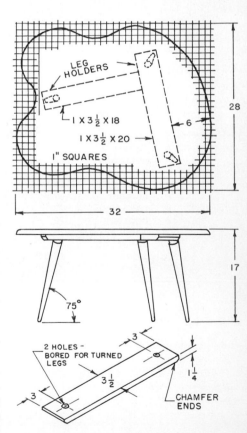

Fig. 6–37 An irregular design, freeform coffee table is enlarged by using coordinate lines.

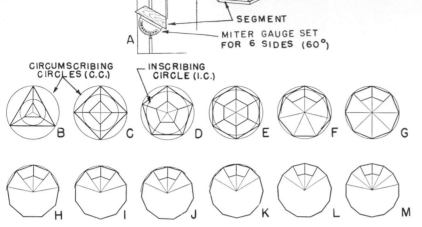

Fig. 6–38 Mitered segments are cut with the use of a miter gage. Angle settings are made according to the information given below as required for the shape to be cut:

LAYOUT FOR CUTTING SEGMENTS OF A HEXAGON (SIX-SIDED FIGURE). SEE A ABOVE.

	Sides	Name	Miter	Bevel	Circumference circle (CC), in.	Inscribing circle (IC), in.
B	3	triangle	30°	cannot be cut	1.732	0.289
C	4	square	45°	45°	1.414	0.5
D	5	pentagon	54°	36°	1.176	0.688
E	6	hexagon	60°	30°	1.000	0.866
F	7	heptagon	64.17°	25.83°	0.868	1.038
G	8	octagon	67.5°	22.5°	0.765	1.207
H	9	nonagon	70°	20°	0.684	1.374
I	10	decagon	72°	18°	0.681	1.538
J	11	undecagon	73.38°	16.62°	0.563	1.702
K	12	dodecagon	75°	15°	0.518	1.866
L	13	sides	76.31°	13.69°	0.479	2.028
M	14	sides	77.14°	12.86°	0.445	2.189

7. Check the two drawings for likeness in shape. When they are similar, darken the lines of the pattern.

8. Cut out the template, and trace around it to make the correct design on the wood.

Layout problems

Various layout problems involve both mathematics and accurate drawing.

Types shown in Figs. 6-38, 6-39, and 6-40 are encountered in performing woodworking operations. In each figure, the letters **C.C.** refer to the **circumscribing** (outside) **circle**. The letters **I.C.** designate the **inscribing** (inside) **circle**.

The tools and procedures for laying out the common hexagon, the octagon, and the ellipse are listed in Unit 13, Laying Out Geometric Designs.

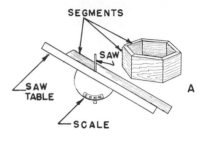

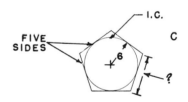

Fig. 6–39 Cutting beveled segments

A. Beveled segments are cut by tilting the saw or saw table to the required angle.

B. Given: Radius of circumscribing circle (CC) and number of sides
Find: Length of side
Rule: Multiply radius of CC by CC factor
Example: 5 sides, 6-inch radius

$1.176 \times 6'' = 7.056''$, $7.056'' = 7\frac{1}{16}''$ length of side

C. Given: Radius of inscribing circle (IC) and number of sides
Find: Length of side
Rule: Divide radius of IC by IC factor
Example: 5 sides, 6-inch radius

$6 \div 0.688'' = 8.72''$ length of side

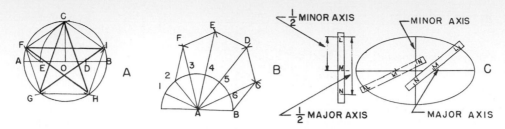

Fig. 6–40 Laying out a pentagon, a polygon (any number of sides), and an ellipse by the trammel method.

Laying out a pentagon

To lay out a pentagon, or star, see Fig. 6-40A, and use this procedure:

1. Divide radius *OB* at *D* (two equal parts).
2. With *D* as center and radius *DC*, draw arc *CE*. Point *C* will be one point of the pentagon.
3. With center *C* and radius *CE*, draw arc *EF*.
4. Line *FC* will be the side of the pentagon and will locate the second point of the star.
5. Continue marking the distance *FC* around the circle to locate points *G, H,* and *I*.

Constructing any polygon

A polygon is a geometric figure having many angles and sides. The length of

the side must be given. The procedure given is for a polygon of seven sides with line *AB* the length of the given side (Fig. 6-40B):

1. With the side *AB* as a radius and *A* as a center, draw a semicircle.
2. Divide the semicircle into seven equal parts by trial and error.
3. Through the second division from the left, draw the radial line *A2*.
4. Extend radial lines through points *3, 4, 5,* and *6*.
5. With *AB* as a radius and *B* as a center, draw an arc to cross line *A6* at *C*.
6. With the same radius *AB,* and with *C* as a center, draw an arc to cross line *A5* at *D*.
7. Continue until points are located at *E* and *F* to form the heptagon (seven-sided figure).

Drawing an ellipse by the trammel method

To draw an ellipse, the major and minor axes must be known:

1. Draw the major and minor axes on a piece of paper or on the wood to be cut (see Fig. 6-40C).
2. On a piece of cardboard, mark distance *LN* equal to one-half the major axis and *LM* equal to one-half the minor axis.
3. Place the cardboard on the axes drawn in step 1, with points *M* and *N* on the major and minor axes.
4. Move the strip, keeping *N* on the minor axis and *M* on the major axis.
5. As the position of the strip is changed, point *L* will locate the points of the required ellipse. Finish by drawing a smooth curve.

unit 7

Selecting an activity project

Skill is as necessary to choosing a project as to constructing it. Deciding on a sound idea for an original piece

of work and then planning it completely are basic to a successful outcome.

Planning

Thorough planning eliminates many mistakes and results in a finished product of superior quality. Complete plans should be made whether the final product is a piece of furniture, a room divider, a boat, a vacation cabin, or a home.

Planning may begin with looking at pictures in your text, other books, magazines, furniture catalogs, and elsewhere. If the project is to be a piece of furniture, visit a furniture store to obtain ideas. As your ideas develop, make rough sketches (Fig. 7-1) of the better ones. After the design becomes completely clear, these ideas are organized into a finished drawing of the project, complete with dimensions and notes.

Choice of an activity project

When designing a project, you should consider several factors:

1. Will the project be an interesting one? Is there a real need and use for it?

2. Is the project well designed? Will it harmonize with its surroundings? Will it be pleasing to the sight? Is it satisfactory as to balance, proportion, color, rhythm, and general appearance?

3. Is it strong enough to withstand the use for which it is intended? If it is to be moved often, will it be too heavy?

4. Is there a reasonable amount of time to plan and make the project? Is it too difficult to construct in the time remaining after proper instruction has been given?

5. Are suitable materials available? Are the plans drawn so that the project is economical in its use of the materials? Is the cost of materials reasonable?

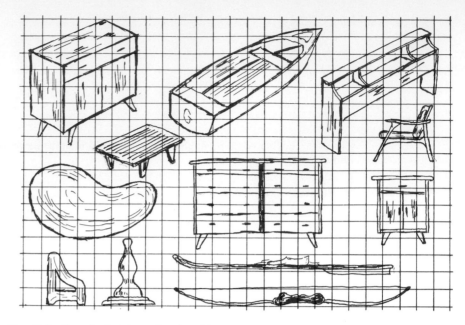

Fig. 7–1 Rough sketches of project ideas and designs.

6. Are tools, machines, and other equipment available to perform the necessary operations?

7. Is the project designed, drawn, and constructed in such a way that many processes of industry will be learned? Will the work involved be valuable in the future for use in a hobby, leisure time activity, or occupation?

unit 8

Project specifications

When a project is planned, creative ideas, sketching, and designing are the necessary steps before it is constructed and finished. The complete drawings are the bases which help to develop and fill in the project plan sheet. The drawings and plan sheets represent some of the same planning steps that are taken in industry to produce a well-designed and functional product.

Cost, time requirements, quality, and quantity of production are essential economic factors in industrial production. Proper selections of wood, hardware, finishes, and construction processes help increase the production quality and quantity of any project.

Estimate as closely as possible the cost and amount of materials needed to construct a project. Keep an exact record, and compare the final figures with the original estimates to determine the accuracy of your estimates. These calculations are made from information given on the multiview, or working, drawing and the materials list.

Working drawing

A detailed **working drawing** gives the information needed to determine sizes and quantities of wood and other materials. It is necessary for complete planning. It saves time and money and helps to eliminate mistakes in construction. Therefore, proper planning includes a multiview drawing of the whole project, one or more pictorial drawings, and sections of parts. Planning may also include making special drawings of parts and developing patterns preliminary to making final plans.

The working drawing shows all necessary joints, all plans for construction, and assembly. Refer to

SECTION 6, "Hardware and Assembly of Cabinetwork."

Selecting the correct wood

Careful selection of wood to be used is very important. A review of the questions in the preceding section will assist in making a wise choice. Also study the information available in SECTION 9, "Technology of Woods." Do this before filling in a project plan sheet like the one on page 42.

Project plan sheets

Most project plan sheets include space for a complete bill of materials, a procedure for doing the operations, and a list of the tools and machines to be used. A suggested project plan sheet is shown in Fig. 8-1. Parts of this unit will help in preparing most of the plan sheet. Unit costs of various materials, either available or to be ordered, are obtained from the instructor and from supply catalogs.

Determining linear, square, and board feet

The quantity of ash, or other wood, necessary to make water skis is simple to determine. However, estimating amounts and figuring costs become more difficult when larger quantities of wood in different shapes and sizes are to be used. The rough sizes of each piece of lumber, plywood, molding, or other wood products are determined from the working drawing.

Molding is sold by the **linear** (running) **foot**. In the metric system it would be sold by the **meter (m)**. For example, a certain molding costs 7 cents per linear foot. If 4 feet are needed, the total cost (4 × 0.07) is 28 cents. All information about quantity, size, shape, length, unit cost, and total cost should be recorded on the project plan sheet.

Plywood is sold by the **square foot (ft²)** or as a standard sheet. The metric measure is a **square meter (m²)**. A standard sheet size is 4 by 8

feet, or 32 square feet (ft²). The cost of a square foot or a sheet depends upon such factors as thickness, grade, type of face veneer, kind of wood, and the bonding agent. The thickness (T) is a preset factor used by the manufacturer to determine the unit cost per square foot or sheet. It is not used in the formula to figure cost. The formula is

$$\frac{\# \text{ Pcs} \times L'' \times W''}{12 \times 12} = \text{ft}^2$$

where: # Pcs = number of pieces
L" = length in inches
W" = width in inches

Example:

$$\frac{\overset{2}{\cancel{3}} \times 8'' \times \overset{5}{\cancel{15}''}}{\underset{\underset{4}{\cancel{6}}}{\cancel{12} \times \cancel{12}}} = \frac{5}{2} \text{ or } 2\frac{1}{2} \text{ ft}^2$$

Most solid **lumber** is sold by the **board foot** (bd ft). A board foot is a piece of material 1 inch thick, 12 inches wide, and 12 inches long, or 144 cubic inches. Lumber that is less than 1 inch thick is usually sold as 1-inch lumber. A piece that was once 1-inch rough stock is usually surfaced to about 3/4-inch thickness. In the formula for figuring board feet, lumber over 1 inch thick is listed by its true thickness in quarters of an inch.

Several tables have been developed to assist in determining board feet. It is best, however, to learn first to compute board measure using one of the formulas given. Thickness (T) and width (W) should always be given in inches ("). Decimal sizes are easier to use than fractions.

When the length is given in feet ('), use the following formula:

$$\frac{\# \text{ Pcs} \times T'' \times W'' \times L'}{12}$$

where: # Pcs = number of pieces
T" = thickness in inches
W" = width in inches
L' = length in feet

Example 1:

$$\frac{\overset{1}{\cancel{3}} \times 1'' \times \overset{1}{\cancel{4}'} \times 2'}{\underset{\cancel{4}}{\cancel{12}}} = 2 \text{ bd ft}$$

Example 2:

$$\frac{6 \times 2'' \times 3\frac{1}{2}'' \times 3'}{12}$$

(Change 3½ to 3.5)

$$\frac{\overset{}{\cancel{6}} \times 2'' \times 3.5'' \times 3'}{\underset{2}{\cancel{12}}}$$

= 10.5, or 10½, bd ft

Example 3:

$$\frac{3 \times 1\frac{1}{4}'' \times 4'' \times 2'}{12}$$

(Use true size of thickness over 1")

$$\frac{\overset{}{\cancel{3}} \times 1.25'' \times 4'' \times 2'}{\underset{3}{\cancel{12}}}$$

= 2.50, or 2½, bd ft

When the length is given in inches ("), use the following formula:

$$\frac{\# \text{ Pcs} \times T'' \times W'' \times L''}{12 \times 12}$$

where: # Pcs = number of pieces
T" = thickness in inches
W" = width in inches
L" = length in *inches*

Example:

$$\frac{4 \times {}^3/_4'' \times 3'' \times 30''}{12 \times 12}$$

(Remember: use 1" as thickness on lumber under 1 inch in size.)

$$\frac{4 \times 1'' \times \overset{}{\cancel{3}''} \times \overset{5}{\cancel{30}''}}{\underset{3}{\cancel{12}} \times \underset{2}{\cancel{12}}}$$

= $\frac{5}{2}$, or 2½, or 2.5, bd ft

The total cost of one kind of lumber is determined by adding the exact board-foot amounts and multiplying by the cost per board foot. The

PROJECT PLAN SHEET

Name_____ Course & Period_____

Name of Project_____ Date Begun_____

Date Completed_____ Estimated Time_____Hrs._____Min.

Actual Time Required_____Estimated Time ÷ Actual Time = _____% Efficiency

Source of the idea & drawing _____

BILL OF MATERIAL

No. of Pieces	Part Name	All Specifications T × W × L Material	Board Feet	Unit Cost	Total Cost
				Total Cost	

STEPS OF PROCEDURE	TOOLS & MACHINES REQUIRED
1.	
2.	
3.	
4.	
5.	
6.	
7.	
8.	
9.	
10.	
11.	
12.	
13.	
14.	
15.	

I. Make detailed working drawing and attach to this plan sheet.

II. Use back for (1) additional steps of construction procedure, (2) finishing procedure, (3) pictorial sketch of project.

Fig. 8–1 A suggested project plan sheet.   Approved By_____

kind of lumber and its grade, thickness, and other factors influence the cost. Lumber prices are most frequently quoted as the price per 100 (*C*) or 1000 (*M*) board feet.

Example 1:

1,000 bd ft of lumber costs $350

$\frac{\$350}{1,000}$ = 0.350, or 35 cents per bd ft

Example 2:

100 bd ft costs $35

$\frac{\$35}{100}$ = 0.35, or 35 cents per bd ft

In the metric system, lumber is sold by the cubic meter (m³) rather than by the board foot. Standard sizes of hardwood will begin at 50 mm wide and increase by 10 mm. Thicknesses will be 19, 25, 32, 38, 50, 63, 75, and 100 mm. Thicknesses beyond 100 mm will increase by 25 mm. Softwood widths will be from 75 to 300 mm in steps of 25 mm. Thicknesses will be 16, 19, 22, 25, 32, 36, 38, 40, 44, 50, 63, 75, 100, 150, 200, and 300 mm. The replacement for a standard two-by-four (2 × 4 inches) should be 50 × 100 mm. Standard lengths will be given in meters; thus an 8-foot 2 × 4 will become a 2.4 meter 50 × 100. These conversions, such as from a 2 × 4 to a 50 × 100, assume that the current standards remain unchanged and are only converted to the closest convenient metric size. It is possible that the standards as well as the measurements will change; for example, instead of being 50 × 100 (2 × 4), a stud could become 40 × 75 or 36 × 63 or whatever the building industry decides is adequate and safe for the job.

Finishing costs

Finishing costs can be estimated in several ways. The price for finishing supplies (including thinner, polishing compound, and wax) is often estimated at 20 to 25 percent of the cost of the lumber. If this method is used, one-fifth to one-fourth of the total lumber cost should be added to the plan sheet.

Finishes are sold in bulk quantities. The common metric liquid measure is the **liter (ℓ).** Usual amounts are one-half pint (1 cup or 0.2366 ℓ), pint (0.4732 ℓ), quart (4 cups or 0.9464 ℓ), and gallon (4 quarts or 3.785 ℓ). The amount needed to finish a project is estimated in these units, or in cups.

A third method is also used: the surface area to be finished is computed in square feet or square meters, and a specific cost per ft² or m² is assigned.

Procedure

The various operations in the work procedure should be listed in numerical order on the plan sheet. The basic processes can be partially determined from the working drawing. Opposite each operation, list the tools and machines for doing the particular job.

unit 9

Discussion topics on designing and planning

1. What is the difference between style and period in furniture design?
2. Name and discuss the relationships among time periods in furniture design.
3. What are the three major fundamentals of modern design?
4. What are the two categories of design?
5. Discuss and explain the necessity of planning and the factors involved in choosing a project.
6. List some professions in which advance planning and design knowledge are absolutely necessary.
7. Identify the primary, secondary, and tertiary colors.
8. What are complementary colors? How are they used?
9. What are the various types of lines found on project drawings?
10. Explain the purposes of the three types of dimensions on drawings.
11. Name the principal drawing views.
12. What is the common method of enlarging and reducing drawings of irregularly shaped objects?
13. How can the internal parts of an object be best represented when they are shown in detail?
14. Why is it necessary to plan and make a drawing of a project before beginning work?
15. Why is time important (1) in building a house and (2) in commercial production of furniture and other wood products?
16. In what metric and customary units of measure are lumber, plywood, and molding sold?
17. Discuss the factors which are essential to industry when workers begin to plan, design, estimate, and select materials for a product.
18. Prepare a sample bill of material of lumber and plywood for a project, giving all necessary information.

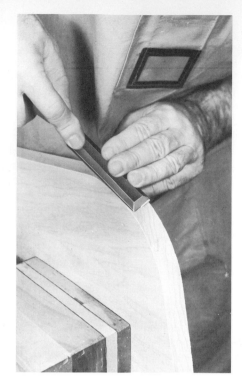

Measurement, Layout, and Hand Tool Processes

unit 10

Safety with hand tools

The safety suggestions given here refer generally to the use of hand tools. Safe practices for using power tools and machinery are included in each tool process section.

Studies made by the National Safety Council indicate that more school shop accidents occur in the forenoon around ten o'clock than any other time of the day. There are also more accidents on Wednesday than on any other day of the week except the working day just before or after a vacation. The wood chisel has caused more injuries than all other hand tools. Fewer accidents occur with sharp tools than with dull ones. These are just a few safety facts gathered from studies and surveys. They indicate that hand tools must be used wisely.

Tool safety

Tool placement. Place tools in an orderly arrangement on the bench top. Point cutting edges away from you.
Screwdriver tips. Keep screwdrivers properly shaped to prevent injuries to hands or to the wood fiber.
Handles. Keep handles firmly fastened on planes, hammers, mallets, chisels, and files.
Correct use of tools. Use all tools properly and only for their intended purpose.

Materials safety

Fastening materials. Always fasten or hold wood properly in a vise, use clamps, or hold firmly on sawhorses.
Waste lumber. Put waste and short pieces of lumber in a storage rack.
Waste rags. Keep oily or finishing rags in closed metal containers.

Physical safety

Lifting. Use your leg and arm muscles to lift heavy objects. Never depend on your back muscles.
Sharpness. Test the sharpness of cutting tools on paper or wood, not on your hand.
Hand protection. Be careful when you use your thumb as a tool guide.

Knives. Always direct the cutting action of knives away from your body.

Personal safety

Clothing. Wear a laboratory or shop apron when you work with wood. Remove your tie and roll up your sleeves when working in the laboratory.
Shoes. Do not wear sandals or open-toed shoes in the laboratory. Low-heel leather shoes offer more protection than sneakers.
Hair. Keep long hair tied back away from your eyes and out of the way of moving machinery.
Jewelry. It is desirable to remove jewelry. A ring could catch under a splinter, or a pendant could catch on a moving piece of machinery.

Laboratory and shop courtesy

Accidents. Report any accident immediately so that first aid can be given.
Carrying stock. Warn others to stand aside when you handle long lumber.
Walking. Walk carefully. Do not run in the industrial laboratory.
Accident prevention. Cooperate with fellow workers to help prevent accidents. Think ahead.

unit 11

Measurement— U.S. customary and metric systems

Knowledge of early civilization indicates that one of the first systems of measurement was based on some assumed lengths, such as lengths of parts of the human body, as shown in Fig. 11-1. As people and their cultures became more sophisticated and greater accuracy was required, it was necessary to adopt a more stable and reliable standard of weights and measures.

The United States acquired the **customary** (or **English**) **system** of weights and measurements as a colony of the British Commonwealth. The English system dates back about five

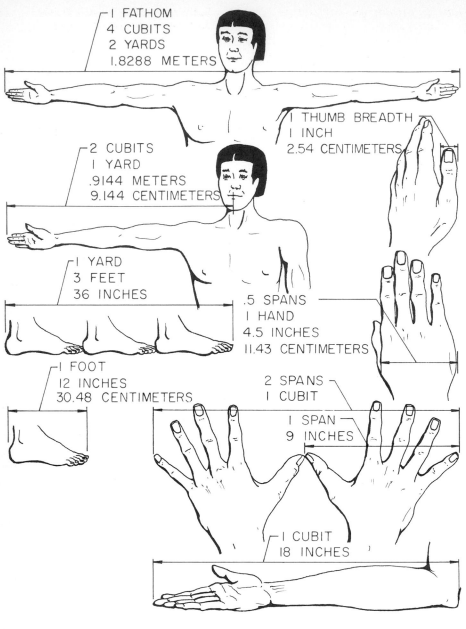

1 FATHOM
4 CUBITS
2 YARDS
1.8288 METERS

2 CUBITS
1 YARD
.9144 METERS
9.144 CENTIMETERS

1 THUMB BREADTH
1 INCH
2.54 CENTIMETERS

1 YARD
3 FEET
36 INCHES

.5 SPANS
1 HAND
4.5 INCHES
11.43 CENTIMETERS

1 FOOT
12 INCHES
30.48 CENTIMETERS

2 SPANS
1 CUBIT

1 SPAN
9 INCHES

1 CUBIT
18 INCHES

CUSTOMARY

METRIC

Fig. 11–1 People, during early civilization, measured by "rule of thumb" based on average lengths of parts of the human body.

Fig. 11–2 Metric and U.S. customary equivalent measures of length.

centuries. It has been refined over a long period but basically evolved from that indicated in Fig. 11-1.

The concept of the **metric system** originated in France during the seventeenth century. Gabriel Mouton, a Lyons vicar, proposed a decimal system having as the basis a measurement of the earth. He suggested Latin prefixes for multiple and submultiple units. It took over 100 years for his ideas to become a reality.

The unit of length of the new system, the **meter,** was equal to one ten-millionth part of the quarter-meridian (North Pole to the equator) passing through Paris. This formed the tentative basis for length, capacity, and mass (weight) for the new measuring system. (The spelling *metre* is used in most English-speaking countries; however, *meter* is used in this text because the suffix *-er* is more common to American English.) Additional refinements have now established that scientifically the meter is an exact number of wavelengths of red-orange light given off by the element krypton 86.

The Emperor Napoleon is credited with spreading the metric system throughout Europe in the early 1800s. The motto for the new system was: "For all people, for all time." The United States is the only major industrialized nation still using the English, or customary, system (Table 11-1).

The United States approved the metric system in 1866. The law passed by Congress stipulated that anyone who so desired was allowed to use the new system, but its use was not mandatory. The United States has participated in several international conferences to foster use of the metric system and is now in the process of converting (changing) to it.

The metric system is based on decimal units of 10. The Système International (SI), or metric system, has seven basic units, with additional ones derived from them (Table 11-2).

The three types of measurement

Table 11-1 METRIC AND CUSTOMARY COMMON UNIT COMPARISON

	Length	Mass	Volume	Temperature	Electric current	Time
Metric	meter	kilogram	liter	Celsius	ampere	second
Customary	inch foot yard fathom rod mile furlong	ounce pound ton grain dram	fluid ounce teaspoon tablespoon cup pint quart gallon barrel peck bushel	Fahrenheit	ampere	second

Table 11-2 SYSTÈME INTERNATIONAL (SI) BASE UNITS

Physical quantity	Name of unit	Symbol
length	meter	m
mass	kilogram	kg
time	second	s
electric current	ampere	A
thermodynamic temperature	kelvin	K
luminous intensity	candela	cd
amount of substance	mole	mol

most important to the woods industries are (1) the **meter** (length), (2) the **kilogram** (mass or weight), and (3) the **liter** (volume), (Table 11-3). The meter is a little longer than the yard; the kilogram is slightly more than twice a pound; and the liter is a little more than a quart. Figure 11-2 presents an accurate comparison of metric and customary (English) systems' length measurements.

The prefixes in the metric system which give the multiples of each unit for length (meter), weight (kilogram), and volume (liter) are the same for all units. These are *kilo* = 1000, *hecto* = 100; *deka* = 10; *deci* = $^1/_{10}$; *centi* = $^1/_{100}$; and *milli* = $^1/_{1000}$ (Table 11-4). Table 11-4 also shows symbols to be used with metric units.

The precision-measurement instruments, now used in the customary system, apply the decimal-inch system of divisions, such as dividing the inch into tenths, hundredths, thousandths, and ten-thousandths.

The metric rule

Metric rules and measuring tapes are available in $^1/_2$- 1-, 3-, 15-, and 30-meter lengths. The meter is divided into 100 centimeters and 1000 millimeters. One inch equals 25.4 millimeters, which is usually interpreted as 25 millimeters. Some common conversions and how to convert to them are shown in Table 11-5.

Table 11-3 METRIC AND CUSTOMARY EQUIVALENT MEASURES

Measures of length

1 meter =	39.37 inches 3.28083 feet 1.09361 yards
0.3048 meter =	1 foot
1 centimeter =	0.3937 inch
2.54 centimeters =	1 inch
1 millimeter =	0.03937 inch or nearly $^1/_{25}$ inch
25.4 millimeters =	1 inch
1 kilometer =	1093.61 yards or 0.62137 mile

Measures of mass (weight)

1 gram =	15.432 grains
0.0648 gram =	1 grain
28.35 gram =	1 ounce avoirdupois
1 kilogram =	2.2046 pounds
0.4536 kilogram =	1 pound
1 metric ton) 1000 kilograms) =	0.9842 ton of 2240 pounds 19.68 hundredweights or 2204.6 pounds
1.016 metric tons) 1016 kilograms) =	1 ton of 2240 pounds

Measures of capacity

1 liter (1 cubic decimeter) =	61.023 cubic inches 0.03531 cubic foot 0.2642 gallon 2.202 pounds of water at 62°F
28.317 liters =	1 cubic foot
3.785 liters =	1 gallon

During the period of conversion, which will take years, many measurement rules and tapes will have a *dual system* of metric and customary units, even though many industries now use the metric system exclusively.

The customary rule

The customary measurement system has been the one used in the United States. It measures in inches, feet, yards, rods, and miles. Measurement

Table 11-4 METRIC DERIVED UNITS WITH SYMBOLS

Quantity	Unit	Symbol
Length	millimeter (one thousandth of a meter) centimeter (one hundredth of a meter) meter kilometer (one thousand meters)	mm cm m km
Area	square millimeter square centimeter square meter square kilometer (one million square meters)	mm² cm² m² km²
Volume	cubic meter milliliter (one thousandth of a liter) liter	m³ ml l
Pressure	pascal	Pa

Quantity	Unit	Symbol
Time	second minute hour (also day, month, and year)	s min h
Speed	meter per second kilometer per hour	m/s km/h
Power	watt kilowatt (one thousand watts)	W kW
Temperature	degree Celsius†	°C
Weight*	gram (one thousandth of a kilogram) kilogram tonne (one thousand kilograms)	g kg t

* Strictly, the gram, kilogram, and tonne are units of mass. For most people and for ordinary trading purposes the distinction between weight and mass is unimportant.

† This unit is often known in the United States as "degree Centigrade." To avoid confusion with a unit used in some other countries, having the same name but used to denote fractions of a right angle, it has been agreed internationally that the name "degree Centigrade" shall be replaced by "degree Celsius."

Table 11-5 CONVERSION FROM CUSTOMARY TO METRIC UNITS

	When you know:	You can find:	If you multiply by:
Length	inches yards miles	millimeters meters kilometers	25.400 0.914 1.609
Area	square inches square feet square yards square miles acres	square millimeters square meters square meters square kilometers square meters	6451.600 0.093 0.836 0.259 4046.856
Mass	ounces pounds	grams kilograms	28.350 0.454
Volume	ounces (fluid) pints quarts gallons board feet cubic feet	milliliters liters liters liters cubic meters cubic meters	29.574 0.473 0.946 3.785 0.002 0.028
Pressure	pounds per square inch (PSI)	Pascals	6894.757
Power	horsepower	Watts	746.000
Speed	miles per hour	kilometers per hour	1.609
Temperature	degree Fahrenheit	degree Celsius	$t_c = (t_f - 32)/1.8$

Fig. 11-3 A typical dual-dimension drawing. Note that millimeters are given above, and inches below, for each measurement. *Beloit Tool Company.*

rules using this system are usually divided into $^1/_2$, $^1/_4$, $^1/_{16}$, $^1/_{32}$, and $^1/_{64}$ inch. Figure 11-2 shows the customary rule measurement divided into $^1/_{16}$, $^1/_4$, $^1/_2$, and 1 inch with each equivalent metric measurement. Measuring tools are shown and used in Unit 12.

Converting to the metric system

It is estimated that approximately ten years will be required for industry in the United States to convert to the

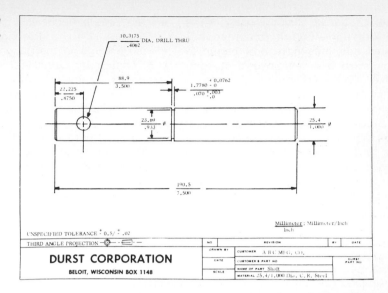

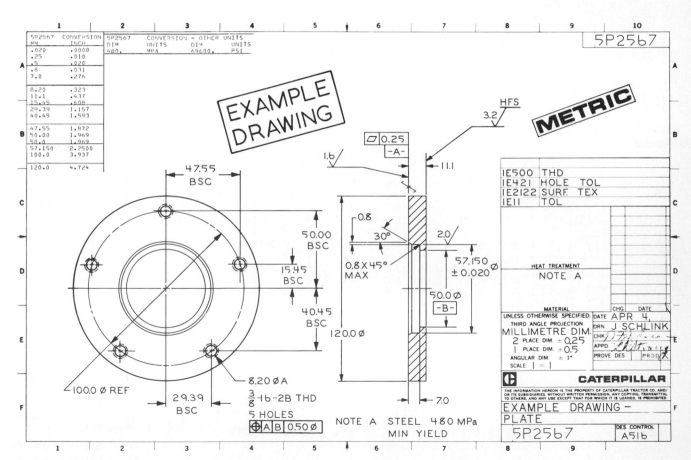

Fig. 11-4 Measurements and other specifications on this drawing are indicated in millimeters. The box at the upper left shows the customary inch equivalents for each metric dimension. *Caterpillar Tractor Company.*

metric system. This is called the period of transition (changeover). Many industries have now begun to familiarize their employees, customers, and suppliers with the changeover. Many drawings and process data use the dual system. Figures 11-3 and 11-4 show two methods now employed in the dual-measurement concept. Figure 11-3 illustrates a dual system with metric units on the top and the customary ones below in the dimensions. Note that the customary dimensions are rendered in decimals.

Figure 11-4 is a drawing with all measurements in metric units. The U.S. customary equivalent for each dimension is given in the upper-left corner of the drawing. Some companies prefer this style of dual dimensioning.

The projects in SECTION 13 employ both systems in order to acquaint you with the metric equivalents for U.S. customary dimensions.

In the dual-measurement method, common fractions are listed in decimals for both the metric and U.S. customary systems: $7/8$ inch reads as 22.225 millimeters, or 0.875 inch. Table 11-6 gives the millimeter equivalents of decimals and fractions of an inch.

An excellent source for detailed information about the SI metric and U.S. customary systems of measure is the National Bureau of Standards, U.S. Department of Commerce, Washington, D.C. 20402.

Table 11-6   MILLIMETER EQUIVALENTS OF DECIMALS AND FRACTIONS OF AN INCH

$1/2$'s	$1/4$'s	8ths	16ths	32ds	64ths	Milli-meters	Decimals of an inch	Inch	$1/2$'s	$1/4$'s	8ths	16ths	32ds	64ths	Milli-meters	Decimals of an inch
					1	= 0.397	0.015 625							33	= 13.097	0.515 625
				1	2	= 0.794	0.031 25						17	34	= 13.494	0.531 25
					3	= 1.191	0.046 875							35	= 13.891	0.546 875
			1	2	4	= 1.588	0.062 5					9	18	36	= 14.288	0.562 5
					5	= 1.984	0.078 125							37	= 14.684	0.578 125
				3	6	= 2.381	0.093 75						19	38	= 15.081	0.593 75
					7	= 2.778	0.109 375							39	= 15.478	0.609 375
		1	2	4	8	= 3.175	0.125 0				5	10	20	40	= 15.875	0.625
					9	= 3.572	0.140 625							41	= 16.272	0.640 625
			5	10	= 3.969	0.156 25							21	42	= 16.669	0.656 25
					11	= 4.366	0.171 875							43	= 17.066	0.671 875
			3	6	12	= 4.762	0.187 5					11	22	44	= 17.462	0.687 5
					13	= 5.159	0.203 125							45	= 17.859	0.703 125
				7	14	= 5.556	0.218 75						23	46	= 18.256	0.718 75
					15	= 5.953	0.234 375							47	= 18.653	0.734 375
	1	2	4	8	16	= 6.350	0.250 0			3	6	12	24	48	= 19.050	0.750
					17	= 6.747	0.265 625							49	= 19.447	0.765 625
				9	18	= 7.144	0.281 25						25	50	= 19.844	0.781 25
					19	= 7.541	0.296 875							51	= 20.241	0.796 875
			5	10	20	= 7.938	0.312 5					13	26	52	= 20.638	0.812 5
					21	= 8.334	0.328 125							53	= 21.034	0.828 125
				11	22	= 8.731	0.343 75						27	54	= 21.431	0.843 75
					23	= 9.128	0.359 375							55	= 21.828	0.859 375
		3	6	12	24	= 9.525	0.375 0				7	14	28	56	= 22.225	0.875
					25	= 9.922	0.390 625							57	= 22.622	0.890 625
				13	26	= 10.319	0.406 25						29	58	= 23.019	0.906 25
					27	= 10.716	0.421 875							59	= 23.416	0.921 875
			7	14	28	= 11.112	0.437 5					15	30	60	= 23.812	0.937 5
					29	= 11.509	0.453 125							61	= 24.209	0.953 125
				15	30	= 11.906	0.468 75						31	62	= 24.606	0.968 75
					31	= 12.303	0.484 375							63	= 25.003	0.984 375
1	2	4	8	16	32	= 12.700	0.500	1	2	4	8	16	32	64	= 25.400	1.000

unit 12

Laying out lumber

Read and study Unit 11 to understand measurement using the metric and customary systems.

Tools

The tools most commonly used for measuring and laying out are the **wooden** or **steel bench rule** (Fig. 12-1), **try square** (Fig. 12-2), **steel framing square** (Fig. 12-3), **combination** or **carpenter's square** (Fig. 12-4), **extension folding zigzag rule** (Fig. 12-5), **flexible steel tape** (Fig. 12-6), **steel measuring tape** (Fig. 12-7), **bevel** (Fig. 12-8), **angle divider** (Fig. 12-9), **marking gage** (Fig. 12-10), **butt gage** (Fig. 12-11), **marking** or **utility knife** (Fig. 12-12), **level** (Fig. 12-13), and **plumb bob** (Fig. 12-14).

Fig. 12–1 A wooden bench rule.

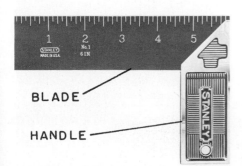

BLADE

HANDLE

Fig. 12–2 A try square.

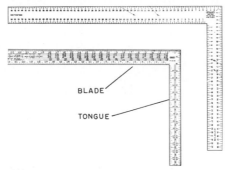

BLADE

TONGUE

Fig. 12–3 A steel framing square. The upper one is metric.

Fig. 12–4 A combination square with metric measurement.

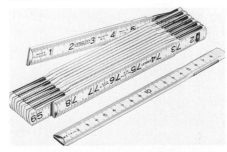

Fig. 12–5 An extension, folding zigzag rule with customary and metric units.

Fig. 12–6 A flexible steel tape with metric and customary scales.

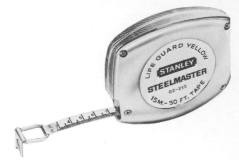

Fig. 12–7 A steel measuring tape available with metric or customary measurements.

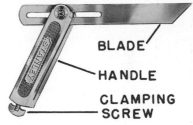

BLADE

HANDLE

CLAMPING SCREW

Fig. 12–8 A bevel tool.

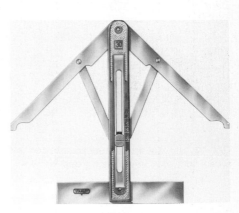

Fig. 12–9 An angle divider.

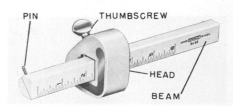

PIN

THUMBSCREW

HEAD

BEAM

Fig. 12–10 A wooden marking gage.

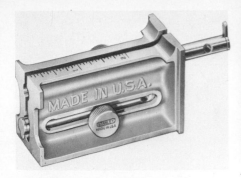

Fig. 12–11 A butt gage for marking hinge gains.

Fig. 12–16 Squaring a line across a board.

Fig. 12–17 Laying out a measurement with the rule on edge.

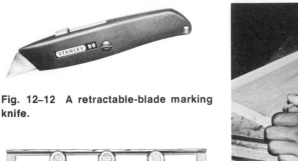

Fig. 12–12 A retractable-blade marking knife.

Fig. 12–18 Measuring and marking with a flexible rule.

Fig. 12–13 An aluminum level for testing horizontal and vertical trueness in carpentry.

Fig. 12–19 Measuring for width.

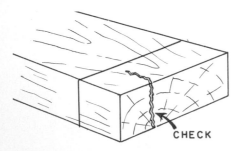

Fig. 12–14 An aluminum plumb bob ensures accuracy in plumbing and leveling.

Laying out length

1. Select the board with the fewest checks, cracks, or blemishes (Fig. 12-15).

2. Square a line across the face (first surface) of the board (Fig. 12-16).

3. Lay out and mark the desired length (Figs. 12-17 and 12-18).

4. Square this line across the board, as in step 2.

Laying out width and thickness

1. Measure and mark the desired width (Figs. 12-19, 12-20, and 12-21).

2. Divide the board into any number of equal parts. Lay the rule on its edge across the board in a diagonal (slanting) direction and mark the divisions (Fig. 12-22).

Fig. 12–15 A board marked to avoid checks or cracks.

CHECK

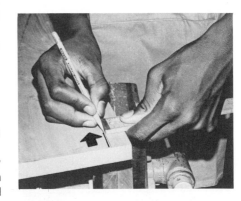

Fig. 12–20 A rule and pencil used for gaging width.

Fig. 12–21 Scribing a line with a marking gage.

Laying out an edge

Extend a line across the edge of the board (Fig. 12-23) by continuing the face line (see Fig. 12-16).

Laying out an angle

1. Adjust the bevel tool to the angle desired (Figs. 12-24 and 12-25).

2. Hold the handle of the bevel against the face, or edge, of the board. Mark along the bevel blade.

Fig. 12–24 Adjusting the bevel to the desired angle against a square.

Fig. 12–22 Dividing a board into equal parts.

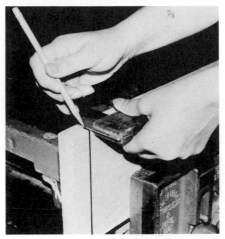

Fig. 12–23 Extending a line across an edge.

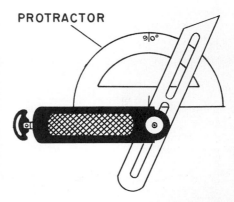

Fig. 12–25 Adjusting a bevel tool to the desired angle with the protractor.

unit 13

Laying out geometric designs

It is frequently necessary to draw arcs and circles, to enlarge patterns, and to trace around a template. Parts of projects often have hexagonal (six-sided), octagonal (eight-sided), and elliptical (oval) shapes. Additional shapes and forms are described in Unit 6, Understanding Working Drawings.

Tools

The **dividers** (Fig. 13-1) is a layout tool used by both wood- and metal-workers.

Trammel points (Fig. 13-2) are movable scribers on a bar. They are used for laying out arcs and circles which are too large for the dividers or compass.

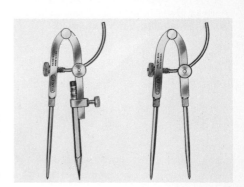

Fig. 13–1 Two types of dividers: one with a pencil and one with a scriber.

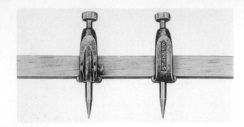

Fig. 13–2 Trammel points.

Fig. 13–3 Setting dividers for a desired radius.

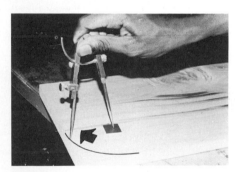

Fig. 13–4 Scribing an arc with dividers. A piece of cardboard under one point protects the wood grain from a dent.

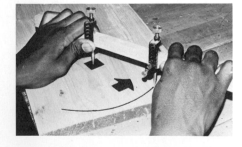

Fig. 13–5 Scribing an arc with trammel points.

Fig. 13–6 Marking off radius lengths on the circumference for a hexagon.

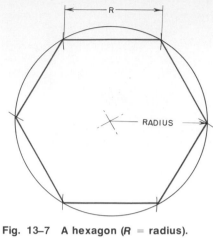

Fig. 13–7 A hexagon (R = radius).

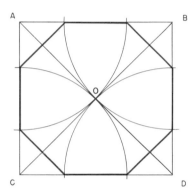

Fig. 13–8 An octagon.

Fig. 13–9 Drawing an ellipse.

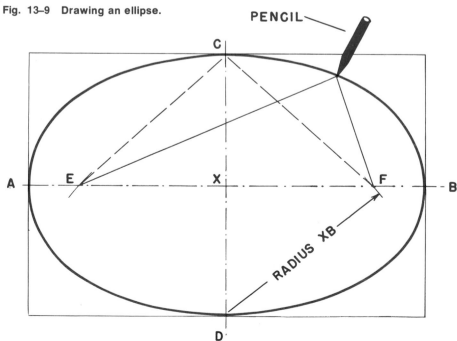

54

Laying out curves, arcs, and circles

1. Set the dividers or trammel points to the desired radius (Fig. 13-3).

2. Scribe (mark) the arc, curve, or circle (Figs. 13-4 and 13-5).

Laying out a hexagon

1. Set the dividers or compass to the length you want for one side of the hexagon.

2. Draw a circle, using the radius set in step 1.

3. Mark off distances on the circumference with the dividers set to the radius length (Fig. 13-6).

4. Connect the intersecting (crossing) points on the circumference with straight lines (Fig. 13-7). This forms a hexagon.

Laying out an octagon

1. Draw a square the size of the octagon.

2. Draw diagonal lines *AD* and *BC* (see Fig. 13-8).

3. Set the dividers to the distance of *A* to *O*. Scribe arcs intersecting the sides of the square. Use the corners as centers (Fig. 13-8).

4. Connect the intersecting points of the square with straight lines (Fig. 13-8). This is an octagon.

Laying out an ellipse

1. Draw a rectangle with the sides representing the width and length of the ellipse (oval) to be drawn (see Fig. 13-9).

2. Divide the rectangle with a horizontal line *AB* and a verticle line *CD* (see Fig. 13-9).

3. Use *C* and *D* as centers. Draw arcs with the dividers set for a radius of *XB*. The arcs will intersect line *AB* at *E* and *F* (see Fig. 13-9).

4. Fasten a string at points *E* and *F* so that it will reach to *C*. This will form triangle *CEF*.

5. Place a pencil against the string, starting at point *C*. Draw half the ellipse *ACB*. Repeat this for the other half.

Fig. 13–10 Tracing around a template.

Tracing around a template

Designs are often transferred by using cardboard or wooden **templates** (patterns). Figure 13-10 shows how to trace a design onto wood by using a template.

unit 14

Crosscutting and ripping

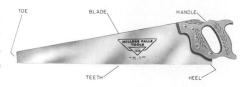

Fig. 14–1 A panel handsaw.

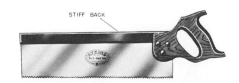

Fig. 14–2 A backsaw.

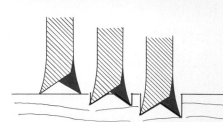

Fig. 14–3 A view of crosscut saw teeth (top) and their cutting action (bottom).

Handsaws are generally classified as either crosscut or rip, according to the cutting action of the teeth. The crosscut is designed to cut *across* the grain (fiber direction) of the wood. The ripsaw cuts *with* the grain. Backsaws, coping saws, and keyhole saws get their names from either their construction or the purpose for which they are intended. These are described in Unit 17, Cutting and Forming Irregular Pieces and Curves.

Tools

The panel **handsaw** (Fig. 14-1) and the **backsaw** (Fig. 14-2) are among the most popular hand tools for the woodworker. Figures 14-3 and 14-4 illustrate and explain the difference be-

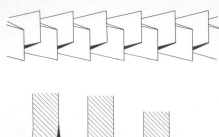

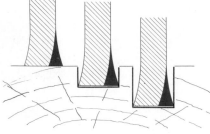

Fig. 14–4 A view of ripsaw teeth (top) and their cutting action (bottom).

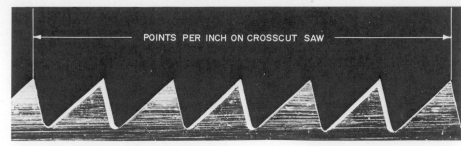

Fig. 14–5 Points per inch on a crosscut saw.

tween crosscut and ripsaw teeth. Figure 14-5 shows how points per inch are counted on handsaw blades. The number of points per inch is usually stamped on the blade near the handle of the saw.

The **miter box** and the **stiff-backed saw** (Fig. 14-6) together make a tool for accurate angle sawing.

Fig. 14–6 A miter box with a backsaw.

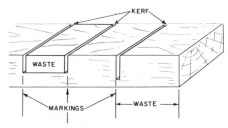

Fig. 14–7 Waste portions of a board.

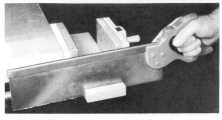

Fig. 14–9 Crosscutting a board held in a bench vise.

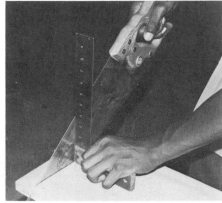

Fig. 14–10 Testing the angle of crosscutting with a try square.

Crosscutting

1. Lay out and mark the board using a sharp pencil and a straight-edge.
2. Fasten the board in a bench vise, or lay it across sawhorses.
3. Crosscut the board on the waste side of the marked line (Figs. 14-7, 14-8, and 14-9).

Ripping

1. Mark the board to be cut.
2. Fasten the board in a bench vise, or lay it on sawhorses.
3. Cut the board by ripping on the waste side of the mark (Fig. 14-10).

Cabinet sawing

1. Lay out and mark the board.
2. Fasten it in a bench vise, or hold it on a bench hook.
3. Saw on the waste side, using a backsaw (Fig. 14-11).

Fig. 14–8 Ripping a board on a sawhorse.

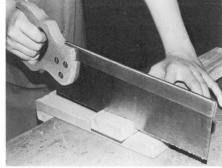

Fig. 14–11 Crosscutting a board on a bench hook.

Planing lumber

Planing a board requires knowledge of types of planes and how they are used. The basic skill of hand planing can be learned in squaring stock (lumber). A board has been "squared" when all its surfaces, edges, and ends are at 90-degree angles to each other. Figure 15-16 shows a sequence (order) of steps in squaring a board. This method is used by many.

Planes

There are many types of planes, but most are assembled, adjusted, and handled the same way. The main parts of a plane are shown in Fig. 15-1.

The illustrations and the brief descriptions of planes which follow will help you to select the best type for a particular job.

The **jack plane** (Fig. 15-2) is the most useful because of its size. It will do the work of the smoothing, jointer, and block planes (mentioned below). The most common jack plane has a bed, or bottom, that is 14 inches (355.6 mm) long.

The **smoothing**, or **bench, plane** (Fig. 15-3) is like the jack plane, but the bed is only about 9 inches (228.6 mm) long.

The **jointer**, or **fore, plane** (Fig. 15-4) is also like the jack except that the bottom is 22 to 30 inches (558.8 to 762 mm) long.

The **block plane** (Fig. 15-5) is approximately 6 inches (152.4 mm) long. It is ideal for planing end grain, because it is easy to handle.

The **bullnose rabbet plane** (Fig. 15-6) has a bed about 4 inches (101.6

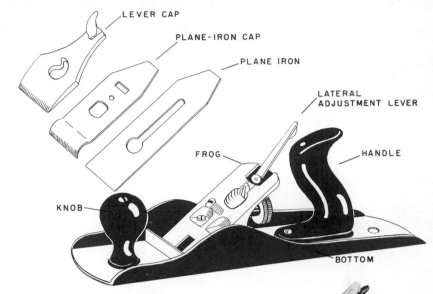

Fig. 15–1 The parts of a plane.

LEVER CAP

PLANE-IRON CAP

PLANE IRON

LATERAL ADJUSTMENT LEVER

HANDLE

FROG

KNOB

BOTTOM

Fig. 15–2 A jack plane.

Fig. 15–3 A smoothing or bench plane.

Fig. 15–4 A jointer or fore plane.

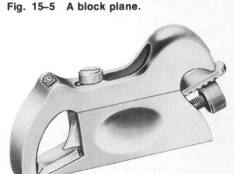

Fig. 15–5 A block plane.

Fig. 15–6 A bullnose rabbet plane.

mm) long. It is ideal for working in close quarters and in corners. A side rabbet plane is illustrated in Figure 15-7. Figure 15-8 shows a **rabbet**, or **fillister, plane.** The adjustable fence makes it possible to plane a rabbet (groove).

A **hand router plane** (Fig. 15-9) can also be used for cutting out rabbets and grooves.

Assembling and adjusting

Planes are assembled as follows:

1. Hone (sharpen) the cutting edge of the plane iron. Refer to Unit 173, Maintaining Basic Hand Tools.

2. Place the plane-iron cap against the flat side of the plane iron with the screw in the slot (Fig. 15-10).

3. Slide the cap to within 1/16 inch (1.5 mm) of the cutting edge of the blade (Fig. 15-11). Tighten the cap with a screwdriver.

4. Place this assembly in the plane with the bevel side of the blade on the frog (see Fig. 15-1).

5. Lay the lever cap over the plane-iron assembly; tighten the cap.

Adjust a plane as follows:

1. Adjust (move) the cutting edge with the lateral lever parallel to the slot in the bottom of the plane.

2. Turn the knurled adjustment nut carefully and precisely right or left to regulate the depth of the cutting edge (Fig. 15-12).

Planing a face surface

1. Fasten the board on the workbench between the vise dog and a bench stop. Place it so that you can plane in the direction of the fibers.

2. Adjust the cutting edge of the plane iron to cut evenly and not too deeply.

3. Plane the surface until it is smooth (Figs. 15-13, 15-14, 15-15). Figure 15-16 presents a set of basic steps in squaring stock. You might

Fig. 15-7   A side rabbet plane.

Fig. 15-8   A rabbet or fillister plane.

Fig. 15-9   An open-throat router plane.

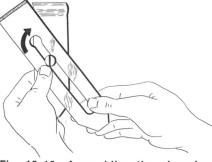

Fig. 15-10   Assembling the plane-iron cap to the plane iron.

Fig. 15-11   Aligning the cap and the plane iron.

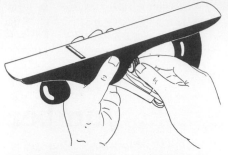

Fig. 15-12   Adjusting for cutting depth.

Fig. 15-13   Planing a surface.

Fig. 15-14   Testing the board for flatness.

Fig. 15-15   Testing diagonally for a wind.

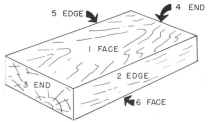

Fig. 15-16   Basic steps in planing a board.

wish to follow these if you are going to hand-plane all faces, edges, and ends of a board.

Planing an edge

1. Fasten the board in a vise with the best edge up. The direction of the grain should be away from you.
2. Plane the edge until it is square with the planed surface (Figs. 15-17, 15-18, and 15-19).

Planing an end

1. Fasten the board in a vise with the best end up.
2. Plane the end. Use one of the three methods suggested in Figs. 15-20, 15-21, and 15-22.
3. Test the end for squareness (Fig. 15-23) to the planed surface (face). Test it for squareness to the planed edge (Fig. 15-24).

Planing the opposite end

1. Measure, mark, and cut the board to the desired length. Allow $\frac{1}{16}$ inch (2 mm) for sawing and planing to the line.
2. Plane the end to the marked line, square with the planed face and the planed edge.

Planing the opposite edge

1. Measure, mark, and rip the board to the desired width. Allow $\frac{1}{16}$ inch (2 mm) for planing to the line.
2. Plane this edge to the line so that it will be squared with the planed face and with both ends.

Planing the last surface

1. Mark the board for thickness, using a marking gage.
2. Plane the last surface (face) to the gage line. Test it for squareness.

Fig. 15–17   Planing an edge.

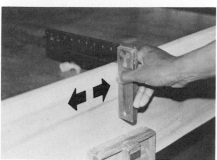

Fig. 15–18   Testing an edge for squareness.

Fig. 15–19   Testing an edge for straightness.

Fig. 15–20   Planing an end by chamfering a corner.

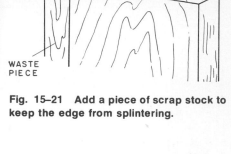

Fig. 15–21   Add a piece of scrap stock to keep the edge from splintering.

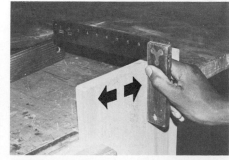

Fig. 15–22   Planing end grain from both directions.

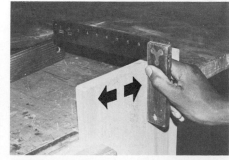

Fig. 15–23   Testing an end for squareness to the face.

Fig. 15–24   Testing an end for squareness against the edge.

unit 16

Planing a chamfer and a bevel

A chamfer and a bevel look similar (Fig. 16-1). A chamfer is an edge decoration; a bevel can be either an edge decoration or a way to fit two boards together at an angle. The chamfer is usually planed to a 45-degree angle; the bevel can be made at any angle.

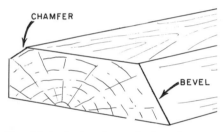

Fig. 16–1 A chamfer and a bevel.

Laying out a chamfer or a bevel

Mark light guidelines for the chamfer or bevel. Use a pencil (Fig. 16-2) or a marking gage.

Planing and testing

1. Fasten the board in a vise. Plane the chamfer or bevel to the marked line (Fig. 16-3).
2. Test the angle of the chamfer or bevel with a sliding bevel (Fig. 16-4).

Fig. 16–2 Gaging a line with a pencil will not damage the end grain of the wood.

Fig. 16–3 Planing a chamfer to a marked line.

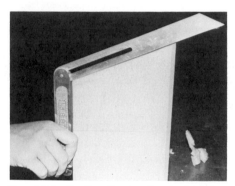

Fig. 16–4 Testing the angle of a bevel.

unit 17

Cutting and forming irregular pieces and curves

Several excellent woodworking tools for sawing, cutting, shaping, and forming irregular parts of projects are listed and illustrated here.

Tools

The **coping saw** (Fig. 17-1) is especially useful for cutting thin boards and plywood.

The **compass saw** (Fig. 17-2) cuts inside curves after a hole has been bored near the line to be sawed.

The **spokeshave** (Fig. 17-3) is used mostly for forming concave (inside-curve) and convex (outside-curve) edges.

A **drawknife** (Fig. 17-4) cuts away waste stock quickly.

Wood, or **cabinet, files** (Fig. 17-5) have various shapes. Their lengths vary from 4 to 14 inches (101.6 to 355.6 mm). They are used to smooth edges. Figure 17-6 shows the patterns of teeth on single- and double-cut files.

Edge-forming tools (Fig. 17-7) can be used for planing, filing, shaping, and smoothing.

The **file card** (Fig. 17-8) has steel bristles that clean the teeth of a file.

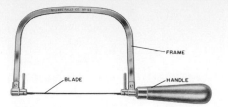

Fig. 17–1   A coping saw.

Fig. 17–2   A compass saw.

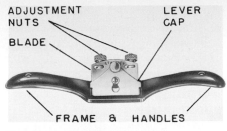

Fig. 17–3   A spokeshave.

Fig. 17–4   A drawknife.

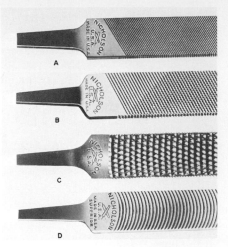

Fig. 17–6   Patterns of file teeth: (A) single-cut, (B) double-cut, (C) rasp (coarse)-cut, and (D) vixen(curved)-cut.

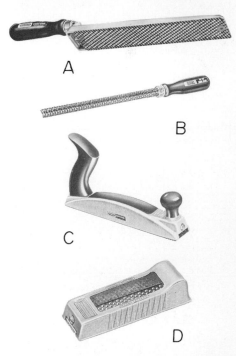

Fig. 17–7   Surface- and edge-forming tools: (A) flat file, (B) round file, (C) plane, and (D) block plane.

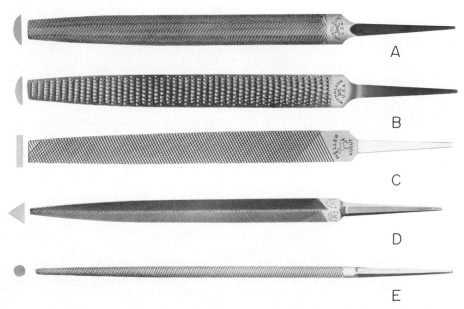

Fig. 17–5   Wood and cabinet files: (A) half-round, (B) rasp, (C) flat, (D) triangular, and (E) round.

Fig. 17–8   A file card.

Cutting with a coping saw

1. Lay out the design directly on the stock, or trace it around a template (see Fig. 14-10).

2. Hold the stock on a V block, or fasten it in a vise. Cut with the coping saw (Figs. 17-9 and 17-10).

Cutting with a compass saw

1. Transfer or draw the design on the wood.

2. Bore a hole in the waste part of the wood. Start the cut.

3. Saw to within $1/16$ inch (2 mm) of the line (Fig. 17-11).

Shaping with a drawknife

1. Fasten the stock in a bench vise so that you will cut in the direction of the grain.

2. Carefully cut away the waste portion of the wood. Use short strokes pulling toward your body (Fig. 17-12). Proceed carefully.

Forming with the spokeshave

1. Fasten the board securely in a bench vise.

2. Pull or push the spokeshave. Smooth the curved edge to the pattern line (Fig. 17-13).

Forming with a file and the forming tool

1. Fasten the board in the bench vise.

2. Push the file or the forming tool over the edge of the wood (Figs. 17-14 and 17-15). Clean the file frequently with a file card (Fig. 17-16).

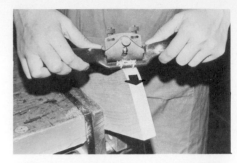

Fig. 17–13 Smoothing a curved edge with the spokeshave.

Fig. 17–14 Filing a curved edge.

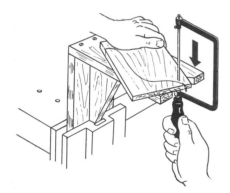

Fig. 17–9 Sawing on a V block.

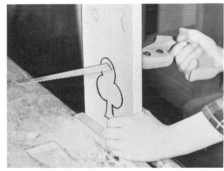

Fig. 17–11 Internal cutting with a compass saw.

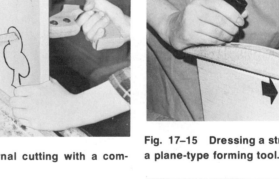

Fig. 17–15 Dressing a straight edge with a plane-type forming tool.

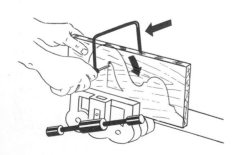

Fig. 17–10 Cutting with a coping saw.

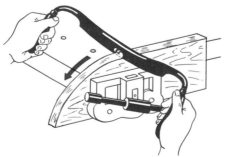

Fig. 17–12 Cutting with a drawknife.

Fig. 17–16 Cleaning a file with a file card.

Trimming with a wood chisel

The wood chisel is used for cutting, trimming, fitting, and shaping. This tool must have a sharp cutting edge with the correct bevel (slant).

Tools

Wood chisels are classified as **socket** or **tang**, depending on how the handle is fastened to the blade (Fig. 18-1). The width of the blade determines sizes, which range from 1/8 to 1 inch (3.18 to 25.4 mm) by eighths and from 1 to 2 inches (25 to 51 mm) by fourths.

A wood or fiber **mallet** (Fig. 18-2) is used to exert additional pressure in chiseling.

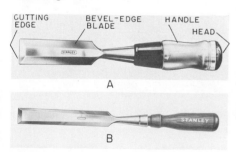

Fig. 18–1 Wood chisels: (A) tang butt and (B) socket firmer.

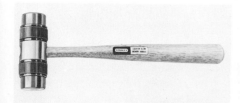

Fig. 18–2 A soft plastic-face mallet.

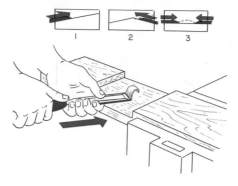

Fig. 18–3 Horizontal chiseling. Note the sequence of steps shown for through chiseling.

Fig. 18–4 Chiseling a mortise vertically.

Horizontal and vertical chiseling

Push the chisel with your right hand. Guide the blade with your left (Figs. 18-3 and 18-4).

Curved chiseling and trimming

1. Push the chisel with a shearing motion when you cut a round corner (Fig. 18-5). Keep the beveled side up.

2. Trim a concave (inside) edge by holding the beveled side of the chisel against the wood (Fig. 18-6). Always cut with the grain.

Fig. 18–5 Trimming an outside curve with a chisel.

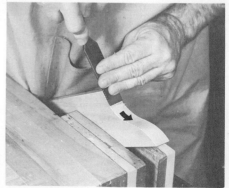

Fig. 18–6 Trimming an inside curve with a chisel.

unit 19

Smoothing a board by scraping

Scrapers are used to remove irregularities and blemishes from surfaces and edges. They smooth with a turned, or **burred,** edge (Fig. 19-1).

Tools

Hand scraper blades are of various shapes (Fig. 19-2). Properly sharpened blades make thin shavings. Hand scrapers are either pulled or pushed.

Other types are the **cabinet scraper** (Fig. 19-3), which must be

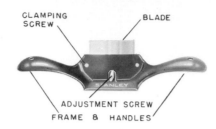

CLAMPING SCREW
BLADE
ADJUSTMENT SCREW
FRAME & HANDLES

Fig. 19-3 A cabinet scraper.

Fig. 19-4 A pull, box, or floor scraper.

pushed, and the **pull, box,** or **floor scraper** (Fig. 19-4), which is pulled across the work.

A **scraper plane** looks like a smoothing plane except that the blade is held forward to scrape rather than to cut.

Hand scraping

Grasp the scraper blade firmly between the thumb and fingers. Spring it to a slight curve. The blade is pushed or pulled (Figs. 19-5 and 19-6).

Smoothing with cabinet scrapers

Scrape the surface of the wood, using long, even strokes. Work with the grain (Figs. 19-7 and 19-8).

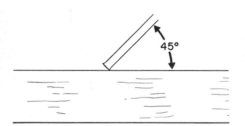

Fig. 19-1 A burred edge and angle for scraping.

Fig. 19-2 Hand scraper blades in various shapes.

Fig. 19-5 Pushing a scraper blade to smooth a surface.

Fig. 19-6 Pulling a scraper blade to smooth a surface.

Fig. 19-7 Smoothing with a cabinet scraper.

Fig. 19-8 Smoothing with a pull scraper.

unit 20

Boring and drilling holes

Holes must be bored or drilled in wood for screws, bolts, dowels, internal sawing, and ornamentation. Some of the tools for performing these processes are described below.

Tools

The **ratchet brace** (Fig. 20-1) holds bits that have a square **tang** (shank).

A **hand drill** (Fig. 20-2) is usually used for drilling holes $1/4$ inch (6 mm) or less in diameter. A straight-shank drill should be used with this tool.

The **automatic push drill** (Fig. 20-3) is sometimes used instead of the hand drill.

Auger bits (Figs. 20-4 and 20-5) vary in length from 7 to 10 inches (178 to 254 mm). Dowel auger bits are only $5 1/2$ inches (140 mm) long. Auger bits are sized by sixteenths ($1/16$) of an inch (1.6 mm) from $3/16$ to 1 inch (4.8 to 25.4 mm). The number stamped on the square tang shows the bit size in sixteenths of an inch.

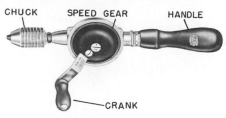

Fig. 20–2   A hand drill.

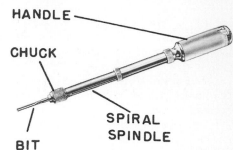

Fig. 20–3   An automatic push drill.

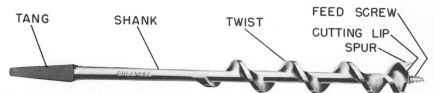

Fig. 20–4   A single-twist auger bit.

Fig. 20–5   A double-spiral electrician's auger bit.

Fig. 20–6   A wood-boring brace drill.

Fig. 20–7   An expansive bit with extra cutter.

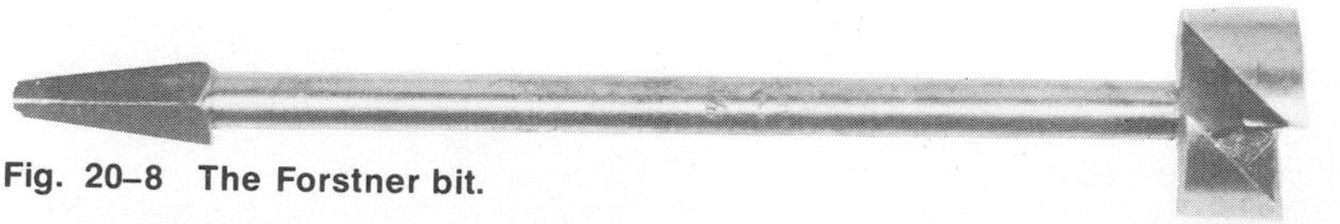

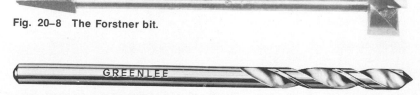

Fig. 20–8   The Forstner bit.

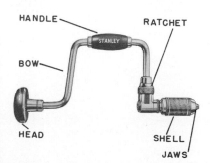

Fig. 20–1   A ratchet brace.

Fig. 20–9   A straight-shank drill.

The **wood-boring brace drill** (Fig. 20-6) makes holes for screws, nails, and bolts.

The **expansive bit** (Fig. 20-7) bores holes from 1/2 inch to 3 inches (13 to 76 mm) in diameter. It has a movable spur, or cutter. Cutters are available to bore holes up to 5 inches (127 mm) in diameter.

A **Forstner bit** (Fig. 20-8) will bore a flat-bottom hole because it has no lead screw.

The **straight-shank drill** (Fig. 20-9) is used with a hand drill. Fractional drill sizes are marked in sixty-fourths (1/64) of an inch (0.4 mm).

Automatic-drill bits (Fig. 20-10) fit into the automatic push drill (Fig. 20-3).

Two types of **depth gauges** are shown in Figs. 20-11 and 20-12. They control the depth of boring by stopping the drill at the desired level.

The **doweling jigs** (Figs. 20-13 and 20-14) are often used to guide and direct a bit for boring holes in dowel joining.

An **awl** (Fig. 20-15) is used for marking the location for boring and drilling holes.

Boring a hole

1. Fasten a suitable bit of the correct size in the chuck of the brace (Fig. 20-16).

2. Mark and locate the center to be bored or drilled, using an awl (Fig. 20-17).

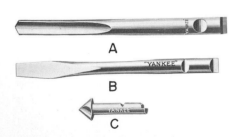

Fig. 20–10 Automatic drill bits: (A) straight bit, (B) screwdriver bit, and (C) countersink bit.

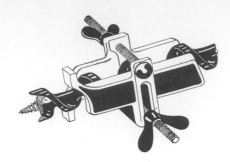

Fig. 20–11 An adjustable depth gage.

Fig. 20–14 A self-centering doweling jig.

Fig. 20–12 A screw-type adjustable depth gage.

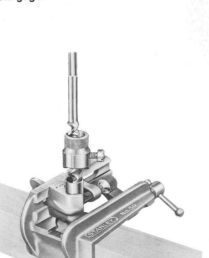

Fig. 20–13 An adjustable doweling jig with depth gage.

Fig. 20–15 An awl.

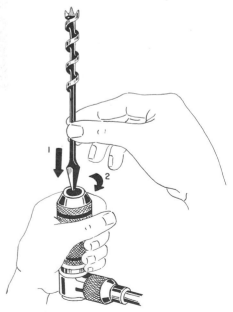

Fig. 20–16 Fastening an auger bit in a ratchet-brace chuck.

66

3. Bore the hole carefully (see Figs. 20-18, 20-19, and 20-20).

4. There are two ways to bore a hole through a board. Fasten a piece of scrap wood on the back, as shown in Fig. 20-18, or follow the two-step procedure shown in Fig. 20-20.

5. Figure 20-21 illustrates the use of a depth gage for boring a dowel hole to a specified depth. Figure 20-22 shows a hole being bored with the aid of a doweling jig.

Drilling a hole

1. Use a straight-shank or automatic drill. Fasten the bit in the chuck.

2. Place the bit on the spot marked as the center of the hole. Drill the hole carefully as shown in Figs. 20-23 and 20-24.

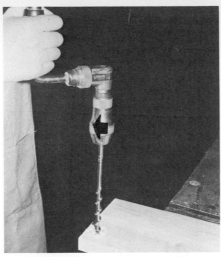

Fig. 20–19 Boring a hole vertically.

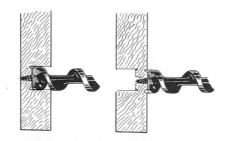

Fig. 20–20 A two-step procedure for boring a hole through a piece of wood.

Fig. 20–17 Starting a lead hole with an awl.

Fig. 20–18 Boring a hole horizontally. (Note the scrap wood on the back to keep the piece from splintering.)

Fig. 20–21 Boring a hole with a self-centering jig and a depth gage.

Fig. 20–22 Boring a hole with a doweling jig.

Fig. 20–23 Drilling a hole with a hand drill.

Fig. 20–24 Drilling a hole with the automatic push drill.

67

unit **21**

Sanding by hand

A completed wood project must be thoroughly sanded before the finish is applied. Sanding is done with any of several abrasive materials. These materials may be made of artificial substances or of natural stone.

Abrasives

Sandpaper is the abrasive most often used on wood. It gets its name from its grit surface, which resembles sand. It is, however, crushed flint or quartz, and it is sometimes called **flint paper**.

Table 21-1   AN ABRASIVE GRADING CHART

Classification and use	Artificial — Silicon Carbide Aluminum Oxide	Natural — Garnet	Flint	Emery
Extra coarse (Sanding coarse wood texture)	12 16 20	16 (4) 20 (3$^1/_2$)		
Very coarse (Second stage in sanding wood texture)	24 30 36	24 (3) 30 (2$^1/_2$) 36 (2)	extra coarse	very coarse
Coarse (Third stage in sanding wood texture)	40 50	40 ($^1/_2$) 50 (1)	coarse	
Medium (Removing rough sanding texture	60 80 100	60 ($^1/_2$) 80 (0) 100 (2/0)	medium	coarse medium
Fine (First stage in sanding before applying finish)	120 150 180	120 (3/0) 150 (4/0) 180 (5/0)	fine	fine
Very fine (Second stage in sanding before applying finish)	220 240 280	220 (6/0) 240 (7/0) 280 (8/0)	extra fine	
Extra fine (Rubbing between finish coats)	320 360 400 500 600	320 (9/0) 400 (10/0)		

Garnet paper is more durable than flint paper. It has a reddish color.

Emery cloth (or paper) is a tough, black abrasive substance. It is usually used for polishing metal.

Abrasive papers and cloth are graded from **coarse** to **fine** as shown in Table 21-1.

Preparing a surface for sanding

1. Use a scraper to remove all planer marks and traces of glue.
2. Raise the dents in the wood by moistening the immediate area.
3. Fill small knots, holes, checks, and cracks by melting in colored stick shellac or lacquer (Fig. 21-1). Colored wood plastic or dough (Fig. 21-2) can be pressed into the defect.

Sanding

1. Tear a piece of sandpaper or other abrasive into four equal parts (Fig. 21-3).
2. Fold the sandpaper around a block of wood, and sand all flat surfaces and edges **with the grain.** Use an even pressure (Fig. 21-4). Sand irregular, concave, or shaped edges as shown in Fig. 21-5.
3. Start sanding with coarse abrasive paper, then medium next, and finish with a fine grit.

Fig. 21-3 Tearing sandpaper against a metal edge.

Fig. 21-4 Sanding a surface with the grain.

Fig. 21-5 Sanding a rounded edge.

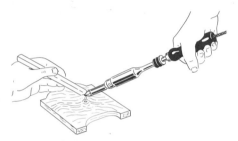

Fig. 21-1 Melting a shellac or lacquer stick to fill a knothole or blemish.

Fig. 21-2 Pressing in dough or wood plastic to fill a defect.

unit 22

Discussion topics on measurement, layout, and hand tool processes

1. List ten safety rules that apply to hand tool woodworking.

2. How many sixteenths ($^1/_{16}$) are there in $^1/_4$, $^3/_8$, $^1/_2$, $^3/_4$, $^7/_8$, 1, $1^3/_8$, and $1^1/_2$?
3. Define and draw each of the following: (a) hexagon, (B) octagon, and (c) ellipse.
4. What are trammel points used for?
5. At what hour of the day, and on what day of the week, do most accidents happen in school industrial laboratories or shops? Why?
6. Illustrate the difference between ripsaw and crosscut saw teeth. Explain and describe the cutting action of each.
7. Name and describe five types of hand planes.

8. What is meant by a "squared" board?
9. List the six general steps sometimes used for squaring a board.
10. Illustrate the difference between a chamfer and a bevel.
11. List and describe the functions of six tools used in cutting and forming irregular pieces and curves.
12. List the two classifications of wood chisels.
13. Give the names of six kinds of drills and bits. Cite a specific use for each.
14. What are the sizes of auger bits which have these numbers stamped on the tang: 4, 7, 9, 11, 13, and 16?

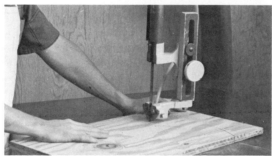

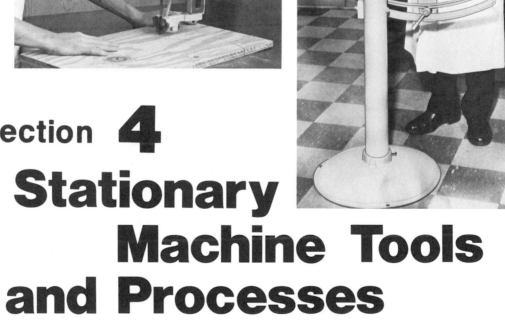

section **4**

Stationary Machine Tools and Processes

unit 23

Safety for stationary machine tools

Stationary machine tools are safe when proper precautions are observed, understood, and followed. The ones listed here apply in general to all types of floor-model power machines. They also pertain specifically to individual machines. Study, review, and use these safety rules before using any machine.

General safety for all power machines

Permission. Always request and obtain permission from the instructor or person in charge before you start to operate the machine.

Clothing. Avoid wearing loose clothing. Button or roll up your sleeves. Remove your necktie.

Jewelry. Remove rings from your fingers. A ring could get caught in splinters and cause serious injury. It can also annoy you while you work.

Eye protection. Always wear safety goggles or a face shield when operating a power-machine tool.

Hand protection. Keep your hands away from moving or operating parts of the machine.

Safety guards. Make certain that safety guards and hold-down devices are in place and properly secured before you start the machine.

Illumination. Direct plenty of shadowfree light on the work to be performed.

Adjustments. Before starting a machine, check all adjustments to see that they are accurately set. Make no adjustments when the machine is in operation.

Instruction manual. Follow the instructions of the manual that applies to the power machine you are using. This is especially true when making certain adjustments or setups for unusual processes.

Material inspection. Inspect lumber before you process it. Remove tacks, brads, nails, finishes, or anything else that might dull or damage blades or cutters.

Accessories. Select and install properly sharpened saw blades, cutters, shaper heads, and other cutting and abrasive devices.

Shavings and sawdust. Remove shavings and sawdust from machine surfaces before turning on the power.

Starting. Allow the machine to come to maximum speed before starting any processes.

Stopping. Shut off the power, and be certain you do not leave the machine until it has come to a complete stop.

Safety for a specific machine. Read and follow the safety precautions that are listed for each specific machine.

Safety for the circular saw

General safety. Observe the general safety precautions given at the beginning of this unit.

Stance. Stand to one side of the saw to avoid a board that may kick back.

Use of guard. Always use a safety guard if the saw teeth extend above the stock being cut.

Saw teeth extension. When using the saw blade, set it to extend approximately $1/8$ inch (3 mm) above the stock.

Blade sharpness. Keep the saw blades sharp.

Teeth and cutter direction. Be sure the saw, dado head, or molding-head teeth and cutters point toward you as you stand on the operator's side of the saw.

Reaching. Never reach behind a saw blade to pull stock through.

Freehand sawing. Always use the rip fence or the cut-off guide. Sawing freehand can be dangerous.

Rip fence. Remove the rip fence when you crosscut.

Splitter attachment. Whenever possible, especially in ripping, use the splitter attachment. It is fitted with antikickback fingers.

Push stick. Use a push stick when you rip narrow stock.

Safety for the radial saw

General safety. Observe the general safety precautions given at the beginning of this unit.

Saw blade and cutters. Make certain that the teeth of the saw blade or cutters point in the direction of the arrow on the saw guard.

Holding stock. Always hold the stock firmly against the table-top guide fence.

Protection of hands. Keep your hands out of the line of the saw blade and cutters. Do not wear rings.

Adjustments. All operating adjustments should be made and secured (locked) before starting the machine.

Antikickback guard. Make sure that this guard is properly adjusted. When ripping and ploughing, always feed the stock from the opposite end of the antikickback guard.

Saw pull. Remember that this saw *pulls* itself *into* the work. It is necessary to *push back* on the handle to prevent the saw blade from cutting too fast and choking.

Push stick. Use a push stick when ripping and cutting grooves and rabbets on narrow stock, even though your fingers may fit between the blade and the fence.

Cutting multiple pieces. When cutting two or more pieces at the same time, never put one piece on top of another. The top one may kick over the fence. Follow the instructions given in this section on gang, or multiple, cutting.

Removing stock. When sawing and cutting across stock, always return the saw cutter head to its starting position before you remove the stock.

Safety for the band saw

General safety. Observe the general safety precautions given at the beginning of this unit.

Blade condition. Examine the blade frequently to make sure it is in good condition. A rhythmic click may indicate that the blade is cracked.

Blade tension. Check the tension of the blade, following the manufacturer's specifications.

Blade lead. Check the blade for lead. An improper set can cause it to pull to one side, thereby cutting in that direction (tapering).

Blade breakage. If the band saw blade breaks while the machine is operating, turn off the power and move away until the machine stops.

Blade size. Use the correct size blade for your cutting.

Table alignment. Check carefully to see that the saw table is square with the blade.

Upper saw guide. Adjust the upper saw guide to within approximately $1/2$ inch (13 mm) of the stock to be cut.

Hand protection. Always keep your hand at least 2 inches (51 mm) away from the blade.

Stance. Take a firm, balanced stance (position of standing) slightly to the

left of the front of the band saw table.

Sawing. Feed the board into the band saw blade firmly, but do not push it too fast.

Freehand sawing. Freehand sawing on the band saw should be attempted only when the work to be sawed rests flat on the table.

Sawing radius. Make sure the radius of the cut is not too small for the width of the blade.

Relief cuts. Study the layout on the board before cutting. Often relief cuts are necessary before the outline cut is made. Make short cuts first, then longer ones.

Curves. Cut curves gradually. A sudden twist may break the blade.

Completing the cut. Be sure to cut through the waste stock when possible, rather than back out of your piece with the blade.

Removing stock. When it is necessary to back the saw blade out of a long cut, turn off the machine and allow the blade to come to a complete stop; then remove the board.

Safety for the jig saw

General safety. Observe the general safety precautions given at the beginning of this unit.

Blade size. Use the proper size blade for the work to be sawed.

Blade teeth. Make certain that the teeth of the jigsaw or saber saw blade are pointing down.

Blade fastening. Fasten the blade correctly in the chuck (or chucks).

Tension. Adjust the tension sleeve properly if the upper chuck is fastened to the blade.

Hold-down clamp. Regulate the hold-down clamp to exert slight pressure on the top of the piece being cut.

Guide adjustment. Adjust the upper guide to about $1/8$ inch (3 mm) above the material being cut.

Plan work. Lay out carefully and plan your work before sawing.

Starting cut. Keep one hand firmly

on the piece to be cut as you turn on the power switch.

Curve cuts. When making curve cuts, *do not* push the stock into the blade. *Turn* it on the table until the curve has been cut.

Safety for the jointer and the jointer/surfacer

General safety. Observe the general safety precautions given at the beginning of this unit.

Sharpness. Check to see that the blades are sharp.

Guard. Keep the safety guard in place and ready to use at all times.

Stance. Take a firm position at the left of the machine. Never stand at the end of the front table.

Planing. Plane only boards longer than 12 inches (305 mm). Shorter boards are unsafe because your hands might get too close to the cutter knives. Plane short boards by hand.

Push block. Use a push block when surfacing boards on the jointer.

Position of work. Always hold the board firmly against the fence or on the table of the jointer.

Warpage. Surface the concave (hollow) side of a warped board first.

End grain. Do not attempt to plane or joint on the regular jointer the end grain of boards less than 8 inches (203 mm) wide.

Direction of cut. Always try to plane in the direction of the grain.

Thickness. Do not surface a board less than $1/2$ inch (51 mm) thick on the jointer. It might split and shatter.

Depth of cut. Do not attempt too deep a cut except for a rabbet cut.

Safety for the planer (surfacer)

General safety. Observe the general safety precautions given at the beginning of this unit.

Board sizes. Do not surface boards less than 14 inches (355 mm) in length and $1/4$ inch (6 mm) in thickness. The board should be sufficiently long for the outfeed roll to start pulling it before the infeed roll releases it.

Stance. Stand at the side of the board to operate the feed control. thickness hand wheel, and switch.

Hands. Keep your fingers away from the top and bottom sides of the board as it is being fed through the planer.

Planing the first surface. When possible, do this on a jointer.

Feeding stock. After the board starts going through the planer, remove your hands from the board and stand aside to avoid possible kickback.

Depth of cut. Do not attempt to make a deep cut. One-sixteenth inch (1.5 mm) is usually satisfactory.

Planed stock. When the board comes through the surfacer, be sure to grasp the board, or see that it feeds onto a table.

Safety for the drill press

General safety. Observe the general safety precautions given at the beginning of this unit.

Speed. Check and adjust the pulley-and-belt combination to see that the correct speed is set up. Use the recommended speeds for the various processes according to the material being bored, such as softwoods or hardwoods.

Interchangeable spindles and chuck. Use the recommended spindle or chuck.

Guard. Keep the guard on the pulleys and belt to prevent your hair and clothing from getting caught.

Chuck key. Always remove the chuck key before starting the drill press.

Attachments. Routing, shaping, and mortising attachments must be properly fastened and adjusted.

Bits and cutters. Use only the recommended bits and cutters for the job to be done.

Clamping small pieces. Clamp small pieces in a drill vise or to the table.

Position of work. Hold the work firmly so that it will not fly or spin off the table to injure you or someone else. Often it is best to fasten the piece securely with clamps.

Boring and drilling. Bore and drill holes without using too much pressure. If the wood smokes, release the pressure temporarily and work more slowly.

Safety for the mortiser

General safety. Observe the general safety precautions given at the beginning of this unit.

Chisels and bits. Make certain that the chisel and bit are the same size and that the bit extends beyond the chisel about $1/16$ inch (2 mm).

Position of stock. Stock must be securely held on the table against the fence.

Safety for the shaper and the router/shaper

General safety. Observe the general safety precautions given at the beginning of this unit.

Cutters. See that the cutter knives or the cutter are *fastened securely* before you use the shaper.

Cutter knives. When using separate cutter knives, check to see that both knives are the same width.

Maintenance tools. Remove all wrenches and special tools used in setting up the machine before you turn on the power.

Spindle. After the cutter head has been securely fastened to the spindle, see that the spindle turns freely *before* turning on the power.

Cutter position. Arrange the cutter head on the spindle so that the unused portions of the cutters or knives are *below* the table.

Direction of rotation. If the shaper has a reversing switch, make certain the direction of feed will *oppose* the direction of rotation. Always feed *into* the cutting edge.

Stance. Maintain a well-balanced position on both feet when operating the shaper.

Handling the work. Hold the board firmly against the fence and the table for straight work. Hold the board firmly against the rub collar on the spindle for irregular pieces.

Starting pin. Be sure the starting pin is securely in place on the table when shaping against the rub collar.

Starting cut. When using the rub collar for a guide, start the cut *away* from any corner.

Moldings. Plan the work carefully to use the correct sequence (order) of cutter forms to produce molding of the pattern desired.

Shaping ends. Boards *less* than 10 inches (254 mm) wide should *not* be shaped on the end, unless the shaper has a sliding jig to clamp on the board and hold it in place.

Safety on the wood lathe

General safety. Observe the general safety precautions given at the beginning of this unit.

Lathe tools. Lathe tools (chisels) must be kept *sharp* at all times.

Tool rest. The tool rest should be kept as *close as possible* to the stock being turned for better leverage. Do not adjust the rest while the lathe is running.

Speed. Run the lathe at the correct speed for the work. Start lathe jobs at the *slowest* speed, and rough the stock down to form before a faster speed is used.

Rough stock. Rotate rough stock *by hand* to be sure it will clear the tool rest.

Tailstock. Adjustments on the tailstock must be secure before you attempt to do spindle turning.

Dead center. Always add a few drops of oil to the dead center before turning on the lathe.

Turning. Hold turning tools firmly with *both hands* while cutting stock.

Spindle turning. Wherever possible, try to cut with the chisels.

Measuring with the caliper. Always stop the lathe before you measure with a caliper.

Faceplate. Be sure to use screws only long enough to hold the faceplate to the wood stock (block). When turning the piece, avoid cutting too deeply and striking the screws.

Sanding and finishing. Always remove the tool rest when sanding or applying finish.

Safety for floor-model sanders

General safety. Observe the general safety precautions given at the beginning of this unit.

Hands. Work safely by keeping both hands away from moving abrasive disks, belts, or drums.

Sanding disk. Be sure the abrasive disk is fastened firmly to the metal plate.

Burning the wood or abrasive. Move the work about to avoid heating and burning any portion of the abrasive disk, belt, or wood.

Belt tension. Check that the sanding belt is neither too loose nor too tight.

Abrasive belts and drums. Select the correct grade of grit and size of belt or drum for the sanding operation to be done.

Belt tracking. Check the installation of an abrasive belt to see that it tracks (runs) evenly on the pulleys.

Belt direction. Note the direction in which the belt, disk, or drum turns. This helps you decide how to hold the piece to be sanded, or how to hold the pressure of the belt on the project.

Disk direction. Sand only on the downstroke half of the disk for better control.

Sanding small pieces. Do not sand small pieces on floor-model sanders without a jig to hold them securely.

Push stick. Use a push stick in sanding small or thin pieces on the small horizontal-belt sander.

section **4a**

Circular saw processes

unit **24**

General information about the circular saw

The circular, or table, saw is one of the oldest known power machines used in woodworking. The modern one (Fig. 24-1) performs many processes. The kind of circular saw most common for the school shop or laboratory and home craft use has one arbor (shaft) and one blade. The universal production models often have a double arbor with two saw blades. Either blade can be raised and put into use without changing blades on the arbor. These are usually ripsaw and crosscut blades.

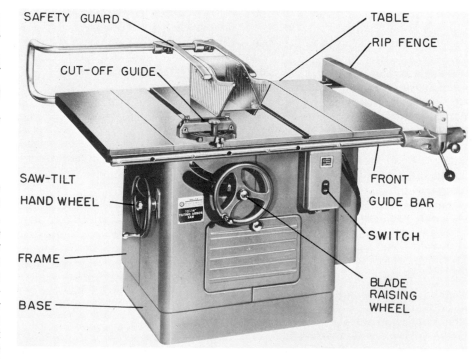

Fig. 24–1 A 12-inch (304.8-mm) circular, table, or variety saw.

Sizes and types

The size of a circular (variety) saw is measured by the largest-diameter saw blade it will accommodate. For school use, the size varies from a 10- to a 14-inch-diameter (254- to 356-mm-diameter) blade. The 10-inch (254-mm) blade runs at a speed of about 3100 revolutions per minute (r/min). The cutting speed, measured in surface feet per minute, is approximately 8100 sfm (2469 meters per minute, m/min). The maximum speed is about 9000 sfm (2743 m/min). Figure 24-1 is a tilting-arbor saw.

Saw parts and uses

The main parts of the circular saw are the arbor, frame, table, rip fence, miter-gage cutoff guide, saw-tilt hand wheel, blade-raising wheel, safety guard, and electric motor.

Arbor. The arbor has a shaft that holds the blade, dado head, or molding head.
Frame. The frame includes the base and the housing for the internal operating mechanisms and the motor.
Table. The table supports the rip fence, cutoff guide, and safety guard.

Rip fence. The rip fence is used as a guide for ripping.
Miter-gage cutoff guide. The miter-gage cutoff guide is used as a guide for crosscutting.
Saw-tilt hand wheel. This is a hand wheel for tilting the saw blade to the correct angle for cutting bevels and miters.
Blade-raising wheel. This is a hand wheel that regulates the cutting height of the saw blade.
Safety guard. The safety guard protects the operator from the saw.
Electric motor. The electric motor drives the circular saw.

unit 25

Circular saw blades and accessories

The two general types of circular saw blades are the **spring set** and the **hollow ground.** Crosscut and ripsaw blades are usually spring set. Combination and carbide-tip blades are hollow ground. Within these two general groups of blades are the crosscut, rip, combination, and carbide-tip blades. A number of accessories and attachments are also available, among which are the dado head and the molding head.

Saw blades

The **circular crosscut,** or **cut-off blade** (Fig. 25-1A) is used for cutting *across* the grain of the wood. On the spring-set blade, the teeth are set alternately right and left so that a cut (kerf) is made that is wider than the thickness of the blade. The hollow-ground blade does not require setting because the blade is thicker at the teeth than it is at the center. Some blades are coated with Teflon fluorocarbon resins to reduce friction (Fig. 25-2).

The **circular ripsaw blade** (Fig. 25-1B) is used for cutting or ripping a board lengthwise (*with* the grain).

The **circular combination saw blade** (Figs. 25-1A and 25-2) has both crosscut and rip teeth. It can be used for either crosscutting or ripping.

The **planer saw blade** is hollow ground, but it looks like the combination blade. It does a smooth job of crosscutting, ripping, and mitering.

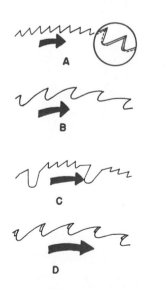

Fig. 25–1 Detail of circular saw blade teeth: (A) crosscut, (B) rip, (C) combination or planer, and (D) carbide-tip.

Fig. 25–2 A Teflon-coated circular combination, or planer, saw blade.

Carbide-tip saw blades (Fig. 25-3) are available in several tooth patterns; the ones shown are typical. This type of blade can be used for all cutting operations. The carbide tips do not dull easily and therefore seldom need sharpening.

Blades vary from 8 to 16 inches (203 to 406 mm) in diameter. The 10- to 16-inch (254- to 406-mm) blades are used in many schools and industries.

Dado head

The dado head is a combination of two outside saws and several inside cutters, which come in various thicknesses (Fig. 25-4). Various combinations of saws and cutters can be used to cut grooves from $1/8$ to $13/16$ inch (3.18 to 20.64 mm).

Figure 25-5 shows how the saw blade and the cutter overlap: A is the outside saw blade, B is an inside cutter, and C is a paper washer or washers, which are sometimes needed to control the exact width of the groove. The outside saw blades are $1/8$ inch (3 mm) thick; hence, two blades fitted together will cut a groove $1/4$ inch (6 mm) thick.

To use the dado head, the throat (opening) plate on the saw table must be replaced with one wide enough for the dado head to come up through it. Figure 25-6 illustrates an adjustable dado cutter that may be used.

Molding head

Straight molding or shaping can be done on the circular saw. Either the saw blade or the dado head is replaced with a molding head, which includes sets of formed knife or cutter shapes (Fig. 25-7). The four shown are standard molding-head cutters. The molding head consists of a cutter head with various shapes of matched steel knives fastened to it.

Many manufacturers make assortments of knife or cutter shapes that fit molding heads. These shapes offer almost unlimited possibilities for

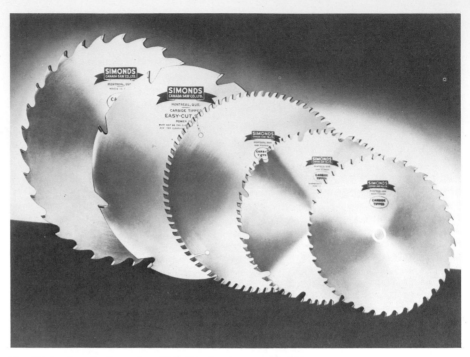

Fig. 25–3 A selection of carbide-tip circular saw blades.

Fig. 25–4 Parts for the dado head: two outside blades and three chipper cutters. The assembled dado head is shown on the left.

making molding shapes on the circular saw.

A special rip fence is required for use with the molding head. It has a cut-out in the center that gives clearance to the cutter head when the knives are at their highest cutting point. A cutout wood facing can also be clamped or screwed to a standard rip fence. Remove the throat plate from the saw table, and replace it with a throat having an opening sufficiently large to accommodate the molding cutters (Fig. 25-7).

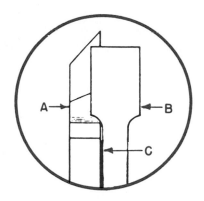

Fig. 25–5 Placement and overlapping of (B) inside chipper cutter with (A) the outside saw blade.

Fig. 25–6 An adjustable dado cutter.

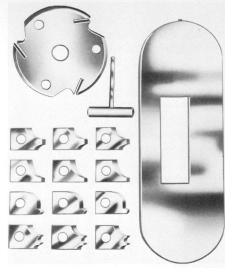

Fig. 25–7 A molding head with four standard knife or cutter shapes. Note the wide-opening throat plate.

unit 26

Operating adjustments

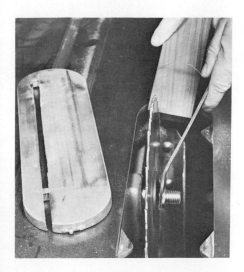

Fig. 26–1 A safe way to loosen the nut that holds the saw blade on the arbor.

The circular saw makes accurate cuts if care is taken to check a few adjustments before using it. Manufacturers make data sheets and operating manuals available for their machines. Study them to learn any special adjustment specifications. The operating techniques described in this unit are basic to most circular saws.

Always make sure that the bearings and other working parts of the machine are properly lubricated according to the operation manual.

Installing saw blades, dado heads, and molding heads

This procedure is for removing a saw blade and installing the dado head assembly or the molding-head cutter on the arbor.

1. Remove the throat plate (see Fig. 26-1).

2. Raise the saw blade as high as it will go, using the hand wheel.

3. Loosen and remove the nut, the outer flange, and the saw blade (Fig. 26-1). As you stand on the work-

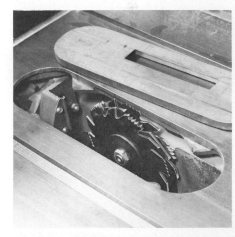

Fig. 26–2 The dado head assembly fastened on the saw arbor. A throat plate with a wider opening is ready to be put in place.

ing side of the saw table, hold a piece of wood in the throat opening against the teeth while loosening the nut.

4. Place the parts of the dado head on the arbor to get the desired thickness: first, one outside blade; next, the chipper blades needed; and last, the opposite outside blade (see Fig. 26-2).

5. Put the flange back on the arbor, and screw on the nut by hand.

6. Adjust the assembly of blades and chippers as shown in Figs. 25-4 and 25-5.

7. Tighten the nut with the wrench.

8. Place the throat plate with the wider opening in position (Fig. 26-2).

Adjusting the rip fence

The typical rip fence has adjustment screws to maintain its parallel alignment with the circular saw blade (Fig. 26-3). The easiest way to check this is to adjust the fence parallel to the table groove and to make the necessary proper positioning (Fig. 26-3).

Adjusting the miter-gage cutoff guide

The miter gage or index on the cutoff guide occasionally gets out of alignment. A simple way to check this is with a square, as shown in Fig. 26-4. The blade, when raised, should be at right angles (90 degrees) to the table top for a square cut.

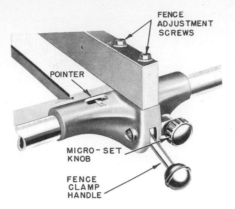

Fig. 26–3 The saw fence assembly.

Adjusting the saw blade

Figure 26-5 illustrates controls for raising the blade and tilting it for a bevel cut.

Fig. 26–4 Checking squareness of the cutoff guide with the saw blade.

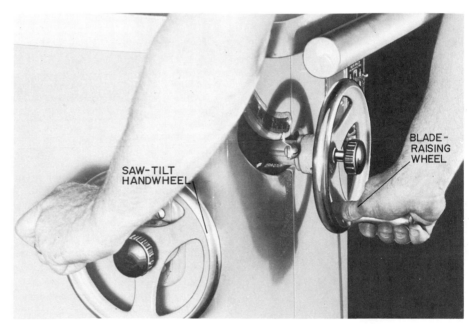

Fig. 26–5 Controls for raising and tilting the saw blade.

unit 27

Crosscutting on the circular saw

Crosscutting is the process of sawing a board *across* the grain (fiber). It is called **square crosscutting** because the board is placed against the cutoff guide and is pushed through the circular saw. Crosscutting short pieces is slightly different from cutting long

ones. A good practice is to remember that any piece shorter than 8 inches (203 mm) must be handled with extreme care.

To handle long pieces of wood, get assistance from someone or use a support to hold the end up, especially the loose end that is cut off. Do not try to crosscut freehand (without a cutoff guide or fence). Always hold the supported piece very securely against the cutoff guide.

Crosscutting

Read and observe the safety precautions in Unit 23.

1. Place the cutoff guide in the slot, or groove, on the table. Usually the left groove is more convenient for crosscutting.

2. Check the cutoff guide to see that it is set at the correct angle of 90 degrees for a right angle.

3. Make certain that the saw blade is set to cut at 90 degrees.

4. Mark the board where it is to be cut off.

5. Hold the board firmly against the cutoff guide (see Fig. 27-1). Place the board so that you saw on the waste side of the marked line.

6. Start the saw, and let it come to full speed.

7. Push the cutoff guide and the board forward (Fig. 27-1), holding the board firmly against the guide. The saw blade should not extend above the board more than 1/4 inch (6 mm).

8. Pull back the board and the cutoff guide at the end of the cut.

9. When several short pieces are to be cut to the same length, clamp a block on the rip fence as shown in Fig. 27-2. This gives sufficient clearance between the saw blade and the rip fence to keep the piece from binding (sticking) between the blade and the fence.

10. Another method of cutting several short pieces to the same length is shown in Fig. 27-3. When crosscutting duplicate long boards, it is easier to fasten a longer wooden facing onto the cutoff guide as shown in Fig. 27-4. A stop attachment can also be used (see Fig. 27-3).

11. A wide board can sometimes be put against the cutoff guide by reversing the guide on the table (Fig. 27-5).

Fig. 27-1 Crosscutting on a circular saw. Hold the board firmly against the cutoff guide. Part of the guard is raised for clarity.

Fig. 27-2 Crosscutting short pieces to the same length. Note the block clamped to the rip fence. The guard is removed for clarity.

Fig. 27-3 Crosscutting duplicate short pieces with the use of a stop attachment on the cutoff guide. The guard is removed for clarity.

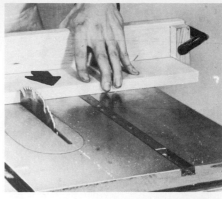

Fig. 27-4 Crosscutting duplicate longer pieces. Note the block fastened at the end of the guide. The guard is removed for clarity.

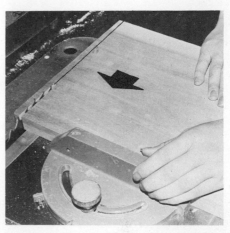

Fig. 27-5 Crosscutting a wide board by reversing the cutoff guide. The guard has been removed to show details.

Sawing a miter

1. Set the guide at the angle desired. Place the guide in the right or left groove, depending upon which is more convenient.

2. Mark the angle to be cut.

3. Hold the board on the table firmly against the cutoff guide so that the saw cut will be on the waste side.

4. Start the saw, and let it come to full speed.

5. Push the guide and the board forward (Fig. 27-6).

Crosscutting a bevel

1. Adjust the saw blade with the blade-tilting wheel to the angle of the bevel. Follow steps 1 through 5 given under "Crosscutting."

2. Push the cutoff guide and the board forward (Fig. 27-7), holding the board firmly against the guide and on the table.

3. When a bevel is cut to a compound angle, the crosscut guide and the saw must be set to the desired angles. The saw must be set to the angle of the bevel.

Fig. 27–6   Making a miter crosscut. Part of the guard is removed to show detail.

Fig. 27–7   Crosscutting a bevel by tilting the saw blade.

unit 28

Ripping on the circular saw

Ripping is the process of sawing a board *lengthwise*. Before attempting to rip a board, make certain that one edge is straight and that one surface is flat. A board with a curved edge can cause the saw blade to stick (bind) and kick the piece back toward the operator. It could also buckle (bend or twist) on the saw blade.

Fig. 28–1   Adjusting the rip fence for the desired distance.

Ripping

1. Adjust the height of the ripsaw or combination blade to approximately $1/4$ inch (6 mm) above the thickness of the lumber stock to be ripped.

2. Arrange and fasten the rip fence at the desired distance from the saw blade (Fig. 28-1).

3. Turn on the switch, stand to one side, and allow the motor to come to full speed.

4. Make a trial cut on a piece of scrap board to check the accuracy. Allow at least $1/16$ inch (2 mm) for dressing (planing) with a jointer or a hand plane.

5. Place the board firmly on the table top. Press it against the rip fence.

6. Push the board with a steady pressure (Figs. 28-2 and 28-3).

7. To rip pieces less than 4 inches (102 mm) wide, use a push stick for safety (Fig. 28-3).

8. To rip a long board, provide a means of handling the long stock (Fig. 28-4).

9. Boards can also be ripped by reversing ends (Fig. 28-5).

Fig. 28–2 Ripping a board to width. Note the guard.

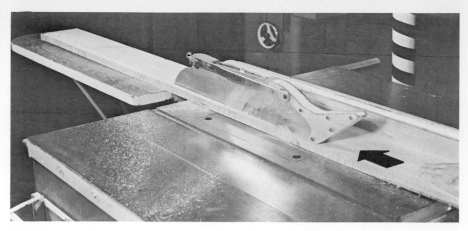

Fig. 28–4 Ripping a long board to width. Note the extension on the saw frame to hold long boards.

Resawing

A thick board can be resawed on the circular saw. To do this completely on this machine, the width must be less than twice the capacity of the blade.

1. Follow steps 1 through 6 under "Ripping." Fasten a feather board firmly on the table top to ensure uni-form pressure against the board being resawed (Figs. 28-6 and 28-7).

2. If the stock is too wide to be resawed completely on the circular saw, a cut can be made on each edge with the circular saw (Fig. 28-7). Then complete the resawing on the band saw. See Unit 42, Straight Sawing and Resawing.

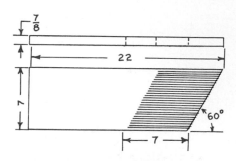

Fig. 28–6 Details for making a feather board.

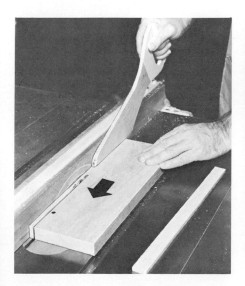

Fig. 28–3 Using a push stick for safety while ripping narrow pieces. The guard is removed for clarity.

Fig. 28–5 Ripping a board by reversing the board ends.

Fig. 28–7 Resawing a wide board to be completed on the band saw. The feather board holds the stock firmly against the rip fence.

Ripping a taper

1. Adjust, or make a jig, to shape the desired taper. Study Figs. 28-8 through 28-10.

2. Mark the line of taper on the board so that you can sight your work.

3. Work the board against the jig.

4. Turn on the switch; allow the motor to come to full speed.

5. Push the jig and the board past the saw blade, making the cut to the desired taper or angle.

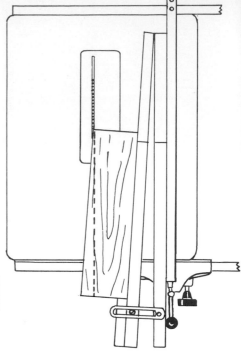

Fig. 28–9 Setting the rip fence for cutting the tapered board.

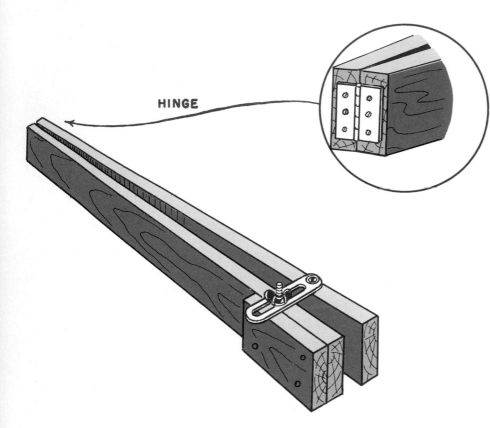

HINGE

Fig. 28–8 Details of an adjustable guide to make a taper cut.

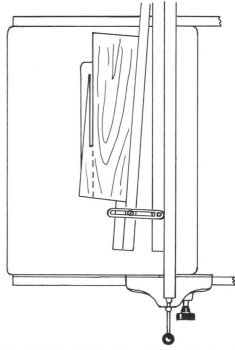

Fig. 28–10 Ripping the taper with the use of a jig.

unit 29

Rabbeting on the circular saw

Rabbeting with the saw blade is the process of making two rip cuts of suitable depth, as shown in Fig. 29-1. One way of doing this is on the circular saw.

Procedure

1. Square the stock to the given dimensions. This entails cutting and planing the board or boards to the required thickness, width, and length.

2. Mark the rabbet cut on the end of the piece (Fig. 29-1A).

3. Set the saw to the width of the rabbet (see Fig. 29-2).

4. Adjust the saw blade for depth.

5. Make a trial cut on a piece of scrap wood.

6. Make the first cut (Fig. 29-2 and 29-1B). Cut the other pieces that have the same rabbet markings.

7. Turn off the saw; readjust it for the final cut (see Fig. 29-1C).

8. Make the final cut on the piece or pieces (see Fig. 29-1C).

A similar procedure can also be used for cutting across the grain.

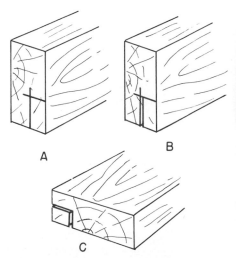

Fig. 29–1 Details of cutting a rabbet: (A) the marked board, (B) the first cut, and (C) the rabbet cut completed.

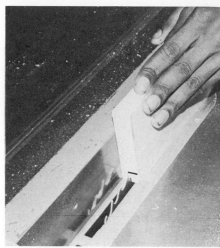

Fig. 29–2 The first cut in making a rabbet. The guard is removed for clarity.

unit 30

Making grooves, dadoes, rabbets, and tenons

The dado head assembly on the circular saw amounts to a thick saw used for making various widths of grooves, dadoes (wide cuts or grooves), rabbets, and tenons. It consists of two outside saws and three or four inside cutters or an adjustable dado head. The outer blades are usually $1/8$ inch (3 mm) thick; therefore, the two used together will cut grooves $1/4$ inch (6 mm) wide to a specified depth. This is the usual groove for recessing $1/4$-inch (6-mm) plywood into panels and doors.

Tenons are easily and quickly made with the dado head. The widest combination is often used. The dado head is usually wide enough to cut the average stub (short) tenon in one pass of the stock (see Fig. 30-5). Tenons can also be made satisfactorily with the crosscut, a combination saw blade, or a commercial tenoning jig (See Fig. 30-8).

Grooving

1. Assemble a dado, or grooving, head with blades and cutters.

2. Fasten the dado head on the saw arbor. Refer to Unit 26, Operating Adjustments. Check to see that the spacer cutters are evenly spaced and that the teeth of the blades and cutters point in the **same direction.**

3. Lay out and mark the groove, or dado, on the stock.

4. To crosscut a dado: place the cutoff guide with the grain of the wood, adjust the rip fence to the desired distance for making the cut.

5. Adjust for the cutting height of the dado head.

6. Turn on the saw, and allow it to come to full speed.

7. Make a trial cut on a piece of scrap wood.

8. Place the board firmly against the cutoff guide or the rip fence. Make the cut with an even pressure (Fig. 30-1). The groove or dado can be made either with or across the grain.

9. A rabbet can also be cut in one operation by using the dado head (Figs. 30-2 and 30-3).

10. A blind dado can be easily made by using stop blocks clamped to the rip fence (Fig. 30-4).

Making tenons with a dado head

1. Assemble and fasten a wide dado head on the saw arbor. See Unit 26.

2. Clamp a wooden block on the rip fence as shown in Fig. 30-5.

3. Set the rip fence to make the desired tenon length. Measure from the wooden block.

4. Adjust the height of the dado head above the table to cut the shoulder of the tenon.

5. Turn on the saw, and make a trial cut on a piece of scrap wood. Check the cuts for measurement accuracy.

6. Hold the rail, or apron, securely against the cutoff guide; the end should be against the wooden block on the rip fence. Push the rail and the cutoff guide slowly over the dado head to make a shoulder cut for the tenon (Fig. 30-5).

7. Turn the rail over; make a corresponding (matching) cut on the other shoulder of the tenon.

8. Make the remaining cuts for the edges of the tenon in a similar manner. This requires resetting the height of the head to fit the tenon.

Making tenons with a circular saw blade

1. Lay out the tenon on the rail, or apron (see Fig. 30-6).

2. Fasten the circular saw blade in place on the arbor.

3. Adjust the saw blade to cut the length of the tenon.

4. Adjust the rip fence.

5. Clamp a feather board on the table. The feathered end should press

Fig. 30–1   Crosscutting a dado with a dado head.

Fig. 30–2   Cutting a rabbet on the dado head.

84

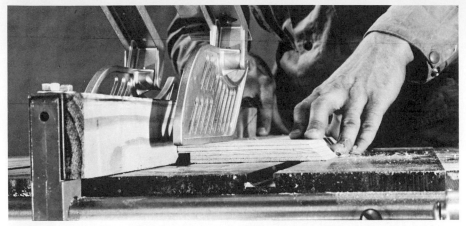

Fig. 30–3 Cutting a rabbet on the dado head by using a board fastened to the rip fence. This board prevents the dado head from cutting into the metal rip fence.

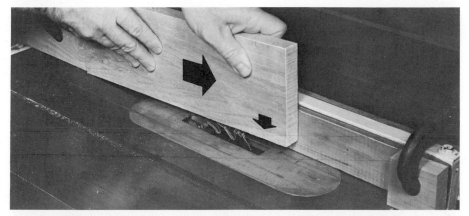

Fig. 30–4 Cutting a blind dado. Note the stop block fastened to the rip fence.

Fig. 30–5 Making the first cut of a tenon on the dado head.

the rail firmly against the rip fence (see Fig. 30-7).

6. Turn on the saw; make a trial cut on a piece of scrap wood. Make any necessary adjustments.

7. Hold the face side of the board firmly against the rip fence. Push it slowly into the saw blade (Fig. 30-7).

8. Repeat this process on other identical tenons to be cut.

9. Stop the machine. Adjust both the rip fence and the feather board to cut the other side of the tenon.

10. Turn on the machine. Make another trial cut on the original piece of scrap wood. Make any necessary adjustments.

11. Again place the tenon piece with the face side against the rip

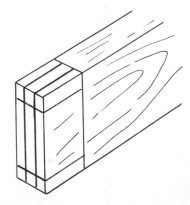

Fig. 30–6 Layout of a tenon.

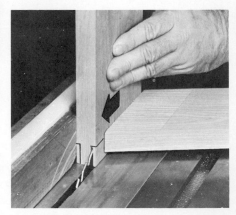

Fig. 30–7 Making the first cut of a tenon. Note the use of the feather board.

fence. Cut as in step 7. Figure 30-8 shows how a tenon may be cut in one pass with a commercial tenoning jig.

12. Shut off the power and reset the rip fence. Make the remaining cuts across the end of the tenon. The feather board is not needed in this process.

13. Place the cutoff guide in the left groove of the table.

14. Adjust the rip fence for cutting away the shoulder (see Fig. 30-9).

15. Set the saw blade at the proper height for cutting away the shoulder.

16. Turn on the saw. Make a trial cut on the original piece of scrap wood. Make adjustments if needed.

17. Place the rail piece against the cutoff guide. The tenon end should be against the wood block on the rip fence.

18. Hold the stock firmly against the cutoff guide. Turn on the power. Push the stock slowly over the saw blade (Fig. 30-9).

19. Repeat this process to cut away the remaining shoulder pieces from the tenon (Fig. 30-10).

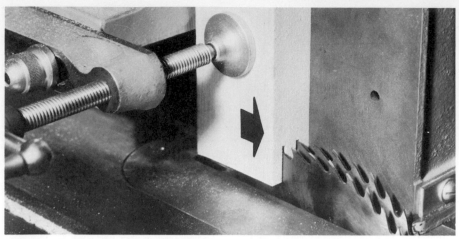

Fig. 30–8   Cutting a tenon with the aid of a tenoning jig.

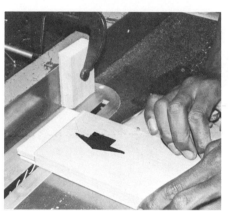

Fig. 30–9   Cutting away the shoulder of a tenon on the circular saw.

Fig. 30–10   Cutting off the remainder of the tenon shoulders.

unit **31**

Shaping straight edges and cutting molding

Shaping straight edges and cutting molding is done quickly and safely with the use of a molding head on the circular saw. The molding head (see Fig. 25-7) has an assortment of molding-head cutters. These fit into molding heads to make almost any pattern on straight shaping or molding. Usually a cutout wood facing is clamped or screwed to a standard rip fence.

Procedure

1. Clamp or screw an extra board to the rip fence (Fig. 31-1).

2. Fasten the desired cutter knives in the molding head. Be certain that the knives make up a matched set.

3. Mount and tighten the cutter head on the saw arbor. Place a throat plate with the proper opening in the saw table.

4. Set the rip fence to the width needed for the shaping operation.

5. Start the machine; gradually raise the molding head until it comes to the desired height for making the cut.

6. Make a trial cut on a piece of scrap wood. Adjust the saw or fence setting if necessary.

7. Place the stock to be shaped or molded on the table. Push it slowly and firmly over the molding head (Fig. 31-2). This makes the shaped edge. Shape the end the same way with the aid of the cutoff guide.

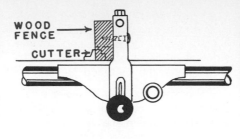

Fig. 31-1 Detail showing an extra wooden facing fastened to the rip fence for shaping and cutting molding.

Fig. 31-2 Shaping the straight edge of a board.

unit 32

Special cuts on the circular saw

The circular saw can be used to make interesting cuts and shapes. Two of the more unusual ones are the cove cut and saw-cut moldings. The **cove cut** is a concave shape, which might be required in the construction of modern furniture (Fig. 32-1). Sometimes the stock is rectangular in cross section, as shown in Fig. 32-1B; it is then cut in half. Also, the two pieces can be fastened together, turned round (split turned) on the lathe, and then separated for cove cutting.

One attractive saw-cut molding, known as the **zigzag shape**, is shown in Fig. 32-8.

Cove cutting

1. Determine the width and depth of the cove cut to be made.

2. Make a wood frame, or use a parallel-rule jig, as shown in Fig. 32-2.

The inside measurement is set for the width of the cut.

3. Set the saw blade at the final height for making the cut (for the intended depth of the cove). This should be half the width of the cove.

4. Place the wood frame, or the parallel-rule jig, over the saw. Turn it until it just touches the front and the rear teeth of the exposed blade (Fig. 32-2). Turn the blade by hand to make certain the teeth barely nick both edges of the frame. This is the proper angle for locating the clamped-on fence (see step 5).

5. Fasten a wooden fence in place on the table top. Use C clamps or hand screws (see Fig. 32-3).

6. Lower the saw blade until it is about $1/8$ inch (3 mm) above the table.

7. Turn on the switch; allow the motor to come to full speed.

8. Feed the work against the wooden fence and across the saw blade slowly but firmly (Fig. 32-3).

9. Repeat this operation each time by raising the saw blade about $1/8$ inch (3 mm).

10. Continue making cuts until the depth and the width of the cove have been reached (Fig. 32-4).

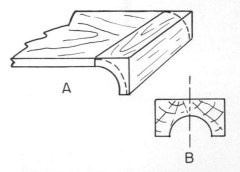

Fig. 32-1 Details of rounded corners for modern furniture construction.

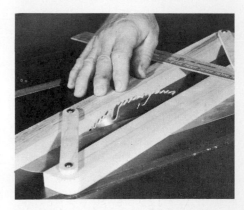

Fig. 32-2 Placing the parallel-rule jig over the saw to determine the angle for making a cove cut.

11. Dress and sand the cove with a swan-neck scraper blade and coarse sandpaper. Continue sanding with finer grades until it is smooth and the saw marks are removed.

The cove can be cut in two and used on the edges of modern furniture, as shown in Fig. 32-1. The outside shaping can be done with a hand plane, scraper blade and sandpaper or by split turning, as mentioned in the first paragraph of this unit.

Saw-cut molding

1. Square the board to the desired thickness, which will later become the width of the molding strips. The board should be longer than the molding.

2. Fasten a wood facing to the cutoff guide (see Fig. 32-5).

3. Drive a small nail into the wood facing to act as a guide pin (Fig. 32-5). The distance from the nail to the blade will determine the spacing of the saw cuts.

4. Set the saw blade to extend above the table the desired height for making the saw kerfs.

5. Place the molding stock against the cutoff guide wood facing. Make the cuts. Repeat cuts are made by alternately turning the work faceup and facedown, as shown in Fig. 32-6.

6. Place an auxiliary wood table on top of the saw table. Fasten it securely with clamps (see Fig. 32-7). The strips that are ripped will be fragile (delicate), so they will need a solid support.

7. Turn on the switch while the saw blade is below the table top.

8. Gradually turn the hand wheel to raise the saw blade. Allow it to cut up through the auxiliary wood table top until it is high enough to cut through the molding stock.

9. Fasten two clamps as shown in Fig. 32-7. These prevent the molding strips from pushing up and breaking.

10. Plane the edge of the molding strip on a jointer.

11. Feed the molding stock through the saw (Fig. 32-7). Each time a strip is cut, plane the edge of the stock. It must have a smooth edge to feed against the rip fence.

This molding can be used as an overlay or it can be applied to a heavier backing piece. It can also be inserted in a recess or groove, making an inlay (Fig. 32-8).

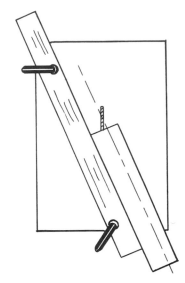

Fig. 32–3 A wooden fence clamped on the table top for making a cove cut.

Fig. 32–4 Cutting a cove by pushing the stock across the saw blade in an angular direction against a wooden fence. This requires a succession of shallow 1/8-inch (3-mm) cuts until the depth has been reached.

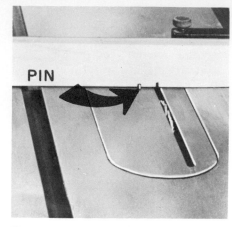

Fig. 32–5 A small nail driven into the wood facing of the cutoff guide serves as a guide pin.

Fig. 32–6 Saw cuts are made by alternately turning the work faceup, and then facedown. The distance from the nail (guide pin) to the blade in Fig. 32-5 determines the spacing of the saw cuts.

Fig. 32–7 One piece of molding stock can be sliced and ripped to produce many feet of molding.

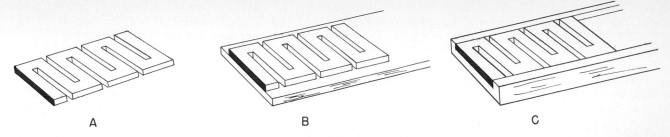

Fig. 32–8   Treatment of saw-cut molding: (A) ripped molding stock, (B) molding fastened onto backing, and (C) molding inserted into a recess or groove.

Radial saw processes

unit 33

General information about the radial (cutoff) saw

The radial (cutoff) saw is a development of the older swing saw, on which the blade swung back and forth above the work table. The modern radial saw (Fig. 33-1) is a precision machine that is capable of doing an amazing variety of operations. It gets its name because the arm can be rotated 360 degrees right or left (Fig. 33-2). It is a versatile tool for the industrial, school, or home workshop.

This machine, with proper adjustment and the many attachments

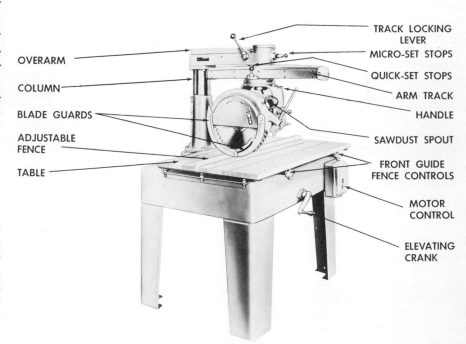

OVERARM
COLUMN
BLADE GUARDS
ADJUSTABLE FENCE
TABLE

TRACK LOCKING LEVER
MICRO-SET STOPS
QUICK-SET STOPS
ARM TRACK
HANDLE
SAWDUST SPOUT
FRONT GUIDE FENCE CONTROLS
MOTOR CONTROL
ELEVATING CRANK

Fig. 33–1   A 14-inch (355.6-mm) radial saw.

available, can be used to crosscut, rip, miter, bevel, and compound-bevel. It can rip tapers; plow; cut dadoes, rabbets, grooves, and tongues; and make tenons. It can also be used for molding and router shaping. It also drills, sands, and grinds.

Types

Radial saws are grouped into three major types, depending upon the design and action of the overarm. The **double-arm** design is shown in Fig. 33-1. On this machine the overarm remains in a fixed lateral position; a second, or turret, arm pivots a full 360 degrees. The pivot action of the second arm (the underarm) always moves the saw toward the work.

A second type has a **stationary overarm** that pivots completely around a support column. This type has distinct disadvantages. The arm projects beyond the front of the saw table and interferes with the operator. It also pivots away from the work and off the table, limiting its capabilities.

The third type is the **sliding overarm** design. This machine requires twice the floor space of the other two. It has a sliding arm that rotates completely around the support column.

Regardless of the arm construction of these three types, radial saws have the same basic parts.

Sizes and speeds

Radial saw sizes are measured by the blade diameter and vary from 8 to 20 inches (203 to 508 mm). The 10- to 14-inch (254- to 356-mm) saws are common in home shops and school industrial laboratories. Larger sizes are more suitable for industrial production. The blade is attached by a direct-drive motor arbor to the motor.

Motor speed on most models is between 3425 and 3450 r/min. The surface speed in sfm varies with the diameter of the blade. This speed can be computed. Multiply the motor r/min

by the blade circumference in inches and divide by 12.

The metric equivalent of surface feet per minute is accurately measured in meters per second (m/s). A meter per minute rate can be easily found by multiplying sfm by 0.3048.

Radial saw parts and uses

Table. The table is a series of boards held in place with guide fence controls.

Guide fence. The guide fence provides backing for crosscutting, ripping, and many other operations. This wooden fence guide is removable. It can be positioned between any of the table boards, depending upon the width of the material to be cut.

Base. The base is usually made of steel. It supports the table and the radial arm.

Yoke. The yoke holds the electric motor, which hangs from the track arm. The yoke can be moved along the

horizontal track arm or held stationary at any point. The blade and other tools are fastened to the arbor.

Track arm. The track arm enables the yoke to move back and forth. It is adjustable through 360 degrees.

Overarm. The overarm is the top horizontal bar which controls the track arm. It is supported by the column at the rear. This arm raises or lowers the cutting blades or tools.

Upright column. The upright column is the steel cylinder that provides support for the overarm at the rear. It holds the radial arm mechanism above the table and base.

Guards. The blade guard protects the operator from the blade and cutters. The antikickback attachment has fingers in front of the blade guard that keep a board from kicking back during ripping operations.

Controls and scales. The several controls are described and illustrated in Unit 35, Operating Adjustments and Care.

Fig. 33–2   Rotational sawing of the radial arm.

Saw blades, cutters, and accessories

Several circular saw blades can be used on the radial saw. There are also a number of accessories and attachments, such as dado, molding, and rafter heads; shaper cutters, routers, and bits; sanding disks and drums; and many specialized and customized production blades and cutters.

Types of saw blades

The types of saw blades used on the radial saw are the same as those used on the circular saw. These are discussed in detail in Unit 25, Circular Saw Blades and Accessories. Make sure that the arbor hole in the blade is the correct size to fit the radial saw arbor.

Dado head

The blades and cutters which make up the dado head are the same as those described in Unit 25.

Molding head

The molding head (Fig. 25-7) is a steel cutter head that holds various shapes of steel knives. The key (wrench) is used to fasten the knives in the grooves. Other cutter blades are illustrated in Fig. 65-4.

Shaper cutters

Figure 65-4, Unit 65, Shaper Cutters, Collars, and Spindles, shows a few of the many three-lip shaper cutters and collars. These offer the possibility of making hundreds of molding shapes on the radial saw. A shaper-cutter adapter (Fig. 34-1) must be used to fit these shaper cutters on the radial saw.

Router bits

Router bits and an adapter (Fig. 34-2) convert the radial saw for router operations.

Rafter-head cutter

A rafter-head cutter (Fig. 34-3) is used for notching rafters.

Sanding disks and drums

Sanding disks and drums (Fig. 34-4) can be used in conjunction with the radial saw. An auxiliary table is needed for disk sanding as is shown in Fig. 38-9.

Fig. 34–1 Shaper-cutter adapter for the radial saw.

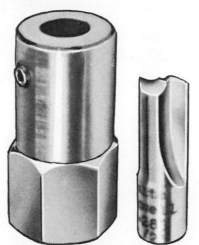

Fig. 34–2 Router bit adapter.

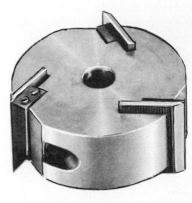

Fig. 34–3 A rafter-head cutter.

Fig. 34–4 Sanding disk and drums.

unit 35

Operating adjustments and care

The versatility, or range of activities, of the radial saw makes it necessary to understand the operation of the various controls and the meanings of the different scales. Controls and scales for a representative type of radial saw are shown in Fig. 35-1. Study the manufacturer's operating manual for the machine in your laboratory before attempting any settings.

Raising or lowering the cutting head

The saw blade and the entire radial assembly above the table can be raised or lowered with the elevating crank handle (Figs. 33-1 and 35-1). On some machines this crank is at the front of the base; on others, it is at the top of the supporting column. One full turn of the crank usually raises or lowers the saw blade or cutting tool $1/8$ inch (3 mm).

Setting for a bevel cut

The blade and motor tilt are controlled for bevel cutting with the bevel-clamp knob or handle and the bevel latch (Figs. 35-1 and 35-2). Pulling out the bevel clamp releases the lock action of the motor **trunnion** (swivel point). The latch changes the position of the motor. The motor can then be moved by hand to any degree of angle on the bevel scale. Most machines have stops which locate the vertical and the 45-degree positions.

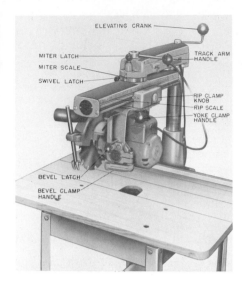

Fig. 35–1 Operating controls and scales of the radial saw.

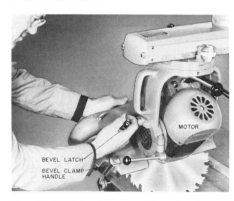

Fig. 35–2 Adjusting for a bevel cut.

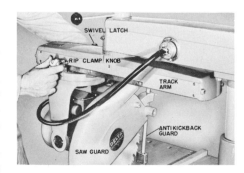

Fig. 35–3 Adjusting the radial saw for ripping.

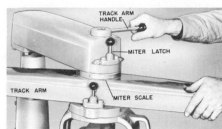

Fig. 35–4 Setting up for cutting miters.

Adjusting the radial saw for ripping

The radial saw can be set for ripping by the yoke-clamp handle, swivel latch, and rip-clamp handle or knob (Figs. 35-1 and 35-3). The yoke-clamp handle releases the carriage lock action. The swivel latch disengages (releases) the swivel. The rip-clamp handle locks the carriage on the arm in the desired ripping position. This can be set by the rip scale.

Setting up for cutting miters

The track-arm clamp handle and the miter latch are used to set up the radial saw for cutting miters (Figs. 35-1 and 35-4). The clamp handle loosens the lock action of the track arm. This arm should now be swung to the desired miter position on the scale and then tightened with the track-arm clamp handle (Fig. 35-4). On most machines there are stops at 0 degrees and at 45 degrees to the right or left.

Squaring the blade to the table and fence

The blade (with guard removed) can be squared to the table with a square (Fig. 35-5). Place the square against the blade and on the table. To square the saw blade with the table, pull the clamp handle to release the lock action of the motor, and make the adjustment.

Square the blade with the guide fence by making a trial crosscut in a fairly wide board that has been jointed on one edge. If an adjustment is needed, loosen the track arm (Fig. 35-6) and make the necessary alignment. The two adjustments of aligning the saw blade with the table and the fence are a little more detailed than this. You should read the manufacturer's manual very carefully to learn the technique required.

Mounting saw blades and cutters

Saw blades and most circular cutting tools are mounted directly on the motor arbor of the radial arm saw. First, loosen and take off the guard. To remove a blade or cutting tool, take off the arbor nut (Fig. 35-7). Use one wrench to hold the motor arbor steady; loosen the arbor nut with a second wrench in a clockwise (right) direction. Follow the opposite procedure for mounting and tightening saw blades, cutters, and dado heads. The

Fig. 35–5 Aligning the blade square with the table.

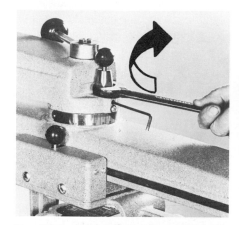

Fig. 35–6 Checking the blade for squareness with the guide fence.

recessed side of the flanges should be against the blade or cutter. Make sure that the teeth point in the direction of the arrow on the guard (see Fig. 33-1).

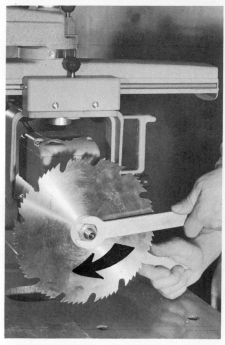

Fig. 35–7 Mounting a saw blade on the saw arbor.

unit 36

Crosscutting, ripping, mitering, and beveling

Basic cutting processes on the radial saw are crosscutting, ripping, mitering, and beveling. Compound-angle cutting and taper ripping are also easy to do on this machine. The 360-degree swing of the track arm makes it possible to cut circles and arcs without a jig. Study Unit 34, Operating Adjustments and Care, before you attempt any of the cuts outlined in this unit.

Crosscutting

Read and observe the safety precautions in Unit 23.

1. Set the track arm at zero degrees on the miter scale. Lock the setting securely (see Fig. 32-1).
2. Set the depth of cut by turning the elevator crank. The teeth of the saw blade should barely scratch the top of the table if you wish to cut entirely through the stock.
3. Place the stock (board) on the table top against the guide fence.
4. Turn on the power switch. Make sure the saw blade is *behind* the guide fence.
5. Pull the yoke handle slowly as the saw cuts across the board (Fig. 36-1). To cut more than one piece to the same length, clamp a stop to the guide fence.
6. Return the saw behind the guide fence before removing the board.
7. Turn off the power switch.

Ripping

1. Set the track arm to the crosscutting position.

2. Adjust the yoke so that the blade is parallel to the guide fence.

3. Set the depth of cut by turning the elevating crank.

4. Push the carriage along the track arm to the ripping width desired. Lock it with the rip-clamp handle.

5. Place the board on the table top against the guide fence.

6. Lower the infeed end of the guard to clear the stock; lock it.

Fig. 36–1 Crosscutting on the radial-arm saw.

Fig. 36–2 Outboard ripping.

7. Adjust the antikickback guard. Make certain that the points of the fingers are set about $1/8$ inch (3 mm) below the surface of the board (see Fig. 36-2).

8. Turn on the power switch.

9. Feed the board into the saw slowly. Make sure that it moves against and along the guide fence (Fig. 36-2). Do *not* feed the stock into the antikickback end of the saw guard.

For **outboard** ripping (Fig. 36-2), the motor is out of the way, and the layout marking is more clearly visible. For **inboard** ripping, the saw head is reversed, and the stock is fed from the opposite direction.

To rip narrow stock, *always* use a push stick to push away the stock that has been cut.

A taper can be ripped by using a specially built jig (Fig. 36-3).

Cutting a miter

1. Loosen and swing the track arm to the desired right- or left-hand angle on the miter scale. Lock it securely.

Fig. 36–3 Ripping a taper.

2. Set the depth of the saw cut by adjusting the elevating crank.

3. Place the stock on the table top against the guide fence (see Fig. 36-4).

4. Turn on the power switch.

5. Pull the saw slowly across the board (Fig. 36-4), as in crosscutting.

6. Return the saw to its position behind the guide fence. Turn off the switch before removing the stock.

Crosscutting a bevel

1. Raise the motor and the cutting head, with the elevator crank, enough to allow the blade to be tilted.

2. Adjust the track arm and yoke for crosscutting; then tilt the blade to the desired angle on the bevel scale. See Unit 35, Operating Adjustments and Care.

3. Set the depth of cut by turning the elevating crank.

4. Place the board on the table top against the guide fence (see Fig. 36-5).

5. Turn on the power switch.

6. Pull the saw slowly across the board (Fig. 36-5), as in crosscutting.

Figure 36-6 shows how to saw a compound angle. This is a combination bevel and miter cut that is made in one pass of the saw blade. It requires both a tilt of the blade and a swing of the track arm, either right or left.

Ripping a bevel

1. Adjust the machine for straight ripping.

2. Position the carriage on the track arm for proper tilt of the bevel.

3. Rip the angle in the stock (Fig. 36-7) by following steps 5 through 9 under Ripping.

Making special cuts

Stock can be cut horizontally, as shown in Fig. 36-8. Set the track arm and yoke as in crosscutting. The blade is then tilted to the 90-degree setting, parallel to the table top.

Fig. 36–4   Making a miter cut.

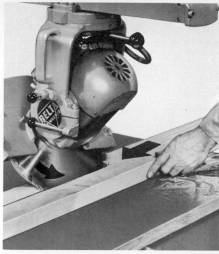

Fig. 36–7   Making an inboard-bevel rip cut.

Fig. 36–5   Crosscutting a bevel.

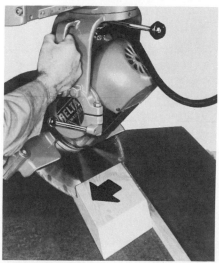

Fig. 36–6   Sawing a compound angle.

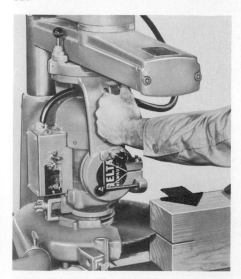

Fig. 36–8   Making a horizontal end cut.

unit 37

Dadoing, ploughing, and rabbeting

The dado head makes it possible to convert the radial saw to do dadoing (grooving across the grain), ploughing (grooving with the grain), and rabbeting. One can also make tenons. Information about dado heads is given in Unit 25.

Crossdadoing

Crossdadoing involves the same machine adjustments, setup procedures, and general processes as in crosscutting. Figure 37–1 shows the process of cutting various widths of cross dadoes.

To cut dadoes in several pieces at the same places, use a stop block clamped to the guide fence.

Angle dadoing

Cutting dadoes, or grooves, at an angle requires adjusting and setting the machine as for cutting miters. Angle dadoes are sometimes also called **gains.** The process of angle dadoing (Fig. 37-2) is the same as for cutting miters except that the dado head does not cut through the board.

Ploughing

Ploughing cuts and shapes a groove lengthwise in a board (Fig. 37-3). The radial saw should be adjusted and set as for ripping. Stock is fed into the dado head the same way as it is for ripping.

Rabbeting

With the dado head, rabbets can be cut in one operation. Set the track arm at zero degrees on the miter scale. Set the yoke to 90 degrees; locate the blade in the inboard position.

Tilt and raise the cutting head to 90 degrees to place the dado head parallel to the table (see Fig. 37-4). Lower the dado head to the desired position for cutting by using the elevating crank.

The cutter head remains stationary, and the stock is pushed along the guide fence to cut the rabbet. A bevel rabbet (Fig. 37-5) requires a slight tilt of the cutting head to the desired angle.

Panel raising

This process (Fig. 37-6) is used considerably in door and cabinet construction.

Cutting tenons

The full width of the dado head is used to cut tenons. This reduces the number of passes (cuts) necessary. When a long tenon is cut, a stop block is used, as shown in Fig. 37-7. The *inside cut* is made first.

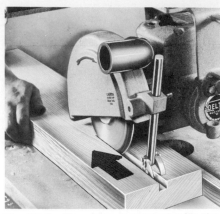
Fig. 37–3 Ploughing (grooving) with the grain of the wood.

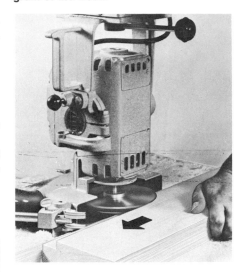
Fig. 37–4 Cutting a rabbet.

Fig. 37–5 Cutting a bevel rabbet.

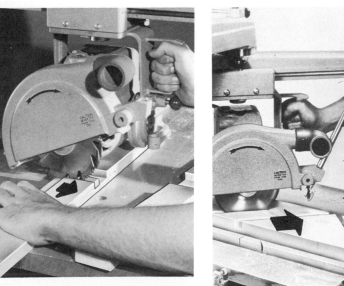
Fig. 37–1 Making several dado cuts on a middle half-lap joint.

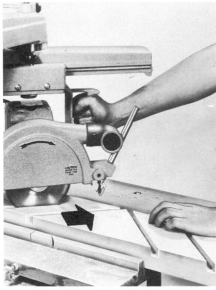
Fig. 37–2 Angle dadoing.

The spacing-collar method is another way to cut tenons. Figure 37-8 shows the arrangement and assembly of this dado head. The procedure for cutting a tenon by this method is shown in Fig. 37-9. Note that the operator is guiding the stock (rail) with a wider squared board to eliminate kickback.

Cutting a tongue-and-groove joint

The dado head and a spacing collar make a good combination for cutting the tongue of a tongue-and-groove joint (Fig. 37-10). The collar thickness should be the same as the tenon thickness.

A specially prepared auxiliary guide fence should be used, as shown in Fig. 37-10. The opening in the fence permits the dado head to come through to the desired depth.

A similar setup is used to cut the groove (Fig. 37-11). The width of the groove should be the same as the width of the tongue. This is achieved by combining the outside blades and the center cutters of the dado head.

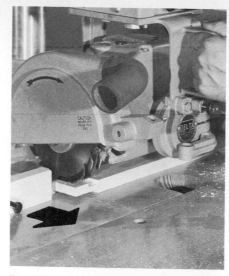

Fig. 37–7 Cutting a tenon with the full dado head.

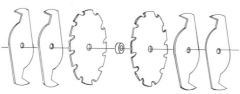

Fig. 37–8 An arrangement of a spacing collar with outside blades and cutters.

Fig. 37–10 Cutting the tongue for a tongue-and-groove joint, using the spacing-collar method.

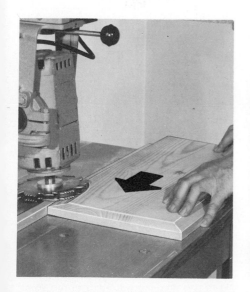

Fig. 37–6 Panel raising with a dado head.

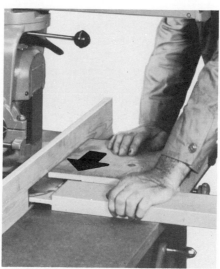

Fig. 37–9 Cutting a tenon by the spacing-collar method.

Fig. 37–11 Cutting a groove for a tongue-and-groove joint.

Cutting a cove

A cove cut is often required for rounding corners in furniture construction and for making molding. Cove cutting can be done either with the regular saw blade or with a dado head. First, decide the width and depth of the cove. Next, set the radial saw to the desired cove measurements.

Cut the cove, making *several* passes, each one cutting 1/8 inch (3 mm) deeper. The dado head is used to make the cove cut shown in Fig. 37-12.

Rafter notching

Several rafters can be notched at the same time (Fig. 37-13). Use the rafter-head cutter shown in Fig. 34-3. It fastens on the arbor like a saw blade or a dado head.

Fig. 37–12 Cutting a cove with a dado head.

Fig. 37–13 Notching several rafters.

unit 38

Molding, shaping, routing, and sanding

The scope of radial saw usefulness extends to such woodworking processes as molding, shaping, routing, and sanding. Unit 25, Circular Saw Blades and Accessories, and Unit 34, Saw Blades, Cutters, and Accessories, describe molding heads, shaper cutters, router bits, and sanding disks and drums. These accessories perform the several processes mentioned.

Molding

The molding cutter head is fastened on the saw arbor. Position the motor vertically, the cutter head parallel with the saw table. The elevating crank lowers or raises the cutter head to the desired height. Slide the carriage forward or backward on the track arm until the knives in front of the fence give the width of the cut planned.

An effective way to determine the shape of the cut that the cutter head will make is shown in Fig. 38-1. Cutting or shaping cuts are made on the side of the stock facing the fence (see Fig. 38-2). Figure 38-3 shows a simple setup for molding circular work. Note that the wooden jig is fastened between the table-top boards in place of the fence guide.

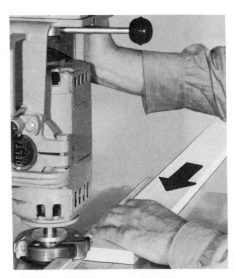

Fig. 38–1 Placing the edge of the stock against the cutter knife to adjust for height and depth of cut.

Shaping

Straight and irregular shaping can be performed on the radial saw. The motor should be adjusted vertically. The stock is fed into and against the cutters from right to left.

Straight shaping is done exactly as that for molding (Fig. 38-4).

Irregular (curved) parts can be shaped by using a rub collar (Fig. 38-5). An auxiliary board fastened to the table top should have a hole for the shaper cutter to work in. Use a guide pin from which to start the cut.

Routing

The routing processes described in this unit are the straight and angular types. **Straight** routing entails moving the piece with the *cutter* remaining stationary (Fig. 38-6). In **angular** routing, the *material* remains stationary and the cutter moves (Fig. 38-7).

Sanding

Figure 38-8 shows how to sand free-hand curves. Tilt the motor to the horizontal position for disk sanding (Fig. 38-9). A sander table should be built for disk sanding. One side is fastened securely to the table between the boards. This auxiliary table provides a surface on which to work.

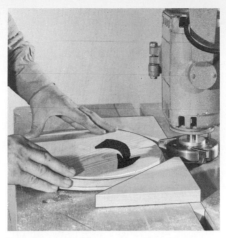

Fig. 38-3   Molding a circular piece.

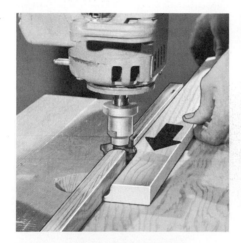

Fig. 38-4   Shaping straight stock.

Fig. 38-2   Cutting a molding on the radial saw.

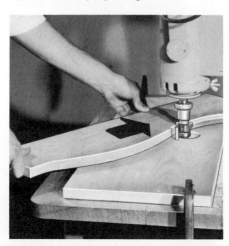

Fig. 38-5   Shaping against a rub collar.

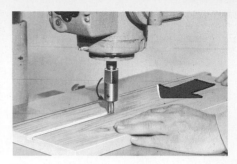

Fig. 38-6   Straight routing.

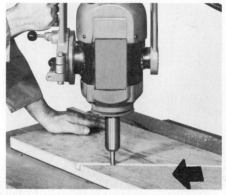

Fig. 38-7   Angular routing.

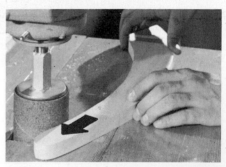

Fig. 38-8   Sanding curved stock free-hand.

Fig. 38-9   Disk sanding on the radial saw.

Band saw processes

unit **39**

General information about the band saw

The band saw (Fig. 39-1) is a machine that performs many sawing operations. The saw itself is a flexible band of steel with teeth cut on one edge. It can be used for straight sawing as well as for cutting curves.

The band saw used in industry is known as a **band mill.** It has a wide blade and is used to saw logs into planks. Lumberyards and millwork factories use a heavy-duty band saw for resawing thick stock into thinner pieces.

Sizes and types

The size of the band saw is measured by the diameter of the wheels around which the band runs. For school use, these vary from 14 to 30 inches (356 to 762 mm). Machines with wheels of less than a 14-inch (356-mm) diameter are suitable for home workshops but are not practical for schools or industrial applications. Smaller wheels tend to crystallize the blades in a relatively short time. They break more easily.

Woodcutting speed varies from 3000 feet per minute (ft/min) to approximately 6000 ft/min (914 to 1829

m/min), depending upon the size of the saw.

Some manufacturers make variable-speed band saws that cut both metal and wood (Fig. 39-1). The speeds are easily changed. The wood-cutting band saw blade can be replaced with a metal-cutting blade.

Parts and uses

The essential parts of the typical wood-cutting band saw are shown in

Figs. 39-1, 39-2, and 39-3. There are numerous parts that require specific adjustments. These are discussed in Unit 41, Operating Adjustments. Descriptions of the basic parts follow:

Wheels. There are two metal wheels whose outer rims are covered with rubber, called **rubber tires.** The band saw blade runs on these rubber tires, which protect the teeth and serve as

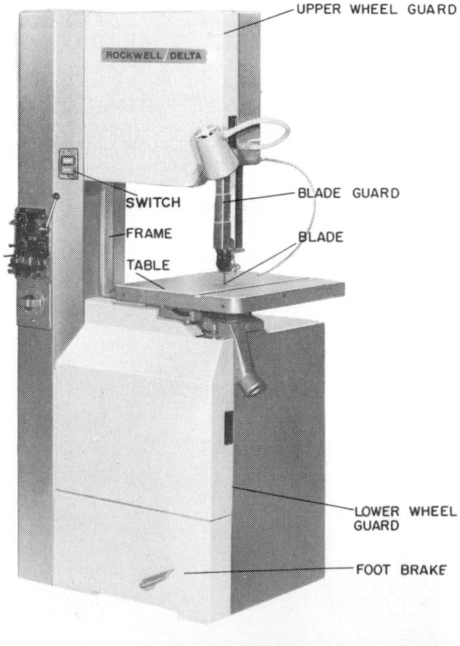

Fig. 39–1 A dual-speed 20-inch (508-mm) band saw. It produces a 4500-feet-per-minute, FPM, (22 860-m/s) speed for cutting wood and a 2000-FPM (10 160-m/s) speed for cutting nonferrous metals.

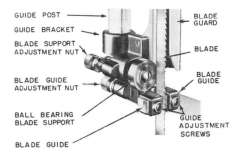

Fig. 39–2 Upper guide assembly for a typical band saw.

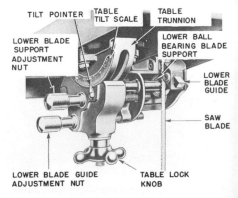

Fig. 39–3 Lower guide and table assembly

cushions, preventing the blade from slipping.

Frame. This is the metal casting that supports the two wheels and all the internal mechanism.

Table. The table supports the work being cut. Most tables are constructed so that they can be tilted to 45 degrees to the right and about 10 degrees to the left.

Upper and lower wheel guards. These guards protect the worker.

Some guards are completely removable; others are hinged to permit access to the blade and to the upper and lower wheels.

Blade guides. There are two blade guides. One is above, the other below, the table (Figs. 39-2 and 39-3). These guide the blade, keeping it from twisting and thus assuring a straight cut. The upper guide is adjustable in height to allow for thickness of cut.

Tension adjustment. This is generally made on the upper wheel. The pressure on the blade is controlled by operating the hand wheel or a small crank.

Base. This is the footing, or metal support, for the machine.

Blade guard. An angular sheet-metal piece, fastened near the upper blade guide, functions as a blade guard. It protects the worker, covering the blade from the upper guide to the upper wheel guard.

unit 40

Band saw blades

The two most popular tooth styles of band saw blades are (1) the standard, or regular, and (2) the skip-tooth, or buttress. Skip-tooth blades cut faster because the teeth do not clog with sawdust. The teeth of both band saw types are set. Figure 40-1 shows how the teeth are set on a regular band saw blade.

Sizes

The thickness of band saw blades averages 0.001 inch (0.025 mm) for each inch of the diameter of the wheels on which they will run. A 20-inch (508-mm) band saw would therefore require blades 0.020 inch (0.508 mm) thick. This is a general way to arrive at blade thickness; however, both thinner and thicker blades are in use.

Teeth are arranged just like those on the handsaw; there is always one more point than teeth per inch. Five teeth per inch will have six points (Fig. 40-2). Figure 40-3 gives a comparison of standard and skip-teeth.

Blades vary in width from 1/8 to 3/4 inch (3 to 19 mm) for home and school use. Width is determined by the diameter of the curve that can be cut on the band saw. Table 40-1 gives data that should be considered before cutting curves. Use a jig saw or drill, or bore curves less than 1/2 inch (13 mm) in diameter.

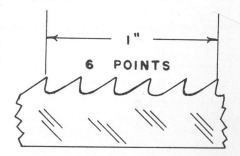

Fig. 40–2 There is always one more point than teeth per inch on the band saw blade.

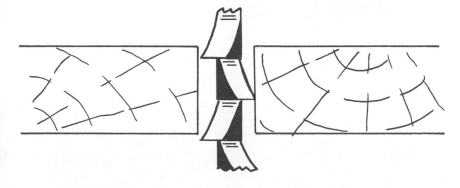

Fig. 40–1   Teeth are set on band saw blades so that the saw kerf (cut) is wider than the blade. This prevents binding.

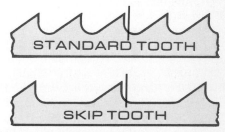

Fig. 40–3   A comparison of standard and skip teeth on the band saw.

Table 40-1 BLADE WIDTHS FOR CUTTING CURVES

Width of blade, in.	Minimum DIA of curve, in.
$\frac{1}{8}$	$\frac{3}{8}$
$\frac{3}{16}$	$\frac{3}{4}$
$\frac{1}{4}$	$1\frac{1}{8}$
$\frac{3}{8}$	$2\frac{1}{2}$
$\frac{1}{2}$	6

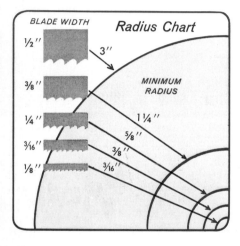

Fig. 40–4 Removing a band saw blade from the band saw. Be sure to release the tension.

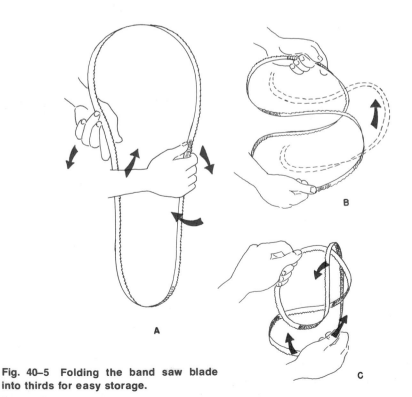

Folding the blade

Band saw blades can be easily folded and stored in minimum space by following these instructions: first, release the belt tension and remove the blade from the band saw (Fig. 40-4). Then, follow steps A, B, and C in Fig. 40-5. This series of steps shows how to grasp the blade (with the thumb of the right hand pointed *up* and the thumb of the left hand pointed *down*). If you do not let the blade slip or turn in your hands, it will probably fall into three loops. The right hand should turn away from your body; the left, toward your body, as shown in Fig. 40-5.

Fig. 40–5 Folding the band saw blade into thirds for easy storage.

unit 41

Operating adjustments

The band saw has several different adjustment devices that must be kept in alignment. Those adjustments described below are typical; they have to be made on most band saws. Before attempting to make adjustments on a particular band saw, be sure to study the manufacturer's data sheet and operating manual. A few of the simpler adjustments are those of the tension on the band saw blade, the blade guides above and below the table, the squareness of the table with the blade, and the cutting action.

Tension adjustment

The various thicknesses and widths of different band saw blades require different degrees of tension (tightness). The tension adjustment is usually made at the top rear of the saw. A hand wheel or handle (crank) is most often used to make this adjustment (see Fig. 41-1). The handle is turned carefully until the index on the scale matches the width of the band saw blade.

Adjusting blade guides

Figure 39-2 shows a detail of the typical blade guide above the band saw table. Figure 39-3 shows the blade guide underneath. Guide pins on either side of the blade are adjusted to allow a slight clearance for the blade on both sides.

The ball-bearing blade support, directly behind the blade, should be adjusted to allow about $\frac{1}{64}$ inch (0.4 mm) of space (Fig. 41-2).

Table adjustment

To obtain right-angle sawing, the band saw table must be at a 90-degree angle to the blade. Check this with a try square (Fig. 41-3). The table lock knob underneath the table usually makes this adjustment.

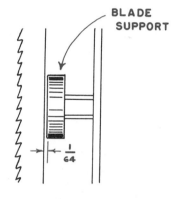

Fig. 41-2 **Proper adjustment of the blade support.**

Fig. 41-1 **The tension-adjustment handle with a tension scale.**

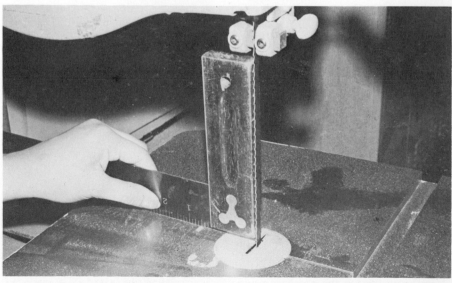

Fig. 41-3 **Checking the squareness of the table and the band saw blade.**

Cutting action of the blade

When a piece of wood is pushed squarely into the band saw blade, it should be cut in a straight line. Sometimes, however, the blade **leads** (pulls) to one side or the other (Fig. 41-4). In Fig. 41-4 the blade leads to the right, making it necessary to check the setting of the guides. The blade may have an improper set. If it is the fault of the guides, adjust them slightly tighter (see Fig. 39-2). If it is improperly set saw teeth, lightly hone the side of the blade. Use a fine stone (Fig. 41-5).

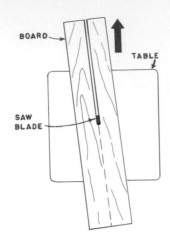

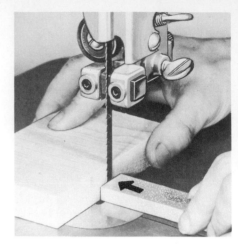

Fig. 41–4 A blade cutting to the side produces a *lead*.

Fig. 41–5 Honing the blade on the lead side.

unit 42

Straight sawing and resawing

The band saw can be used for straight sawing as well as for cutting curved pieces. Most band saws are fitted with a rip fence and a miter-gage cutoff guide. The widest band saw blade available should be used for both straight sawing and resawing. (Resawing is cutting stock to a narrower thickness.) Resawing is a job that the band saw does better than any other machine.

Straight freehand sawing

Read and observe the safety precautions in Unit 23.

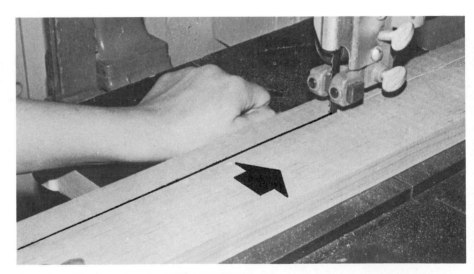

Fig. 42–1 Making a hand-guided straight cut.

1. Raise the upper blade guide to clear the lumber being cut. The guide should clear the stock by approximately 1/2 inch (13 mm).
2. Mark the board.
3. Turn on the switch. Make certain that you allow the blade to come to full speed.
4. Now feed the lumber slowly through the saw. Guide it gently with one hand; push it with the other (Fig. 42-1). Saw slightly on the waste side.

Ripping

1. Repeat the first two steps of freehand sawing.

2. Attach the rip fence to the band saw table. Set it to the desired width of the cut to be made (Fig. 42-2).

3. Turn on the switch, and allow the blade to come to full speed.

4. Feed the piece into the saw (Fig. 42-2). Hold it firmly against the fence while pushing it into the saw blade.

5. A square length of wood can be split or ripped in two diagonally. Tilt the table to 45 degrees; push the stock along the rip fence (Fig. 42-3).

6. The band saw is excellent for removing corners of turning squares (Fig. 42-4).

Crosscutting

1. Repeat the first two steps of freehand sawing.

2. Place the cutoff guide on the table in the groove. If the band saw does not have a groove, a wooden extension table can be grooved and fitted to the side, as shown in Fig. 42-5.

3. Turn on the switch, and allow the blade to come to full speed.

4. Hold the stock firmly against the cutoff guide, and feed it slowly into the band saw blade (Fig. 42-5).

5. Crosscut wide boards by reversing the cutoff guide (see Fig. 27-5).

Resawing

1. When possible, make preliminary ripsaw cuts on the circular saw before resawing on the band saw (Fig. 42-6).

2. Repeat the first three steps of freehand sawing.

3. Turn on the switch, and allow the blade to come to full speed.

4. Feed the stock very slowly into the band saw (Fig. 42-7). The edge of the piece being resawed should be planed at right angles to the face.

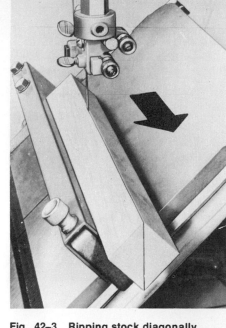

Fig. 42–3 Ripping stock diagonally.

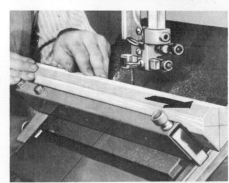

Fig. 42–4 Ripping off corners of turning-square stock.

Fig. 42–5 Crosscutting with the aid of a cutoff guide.

Fig. 42–2 Ripping stock against a ripping fence.

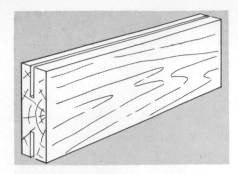

Fig. 42–6 Ripsaw cuts made on the circular saw make resawing easier.

Fig. 42–7 Resawing along a ripping fence.

5. A wooden or metal pivot-block jig fastened onto the saw table is perhaps the simplest guide when resawing stock (Figs. 42-8 and 42-9). The operator can feed the stock in such a way as to offset any lead in the band saw blade. The wooden pivot block or guide can be made easily. The end that serves as the rip guide should be rounded.

Fig. 42–8 Resawing against a wooden pivot-block jig for a guide.

Fig. 42–9 Resawing stock with a metal revolving pivot block for a guide.

unit 43

Curved and irregular sawing

The band saw is basically designed to cut curves and irregular shapes. Many persons consider this its primary function. Sometimes helpful jigs can be built. Duplicate parts can most easily be made by fastening or nailing several pieces together and then cutting them at one time. It is even desirable to leave the pieces fastened together while dressing down the edges by filing or sanding. This assures that they will be identical.

When cutting circles, be sure that you watch the sawing very carefully. The band saw blade cuts across a grain easily, but it has a tendency to follow the grain when cutting with it. Before sawing curves, circles, or irregular parts, study Table 40-1 for the minimum diameters of curves which can be made easily with different widths of blades.

Freehand sawing of curves

1. Raise the upper blade guide to clear the piece being cut.
2. Mark the layout on the board.
3. Turn on the switch, and allow the blade to come to full speed.
4. Study the piece to determine whether relief cuts should be made first (Fig. 43-1). For sharp curves, some relief cuts should be made as shown in Fig. 43-2.
5. Feed the piece into the saw blade. Make the cut on the waste side of the marked line (Fig. 43-3).

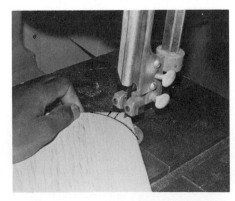

Fig. 43–1 Making relief cuts before sawing the curve.

6. To saw a circle or a disk, start the cut from the end grain; follow around the marking (Fig. 43-4).

Irregular and circular sawing using jigs

1. If many identical circular pieces are to be sawed, make a ³/₄-inch-thick (19 mm-thick) plywood jig, as illustrated in Fig. 43-5. Fasten or clamp it to the band saw table (see Fig. 43-6).

2. Select the stock from which the circles are to be made.

3. Repeat steps 1 through 3 of "Freehand Sawing of Curves."

4. Place the material on the pivot point of the jig; cut out the circular piece (Fig. 43-6). Cut the other pieces the same way.

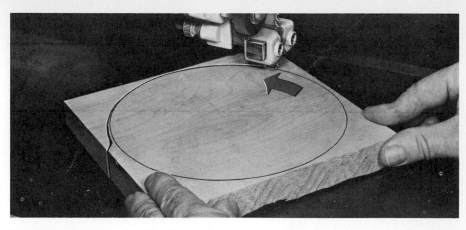

Fig. 43–4 Sawing a circular piece.

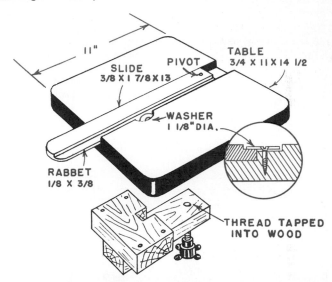

Fig. 43–5 A plywood jig to be fastened on the band saw table for cutting a circular piece. This one has a sliding pivot bar that can be adjusted to the desired radius.

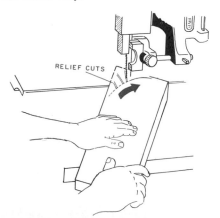

Fig. 43–2 Relief cuts are desirable when sawing sharp curves.

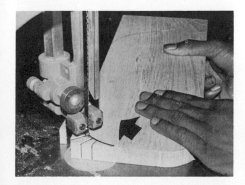

Fig 43–3 Sawing to a curved line. Note the relief cuts.

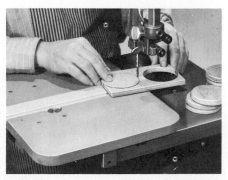

Fig. 43–6 Cutting identical circles with the use of a jig.

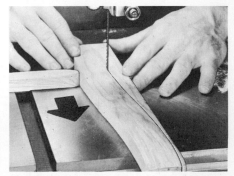

Fig. 43–7 Sawing parallel curves with a pivot guide as a jig.

5. Curved work that is to be ripped to an equal width can be cut on the band saw. Use a pivot guide clamped on the table (Fig. 43-7).

6. A pattern can be used where a number of similar pieces are to be cut. Figure 43-8 shows a wooden arm jig clamped to the saw table. The end of the arm is cut to a curve, either concave or convex. Center the curve in line with the teeth of the blade. Cut a slight notch at this point for the blade. Fit the pattern with anchor points or brads so that it can be pressed down and held to the piece that is to be cut.

7. Push the pattern and the piece to be cut gently into the band saw blade (see Fig. 43-8).

8. Some work pieces require compound cuts. This means cutting from two or more sides. Figure 43-9 shows how the template, or pattern, was first marked on the wood stock. Figure 43-10 shows this type of freehand sawing.

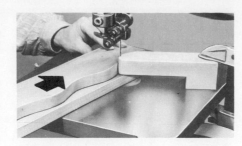

Fig. 43–8 Sawing duplicate parts with a pattern and wooden arm jig.

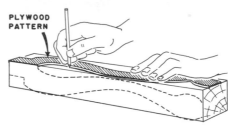

Fig. 43–9 Marking compound cuts on wood stock, following a pattern.

Fig. 43–10 A board with compound cuts made on the band saw.

Jig (scroll) saw processes

unit 44

General information about the jig (scroll) saw

The jig (scroll) saw (Fig. 44-1) is used mostly to cut internal (inside) or external (outside) curves in thin wood. The operating principle of this machine is that it changes **rotary motion** (round and round) to **reciprocal action** (up and down). The reciprocal action operates a moving plunger that has a small, narrow, short saw blade fastened in it.

Sizes and speeds

The size of the jig saw is measured by the distance from the saw blade to the inside of the curved portion of the overarm. Common sizes are 18 and 24 inches (457 and 610 mm). The latter has the capacity to cut a circle 48 inches (1219 mm) in diameter within the overarm. The usual maximum thickness of stock that a jig saw will cut is 2 inches (51 mm); however, most jig saws are used to cut thin pieces. Their speeds vary from 650 to 1700 cutting strokes per minute (csm).

Parts and uses

The main parts of the jig saw are shown in Fig. 44-1. There are also other parts that make specific adjustments. These are discussed in Unit 45, Jig Saw Blades and Operating Adjustments. Basic parts are listed here.

Base. The base contains the mechanism that converts rotary motion into reciprocal action. It serves as a mounting for the motor and the table, and it supports the overarm.

Overarm. Fastened to the base, the overarm holds the upper head, tension sleeve, upper chuck, and other attachments.

Table. The table is the support for the lumber being cut. It can be tilted 45 degrees to the right or left of horizontal. The table operates on a trunnion, or table tilt (Fig. 44-2). This is part of the table assembly, which also includes the lower plunger mechanism.

Tension sleeve and upper chuck. The sleeve usually contains a tension spring that pulls the blade up each time after the motor pulls it down. A guide assembly (Fig. 44-3) fastened onto this head has a hold-down guard to keep the stock firmly on the table. Each manufacturer has instructions for adjusting blade tension.

Belt and pulley guard. This guard is a metal protective cover that encloses the V belt and the pulleys of the motor and the jig saw. Most guards can be removed by loosening one hand-operated screw or nut. This is usually necessary when changing the V-belt arrangement to vary the cutting speed of the blade.

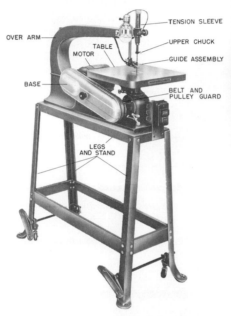

Fig. 44–1 A 24-inch (609.6-mm) jig saw.

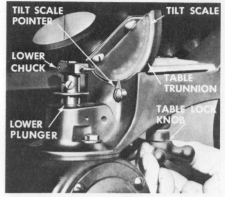

Fig. 44–2 A jig saw table assembly and lower plunger.

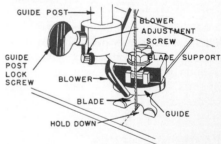

Fig. 44–3 A guide assembly for the jig saw.

unit 45

Jig saw blades and operating adjustments

The jig saw is one of the simplest and safest machines on which to work. Some adjustments must be made and checked each time the machine is used. The few described here are general, so the data sheets and operating manual of the manufacturer should be studied thoroughly. Adjustments require basic knowledge of types of blades and their functions.

Blades

Many different sizes and styles of blades are available for the jig saw. Figure 45-1 pictures seven common sizes. They are classified in two groups: (1) blades that are gripped by both upper and lower chucks, generally known as **jeweler's blades**, and (2) blades held in the lower chuck only. These are called **saber blades.**

Jeweler's blades are sometimes called **piercing blades;** they also cut metal. Often the pins are removed from ordinary coping saw blades and the blades used on the jig saw, instead of the jeweler's blades. They are satisfactory and inexpensive.

Fine work, especially on tight curves, is most satisfactorily done using jeweler's and coping saw blades. They can cut material up to the full capacity of the saw. Saber blades are heavier and cut faster, so they are used where curves are not too abrupt. A general rule is to use finer teeth for the harder woods and coarser teeth for softer ones.

Speed of cutting

Most jig saws regulate speed with three- or four-step pulleys. This is referred to as a **multispeed drive.** Slow speeds produce a rough cut; higher speeds result in smoother, finer edges.

Fastening blades

Chucks are used to hold blades. There are two chucks for this purpose: one is beneath the table, fastened to the driver plunger; the other, an upper one, is attached to the spring tension sleeve.

Jig saw and jeweler's saw blades are fastened in both chucks (Fig. 45-2). Saber blades are held in the lower chuck only. When using a saber blade, it is desirable to add a special guide directly under the table, as shown in Fig. 45-3. This extra guide gives more support to the upper guide, since the saber blade is held by only one chuck.

Each jig saw manufacturer provides chucks that adjust a little differently, but the general principle is the same. The blade must be centered in the chuck to make it cut vertically and in straight alignment. Self-centering chucks are available for both the upper and the lower plungers (Fig. 45-4).

Installing a regular jig saw blade

1. Remove the throat plate from the table (refer to Fig. 45-2).
2. Loosen the adjustment on the lower chuck. This will require either a screwdriver, an Allen-head wrench, or a special tool that comes with the jig saw.
3. Insert the jig saw blade from the top of the opening on the table. Fasten it securely about 3/8 inch (10 mm) deep in the lower chuck (see Fig. 45-2). The teeth should point *down*.
4. Loosen and push down the plunger and the tension sleeve attached to the overarm so that the upper chuck grasps about 3/8 inch (10 mm) of the blade.
5. Fasten the blade in the upper chuck as you did in the lower one.
6. Pull up the plunger and the tension sleeve until the proper tension is obtained on the blade. Fasten the assembly in the upper arm. Follow the manufacturer's suggestions on the correct amount of blade tension.

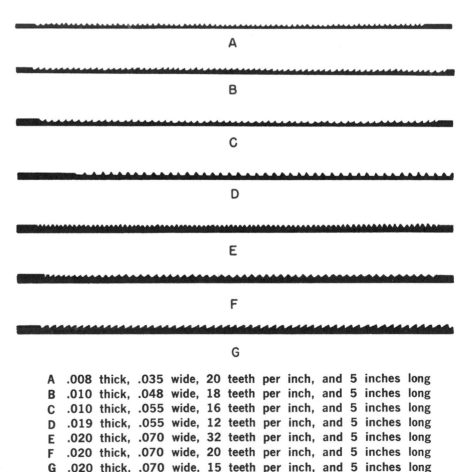

A

B

C

D

E

F

G

A .008 thick, .035 wide, 20 teeth per inch, and 5 inches long
B .010 thick, .048 wide, 18 teeth per inch, and 5 inches long
C .010 thick, .055 wide, 16 teeth per inch, and 5 inches long
D .019 thick, .055 wide, 12 teeth per inch, and 5 inches long
E .020 thick, .070 wide, 32 teeth per inch, and 5 inches long
F .020 thick, .070 wide, 20 teeth per inch, and 5 inches long
G .020 thick, .070 wide, 15 teeth per inch, and 5 inches long

Fig. 45–1 Seven common sizes of jig saw blades.

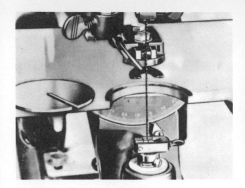

Fig. 45–2 The table cut away and the throat plate removed to give an exposed view of a jig saw blade fastened in both chucks.

7. Turn the pulley or V belt by hand to make sure that everything is working smoothly.

8. Replace the throat plate.

The procedure of installing a saber blade is similar except that it is fastened in the lower chuck only. Add a special guide, as shown in Fig. 45-3.

Table adjustments

Most jig saws have a table that can be tilted in either direction to permit bevel cutting.

Tilting is easily controlled by the table lock knob under the table (Fig.

Fig. 45–3 The table cut away and the throat plate removed to give an exposed view of a saber saw blade fastened in the lower chuck. Note the addition of a special guide under the table.

Fig. 45–4 A self-centering chuck.

44-2). The table can be tilted 45 degrees to the right or left. Figure 44-2 shows in the foreground one of two capscrews on the tilt-scale pointer. Zero on the scale indicates the table is at a right angle to, and perfectly square with, the blade. Each line on the scale represents one degree of tilt.

Closely allied with adjusting a table is regulating the hold-down attachment (clamp) on the upper guide assembly. This should always be adapted to the top surface of the work being cut. The hold-down clamp can be shifted to fit the piece that is being cut at an angle or a bevel (see Fig. 44-3).

unit 46

External and internal sawing on the jig saw

The jig saw is ideally suited to making both external and internal cuts. Inter-

nal sawing is sometimes called **piercing**. A $1/8$-inch-wide (3-mm-wide) blade is an average size for doing almost all cutting on the jig saw. It is not limited to cutting wood only; with blades of the correct thickness, it can cut metal, plastics, and cardboard.

Irregular external sawing

Read and observe the safety precautions in Unit 23.

1. Mark, layout, or transfer the design to the board or boards. Identical pieces can be cut at the same time by fastening them together with brads.

2. Check to see that the jig saw blade is properly fastened in both chucks. The saber blade is held only by the lower one. Make certain that the teeth *point down*.

3. Place the board or boards on the saw table against the saw blade. Lower and adjust the hold-down clamp so that it barely clears the work.

Be sure that the blade is square with (at 90 degrees to) the table.

4. Turn on the power. Gently but firmly move the stock into the saw blade. Start the cut outside the mark or pattern line (Fig. 46-1). This allows for edge dressing (smoothing). When sawing sharp turns, apply very little forward pressure and turn the work slowly.

5. Continue sawing until all outside cutting is completed.

Irregular internal sawing

1. Repeat step 1 of "Irregular External Sawing."

2. Drill or bore a hole in the waste portion of the design.

3. Insert the blade through this hole. Fasten it firmly in the chucks. The saber blade is held only by the lower one.

4. Repeat steps 3, 4, and 5 of "Irregular External Sawing" (see Fig. 46-2). Internal sanding can also be performed on the jig saw (Fig. 46-3).

Straight sawing

Freehand straight sawing can easily be done on the jig saw. Figure 46-4 shows straight sawing a board with the chucks and blade turned to the side. This adjustment is necessary when the board is too long to clear the overarm. The chucks of most jig saws can be adjusted to this position.

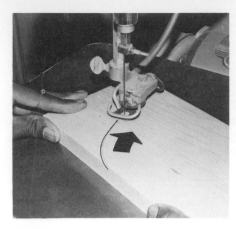

Fig. 46–1 Irregular external sawing on the jig saw.

Fig. 46–2 Irregular internal sawing on the jig saw.

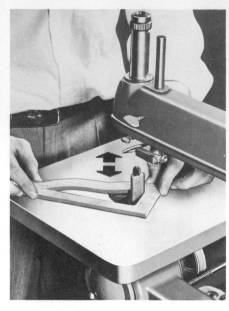

Fig. 46–3 Sanding can also be performed on the jig saw. This requires a special sanding accessory.

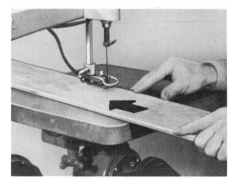

Fig. 46–4 Straight-sawing a long board from the side of the jig saw.

unit 47

Making inlay designs or pictures

Making inlay designs or pictures from wood veneers is fascinating. It is not difficult, but it does require accuracy. Inlay pictures or designs make excellent decoration for bookends, trays, coffee and end table tops, and covers of useful small boxes (Fig. 47-1). If a dark and a light piece of veneer are cut on the jig saw at the same time, any piece from one will fit into the corresponding space in the other. That is, the pieces are interchangeable.

Making inlay pieces on the jig saw

1. Transfer the design or picture, using carbon paper, to a piece of ¹/₈-inch (3 mm) plywood. Figure 47-1 shows a finished inlay picture on a wooden bookend.

2. Study and plan the most effective color and grain of veneer to use to represent the parts of the picture. Different colors and grains provide the contrast that helps make the design effective.

3. Arrange the pieces of veneer in cross bands between two pieces of plywood, as illustrated in Fig. 47-2. The ¹/₈-inch (3-mm) plywood with the transferred design marked on it is on the top. A piece of the same size is on the bottom. Nail this assembly together for sawing. The two pieces of plywood merely serve to hold the decorative veneers together while they are being cut.

4. Using a very thin jeweler's blade, cut out the design or picture on the marked lines.

5. Assemble the pieces face down

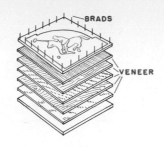

Fig. 47–2 An exploded view of plywood and veneer pieces to be nailed together for sawing.

Fig. 47–3 Assembling the various inlay pieces (using rubber cement) on a temporary cardboard mount.

on a sheet of cardboard, using rubber cement to hold them in place (Fig. 47-3). They are arranged like a jigsaw puzzle. There will be enough pieces of veneer stock to plan and arrange as many veneered designs as there are sheets of veneer. The contrasts of veneers will be different for each arrangement.

6. Lay out and cut the base to which the inlay assembly is to be permanently glued.

7. Apply glue to the base. Place the inlay assembly on the glued surface (Fig. 47-4). The cardboard should be on top. Clamp the glued assembly (veneer, design, and base) between two pieces of ³/₄-inch (19-mm) plywood until the glue is dry.

8. Remove the assembly from the clamps. Lift off the cardboard sheet. It will pull off because rubber cement separates easily.

9. Sand the veneered surface until it is smooth.

10. Shape the outside of the piece. Complete the bookend. It should be similar to Fig. 47-1.

11. Apply a clear finish.

Fig. 47–1 An inlaid bookend.

Fig. 47–4 Placing the cardboard with veneer on the glued, permanent base.

Jointer and rotary jointer/surfacer processes

unit 48

General information about the jointer and the rotary jointer/surfacer

The jointer (Fig. 48-1) is an electrically driven power planer. This tool is used mainly to plane the surfaces and edges of boards. It can also be used to plane tapers, chamfers, and bevels; cut rabbets; and make other specialty cuts.

Sizes and types of jointers

The capacity (size) of the jointer is usually determined by the cutting widths of the knives used in the cutter head. These range from 4 inches (102 mm) in even numbers through 16 inches (406 mm). Most cutter heads have three or four knives which revolve at a speed between 3600 and 4000 r/min.

The **table** of the jointer consists of two parts: the front, or **infeed**, and the rear, or **outfeed**. Both are usually adjustable for levelness and cutting height. The surface of the rear table must be level (even) with the cutting edges of the knives. If it is higher or lower, the planed edge or surface will not be straight and accurate. The front table is easily adjustable. It can be lowered to provide the depth of cut on the stock.

Jointers used in school laboratories and home workshops are usually handfed. Large industrial jointers usually have self-feeding mechanisms.

Jointer parts and uses

The main parts of the jointer are the cutter head, front and rear tables, fence, guard, table adjustments, and base.

Cutter head. The cutter head (Fig. 48-2) has three and sometimes four fitted knives. Other parts of this portion of the tool are also shown.

Front table. This is the infeed table, which is easily adjustable for the depth of the cut. It supports the board, which is fed into the knives.

Rear table. The rear table is usually adjustable. For most cuts, it should be even with the cutting edges of the knives. It supports the board after it is planed.

Fence. The fence is used as a guide. It is usually set at a 90-degree angle to the table to get edges planed at a right angle to the face. It can be set at an angle to produce a chamfer or a bevel.

Guard. The guard covers the cutting knives. It swings out or up as the board is planed, thereby protecting the operator.

Table adjustments. These are conveniently located under or to one side of the front and the rear tables. They raise or lower the tables, according to the type of cut desired.

Base. The base is the stand, or support, which holds the jointer.

The **rotary jointer/surfacer** (Fig. 48-3) is a relatively new machine designed for surface or edge planing up to 6 inches (152.4 mm) in width or thickness. It has the trade name of *Uniplane*. One can plane, joint, bevel, chamfer, trim, taper, and do almost any process on this machine that can be done on a jointer.

Parts and uses of the rotary jointer/surfacer

The essential parts are the table, fence (infeed and outfeed), cutter head, cutter-head guard, miter gage, and stand or cabinet.

Cutter head. The cutter head (Fig. 48-4) rotates at a speed of 4000 r/min, or 32 000 csm. There are eight cutters:

four for rough cutting and four for finishing. These are alternately spaced on the cutter head, first making a rough, then a finish, cut.

Table. The table can be tilted and locked in any position between 0 and 45 degrees.

Fence. This part consists of two pieces: the adjustable infeed and the stationary outfeed.

Cutter-head guard. This protects the operator from possible injury.

Miter gage. The miter gage operates in a slot on the table. Its graduated index determines the angle of cut.

Stand, or **cabinet.** This is the base, or stand, which supports the rotary jointer/surfacer.

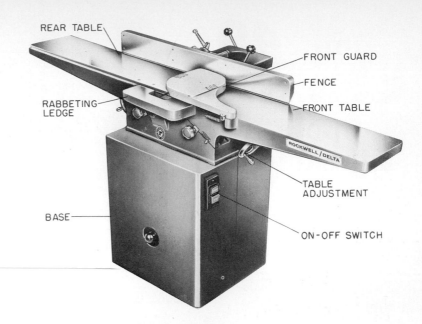

Fig. 48–1   An 8-inch (203.2-mm) jointer.

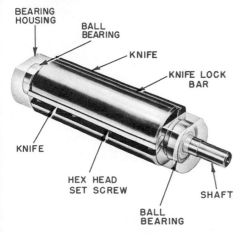

Fig. 48–2   A jointer cutter head.

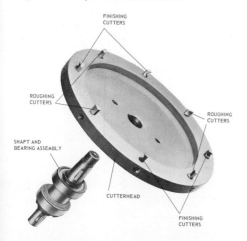

Fig. 48–4   The cutter head, showing the relation of roughing and finishing cutters.

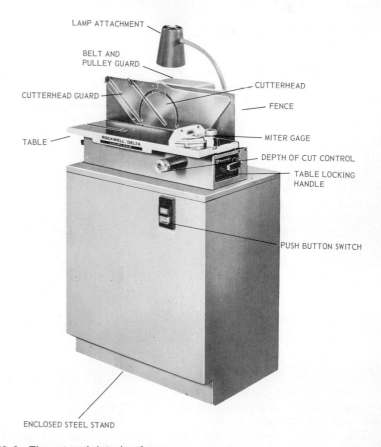

Fig. 48–3   The rotary jointer/surfacer.

unit 49

Jointer operating adjustments

The jointer is a precision machine. When perfectly adjusted, it can perform many time-saving planing processes.

Rear-table adjustment

To do satisfactory work, the rear table must be even and *exactly* level with the cutting edge of the knives in the cutter head, as shown in Fig. 49-1.

1. Release the hand wheel or handle at the back of the jointer.
2. Raise or lower the rear table until it is even with all the knives (Fig. 49-2).
3. If a knife is out of alignment, tap it down lightly, or pry it up. To make this adjustment, slightly loosen the screws that hold the knife in the cutter head so that the knife can be aligned, as shown in Fig. 49-3.
4. When the *rear table* has been adjusted accurately in relation to the knives, tighten the hand or locking wheel. If the rear table is higher than the knives, the jointer will cut a taper on the board, as shown in Fig. 49-4. If the rear table is lower, the knives will make a gouge at the end of the cut, as shown in Fig. 49-5.

Other adjustments

Check the fence with the table to make sure it is at a right angle with (90 degrees to) the table, as in Fig. 49-6.

The **rotary jointer/surfacer** has adjusting devices for both depth and angle of cuts. The infeed fence is adjustable for depth of cut by turning the depth-of-control knob, which is calibrated in 64ths of an inch (0.39 mm). The maximum depth of cut is $1/8$ inch (3 mm).

The table adjusts from 0 to 45 degrees by a tilt scale and table lock (Fig. 49-7); 0 means a cut 90 degrees to the table. Study the service manual, or follow instructions given by your teacher, when making adjustments.

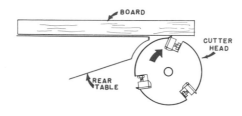

Fig. 49-1 The correct adjustment of the rear table of the jointer with the cutting edge of the knives.

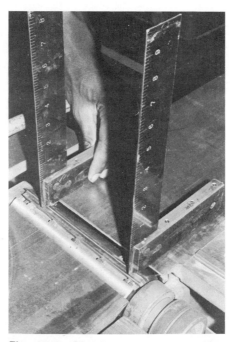

Fig. 49-2 Checking the rear table against the cutter knives for evenness.

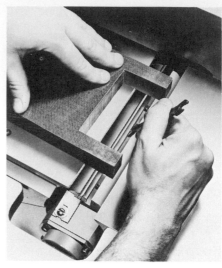

Fig. 49-3 Adjusting the alignment of the cutter knife with the rear table.

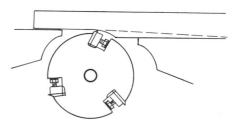

Fig. 49-4 A taper cut made with the rear table too high.

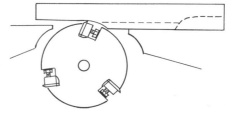

Fig. 49-5 A gouge cut results when the rear table is set too low.

Fig. 49–6 Checking the squareness of the fence and the table.

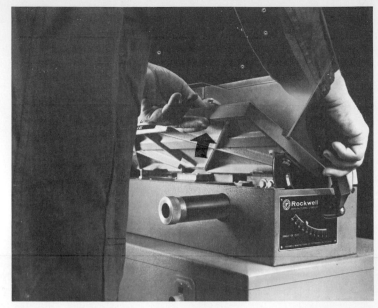

Fig. 49–7 Adjusting the table on the jointer/surfacer for a bevel cut.

unit **50**

Planing surfaces, edges, and ends on the jointer

A board can be completely planed on the jointer if the cutter knives can cut the entire width of the board at one time. An 8-inch (203-mm) jointer, for instance, can easily plane the entire width of an 8-inch board because this size of lumber usually measures only 7^1/$_2$ inches (190 mm) in width.

Figure 50-1 shows the steps (sequence) in planing the ends and edges of a board after the faces have been planed. It is considered unsafe to plane the end of a board that is not *at least* 8 inches (203 mm) wide.

Planing a surface

Read and observe the safety precautions in Unit 23.

1. Adjust the front (infeed) table for a cut of about ^{1}/$_{16}$ inch (2 mm).

2. Check to see that the guard is in place and is working properly.

3. Check the surface of the board for a warp (Fig. 50-2) and/or a wind (slight twist). The concave (hollow) face should be placed down and planed first.

4. Turn on the switch, and allow the machine to come to full speed.

5. Push the stock forward firmly with both hands (Fig. 50-3). Stand at the left of the front table as you plane.

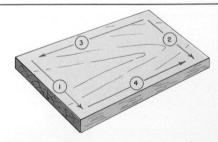

Fig. 50–1 Steps, or sequence, in planing and squaring a board on the jointer.

Fig. 50–2 A warped board. The cupped face should be planed first.

117

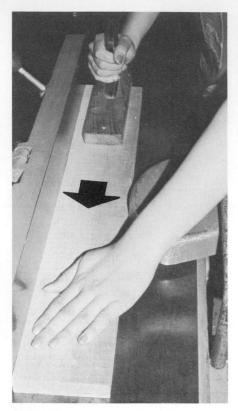

Fig. 50–3 Planing the surface with the aid of a push stick for safety.

Plane in the direction of the grain. Use a push block for planing surfaces.

6. Check the planed surface to see that it has been fully planed and is smooth. It may be necessary to make additional cuts to remove the warp, wind, or rough-sawed finish. The final cut should be very shallow.

Jointing an edge

1. Check the fence with a try square to make certain it is set at a right angle to the table (see Fig. 49-6).

2. Select the best edge of the board to be planed. This should be the one that has the fewest irregularities and that is the straightest.

3. Adjust the depth of the cut to approximately $1/16$ inch (2 mm). This is done by lowering the front table.

4. Turn on the switch, and allow the motor to come to full speed.

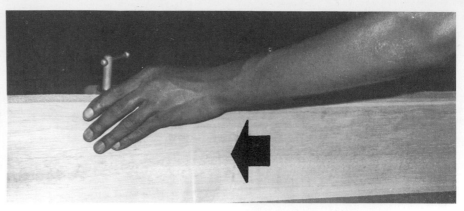

Fig. 50–4 Planing an edge. The guard is removed to show cutting action.

5. Place the board on the front table with the best surface (face side) against the fence. Make certain that you plane *with* the grain.

6. Hold the board against the fence firmly with both hands, and slowly push it over the cutter head (Figs. 50-4 and 50-5).

Joint an end

1. Check the end of the board with a try square or a framing square.

2. Adjust the depth of the cut by raising or lowering the front table. The depth of the cut should be very shallow: approximately $1/32$ to $1/16$ inch (1 to 2 mm). A deeper setting will tear the grain at the end of the cut.

3. Turn on the switch, and allow the motor to come to full speed.

4. Place the end of the board on the front table with the best face against the fence. Remember: never plane end grain on the jointer if the width is less than 8 inches (203 mm).

5. Hold the board firmly with both hands; slowly push it forward over the cutter head (Fig. 50-6). Jointing completely across the end of a board is satisfactory when squaring up stock, as shown in Fig. 50-1.

6. Another method of jointing an end is first to make a short cut of about 1 inch (25 mm) along one end.

7. Reverse the board and joint the end to blend with the cut made in step 6 (Fig. 50-7).

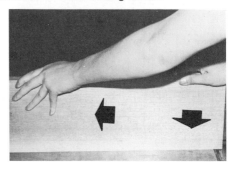

Fig. 50–5 Completing the edge cut on the jointer. The guard is removed to show cutting detail.

Fig. 50–6 Jointing (planing) the end of a board.

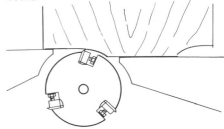

Fig. 50–7 An alternate method of jointing an end.

unit 51

Planing chamfers, bevels, rabbets, and tapers on the jointer

Fig. 51–2 Planing a chamfer or bevel on the jointer with the fence tilted backward (out). Guard removed for clarity.

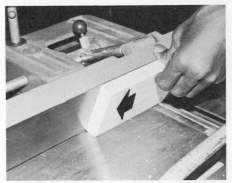

Fig. 51–3 Planing a chamfer or bevel on the jointer with the fence tilted forward (in). Guard removed for clarity.

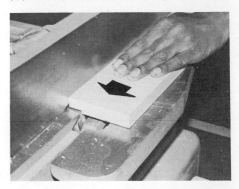

Fig. 51–4 Planing a rabbet on the jointer.

Although the jointer is primarily used to plane the surfaces and edges of boards, it has other uses. The jointer can be used to make a number of specialty cuts in addition to ordinary planing. This versatile machine can be adapted to plane chamfers, bevels, rabbets, and tapers.

Planing a chamfer or a bevel

1. Set a sliding bevel to the desired angle for the chamfer or bevel. An angle of 45 degrees is often used for chamfers.
2. Adjust the fence to fit the angle of the sliding bevel (Fig. 51-1).
3. Adjust the depth of the cut.

Fig. 51–1 Adjusting a fence to the desired angle for the chamfer or bevel.

4. Turn on the switch, and allow the motor to come to full speed.
5. Make a trial run on a piece of scrap wood; test the angle with the sliding bevel. Make adjustments if necessary.
6. Plane the chamfer or bevel as shown in Figs. 51-2 and 51-3. Make the number of cuts necessary to shape them. If the chamfer or bevel is to be cut on the ends, as well as the edges, shape the *ends* first, then the edges.

Planing a rabbet

1. Lay out and mark the exact size of the rabbet on the front edge of the board (see Fig. 51-4).
2. Move the fence over to the front edge of the table.
3. Move the guard out of position so that you can see the knives in the cutter head.
4. Turn the cutter head *by hand* until the cutting edge of one of the knives is at the top.
5. Measure in the distance for the width of the rabbet along the top edge of the cutter knife. Move the jointer fence to this point; fasten it to this measurement. Make sure the fence is parallel to the edge of the tables.
6. Adjust the depth of cut by low-

ering the infeed (front) table to the desired depth of the rabbet. If the depth is greater than $3/8$ inch (10 mm), it will be necessary to take more than one cut.
7. Check to see that all adjustments have been secured.
8. Turn on the jointer. Make a trial run for the rabbet cut on scrap.
9. Check the rabbet cut for accuracy. Make adjustments if needed.
10. Plane the rabbet (Fig. 51-4).

Planing a taper

1. Mark the taper on the stock.
2. Adjust the depth of the cut to the same depth as that of the taper cut. Raise or lower the front table if it

is not greater than 1/4 inch (6 mm). Otherwise, more than one cut should be taken.

3. Turn on the motor, and allow it to come to full speed.

4. In tapering the full length of the edge, handle the board in the manner shown in Fig. 51-5. Drop the front edge of the board so that it barely falls on the back table; push it forward to make the taper cut.

5. When tapering only a part of the edge, mark the front line of the taper on the stock (Fig. 51-6).

6. Plane the taper (Fig. 51-7). Use a push block for safety.

7. Very short tapers are most easily cut by *pulling* the work over the cutter head, as shown in Fig. 51-8. The front table should be lowered to the desired depth. The stock is placed on the table so that the start of the taper comes over the knives (Fig. 51-8).

8. Push the stock down so that the end makes contact with the front table. Slip a block under the free end of the stock to maintain this position, and then pull the piece toward you (see Fig. 51-8).

Fig. 51–5 Planing a taper to the full length of the board. The guard is removed to show detail.

Fig. 51–7 Tapering a part of an edge, such as on a square leg.

Fig. 51–6 Setting a stop with the table adjusted for tapering a portion of an edge or a leg. The guard is removed for clarity.

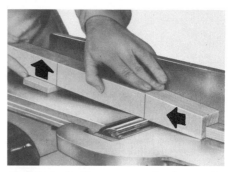

Fig. 51–8 Cutting a very short taper by pulling the piece toward you.

unit 52

Planing on the rotary jointer/ surfacer

Planing

Read and observe the safety precautions in Unit 23.

1. Adjust the infeed fence to the desired depth of cut.

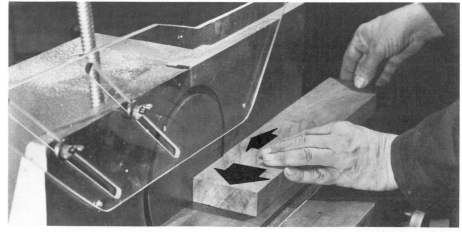

Fig. 52-1 Planing an edge.

Fig. 52–2 Planing a face with the aid of a push stick.

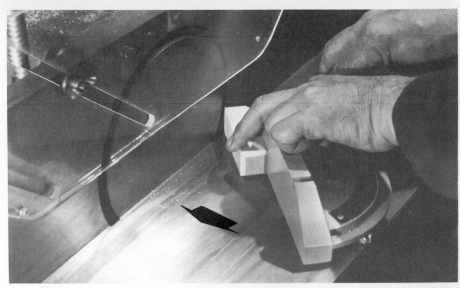

Fig. 52–4 Cutting chamfers with the use of a miter gage.

Fig. 52–3 Trimming an end by using the miter gage.

Fig. 52–5 Trimming a compound cut.

2. Test the fence for squareness to the table surface. Use a try square. This adjustment should be for a 90-degree angle, unless a bevel is to be cut (see Fig. 49-7).

3. Check to see that the cutter guard is working properly.

4. Turn on the switch. Allow the machine to come to full speed.

5. Firmly push the stock forward from right to left. Use both hands (Fig. 52-1).

6. Hold thin stock in place with a push block for safety (see Fig. 52-2).

7. Use the miter gage when cutting or trimming the end of stock (Fig. 52-3).

8. Chamfers, bevels, and angle cuts can be made by setting the miter gage at the desired angle to be cut (Fig. 52-4).

9. A compound cut requires adjustment of both the table and the miter gage (Fig. 52-5).

10. Turn the machine off immediately after the cuts have been completed.

Surfacer processes

unit 53

General information about the thickness planer (surfacer)

The planer is also called the thickness planer or the surfacer (Fig. 53-1). It is a single-purpose woodworking machine used for making a smooth planed surface on a piece of stock. The thickness planer planes, or surfaces, the stock to an even thickness.

Planers are either double or single. The size is determined and listed by the maximum thickness and width of board it can handle. The single surfacer planes one face of a board at a time. It is the most frequently used type in school industrial laboratories. The 12-inch (305-mm) surfacer can plane stock up to 4 inches (102 mm) thick and 12 inches (305 mm) wide. Larger single surfacers can plane stock up to 9 inches (229 mm) thick and 42 inches (1067 mm) wide.

Double surfacers plane both surfaces of the stock at the same time.

Most planer cutter heads have three evenly spaced knives (see Fig. 53-2). Successive cuts are made as the corrugated infeed roll pushes the board through the planer head. The outfeed roll holds the board against the table, and the table rolls as it moves forward (Fig. 53-2). The speed of the cutter head varies from 3600 to 6000 r/min.

Operating adjustments

The operating controls of the surfacer are few and simple. An electric switch turns on the power for the machine. A hand wheel or electrical control raises and lowers the table to adjust for stock thickness (Fig. 53-3). A feed control can be cut on and off to move the board into the cutter head. On some machines this control also regulates the speed from slow to fast. There is a thickness gage with an indicator (index) that shows the thickness to which the board is being planed.

Other adjustments are considered as maintenance, and these vary according to the sizes and different makes of machines. You should study the manufacturer's manual carefully before making such adjustments.

Parts and uses

Feed mechanism. The head of the planer contains the feed roll, chip

CONTROL PANEL

MANUAL THICKNESS CONTROL

ROCKWELL

FEED AND CUTTER ROLLS

TABLE

BASE

Fig. 53–1 A 24- by 9-inch (609.6- by 228.6-mm) single planer (surfacer).

breaker, cutter head, and outfeed roll. These parts are illustrated in Fig. 53-2. A direct feed motor is usually attached to the planer head.

Table. The flat surface on which the lumber rides.

Base. The frame which serves as a mounting for the working parts.

Thickness-control hand wheel or electrical control. This adjusts the table, which controls the thickness remaining after the cut.

Feed control. This operates the infeed and outfeed rolls that move the stock through the rolls and under the cutter head. On some machines it also determines the speed at which the piece is fed into the planer head.

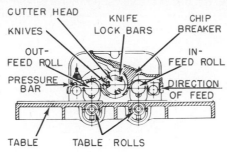

Fig. 53–2 Detail of the cutter head and rolls on the typical planer.

Fig. 53–3 Adjusting the surfacer table with an electrical control for thickness of cut.

unit 54

Planing to thickness

Very accurate and "true" surfacing of stock on a planer can be done if one side (face) of the board has first been planed on the jointer. This is especially desirable if the board is warped or twisted. A warped board (Fig. 54-1) should have the cupped (warped) face planed first. A board having a *wind* (twist) should have one face planed flat before it is surfaced.

Boards can be edge-glued together and surfaced to uniform thickness (Fig. 54-2). The width must, of course, be within the capacity of the surfacer.

Lumber that is less than 14 inches in length or $1/4$ inch (6 mm) thick *should not be planed* in the surfacer. The board should be sufficiently long that the outfeed roll starts pulling it before the infeed roll releases it. Inspect boards to make certain that they are clean and free from tacks, brads, nails, screws, or paint or other finishing materials.

Planing

Read and observe the safety precautions in Unit 23.

1. Plane one face of the board on the jointer. This can be done, however, only if you have a jointer that is wide enough. If not, follow the procedure given in the next step.

2. Adjust the table to the desired thickness. The first cut should be $1/16$ inch (2 mm) *less* than the maximum thickness of the board. Take a shallow cut on hardwoods and a slightly heavier (deeper) one on softwoods. A good average depth is $1/16$ inch (2 mm). If the first face cannot be planed on the jointer, it can be done on the surfacer by placing the cupped face (concave) down (see Fig. 54-1).

3. Check the direction of the wood grain. Try to feed the board so that the cut will be made *with* the grain.

4. Turn on the electric power, and adjust the feed control so that the rollers and the cutter head are turning.

5. Place the board flat on the infeed side of the table. Push it straight forward until the feed rolls pull it (Fig. 54-3).

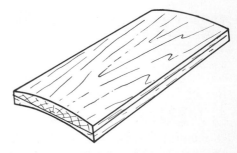

Fig. 54–1 Plane the cupped face of a warped board first.

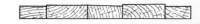

Fig. 54–2 Boards edge-glued for planing.

Fig. 54–3 Feeding a board into the thickness planer.

Fig. 54–4 Removing a surfaced board from the planer.

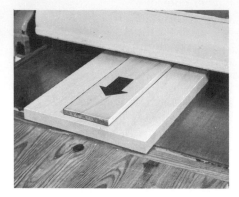

Fig. 54–5 Planing a thin board.

6. Grasp the surfaced board as it comes off the back table (Fig. 54-4). Do not allow the surfaced board to fall to the floor.

7. Run the stock through the sur- facer as often as necessary. Reduce the board to the planned thickness. Thin boards can be surfaced by plac- ing them on top of thicker ones (Fig. 54-5).

Drill press processes

unit 55

General information about the drill press

The drill press was originally designed for the metalworking trades, but it has been adapted for woodworking, plas- tics, and composition materials. It is most frequently used for drilling and boring holes. The term **boring** usually implies cutting holes in wood, even though twist drill bits are used. The term **drilling** is usually associated with the process of machining holes in metal. However, the two terms are used interchangeably in modern wood- working using the drill press.

Drill presses are made in bench and floor models (Fig. 55-1). The only difference between the models is the length of the upright column.

The many available attachments make it possible to do operations in woodworking other than boring and drilling holes. These are mortising, shaping, routing, and sanding. The process of mortising on the drill press is almost identical to that of mortising on the mortiser. See Unit 63, Mortising on the Drill Press.

Sizes and speeds

The more practical sizes of drill presses vary from 12 to 20 inches (305 to 508 mm). The size is determined by measuring twice the distance from the center of the chuck to the front of the vertical column.

The speed of this machine varies from approximately 300 to 6000 r/min. On most drill presses, the speed is controlled by shifting the drive belt, or belts, on a set of cone pulleys located in the head. Slow speeds are used for metalworking; faster ones are for woodworking.

The manufacturers' manuals contain charts and tables that show the speeds of numerous belt-and-pulley combinations. On the drill press shown in Fig. 55-1, only a handle on the head is changed to vary the speed. The speed-guide index indicates the speed.

Parts and uses

Base. A heavy cast-iron footing, or support, usually forms the base of the drill press.

Column. The column is a hollow, rigid tube that fits into the base. It supports the table, motor, and head.

Table. The flat table holds the work. It is adjustable for angle, and it moves up and down on the column.

Head. The top assembly is the head. It has the spindle, pulleys, bearings, and belt. It also supports the motor.

Chuck. The chuck is usually a geared and keyed device that is fastened to the spindle. It holds the bits. Its capacity ordinarily varies from 0 to 1/2 inch (0 to 13 mm).

Feed lever or handle. This part raises or lowers the spindle during drilling.

Depth stop. This consists of double-locking nuts that are used to adjust the depth of the drilled hole.

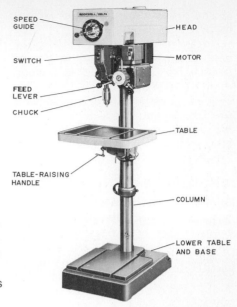

Fig. 55–1 A 17-inch (431.8-mm) floor-model drill press.

unit 56

ily are shaper cutters and small sanding drums.

On some drill presses, the spindle must be changed to attach the accessories. Many are now designed with

The numerous jobs the drill press can do depend upon the many types of bits, cutters, and accessories that are available (Figs. 56-1 through 56-14) Several types of bits bore and cut holes in wood. Mortising bits and chisels, along with the mortising attachment, readily convert the drill press into a mortiser (see Unit 63). Other accessories that fasten on it eas-

Fig. 56–1 A straight-shank twist drill bit is available in decimal, number, and letter sizes.

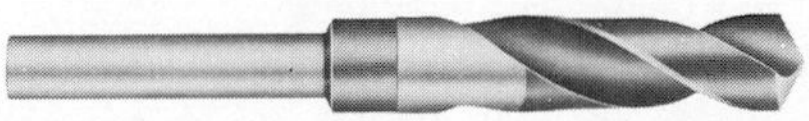

Fig. 56–2 A machine bit for wood with reduced shank.

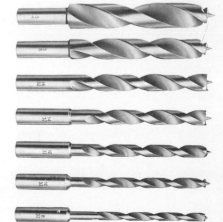

Fig. 56–3 The double-spur twist bit.

125

special arbors that fit into the conventional geared chuck.

The manufacturer's manual gives detailed instructions on the proper spindles to use and how to change them. The manual should also be studied for setting correct speeds and for assembling and fastening the many bits, cutters, and accessories that are illustrated and described.

Accessories and attachments

Shaper cutters, collars (see Fig. 65-1), and a **spindle adapter** convert a drill press into a shaper. It is desirable that an auxiliary wood table with a center hole be attached to the metal table of the drill press for this operation. A fence and hold-down clamps are other accessories used in converting the drill press into a shaper. Figure 59-14 shows a drill press converted for use as a shaper.

Sanding drums of various sizes can be used on a drill press (Fig. 56-14). These are especially useful for sanding curved work. The drum shanks fit interchangeable spindles or chucks.

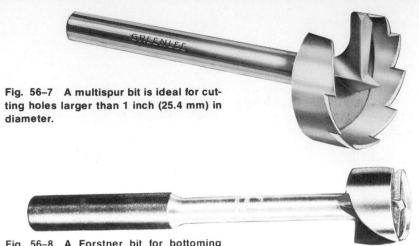

Fig. 56–7 A multispur bit is ideal for cutting holes larger than 1 inch (25.4 mm) in diameter.

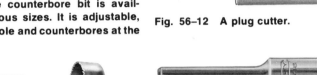

Fig. 56–8 A Forstner bit for bottoming holes.

Fig. 56–9 The counterbore bit is available in numerous sizes. It is adjustable, and it drills a hole and counterbores at the same time.

Fig. 56–12 A plug cutter.

Fig. 56–13 A countersink bit.

Fig. 56–4 A wood auger bit with threads filed off the feed screw may be adapted for the drill press.

Fig. 56–5 A spade- or power-type wood bit.

Fig. 56–6 A power bore bit.

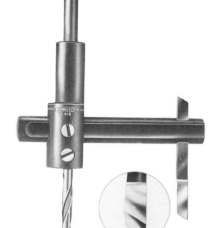

Fig. 56–11 An adjustable circle cutter.

Fig. 56–10 A quick-cut hole saw.

Fig. 56–14 A sanding drum.

unit 57

Operating adjustments

A few basic adjustments are required before the drill press is used to bore or drill holes. These also apply to other drill press operations when the various attachments are used.

Boring to depth

Holes are often bored to a specified depth. The best and most accurate method is to use the stop-rod nuts shown in Fig. 57-1. Determine the setting by bringing the drill down alongside the work to a pencil mark showing the desired depth. Adjust and tighten the stop-rod nuts.

Another method is to bring the bit into contact with the wood and then set the depth pointer at a specified mark. The depth of the hole can be figured from this marking as the bit cuts into the wood. Watch the index marking for accurate depth of hole.

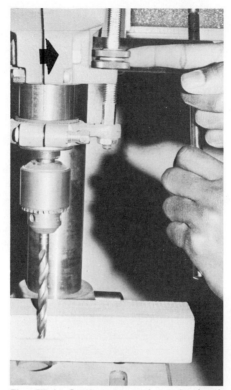

Fig. 57–1 Setting stop-rod nuts for depth of hole by bringing the drill down alongside the work to a pencil mark showing the desired depth. Also, tightening the stop-rod nuts.

Adjusting the drill press table

Most processes require the drill press table to be set at a right angle (90 degrees) to the bit. Check this with a try square (Fig. 57-2). An adjustment nut underneath the table holds it in the desired position.

Some boring jobs require that the table be set at a tilt. Tilt the table to the desired angle by aligning it to the bit, using a bevel tool.

The table is adjusted for height by sliding it up or down and then fastening it to the column.

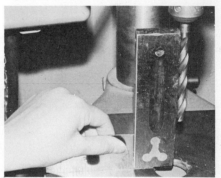

Fig. 57–2 Checking the squareness of the drill table and the bit.

unit 58

Boring and cutting holes

Any of the bits illustrated and described in Unit 56, Bits, Cutters, and Accessories, can be used to bore and cut holes in wood.

Large-diameter holes are often made with cutting bits and other special tools. The plug cutter, though it cuts holes, is actually used to cut dowels of various diameters, depending on the size of the cutter. These vary from $3/8$ to 1 inch (10 to 25 mm).

It is always advisable to put a piece of scrap wood on the table directly under the piece of wood being bored. Fasten the bit securely in the chuck or spindle before boring.

Boring a hole

Read and observe the safety precautions in Unit 23.

1. Lay out and mark the center of the hole. Use an awl.

2. Select the drill or bit of the correct size. Fasten it in the chuck. Make sure it does not wobble.

3. Place the board on the table of the drill press. Put a piece of scrap wood underneath the board.

Fig. 58-1 Boring a hole with a twist drill.

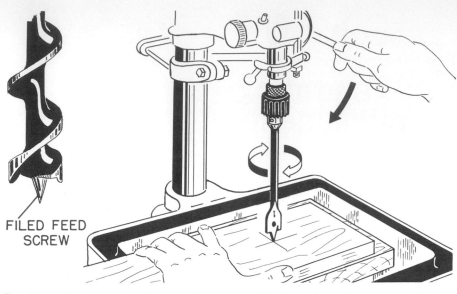

FILED FEED SCREW

Fig. 58-3 Boring a hole with a spade-type wood bit. Note the ordinary auger bit at the left with a filed feed screw. With the tang cut off, this altered wood auger bit may be used in a drill press.

Fig. 58-2 Drilling a hole with a double-spur twist bit.

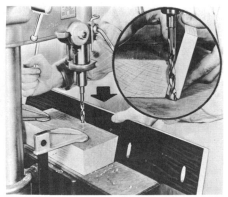

Fig. 58-4 Boring a pocket hole into the side rail of a table with the aid of a wooden jig.

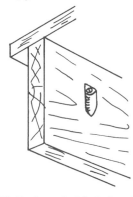

Fig. 58-5 A pocket hole in a table rail.

4. Adjust the table to the correct height and tilt angle. The tilt, of course, depends on the angle at which the hole is to bored.

5. Adjust for depth of boring.

6. Turn on the power switch.

7. Hold the board, or stock, securely by hand (or with clamps, if necessary). Apply an even pressure in feeding the bit into the wood slowly (Figs. 58-1, 58-2 and 58-3).

8. Figure 58-4 illustrates a unique technique for boring pocket holes (for recessing screws) into the side rail of a table to fasten the top. Note the inset, which shows an end view (see also Fig. 58-5).

9. Figure 58-6 shows a simple method of clamping stock to bore a hole at an angle. Note that the table has been tilted to obtain the desired angle. Figure 58-7 shows how to tilt the head to bore at an angle.

10. Figure 58-8 describes how to bore a series of holes freehand for a mortise. This method can be used if a mortising attachment and bits are not available.

11. Figure 58-9 presents a way to bore a hole that is deeper than the length of the drill bit. The simplest

method is to work from opposite ends. The table is tilted vertically; the wooden cylinder is aligned and held in place with a V block. The hole is bored first from one end, then from the other. In this way the capacity of a 4-inch (102-mm) twist drill is increased to 8 inches (204 mm).

Cutting a hole

1. Figure 58-10 shows a multispur bit cutting a 2-inch (51-mm) hole. The work is clamped to the table because a large bit makes it difficult to hold the work by hand.

2. A large hole can also be cut with a quick-cut hole saw (Fig. 58-11) or a circle cutter (Fig. 58-12).

Cutting dowels and circular plugs

The plug cutter makes it easy to cut dowel pins (see Fig. 58-13). In addition, cross-grain plugs can also be made with this cutter. Cross-grain plugs are especially useful for plugging holes in the surfaces, or the edges, of wood. Cross-grain plugs are also used where heads of screws and bolts are recessed below the surface.

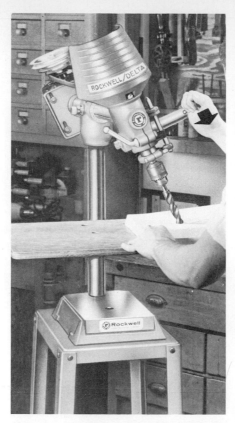
Fig. 58-7 Boring a hole by tilting the head of a radial drill press.

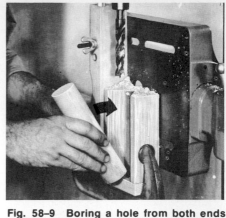
Fig. 58-9 Boring a hole from both ends with the aid of a V block clamped on a tilted table.

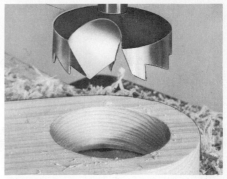
Fig. 58-10 Cutting a large hole with a multispur bit.

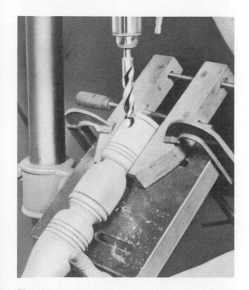
Fig. 58-6 Boring a hole at an angle. Note method of clamping stock in position.

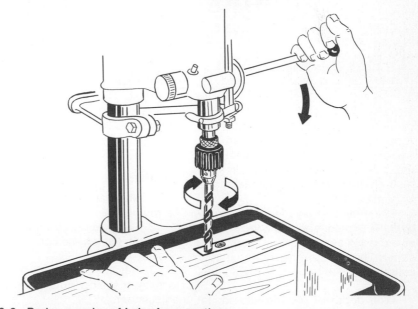
Fig. 58-8 Boring a series of holes for a mortise.

Fig. 58–11 Cutting a large hole with a quick-cut hole saw.

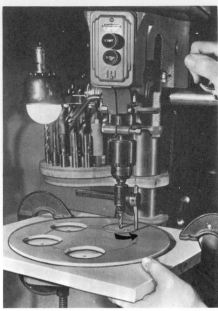

Fig. 58–12 Cutting a hole with an adjustable circle cutter.

Fig. 58–13 Making dowel plugs with a plug cutter.

unit 59

Routing, inlaying, and shaping

Routing and shaping can easily be done on the drill press when the proper bit and cutters are used. The speed is increased to approximately 5000 r/min in order to get a clean and smooth cut.

Material is always fed from *left to right*. This means that the work must be moved in against the rotation of the cutter. The thrust of the cutter should cause the piece to be pressed against the fence.

The depth of routing should not exceed $^1/_8$ inch (3 mm) per cut, or pass. If a deeper cut is required, repeat the cut with the bit set deeper each time.

Use only small shaper cutters for shaping because most drill press spindles will not withstand a side load, or thrust. The shaping procedure is generally very similar to the procedure that is recommended in Units 64 through 71.

Routing

1. Mark and lay out the piece to be routed.

2. Select the correct router or cutter bit. Fasten the correct bit in the chuck.

3. Set the depth of the cut by locking the stop nuts on the depth adjustment.

4. Fasten a fence to the table. Adjust it for the location of the cut (see Figs. 59-1 and 59-2).

5. Turn on the power switch.

6. Hold the work firmly against the fence. Feed it slowly into the router bit from *left to right* (Figs. 59-1 and 59-2).

Routing ornamental molding

Figure 59-3 shows a setup, or jig, for cutting ornamental molding. The spacer board is butted against the fence, and the piece is nailed to this board. The pin in the fence fits into the saw cuts of the spacer board and controls the repeat router bit cuts.

Figure 59-4 illustrates another method of routing molding. In this method, the work is simply pivoted on the guide pin.

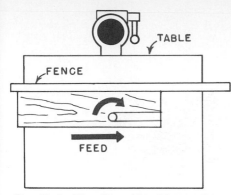

Fig. 59-1 Direction of feed for routing.

Fig. 59-2 Routing on the drill press.

Fig. 59-3 Routing ornamental molding with the use of a spacer-board jig.

Fig. 59-4 An alternate method of routing molding.

Fig. 59-5 Three molding designs made by routing.

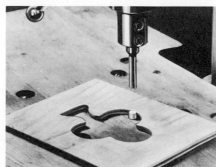

Fig. 59-6 The pin-and-pattern method of routing.

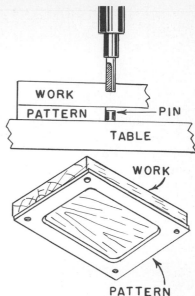

Fig. 59-7 Detail of the pin-and-pattern method of routing.

Figure 59-5 shows three interesting molding designs that can be made with these router-cutting methods.

Routing with a pattern

1. Lay out and cut a full-size template from $1/4$-inch-thick (6-mm-thick) plywood (see Fig. 59-6).

2. Fasten a suitable router bit into the chuck.

3. Drill a hole and insert a pin (dowel) into an auxiliary wood table. This pin must be the same diameter as that of the router bit, must be in line with the bit, and must project above the table about $3/16$ inch (5 mm) (Figs. 59-6 and 59-7).

4. Fasten the plywood pattern to the underneath side of the piece to be routed (see Fig. 59-7). Use short brads.

5. Adjust and lock the router bit cutting depth (see Figs. 59-7 and 59-8).

6. Place the work on the table. Turn on the power. Follow the template design to rout the surface piece (Fig. 59-8).

Fig. 59–8 Cutting (routing) a circular recess by the pin-and-pattern method.

Fig. 59–9 Making an intricate routing for inlay.

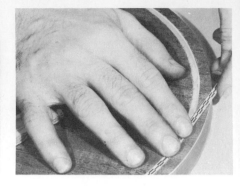

Fig. 59–12 Laying an inlay strip in place.

Routing for inlay

1. Follow steps 1 through 6 above.

2. Figure 59-9 shows the process of routing a groove for inlay work. Always guide the work along a fence. The router bit should be the same diameter as the width of the inlay band (strip). The depth of the cut should be slightly *less* than the thickness of the inlay strip.

3. Make the routed corners square with a wood chisel (Fig. 59-10). The router bit leaves rounded corners.

4. Cut inlay strips long enough to fit the routed grooves (Fig. 59-11). A mitered guide block helps to get accurate joints.

5. Lay the inlay strip in place (Fig. 59-12). Check to see that all joints fit perfectly. The inlay is now ready to be glued in place permanently.

Shaping on the drill press

An auxiliary plywood shaping table, fence, and hold-down clamps should be fastened to the drill table for shaping a straight edge (Fig. 59-13). Note that the operator is guiding the narrow strip, which is being shaped on the end, with a larger square piece. Figure 59-14 illustrates a method of shaping or smoothing the inside edges of a curved piece. Irregular pieces can also be shaped on the drill press by using a rub collar to control the depth of cut.

Fig. 59–10 Chiseling a routed corner square for inlay.

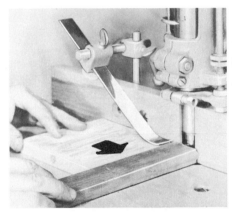

Fig. 59–13 Straight-edge shaping on the drill press.

Fig. 59–11 Cutting inlay strips to length using a wood chisel and a miter block.

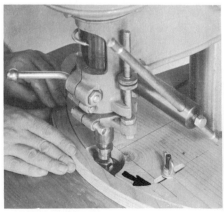

Fig. 59–14 Shaping the inside edge of a curved piece.

unit 60

Sanding on the drill press

Drum sander attachments for the drill press are described in Unit 56, Bits, Cutters, and Accessories.

Many sanding operations can be done with this assortment of drums. Figure 60-1 shows a very useful custom-made raised sanding table. It can be attached to an auxiliary wood table or directly to the cast-iron drill press table. The several different sizes of holes in the top are for the sanding drum to work up and down in.

Sanding

1. Cut wood pieces approximately to outline.

2. Next, dress the sawed edges carefully with a spokeshave, file, or other similar tool. You are now ready to sand them.

3. Fasten a suitable size of sanding drum in the drill press chuck or spindle.

4. Clamp the sanding table to the drill press table (see Fig. 60-1). Locate it so that the sanding drum will go into the correct hole.

5. Place the piece to be sanded on the table. Raise the table so that the drum drops into the hole and lock the spindle.

6. Turn on the power and sand the edges of the piece, as desired (see Fig. 60-1). The sanding drums can be used to dress inside cuts and holes as well as to smooth outside edges.

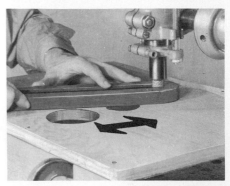

Fig. 60–1 Drum sanding an edge on the drill press.

Mortising processes

unit 61

General information about the hollow-chisel mortiser

The hollow-chisel mortiser (Fig. 61-1) performs two operations at the same time: as the bit bores the hole, the hollow, square chisel that surrounds it trims the wood further, making a square opening. Vertical and horizontal mortisers are used extensively in such industries as sash-and-door plants and furniture factories. Chisel-and-bit combinations make possible efficient production of various sizes of holes.

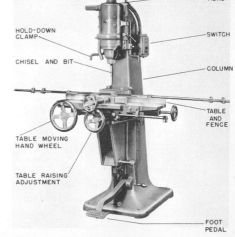

Fig. 61–1 A hollow-chisel mortiser.

133

Types of mortisers

Many mortisers are equipped with a table that can be adjusted horizontally by means of a hand wheel; the stock is moved back and forth by the action of the table. Most mortisers have an automatic mechanism that moves the head assembly (motor, chuck, chisel, and bit) up and down to cut the mortise (square opening) as pressure is applied on the foot pedal. The usual mortiser operating speed is 3600 r/min.

Figure 61-2 is a cross-section detail showing the hollow-chisel and bit assembly fastened in place on the commercial mortiser. There should always by a $1/16$-inch (2-mm) operating clearance between the bit and the end of the chisel, as shown in Figs. 61-2 and 61-3.

Figure 61-4 shows a mortising attachment fastened to a drill press. This converts the drill press into a manually operated mortiser. The stock must be moved back and forth on the table by hand. The cutting of the mortising chisel and bit is controlled by a feed lever.

Mortising tools for the drill press consist of a hollow chisel with four cutting edges that cut a square hole, a bit without a point that works inside the chisel (Fig. 61-5), and a chisel adaptor, or bushing. Chisel-and-bit sets vary in size from $1/4$ to $1/2$ inch (6.35 to 12.70 mm) for mortising on the drill press. Bushings are usually supplied that permit any size of bit to be mounted in the $1/2$-inch (12.7-mm) hole spindle. In many cases the bit fits directly into the chuck. When this happens, it does not require a bushing.

Parts and uses

Motor head. The motor head consists of a direct-drive motor, chuck, chisel, and bit. It is this motor head mechanism that moves the bit and chisel vertically along the ways (guides).

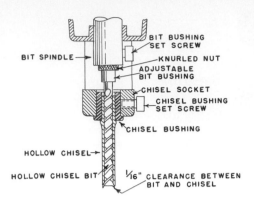

Fig. 61–2 A cross section of a chisel-and-bit assembly.

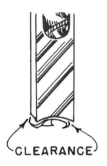

Fig. 61–3 The operating clearance between the end of the chisel and bit should be $1/16$ inch (2 mm).

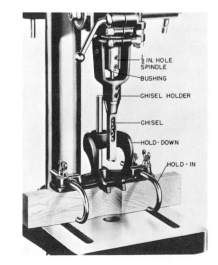

Fig. 61–4 The drill press converted for mortising.

Fig. 61–5 A hollow-chisel mortising bit, and bushing to use on a drill press for mortising.

Table and fence. This unit moves horizontally; however, on some machines it can be tilted to the right or left 45 degrees so that holes can be cut at an angle. A clamp is provided on the table to hold the stock against the fence.

Column. The head, table, foot lever, and other parts are rigidly supported by this one-piece casting.

Foot lever. The purpose of the foot lever is to control the action of the motor head.

Chisel and bit. Chisels, with companion bits, vary in size according to the capacity of the mortiser. For school use, this is usually $1/4$ to $3/4$ inch (6.35 to 19.05 mm).

Horizontal adjustment. The hand wheel that is used to control the movement of the table is the horizontal adjustment.

Depth adjustment. A hand wheel is used to make the depth adjustment. The hand wheel raises or lowers the table to the correct cutting depth of the chisel.

Mortising on the hollow-chisel mortiser

Mortising is a relatively simple process. The machine must be set with the correct size of chisel and bit, and the table must be adjusted for depth.

Mortising

Read and observe the safety precautions in Unit 23.

1. Square the stock to the desired size. Mark the location of the mortise (Fig. 62-1).

2. Install the correct size of chisel and bit into the mortise head. The bit should extend about $1/16$ inch (2 mm) beyond the chisel (see Fig. 61-2).

3. Clamp the stock securely in place on the table against the fence.

4. Mark a line on the end of the piece to indicate the depth of the cut. Adjust the vertical height of the chisel to the proper depth (Fig. 62-2).

5. Move the table into line with the chisel to make the first cut.

6. Turn on the motor, and make the first cut to only half the final depth. This procedure prevents burning the chisel and bit (Fig. 62-3). The chisel and bit can be made to cut into the wood by the action of the foot lever or the hand control, depending upon the machine.

7. Move the stock over slightly. Make the second cut to the full depth (Fig. 62-4), and then clean out the first cut. Continue making cuts until the mortise has been completed.

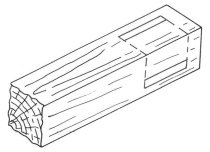

Fig. 62–1 Stock squared and marked for a mortise.

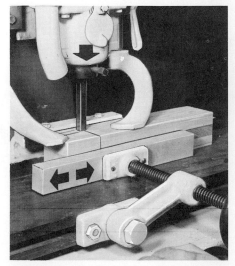

Fig. 62–3 The first cut on the mortiser.

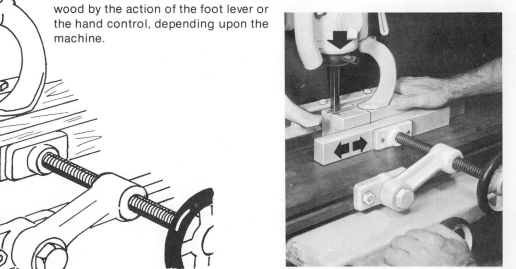

Fig. 62–2 Adjusting the cutting depth of the chisel.

Fig. 62–4 The second cut on the mortiser.

Figure 62-5 shows another method of making a series of first passes (cuts). After these have been completed, clean out the remaining portions of the mortise with a final series of passes.

A mortise that is wider than the chisel can be cut as shown in Fig. 62-6.

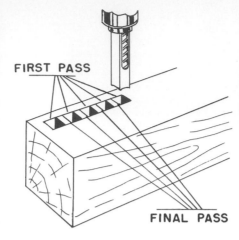

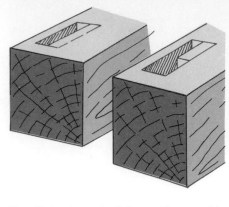

Fig. 62–5 An alternate method of making mortise cuts.

Fig. 62–6 A method for cutting a wide mortise with a narrow chisel.

unit 63

Mortising on the drill press

Fig. 63–2 Detail of a completed mortise cut.

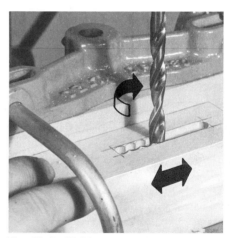

Fig. 63–3 Making a mortise with a drill bit.

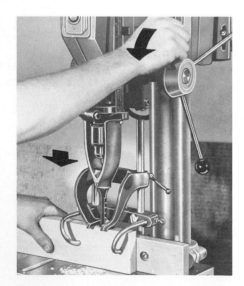

Fig. 63–1 Cutting a mortise on the drill press.

The drill press can be conveniently converted into a mortiser (see Fig. 61-4). Use the chisel-and-drill bit shown in Fig. 61-5. The instruction sheet or manual that accompanies the drill press and mortising attachments will provide specific instructions for assembling the mortising kit on the drill press and for operating it after assembly.

The speed of the drill press for mortising should be about 2250 r/min for softwoods and approximately 1500 r/min for hardwoods.

Mortising

1. Check the clearance between the chisel and the bit. It should be about $\frac{1}{16}$ inch (2 mm) (see Fig. 61-3). If the bit extends below the chisel too far, the chips may be too large to pass through the chisel. The bit should not touch the chisel.

2. Lay out and mark the mortise cut (see Fig. 62-1).

3. Fasten the piece to be mortised on the table against the mortising fence. It should be held down with the hold-down clamp and firmly against the fence with the hold-in clamps (see Fig. 61-4).

4. Adjust the position of the fence on the drill press table.

5. Adjust the two lock nuts for the depth of the mortise cut (see Unit 57).

6. Turn on the power and make the first mortise cut. Bring the chisel down to the end of the mortise, and then apply pressure gradually as the drill cuts the wood out and brings it up through the chisel (Fig. 63-1).

7. Continue making cuts until the mortise is cleanly cut (Fig. 63-2).

8. Mortises can be cut as shown in Fig. 63-3. Bore a series of holes with the drill bit; clean out the mortise by pushing the piece back and forth, increasing the depth of the drill bit about $1/8$ inch (3 mm) on each pass. The ends of the mortise can be cut square with a wood chisel, or else the tenon can be rounded to fit the mortise.

Wood shaper and router/shaper processes

unit 64

General information about the shaper and the router/shaper

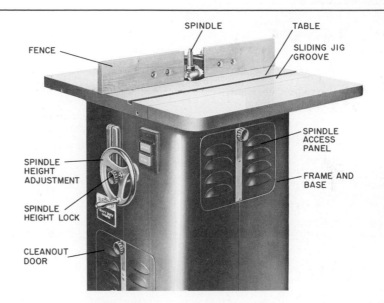

Fig. 64–1 A heavy-duty woodworking shaper.

Labels: FENCE, SPINDLE, TABLE, SLIDING JIG GROOVE, SPINDLE ACCESS PANEL, FRAME AND BASE, SPINDLE HEIGHT ADJUSTMENT, SPINDLE HEIGHT LOCK, CLEANOUT DOOR

The shaper (Fig. 64-1) is used in woodworking for grooving and shaping on straight or curved edges, for making molding and paneling, and for making almost limitless combinations of decorative cuts. Shaping is done with guides, collars, and patterns and with the aid of forms, jigs, and fixtures.

Sizes and types of shapers

The size of a shaper is measured by the diameter of the spindle and the size of the table. Most machines used in school industrial laboratories are equipped with $5/16$- to $3/4$-inch (7.9- to 19.0-mm) spindles. The spindles are usually interchangeable. See Unit 65, Shaper Cutters, Collars, and Spindles.

The vertical spindle (Fig. 64-2) rotates at a speed of from 7000 to 10 000 r/min. This makes it important to observe every safety precaution when using the shaper.

Many shapers have reversible motors to provide rotation in two directions. This rotation permits additional combinations of shapes from the cutters because they must be turned over. The reversing mechanism is usually controlled by a switch.

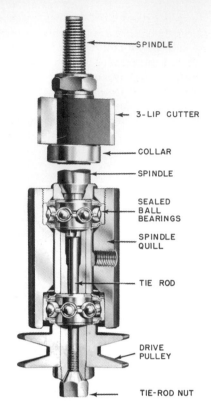

Fig. 64–2 A shaper-spindle assembly.

Labels: SPINDLE, 3-LIP CUTTER, COLLAR, SPINDLE, SEALED BALL BEARINGS, SPINDLE QUILL, TIE ROD, DRIVE PULLEY, TIE-ROD NUT

Parts and uses of the shaper

Table. The shaper table supports the guide or fence and the stock to be shaped.

Frame and base. The frame and base enclose the motor and shaping mechanism and hold up the table.

Spindle. The shaper spindle is the round vertical drive shaft. The cutter head, or cutters, are attached to the spindle.

Spindle height adjustment wheel. This controls the spindle to which the cutters are fastened.

Fence. The fence or guide is adjustable. It is used for guiding straight stock.

The **router/shaper** is a versatile overarm machine well suited for working wood, plastic, and nonferrous metals (Fig. 64-3). It can be used as a router or as a shaper for routing, molding, grooving, mortising, tenoning, and rabbeting. These processes can be done with guides, collars, patterns, and jigs.

Sizes and types

The 2-horsepower (hp), or 1492-watt (W), motor of this machine produces a high speed of 20 000 r/min. A wide variety of processes can be performed with the use of the $1/2$-inch (12.7-mm) collet chuck and the three adapters that hold $1/4$-, $5/16$-, and $3/8$-inch-diameter (6.4-, 7.9-, and 9.5-mm-diameter) bits.

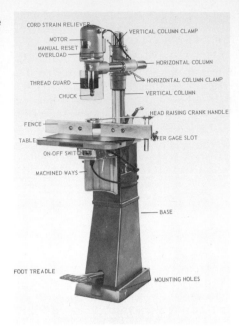

Fig. 64–3 A router/shaper.

Labels: CORD STRAIN RELIEVER, MOTOR, MANUAL RESET OVERLOAD, THREAD GUARD, CHUCK, FENCE, TABLE, ON-OFF SWITCH, MACHINED WAYS, FOOT TREADLE, VERTICAL COLUMN CLAMP, HORIZONTAL COLUMN, HORIZONTAL COLUMN CLAMP, VERTICAL COLUMN, HEAD RAISING CRANK HANDLE, MITER GAGE SLOT, BASE, MOUNTING HOLES

Parts and uses of the router/shaper

The numerous parts are identified in Fig. 64-3. They are reasonably similar to those of the shaper in use and performance.

unit 65

Shaper cutters, collars, spindles, and accessories

There is a wide variety of cutter combinations available. Together, they can do almost any type of shaping. The hollow spindle allows the use of interchangeable spindle heads, which can accommodate many sizes and types of solid-lip cutters, three-knife cutter heads, and open cutter knives in slotted collars.

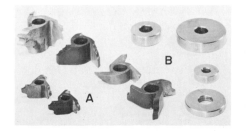

Fig. 65–1 (A) Solid three-lip cutters and (B) various sizes of rub collars.

Cutters and collars

Solid three-lip cutters, with $5/16$- or $1/2$-inch (7.9- to 12.7-mm) holes, are available in a wide selection of shapes. They offer almost unlimited possibilities for making molding designs (Figs. 65-1 through 65-3). These are solid, one-piece cutter knives that can be used singly or together to make intricate molding patterns in one pass through the shaper. Figure 65-3 shows the profiles of many standard solid three-lip cutters.

Another type of cutter head is the three-knife safety assembly (Fig. 65-4). It fits a $1/2$- or a $3/4$-inch (12.7- or 19.0-mm) spindle. There are interchangeable three-knife sets for this head (Fig. 65-5). The knives can be removed and installed with an Allen-head wrench.

Open knives that fit slotted collars are available for the craftsmen who desire to make molding of their own design. The edges of the knives have been ground (beveled) at a 30-degree angle. This has been done so that they will clamp safely between slotted collars (Fig. 65-6). These knives are also available as blanks in matched pairs. The cutting edge of a blank must be ground.

On the right in Fig. 65-1 are various sizes of collars that can be used for spacing or for rub collars when shaping curved pieces. These sometimes vary in thickness and come in an assortment of diameters.

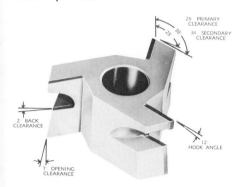

Fig. 65–2 Carbide-tip three-lip cutters retain their sharpness a long time.

Fig. 65–4 A three-knife safety cutter head.

Fig. 65–6 Slotted collars and bevel-edge knives.

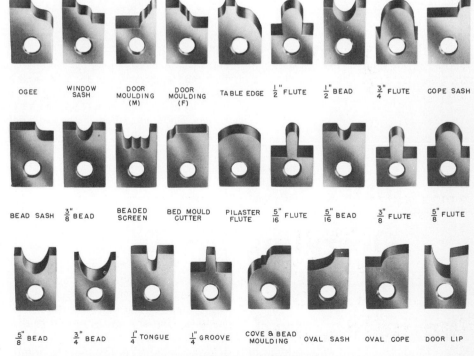

Fig. 65–3 Profiles of standard solid three-lip cutters.

Fig. 65–5 An assortment of three-knife safety cutters.

Spindles

Most shapers have several easily interchanged spindles (Fig. 65-7). They permit the use of a rather complete range of cutters. Included, usually, are the 5/16-inch (7.9-mm) spindle for small cutters, with 5/16-inch holes; the 1/2- and 3/4-inch (12.7- and 19.0-mm) spindles for regular cutters, with 1/2- and 3/4-inch holes.

Accessories

The versatility of the **router/shaper** enables the operator to make almost unlimited cuts. Adapting spindles permits the operator to use the many shaper cutters listed in this unit and the router bits described in Unit 102. Figure 65-8 shows the accessories for the router/shaper. These accessories permit the overarm machine to be used either as a router or as a shaper.

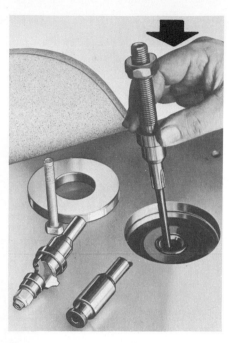

Fig. 65-7 Interchangeable spindles.

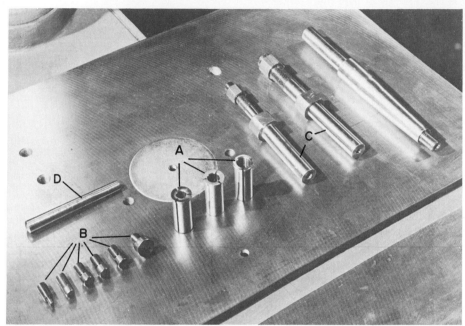

Fig. 65-8 Accessories for the router/shaper: (A) router bit adapters for use with 1/4-, 5/16-, and 3/8-inch-shank (6.35-, 7.94-, and 9.52-mm-shank) router bits, (B) six various-size guide pins for use when routing with a guide pin, (C) two shaper spindles for use with 5/16- and 1/2-inch-hole (7.94- and 12.7-mm hole) shaper cutters, and (D) tapered starting pin for use when shaping with collars.

unit 66

Operating adjustments

The **shaper,** like all other machine tools, requires certain adjustments to stay efficient, reliable, versatile, and aligned. The operator should always study the manufacturer's data sheet and operating manual before attempting to make any of the various adjustments on the shaper. Although these adjustments are similar on most shapers, the technique for making them will be different.

Interchange of spindles

Many shapers have hollow vertical shafts that allow interchange of spindles (see Fig. 65-6). The several types of spindles, and their specific purposes, were explained in the previous unit.

Each spindle is fitted with a tie rod

(Fig. 66-1) that is threaded at both ends. One end is fitted to the spindle; the opposite end is capped with a tapered nut after it passes through the hollow main spindle. The shank of each spindle is fitted with a keyway that prevents the auxiliary spindle from slipping or turning on the hollow main spindle.

Figure 66-1 shows the mechanism and parts of a heavy-duty shaper. This indicates the location of the spindle assembly. Figure 64-2 shows a detail of the shaper spindle and assembly. On lighter shapers, this assembly is slightly different; however, the same principles of operation apply. The shaper manual will give detailed instructions on loosening any specific spindle. Figure 66-1 also shows the spindle height-control hand wheel.

Assembling solid three-lip and three-knife safety cutters

The several types of cutters and cutter blades discussed in the previous unit require different methods of assembly. Figure 66-2 shows how to mount a solid three-lip cutter. The same method is used in mounting the three-knife safety cutter head on the spindle (see Fig. 65-3).

The remainder of the spindle, either above or below the cutter, is filled in with spare collars before the nut is fastened to the top. Collars should be of smaller diameter than the cutting edges of the cutter if a fence is to be used.

If you are using one of the collars as a rub collar, place it either directly above or directly below the cutter, depending on where it makes contact with the wood edge to be shaped. There the diameter should be large enough to serve as a fence to be used for curved and irregular edges.

Assembling open-face knife cutters

Open-face knife cutters make possible custom grinding of the cutting edges.

Once their edges have been ground and honed, they are fastened between slotted collars.

The ground knife cutters should be fastened firmly between the slotted grooves of the collars, as shown in Fig. 66-3. Figure 66-4 gives a typical setup of open-knife cutters fixed between slotted collars (see also Fig. 65-6).

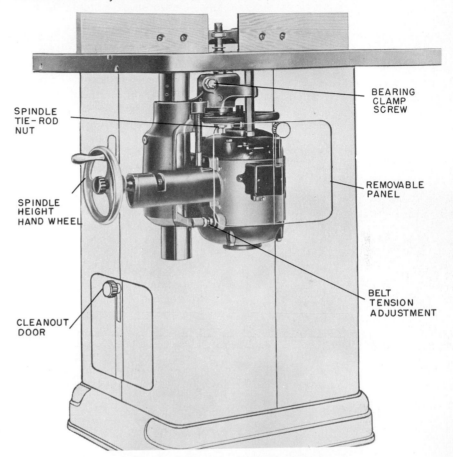

Fig. 66–1 The mechanism and parts of a heavy-duty shaper.

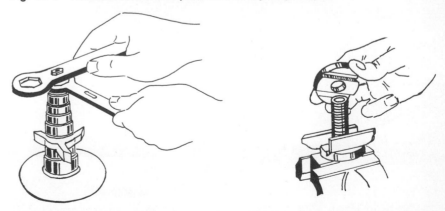

Fig. 66–2 A method of mounting a solid three-lip cutter on the spindle.

Fig. 66–3 Knife cutter blades assembled between slotted collar grooves.

141

Fig. 66–4 A typical setup of open-knife cutters fastened between slotted collars.

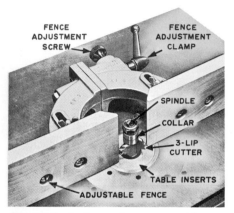

FENCE ADJUSTMENT SCREW
FENCE ADJUSTMENT CLAMP
SPINDLE
COLLAR
3-LIP CUTTER
TABLE INSERTS
ADJUSTABLE FENCE

Fig. 66–5 A shaper fence assembly.

Fastening the fence guide

The fence guide is secured to the table with either stud bolts or a fence-clamp stud (Fig. 66-5). Figure 65-7 shows two fence-clamp studs fastened in place without the fence.

The fence is so constructed that either half can be adjusted. For most work, the halves are in line. The wood faces are usually adjustable, in or out, to accommodate various cutter sizes. The opening should never be any larger than is needed to clear the cutter.

Figure 66-6 shows a situation in which the fence guide should not be in line. Here the rear (left half) must be adjusted forward to form a support. The process shown would involve cutting away the original edge.

Adjusting safety clamps

Most shapers are equipped with hold-down devices, such as spring-type clamps, that provide safety as well as tension against the piece being shaped (Fig. 66-7). Sometimes the work does not permit using either or both.

When the rub collar serves as a fence guide during the shaping of ir-regular edges, use a circular fiber ring guard for safety (see Fig. 68-7).

Adjustment of the horizontal-column clamp on the **router/shaper** quickly raises or lowers the overarm and head to the exact height required. The head can be rotated a full 360 degrees around the column and positioned anywhere (Fig. 66-8). The head can be tilted to any angle (Fig. 66-9).

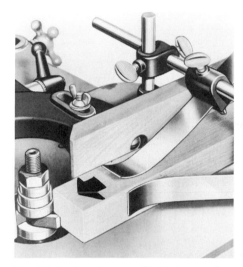

Fig. 66–7 A spring-steel hold-down safety clamp.

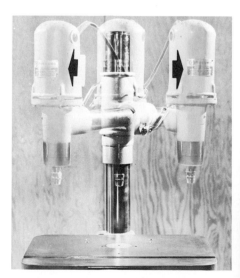

Fig. 66–8 The head is easily raised to rotate a full 360 degrees around the column.

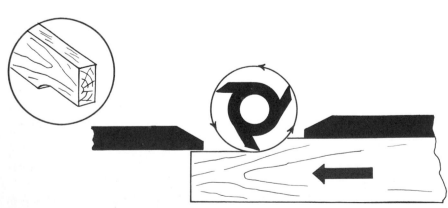

Fig. 66–6 Top view of the fence-guide adjustment to support an unusual cut.

Because of the flexibility of the router/shaper, there are many adjustments that must be made. It is advisable to study the operating manual that accompanies this machine.

The overarm router/shaper can perform many processes of routing and shaping when the motor head is set up for routing, as shown in Fig. 64-3. For shaping, the machine can also be set up with the motor under the table (Fig. 66-10).

Figure 66-11 illustrates how the work must be fed into the cutter when the motor is above the table for routing. Always feed *against* the cutter rotation, from left to right. When the motor is mounted *below* the table, always feed the work from *right to left* (Fig. 66-12).

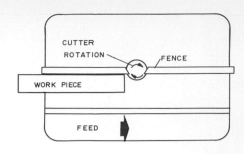

Fig. 66–11 The direction of feed when the motor is mounted above the table for routing.

Fig. 66–9 The head may be tilted to any angle.

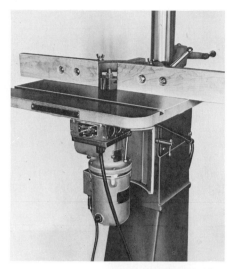

Fig. 66–10 The motor mounted under the table for shaping.

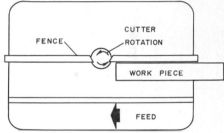

Fig. 66–12 The direction of feed when the motor is mounted below the table for shaping.

unit 67

Shaping straight edges on the shaper

Shaping straight edges will require alignment of the adjustable fence. Using a fence is the fastest, most satisfactory, and perhaps the safest method of shaping. There are only two adjustments: the first aligns the fence (see Figs. 67-1 and 67-2); the second adjusts the height of the cutter (see Figs. 67-3 and 67-4). This type of shaping might cut rabbets and grooves as well as shape edges. The guard and

Fig. 67–1 Adjusting and fastening the fence guide.

Fig. 67–2   Aligning the two parts of the fence with a framing square.

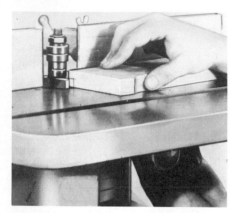

Fig. 67–3   Adjusting the cutter height of a light-duty shaper.

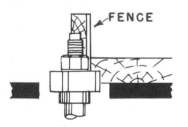

Fig. 67–4   Detail of shaping a straight edge against a fence guide.

Fig. 67–5   Starting to shape an edge.

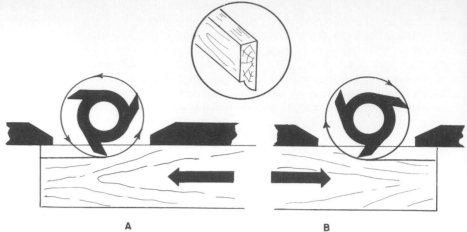

A   B

Fig. 67–6   Top view showing (A) the stock fed conventionally from right to left and (B) the stock fed from left to right. The insert shows the shaped edge.

hold-down clamps do not appear in many of the illustrations in this unit so that cutting details can be shown more clearly.

Procedure

Read and observe the safety precautions in Unit 23.

1. Select the cutter, cutter head, or knife assembly. Fasten it securely on the spindle (see Unit 66).

2. Sketch the planned cut on the end or the edge of the wood.

3. Adjust the fence guide and fasten it securely (Fig. 67-1). Make sure the two parts of the fence are in alignment. Check this with a framing square (Fig. 67-2).

4. Adjust the cutting height of the spindle for the planned cut (Figs. 67-3 and 67-4).

5. Place hold-down clamps for safety and tension. Adjust these with the work on the table (see Fig. 66-7).

6. Turn on the power. Allow the shaper to come to full speed.

7. Make a trial run on a piece of scrap wood. Hold it firmly in position against the fence. Feed it into the cutter head from *right to left*. Figure 67-5 shows the bottom part of the edge being shaped. Occasionally the

shaper cuts may be such that the motor should be reversed through the switch, the cutter head inverted (turned upside down), and the piece fed from *left to right*. Figure 67-6 illustrates the difference in making cuts from right to left and left to right. It also shows the direction of the cutter blade.

8. Shape the edge if the trial cut is accurate.

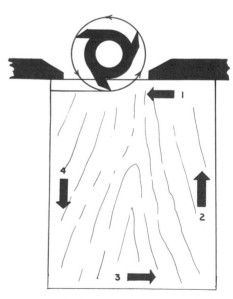

Fig. 67–7   Steps in shaping all four straight edges of a board.

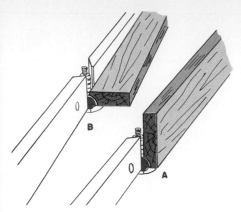

Fig. 67–8 The similarity of face and straight-edge shaping: (A) the face of the board and (B) the edge.

9. When shaping all four straight edges on a board, follow the sequence of cuts shown in Fig. 67-7.

10. Shaping the edge of a wood face is very similar to that of shaping a straight edge. Figure 67-8 illustrates the similarity. It is a matter of how the board is placed against the fence and table.

11. Figures 67-9 through 67-12 show how moldings can be cut by planning the sequence from available shaper forms (patterns).

Fig. 67–11 The final molding cut.

Fig. 67–9 Making the first molding cut.

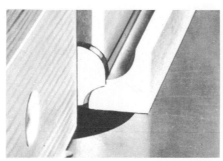

Fig. 67–10 Making the second molding cut.

Fig. 67–12 Two cutters used for molding.

unit 68

Shaping irregular and circular edges on the shaper

Most irregular shaping requires the use of the rub collar to serve as the guide in place of the straight fence. The rub collar can be used above, below, or between two cutters, as illustrated in Figs. 68-1, 68-2, and 68-3. Work that cannot be shaped against a fence guide is usually shaped against a rub collar. The collar rim rides against the piece and limits the depth of cut.

Circular pieces are shaped much as irregular ones are. However, a wooden jig such as the one in Fig. 68-10 is a very useful guide.

The guard and hold-down clamp do not appear in many illustrations in this unit so that setting and cutting details can be more clearly shown.

Shaping irregular edges

1. Select the cutter, or knife blade assembly, and also a rub collar of the

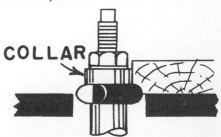

Fig. 68–1 Detail showing a rub collar above the cutter. This shapes the lower side of the edge.

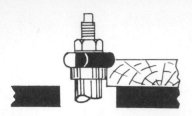

Fig. 68–2 Detail showing the rub collar below the cutter. This shapes the top side of the edge.

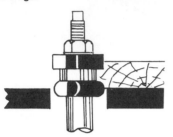

Fig. 68–3 Detail showing the rub collar between two cutters. This shapes both top and bottom sides with one pass.

correct diameter. Fasten these securely on the spindle. See Unit 66, Operating Adjustments. In selecting the collar size, remember that the rub collar will serve as a depth gage for the cut (see Figs. 68-1, 68-2, and 68-3).

2. If possible, sketch the planned cut on the end of the board.

3. Adjust the cutting height of the spindle so that the shaper cut or cuts will be made where they were planned. Adjust the circular fiber ring guard so that it barely clears the work (see Fig. 68-7).

4. Fasten the starting pin securely in the table (see Fig. 68-4).

5. Turn on the power and allow the shaper to come to full speed.

6. Make a trial cut on a scrap piece of wood. Place the piece to be shaped firmly in position against the starting pin (Fig. 68-4). Gradually, but

firmly, push the wood into the revolving cutter head so that it makes contact with the rub collar (Figs. 68-5, 68-6, and 68-7).

After making full contact with the starting pin and the rub collar, gradually move the board so that you will move away from (not depend upon) the starting pin (Fig. 68-8).

7. Shape the entire edge if the trial cut is accurate.

8. When shaping the entire edge of an irregular piece, start the cut as illustrated in Fig. 68-9.

9. Continue to cut carefully and accurately until the desired shaping has been completed.

Shaping circular pieces

An excellent guide, which can be used for a wide variety of circle sizes, is shown in Fig. 68-10. It is a flat piece of wood that is as thick as, or thicker than, the piece being shaped. It has a 90-degree V opening cut in the center. The size of the opening should conform, generally, to the size of the circular piece. This guide (wooden jig) can be set for use with pieces of many different diameters. It must, however, provide two contact points for the circular work.

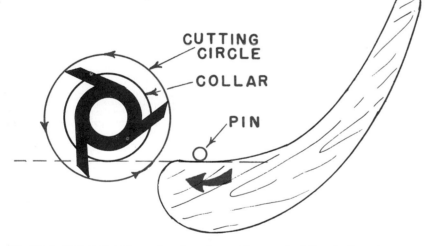

Fig. 68–4 Detail of an irregular piece in position against the starting pin.

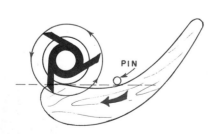

Fig. 68–5 Detail of an irregular piece which is making contact with the rub collar.

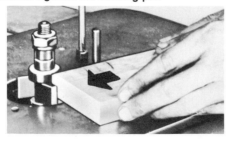

Fig. 68–6 A board placed against the starting pin and the rub collar. The guard is removed for clarity.

Fig. 68–7 Shaping an irregular edge. Note the circular fiber ring guard for safety purposes.

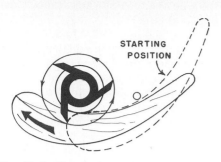

Fig. 68–8 Detail of a piece being moved into cutting position and away from the starting pin.

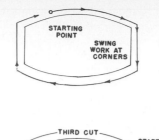

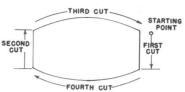

Fig. 68–9 Detail of continuous shaping around an irregular edge.

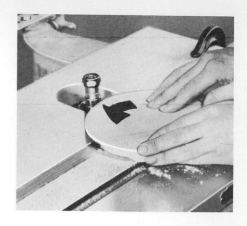

Fig. 68–10 Shaping a circular piece against a wooden, custom-made guide.

unit 69

Shaping with an outline pattern on the shaper

Shaping that is guided by an outline pattern (template) is similar to irregular-edge shaping against a rub collar. In this method, however, the *pattern rides against* the collar; the work does not. This eliminates burning, or scoring, of the edges of the piece by friction with the rub collar. The pattern method ensures accuracy for duplicate pieces.

Figure 69-1 shows a detail of shaping when the pattern is fastened to the *top* of the work. Note that the rub collar is fixed on the shaper spindle and that the pattern rubs against it. In Fig. 69-2 the pattern is shown fastened *underneath* the work being shaped, and the rub collar is placed underneath the shaper cutter.

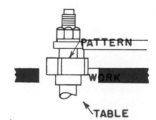

Fig. 69–1 Detail showing a pattern fastened to the top of the work.

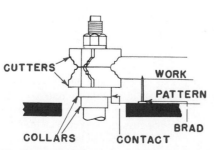

Fig. 69–2 Detail showing a pattern fastened underneath the work. Note the brad anchor point.

Making the pattern

The pattern is usually made of $3/4$-inch-thick (19-mm-thick) hardwood. It can be a solid piece, or it can be built up as shown in Fig. 69-6. The pattern form must be the exact outline of the work that is to be shaped or molded. The edges must be dressed smooth and oiled or waxed so that the piece will move smoothly and easily against the rub collar without edge burning.

The pattern is fastened with anchor points to the board to be shaped. The simplest of these is a small brad which will go through the pattern and extend $1/8$ to $1/4$ inch (3 to 6 mm) into the bottom side of the piece to be shaped (see Figs. 69-2 and 69-3). The guard and the hold-down clamp do not appear in many illustrations so that setting and cutting details can be shown more clearly.

Shaping with an outline pattern

1. Mark, cut, and dress (smooth) the pattern from hardwood. Maple and

birch are good woods for this purpose.

2. Drive at least four brads (anchor points) through the bottom side of the pattern. They should extend

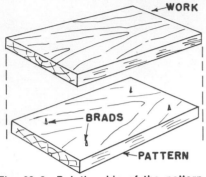

Fig. 69–3 Relationship of the pattern to the piece being shaped.

about $1/8$ to $1/4$ inch (3 to 6 mm) above the pattern (see Fig. 69-2).

3. Mark, cut, and dress the edges of the board to be shaped. If only a portion of the edge is to be shaped, this piece should be exactly the size of the pattern (see Fig. 69-1).

4. If the entire edge of the board is to be shaped, it should be roughly sawed about $1/16$ to $1/8$ inch (2 to 3 mm) oversize (see Fig. 69-2).

5. Anchor (fasten) the pattern to the board to be shaped. Figure 69-3 shows this assembly.

6. Follow steps 1 through 5 in Unit 68, Shaping Irregular and Circular Edges. Fasten the pattern either below

or above the stock, depending upon the type of edge cut planned (see Figs. 69-1 and 69-2).

7. Place the pattern and the piece to be shaped firmly in position against the starting pin. Firmly push the assembly into the revolving cutter head until it makes contact with the rub collar (Fig. 69-4). After making full contact with the starting pin and the rub collar, gradually move the assembly away from the starting pin (Fig. 69-5). Figure 69-6 shows a built-up outline pattern (template) for shaping the edge of an end table top.

8. Continue the cut until the shaping is completed.

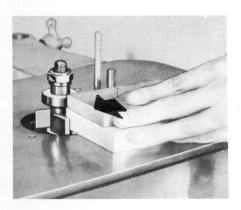

Fig. 69–4 Shaping an edge following a pattern (template). Note that only a portion of the edge is being cut. The guard is removed to show detail.

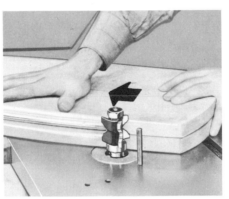

Fig. 69–5 Shaping an edge following a pattern. Note that the entire thickness of the edge is being cut. The guard is removed to show detail.

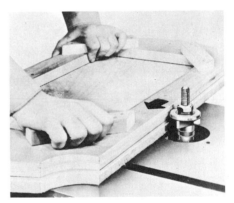

Fig. 69–6 Shaping an edge of an end-table top following a built-up outline template.

unit 70

Shaping with jigs and special forms on the shaper

There are some special cuts and grooves that involve the use of jigs and special types of forms. Some of these can be custom-made for the particular job; others are standard accessories that are available from shaper manufacturers. The variety of such cuts and grooves is dependent entirely

upon the ingenuity of the operator, the cutters available, and the shape of the specially built forms.

In general, a jig or a form is any device upon which the work is securely fastened by means of clamps, screws, or wedges. Special forms must be built to support irregular

Fig. 70–1 Shaping with a sliding jig. The front supporting arm is removed to show the cut more clearly.

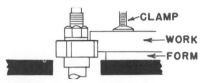

Fig. 70–2 Detail of shaping with a sliding jig.

Fig. 70–3 Holding stock with a jig while cutting a 45-degree end chamfer.

Fig. 70–4 Cutting a tenon with a sliding tenoning jig.

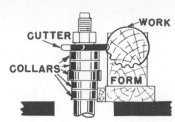

Fig. 70–6 Detail of the fluting process.

Fig. 70–5 A special fluting (grooving) jig for making flutes in a table leg.

pieces, such as legs that require fluting (grooving).

Procedures for making many types of cuts will not be outlined. Each requires an order of procedure developed by the operator for that specific job. A few of the more common cuts, however, are described and illustrated. The guard and the hold-down clamp do not appear in many illustrations in this unit in order to show setting and cutting details.

Shaping with jigs

Most manufacturers of wood shaper equipment make available mechanical clamps that can be used as jigs. These clamps hold the work while the special cuts are made. Figure 70-1 shows a sliding jig that holds the piece while it is advanced to the cutter head. Figure 70-2 gives the detail drawing to demonstrate this process.

The **sliding jig** is an excellent accessory with which to hold narrow stock that is being shaped on the end. Figure 70-3 illustrates how to cut a 45-degree chamfer on the end of a square piece.

A **sliding tenoning jig** can be used to good advantage for many shaper operations. Figure 70-4 shows the use of one for cutting the tenon on the end of a formed (bent) laminated leg.

Shaping with specially built forms

Fluting (grooving) a round table leg requires a specially built jig. Figure 70-5 pictures the **fluting jig** (special form) being used to cut flutes in a table leg. Note the stop assembly, which is clamped to the shaper table. This controls the beginning and the end of the cutting operation so that all grooves will be the same length.

The circular piece at the right of the jig is a disk that has equally spaced holes drilled in it. These mark the location for each flute. See Fig. 70-6.

Routing and shaping on the router/shaper

Routing with the fence as a guide

Read and observe the safety precautions in Unit 23.

1. Place the motor and spindle assembly in the overarm position (see Fig. 66-8). For 90-degree routing, make certain the spindle is in a vertical position.

2. Select the proper size router bit and adapter. If a 1/4-inch (6.3-mm) shank router bit is to be used, insert the 1/4-inch (6.3-mm) router bit adapter into the cutter spindle. However, if a 1/2-inch (12.7-mm) shank router bit is to be used, it is not necessary to use an adapter because the spindle is bored for 1/2 inch (12.7 mm).

3. Tighten the chuck "finger tight" and insert the shank of the router bit inside the adapter or spindle.

4. Fasten the bit, or bit adapter, in the chuck securely.

5. Assemble and fasten the fence guide to the table top with either stud bolts or a fence-clamp stud. Make sure the two parts of the fence are in alignment.

6. Adjust the cutting height of the cutter and spindle for the planned cuts.

7. Turn on the power. Allow the motor to come to full speed.

8. Make a trial run on a piece of scrap wood, holding it firmly in position against the fence.

9. Make needed adjustments. *Always feed the work piece from left to right against the cutting action of the bit* (see Fig. 66-11).

10. Place the work piece on the table. Hold it firmly against the fence guide.

11. Make the desired cut by pushing the piece from *left to right* (Figs. 71-1 and 71-2).

12. Turn off the power of the machine.

Guide-pin routing

Routing with the guide pin is a simple fast method of making duplicate cuts. A guide pin, usually the same diameter as the router bit, is used. A full-size template of the work is necessary. This template may be cut from 1/4-inch-thick (6-mm-thick) plywood.

1. Repeat steps 1 through 4 under "Routing with the Fence as Guide."

2. Place the guide pin into the table insert.

3. Lock it in place with the locking nut.

4. Adjust the motor head so that the router bit is in alignment with the guide pin in the table top. Study the manufacturer's manual to make the proper adjustments.

5. Fasten the template to the bottom of the work piece (see Fig. 71-3).

6. Place the template and work piece over the guide pin with the template *face down* (Fig. 71-3).

7. Turn on the motor and allow it to come to full speed.

8. Lower the cutter bit and motor head to the desired cutting depth. Hold the work piece securely during this process.

9. Following the template, push

Fig. 71-1 **Routing a rabbet using the fence as a guide.**

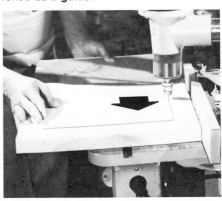

Fig. 71-2 **Routing a decorative design on a door panel.**

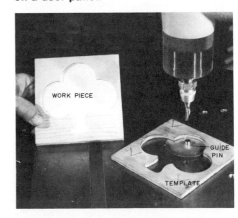

Fig. 71-3 **A template, work piece, and guide pin.**

the work piece in a *counterclockwise* path against the cutting action of the bit. Go around the entire perimeter of the template first (see Fig. 71-4).

10. Clean out the inside of the cavity (groove) using a series of back-and-forth passes and going with the grain of the wood (Fig. 71-4).

11. Turn off the power of the machine.

12. Lift the head to remove the work piece.

Shaping with the fence as a guide

The shaping procedure on the router/shaper is very similar to the procedure used on the heavy-duty shaper. Study Units 67 and 70.

1. Change the machine from router to shaper position. The motor-and-spindle assembly is switched from the overarm position to the under-the-table one (see Fig. 66-12).

2. Repeat steps 2 through 6 under the heading "Routing with the Fence as a Guide."

3. Turn on the power and allow the motor to come to full speed.

4. Make a trial run on a piece of scrap wood, holding it firmly on the table top and in position against the fence (Fig. 71-5).

Fig. 71–4 Routing a design with the guide-pin–template method.

5. Make the needed adjustments.

6. Always feed the work piece from *right to left*, against the cutting action of the bit, when the motor assembly is under the table top.

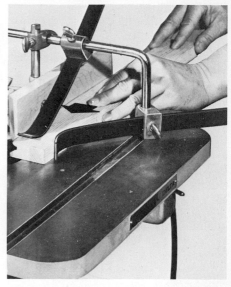

Fig. 71–5 Shaping on the router/shaper with the aid of a fence.

Lathe processes

unit 72

General information about the wood lathe

The wood lathe is one of the oldest types of power equipment used to fashion wooden objects. Woodturning is an interesting woodworking skill. The lathe, more than any other tool, is in itself a complete unit, capable of producing finished work. Modern lathes (Fig. 72-1) enable craftsmen to produce beautifully formed pieces.

Sizes, types, and speeds

Two factors usually determine the size of a wood lathe: (1) the swing of the faceplate, which indicates the maximum diameter of the piece that can be turned (faceplate turning), and (2) the maximum length of a piece that can be turned between centers (spindle turning). A lathe capable of turning 30-inch-long (762-mm-long) stock must have a bed long enough to support the tailstock assembly (and on some lathes also the headstock assembly) in addition to the length needed for holding the wood.

A typical industrial laboratory, school-size lathe is a 12-inch (305-mm) wood lathe with a 4-foot (1219-mm) bed.

The turning speed is controlled by either (1) a multispeed motor, (2) a variable-speed control, (3) spring-loaded pulleys, or (4) three- or four-step pulleys. When step pulleys are used, a V belt must be changed manually for any desired speed. The first three methods of controlling speed usually employ a dial speed control. The speed range of the wood lathe is from approximately 350 to 3600 r/min. The larger the stock to be turned, the slower the speed.

Parts and uses

Headstock assembly. This assembly contains the driving mechanism; the spindle for the live, or spur, center; and, on some lathes, the speed control. The headstock of many lathes also includes the motor.

Tailstock assembly. The tailstock assembly includes the dead center

spindle, the dead center, and the hand wheel and locking adjustments.

Lathe bed (ways). This is the supporting body of the lathe. It holds the head- and tailstock assemblies. It also holds the tool rest and support.

Frame or legs. The upright support on which the lathe stands consti-

tutes the frame. On some lathes, this is a complete base; on others, legs are fastened to the lathe bed.

Tool rest. This is a horizontal guide. It is held in a tool-rest holder or support. The turning tool is worked back and forth along the tool rest during the woodturning operation.

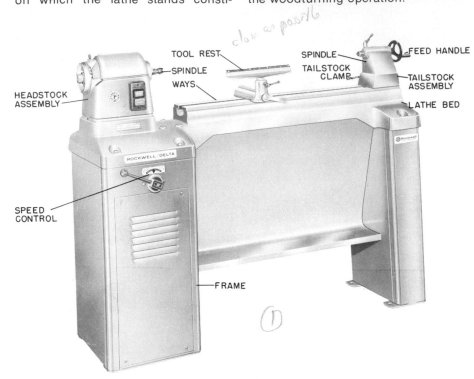

Fig. 72–1   A 12-inch (304.8-mm), variable-speed, wood-turning lathe.

unit 73

Woodturning chisels and accessories

A standard set of tools (chisels) used in woodturning consists of five basic

shapes (Fig. 73-1). There are several sizes for some of these shapes, as described below. These cutting tools are fitted with long hardwood handles. Several accessories are also available; they are illustrated and discussed.

Turning chisels

Gouge. This is the most frequently used lathe tool. It is a roundnose, hol-

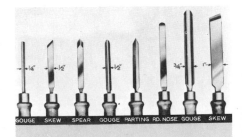

Fig. 73–1   A set of standard wood-turning chisels.

152

low chisel used for rough-cutting and for cutting coves. Gouge tools come in several sizes.

Skew Chisel. This is a double-ground flat chisel whose end is ground to an angle. It is used to smooth cylinders and to cut beads, V grooves, shoulders, and similar cuts. See Unit 75, Practice Turning between Centers.

Diamond or spear-point chisel. The diamond-point (spear-point) chisel is a scraping tool. It is used whenever its shape fits the contour of the piece.

Roundnose chisel. This is also a scraping tool.

Parting tool. The parting tool is also a double-ground chisel. It is used to cut off the ends and to make cuts to required diameters.

Accessories

The **12-inch (305-mm) tool support** is the most conventional size of this attachment (Fig. 73-2). It is ideal for general lathework because it can be adjusted to any angle (Fig. 73-3).

The **right-angle tool rest** (Fig. 73-4) is used to turn edges and faces without adjusting the tool rest.

The **24-inch (610-mm) tool rest** (Fig. 73-5) is convenient for doing long turnings if you do not wish to move the shorter tool rest. This support requires an extra tool holder or support base.

Figure 73-6 shows 6- and 3-inch-diameter (152- and 76-mm) **faceplates.** These permit the turning of different sizes of faceplate pieces.

The **screw-center faceplate** (Fig. 73-7) affords quick mounting (fastening) of small faceplate turnings.

The **drive (spur) center** (Fig. 73-8) and the **cup (dead) center** (Fig. 73-9) are used for all spindle turnings.

Horizontal drilling or boring can easily be done on the lathe with the addition of a special **geared chuck.** The geared chuck is inserted either into the headstock of the lathe or the tailstock spindle (Fig. 73-10).

Sanding drums, fitted into the headstock spindle, are excellent for sanding irregular edges (Fig. 73-11).

Fig. 73–2   A 12-inch (304.8-mm) tool support.

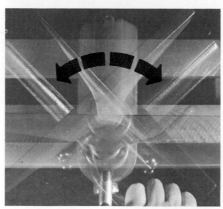

Fig. 73–3   Phantom view of a tool rest showing many angle adjustments.

Fig. 73–4   A right-angle tool rest.

Fig. 73–5   A 24-inch (609.6-mm), double-post tool rest.

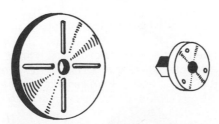

Fig. 73–6   Six- and three-inch–diameter (152.4- and 76.2-mm-DIA) faceplates.

Fig. 73–7   A screw-center faceplate.

Fig. 73–8   A drive, or spur, center.

Fig. 73–9   A cup, or dead, center.

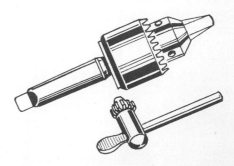

Fig. 73–10   A geared chuck.

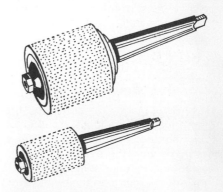

Fig. 73–11   Sanding drums.

Fig. 73–12   An outside spring caliper.

Fig. 73–13   An inside spring caliper.

An **outside spring caliper** (Fig. 73-12) and the **inside spring caliper** (Fig. 73-13) check the correct diameters for spindle and faceplate turning.

The **slip stone** (Fig. 73-14) is an absolute necessity for whetting (sharpening) turning chisels.

Fig. 73–14   A slip stone.

unit 74

Setting up to turn spindles

Turning done between lathe centers is called **spindle,** or **between-center, turning.** This method is followed to turn any round shape, such as chair and table legs, or other pieces requiring the use of both lathe centers. It is important to know how to center the work and mount it on the lathe.

Centering the wood piece

1. Select and cut stock for the spindle turning. It should be approximately square. The ends should also be square with the sides. The thickness should be approximately 1/4 inch (6 to 7 mm) larger than the diameter of the finished spindle. The length can be the exact length of the desired turning, or it can be 1/2 inch (13 mm) longer if you wish to cut the ends smooth after the turning is completed.

2. Draw diagonal lines across both ends of the piece (Fig. 74-1). The point of intersection (crossing) is the center. Some woodworkers prefer to do this only on the live center end and then dent the dead center with an awl.

3. Cut a 1/8-inch-deep (3-mm-deep) saw kerf on the diagonal lines on both ends of the piece (Fig. 74-2).

4. Remove the live center from the headstock of the lathe. Use the pin or rod provided for that purpose.

5. Place the live center (spur point) in the saw grooves. Tap it firmly a couple of times with a mallet to drive it in (Fig. 74-3). This will seat (sink) the prongs (spurs) of the live center in the saw cut.

6. Remove the live center from the wood. Replace it in the headstock of the lathe.

Fig. 74–1   Drawing diagonal lines to locate the center.

Fig. 74–2   Sawing on the diagonal lines.

154

Mounting stock on the lathe

1. Place the stock with the grooved end against the live center. Hold it carefully and firmly in position with your left hand.

2. Move the tailstock up to within 1 inch (25 mm) of the end of the wood.

3. Lock the tailstock to the lathe.

4. Turn the hand wheel on the tailstock until the point of the dead center fits either into the hole made with the awl or the center made with the saw cut (see Fig. 74-4).

5. Tighten the hand wheel on the tailstock until the piece to be turned is fastened securely. Lock the hand wheel using the adjustment lever. Figure 74-4 shows the piece located between centers.

6. Put two or three drops of lubricating oil on the dead center (Fig. 74-5). Lubricant is not needed if this center is of the ball-bearing type. Oil lessens burning caused by friction.

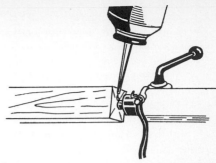

Fig. 74–5 Adding drops of oil to the dead center.

Fig. 74–3 Driving the live center (spur point) into place.

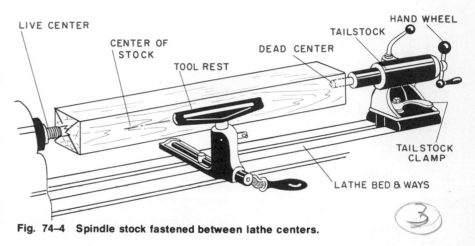

Fig. 74–4 Spindle stock fastened between lathe centers.

unit 75

Practice turning between centers

Turning spindles between centers can be done with either a cutting or a scraping action. The chisels that are used for turning are described and illustrated in Unit 73, Woodturning Chisels and Accessories. The cutting method is faster and makes a cleaner surface. Much practice is required to learn how to cut; for this reason, many beginners use the scraping method. Most of the processes described and illustrated in this unit use the cutting technique. After you have practiced these cuts, you should be able to make a spindle turning as outlined and illustrated in the next unit.

Roughing the stock

Read and observe the safety precautions in Unit 23.

1. Carefully adjust the position of the tool rest until it is about 1/8 inch (3 mm) away from the piece to be turned and 1/8 inch (3 mm) above the center line (Fig. 75-1).

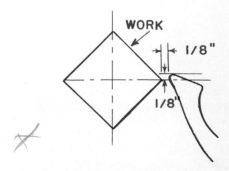

Fig. 75–1 The position of the tool rest in relation to the spindle turning.

155

2. Move the spindle stock by hand. Make sure that there is at least a 1/8-inch (3-mm) clearance between all edges of the wood and the tool rest.

3. Turn the speed control to a low speed.

4. Place the 3/4-inch (19-mm) gouge on the tool rest. Move it on the tool rest and against the revolving spindle to make the first cut (Fig. 75-2). This cut starts about 2 inches (51 mm) from the tailstock end. Note in Fig. 75-3 that the gouge is rolled over slightly in the same direction as the cut.

5. Make a second cut, starting about 3 inches (76 mm) to the left of the first one. Advance toward the tailstock until you feed into the first cut (Fig. 75-2).

6. Continue to make this series of cuts until you reach a point about 2 inches (51 mm) from the live center end; then *reverse* direction and cut off the remainder. After some experience, you should be able to start at one end and make a continuous cut to the other.

7. Continue the rough-cutting until the spindle is round and still slightly larger than the maximum diameter of the finished piece (Fig. 75-4). You can move the gouge from left to right or from right to left, whichever is most convenient.

Smoothing the wood spindle with a skew chisel

1. Set the caliper to the maximum diameter desired (see Fig. 75-7).

2. Place the large skew chisel on the tool rest; make the fine (accurate) shearing cut, as shown in Fig. 75-5. This cut requires much careful practice. The center of the skew chisel cutting edge should be used for making skew cuts, not the point.

Figure 75-6 shows a common way of scraping with the skew chisel. This method is often used by beginners.

3. Make cuts until the spindle is formed to the desired diameter.

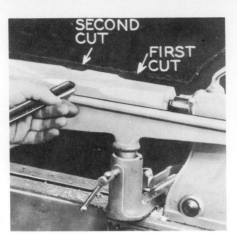

Fig. 75–2 The sequence of cuts for rough turning with the gouge.

Fig. 75–3 The correct way to use the gouge for a shearing cut.

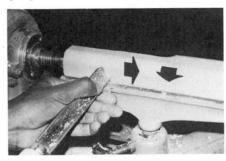

Fig. 75–4 Rough-cutting the stock to the approximate diameter.

Fig. 75–5 Making a cut using the skew chisel.

Fig. 75–6 Smoothing by scraping.

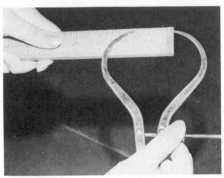

Fig. 75–7 Setting a caliper to the desired dimension.

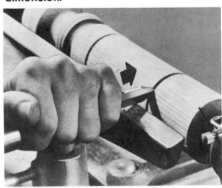

Fig. 75–8 Making a parting cut.

Fig. 75–9 Cutting and gaging for diameter.

Making a parting cut

1. Speed the lathe slightly.
2. Set the caliper to the desired diameter (Fig. 75-7).
3. Place the parting tool on its edge on the tool rest (see Fig. 75-8).
4. Grasp the parting tool firmly with one hand; push it *directly into* the revolving spindle (Fig. 75-8) to make a scraping groove cut. Use this for cutting to depth or for squaring ends.
5. Cut until the desired diameter of the spindle has been reached (Fig. 75-9). Hold the tool in one hand while gaging with the caliper. Figure 75-10 shows how to make a clearance cut when the groove is over $^3/_8$ inch (10 mm) deep. This prevents burning the point of the parting tool.

Making a cove (concave) cut

1. Lay out, or mark, the width of the cove with a pencil.
2. Place a gouge (narrower than the cove) on the tool rest. Push it into the stock to remove the surplus wood (Fig. 75-11). This is a scraping action.
3. Finish cutting the cove with the same gouge (Fig. 75-12).

Cutting a shoulder

1. Cut the wood to within $^1/_{16}$ inch (2 mm) of the required shoulder diameter with a parting tool.
2. Smoothing the shoulder with the point of the skew chisel (Fig. 75-13) makes a clean-cut shoulder face.

Beads and V cuts

1. Mark the cylinder the width of the beads or Vs (see Fig. 75-14).
2. Make the first cut for the beads with the *point* of a skew chisel (Fig. 75-14).
3. Round the beads with the *edge* of the skew chisel (Fig. 75-15).
Figure 75-16 shows how beads and Vs are cut with a skew chisel or are scraped with a spear-point chisel. Beginners often prefer scraping.

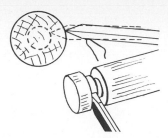

Fig. 75-10 Making a clearance cut to prevent burning the point of the parting tool.

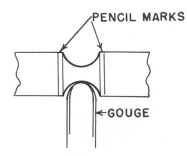

Fig. 75-11 Removing surplus wood in a cove with a gouge.

Fig. 75-12 Finishing a cove cut.

Fig. 75-13 Making a side cut, with a skew chisel, squaring a shoulder.

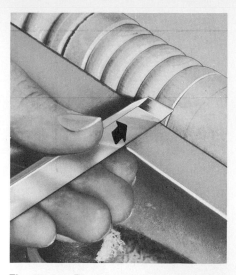

Fig. 75-14 The first cut in turning beads using a skew.

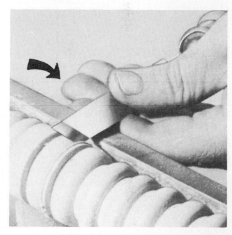

Fig. 75-15 Rounding beads with a skew.

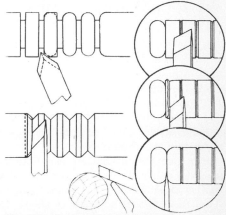

Fig. 75-16 Beads and V cuts.

unit 76

Spindle turning

The previous unit described and illustrated some of the more common shapes that can be cut between centers on the wood lathe. Spindle turning (between centers) requires a general procedure, as presented in this unit. You will find it necessary to refer to the previous unit for details of the various cuts.

Included here is information on **post blocking.** In this process, some extra wood is added to the portions of the spindle where the diameters are greater than the main part of the piece, as is often the case with a lamp column or a table leg. Figure 76-14 shows the effect obtained by use of contrasting woods. The work should be perfectly centered to avoid a lopsided appearance or pattern. Figure 76-1 illustrates how spindle turning is done industrially on an automatic lathe.

Fig. 76–1 **Industrial method of mass producing identical spindles (turnings) on an automatic lathe.**

Straight, or spindle, turning

Read and observe the safety precautions in Unit 23.

1. Turn to the maximum diameter. See "Roughing the Stock" and "Smoothing the Wood Spindle with a Skew Chisel" in the preceding unit.

2. Mark the required dimension lines along the turning. Use a pencil and a rule (Fig. 76-2). You can also use a full-size template (Fig. 76-3).

3. Cut to the pattern diameters (depths) using the parting tool (cut-off tool) and a hardboard diameter gage (Fig. 76-4). These are the basic cuts that locate the different diameters.

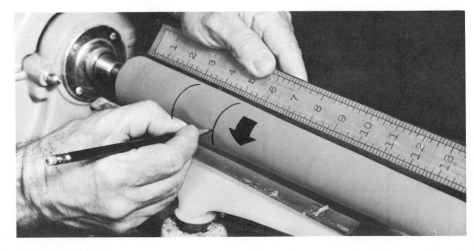

Fig. 76–2 **Marking dimension lines with a pencil and a rule.**

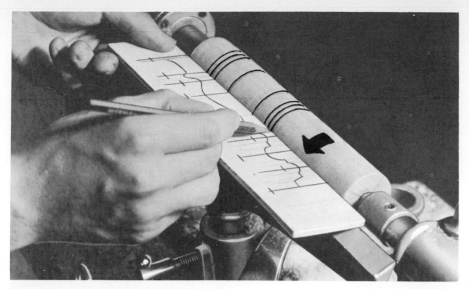

Fig. 76–3 Marking dimension lines with a pencil and a full-size template.

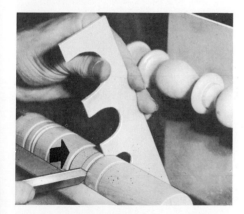

Fig. 76–4 Cutting and gaging to the various diameters (depths).

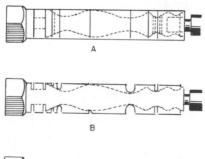

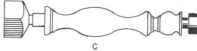

Fig. 76–5 The steps in making a spindle turning.

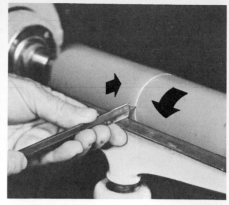

Fig. 76–6 Cutting with the parting tool to separate the square portion from the part to be turned.

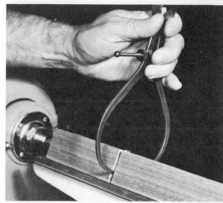

Fig. 76–7 Gaging the diameter with a caliper.

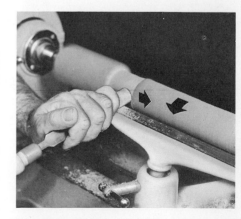

Fig. 76–8 Rough-cut turning with the gouge. Note that the square portion (on the left) will not be cut.

They can also be gaged with the caliper. Figure 76-5 illustrates these cuts on a typical turning design: (A) lines marked on the spindle, (B) first cuts in the spindle, and (C) the completed spindle turning.

4. Finish the spindle turning by using any of the cuts described and illustrated in Unit 75, Practice Turning between Centers.

5. Turned legs may have to have a square portion left at the top, particularly if mortise-and-tenon joints are to be used to fasten them to rails. In this case, all turning should begin from the square part, as illustrated in Figs. 76-6, 76-7, and 76-8. The procedure will then be the same as for any straight turning.

Sanding

1. Use a quarter of a sheet of medium-grit abrasive paper.

2. Move the tool rest away from the work.

3. Start the lathe turning at low speed.

4. Sand all shoulders first with the abrasive paper folded. Make sure

to hold the abrasive paper so that the shoulders will *not* get rounded (Fig. 76-9).

5. Use extra-fine abrasive paper for final sanding.

6. Stop the lathe. Sand the turning *lengthwise* by hand. This removes cross-grain scratches which were made while the work was revolving (Fig. 76-10).

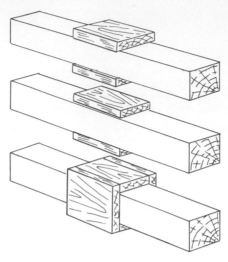

Fig. 76–11 Steps in gluing on blocks of wood for post blocking.

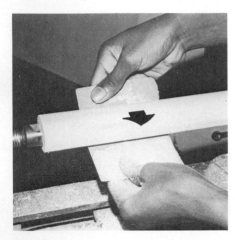

Fig. 76–9 Sanding a straight turning on the lathe.

Fig. 76–10 Sanding a straight turning lengthwise to remove circular abrasive (sanding) marks.

Post-block turning

1. Make, locate, and glue extra wood blocks onto the main spindle, as illustrated in Fig. 76-11. These should be glued on where extra material is needed. Allow the glue to dry thoroughly before any turning is done.

2. Center and mount the spindle on the lathe (see Fig. 76-12).

3. Shape the spindle (Figs. 76-12, 76-13, and 76-14). The post-block portion should be rough-turned before the remainder of the spindle is turned (see Fig. 76-14).

4. Complete all turning on the spindle as explained in the steps in this unit under "Straight, or Spindle, Turning."

Fig. 76–12 Starting the rough cut on a post-block spindle.

Fig. 76–13 Smoothing the post-block turning with a skew chisel.

Fig. 76–14 Post-block rough turned. The remainder of the spindle can now be cut.

unit 77

Setting up for faceplate turning

Faceplate turning is accomplished with the use of either 3- or 6-inch-diameter (76- or 152-mm-diameter) or screw-center faceplates. These are screwed to the headstock spindle. Wood projects that are most often turned on the faceplate base are bowls, circular trays, and bases for lamps. The several common methods of fastening wood stock to faceplates are described.

Preparing stock for the faceplate

1. Select the stock according to the type of wood, thickness, width, and length. Be sure to allow a surplus of approximately $1/2$ inch (13 mm) in both width and length and $1/8$ inch (3 mm) in thickness.
2. Rough-cut this piece (see Fig. 77-1).
3. Plane one face smooth.
4. Draw diagonals on the block to locate the center (Fig. 77-1).

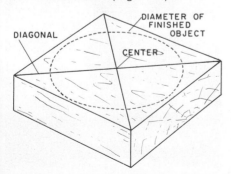

Fig. 77–1 Stock marked for faceplate turning.

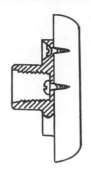

Fig. 77–2 Direct fastening on a faceplate.

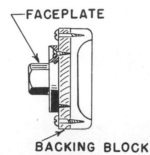

Fig. 77–3 Using a backing block for fastening stock to a faceplate.

5. Lay out a circle to represent the diameter of the bowl or other faceplate turning. The center is the point where the diagonals cross.
6. Cut out the turning disk on the jig or band saw (see Fig. 77-4).
7. Then select a size of faceplate that is suitable to fit the wood block.

Fastening stock or a turning disk to the faceplate

1. Fasten the faceplate with screws to the *smooth face* of the wood block that is to be turned (Figs. 77-2 and 77-3). Figure 77-2 shows a direct fastening that can be used where the inside of the turning is not to be cut out. Figure 77-3 illustrates the use of a backing block for internal cutting. Be

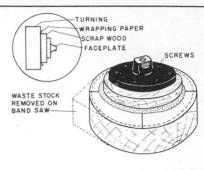

Fig. 77–4 Turning stock that is glued to the backing block of a faceplate.

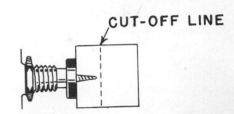

Fig. 77–5 Fastening a screw-center faceplate to a small-diameter turning.

sure the screws *do not go through* the block.
2. Figure 77-4 shows another method of fastening a faceplate to the block of wood. Glue the backing block (scrap wood) to the turning stock with a heavy sheet of wrapping paper between them. When the turning is completed, the project can be pried away from the scrap wood easily, since only paper is between the two pieces.
3. Figure 77-5 illustrates how to fasten a screw-center faceplate to a small-diameter (less than 3-inch or 76-mm) turning block.

Mounting stock

Mount (fasten) the faceplate and the wood block assembly on the live center spindle of the lathe head.

161

unit 78

Faceplate turning

Most of the cutting in faceplate work is done with a scraping action. Rough-forming (cutting), using a gouge, is similar to that used for spindle cutting. Figure 78-1 shows the correct cutting tools (chisels) to use to make different cuts. Always use the largest faceplate that can be fastened to the block being turned. The processes explained and illustrated in this unit are basic. They can be combined to make intricate faceplate turnings.

Usually, the first cutting shapes the mounted disk (block) of wood to the approximate final diameter. This reduces, and practically eliminates, noticeable vibration.

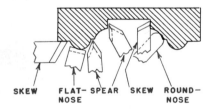

Fig. 78-1 The use of chisels for faceplate turning.

Turning a bowl or tray

1. Fasten the faceplate and the wood block assembly on the spindle of the lathe head.

2. Adjust the tool rest parallel with the *ways* of the lathe bed. Set it 1/4 inch (6 mm) from the outer edge and down 1/8 inch (3 mm) from the center (see Fig. 78-2).

3. Turn the work *by hand* to see that the wood block assembly does not hit the tool rest.

4. Turn the speed control to its low speed. Smooth (shape) the edge with either a gouge (Fig. 78-2), a squarenose chisel (Fig. 78-3), a spear-point chisel (Fig. 78-4), or a parting tool (Fig. 78-5). Note that a right-angle tool rest is used in two of the illustrations.

5. Next, turn off the motor. Adjust the tool rest so that it is parallel with the piece being worked.

6. Turn on the motor to a faster speed than the speed you used for rough-shaping.

7. Smooth the wood face with a gouge (Fig. 78-6), a roundnose turning

Fig. 78-2 Shaping the edge with a gouge.

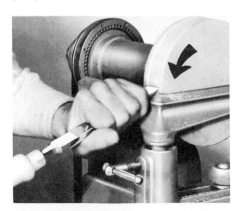

Fig. 78-3 Shaping the edge with a squarenose chisel.

Fig. 78-4 Shaping the edge with a spear-point chisel.

Fig. 78-5 Truing the edge with a parting tool.

Fig. 78-6 Smoothing the face with a gouge.

Fig. 78–7 Smoothing the face with a squarenose chisel.

tool, or a squarenose chisel (Fig. 78-7).

8. Finish the turning (cutting) according to the design or drawing (Fig. 78-8). Use appropriate turning chisels for each type of cut (see Fig. 78-1). Those turnings that are too large to be cut over the lathe bed can be fastened on the *outboard end* of the spindle, as shown in Fig. 78-9. A floor stand will be needed to hold the tool rest.

9. Sand the completed faceplate turning (see Figs. 76-9 and 76-10).

Cutting a deep bowl

Deep bowls and turned jewel boxes (Figs. 78-10 and 78-11) can best be made by using the drill press to bore a hole to the required depth. Turning chisels can then be used off this deep

Fig. 78–9 Large faceplate work turned on the outboard end of the spindle.

Fig. 78–8 Shaping or cutting the design into the wood block.

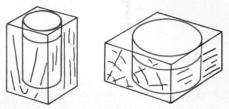

Fig. 78–10 Novelty boxes can be turned with the grain of the block either vertical or horizontal.

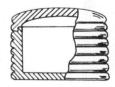

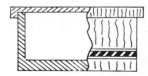

Fig. 78–11 Design suggestions for turning jewel boxes.

163

hole to widen the opening. Figures 78-12 through 78-15 show the steps in doing this. An inside caliper may be used to ensure proper dimensions (Fig. 78-14).

Fig. 78-12 Cutting the inside for depth using the skew chisel.

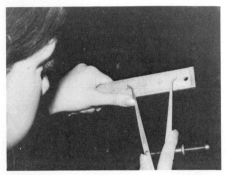

Fig. 78-14 Setting an inside caliper to a measurement.

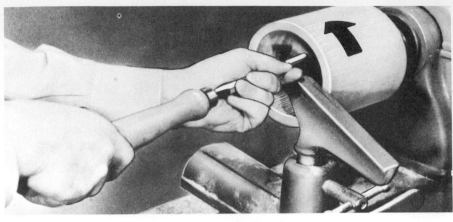

Fig. 78-13 Smoothing the inside bottom by scraping.

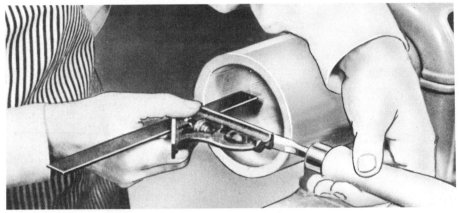

Fig. 78-15 Measuring for depth.

unit **79**

Finishing lathe turnings

When the entire project is made on the lathe, it can be finished satisfactorily before it is taken off. One of the best finishes put on in this manner is called **French polish.** The ingredients of French polish are pure white shellac, boiled linseed oil, and denatured alcohol. They are not mixed together but are kept in three separate bottles. A soft rag is used to apply the finish.

Applying a French finish

1. Place the cloth pad over the mouth of the shellac bottle, and tip the bottle until the rag is almost saturated with shellac.

2. Add some denatured alcohol to the pad. Add about half as much alcohol as you did shellac.

3. Then add two or three drops of boiled linseed oil to the pad.

4. Run the lathe at low speed. Hold the pad to the spindle or faceplate turning (Fig. 79-1). Hold it lightly at first, and then increase the pressure until the cloth is almost dry. Move it back and forth along the work while it is turning (revolving).

5. Repeat this process until the surface of the piece is evenly coated.

6. Allow the first coat to dry and harden 24 to 48 hours, and then apply a second one. On successive coats, increase the proportion of shellac, using just sufficient alcohol and oil to prevent rings from forming on the piece. It requires some experience to obtain a smooth, even coating, but the final result will be a smooth, lustrous sheen of pleasing quality.

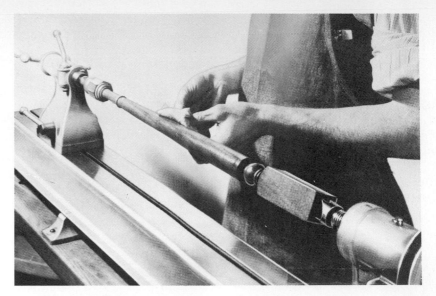

Fig. 79–1 Applying a French finish.

section 4k

Stationary sanding machine processes

unit 80

General information about sanding machines

Power sanders are used extensively. The stationary model sanders which you may have available are (1) the horizontal-belt table sander (Fig. 80-1); (2) the small vertical-belt sander

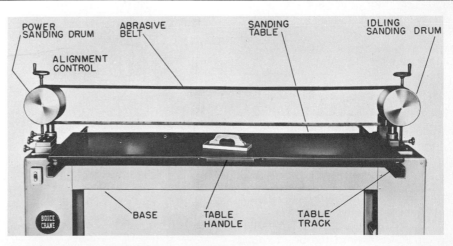

Fig. 80–1 A school-size, table-model belt sander.

165

(Fig. 80-2); (3) the disk sander (Fig. 80-3); (4) the spindle sander (Fig. 80-4); and (5) the sander/grinder (Fig. 80-5).

There are many variations of each of these machines, ranging from those illustrated to fully automatic ones that require no manual skills. Sanders are sometimes referred to as **finishing machines**.

Horizontal-belt table sander (parts and uses)

A horizontal-belt sanding machine smooths any large-surface items that can be held on a sanding table (Fig. 80-1).

Table. The sander model shown has a stationary table with respect to height, but it slides forward and backward on rollers. The table supports flat surfaces and boards while they are being sanded.

Pulley columns. Hand wheels on the pulley columns move the pulleys up or down to raise or lower the sanding belt. Figure 80-1 shows a common horizontal table sander for school use.

Idler pulley. One of the regular pulleys has a tension adjustment that makes it the idler pulley.

Abrasive belt. The machine shown in Fig. 80-1 uses a continuous sanding belt in any width not exceeding the width of the pulleys, which are usually 8 inches (203 mm) wide. The abrasive-belt speed varies from 900 to 1800 feet per minute, ft/min (274 to 549 m/min).

Small vertical and horizontal sanders (parts and uses)

Vertical or horizontal sanders may be combined with a disk sander as shown in Fig. 80-2. These machines are used to sand flat or curved surfaces.

Table. The table may be adjusted to hold the piece being sanded in a vertical or horizontal position. It also tilts away from or toward the belt to sand bevels.

Fence. The fence is used only on the horizontal-belt sander. It can be tilted to sand a bevel.

Sanding belts. Belt sizes vary according to the capacity of the machine. Belt speed is around 3450 ft/min (1052 m/min).

Base. The base is a cast-iron or steel support on which the machine rests.

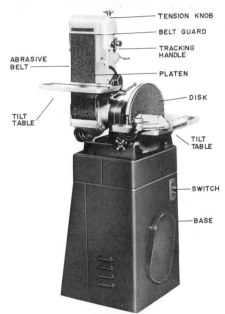

Fig. 80-2 A combination belt-and-disk sander.

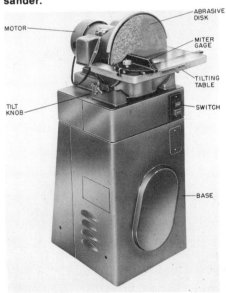

Fig. 80-3 A disk sander.

Disk sander (parts and uses)

The disk sander (Fig. 80-3) is used to sand straight and convex (outward-curved) edges. The disk diameters range from 8 to 18 inches (203 to 457 mm). Frequently the disk sander is one part of a dual machine, the other part being a small belt sander (see Fig. 80-2).

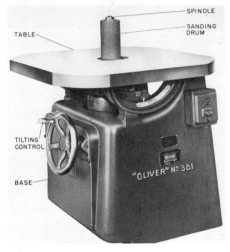

Fig. 80-4 A spindle sander.

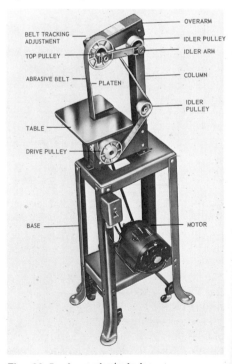

Fig. 80-5 A sander/grinder.

Table. The table on most sanding machines can be tilted to sand beveled edges.

Miter gage. A miter gage makes it possible to hold stock at various angles.

Frame. The disk sander frame is the stand that supports the machine.

Motor. The speed of the motor is usually 1725 r/min; the disk is directly attached.

Abrasive disk. The abrasive disk is a sheet of abrasive paper on a metal disk. The paper is fastened to the disk with a special abrasive-disk cement, or adhesive.

Spindle sander (parts and uses)

The spindle sander (Fig. 80-4) is sometimes called a **vertical-drum sander.** It smooths concave (inside-curved) edges. Detachable spindles hold drums that vary from $1/2$ inch by 6 inches (13 by 152 mm) to 6 by 9 inches (152 by 229 mm). On some machines, the table tilts; on others, the spindle.

Table. This is a metal plate on which the piece being sanded rests.

Spindle. The spindle is a rotating shaft that supports the sanding drums. Most spindles are detachable and operate with an oscillating (up-and-down) action. The speed varies from 1800 to 3600 r/min.

Base. This is a cast-iron or steel frame that supports the table and the entire working mechanism.

Sanding drums. Steel or rubber sanding drums are used on the spindle sander. The sanding sleeves are held tight on rubber drums by means of the air or mechanical pressure expansion of the rubber.

Sander/grinder (parts and uses)

The sander/grinder (Fig. 80-5) is intended for small or detailed sanding and grinding. The sanding speed is rated at 4000 sfm (1219 m/min). Internal, or pierced (cutout), sanding is done by inserting the sanding belt through the work and in front of both idler pulleys.

Table. The table is a metal plate on which the piece being sanded is fastened.

Drive pulley. The drive pulley receives power directly from the motor, then operates the abrasive belt.

Top pulley. The top pulley holds the abrasive belt taut (tight) and in place. It also serves as an idler, because of the tension built into the overarm. There is a tracking adjustment on the shaft housing of this pulley to keep the belt running true on the pulley.

Platen. A strip of metal backing up the abrasive belt.

Column and frame. This is of channel construction, which gives rigidity.

unit 81

Abrasives and adjustments

Adjustments on the several types of stationary sanders vary according to the manufacturer's specifications and the sizes of the machines. The adjustments usually consist of replacing the sanding belts or drums, aligning the idler pulley (the other pulley drives the belt), and regulating the angle of the table or the spindle. The suggestions in this particular unit are general, as they apply to each of the types of machines discussed.

Abrasives

Abrasive belts and sheet material for use on floor and portable sanders are classified by **grits.** Generally, Nos. 36 to 50 are considered suitable for roughing wood stock, 60 to 100 for medium finishing (smoothing), and 120 to 180 for fine sanding. Table 21-1, page 68, gives a detailed classification of abrasives.

Large belt table sander

The main adjustments on this machine include *raising and lowering* each of the two pulleys (Fig. 81-1), *tightening* the sanding belt with tension screws, and *aligning* the idler pulley to make the sanding belt track properly. These

Fig. 81-1 Adjusting a belt pulley for height above the sanding table.

are all controlled with handles and hand wheels.

Small vertical and horizontal sanders

The angle **tilt** (of the table for the vertical sander and of the fence for the horizontal one) is made with a hand adjustment under the table or at the end of the fence. Both are similar in operation.

Replacement of the sanding belt entails loosening the tension on the idler pulley, removing the outside of the case, and then taking off the worn belt. The new sanding belt should be put over the two pulleys and then the case is placed back on.

The idler pulley should be carefully **regulated** to align the abrasive belt (Fig. 81-2).

Fig. 81-2 Regulating the idler pulley to align the abrasive belt.

Disk sander

The **tilt** of the disk sander table is adjusted with the handle, which is usually underneath the table. This can be loosened and tightened to adjust the angle. The table is usually set at 90 degrees to the disk (Fig. 81-3).

Installing a new sanding disk requires removing the worn abrasive paper on the metal disk plate. Usually the worn disk can be peeled off. If it does not loosen, hold the end of a

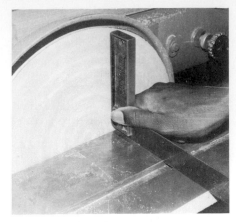

Fig. 81-3 Checking the 90-degree alignment of table and disk.

wooden block against the sanding disk while the disk is revolving. The heat of friction tends to loosen the paper.

Manufacturers recommend applying a commercial stick cement to the revolving plate (Fig. 81-4) to fasten the new paper disk to the metal plate (Fig. 81-5). A band of the stick cement is also rubbed on the outer edge of the paper disk to make it adhere to the metal plate.

Spindle sander

The angle of **table tilt** is usually the only adjustment that is made on the spindle, or drum, sander.

Replacing sanding drums is also an adjustment. On some machines, the sleeves are slipped over rubber drums that are held tight by expansion of the rubber under pressure.

Sander/grinder

The angle of table tilt may be adjusted easily by loosening and then tightening the supporting belt (Fig. 81-6). The abrasive belt-tracking adjustment on the housing for the top pulley keeps the belt in alignment on the pulleys. Replacing the abrasive belt is a very simple matter. It requires only pressing down the tension on the overarm.

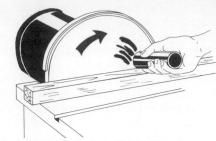

Fig. 81-4 Applying disk adhesive to the metal plate for fastening the abrasive sheet.

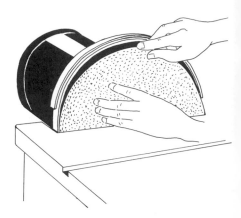

Fig. 81-5 Fastening an abrasive sheet on the disk.

Fig. 81-6 A table adjusted for the desired angle of sanding.

unit 82

Sanding on stationary model sanders

Sanders smooth wood in preparation for applying finishes. It must be remembered that the piece being sanded must be continuously moved for even sanding.

Sanding on the large belt table sander

Read and observe the safety precautions in Unit 23.

1. Adjust the height of the pulleys operating the sanding belt to the desired clearance from the work. The sanding belt should be about 1 inch to 2 inches (25 to 51 mm) above the piece being sanded.

2. See that the correct abrasive grit is on the sanding belt.

3. Press down on the inside of the moving sanding belt. Use the hand-stroke belt sander block (Fig. 82-1).

Continue moving the block and the piece back and forth, and lengthwise, until the surface is smooth and evenly sanded.

Sanding on small vertical and horizontal sanders

1. Adjust the table (of the vertical sander) or the fence (of the horizontal sander) for the sanding angle desired. This will usually be 90 degrees to the sanding belt.

2. Be sure that the abrasive belt is of the correct grit. Also check that the alignment of the belt on the pulleys is proper.

3. Move the work on the table slowly into contact with the moving sanding belt. (Figs. 82-2, 82-3, and 82-4).

Sanding on the disk sander

1. Adjust the table for the sanding angle desired. For most work it should be at a 90-degree angle to the disk.

2. See that the abrasive disk is of the correct grit.

3. Move the piece on the table slowly into contact with the revolving

Fig. 82–3 Sanding a bevel on a small belt sander.

Fig. 82–1 Sanding an end table top on a large horizontal-belt sander.

Fig. 82–2 Sanding a smooth face on a small horizontal-belt sander.

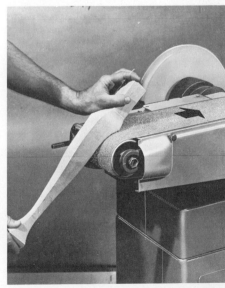

Fig. 82–4 Sanding concave (inside) edges on the small belt sander.

disk. Continue moving it until the edge or end is smooth and even (Figs. 82-5 and 82-6). Feed the work into the disk on the down side of the rotation.

Sanding on the spindle sander

1. Adjust the table or the spindle for the sanding angle desired.
2. See that the correct grade of grit is on the abrasive drum.

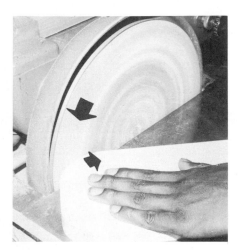

Fig. 82–5 Sanding a convex (outside) edge on the disk sander.

Fig. 82–6 Sanding an end on the disk sander.

3. Move the piece on the table slowly into contact with the revolving sanding drum. Continue moving the piece until the edge is smooth and even (Fig. 82-7).
4. Figure 82-8 shows a special sanding attachment fastened on a motor for final finishing of turned spindles.

Sanding on the sander/grinder

1. Adjust the table for the desired angle of sanding.
2. Check the belt for the correct abrasive grit.
3. Turn on the switch. Allow the abrasive belt to come to full speed.
4. Move the board (stock) slowly on the table against the sanding belt (Fig. 82-9).
5. Sand intricate and internal designs by using the two idler pulleys to redirect the abrasive belt (Fig. 82-10).

Fig. 82–7 Sanding a curved edge on the spindle sander.

Fig. 82–8 Sanding a turned spindle.

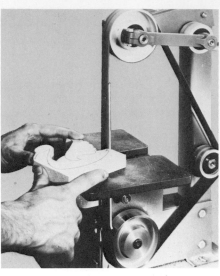

Fig. 82–9 Sanding an edge freehand on the sander/grinder.

Fig. 82–10 Sanding an internal, or pierced, cutout on the sander/grinder.

unit 83

Discussion topics for stationary machine tools and processes

1. List at least six safety rules that should be observed when using each machine in Section 4.
2. What are the two general types of circular saw machines? What makes them different?
3. What is a dado head?
4. How is the feather board used in connection with sawing on the circular saw?
5. How far should a saw blade extend above the work for safe operation of the circular saw?
6. Describe three major types of radial saws. Which type is in your industrial laboratory?
7. What determines the size of the radial-arm saw?
8. Give the formula for determining the surface speed (in ft/min) of the radial saw blade.
9. Name six types of cutters and other accessories that can be used on the radial-arm saw. List a process that each can perform.
10. Describe the difference between outboard and inboard ripping on the radial-arm saw.
11. List the sizes of the outside blades and inside cutters of a dado head for cutting a $5/8$-inch dado.
12. How is the size of a band saw measured? What is the size of the one in your school shop or laboratory? If you have one in your home workshop, what is its size?
13. What is the variation in cutting speeds in band saws? What determines the speed?
14. What are the minimum diameters of curves that can be cut with $1/8$-, $1/4$-, $1/2$-, and $3/4$-inch-wide band saw blades?
15. What is the purpose of relief cuts?
16. What is the purpose of the feather board during resawing?
17. What are the gullets of band saw teeth?
18. How is the size of a jig saw measured?
19. Give the general rule with respect to speed of cutting hardwoods and softwoods on the jig saw.
20. What is the general rule for the types of jig saw blades to use?
21. What is the process called which involves the fitting together of several types of thin wood, or veneers?
22. How is the size of a jointer determined? What size or sizes are in your school shop or laboratory?
23. Explain what will happen if the rear table is lower than the cutting edge of the knife blades on the jointer. What will happen if it is higher?
24. Define the terms **warp** and **wind** in boards.
25. What is the narrowest board that can be safely planed on the jointer and the rotary jointer/surfacer?
26. Which table do you adjust to set the depth of cut on the jointer?
27. List five unusual types of cuts that can be made on the jointer and the rotary jointer/surfacer.
28. Why should you stand aside while feeding a board into the planer? To which side of the board should you stand?
29. How is the size of a thickness planer determined? What is the size of the one in your school shop or laboratory?
30. What are the minimum length and thickness which can be safely handled in a planer? Why are they the minimums?
31. What are the two general models of drill press?
32. List five operations other than drilling for which the drill press can be used.
33. How is the size of a drill press measured?
34. Describe how you would adjust a drill press to bore to a particular depth and at a particular angle.
35. List and describe four kinds of bits that can be used for boring holes and drilling on the drill press.
36. What two kinds of machines can be used for mortising?
37. What is a mortise?
38. Describe the action that takes place when a mortise is cut on a hollow-chisel mortiser.
39. How is the size of a shaper determined?
40. Name and describe three types of shaper-cutter heads.
41. What is the purpose of a jig when using a shaper?
42. Describe two kinds of shaping which depend upon the rub collar as a depth guide.
43. Name and describe five basic turning chisels. When can each be used to best advantage?
44. What are the two general kinds of turnings that can be made on the wood lathe?
45. What is the general rule regarding speed in woodturning?
46. What is the name of a finish that can be applied on the turning before it is taken from the lathe? What are the ingredients of this finish?
47. Why is it dangerous to use a disk sander that has a loose disk?
48. What is the purpose of the idler pulley on a belt sander?

section **5**

Portable Power Tools and Processes

Safety for portable power tools

Portable power tools are efficient and safe to use when proper precautions are observed, understood, and followed. Those given here apply both to general safety and to the specific individual portable power tools you use. Study, review, and use these safety rules before working with any portable power tool.

General safety for all portable power tools

Permission. Always secure permission from your instructor, or from the person in charge, before using any portable power tool.

Clothing. Avoid wearing loose clothing. Button or roll up your sleeves. Remove your necktie or scarf.

Jewelry. Remove rings and pendants before using these tools.

Planning. Lay out and carefully plan your work before using these tools.

Stance. Maintain a well-balanced position on both feet when operating a portable power tool.

Illumination. There should be plenty of shadowfree light on the work.

Eye protection. Always wear safety goggles or a face shield.

Attachments and accessories. It is desirable to read the manufacturer's manual for the power tool. It often suggests special jigs and setups.

Safety for electric power tools

Adjustments. Disconnect the plug from the electric power outlet before making adjustments or changing accessories.

Electrical grounding. The electrical connection for every portable power tool equipped with a three-pronged plug should be grounded. Many portable power tools are double insulated to reduce shock hazards. These tools may be used with any outlet.

Electric cord. Arrange the flexible electric cord so that it will not interfere with your work and will not become damaged. If convenient, a good safety arrangement is to hang the cord over your shoulder.

Stopping. When you release the switch to the power, be sure to hold the portable power tool in your hands until all action stops. You may then return it to its proper place or lay it on the bench in the correct position.

Safety for pneumatic air-power tools

General safety. Observe the general safety precautions given at the beginning of this unit.

Power. Make certain all hose and pipe fittings are tightened securely before opening the valve in the air line. The recommended air-line pressure is 90 to 100 pounds per square inch (psi). In the metric system, pressure is measured in units called *pascals* (Pa). Pounds per square inch can be converted to pascals by multiplying by 6894.757; thus 90 to 100 psi becomes 620 528.13 to 689 475.70 Pa. Use your knowledge of the metric system to obtain the more convenient unit of kilopascals (kPa).

Direction of rotation. Set the reversing valve for the proper direction of rotation.

Speed of operation. Avoid short bursts of speed which might damage tool operation.

Torque. Adjust the output torque control screw for proper torque. (Torque is a turning or twisting force).

Stopping. When the work is completed: (a) shut off the air supply to the tool hose, (b) vent (release) the compressed air in the hose by squeezing the trigger, and (c) disconnect the air-powered tool from the hose.

Safety for the portable electric handsaw and the motorized miter-box saw

General safety. Observe the general safety precautions given at the beginning of this unit.

Blade. Make certain that the teeth of the blade are sharp. Study the manufacturer's manual for definite instructions on changing the saw blade.

Cutting depth. Always check for the correct depth adjustment before cutting.

Bevel. Check for the correct bevel adjustment before making a cut.

Ripping. When possible, use a guide or a fence for ripping.

Safety with the saber saw

General safety. Observe the general safety precautions given at the beginning of this unit.

Blades. Select the correct type and size of blade for the job planned.

Holding material. Hold or clamp the board to be cut so that it cannot vibrate.

Safety for the portable electric power plane

General safety. Observe the general safety precautions given at the beginning of this unit.

Cutter replacement. Do not attempt to replace the cutter, or to sharpen it, without carefully studying the manufacturer's manual.
Cutting depth. Always check for correct depth adjustment before making a cut.
Bevel. Check for the correct bevel depth adjustment before making a cut.

Safety for the electric hand drill

General safety. Observe the general safety precautions given at the beginning of this unit.
Drill bits. Select the proper size and type of bit for the job. Do not use larger bit sizes than are recommended by the drill press manufacturer.
Chuck. Fasten the bit securely in the jaws of the chuck before drilling.
Holding material. Hold or clamp the material firmly before drilling holes.
Drilling. Hold the hand drill with either hand, or both, while drilling. Do not force and break the bit.

Safety for the router

General safety. Observe the general safety precautions given at the beginning of this unit.
Hands. Keep both hands on the handles of the portable electric router when you use it.
Bits and cutters. Make sure the bits and cutters are sharp. Know the purpose of each one before using it.
Cutting depth. Always check for the correct depth adjustment before making a cut.
Direction of movement. Move the router from *left to right* when you cut straight edges. Move it from *right to left* when you cut curved edges.

Safety for portable electric sanders

General safety. Observe the general safety precautions given at the beginning of this unit.
Hands. Keep both hands on the handles of the belt sander while operating it.

Machine protection. Hold onto the handle of the sander when you plug the sander into the electrical circuit. If the switch happened to be on, the machine could "walk off" the bench and become damaged.
Belt direction. When installing an abrasive belt, point the arrow on the belt in the direction it will turn.
Abrasive belts and sheets. Make certain that you select the correct size of belt or sheet and the proper grade of grit to do the job.
Changing belts and sheets. Disconnect the plug from the power outlet before changing abrasive belts or sheets.
Belt tracking. Check the installation of an abrasive belt after it has been installed. Make certain it tracks properly (is in alignment with the edge).
Starting. Always lift the sander before starting to sand, and also before cutting off the power.
Sander weight. The weight of either sander is sufficient for most sanding.
Sander at rest. Lay the belt sander on its side when you are not using it.

unit 85

Pneumatic (air-powered) tools

The uses of pneumatic (air-powered) portable tools have increased steadily in all phases of the manufacturing and construction industries and in instructional programs. Since this power source is becoming common, it is important to understand pneumatic operating principles. Compressed air is an easily adapted source of power. The main advantage is that the tools are lightweight, powerful, and rugged and require less maintenance than comparable portable electric power tools.

Portable air tools are less complicated than most conventional electric ones performing similar operations. Some of the more common portable air-powered tools for use in woodworking are (1) the air drill with offset handle (Fig. 85-1), (2) the portable circular saw (Fig. 85-2), (3) the router (Fig. 85-3), (4) the screwdriver (Fig. 85-4), and the belt sander (Fig. 85-5).

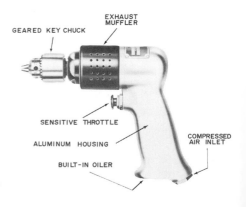

Fig. 85-1 An air drill with offset handle.

Air motor components

Figure 85-6 shows an impact wrench in cross section, with typical air motor components (parts) labeled.

Air motor. This is a relatively simple assembly, although built to extremely close tolerances. Figure 85-7 is an exploded view of the basic parts of the heart of an air-powered tool.

With normal wear, the air motor cannot be damaged by overload. This motor has a minimum of working parts which are moved by air.

Fig. 85—4 An air-powered screwdriver.

Fig. 85—2 A portable air-powered circular saw.

Fig. 85—5 An air-powered belt sander.

Fig. 85—3 An air-powered router.

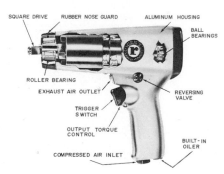

SQUARE DRIVE   RUBBER NOSE GUARD   ALUMINUM HOUSING
BALL BEARINGS
ROLLER BEARING
EXHAUST AIR OUTLET
REVERSING VALVE
TRIGGER SWITCH
OUTPUT TORQUE CONTROL
BUILT-IN OILER
COMPRESSED AIR INLET

Fig. 85—6 An air-powered impact wrench with a cross-section view.

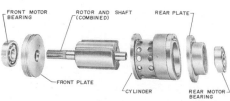

FRONT MOTOR BEARING   ROTOR AND SHAFT (COMBINED)   REAR PLATE
FRONT PLATE
CYLINDER
REAR MOTOR BEARING

Fig. 85—7 An exploded view of the basic parts of an air motor.

Planetary gearing. Figure 85-8 shows this component available on drills, fastening tools, and some abrasive tools. Planetary gears can carry high speed and power transmission in a small space. The entire planetary gearing system is supported on antifriction bearings and it can be externally lubricated.

Governor. Figure 85-9 shows a positive-speed governor, which provides maximum operating efficiency at minimum cost. Safety is achieved by controlling air consumption so that the right amount of air is admitted to the tools as the load is applied. This type of governor is used on many air grinders.

Fig. 85—8 Planetary gearing for air-powered tools.

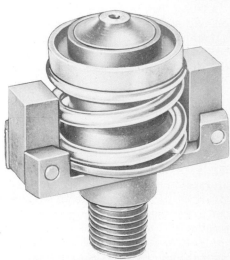

Fig. 85—9 A positive-speed governor.

175

Clutches

Most manufacturers of air-powered screwdrivers and wrenches provide three types of clutches: (1) positive, (2) adjustable, and (3) torque-control system.

Positive clutch. This type has one set of jaws held apart by light spring pressure (Fig. 85-10). The output of this clutch is largely dependent upon the pressure exerted by the operator and the length of time the jaws are allowed to remain engaged. The operator can further tighten the jaws by easing back on the tool, permitting an impacting action because of ratcheting of the clutch jaws.

Adjustable clutch. The drawing in Fig. 85-11 illustrates the action of this type of clutch. It has two sets of jaws. The first set is held apart by light spring pressure. This permits the motor and gears to revolve without rotating the bit until sufficient forward pressure has been exerted to close the gap and engage the jaws.

The second set of jaws is held together by heavier spring pressure. These jaws disengage and ratchet (make a grasping motion in one direction) when resistance to turning of the work exceeds the spring setting. The operator can permit the clutch to ratchet, which will give a slight impacting action that tends to continue tightening. Output torque (twist) can be increased or decreased by turning the adjusting nut, which controls the amount of compression on the spring.

Torque-control system clutch. Figure 85-12 portrays the mechanism of this system. Tension in a fastener (caused by stretching of the threaded portion of a fastener), and not torque, holds material together. As more torque is applied, more fastener tension is developed. Fastener tension can be regulated by controlling the torque.

Torque is controlled by a heavy torsion spring that acts as a torque-sensing device between driven, and driving, members in a screwdriver. When the screw is being driven (see Fig. 85-9), torque is transmitted from the driving member through the torsion spring to the driven member. When torque exceeds a preset amount, the torsion spring begins to wind up, permitting relative rotation between driving and driven members. This rotation causes the actuating ball in the driven member to control a valve that stops the tool.

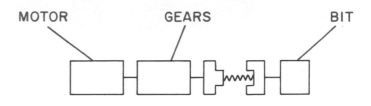

Fig. 85–10   A diagram of a positive clutch.

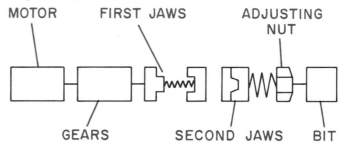

Fig. 85–11   A diagram of an adjustable clutch.

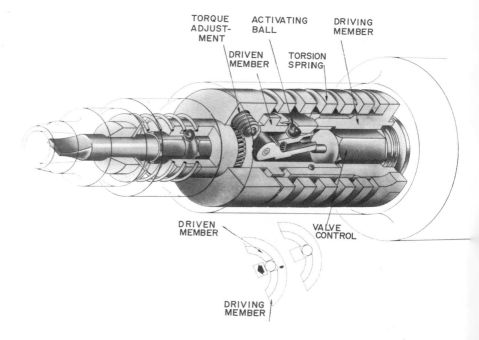

Fig. 85–12   A torque-control system clutch.

176

Portable power handsaw and motorized miter-box saw processes

unit 86

General information about the portable electric handsaw and the motorized miter-box saw

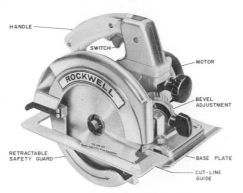

HANDLE
SWITCH
ROCKWELL
MOTOR
BEVEL ADJUSTMENT
RETRACTABLE SAFETY GUARD
BASE PLATE
CUT-LINE GUIDE

Fig. 86–1 A portable electric handsaw with a built-in blade brake and other safety features.

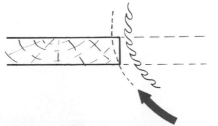

Fig. 86–2 The cutting action of saw teeth.

The **portable power handsaw** (Fig. 86-1) is sometimes called an **electric circular handsaw.** It is used extensively in building construction. This power tool has been improved with the development of a built-in blade brake. This is a good safety factor and also saves time by stopping the blade quickly so that either adjustments or succeeding cuts can be made. Other safety devices include a kick-proof clutch, nondragging telescoping guards, auxiliary front blade guard, and built-in insulated trigger switch. Its balance makes it easy for the operator to use for hours without fatigue.

The cutting action of the blade is up from the underside of the board (Fig. 86-2). It is exactly opposite from the cutting action of the handsaw. The portable electric handsaw is also useful for cutting grooves, dadoes, and rabbets.

Sizes

The size of the portable electric handsaw is determined by the diameter of the blade it uses. Blades range from $4^1/_4$ to 12 inches (114 to 305 mm) in diameter. The depth of cut varies from slightly over 1 inch (25 mm) to about $4^1/_2$ inches (114 mm).

Electric power handsaws are considered tools rather than machines because they are portable and light in weight. Weighing from 6 to 12 pounds (2.7 to 5.4 kilograms, kg), they are convenient to carry and to operate. The horsepower rating of the electric motor varies from $^1/_6$ to $1^1/_2$ hp (124 to 1119 W).

Parts and uses

Base plate. The base plate supports the motor, the handle, the blade, and the entire mechanism of the tool. It is adjustable, controlling the depth and tilt angle of the cut.

Handle. The handle is contoured (shaped) to give perfect balance in operation. Most handles have a self-contained, insulated, safety trigger switch.

Motor. The motor is contained in a body housing that also includes the gear drive that turns the blade.

Retractable safety guard. This spring guard lowers, covering the lower saw teeth when the tool is not in operation. The guard retracts when the tool is in use.

Bevel adjustment. An index, or bevel scale, is usually found on the front of the tool. It shows when the saw blade is set at any angle from 45 to 90 degrees to the base plate.

Blade. The combination blade is most frequently used because of the versatility of the portable electric handsaw. This blade is designed for rough and semismooth cutting. A planer blade is used when the cut must be very smooth. For prolonged crosscutting or ripping, a regular crosscutting or ripping blade should be used.

The **motorized miter-box saw** (Fig. 86-3) is a relatively new portable machine. It produces accurate miters and square cuts. The cutting action of the blade is from the underside, thereby pulling the work piece against the fence.

This portable unit weighs only 43 pounds (19.5 kg), making it easy to move. A 9-inch-diameter (229-mm-diameter) crosscut circular saw blade will produce a clean cut. A unique feature is that the blade may be stopped quickly by pressing the brake button on the handle. The protractor scale and the miter control are very similar to those of the manually operated miter box.

Fig. 86–3 A motorized miter-box saw.

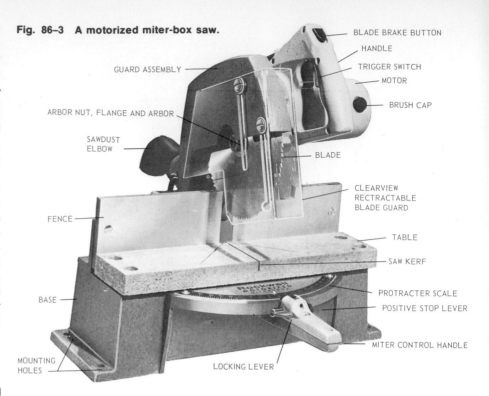

BLADE BRAKE BUTTON
HANDLE
TRIGGER SWITCH
MOTOR
BRUSH CAP
GUARD ASSEMBLY
ARBOR NUT, FLANGE AND ARBOR
SAWDUST ELBOW
BLADE
CLEARVIEW RECTRACTABLE BLADE GUARD
FENCE
TABLE
SAW KERF
BASE
PROTRACTER SCALE
POSITIVE STOP LEVER
MITER CONTROL HANDLE
MOUNTING HOLES
LOCKING LEVER

unit 87

Operating adjustments and maintenance on the power handsaw

The various adjustments on the portable electric handsaw make possible several different positions. It is possible, for example, to change the depth of cut and also to make different bevel cuts. Figure 87-1 shows a cross section of the various parts and adjustment controls. It is a relatively simple

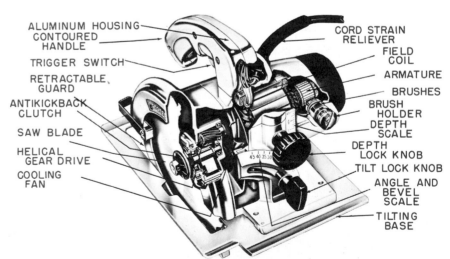

ALUMINUM HOUSING
CONTOURED HANDLE
TRIGGER SWITCH
RETRACTABLE GUARD
ANTIKICKBACK CLUTCH
SAW BLADE
HELICAL GEAR DRIVE
COOLING FAN
CORD STRAIN RELIEVER
FIELD COIL
ARMATURE
BRUSHES
BRUSH HOLDER
DEPTH SCALE
DEPTH LOCK KNOB
TILT LOCK KNOB
ANGLE AND BEVEL SCALE
TILTING BASE

Fig. 87–1 A cross section of the parts and adjustment controls of the portable electric handsaw.

matter to change blades (Fig. 87-2). The motor will give maximum wear if its carbon brushes are inspected often (Fig. 87-3).

Changing a blade

1. Disconnect the electric cord from the power source.

2. Set the portable electric hand-

saw on blocks of wood sufficiently high to clear the retractable guard (see Fig. 87-2).

3. Loosen the retaining screw by turning it counterclockwise (to the left). Use the wrench that comes with the saw (see Fig. 87-2). Hold the blade securely with the front block. This keeps it from turning. Some saws have a built-in blade lock, which holds the shaft stationary while the screw is loosened.

4. Push back the retractable guard so that you can lift off the blade and slide it down through the bottom opening.

5. Clean the surfaces of the collars. Make certain that you remember to add a thin film of grease.

6. Place the new or sharpened blade on the arbor. Tighten the retaining screw by turning it clockwise, or to the right (Fig. 87-2). Make it secure with the wrench. The teeth of the blade should point up, toward the front of the saw.

7. Return the retractable blade guard to its proper position.

Adjusting for depth of cut

1. Loosen the large, round depth lock knob on the front of the saw by turning it counterclockwise about three-fourths of a turn (see Fig. 87-1). This unlocks the slide.

2. Raise or lower the slide until the blade extends the desired distance below the base plate.

3. Tighten the depth lock knob by turning it clockwise until it is secure. Each manufacturer has specific instructions for making very slight depth adjustments.

Adjusting for bevel cuts

1. Loosen slightly the tilt lock knob on the front of the portable electric handsaw (see Fig. 87-1).

2. Swing the body of the saw until the desired angle is obtained.

3. Tighten the tilt lock knob to hold the base in the selected position.

Motor brush inspection

1. Remove one brush holder with a screwdriver.

2. Withdraw (pull out) the spring and the brush (Fig. 87-3). Note the position of the brush. If the carbon is worn to less than $1/4$ inch (6 mm) in length, it should be replaced.

3. If the old carbon is not worn too much and the spring is not damaged, broken, or burned, you may reinstall it in its former position. Do not turn it over, however.

4. Be sure to fasten the brush holder securely.

5. Check the opposite brush.

Fig. 87-2 Tightening the saw blade.

Fig. 87-3 Checking motor brushes for wear.

unit 88

Crosscutting and ripping with the power handsaw

The portable electric handsaw is designed to be used with the right hand. The left hand holds the work on sawhorses or on other rigid supports, and the right hand guides the saw across or with the work. Keep in mind that the saw teeth cut *from the bottom* of the board to the top (see Fig. 86-2). Crosscutting and ripping are done very much the same way; however, ripping is a little more difficult, espe-

cially when the saw is operated freehand.

Crosscutting

Read and observe the safety precautions in Unit 84.

1. Adjust the depth of the cut so that the blade saws just through the board.

2. Lay out or mark the board.

Fig. 88–1 Crosscutting with the portable power handsaw.

3. Plug the cord into an outlet.

4. Put the front of the base plate squarely on the edge of the board. Move the saw forward until the blade just touches the wood at the marked line for the cut. The alignment is made with the cut-line guide, or notch (see Fig. 86-1).

5. Back the saw slightly away from the work. Start the motor with the trigger switch.

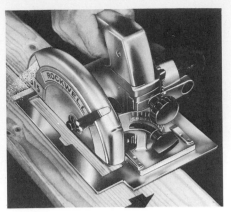

Fig. 88–2 Freehand ripping.

6. When the saw has reached full speed, move the blade steadily forward through the board (Fig. 88-1). Do not force the motor. Move the saw only fast enough to keep it cutting.

7. Cut off the power with the trigger switch when the cutting is completed.

8. Stop the blade by pressing down on the blade brake button if the tool is equipped with a brake stop.

Ripping

1. Follow steps 1 through 8 as in crosscutting with this exception: in step 4 the base plate should be put squarely on the end of the board for ripping. It is quite possible to rip *freehand* while following a straight line (Fig. 88-2), but the use of a guide is recommended for greater accuracy.

2. Attach the rip guide, and set it to the desired width of the cut. This guide is particularly useful in making narrow rip cuts (Fig. 88-3).

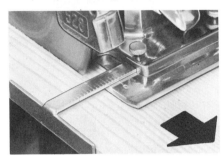

Fig. 88–3 The rip guide helps make accurate rip cuts.

unit 89

Making pocket and bevel cuts with the power handsaw

The portable electric handsaw can be used to cut pockets. It also makes miter, bevel, and compound cuts. The procedure for handling this tool is like that for crosscutting and ripping.

A pocket cut is one that must be made *inside* the area of the material; it does not start from an edge or an end. A bevel cut can be made straight across or at an angle.

Pocket cut

1. Mark the area to be cut with clear lines on all sides.

2. Plug the cord into an electric outlet.

3. Start near the corner of one side by placing the front edge of the saw base plate firmly on the work (see Fig. 89-1).

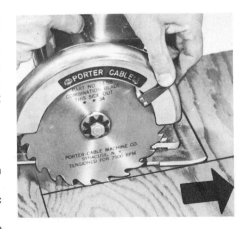

Fig. 89–1 Starting the pocket cut. Note that the retractable guard is pulled back with the left hand.

4. Hold the saw up so that the blade clears the material. Be sure you have adjusted the blade for the proper depth of cut.

5. Push the retractable lower guard all the way back so that the blade is exposed (Fig. 89-1).

6. Start the motor, and lower the blade into the board. The front of the tilting base serves as a pivot as the saw blade is lowered.

7. Follow the marked line right up to the corner.

8. Use the procedure described above for sawing the other lines of the pocket cut.

9. Use a compass saw to cut the corners cleanly and accurately.

Bevel cut

1. Set the blade at the desired angle to the base.

2. Adjust the depth of cut so that the blade cuts just through the piece.

3. Mark the board where it is to be cut.

4. Follow steps 3 through 8 under crosscutting in Unit 88 (see Fig. 89-2).

Special cuts

The portable electric handsaw can also be used for cutting grooves, dadoes, and rabbets. See Unit 25, Circular Saw Blades and Accessories, which gives information concerning special cuts.

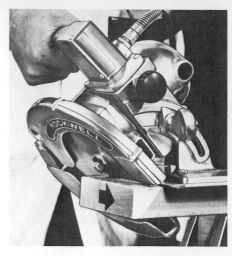

Fig. 89–2 Crosscutting a bevel cut.

unit 90

Sawing on the motorized miter-box saw

1. Adjust and set the angle of the cut with the locking lever and miter control handle (see Fig. 86-3).

2. Mark the work for desired cut.

3. Place the work piece on the miter-box table against the fence.

4. Turn on the motor switch and allow the motor to come to full speed.

5. Using the saw handle, pull the revolving blade across the work piece while holding the piece firmly against the fence (Figs. 90-1 and 90-2).

6. Turn off the power. Allow the blade to come to a complete stop before removing any of the cut stock.

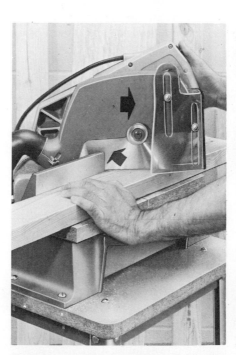

Fig. 90–1 Sawing a 45-degree cut to the right, across a flat surface.

Fig. 90–2 Cutting 45 degrees to the left, across an edge.

Saber saw processes

unit 91

Information about the saber (bayonet) saw

The saber (bayonet) saw (Figs. 91-1 and 91-2) is actually a portable electric jig saw. Portable and very versatile, it cuts all kinds of wood, plastic, composition board, veneer material, thin metal, cardboard, and even leather. This broad range of work makes it an ideal portable electric saw.

Sizes, speed, and action

The general appearance of most saber saws would seem to indicate that all are of the same capacity. The difference lies in sturdiness of construction, cutting ability, and motor power. The heavy-duty machine (Fig. 91-2) readily cuts up to 2-inch-thick (51-mm-thick) stock. Thus, it is particularly useful in building construction.

Most are designed to operate on normal household electric current. The cutting speed is approximately 4200 strokes per minute (spm).

The action of the better saber saws is an **orbital** (oval) blade motion (Fig. 91-3). In this design, the blade cuts only on the up stroke, backing away on the return stroke. This eliminates return-stroke blade drag. As a result, the teeth may stay sharp longer, and the blade does not heat up quickly.

Fig. 91–1 A saber (bayonet) saw.

Fig. 91–2 A heavy-duty saber saw.

Parts and uses

The main parts of the saber saw are shown in Figs. 91-1 and 91-4.

Case. This housing of lightweight-alloy metal or high-impact–resistant plastic contains the working mechanism.

Handle. The handle is the sturdy piece on top which allows the operator to manipulate the saw with ease. It usually includes a fingertip switch. Some models of saws attach an auxiliary handle on the side (Fig. 91-2).

Brushes. These are at the back of the motor housing. They are easily taken out when the cap is removed.

Base. The base serves as an inverted (upside-down) table. It provides a surface to guide the saw on the work. On most models, the base can be tilted.

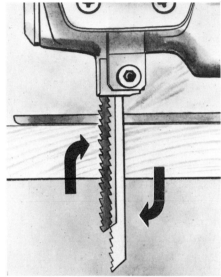

Fig. 91–3 Orbital (oval) blade motion (action) of a quality saber saw.

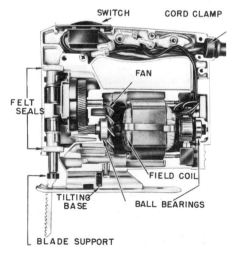

Fig. 91–4 A cross section of a typical saber saw.

unit 92

Saber saw blades and operating adjustments

It is important to select the right blade (Fig. 92-1) for use with the portable jig (saber) saw. The variation in type of blade used depends upon the kind of material to be cut.

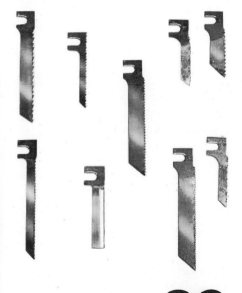

Blades

The 10-tooth long blade can be used to cut lumber up to 2 inches (51 mm) thick. The 10-tooth short blade is used to cut small-radius curves and intricate designs. It should be used for material up to only 1 inch (25 mm) thick. Both 10-tooth blades give a reasonably fine-cut (smooth) finish. The 6-tooth long blade is similar to the 10-tooth long blade except that it makes a rougher cut.

This is general information to guide you in selecting blades for working with wood. Table 92-1 gives a partial listing of blade requirements for other types of materials.

Adjustments

Aside from motor maintenance, only a few adjustments are needed to make cuts with the saber saw. The installation of the correct type of saw blade for the work to be cut is one. Another adjustment is tilting or replacing the base on some tools.

Each manufacturer's product requires a slightly different blade-fastening method. The operator's manual that comes with each saber saw should be studied very thoroughly before attempting to operate the tool. The manufacturer's manual gives specific instructions that are unique to each brand.

Table 92-1 SELECTION OF BLADES FOR CUTTING VARIOUS MATERIALS

Material to be cut	Number of teeth per inch	Type of blade
Aluminum sheet and tubing	14	high-speed steel
Brass sheet and tubing	14	high-speed steel
Copper sheet and tubing	14	high-speed steel
Formica	10	high-carbon steel
Masonite	10	high-carbon steel
Plexiglas and Lucite (acrylics)	10	high-speed steel
Plastics (other types)	14	high-speed steel
Plywood	10	high-carbon steel
Steel sheet and tubing	14 or 24	high-speed steel
Wood (general cutting)	10 or 6	high-carbon steel

Fig. 92–1 A typical assortment of blades for a saber saw.

unit 93

Cutting with a saber saw using guides

Some saber saws are equipped with a guide to aid both straight ripping cuts and crosscutting. When the guide is turned over and fitted onto a steel guide pin, this saw cuts perfect circles up to the capacity of the guide.

Ripping and crosscutting with a guide

Read and observe the safety precautions in Unit 84.

1. Fasten the correct blade on the

saw. Select it for the material to be cut. See Unit 92.

2. For ripping or crosscutting narrow stock, fasten the guide in place and adjust it to the desired width (see Fig. 93-1). If the piece to be cut off is wider than the guide permits, clamp a wooden fence (guide) on the board (see Fig. 93-2).

3. Hold the board so that the blade can cut through freely.

4. Start the motor. Slowly saw the board. Keep the guide firmly against the edge or the end of the stock, or keep the saw against the wooden fence or guide (Figs. 93-1 and 93-2).

Sawing circles

1. Place the board securely in some position, such as on sawhorses, that allows space underneath for the blade.

2. Lay out the circumference of the circle. Use a compass or dividers.

3. Drill a $3/16$- or $1/4$-inch (5- to 6-mm) starting hole through the board. This should touch the circle line on the waste side.

4. Fasten the correct blade on the saw for the material to be cut.

5. Drive the circle guide pin into the board at the center of the circle (see Fig. 93-3).

6. Turn the rip guide over, and fasten it in the saw to the radius desired (see Fig. 93-3).

7. Start the motor with the saw in place. Slowly push the saw as it makes the circular cut (Fig. 93-3).

Fig. 93–1 Ripping a board with a saber saw and metal guide.

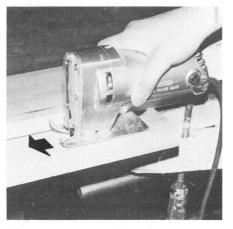

Fig. 93–2 Ripping with the saber saw using a wooden guide.

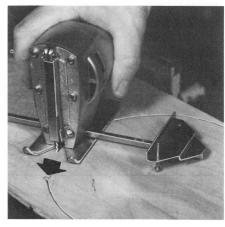

Fig. 93–3 Cutting a circle with a saber saw using a circular guide and pin.

unit 94

Freehand sawing to marked lines

This unit illustrates and explains many uses for freehand sawing to marked lines with the saber saw. These kinds of cuts are used by the cabinetmaker, carpenter, contractor, home owner, and hobbyist.

Sawing to marked lines

1. Fasten the material to be cut in a bench vise, use clamps to fasten it to a worktable, or place it on sawhorses. This is especially important when sawing small pieces. Some cutting will be done directly on floors, walls, and other fixed surfaces.

2. Mark the area to be cut.

3. To start an internal cut, place the forward edge of the saw base firmly on the edge of the material so that the saw is *tilted* (Fig. 94-1). This is called **plunge cutting.** Do this only when the wood is 1 inch (25 mm) thick or *thinner.*

4. Turn on the motor, and move the saw into the piece of material (Figs. 94-1 and 94-2). Do not force the saw. Let the blade and the saw do the work.

5. Move the saw forward rapidly enough to keep the blade cutting.

6. The saber saw is ideal for making wall pockets for electric outlets (Fig. 94-2).

7. Figures 94-3 and 94-4 show the use of saber saws to make freehand cuts.

8. Figure 94-5 illustrates the use of the saber saw to cut notches and to fit rafters.

9. Letters or numerals are easy to cut out, and they can be fashioned very smoothly by using the plunge cut (Fig. 94-6).

10. Cutting angles and making compound cuts up to 45 degrees can be done on some saws (Fig. 94-7).

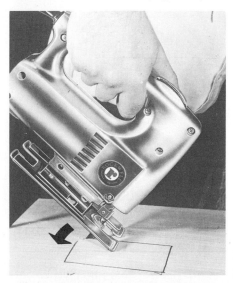

Fig. 94–1   Starting to saw an internal design with a plunge cut.

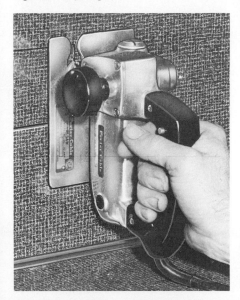

Fig. 94–2   Cutting a wall pocket for an electric outlet with a saber saw.

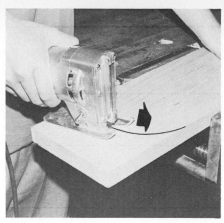

Fig. 94–3   Making a freehand curved cut.

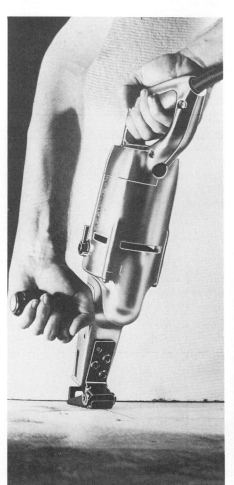

Fig. 94–4   Sawing freehand with a heavy-duty saber saw.

Fig. 94–5   A roof rafter notched with a saber saw.

Fig. 94–6   Cutting out letters with the saber saw.

Fig. 94–7   Sawing a compound cut with the saw base tilted.

Portable power plane processes

unit 95

Information about the portable power plane

The portable power plane (Fig. 95-1) is actually a portable electric jointer. This plane is being used increasingly by contractors, carpenters, builders, home renovators, and cabinetmakers. A power block plane, weighing only 3¾ pounds (1.7 kg), is shown in Fig. 95-2.

Types, sizes, and speeds

Electric plane sizes range from power block planes of 3¾ pounds (1.7 kg) to heavy-duty planes weighing as much as 16 pounds (7.3 kg). Speeds vary from 18 000 to 25 000 r/min.

The cutter used in most machines is a solid body with two spiral cutting edges ground on them. This cutter body can be removed and sharpened with a special tool, which is available from the manufacturer.

The width of the cut in planing varies from $1^{13}/_{16}$ to $2^{1}/_{2}$ inches (46 to 64 mm). The depth of cut on some power planes is from $^{1}/_{16}$ to $^{3}/_{16}$ inch (1.6 to 5.0 mm) maximum, depending upon the machine.

Parts and uses

Body. The aluminum alloy body is the housing that encloses the motor and the spiral cutter. It is located so that the operator can handle the tool easily and have control of the trigger switch.

Depth adjustment. The depth adjustment lever controls the depth of cut. The markings are calibrated (indexed) to show the exact depth of cut.

Cutter blade. The cutter blade is a solid piece of specially hardened steel upon which are ground two spiral edges.

Chip deflector. This is a part of the body (frame) which throws chips out to the side.

Bevel adjustment. The bevel adjustment permits setting a plane bed (body) or fence to make outside bevel cuts from 0 to 15 degrees and inside ones from 0 to 45 degrees.

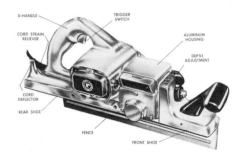

Fig. 95–1   A portable power plane.

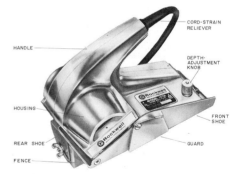

Fig. 95–2   A portable power block plane.

unit 96

Operating adjustments

Adjustments differ on the portable power plane according to specifications of the manufacturer. Study the operating manual very thoroughly, especially with respect to removing, sharpening, and assembling the cutter. Other adjustments deal with setting the depth and bevel for cutting.

Setting the cutter

1. Set the depth adjustment on the plane to zero (0). Use the adjustment lever located at the front end of the plane (see Figs. 95-1 and 95-2).

2. Turn the plane over (upside down).

3. Place a straightedge (or a try square) across the cutter opening so that it rests on both the front and the rear shoes (see Fig. 96-1).

4. Turn the cutter by hand until it lifts the straightedge (Fig. 96-1).

5. Adjust the lever until the tip of the cutting edge barely touches the straightedge. The cutter is now set at zero. This adjustment must be made every time the cutter has been sharpened and fastened on the plane.

Depth and bevel adjustments

1. Advance (turn) the depth adjustment lever at the front end of the plane to obtain the cutter depth desired (Fig. 96-2). Most markings are in sixty-fourths of an inch. There are usually two to each number. Placing the lever marking at 1 would make a $1/32$-inch cut. Halfway between 0 and 1 is a marker indicating a $1/64$-inch cut.

Setting the lever halfway between 1 and 2 makes a $3/64$-inch cut (see Fig. 96-2). To make a $1/16$-inch cut, set the lever at 2. At some future time the portable power plane will probably have metric dimension settings.

2. The bevel adjustment is shown in the lower right in Fig. 96-2. It is made by loosening the two wing nuts on the graduated apron hinges and tilting the apron to the desired angle. Most electric power planes can be quickly set for outside bevel cuts from 0 to 15 degrees and for inside bevel cuts from 0 to 45 degrees. The wing nuts should be tightened securely.

Fig. 96–1 Setting the portable power plane at zero (0) while turning the cutter.

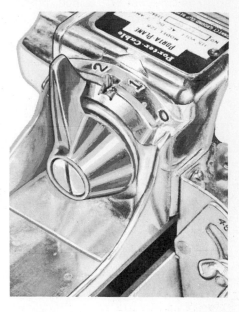

Fig. 96–2 Depth and bevel adjustments.

unit 97

Planing with the portable power plane

Planing with the portable power plane requires a stance (position of standing) similar to that used with regular hand planing. The difference, however, is that the portable power plane must be properly handled and advanced steadily and evenly along the work.

Procedure for planing

Read and observe the safety precautions in Unit 84.

1. Adjust the depth for making the cut.

2. Plug the electric cord into a power outlet. The cord should be grounded for safety.

3. Grasp the plane as shown in Figs. 97-1 and 97-2. The right hand should be on the handle, and the forefinger should be free to control the switch.

Fig. 97–1 Planing an edge with the portable power plane.

4. Place the plane on the board with the cutter slightly back from the edge or surface of the wood. Make certain that the electric cord cannot interfere with the planing process.

5. Turn on the switch. Push the plane to make the cut (Figs. 97-1 and 97-2).

6. A final cut of $\frac{1}{32}$ inch (practically 1 mm) will give a smooth surface that will probably require no sanding.

7. A bevel or a chamfer can be cut by adjusting the fence to the desired angle marking (Fig. 97-3). The procedure is similar for straight planing.

Fig. 97–2 Planing the surface of a board.

Fig. 97–3 Planing a chamfer with a power block plane. Note the angle of the fence.

section 5d

Portable power hand drill processes

unit 98

Information about the power hand drill

The portable power hand drill (Fig. 98-1) is one of the most popular and useful of all portable power tools. It is manufactured in a variety of types, sizes, and capacities. This handy tool is used extensively by building contractors and home owners and in school shops and laboratories.

This tool is usually equipped with an electric motor that operates on normal house electrical voltage. It is of the utmost importance, however, that portable tools be used only where they

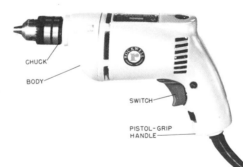

CHUCK
BODY
SWITCH
PISTOL-GRIP HANDLE

Fig. 98–1 A pistol-grip portable power hand drill.

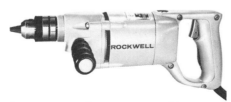

ROCKWELL

Fig. 98–2 A D-handle portable power hand drill.

can be grounded, unless they are double insulated.

Types and sizes

There are three basic types of portable power hand drills: (1) the pistol-grip drill, (2) the D-handle drill, and (3) the spade-handle drill. These are illustrated in Figs. 98-1, 98-2, and 98-3.

ROCKWELL

Fig. 98–3 A spade-handle portable power hand drill.

188

The **pistol-grip drill** (Fig. 98-1) is perhaps the most common because it is designed for one-hand operation. It is economical and compact. Various models of this drill have different chuck capacities and run at different speeds. The average drill speed is rated about 2000 r/min without a load. This lightweight drill has a drill bit capacity of up to $1/4$ inch (6.35 mm).

The **D-handle drill** (Fig. 98-2) has an advantage over the pistol-grip drill. Its auxiliary handle permits more accurate drilling control.

The **spade-handle drill** (Fig. 98-3) has the largest chuck capacity, taking drill bits up to $1/2$ inch (12.7 mm). It operates at a slower speed than the other two types of drills because it is designed for heavier duty. Its average drill speed is rated at about 600 r/min without a load. Because of its size, both hands are required to use it.

Portable power drills are designated by the maximum drill diameter that the chuck can accommodate. Sizes vary from $1/4$ to 1 inch (6.35 to 25.4 mm). The drill speed decreases as the size of the drill chuck increases because of the purpose and motor capacity of the drill.

Portable electric hand drills with self-contained power packs are available for use where electric power sources are not available or convenient.

Drill parts and uses

Body or housing. This part (Fig. 98-4) is often made of lightweight aluminum alloy. The body can also be made of impact-resistant plastic. This is the usual material when the tool is double insulated. Double insulation allows the use of a two-prong plug instead of a three-wire grounded plug.

The body encloses the power mechanism, which includes the motor and the gears that give the drill the desired speed and power.

Handles. There are several shapes of handles. All are located to give the operator easy control of the power switch.

Chucks. Chucks are described and illustrated in Unit 99.

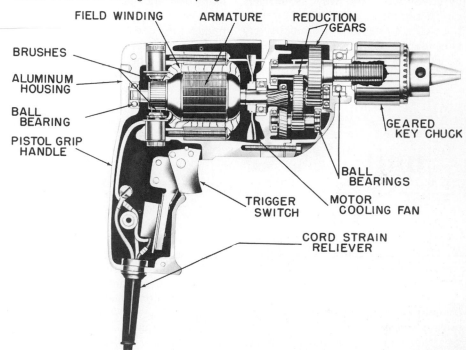

Fig. 98–4 **A cross section with the parts of a pistol-grip portable electric hand drill.**

unit 99

Chucks and drill bits

Chuck sizes are measured by the sizes of the drill bits they can handle. Portable electric hand drills use either key or keyless chucks (see below). Several types of round-shank bits can be used effectively with power hand drills.

Chucks

The three-jaw key chuck is designed to center the drill bit (Fig. 99-1). The jaws are opened by turning the sleeve counterclockwise (as seen from the bit end). After the bit is inserted in the chuck opening, the sleeve should be

Fig. 99–1 **A key chuck for the portable power hand drill.**

turned clockwise until the bit is gripped in the chuck jaws.

The chuck key should be inserted in one of the three holes of the chuck body and turned clockwise until the jaws are tight. It should then be fitted into each of the other two holes until the bit is secure.

A keyless chuck (Fig. 99-2) works in much the same way as the key chuck, but the bit is tightened firmly in the chuck by hand. This chuck is very serviceable, especially when using small-diameter drill bits which may not stay tight in a keyed chuck.

Drill bits

The types of drill bits that can be used successfully with the portable hand drill are (1) straight-shank twist drill bits, which are used in metalworking as well as woodworking; (2) spade, or power, bits which are used to bore holes in wood; (3) combination wood-drill and countersink bits, which make pilot and shank holes for screws and which countersink for screwheads in one drilling operation; and (4) countersink bits, which set screwheads. These bits are illustrated and discussed in detail in Unit 56.

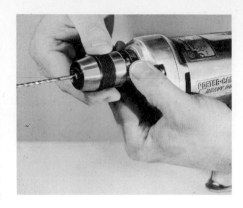

Fig. 99–2 Tightening a bit in a keyless chuck.

unit 100

Drilling holes

Drilling holes, countersinking, and driving screws are some of the many jobs that can be performed with the portable electric hand drill. With the correct bits, this tool can be used to drill holes in metal, plastics, concrete, and composition materials.

Procedure

1. Mark the center point of the hole. Use an awl or a nail. This prevents the bit from wandering (slipping).

2. Select the correct size and type of bit. Fasten it in the chuck.

3. Connect the electric drill to a properly grounded wall receptacle if it is not double insulated.

4. Put the point of the bit in the dent made in step 1. Do this before you turn on the motor.

5. Hold the drill perpendicular to the work. Start the motor (Fig. 100-1).

6. Drill the hole. Use just enough pressure to keep the drill cutting into the wood. Let the tool do the work while you use a steady, even pressure.

7. Use a block of wood to back (reinforce) the board, if the hole is to be drilled completely through (Fig. 100-2).

8. Withdraw the bit from the hole with the motor still on; then turn off the switch.

Fig. 100–1 Drilling a vertical hole. A try square helps align the power hand drill perpendicular to the board.

9. Figure 100-3 shows a hole being drilled with a D-handle power drill.

10. Screws can be driven with a portable power hand drill by using a speed-reduction ratchet (Fig. 100-4).

11. Building tradesmen find the self-contained power-pack electric drill extremely convenient and satisfactory for working in places that do not have regular electric power.

Fig. 100–2 Drilling a hole horizontally using a block of wood to back (reinforce) the board.

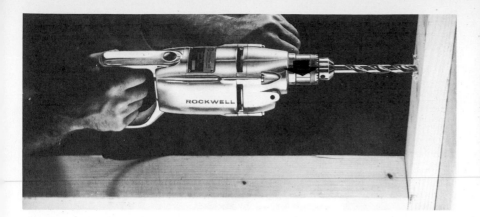

Fig. 100–3 Drilling a hole with a D-handle power drill.

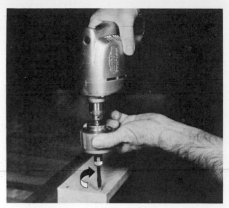

Fig. 100–4 Driving a screw with a speed-reduction ratchet.

Portable power router processes

unit 101

General information about the portable power router

The portable power router (Fig. 101-1) is probably the safest of all portable power tools. It is a precision-built piece of portable equipment. The router cuts to a desired thickness and depth into, and through, wood and many other materials. Accessories make it possible to produce intricate joints, decorative cuts, and inlays. It can also be used to shape edges, cut recesses (gains) for door hinges, and make dovetail joints.

The wide selection of bits and cutters makes the portable power router an extremely versatile tool. It can be used for freehand cutting by being guided with the hands alone. It can also be used with various templates.

Sizes and speeds

The size of the portable electric router is measured by the horsepower rating of its enclosed motor, which varies from $1/4$ to 3 hp. The 3-hp motor is a heavy-duty, industrial size. The speed range is from 16 000 to 27 000 r/min. The metric equivalent of 1 hp is 746 W.

The above motor speeds will vary from 186.5 to 2238 W if rated metrically.

Fig. 101–1 A portable electric power router.

191

Parts and uses

Motor unit. The router motor is self-contained. Figure 101-2 shows a cutaway view of the many parts, including the motor.

Base. The base is the platform, which rides the surface of the wood and controls the depth of cut.

Hand knobs. The two knobs or handles are conveniently located for easy grasp and control. Some routers have a handle and a knob, in which case the trigger switch is usually located in the handle (see Fig. 101-2).

Depth adjustment ring. This is a micrometer depth adjustment control, usually fastened to the base.

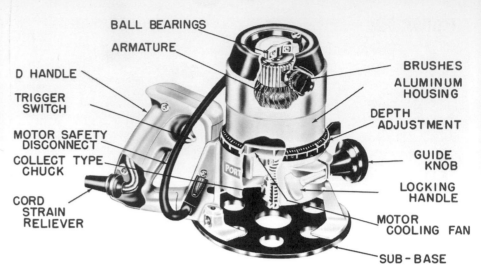

Fig. 101–2 A cutaway view of a portable electric power router.

unit 102

Router bits, cutters, accessories, and adjustments

There are router bits and shaper cutters in sizes and shapes to permit almost any cut desired. Figures 102-1 through 102-4 show a few of the bit shapes and the cuts they make. The several units in this section discuss and show these and other bits, cutters, and accessories that are used for specific operations.

Inserting a bit into the router chuck

1. Insert the bit all the way into the chuck, and then back it out about $1/16$ inch, or 2 mm (Fig. 102-5).

2. Fasten the chuck with the wrenches furnished with the router. Some chucks require two wrenches.

3. The depth of cut can be set by measuring with a rule and then adjusting the depth ring (Fig. 102-6).

4. Reverse this procedure when removing the bit or cutter.

Router accessories

An important router accessory is an **edge guide,** which can be used in cutting an edge, a radius, a groove, or a circle. Figures 104-1 through 104-4 show how it is used.

A highly developed **template** used for making dovetail joints for drawers is shown in Fig. 106-2.

shaper cutters

Fig. 102–1 Shaper cutters for the router: (A) weather strip for narrow groove cutting, (B) straight face for grooving, (C) 45-degree bevel chamfer for bevel cutting, (D) cove for cove cutting edges, (E) corner round for edge rounding, (F) carbide-tip door-lip cutter, (G) surface bead for decorative beading, (H) corner bead for decorative edging, and (I) cove and bead for decorative edging.

router bits

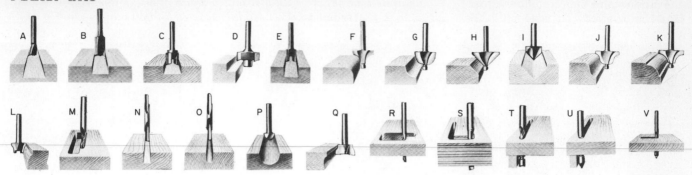

Fig. 102–2   A selection of router bits: (A) dovetail for dovetailing joints; (B) straight for general stock removal, slotting, grooving, and rabbeting; (C) stair router for routing stair tread and riser grooves; (D) rabbeting for rabbeting or step-cutting edges; (E) mortise for stock removal, dadoes, rabbets, and hinge-butt mortising; (F) corner round for edge rounding; (G) cove for cutting inverted radii; (H) 45-degree bevel for bevel cutting; (I) V groove for simulating plank construction on panels; (J) roman ogee for decorative edging; (K) bead for decorative edging; (L) sash bead for beading the inner side of window frames; (M) straight spiral for slotting and mortising (particularly aluminum door jambs); (N) straight double-ended for general routing, inlay, and scrollwork; (O) veining for decorative freehand routing, carving, and inlay work; (P) core box for reeding, fluting, carving, and general ornamentation; (Q) sash cope for coping window rails to match bead cut; (R) straight spiral for deep slotting; (S) stagger tooth for through cutting, such as sink cutouts and door lights; (T) pilot spiral, with mortising boring point, for panel pilot routing where it is necessary to pull chips out of the cut; (U) pilot spiral for plunge cutting; and (V) panel pilot for cutting openings and for all through cutting.

bits and cutters

FOR TRIMMING PLASTIC LAMINATES AND WOOD VENEERS

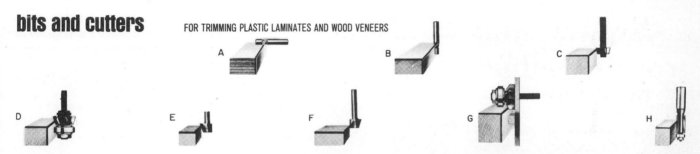

Fig. 102–3   Router bits and cutters for trimming plastic laminates and wood veneers: (A) flush-cut trimming bit for trimming laminates; (B) 7-degree bevel trimming bit for trimming laminates; (C) 10-degree bevel trimming bit for trimming laminates; (D) 25-degree bevel cutter with bearing guide for trimming laminates; (E) 25-degree bevel trimming bit for trimming laminates; (F) flush-cut trimming bit for trimming laminates; (G) 15-degree backsplash trimmer for trimming laminates; and (H) carbide-tip, ball-bearing, flush-cut trimming bit for trimming laminates.

miscellaneous accessories

Fig. 102–4   Miscellaneous accessories for the router: (A) one-piece and screw-type bit units; (B) adapter to increase diameter of shank to fit various-diameter router collets; (C) pilot to control horizontal depth of cut of router bit; (D) shaper collar; (E) arbors for use with screw-type router bit; (F) bushing used to reduce hole diameter of shaper cutter; and (G) spindles for use with shaper cutters and some plane cutters.

Some router manufacturers make a **shaper stand** that permits the router to be inverted and fastened in the stand, becoming a shaper (Fig. 102-7).

Another important mechanical aid is the **hinge-butt template.** It is used to locate and to serve as a guide in cutting notches (gains) in doors and door frames for butt hinges (see Fig. 107-1).

Fig. 102–5 Inserting a bit into the router collet (chuck).

Fig. 102–6 Checking bit depth adjustment.

Fig. 102–7 Grooving for a drawer bottom with an inverted router on a shaper stand.

unit 103

Shaping and routing edges

One of the most common uses of the router is to cut decorative edges on wood. The wide range of available bits and cutters makes it possible to cut a simple corner round and to make decorative cove and bead edges. When making cuts on all four edges of a board, make the first cut on the end *across* the grain. If any chipping occurs at the end of a cut, remove it by making the next cut *parallel* to the grain. Tongue-and-groove joints, edge joints, and rabbets can be edge-cut.

Shaping an edge

Read and observe the safety precautions in Unit 84.

1. Decide on the bit or cutter you will use.

2. Fasten the cutter in the chuck, as outlined in the previous unit.

3. Adjust the router for the correct depth of cut. Follow the instructions given in the manufacturer's manual.

4. Make a test cut on a piece of scrap wood.

5. Fasten the board or the project firmly.

6. Place the router base on the board with the cutter or the bit over the edge.

Fig. 103–1 Pushing the router to shape an edge.

7. Turn on the switch. Push or pull the router against the edge of the board until it hits the bit or the cutter collar.

8. Push or pull the router from left to right (Fig. 103-1).

9. Finish shaping the edge.

10. Turn off the power. Remove the router from the board or project.

Routing an edge for a joint

1. Follow steps 1 through 9 above.

2. Figure 103-2 illustrates cutting a rabbet on the edge of a board.

Fig. 103–2 Pulling the router to rabbet on an edge.

Cutting grooves and dadoes with a guide

The router edge guide is a useful attachment which may be simple or elaborate. It is used as an aid in cutting a radius or a circular groove and in cutting grooves, veins, and dadoes parallel to edges and ends. Grooves can also be cut in a similar manner for inlaying.

Cutting grooves, veins, and dadoes

1. Decide on the suitable cutter or bit for the job.
2. Fasten the cutter in the chuck.
3. Adjust the router for correct depth of cut.
4. Attach the edge guide; make the necessary adjustments. Study the manufacturer's manual for specific directions about the router (see Fig. 104-1).
5. Make a trial cut on a piece of scrap wood. Make all the necessary adjustments.
6. Place the router base on the board. Be very careful: be very sure to see that the cutter or the bit is over the edge.
7. Turn on the switch. Next, begin to move the router slowly and carefully from left to right.
8. Continue making all necessary grooves, veins, and cuts.
9. Turn off the switch. After the router has stopped, you may remove it from the piece of wood.
10. In addition, it is also possible to cut dadoes with the edge guide. However, a slight adaptation is necessary on the guide (see Fig. 104-2).

Cutting curved and circular grooves

1. Follow steps 1 through 9 under "Cutting Grooves, Veins, and Dadoes."
2. Curved cuts can be made parallel to a curved or an irregular edge by using the edge guide (Fig. 104-3).
3. Figure 104-4 shows some circular cuts that were made by using a guide. The router has been removed, leaving only guide and cutter bit.

Fig. 104–3 Cutting a curved groove parallel to a curved surface.

Fig. 104–1 Cutting a groove with the aid of an edge guide.

Fig. 104–2 A router edge guide adapted for cutting dadoes.

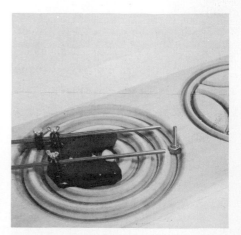

Fig. 104–4 Circular cuts made with the router using an edge guide.

unit 105

Freehand routing

There are a number of routing operations that can be performed by the freehand method. One example is routing letters or patterns directly into the surface of a board. Another is cutting out stock from the surface of wood following a penciled layout.

An example of freehand routing is cutting a groove or dado by simply guiding the router base along a straight piece of wood. On the other hand, one can use a wooden template to cut out the contour of the design and then work the router cutter collar against the template.

Freehand routing without a template

1. Mark or lay out the design to be cut on the surface of the wood.
2. Select a suitable bit.
3. Fasten the bit in the chuck of the router; adjust it for the correct depth.
4. Try out the cut on a piece of scrap wood.

5. Turn on the power with the trigger switch. Slowly place the base of the router onto the surface of the wood. Cut out the background as desired (Fig. 105-1).
6. To achieve a carved effect, use chisels and carving tools to shape the parts of the design and to cut accurately and cleanly to the corners.
7. A name plate can be made in a similar manner.

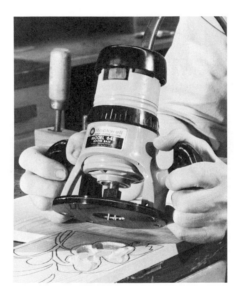

Fig. 105–1 Freehand routing a wood carving.

Freehand routing with a template

An irregular pattern or design can be cut into a surface with the router by using a precut wooden template as a guide (Fig. 105-2). This could involve cutting a vein (grooved) outline of the design or cutting out (recessing) the entire background to a given depth by using correct bits and cutters.

Fig. 105–2 Freehand routing an irregular pattern using a wooden template.

unit 106

Making a dovetail joint

A dovetail joint (Fig. 106-1) usually indicates well-constructed furniture.

Most router manufacturers make available an inexpensive dovetail template that can be used in conjunction with their tool to make these joints (Fig. 106-2). The one shown will handle stock up to 12 inches (305 mm) wide and from $5/16$ to 1 inch (8 to 25 mm) thick. A **flush** dovetail joint or a rabbeted (overlapping) one can be made with this template (see Fig. 106-1). It is always a good idea to practice making a dovetail joint first. You may use pieces of scrap wood for this important exercise.

Fig. 106–1 Rabbeted (overlapping) dovetail drawer construction.

Fig. 106–2 A dovetail joint template kit with its parts.

2. Insert and fasten the proper template guide into the router sub-base.

3. With the motor in the base, fasten the dovetail bit through the template guide and into the router collar. Tighten the collar.

4. Adjust the depth of the bit. The tip should be exactly 19/32 inch (15.08 mm) from the bottom of the router base. This 19/32-inch depth cuts a 1/2-inch (12.7-mm) flush dovetail joint, assuming that the sides of the drawer are 1/2 inch (12.7 mm) thick. Different thicknesses require other settings, according to the manufacturer's manual.

the front clamping bar (Fig. 106-3).

7. Readjust the side of the drawer (the vertical piece). It should now fit snugly against both the left work stop and the plastic template (Fig. 106-4).

8. Plug the cord of the router into the power outlet.

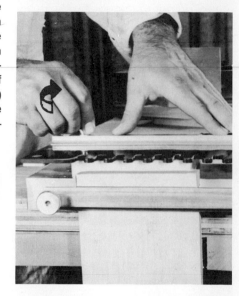

Fig. 106–3 Clamp the front and side to the template.

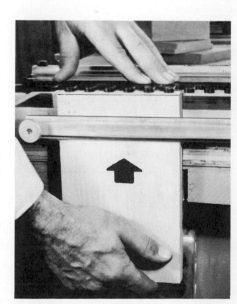

Fig. 106–4 Fasten the side flush to the template.

Making a flush dovetail drawer joint

1. Fasten the broad aluminum base of the template to the workbench or to a piece of plywood. The front overhanging apron of the template base should butt snugly against the front edge of the workbench or the plywood board. Read the instructions that come with the kit on how to assemble the template. These vary with the manufacturer.

5. Fasten the side piece of the drawer vertically against the front apron. The side of the drawer should be temporarily tightened in the template. Butt (press) it firmly against the left stop. About 1/2 inch (13 mm) of stock should show above the aluminum base.

6. Place the front of the drawer horizontally underneath the plastic "finger" template. Butt it firmly against the left stop and flush against the side of the drawer, which is held by

9. As you stand facing the template, place the router firmly on the finger template. The work to be cut is at the left of it (see Fig. 106-5).

10. Turn on the switch. Make the first cut along the entire outside edge of the drawer side, working from *right to left*. Do not rout (cut) into the openings of the finger template (Fig. 106-5). This preliminary cut tends to prevent chipping the edge when the router is moved around the template fingers.

base. Match the right-side piece of the drawer against it on the front apron (Fig. 106-9). Proceed to make the dovetail joint for this corner as you did the first one.

15. Make other necessary cuts in the drawer pieces to receive the bottom and the back portions. These will probably be dado cuts, especially for the bottom piece.

16. The drawer parts are now ready for assembly.

Fig. 106–8 Fitting a dovetail joint for snugness.

Fig. 106–5 Cut the outside edge from right to left.

Fig. 106–6 Cut between the finger slots from left to right.

Fig. 106–9 The other end of the drawer front and the right drawer side fastened in the template, ready for routing.

11. Rout between the finger slots. Move the router carefully from *left to right* around the outline of the template (Fig. 106-6). The joint in both the side and the front pieces is now cleanly cut (see Fig. 106-7). It is ready for fitting.

12. Carefully remove the two sections of the drawer, that is, the front and the side sections, from the template (refer to Fig. 106-7).

13. Fit the front and side drawer pieces together to test snugness (Fig. 106-8). If the fit is *loose, drop* the router bit approximately $1/64$ inch (0.5 mm). On the other hand, if it is *tight, raise* the router bit approximately $1/64$ inch (0.5 mm).

14. Reverse the end of the front drawer piece and move it to the right-hand side of the template aluminum

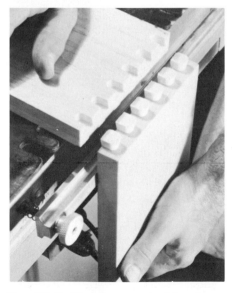

Fig. 106–7 The front and side pieces removed from the template.

Making a dovetail joint for a rabbeted drawer front

1. A rabbeted, or overlapping, drawer front requires adding $3/4$ inch (19 mm) to both the length and the width of the drawer front. The more practical metric size would be 20 mm.

2. Cut a $3/8$- by $3/8$-inch (9.5 by 9.5 mm) rabbet completely around the inside of the drawer front. The practical metric size would be 10 mm.

3. Set the stops on the aluminum base and the other parts of the template for making such a joint. Be sure to follow the manual instructions.

4. To cut the overlapping dovetail joint, follow a similar procedure to that for the flush joint. The finished overlapping dovetail joint will look like that in Fig. 106-1.

Routing a hinge gain using a template

The hinge-butt template is widely used with a router to cut hinge gains (recesses) on doors and jambs. The hinge template is like other templates; when properly set, it eliminates guesswork.

Most hinge-butt templates and frame assemblies include three separate hinge-butt sections fastened to a long adjustment rod. This makes it possible to cut out one, two, or three hinge placements alike in several doors or jambs without resetting the template. The illustrations in this unit, however, show the use of only one single hinge-butt template section. The complete template can be adjusted for practically any standard door hinge size, as well as for standard thickness and height.

Routing a door edge for hinges

1. Determine the size of the hinge and the thickness and height of the door. Also find out whether this is to be a right- or a left-hand opening door.
2. Insert two guide pins in each hinge-butt template section (Fig. 107-1). The pins determine the size of the recess (cutout area) for the hinge. The holes in the template are marked for size.
3. Select the correct template section for either a right- or a left-hand-opening door.

Fig. 107–1 Locating hinge-size guide pins in the template section.

4. Insert the end-gage rod through the template clamp of the hinge template. It should touch the guide pin that was inserted in step 2. Tighten it with the wing nut. This automatically provides proper clearance between the top of the door and the jamb.
5. Place this template section on the door edge. Hook the end-gage plate tightly over the top of the door. Hold the two edge gages tightly against the door face (Fig. 107-2).
6. Fasten the template to the edge of the door with nails.
7. Locate and fasten the other hinge-butt templates and adjustment rods on the edge of the door in the same way (Fig. 107-3).

Fig. 107–2 Locating the top hinge template on the edge of the door.

8. Fasten the correct hinge template guide to the base of the router. Install the routing bit in the column. The depth of the bit should be adjusted to cut the thickness of the hinges being used. About $1/8$ inch (3 mm) is the thickness of most hinges.
9. Place the router in position on one of the template sections so that the bit is clear of the door (Fig. 107-4). Turn on the motor.
10. Move the router into the door edge, along the right-hand guide pin, about $1/2$ inch (13 mm). Pull the router back from the door. Take a light cut of about $1/4$ inch (6 mm) along the edge of the door. Work from right to left until you reach the left-hand guide.

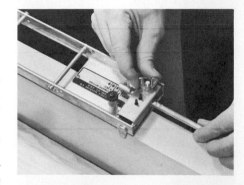

Fig. 107–3 Fastening the adjustment rod into the first template section. Add other section templates and rods as needed.

Fig. 107–4 A router on the template, ready to start the hinge cut.

Fig. 107–5 A router in position after the hinge butt (gain) has been cut.

Fig. 107–6 Using a claw hammer to remove the hinge template from the edge of the door.

Fig. 107–7 Fitting a round-corner hinge into the gain.

Move the router along the door into the left-hand guide pin until you reach the back of the template. Then move the tool along the back of the template until it rests against the right guide pin. Slide the router over the template to remove all the remaining stock (Fig. 107-5).

11. Repeat this process on the remaining hinge sections.

12. Pull out the nails (Fig. 107-6) which hole the template assembly on the edge of the door. Use a claw hammer. Remove the template assembly.

13. Check the fit of the hinge in the gain (recess) of the door edge (Fig. 107-7). The router bit leaves round corners which fit round-cornered hinges. Square the corners with a chisel if the hinges are square.

Routing a door jamb for hinges

1. Loosen the wing nut that holds the end gage. Rotate the end gage

Fig. 107–8 Jamb-gage pins locate the template.

until it is parallel with the bottom of the template. Tighten the wing nut.

2. Slide the edge of the template (without the end gages) over the face of the jamb (frame) until the first or the second row of six jamb-gage pins is aligned against the edge (Fig. 107-8). The first row is used for $1^3/_8$-inch-thick (35-mm-thick) doors; the second, for $1^3/_4$-inch-thick (44-mm-thick) doors.

3. Butt the end gage against the top of the jamb (Fig. 107-9). Fasten the template with nails. When door stops are already in place, simply fasten the template with the edge against the stop.

4. Rout the hinge mortises in the jamb as you did when you routed the hinge gains on the door edges.

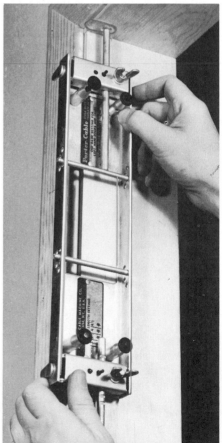

Fig. 107–9 A template nailed to the door jamb.

Portable power belt and finishing sander processes

unit 108

General information about portable power sanders

Portable power sanders are used to sand wood surfaces smooth. The two described and illustrated in this unit are (1) the belt (Fig. 108-1) and (2) the finishing (Fig. 108-2) sanders.

Information on the selection of correct abrasives and grits is given in Unit 81, Abrasives and Adjustments. Each manufacturer has ready-made abrasive sheets to fit each particular brand and model. Replacements can be cut from standard abrasive sheets. Garnet and manufactured abrasives usually make the best coatings for the sheets.

Portable belt sander (parts and uses)

This lightweight machine is probably the most useful of all the portable sanders.

The portable belt sander (see Fig. 108-1) has an abrasive belt that

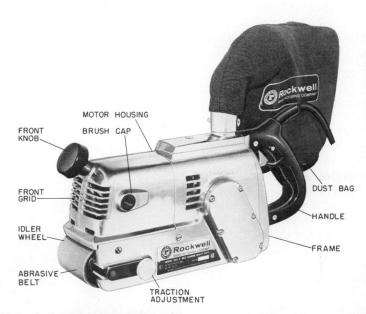

Fig. 108–1 A portable power belt sander.

runs continuously over pulleys situated at both ends. The average portable model weighs between 10 and 20 pounds (4.5 and 9 kg). Its size is usually determined by the size of the belt. Two typical sizes are 3 by 24 inches (76 by 610 mm) and 4 by 27 inches (102 by 686 mm). The heavier machine, which is more useful for school and industrial work, is usually equipped with a dust bag.

Figure 108-3 is a cutaway view of a 3- by 24-inch (76- by 610-mm) dustless belt sander.

Motor housing. The housing is usually made of cast aluminum to reduce the weight of the machine.

Frame. The frame is an aluminum casting to which is fastened the motor housing and the other parts of the machine.

Traction wheel. The traction wheel is the rear pulley, which drives the abrasive belt.

Idler wheel. The idler wheel is the front pulley. It provides tension on the abrasive belt.

Handle. The handle is usually made

201

of composition or plastic (shockproof) material; it contains the trigger switch. A ball knob or a front handle is also mounted because operation of the sander requires use of both hands for good control.

Dust bag. This is a removable bag which catches the dust and which can be emptied when full.

Shoe base. The shoe base is a metal plate over which the back of the abrasive belt moves. It forces the belt to make contact with the wood.

Abrasive belt. Belts are available in many grits (rough to fine) to fit portable belt sanders of different sizes.

Finishing sander (parts and uses)

Finishing sanders are either orbital (circular) or oscillating (back and forth, or vibrating) in motion. Figure 108-2 pictures an orbital sander.

The designation *finishing sander* means that this tool is used for fine sanding. It is sometimes used to obtain a finer surface finish after using the belt sander.

Finishing sanders vary in size to take one-fourth-, one-third-, or one-half-sheet sizes of abrasive paper or cloth. Their weights vary from 4 to 10 pounds (1.8 to 4.5 kg).

Figure 108-4 is a cutaway view of a finishing sander.

Motor housing. This housing is usually made of cast aluminum to reduce the weight of the machine. It houses the motor and all other parts of the sander.

Pad plate. Abrasive sheets are fastened and locked to the pad plate, which forces them to make contact with the wood.

Clamps. The pad plate has a clamp at each end which holds the abrasive sheet.

Handle. The hand-fitting aluminum handle includes the trigger switch. There is usually a second handle on the front so that this tool can be operated with both hands.

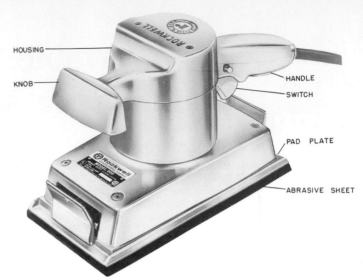

Fig. 108–2 An orbital finishing sander.

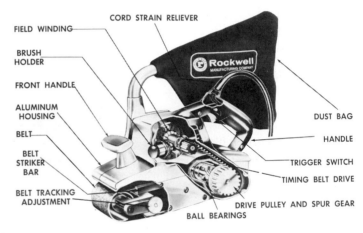

Fig. 108–3 A cutaway view of a dustless belt sander.

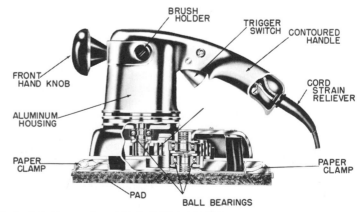

Fig. 108–4 A cutaway view of a finishing sander.

Operating adjustments

Portable sanders require adjustments when the sanding belt on the belt sander and the abrasive sheet on the finishing sander need replacing. An additional adjustment on the belt sander is a periodic inspection of its carbon brushes. The finishing sander has fewer adjustments.

Adjustments on the belt sander

Installing an abrasive belt. Abrasive belts are installed as described below.

1. Lay the sander on its left side. Make sure it is *disconnected* from the power outlet.

2. Release the tension from the idler pulley (wheel). This should be done according to the manufacturer's instructions.

3. Remove the worn-out belt.

4. Slip the new belt over the traction and idler pulleys (Fig. 109-1). The arrow printed on the inside of the belt should point *in the direction* the belt

will turn. Be sure that you have the right belt size and the correct grit.

5. Position the belt so that the outer edge is even with the ends of the wheels.

6. Reinstate the tension so that the idler wheel puts pressure on the sanding belt.

7. Adjust the belt tracking. Tilt the sander back, start the motor, and turn the belt alignment screw so the outer edge of the belt runs even with the ends of the wheel (Fig. 109-2).

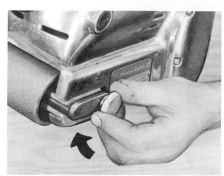

Fig. 109–2 "Tracking" the sanding belt.

Fig. 109–3 Inspecting a brush (carbon) on a portable belt sander.

Checking the switch. Many sanders have a locking trigger in the handle. Learn how to use this before sanding.
Brush inspection. The motor brushes should be inspected often for wear. Remove one brush cap; withdraw the spring and brush (carbon) (see Fig. 109-3). If the carbon is $3/16$ inch (5 mm) or longer, put it back exactly as it was. If not, put in a new one. Check the brush on the opposite side.

Adjustments on the finishing sander

Installing an abrasive sheet. Abrasive sheets are installed as described below.

1. Release the clamps that hold the worn abrasive sheet. Remove it.

2. Slip one end of the new abrasive sheet around either end of the base pad (see Fig. 109-4). Check to see that you have the proper size and the correct grit.

3. Clamp this end of the sheet in place.

4. Stretch the sheet tightly over the pad (Fig. 109-4).

5. Insert the free end of the abrasive sheet under the clamp at the other end.

6. Fasten the clamp in place.

Fig. 109–4 Stretching and fastening an abrasive sheet over the base pad of a finishing sander.

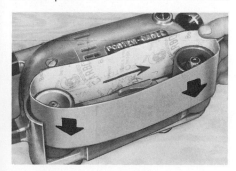

Fig. 109–1 Installing an abrasive belt on a portable belt sander.

unit 110

Sanding with portable power sanders

Sanding with portable power machines requires carefully planned

Fig. 110–1 Lift the sander from the work before starting or stopping the motor.

procedures. Belt and finishing (orbital and oscillating) sanders are easy to operate and control. However, it is important to remember to keep the machines *moving* when they are in use. These sanders have sufficient weight; thus no additional pressure should be applied. They are guided over the surface of the piece by the operator's hands. *Always lift* the sander from the work before starting and stopping the motor, as shown in Fig. 110-1.

Portable sanders, with proper abrasive materials, can be used on metal, slate, marble, or plastic.

Sanding with a belt sander
Read and observe the safety precautions in Unit 84.

1. Fasten the board or project firmly.
2. Select an abrasive belt of the proper grit.
3. Install the belt. Follow steps 1 through 7 under "Adjustments on the Belt Sander" in Unit 109.
4. Using both hands, place the sander on the board or project to get the "feel" of it.
5. Lift the sander with both hands, and turn on the trigger switch.
6. Lower the sander to the wood surface. Guide it over the piece with both hands. Work the machine in the direction of the grain (Fig. 110-2).
7. Move the sander forward, backward, and sideways. Do not pause in any one spot while sanding.
8. Turn off the power. Change the abrasive belts. Continue with the finer

grits until the surface has been smoothed for final finishing.

Sanding with a finishing sander

1. Fasten the board or project firmly.
2. Select an abrasive sheet of the correct grit.
3. Fasten the abrasive sheet on the base pad. Review the six steps for installing abrasive sheets listed in Unit 109, Operating Adjustments.
4. Connect the plug to the power outlet.
5. Lift the finishing sander off the board. Start the motor.
6. Set the sander down evenly on the project or piece. Move it back and forth (Fig. 110-3).
7. Guide the sander with the handle. Use both hands until you get the feel of its operation. The weight of the machine itself exerts sufficient pressure for most sanding.
8. Turn off the power. Change abrasive sheets. Continue with finer grits until the surface is smooth.

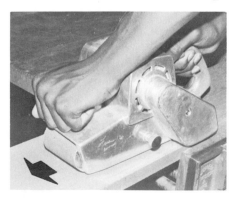

Fig. 110–2 Sanding with a portable belt sander.

Fig. 110–3 Sanding with a finishing sander.

unit 111

Discussion topics on portable power tools and processes

1. List six safety rules to follow in using the portable power handsaw and the motorized miter box.
2. List eight materials the power handsaw can cut when fitted with the proper blades or disks.
3. Explain two types of adjustments that are readily made on both portable saws.
4. Explain how you can make a rip guide if the regular one does not extend far enough on the power handsaw.
5. How is the size of a portable electric handsaw determined?
6. Explain a pocket cut. Describe the procedure for making a pocket cut with the power handsaw.
7. List six safety rules to be observed when using the saber saw.
8. Why do the teeth of the portable power jig saw point up?
9. Approximately how many strokes per minute does the average saber saw make?
10. List four advantages the orbital-motion portable jig saw has over the jig saw with a straight up-and-down (reciprocal) motion.
11. Explain the term *plunge cutting* with the saber saw.
12. Explain the advantage of a saber saw base that has angle adjustment.
13. List six safety rules to observe when using the portable power plane.
14. Discuss the advantages of the portable power plane over conventional hand planes.
15. Describe the cutter used in most portable power planes.
16. How is the depth of the portable power plane cut adjusted?
17. List six safety rules to observe when using the portable power hand drill.
18. What is the source of power when using the portable drill without a regular electrical system? Where would this tool be most useful?
19. Name three general types of portable electric hand drills. What is the distinguishing feature of each?
20. Name three advantages of the portable power hand drill over the drill press.
21. What is the relationship of cutting speed to the size of the drill bit?
22. What is meant by *grounding* a portable electric tool?
23. List five safety features in using the router.
24. What makes the router one of the safest portable electric tools?
25. List eight jobs you can do with the router if you have the necessary bits, cutters, and accessories.
26. Name and illustrate six router cuts.
27. Name and describe the uses of the most important router templates for cabinetwork and carpentry.
28. What are two other names or terms that designate the hinge recess, or cutout?
29. List 10 safety rules for the portable sander.
30. Why is it advisable to lift the belt sander when starting it and when turning it off?
31. Why should you keep a portable sander moving continuously while it is in use?
32. List three general grit classifications for abrasive belts and sheets.
33. Visit a building contractor, mill and sash company, furniture manufacturer, or other wood-products manufacturing plant. Report on the types and sizes of portable power tools in use. List the purposes for which they are used.

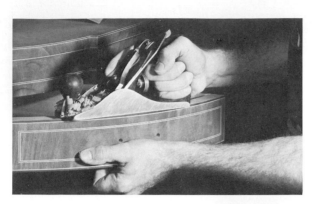

Hardware and Assembly of Cabinetwork

unit 112

Fastening with screws

Wood screws are better than nails as fasteners because they hold better over a longer period of time. To increase their usefulness still more, screws are often used with glue.

Origin of screws

It is thought that the screw, or spiral, was invented in Greece by Archimedes in approximately 250 B.C. The spiral was used in a pipe to raise water for irrigation. Several hundred years later it was found that screws could be used to exert pressure. They were used in wine and coin presses and eventually in the first printing press, which was made by Johann Gutenberg in 1450. This use of screws led to the development of screw clamps. Wooden screws (pressure clamps) have been used in veneer presses for centuries.

Types

The most common types of screws for woodworking are slotted and have **flat, round,** and **oval heads** (Fig. 112-1C, D, and E). This slotted-type head is very old. Another type is the Phillips, or cross-point, screw (Fig. 112-1A and B). It, too, has flat, oval, and round heads. It holds the tip better and gives more driving surface when the screw is turned into the wood. Phillips-head screwdrivers or bits are required to drive (turn) these screws (see Fig. 112-9).

Wood screws are made from mild (soft) steel, stainless steel, brass, aluminum, and siliconbronze (an alloy, or mixture, of silicon, copper, tin, and sometimes zinc). Common steel

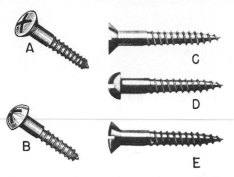

Fig. 112–1 Types of wood screws: (A) flat Phillips head, (B) round Phillips head, (C) flat slotted head, (D) round slotted head, and (E) oval slotted head.

Fig. 112–2 Boxes of wood screws contain 100 or 144 (1 gross) screws.

screws may rust if used where humidity (moisture content) is high. To avoid rust, screws are often made from brass or are steel-plated (coated) with a rust-resistant metal such as cadmium (a zinc ore), nickel, or chromium (a metallic chemical element). Brass and rust-resistant plated screws are especially useful on boats and for ornamentation on projects where the head of the screw is visible.

Screws are usually packaged in boxes containing either 100 or 1 gross (144). The boxes (Fig. 112-2) are labeled to show quantity, length, gage (diameter of the shank), type of head, material, and the finish when necessary. Flat-head steel screws are often **bright** finished; round-head screws are often **blued.**

There are 20 common lengths of screws (Table 112-1). They range from

$1/4$ inch (6.35 mm) to 6 inches (152.4 mm) in length. Shank gages range from number zero (No. 0), which is about $1/16$ inch (1.59 mm) in diameter, to number 30 (No. 30), about $7/16$ inch (11.11 mm) in diameter. The relationship of these sizes is shown in Fig. 112-3. The length is usually measured from the point to the bottom of the slot.

Numerous other types of heads and sizes and shapes of screws are available (Fig. 112-4). **Square,** or **hex-head, screws** (Fig. 112-4C and D) are called **lag screws** or **lag bolts;** they are used where greater holding power is needed. A wrench (see Fig. 112-15) is used to drive these into a pilot hole that has been drilled into the wood. A **dowel screw** (Fig. 112-4E) is convenient to use to fasten a small post and shelf (Fig. 112-5).

Table 112-1   LENGTH OF SCREWS MADE IN EACH GAGE

Length	Gage	Length	Gage	Length	Gage	Length	Gage	Length	Gage	Length	Gage
$1/4$	0–4	$3/4$	2–16	$1^1/2$	3–24	$2^1/2$	5–24	4	8–30
$3/8$	0–9	$7/8$	2–16	$1^3/4$	5–24	$2^3/4$	6–24	$4^1/2$	12–30
$1/2$	1–12	1	3–20	2	5–24	3	6–26	5	12–30
$5/8$	1–14	$1^1/4$	3–24	$2^1/4$	5–24	$3^1/2$	8–26	6	12–30

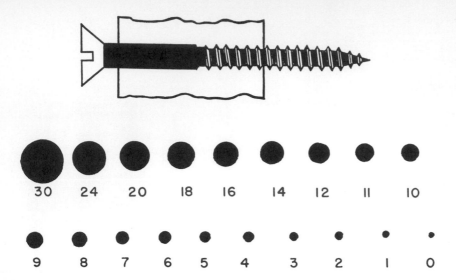

Fig. 112–3 Shank (body) sizes of wood screws range from No. 0 to No. 30 ($1/16$ to $7/16$ inch, 1.59 mm to 11.11 mm, in diameter).

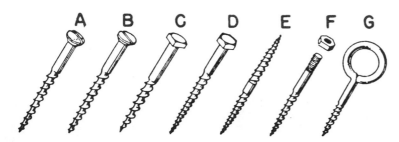

Fig. 112–4 Special types of screws are used for many purposes in woodworking: (A) oval fillister head, (B) flat fillister head, (C) square head, (D) hex head, (E) dowel screw, (F) hanger bolt, and (G) screw eye.

The **hanger bolt** (Fig. 112-4F) or screw has regular wood screw spirals on one end and standard bolt threads on the opposite end. It is available in a variety of sizes, and it is especially useful for connecting a complete table top, such as a round, or drum, top to one or more posts (Fig. 112-6). A special shop-made tool (Fig. 112-7) drives the hanger bolt easily into the wood after a pilot hole of the correct size has been drilled.

Tools

Hand and portable power tools to drive screws include the ordinary screwdriver (Fig. 112-8), Phillips-head (cross-point) screwdriver (Fig. 112-9), offset screwdriver (Fig. 112-10), screwdriver bit (Fig. 112-11), countersink bit (Fig. 112-12), and automatic spiral (ratchet) screwdriver (Fig. 112-13). The brace, bits, and drills are discussed in Unit 20.

A combination wood-drill and countersink (Fig. 112-14) is available in 24 sizes. The sizes range from $1/2$ inch (12.7 mm) No. 5 to $2 1/2$ inches (63.5 mm) No. 12. It drills the pilot (lead) hole, shank (body) clearance hole, and the countersink enlargement in one drilling operation. It can be held either by hand or in a power tool.

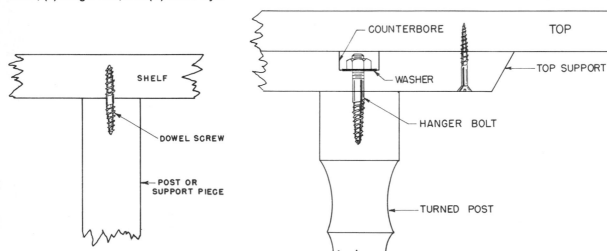

Fig. 112–5 Posts are sometimes fastened to shelves with dowel screws.

Fig. 112–6 A table top may easily be connected to a post with a hanger bolt.

208

Open-end adjustable wrenches (Fig. 112-15) can be used to turn lag screws or bolts into the work.

Fastening

1. Using an awl, locate and mark the points where screws are to be inserted. Select the type and size of screw. (If the combination drill and countersink is used, steps 2 through 4 can be omitted.)

Fig. 112–9 A short Phillips-head screwdriver is useful for driving Phillips-head screws in close places.

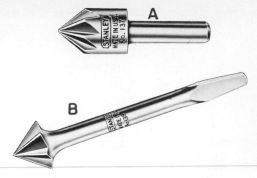

Fig. 112–12 Countersink bits fit many tools: (A) hand and portable electric drills or drill press, and (B) brace.

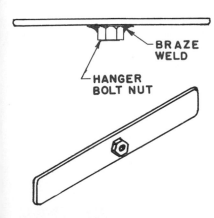

Fig. 112–7 A specially made tool can assist in driving the hanger bolt.

Fig. 112–10 An offset screwdriver may be used in close places.

Fig. 112–13 An automatic spiral, or ratchet, screwdriver.

Fig. 112–11 A screwdriver shank for a brace.

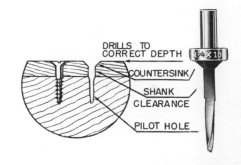

Fig. 112–14 The combination wood-drill and countersink is useful for drilling and countersinking holes in a single operation.

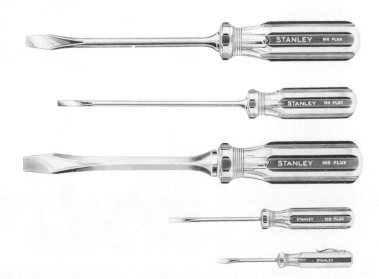

Fig. 112–8 Common screwdriver sizes.

Fig. 112–15 An open-end adjustable wrench is useful for driving lag screws or bolts into wood.

Table 112-2 PILOT-HOLE SHANK-CLEARANCE-HOLE BORING RECOMMENDATIONS

Screw no.	Bit or drill sizes						
	For shank-clearance holes		For pilot holes				
			Hardwoods		Softwoods		
	Twist bit (nearest size in fractions of an inch)	Drill gage no. or letter (to be used for maximum holding power)	Twist bit (nearest size in fractions of an inch)	Drill gage no. (To be used for maximum holding power)	Twist bit (nearest size in fractions of an inch)	Drill gage no. (to be used for maximum holding power)	Auger bit no. (to counterbore for sinking head by 16ths)
0	$1/16$	52	$1/32$	70	$1/64$	75	
1	$5/64$	47	$1/32$	66	$1/32$	71	
2	$3/32$	42	$3/64$	56	$1/32$	65	3
3	$7/64$	37	$1/16$	54	$3/64$	58	4
4	$7/64$	32	$1/16$	52	$3/64$	55	4
5	$1/8$	30	$5/64$	49	$1/16$	53	4
6	$9/64$	27	$5/64$	47	$1/16$	52	5
7	$5/32$	22	$3/32$	44	$1/16$	51	5
8	$11/64$	18	$3/32$	40	$5/64$	48	6
9	$3/16$	14	$7/64$	37	$5/64$	45	6
10	$3/16$	10	$7/64$	33	$3/32$	43	6
11	$13/64$	4	$1/8$	31	$3/32$	40	7
12	$7/32$	2	$1/8$	30	$7/64$	38	7
14	$1/4$	D	$9/64$	25	$7/64$	32	8
16	$17/64$	I	$5/32$	18	$9/64$	29	9
18	$19/64$	N	$3/16$	13	$9/64$	26	10
20	$21/64$	P	$13/64$	4	$11/64$	19	11
24	$3/8$	V	$7/32$	1	$3/16$	15	12

2. Select the correct size of bit or drill for the pilot hole (Table 112-2).

3. Fasten the drill in the chuck of a hand or power tool. Drill through the first piece of wood and into the second one. This aids in aligning all holes correctly when the screws are no larger than about 10 gage.

When large shank holes are made with auger bits, it is preferable to perform step 4 *before* performing step 3. The tip of the auger bit then marks the location of the pilot hole in the second piece of wood.

4. Select the correct size of drill or bit for the shank hole (Table 112-2). Place it in the chuck. Remove the top piece of wood, and drill the shank hole through it.

5. Countersink the shank hole (Figs. 112-16, 112-17, and 112-18) if an oval- or flat-head screw is to be used. Counterbore the hole if the screw is to be capped, or plugged, with a screw-hole button or plug (Fig. 112-19).

6. Select a screwdriver or screwdriver bit to fit the crossed-recess (Phillips-head) or the straight-slot screwhead (Fig. 112-20).

7. Coat the screw lightly with

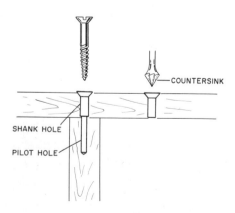

Fig. 112–16 The proper size of pilot and shank clearance holes and proper countersinking are important for a good fit.

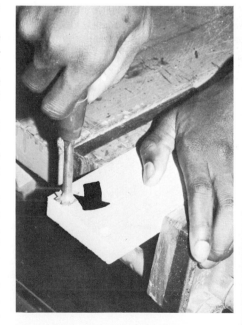

Fig. 112–17 The countersink bit is easily used in a file handle.

soap, wax, or paraffin to make it turn easily.

8. Hold the screwdriver tip firmly in the slot; drive the screw into place (Fig. 112-21). The brace with the screwdriver bit (Fig. 112-22) and the automatic spiral (ratchet) screwdriver (Fig. 112-23) both speed up the job of inserting screws.

Figure 110-4 shows the reduction gear (reduced-speed) ratchet being used with a portable drill to drive a screw.

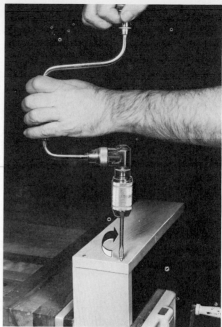

Fig. 112–22 **Driving a screw with the brace and screwdriver bit. This device speeds up the process considerably.**

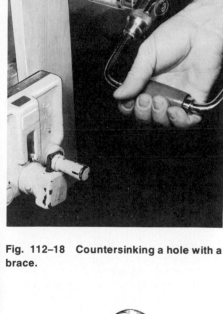

Fig. 112–18 **Countersinking a hole with a brace.**

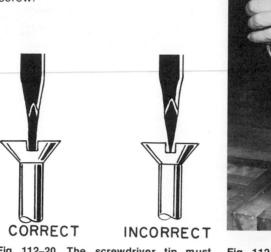

Fig. 112–20 **The screwdriver tip must fit in the straight or crossed slot of the screw.**

CORRECT   INCORRECT

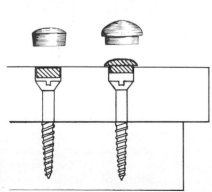

Fig. 112–19 **Counterbored holes are filled with plugs or screw-hole buttons. Note the oval-head plug.**

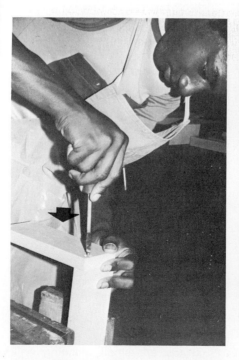

Fig. 112–21 **Hold the screwdriver firmly.**

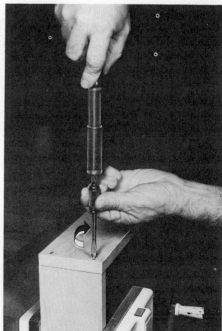

Fig. 112–23 **Driving a screw with the automatic ratchet, or spiral, screwdriver.**

Assembly with nails and brads

The most widely used nail sizes, lengths, gages, and diameters and the approximate number per pound of common, casing, box, and finishing nails, and flooring brads are shown in Tables 113-1, 113-2, 113-3, and 113-4. The common size used and the type of head usually determine the use of a nail. Nails are not often used for cabinetwork. They are usually used in rough construction, where they do not detract from good appearance and craftsmanship.

Sizes and kinds

Nail sizes are indicated by the term **penny**, abbreviated **d**, which designates the weight of 1000 nails. Sizes range from 2 penny (2d) to 60 penny (60d). For example, one thousand 2-penny nails weigh 2 pounds.

Common nails (Table 113-1) have relatively thick heads and are larger in diameter than most nails. They are used for all forms of general nailing and especially for construction purposes.

Casing and **box nails** (Table 113-2) generally have the same size designation, but both are smaller in diameter than the common nail. Casing nails have cone-shaped heads. They are used mainly to nail interior trim and painted cabinetwork. Box nails have thin, flat heads that are similar to common nail heads. They are sometimes coated or barbed to increase their holding power. Coated or

barbed nails are often used for nailing boxes and light crates.

Finishing nails (Table 113-3) have small heads which are frequently set below the surface. The holes this leaves are then filled with putty, wood plastic, or other suitable filler.

Brads are small finishing nails which vary from $1/4$ to $1\,1/4$ inches (6.35

to 31.75 mm) in length for smaller sizes. They are useful when small, thin pieces of wood are to be assembled. Larger forms are called **flooring brads** (Table 113-4); these range in length from 2 to 4 inches (50.8 to 101.6 mm). Corresponding sizes are the same as for common nails, but the brad head is similar to the casing head.

Table 113-1 COMMON WIRE NAILS

Size	Length, in.	Gage, no.	Diameter, in.		Approx. no. per lb
			Actual	Approx.	
2d	1	15	0.072 0	$5/64$	876
3d	$1\,1/4$	14	0.080 0	$5/64$	568
4d	$1\,1/2$	$12\,1/2$	0.098 5	$3/32$	316
5d	$1\,3/4$	$12\,1/2$	0.098 5	$3/32$	271
6d	2	$11\,1/2$	0.113 0	$7/64$	181
7d	$2\,1/4$	$11\,1/2$	0.113 0	$7/64$	161
8d	$2\,1/2$	$10\,1/4$	0.131 3	$1/8$	106
9d	$2\,3/4$	$10\,1/4$	0.131 3	$1/8$	96
10d	3	9	0.148 3	$5/32$	69
12d	$3\,1/4$	9	0.148 3	$5/32$	63
16d	$3\,1/2$	8	0.162 0	$5/32$	49
20d	4	6	0.192 0	$3/16$	31
30d	$4\,1/2$	5	0.207 0	$13/64$	24
40d	5	4	0.225 3	$7/32$	18
50d	$5\,1/2$	3	0.243 7	$1/4$	14
60d	6	2	0.262 5	$17/64$	11

Table 113-2 CASING NAILS; SMOOTH AND BARBED BOX NAILS

Size	Length, in.	Gage, no.	Diameter, in.		Approx. no. per lb
			Actual	Approx.	
2d	1	$15\,1/2$	0.067 2	$1/16$	1010
3d	$1\,1/4$	$14\,1/2$	0.076 0	$5/64$	635
4d	$1\,1/2$	14	0.080 0	$5/64$	473
5d	$1\,3/4$	14	0.080 0	$5/64$	406
6d	2	$12\,1/2$	0.098 5	$3/32$	236
7d	$2\,1/4$	$12\,1/2$	0.098 5	$3/32$	210
8d	$2\,1/2$	$11\,1/2$	0.113 0	$7/64$	145
9d	$2\,3/4$	$11\,1/2$	0.113 0	$7/64$	132
10d	3	$10\,1/2$	0.127 7	$1/8$	94
12d	$3\,1/4$	$10\,1/2$	0.127 7	$1/8$	88
16d	$3\,1/2$	10	0.135 0	$9/64$	71
20d	4	9	0.148 3	$5/32$	52
30d	$4\,1/2$	9	0.148 3	$5/32$	46
40d	5	8	0.162 0	$5/32$	35

Table 113-3 FINISHING NAILS

Size	Length, in.	Gage, no.	Diameter, in.		Approx. no. per lb
			Actual	Approx.	
2d	1	16$\frac{1}{2}$	0.058 2	$\frac{1}{16}$	1351
3d	1$\frac{1}{4}$	15$\frac{1}{2}$	0.067 2	$\frac{1}{16}$	807
4d	1$\frac{1}{2}$	15	0.072 0	$\frac{5}{64}$	584
5d	1$\frac{3}{4}$	15	0.072 0	$\frac{5}{64}$	500
6d	2	13	0.091 5	$\frac{3}{32}$	309
7d	2$\frac{1}{4}$	13	0.091 5	$\frac{3}{32}$	238
8d	2$\frac{1}{2}$	12$\frac{1}{2}$	0.098 5	$\frac{3}{32}$	189
9d	2$\frac{3}{4}$	12$\frac{1}{2}$	0.098 5	$\frac{3}{32}$	172
10d	3	11$\frac{1}{2}$	0.113 0	$\frac{7}{64}$	121
12d	3$\frac{1}{4}$	11$\frac{1}{2}$	0.113 0	$\frac{7}{64}$	113
16d	3$\frac{1}{2}$	11	0.120 5	$\frac{1}{8}$	90
20d	4	10	0.135 0	$\frac{9}{64}$	62

Table 113-4 FLOORING BRADS

Size	Length, in.	Gage, no.	Diameter, in.		Approx. no. per lb
			Actual	Approx.	
6d	2	11	0.120 5	$\frac{1}{8}$	157
7d	2$\frac{1}{4}$	11	0.120 5	$\frac{1}{8}$	139
8d	2$\frac{1}{2}$	10	0.135 0	$\frac{9}{64}$	99
9d	2$\frac{3}{4}$	10	0.135 0	$\frac{9}{64}$	90
10d	3	9	0.148 3	$\frac{5}{32}$	69
12d	3$\frac{1}{4}$	8	0.162 0	$\frac{5}{32}$	54
16d	3$\frac{1}{2}$	7	0.177 0	$\frac{11}{64}$	43
20d	4	6	0.192 0	$\frac{3}{16}$	31

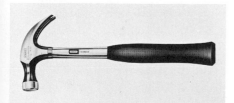

Fig. 113–1 A typical claw hammer with a rubber-covered steel handle.

Fig. 113–2 A nail set.

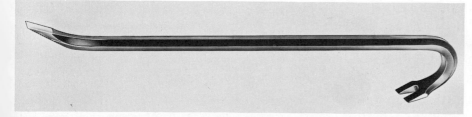

Fig. 113–3 A wrecking bar is used to pull large nails and to pry pieces apart.

Notice in the tables that nails up to 3$\frac{1}{2}$ inches (88.9 mm) in length increase $\frac{1}{4}$ inch (6.35 mm) per size. Sizes 20 penny and above increase by $\frac{1}{2}$ inch (12.7 mm) for each size.

Tools

The **claw hammer** (Fig. 113-1) is the proper tool for driving a nail. Hammer sizes are measured by the weight of the head. The 12- and 16-ounce sizes are the most popular.

A **nail set** (Fig. 113-2) is used to set (drive in) finishing and casing nails below the surface of the board. They are available in different concave-tip sizes to fit the heads of different sizes of nails.

The **wrecking bar,** sometimes called a **crowbar** (Fig. 113-3), is used to pull very large nails and to help pry large nailed pieces apart.

Driving nails

1. Select the correct type and size of nail for the job.

2. Drive the nail with the hammer until it is practically flush (smooth) with the wood (Fig. 113-4). Hold the nail when first starting the driving.

The length of the nail should be about three times the thickness of the first board. If a nail is to be driven through hardwood, drill a very small

Fig. 113–4 Continue driving a finishing nail until it is almost flush with the wood surface.

213

pilot hole through the first board to prevent splitting (Fig. 113-5).

3. When desired, set the head of the nail about 1/16 inch (2 mm) below the surface of the wood (Fig. 113-6). Use a nail set. Fill the hole with putty or wood plastic.

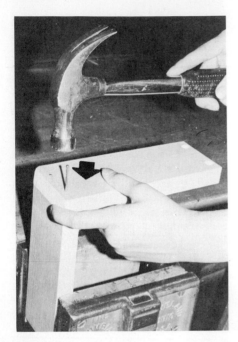

Fig. 113-5 A small pilot hole should be drilled before nails are driven into hardwood.

Fig. 113-6 Set a finishing nail below the wood surface with a claw hammer and a nail set.

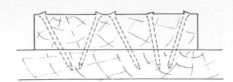

Fig. 113-7 Driving nails at an angle helps give more holding power.

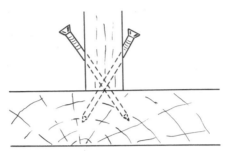

Fig. 113-8 Driving nails at angles, joining two pieces perpendicularly, is called *toenailing.*

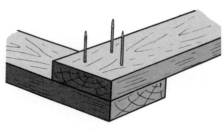

STEP 1

STEP 2

STEP 3

Fig. 113-9 Nails should be clinched after they are driven through pieces.

Special nailing methods

Figure 113-7 shows how to get increased holding power by driving nails at an **angle.**

Driving nails as shown in Fig. 113-8 is **toenailing.**

Figure 113-9 describes three steps in **clinching** nails to hold two or more boards securely.

Air-driven staples are also used to attach solid wood braces and panels of plywood (Fig. 113-10) and hardboard (Fig. 113-11).

Pulling nails

1. Slip the claws of the hammer under the head of the nail. Pull the handle until it is at about a 90-degree angle to the board (Fig. 113-12).

If the nail is too long to pull, slip a block of wood under the head of the hammer to increase leverage (Fig. 113-13).

2. Use a wrecking bar to pry pieces apart or to pull out very large nails (see Fig. 113-3).

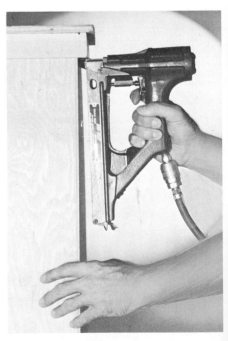

Fig. 113-10 Attaching a plywood side panel with staples.

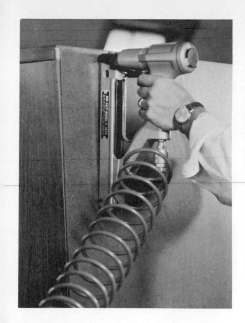

Fig. 113–11 Air-driven staples can speed construction and are said to have more holding power.

Fig. 113–12 Drawing or pulling a nail.

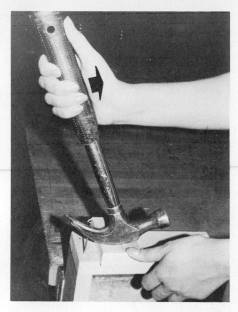

Fig. 113–13 A scrap block increases leverage for pulling larger nails and prevents marring.

unit 114

Application of plastic laminates

Laminated plastic sheets *bonded* (cemented) to plywood and particle board have become especially suitable for many residential, commercial, institutional, and furniture uses. The sheets are made of several layers of strong kraft paper which have been impregnated (soaked) with synthetic resins (Fig. 114-1). The finished decorative sheet is extremely durable when used to cover surfaces for furniture and furnishings. Some of the familiar trade names are Formica, Micarta, Textolite, and Nevamar.

Laminates are often used on flat areas but can also be attached to curved surfaces. This covering can be sawed, drilled, punched, filed, routed, shaped, sanded, and polished. Woodworking and metalworking tools and machines can be used; however, special saw blades and bits will cut more effectively and will not be dulled as easily. Two special tools designed for use on laminates are a carbide-tip knife (Fig. 114-2) for scoring (marking) and a special router cutter (see Fig. 102-3).

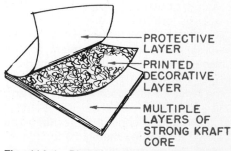

PROTECTIVE LAYER
PRINTED DECORATIVE LAYER
MULTIPLE LAYERS OF STRONG KRAFT CORE

Fig. 114–1 Plastic laminates are made of layers of strong kraft paper, a decorative sheet, and a protective top sheet.

Numerous colored and patterned plastic sheets are available. These range from solid and multicolors to marble and metallic effects, various abstract patterns, and wood-grain designs.

Each laminate manufacturer will recommend a bonding or cementing material for use on a specific product. Contact cement is one of the more commonly used adhesives.

Edges of counter tops and tops for coffee, end, and occasional tables usually will have the plastic laminate applied first to the edge, after which the top covering is bonded in place. The following instructions outline the steps of this procedure in this sequence.

Applying plastic laminate on edges

1. Fill all holes in the edges and surfaces of the board to be covered with wood dough or other filling compound. Allow hole and crack filler to dry thoroughly.

2. Sand all edges and surfaces smooth.

3. Using a carbide-tip knife or a sturdy, sharp awl, mark (score) the laminate strips a *little wider* than the edges that are to be covered (Fig. 114-3).

4. Break or snap the scored laminate piece (Fig. 114-4), or cut the strip using a fine-tooth handsaw or a circular saw (Fig. 114-5). If the laminate is to be snapped, as shown in Fig. 114-4, make certain that the scoring has cut through both the top protective layer and the printed decorative layer (see Fig. 114-1).

5. Apply contact cement to the edge of the plywood panel, or particle board, and also to the rough side of the laminate strip (see Figs. 114-9) and 114-10).

Allow the cement to *set* (become tacky) for approximately 20 to 30 minutes. Follow the directions given on the container for the time to be allowed.

6. Press the laminate strip firmly to the edge (Fig. 114-6). Allow a slight overlap for dressing down. Tap with a rubber mallet to help set the strip firmly to the edge.

7. Dress down (smooth) the laminate edge even with the surface of the top. Use a flat-face file (Fig. 114-7) or a router with a special bit for this purpose (Fig. 114-8).

Fig. 114–2 Scoring tool for plastic laminate.

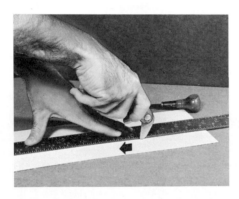

Fig. 114–3 The cut should be made through both the top and the decorative layer when using a scoring tool or an awl.

Fig. 114–4 Bend the laminate toward the decorative surface to secure a sharp break after scoring.

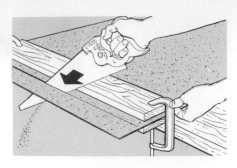

Fig. 114–5 A fine-tooth handsaw can be used to cut straight pieces of laminate.

Fig. 114–6 Cover the edges first, beginning at one end and following through to the opposite end.

Fig. 114–7 A flat wood file is used to smooth the edges flush with the surface.

Fig. 114–8 A special laminate cutter may be used with the router to cut edge strips flush with the top.

216

Applying plastic laminate on a surface

8. Follow preceding steps 1 through 4.

9. Apply contact cement (or other recommended adhesive) to the entire surface of the panel or board (Figs. 114-9 and 114-10) and also on the rough side of the plastic laminate. Allow the cemented surface to dry and become *tacky* (sticky), as in step 5.

10. Hold the cemented laminate sheet in the correct position over the cemented plywood or board surface (Fig. 114-11). Allow for slight overlap.

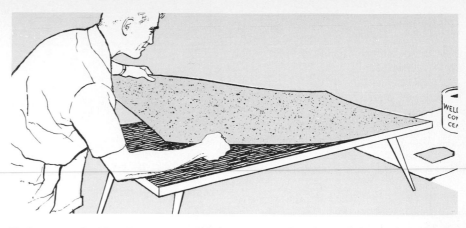

Fig. 114–11 Position the surface laminate sheet to allow for a slight overlap.

Fig. 114–9 A serrated (notched) metal spreader applies contact cement evenly on the surface.

Perfect positioning can be attained by laying some scrap pieces of laminate, or a sheet of heavy kraft paper, on the top to be covered, as shown in Fig. 114-12. These strips of paper will not stick and can be pulled out as the laminate sheet is held in the correct position.

11. Apply uniform pressure over the positioned laminate surface to ensure complete contact with the base (Fig. 114-13). A rolling pin or rubber mallet will make a tight bond.

12. Remove the plastic laminate overlap with a router using a special bit (Fig. 114-14) or with a flat file (see Fig. 114-7).

13. Clean excess adhesive or cement from the laminate surfaces. Use the thinner recommended by the manufacturer. A cloth moistened with lacquer thinner will clean contact cement from plastic laminate and tools.

Fig. 114–13 A rolling pin is an excellent tool to apply pressure for bonding.

Fig. 114–10 A roller or a large brush may be used to apply cement over a large surface.

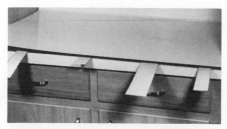

Fig. 114–12 Scrap laminate strips, or heavy kraft paper, will prevent the surface laminate sheet from bonding (sticking) while it is being positioned in place.

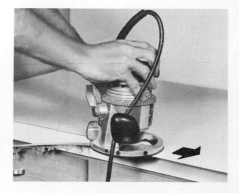

Fig. 114–14 Excess overlap is easily smoothed and made flush with the edges by using the router and a laminate cutter.

Supplementary procedures

1. Plastic laminate sheets can also be cut with a special laminate cutter (Fig. 114-15).

2. External cuts or curves can be made with sharp tin snips (Fig. 114-16).

3. Excess laminate edging can be removed with a common metal nippers, then filed smooth in corners where a router cannot function (Fig. 114-17).

4. Pieces of plastic laminate may be butt-joined, as shown in Fig. 114-18.

5. An opening for an electrical wall outlet can be made with a hammer after the laminate has been fastened (Fig. 114-19).

Fig. 114–15 A special laminate cutter can be used to cut straight across large or small pieces.

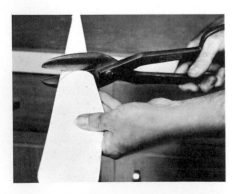

Fig. 114–16 External curves can be cut with a sharp tin snips. Remove only small amounts on each cut to prevent chipping.

Fig. 114–17 Use metal nippers to remove excess plastic in corners; then smooth the edge by filing.

Fig. 114–18 Laminate sheets may be butt-joined if necessary.

Fig. 114–19 Holes over electrical outlets may be broken out after the laminate has been securely bonded to the backing.

6. Internal cuts, such as for a sink opening in the kitchen, can be done with the drill and keyhole saw (Fig. 114-20) or with a jigsaw.

7. A special metal or plastic corner or cove molding may be attached and used when providing for a backsplash of a sink (Fig. 114-21).

8. If metal edge banding is used instead of plastic laminate, attach it as illustrated in Fig. 114-22.

9. If a seam or butt joint is necessary around the sink, try to locate it at the center of the sink (Fig. 114-23). The joints must be absolutely tight fitting.

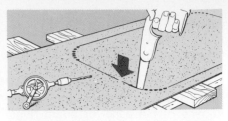

Fig. 114–20 The drill and the keyhole saw are valuable for cutting internal curves.

Fig. 114–21 Attaching a laminate backsplash by using metal or plastic cove molding fastened to plywood.

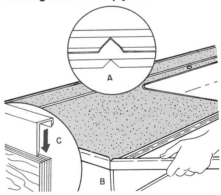

Fig. 114–22 Metal edge molding is attached after the top surfaces are covered. (A) Miter cut in molding for a corner, (B) bending around corner, and (C) cap molding for top and edges of backsplash.

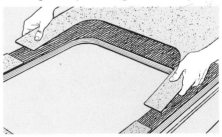

Fig. 114–23 If joints are absolutely necessary, make them near the center of the sink to minimize the fitting of pieces.

unit 115

Building up custom plywood and veneering

It is frequently desirable to create and veneer curved plywood parts and to veneer flat surfaces. Much of this can be accomplished in the school industrial woodworking laboratory. The production of plywood and veneer on a commercial basis is described and illustrated in Unit 148. This unit gives instruction on applying veneer, preparing lumber and veneer for building up the core, crossbanding, and preparing veneer for the surfaces of both curved and flat pieces (Fig. 115-1).

Clamping facilities must be available for curved and flat forming. Figure 115-2 shows excellent shop-built clamp units for gluing veneer on flat sheets of plywood. Curved, or formed, laminated pieces can be constructed by using specially built forms, or jigs, made for specific shapes (Figs. 115-3 and 115-4).

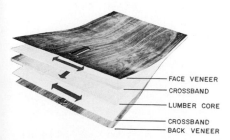

Fig. 115–1 Plywood and veneer construction.

FACE VENEER
CROSSBAND
LUMBER CORE
CROSSBAND
BACK VENEER

Fig. 115–2 Shop-built clamp units for flat veneering. Note how upright end pieces open out.

Fig. 115–3 A curved form made of glued-up lumber. The glued-up veneered plywood piece in front was pressed in this form.

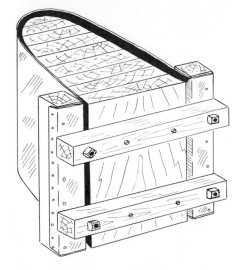

Fig. 115–4 Form for building a curved plywood panel for a magazine rack. This form uses a piece of metal around the outside for exerting uniform pressure.

Fig. 115–5 Several laminated pieces made with specially built forms.

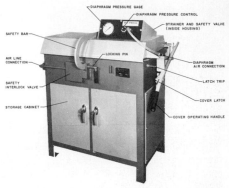

DIAPHRAGM PRESSURE GAGE
DIAPHRAGM PRESSURE CONTROL
STRAINER AND SAFETY VALVE (INSIDE HOUSING)
SAFETY BAR
LOCKING PIN
AIR LINE CONNECTION
DIAPHRAGM AIR CONNECTION
LATCH TRIP
SAFETY INTERLOCK VALVE
COVER LATCH
STORAGE CABINET
COVER OPERATING HANDLE

Fig. 115–6 A commercial veneering and laminating press designed for school use.

Figure 115-5 shows laminated pieces built up by using specially built forms.

There is an excellent commercial veneering and laminating press (Fig. 115-6) that can be used to do specialty plywood construction and veneering.

Preparing veneer surfaces

Interesting patterns can be achieved through the arrangement of veneer pieces (Fig. 115-7). Exotic and colorful woods for veneering are available at a cost much less than that for solid woods. Most veneer stock is $1/28$ to $1/35$ inch (0.907 to 0.726 mm) thick. If carefully handled, this is ample material to achieve maximum value from wood grain.

Fig. 115–7 Arranging veneer pieces for matching.

1. Decide on the pattern and sizes of veneer matching (Figs. 115-8 through 115-11). The following steps are for the side-to-side match (Fig. 115-8); however, similar treatment would do for the various other kinds of matches.

2. Select two pieces of veneer having an almost identical pattern. Lay them on top of each other so that the patterns practically match.

3. Place a steel square straight-edge along the line for matching.

4. Cut away the surplus with a sharp knife, chisel, or veneer saw.

5. Clamp the two pieces of veneer between two boards that have straight edges. The edges of the veneer should project slightly beyond the edges of the clamping jig (Fig. 115-12).

Fig. 115–10 Four-piece veneer match.

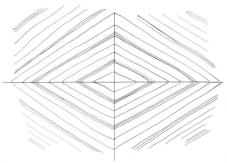

Fig. 115–11 Diamond match.

Fig. 115–8 Side-to-side veneer match.

Fig. 115–9 End-to-end veneer match.

6. Plane the matched edges to form a perfect joint (Fig. 115-12).

7. Remove the veneer pieces from the clamp and lay them on a smooth surface with the planed edges together.

8. Cut a piece of 1-inch-wide (25-mm-wide) gummed paper tape long enough to cover the joint.

9. Moisten the gummed side of the tape with a damp sponge. Press the tape over the matched joint (Fig. 115-13). Allow the gummed paper to dry before handling the matched pieces. The matched veneer is now ready for gluing to a flat plywood or particle board surface or for use in building up laminated, curved pieces, such as the one that is shown in Fig. 115-3).

10. Cut a piece, or pieces, of veneer for the back of the panel. Unless the back surface will be visible, use a less expensive veneer material. Veneer is needed on the back of the panel to prevent warping.

Gluing veneer pieces

The veneer pieces, matched and assembled in the previous steps, are now ready to be glued as face plies onto flat panels or formed laminated, built-up plywood. The steps listed are for gluing veneer to the desired thickness of flat plywood or particle board.

1. Smooth the surfaces of the panel to be veneered. They must be free of finishing materials or other foreign matter. Sanding with 80- to 100-grit abrasive paper will prepare the surface.

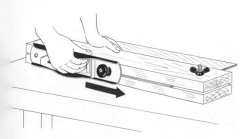

Fig. 115-12 Planing veneer edges for matching.

Fig. 115-13 Pieces of veneer being taped together for the final gluing on the surface of plywood.

2. Spread glue on one surface of the sanded panel to which the veneer will be fastened.

Weldwood brand plastic resin glue is an excellent adhesive. Follow the instructions on the container. Most veneer suppliers also have excellent similar adhesives.

One may wish to apply edge banding of a solid wood the same as the veneer, rather than to use one of the edgings recommended later in this unit. If this is preferred, the solid-wood edge banding should be fastened on the panel or board with a spline joint prior to veneering the surfaces.

3. Spread glue on the *untaped* face of the veneered pieces. Be sure that the tape side of the veneer is out.

4. Press the matched veneer to the glued surface of the panel.

5. Turn the board over while holding the veneer so that it will not slip or fall off.

6. Repeat steps 1 through 4 to glue the reverse side.

7. First place lengths of wax paper over both veneered surfaces. It is also good practice to put sheets of newspaper over the wax paper. Wax paper prevents the board from sticking to the newspaper.

8. Put the glued-up panel with paper between two *cauls* (pressboards of panels).

9. Apply pressure with a veneer press or hand clamps (Fig. 115-14). Allow the glued assembly to dry overnight or for the recommended time for the adhesive used.

10. Remove the built-up panel from the press or clamps.

11. Clean off any newspaper, excess glue, or wax paper sticking to the surface of the veneer. The gummed tape can be removed with a wet sponge or can be sanded off.

12. Sand the veneered surfaces for final finishing. Use a fine-grade abrasive paper and sand *only* in the direction of the grain.

13. Cut and square the glued-up veneer panel to the required size.

14. The panel is now ready for edge banding, if necessary, and/or finishing.

Forming laminated, curved plywood

Forms must be available for the desired shape of the planned panel (see Figs. 115-3 and 115-4). These can readily be made. Often it requires gluing up thicknesses of stock, then band sawing and sanding to the desired curved form.

1. Prepare the stock for making the core. This will usually consist of one, three, or five layers of single-ply poplar or basswood $1/8$ to $3/16$ inch (3 to 5 mm) thick. Stock of this thickness can be obtained from some veneer suppliers.

Fig. 115-14 Flat veneered plywood sheet in clamps.

2. Apply glue to the surfaces of the core stock pieces. Place these pieces one on top of the other, with the grain alternating at right angles. These bonded pieces form the core onto which the veneer is glued.

3. Spread glue on the back surfaces of the thin veneer pieces. Arrange them in their proper positions on the core material.

4. Place lengths of wax paper first and then newspaper over and under the glued assembly.

5. Place the glued material, with wax paper and newspapers, in the form and clamp it securely (see Fig. 115-15).

6. Follow steps 10 through 12 under "Gluing Veneer Pieces."

Fig. 115-15 Curved veneered plywood in clamps.

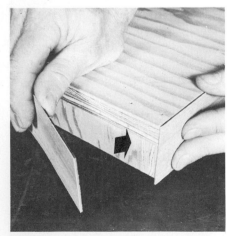

Fig. 115-16 Strips of two plies of veneering may be glued together to make satisfactory edging on flat panels.

Fig. 115-17 Specially prepared veneer tapes, matched to the surface veneer, are suitable for edge gluing on a finished plywood panel.

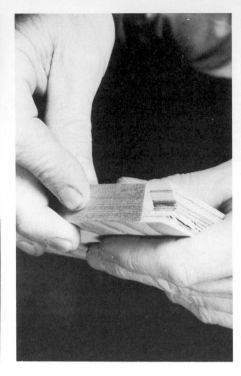

Fig. 115-18 A satisfactory edging may be made to fit a V groove that has been cut on the edge of the plywood.

Finishing the edges

Edges of plywood or particle board should be treated with some type of edging to give a finished appearance (Figs. 115-16 through 115-19). In Fig. 115-17 the edge band is put on with contact cement. Figure 115-18 shows a specially prepared edge-banding veneer tape available in almost any kind of wood grain. This tape comes with the adhesive already applied to it. Figure 115-19 pictures the use of solid wood to match the surface veneer. It is cut to fit a V groove in the edge of the plywood. A molding, such as that illustrated in Fig. 115-19, also makes a good edge banding, especially for coffee and end table tops.

Fig. 115-19 Molding makes an excellent edge banding on veneered panels.

unit 116

Gluing and clamping

Joints that have been well made, coated correctly with a properly prepared glue, and clamped securely are as strong as, or stronger than, the wood itself. Glue is applied to face surfaces of boards that are clamped together for increased thickness (see Fig. 116-5). Board edges are coated with glue and clamped to form wider surfaces (see Fig. 116-11). Table 116-1 offers suggestions on the type of cement or glue to use.

Table 116-1 GUIDE FOR USING GLUE

X—Best product for this use X—Acceptable for this use Adhesive / Properties	Wood to wood and plywood	Wood veneering	Plastic laminates to wood	Wood boats and marine uses	Wood for outdoor use	Metal to wood	China repair	Patch seal solder	Metal to metal	Paper to paper or cloth	Leather to leather or wood	Rubber to wood or metal	Cloth to cloth or wood
Aliphatic resin — Liquid, ready-to-use aliphatic resin. Tacky, highest strength. Good heat resistance. Durable, tough bond.	X	X	X							X	X		X
White glue — Liquid ready-to-use polyvinyl acetate resin. Sets fast (20–30 min clamp). Dries clear.	X	X	X							X	X		X
Liquid hide glue — Liquid, ready-to-use brown animal glue. Reliable. Clamping time 40–50 min.	X	X	X							X	X		X
Contact cement — Liquid, ready-to-use neoprene-based adhesive. No clamping needed. Water resistant.		X	X						X		X	X	X
Plastic resin — Powdered, urea based. Mixes easily with water. Good water resistance. Requires 6–8 hours clamping.	X	X	X		X								
Waterproof — Two-part resorcinol resin adhesive. Fully waterproof. Requires overnight clamping.	X	X	X	X	X								
Casein — Powdered glue. Mix with water. Water resistant.	X	X	X										
Epoxy cement — Two part: resin and hardener. Bonds almost anything. Requires 8–10 hours setting time.						X	X	X	X				
Household cement — Liquid: clear and fast drying (5–15 min). Vinyl base. Water resistant.							X			X			X
Liquid solder — Liquid—requires no heat or mixing. Water resistant.								X					

Types of glue

Glues, cements, or adhesives for woodworking can be classified in six categories. Three that are well adapted for use in most woodworking are (1) animal, (2) casein, and (3) synthetic resins. Those that are less frequently used are (4) vegetable (plant starch), (5) fish, and (6) blood albumin. The all-purpose epoxy (plastic) resin and household cements are used for general bonding.

Animal glue is one of the oldest used in woodworking. It is made principally from hides and hooves of cattle. It is available in flake, powder, and liquid forms. Flake and powder forms must be mixed with water and heated before use. Their strength decreases with repeated heatings. This type of glue is *not* highly water resistant and should not be used on outdoor furniture, boats, or anything else that is exposed to considerable moisture.

Casein glues are made from casein (powdered milk curd) and certain chemicals. They are made in powder form and are prepared for use by adding water to form a pastelike mixture. Good casein glues are highly water resistant, but they have a tendency to stain woods.

Polyvinyl-resin is a white liquid glue. It sets quickly and makes a strong bond. It is easy to use by direct application from its plastic squeeze container.

Synthetic resins, which form the basis for a number of plastics, are very popular and durable wood adhesives. The types of resins involved are the **thermoplastic** and **thermosetting.** Thermoplastic resins are not practical for use in most general woodworking because they often require special handling and equipment. Thermosetting resins are used very successfully for gluing wood. They include the formaldehyde group: urea, phenol, resorcinol, and melamine.

Urea formaldehyde resin is probably the most popular with wood-

workers. It is marketed in both powder and liquid forms. The powder type contains wood flour or walnut shell flour as a filler. Urea resin glue possesses high moisture resistance and sets cold. That is, it cures (sets, or hardens) at room temperature.

Phenol formaldehyde resin glue is used in the high-pressure, hot-press method of manufacturing plywood that is intended for use under extreme moisture conditions.

Resorcinol formaldehyde resin comes in liquid form only. A catalyst (substance to speed the process) must be used to prepare this glue. Resorcinols set at room temperature, but they set more quickly at high temperatures.

Melamine resin glue is available in powder form and is very similar to the phenol type in use, strength, and other characteristics.

Vegetable glue is made in powder form from starches derived from plants. It lacks water resistance, tends to stain, and sets slowly.

Fish glue comes in prepared liquid form, ready to use. It is made from the heads, skin, and bones of fish. It lacks water resistance and is used mostly for small repair jobs that do not require strength.

Blood albumin glue is made from the soluble albumin of beef blood. It is highly resistant to moisture.

Types of clamps

Clamps most often used in furniture and cabinetmaking are the **cabinet,** or **carriage** ("C"), clamp (Fig. 116-1); the **bar clamp** (Fig. 116-2); the adjustable,

Fig. 116–1 C clamp.

parallel-jaw **hand-screw clamp** (Fig. 116-3); and the **band clamp** (see Fig. 116-18). An adaptation of the bar clamp is called the **multiple-disk clutch clamp** (Fig. 116-4). It can take the place of either the C or the hand-screw clamp.

Fig. 116–2 Bar clamp.

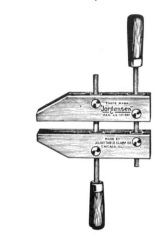

Fig.116–3 Parallel-jaw hand-screw clamps.

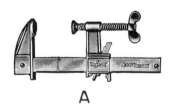

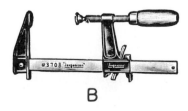

Fig. 116–4 A special bar clamp called a *multiple-disk clutch clamp.*

Gluing and clamping precautions

1. Remove dust, oil, wax, or finishes from the surfaces or edges to be glued.

2. Glue and clamp only if the temperature is above 70 degrees Fahrenheit (70°F). The metric equivalent temperature is 21 degrees Celsius (21°C).

3. Size (pretreat) the end grain of the wood to be glued. Apply a water-thin mixture of glue to the board ends 10 to 15 minutes before spreading on the main film of glue. End grain is absorbent, and the moisture from the main glue layer will soak in if it is applied without preliminary sizing.

4. Put equal pressure on clamps.

5. If possible, use scrap pieces of wood between the metal clamp jaws and the wood being clamped.

6. Apply a thin, even glue coat to surfaces or edges to be clamped.

7. Space the bar clamps 12 to 15 inches (305 to 381 mm) apart.

8. Always clean off excess glue before it dries.

Gluing and clamping for thickness

1. Mix or prepare the glue according to the manufacturer's directions.

2. Adjust the clamps to fit the job.

3. Make protective blocks for C, hand, and bar clamps.

4. Spread the glue rapidly and evenly on the surfaces of the pieces.

5. Place the glued surfaces together; assemble the hand or C clamps (Figs. 116-5 through 116-8). The correct method of fastening hand clamps is shown in Fig. 116-5. The others show the use of the various clamps for gluing up stock to increase the thickness.

Gluing and clamping for width

1. Follow steps 1 through 3 above.

2. Spread glue rapidly and evenly on the edges of the boards.

3. Assemble the boards. The end grain should be arranged as indicated in Fig. 116-9. This reduces the wood's tendency to warp.

Fig. 116–6 Increasing the thickness of long, narrow pieces can be easily done by using parallel-jaw clamps.

4. Fasten the clamps lightly and then tap the boards, as shown in Fig. 116-10. This aligns the boards. Note especially that the clamps are fastened on both sides.

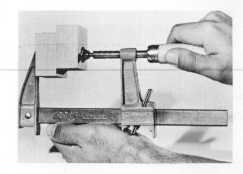

Fig. 116–8 Small pieces are easily glued with special clamps.

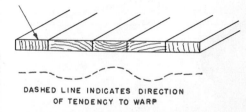

DASHED LINE INDICATES DIRECTION OF TENDENCY TO WARP

Fig. 116–9 Alternate the annual rings of wood pieces to help prevent warping.

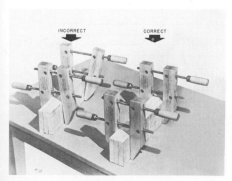

Fig. 116–5 Hand-screw clamps must be adjusted properly to clamp materials.

Fig. 116–7 C clamps can be used if parallel-jaw clamps are not available.

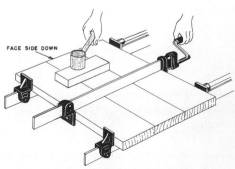

Fig. 116–10 Level the boards with a mallet and a scrap block.

5. Tighten the clamps to uniform pressure (Fig. 116-11). If the boards tend to buckle, keep them aligned as shown in Fig. 116-12. Use multiple-disk clamps, C clamps, or hand clamps.

6. Spot electronic gluing will hold joints sufficiently so that clamps can be removed within 30 minutes (Fig. 116-13). In electronic gluing, an electrode (lead) from the machine is placed on each side of the joined pieces. An electric current is applied from the machine which produces a magnetic field and quick heat between electrodes on the joint. As a result, the glue sets (dries) quickly.

Special gluing clamping

1. Follow steps 1 through 3 under "Gluing and Clamping for Thickness."

2. Put the parts together and make a trial assembly using the most suitable clamps for the job.

3. Spread glue rapidly and evenly on all parts to be assembled. Apply glue on dowel pins, splines, and other wooden parts for joints.

4. Assemble all parts and fasten the clamps in place (Figs. 116-14 through 116-16). Figure 116-16 shows the use of a shop-made jig for clamping cabinet parts. Figure 116-17 is a

Fig. 116-11 Bar clamps are placed above and below pieces that are glued edge to edge to prevent buckling.

Fig. 116-12 The multiple-disk clutch grips the bar automatically at any point. The holding platen helps to level the boards.

Fig. 116-13 An electronic gluing machine spot-heats and speeds up the work.

Fig. 116-14 "I" bar clamps used to clamp a frame.

Fig. 116-15 Long, flat, steel bar clamps are used to clamp oversize frames in both directions.

Fig. 116-16 Special fixtures help perform clamping operations on large projects.

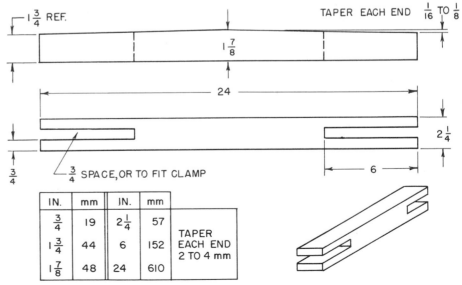

IN.	mm	IN.	mm	
$\frac{3}{4}$	19	$2\frac{1}{4}$	57	
$1\frac{3}{4}$	44	6	152	TAPER EACH END
$1\frac{7}{8}$	48	24	610	2 TO 4 mm

Fig. 116-17 Details for a special bar-clamp device.

detail drawing for making this special bar-clamp device.

5. Irregularly shaped assemblies can be clamped and held securely with the canvas-or steel-band clamp (Fig. 116-18). A canvas-band clamp is similar to a steel-band clamp but uses cloth in place of steel.

6. Miter joints can be held with the miter jig and a hand-screw clamp, as shown in Fig. 116-19, or with a special miter clamp (Fig. 116-20).

Fig. 116–18 The steel-band clamp holds irregular parts together.

Fig. 116–19 The hand-screw clamp is easily used with the miter jig.

Fig. 116–20 A splined miter joint is held for gluing with a miter clamp, which is adaptable for clamping in either two or four directions.

unit 117

Joints and joint strengtheners

It is very important to designate the types of joints for use in a project during the stages of planning and making a working drawing. The joints selected for assembly of a project or its parts affect such factors as eventual strength, beauty, and construction time. Drawer construction is a good example (Fig. 117-1).

Types of joints and uses

The basic types of joints are (1) butt, (2) dado, (3) rabbet, (4) lap, (5) dovetail, (6) mortise and tenon, (7) miter, and (8) tongue and groove (Fig. 117-2).

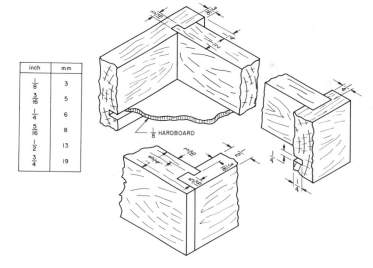

inch	mm
$\frac{1}{8}$	3
$\frac{3}{16}$	5
$\frac{1}{4}$	6
$\frac{5}{16}$	8
$\frac{1}{2}$	13
$\frac{3}{4}$	19

Fig. 117–1 Examples of typical drawer construction, showing several kinds of joints.

The dowel and the spline are used to strengthen some of these basic types of joints. Most joints have numerous variations.

Butt joints are used for simple construction. Dowels strengthen this type of joint when it is used. However, the doweled butt joint is not as strong as the mortise-and-tenon joint. Butt joints are also doweled to strengthen materials glued edge to edge to form large surfaces (Fig. 117-3).

227

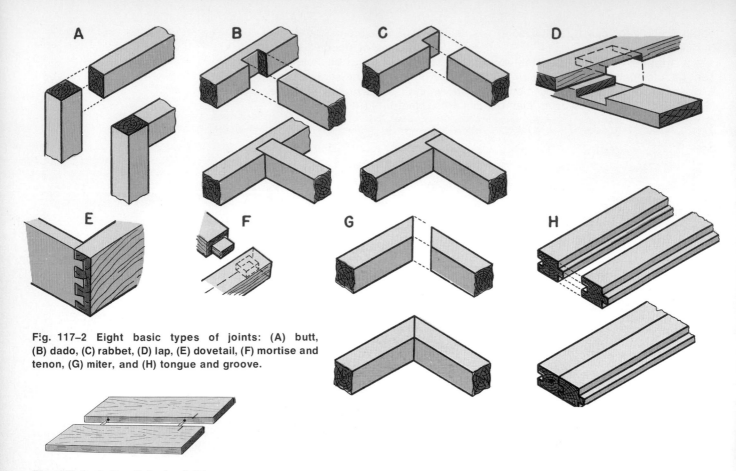

Fig. 117–2 Eight basic types of joints: (A) butt, (B) dado, (C) rabbet, (D) lap, (E) dovetail, (F) mortise and tenon, (G) miter, and (H) tongue and groove.

Fig. 117–3 A doweled edge joint.

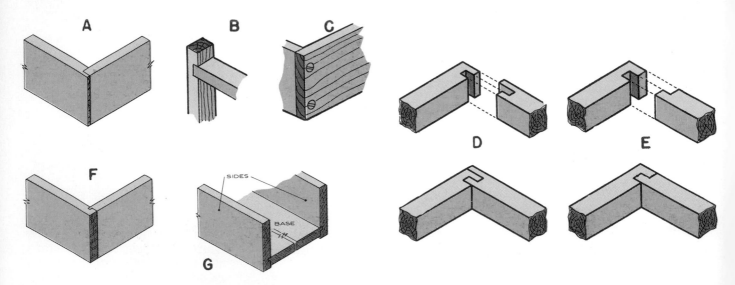

Fig. 117–4 Combinations of joints are often stronger than individual joints: (A) rabbet; (B) dado; (C) butt with screws; (D) dado, tongue, and rabbet; (E) dado and rabbet; (F) barefaced tongue and dado; and (G) barefaced tongue and groove.

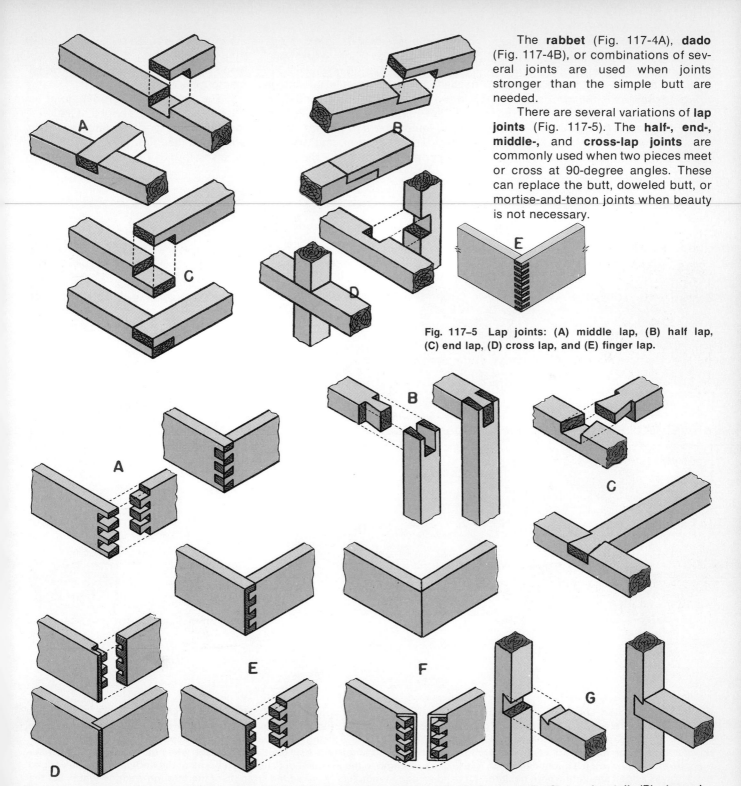

The **rabbet** (Fig. 117-4A), **dado** (Fig. 117-4B), or combinations of several joints are used when joints stronger than the simple butt are needed.

There are several variations of **lap joints** (Fig. 117-5). The **half-, end-, middle-,** and **cross-lap joints** are commonly used when two pieces meet or cross at 90-degree angles. These can replace the butt, doweled butt, or mortise-and-tenon joints when beauty is not necessary.

Fig. 117–5 Lap joints: (A) middle lap, (B) half lap, (C) end lap, (D) cross lap, and (E) finger lap.

Fig. 117–6 Types of dovetail joints: (A) through multiple dovetail; (B) through single dovetail; (C) lap dovetail; (D) stopped lap dovetail; (E) lap, or half-blind, dovetail; (F) blind miter, or secret, dovetail; and (G) dovetail dado.

229

Dovetail joints (Fig. 117-6) are made on corners where much strength is desired and where pulling strain is involved. Joining sides and fronts of drawers is the most common use of dovetails in furniture construction. The dovetail joint is usually made with a router. See Unit 106, Making a Dovetail Joint.

Mortise-and-tenon joints (Fig. 117-7) are made when exceptional strength and wearing qualities are needed. They are used especially to join two pieces, such as legs and rails.

Miter joints (see Fig. 117-2G) are used to join corners of picture frames or two pieces of trim, molding, or larger surfaces. The ends of the pieces are cut at 45-degree angles. The miter joint is strengthened by using either wood dowels, splines, or special metal clamp nails.

The **tongue-and-groove joint** is often used when the edges of material for table tops or other large surfaces are joined (see Fig. 117-2H). This joint is also found on flooring, center-

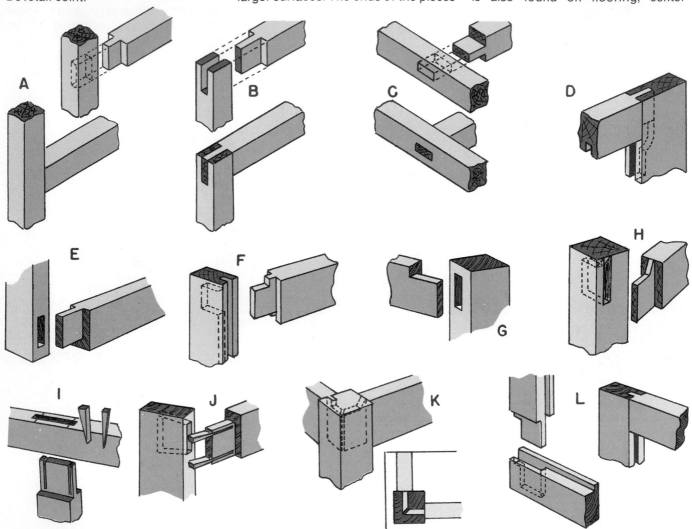

Fig. 117–7 Common and special mortise-and-tenon joints and their application: (A) blind mortise-and-stub tenon; (B) through mortise-and-stub tenon, (C) open through mortise-and-stub tenon; (D) stub tenon in slot (not a true mortise-and-tenon, but easily made for light framing); (E) simple mortise-and-tenon joint used for framing; (F) haunched tenon used for grooved framing (the haunch fills the gap made by the full-length groove); (G) barefaced tenon (has only one shoulder used when the tenon piece is thinner than the mortised one); (H) haunched tenon (gives extra strength to the joint without showing a break at the end); (I) through-wedged tenon (gives added strength where desired); (J) blind-wedged tenon (gives the added strength of the through-wedged tenon, but the joint is not seen); (K) mitered tenon (used to secure maximum length on tenon); and (L) tenon with long-and-short shoulder (used in framework or sash where a rabbet is required).

matched siding, fencing, and some roofing materials. The tongue is frequently used in combination with the dado and the rabbet (see Figs. 117-4D, F, and G). The basic joint, as it is cut and fitted, may need additional strengthening. To provide the extra reinforcement, metal fasteners, wood dowels, splines, and braces are sometimes added.

Metal strengtheners

Several forms of metal fasteners can be used to strengthen joints. Three of these are the **corrugated fastener** (Fig. 117-8), a special **four-pronged fastener** (Fig. 117-9), and the **clamp nail** (Fig. 117-10B). Metal fasteners detract from the general beauty of the object, and they do not have the holding power of properly used wood strengtheners. They are sometimes convenient, however.

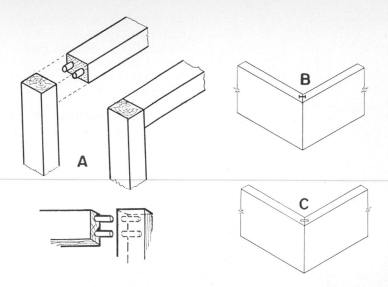

Fig. 117–10   Joint strengtheners: (A) doweled butt joint, (B) miter joint with a clamp nail, and (C) miter joint with a wood spline.

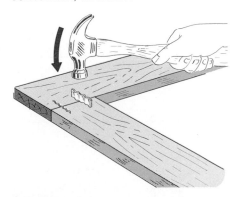

Fig. 117–8   Driving a corrugated fastener.

Fig. 117–9   Driving a four-prong metal fastener.

Dowels as strengtheners

Wood dowels are frequently used in furniture construction. They strengthen joints when one end of a board is butted to the edge of a second (Fig. 117-10A) and when pieces are glued edge to edge (see Fig. 117-3). Dowels are also used in miter joints.

The best dowel rods are made from birch and maple and come in several lengths and sizes (diameters). The 30- and 36-inch (762- and 914-mm) lengths are common. Many sizes are made, but the usual sizes are $1/4$, $3/8$, $1/2$, $3/4$, and 1 inch (6.35, 9.53, 12.70, 19.05, and 25.40 mm). Special grooved and ungrooved dowel pins (often $3/8$ by $1^1/2$ inch or 2 inches) can be obtained (Fig. 117-11). The spiral-groove pins hold glue better and strengthen the joint more than smooth pins. When necessary, dowels can be made as shown in Fig. 117-12. Square pieces of wood are driven through a nut having the correct opening for the dowel. The nut is held securely in a vise.

If dowels do not have spiral grooves, they should have a flat place or a straight groove on one side to

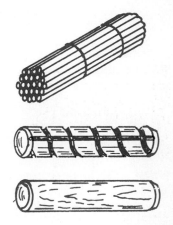

Fig. 117–11   Grooved and ungrooved dowel pins.

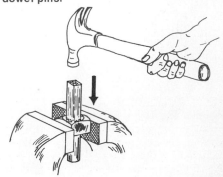

Fig. 117–12   Making a dowel in a jig.

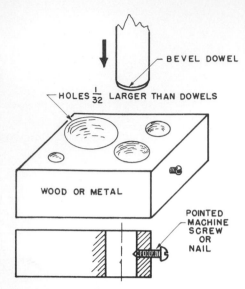

BEVEL DOWEL

HOLES $\frac{1}{32}$ LARGER THAN DOWELS

WOOD OR METAL

POINTED MACHINE SCREW OR NAIL

Fig. 117–13 Grooving a dowel.

Fig. 117–14 Cutting kerfs for splines. Note attachment for holding the piece.

allow excess glue to escape from the hole made for the dowel. A groove can be made in almost any length of dowel by driving the dowel through a special jig (Fig. 117-13).

Splines as strengtheners

A **spline** is a thin strip of wood, plywood, or single piece of veneer glued into a special groove (saw kerf) to strengthen joints. A saw cut may run all the way across a joint or only partially into it (Fig. 117-15). The circular (table) saw can be used (Fig. 117-14) to make matching cuts in two pieces that are to be joined with a spline. The thickness and the width of the cut are determined by the size of the spline and the extra strength needed.

Braces and strengtheners

Wood braces are frequently used to strengthen joints. They add additional strength to any type of corner joint, even when mortise-and-tenon joints, dowels, or splines have been used.

Triangular and flat corner braces (Figs. 117-16 and 117-17) add support to the corners of wooden objects. The flat corner brace (Fig. 117-18) strengthens the corner and provides a surface to which leg hardware is attached.

Special connectors and strengtheners

Knock-down designs and **on-site** assembly of wood products cause special problems of construction and transportation. Special connectors and strengtheners solve some of these.

The **self-tapping insert and screw** (Fig. 117-19) is adaptable for joining legs to bases. The **fishbone connector** offers ease of joint construction (Fig.

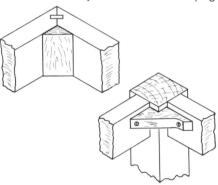

Fig. 117–16 Triangular corner braces.

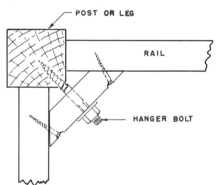

POST OR LEG

RAIL

HANGER BOLT

Fig. 117–17 A flat corner brace.

Fig. 117–18 Flat corner braces make surfaces on which to attach leg hardware.

Fig. 117–15 The saw kerf (cut) for a spline partially cut across a joint.

117-20). It is often used with lumber, plywood, and particle board where the capscrew head is visible only from the back.

The **dovetail fastener** (Fig. 117-21) is a wedge-shaped metal tenon that is tapped for a bolt. The wood is routed and the bolt connects the pieces.

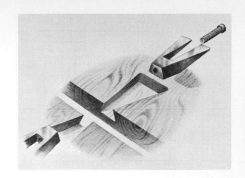

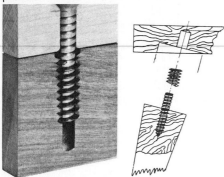

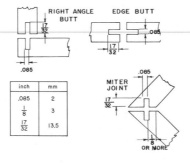

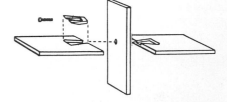

Fig. 117–19 Self-tapping insert and screw. First, counterbore base; second, drill hole partially into base; and third, install insert for assembly.

Fig. 117–20 Insert the fishbone connector. First, saw grooves; second, cement receiving strips in place; third, recess for capscrew; and fourth, assemble.

Fig. 117–21 A dovetail fastener permits knock-down construction, flat shipping, and assembling with a screwdriver.

unit 118

Cabinet hardware

There is an almost unlimited selection of hardware items for furniture, cabinetwork, and building construction. Larger pieces of very useful hardware are drawer rollers, ball-bearing swivels for lazy susans and chairs, bases to support swivel chairs, and hardware for reclining chairs and platform rockers.

Practically all the hardware is obtainable in many sizes and designs. When hardware is purchased, the necessary screws, pins, and other fastening devices are usually supplied with it.

Furniture and cabinet hardware is used for both decoration and function. It is necessary to be very accurate when locating, drilling, and chiseling the recesses and when making the final attachments (Fig. 118-1). This is usually one of the last operations performed. If hardware is attached before the finish is applied, it is often removed again until all finish work is done. It is then replaced.

Round tapered legs

Round tapered legs for tables, chests, and other pieces of furniture can be

Fig. 118–1 Fitting doors for hinges before finishing.

made or purchased in many materials and sizes. Necessary parts are shown in Fig. 118-2. Combination brackets, as illustrated, allow the leg to be inserted either vertically or at a standard 15-degree angle. Single brackets are also available.

A leg is turned and fitted to the metal cap or ferrule on the tip of the

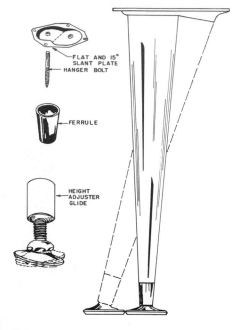

Fig. 118–2 Typical hardware for round tapered legs.

leg. This cap may be plain, or it may have a self-leveling swivel base, or glide.

The top of the leg is prepared for the hanger bolt by drilling a pilot hole. Put soap, wax, or paraffin on the screw threads of the bolt, and use the device shown in Fig. 112-7 to aid in screwing the bolt into the wood easily.

Angle irons, plates, braces, and fasteners

Flat T and 90-degree flat angle fasteners (Fig. 118-3A and B) are used to strengthen butt joints on the face surface and where edges join at 90 degrees. The bent angle iron is sometimes used to attach table tops. Corner plates and braces (Fig. 118-3C and D) are used for attaching legs to the rails of tables and to strengthen similar corners. Table-top fasteners (Fig. 118-3E) are commonly used to attach a table top to the rails.

Hinges

A few of the many types of common and special hinges in use are shown in Figs. 118-4 and 118-5. A large number of shapes, designs, and finishes are available.

The unswaged, partial-, or full-swaged **butt hinge** has always been popular and practical. The type of

swage (shape) (Fig. 118-4A) determines to a large extent the amount of gain (chiseling out) required. For cutting gains, refer to Unit 107.

The names of the **half-surface** and **full-surface** (offset) **hinges** (Fig. 118-5H and I) indicate their placement on doors. The hinge is either fully visible on the surface or half hidden behind a door. Surface hinges range from the many-shaped, ornamental types to heavy, rough strap hinges that are found on farm and ranch gates and barn doors.

Invisible hinges are mounted so that they are concealed from view when doors are closed (Fig. 118-6). These are frequently used on quality furniture, such as drop-leaf tables. This hinge permits perfectly flush mounting, so that no hinge parts show. Holes are bored to accommodate the hinge.

Combination hinges (Fig. 118-5M) are often used on desks and chests. They are sold in pairs.

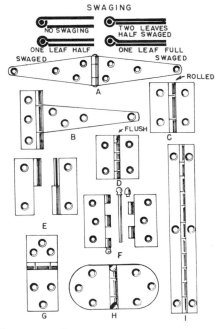

Fig. 118–4 Common hinges: (A) plain strap, (B) T, (C) tight-pin butt, (D) plain-pin butt, (E) loose-joint butt, (F) loose-pin butt, (G) table leaf, (H) round-and-flush, and (I) continuous (piano).

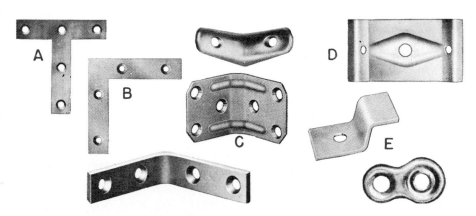

Fig. 118–3 Fasteners and braces: (A) T plates, (B) flat corner iron, (C and D) corner braces, and (E) table top fasteners.

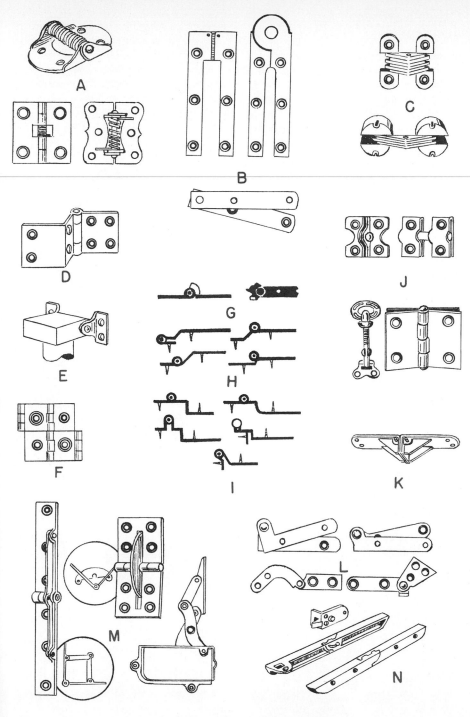

Cabinet catches

Four of the many kinds of cabinet catches are shown in Fig. 118-7. These are (1) friction, (2) magnetic, (3) roller, and (4) spring-wedged catches. The magnetic catch is noiseless and is a very practical way of keeping cabinet doors closed. A spring-wedged catch, offset hinges, and drawer and door pulls are shown in Fig. 118-8.

Drawer and door pulls

Drawer pulls, door handles, and knobs are made in a great variety of materials, finishes, sizes, and patterns (Fig. 118-9). People can design and make

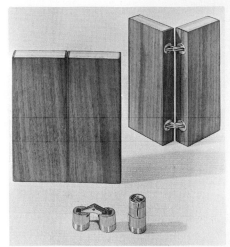

Fig. 118–6 Invisible hinges and their installation.

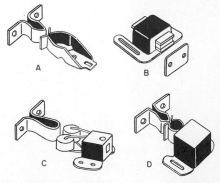

Fig. 118–7 Typical cabinet catches: (A) friction, (B) magnetic, (C) roller, and (D) spring-wedged.

Fig. 118–5 Special hinges: (A) spring, (B) knife, (C) invisible link, (D) chest, (E) tilt-top table, (F) double action, (G) stop, (H) visible offset, (I) semiconcealed offset, (J) friction, (K) built-in fixture, (L) semiconcealed, (M) combination, and (N) drop-front drawer with catch.

their own pulls, but commercially made ones come complete and ready for mounting and are made of wood, plastic, nylon (Fig. 118-10), metal, and composition materials.

Single-post knobs and **pulls** are usually put on small drawers or on doors that open easily. They are installed by marking the location desired and drilling a hole to accommodate the correct size of screw. Drawer and door pulls with **two posts** and screws require very accurate centering and drilling to make the handle align for a correct fit.

Other hardware and accessories

Metal or **nylon glides** (Fig. 118-11) are added to the bottoms of chair and table legs and to other furniture to prevent chipping and wear. **Rollers** mounted in kitchen cabinets and on drawer frames permit easy drawer opening and closing (Fig. 118-12). **Nylon tape** (Fig. 118-13) and **self-adhering plastic glides** are also available for mounting on drawer frames to allow drawers to open and close easily.

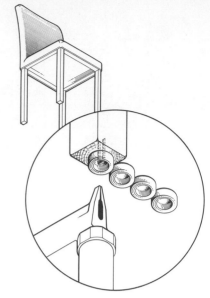

Fig. 118–11 Installing a nylon chair glide with a special staple.

Fig. 118–8 A spring-wedged catch, offset hinges, and metal drawer and door pulls, shown as a typical cabinet installation.

Fig. 118–9 Antique brass and French gilt (old gold) drawer pulls and knobs.

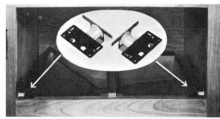

Fig. 118–12 Rollers mounted on drawer frames.

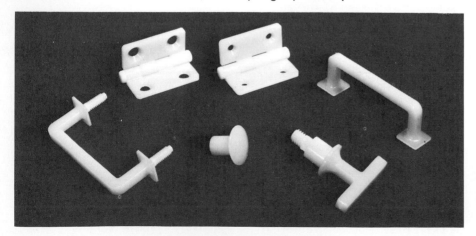

Fig. 118–10 Nylon handles, knobs, and hinges are available. They can be dyed to match wood colors with common household dyes.

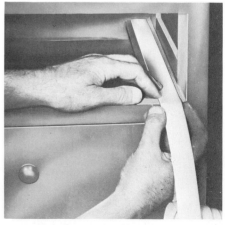

Fig. 118–13 Nylon tape can be attached to drawer frames for easy drawer glide.

unit 119

Discussion topics on hardware and assembly of cabinetwork

1. Make a sketch to show how the lengths of the different types of screws are measured. Make another one to show how an ordinary screwdriver should be shaped for driving slotted screws.
2. What are the advantages of using screws instead of nails?
3. List the information you should have when you buy wood screws.
4. Sketch the heads, list the names, and explain the uses of the common types of nails and brads.
5. What do **6d** and **10-penny** mean?
6. What must you know about nails before ordering (buying) them?
7. Tell how plastic laminate is composed and manufactured.
8. Why is the back side of laminates sanded and roughened?
9. What are some common tools used to work and apply plastic laminates?
10. Contact a materials dealer and collect several designs and types of plastic laminates for class inspection.
11. What are some reasons for building up custom plywood from veneers?
12. What are the common thicknesses of veneer stock?
13. If a solid edge banding is desired, why should it be fastened to the panel or board prior to veneering?
14. What type of joint is best to use in attaching a solid edge banding to a panel before veneering?
15. What kind of material may be used to cover edges of veneered plywood or particle board?
16. What are the five common types of "natural-product" glues?
17. How are the more recently developed synthetic resins classified?
18. Name three kinds of clamps most often used in woodworking. List their specific uses.
19. What is meant by **sizing end grain?** How is it done? Why?
20. Why is it recommended that only pieces that are 4 or 5 inches (102 or 127 mm) wide be used in gluing together several boards edge to edge?
21. Sketch one kind of joint in each of the eight categories. Discuss its use in wood construction.
22. List several types of joints used in drawer construction.
23. What are the usual forms of joint strengtheners?
24. From what kinds of wood are the best dowels made?
25. Where are splines used?
26. Explain the purpose of alternating the direction of the annual rings of end-grain pieces being doweled or glued edge to edge.
27. Why are wooden corner braces of value in furniture construction?
28. Name five types of hinges. Where can each be used?
29. Sketch several ways of attaching table tops with metal hardware.
30. What are several types of cabinet catches?
31. List the kinds of hardware used on furniture in your home.

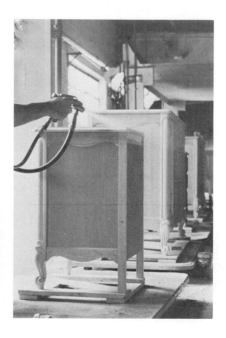

Preparation of Wood and Application of Finishes

unit 120

Preparing wood surfaces and selecting a finish

Preparing wood surfaces and selecting the finish the wood will take best are important parts of planning. Each craftsman has personal preferences and methods.

Woods and finishes

The woodworker soon learns that the quality of a finish can be no better than the surface to which it is applied. Stains and natural finishes bring out the beauty of wood grain, but they also magnify defects instead of covering and minimizing them. Minor blemishes, scratches, and planer and jointer marks may appear slight in bare wood, but they are emphasized when the finish is put on.

The design and construction of a project determine whether the entire project can be sanded after assembly or whether parts are more conveniently sanded first.

Sanding surfaces

Sanding operations are divided into four general categories. The first three are **rough, preparatory,** and **prefinish.**

The fourth category of sanding is **finish.** The final cleaning is done (Fig. 120-1) and the surface is finished "in the white." This expression means that all surfaces are completely sanded and ready for bleaching, staining, filling, or other finishing operations.

Finishing abrasives

Pumice, rottenstone, and tripoli are special powdered abrasives that are derived from natural sources.

Pumice is a powdered volcanic lava that makes a relatively coarse abrasive. It is used for rubbing final finishes to help smooth the surface before using rottenstone or tripoli.

Rottenstone is very fine and much softer than other abrasives. It is made from decomposed limestone shale (fossilized rock); it has a dark grayish color. The name comes from the offensive odor given off when the shale is broken and ground into powder.

Tripoli is rottenstone that owes its name to Tripoli, Libya, where it is found. It is used with a lubricant, such as lemon oil, for rubbing finishes.

Man-made abrasives for final finishes are **boron carbide** (B_4C), which is next to the diamond in hardness; **silicon carbide** (SiC); and **aluminum oxide** (Al_2O_3).

Steel wool is an abrasive of a different type. It is used to remove, clean, or rub and polish finishes. Its grades are No. 3 (coarse), No. 2, No. 1, and Nos. 0 to 4/0 (extra fine). Grades No. 3/0 and No. 4/0 are used to buff and rub down final coats of finish.

Because this material is made of fine steel shavings, there are some

Fig. 120–1 Many furniture manufacturers hand-clean and sand their products before a finish is applied.

disadvantages in using it. For example, the coarser grades can easily cut your hands. The fine grades, on the other hand, permit steel dust particles to fly free in the air, where they can be inhaled. Also, steel wool rusts where there is considerable humidity.

The disadvantages of steel wool have been overcome by the development of the ultrafine **garnet pad.** It resembles steel wool and is used for the same purposes. It is soft, resilient, nonrusting, long-lasting, and easy on the hands; it produces a uniformly smooth finish.

Repairing blemishes before finishing

Holes from knots and other causes, cracks, scratches, and other imperfections should be repaired either during the initial (first) sanding operation or before the prefinish operation. The surfaces can be smoothed and the blemishes made less noticeable. Many blemish-repair materials are shown in Fig. 120-2.

Raising the grain. Serious scratches and deeper impressions can be raised by sponging them with very warm water and then steaming them with a warm iron. An electric iron is useful for this purpose, but do not burn the wood.

Large holes and small, rough knots. These can be made uniform size by using a wood auger or a Forstner bit. A plug cutter is used to cut a round plug from a similar piece of wood. Be sure the grain in the plug runs in the same direction as the grain in the area where the plug is inserted.

Cracks. Favorite materials to fill cracks and other blemishes are stick shellac and lacquer. These sticks can be purchased in solid white, natural, clear, and in more than 70 colors. Stick shellac is heated and worked

239

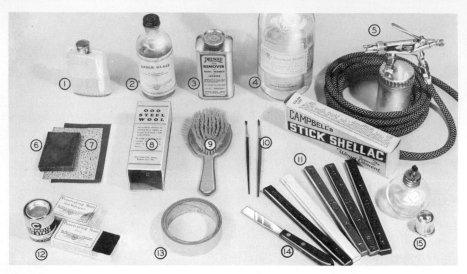

Fig. 120–2 Blemish-repair materials: (1) lemon oil; (2) French polish; (3) varnish remover; (4) denatured alcohol; (5) touch-up gun; (6) felt; (7) abrasive papers; (8) steel wool; (9) dulling brush; (10) pencil brushes; (11) stick shellac; (12) spirit stain; (13) masking tape; (14) burning-in knife; and (15) alcohol lamp.

into the crack or opening with a heated spatula, flat knife, electric soldering iron, or special heating device. The process of repair after finishing is called **burning in.**

These repairs should *not* be done in the finishing room because the materials are flammable. Practice on scrap material to determine the heat needed. It is best to repair the surface *before sanding:*

1. Mask the crack with masking tape (Fig. 120-3).

2. Heat the end of a flexible spatula or knife, and apply the stick shellac (Fig. 120-4).

3. Pack the shellac into the crack until it is full (Fig. 120-5).

4. Remove the tape and cut off the excess shellac (Fig. 120-6).

5. Back up No. 6/0 finish paper with a felt or cloth pad. Dip the paper in alcohol; then in rubbing oil or water. Rub the patch quickly and firmly with a few strokes (Fig. 120-7).

6. Dull the patch by rubbing lightly with No. 3/0 steel wool.

Fig. 120–5 Packing stick shellac into a crack.

Fig. 120–6 Removing excess shellac.

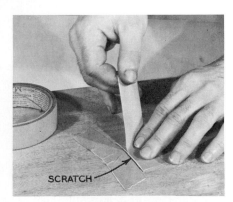

Fig. 120–3 Masking a crack or blemish for repair.

Fig. 120–4 Heating a spatula, or flexible knife, and stick shellac to prepare for filling a crack.

Fig. 120–7 Rubbing the patch or repair mark with rubbing oil, alcohol, and water.

7. If a thin coat results because of rubbing, use spray equipment and spray on a coat of clear lacquer or ether varnish (Fig. 120-8), and rub down the entire surface.

Wood plastic, wood dough, and water putty (a dry powder which is mixed with water) are especially useful for repairing deep blemishes. A prepared surfacing putty can be purchased for use on small imperfections.

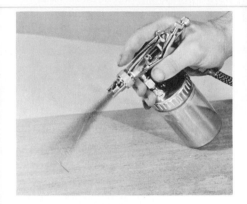

Fig. 120–8 Spraying on a thin coat of clear lacquer to build up a finish coat over a blemish.

Selecting final finishes

A final finish can be selected from among oils, waxes, shellacs, lacquers, varnishes, paints, and enamels (Fig. 120-9). Several of these permit different mixtures for special purposes. The choice of a final finish is very im-portant to protect and beautify the wood in the project.

Fig. 120–9 Lacquer enamels give a bright, clean appearance to older kitchen furnishings.

Brush and spray finishing at room temperature are the methods most often used in the school industrial laboratory and the home workshop. Industries often use hot-spray finishes and infrared drying (Fig. 120-10).

Fig. 120–10 Hot-spray finishes and in-frared drying are used by many modern furniture manufacturers.

unit 121

History of finishes

Asphalt or bituminous (tarlike natural substance) coatings have been known and used as preservatives for centuries. Skeletons of prehistoric animals were found perfectly preserved in the La Brea asphalt pits near Los Angeles, California. Pitch, asphalt, wax, and paint were used many thousand years ago to protect and preserve surfaces.

History of varnish

The word *varnish* is derived from the Latin word *vernix*. A translucent fossilized resin that we know as amber was transported from the North Sea to Egypt. It is believed that this substance was named "Berenice" after the Queen of Cyrene, who was married to an Egyptian pharaoh. (Cyrene was a Greek city and colony in Cyrenaica, North Africa, about 550 B.C.)

These **fossilized resins** and **co-pals** (fossilized tree resins) were once favored in the manufacture of varnish. Copals were dug from the earth in the upper African Congo and in India.

Chemists have now, however, developed synthetic resins that are more durable than the original fossil gums.

History of shellac

Natives of India were using shellac to protect surfaces in their homes and temples before the time of Julius Caesar (100–44 B.C.) Europeans did not use this substance until just before 1600, although Marco Polo had introduced shellac several hundred years before.

Once a year, tiny insects swarm on the **lac trees** in India. These small bugs are scientifically called *Tachar-*

dia lacca. They often cluster so thickly that the trees appear reddish in color. By sucking the tree sap into their bodies they literally eat themselves to death.

During this time, the female lays about 1000 eggs at a time. The sap of the tree is secreted as a gum, which covers both the bugs and the eggs. This liquid hardens and several months later is broken as the eggs hatch and the young move to other trees. The crust is harvested from the tree twigs, put through several purifying processes, and made into a gum that is the basis of commercial shellac.

History of lacquer

Lacquer is a quick-drying product that plays a very important role in wood finishing.

Records show that the Japanese and the Chinese were using lacquer over 2000 years ago. Plain wooden pieces were often covered with several hundred layers of lacquer until the coating was thick enough to carve.

Ancient Chinese lacquer was obtained from the sap of a tree. The tree was tapped, and the sap emerged as a grayish-white liquid that darkened to black when exposed to air. It was eventually pounded, heated, stirred to evaporate excess moisture, and then stored in airtight containers.

Using gun cotton (nitrocellulose) and butyl alcohol with its esters and other chemicals, chemists have developed a synthetic lacquer that dries rapidly.

History of paint

Paints have been used through the years for decoration and for weather protection. Paint has been used to improve working conditions by promoting safety, cleanliness, and sanitation and by improving the effects of lighting and heating.

Water-thinned paints, made from casein and egg white or glue, were used by the Egyptians as early as 3000 to 2000 B.C. Very little progress was made in paint for centuries. In the early colonial days in America, lime and water made a whitewash mixture that was used as paint. In the early part of the twentieth century, animal glue and whiting (chalk from the White Cliffs of Dover, England) were mixed to use as a binder for pigment. This calcimine paint was not highly washable or durable.

Casein paint was developed about the same time as calcimine paint. It was composed of casein, whiting, preservatives, and a hiding pigment (coloring substance).

Vegetable oils made possible the oil-resin and latex-emulsion paints. *Latex* once referred only to a substance extracted from the rubber plant, but it now refers to a variety of synthetic resins.

Oil-base paints are extremely popular. They consist mainly of either white or colored pigments and certain vehicles, or liquids. These paints are used extensively for both exterior and interior work. A good house paint should contain at least 65 percent pigment; the remaining 35 percent or less should be the vehicle. Linseed oil is the most important of all drying oils; it is obtained from flax seed. Drying oil is an oily liquid which, applied as a thin film, dries or hardens within 48 hours when exposed to normal weather. This oil should compose 80 to 90 percent of the vehicle, with thinners (turpentine and mixed spirits) and driers making up the remainder.

Vegetable, animal, or mineral color pigments are added. Extender pigments do little in covering a surface, but they are necessary to prevent the other pigments from settling into a hard mass.

Various formulas are derived for different paints. Materials are added to prevent such common paint failures as chalking, checking, cracking and scaling, mildewing, blistering, and discoloring.

Paint: a world development

Materials for paints from the animal, vegetable, and mineral kingdoms have been obtained from every part of the world. Linseed oil from the flax fields. varnish gums from buried prehistoric forests, and tung oil from China and later from the southern United States are some of the ingredients used to manufacture paint. Oil and gas fields produce their share of mineral spirits, carbon and lamp blacks, and benzene.

Beeswax, shellac gum, and some lime from oyster shells are also used in paints.

unit 122

History, use, and care of brushes

The ancient Egyptians were the first to use paintbrushes made from split reeds soaked in water (Fig. 122-1). The Greeks later utilized the tails and feet of small fur-bearing animals for brushes.

In the thirteenth century, castle walls were whitened by using a pound of bristles tied to a stick to spread the finish. Brush makers' guilds were formed in England and France, and they were given special privileges. Flat brushes did not appear until after 1840. The American brush industry

Fig. 122–1 Brushes used by ancient Egyptians were made of split reeds soaked in water.

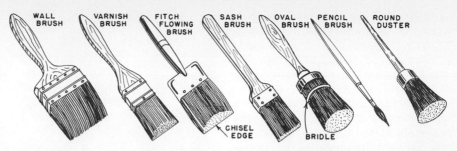

WALL BRUSH   VARNISH BRUSH   FITCH FLOWING BRUSH   SASH BRUSH   OVAL BRUSH   PENCIL BRUSH   ROUND DUSTER

CHISEL EDGE   BRIDLE

Fig. 122–3 Many shapes and sizes of brushes are made for amateur and for professional painters and finishers.

Fig. 122–4 The bristle of the wild boar is the best hair for brush making.

Fig. 122–5 Eight to twelve types of either boar bristle or synthetic filament are required for mixing a good paintbrush.

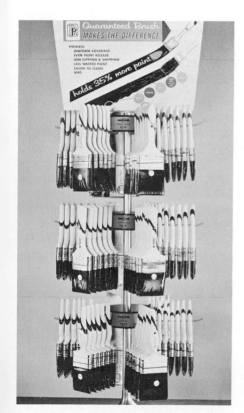

Fig. 122–2 Brushes for home craftsmen are made in many sizes. Professional painters use more expensive tools.

Fig. 122–6 Stock for a medium-cost brush is weighed and placed in a ferrule, or metal band. A machine performs similar operations to make smaller, low-cost brushes.

efficiently designed and developed the modern metal-bound paintbrushes and varnish brushes during the early part of this century (Fig. 122-2).

Finishing brushes are made in numerous shapes and sizes for specific purposes (Fig. 122-3). Most finishers, however, prefer a chisel-edge brush.

Brush making

Bristle is the name given to the hair of the wild boar. The unique characteristics of the hair (Fig. 122-4) are not found in the hair of any other animal. The **split end,** or **flag,** and the **taper** from the root to the flag make this hair the most important material used in brush manufacture. The bristle (hair) is tapered like a flagpole. These qualities of bristle give a bristle brush the ability to hold and carry paint. No natural substitute has been found that is more satisfactory for making brushes than the bristle. The bristle or hair is collected, cleaned, tied in batches, transported, sorted, mixed (Fig. 122-5), weighed (Fig. 122-6), and

Fig. 122–7 High-quality paintbrushes are assembled by individual workers.

combed. Eventually a well-designed brush is assembled by hand (Fig. 122-7) from a mixture of many kinds and lengths of bristle. Some brushes are manufactured by automation (Fig. 122-8).

Coarse brushes (not classified as paintbrushes) are made from many materials other than bristles and soft hair. Some of the materials are horsehair, istle or tampico fibers (cactus family), palmetto and other palms, and rice root. Thousands of different grades of brushes are made from tampico fiber. Rice root is a crinkly root of a large bunch grass that grows in Mexico and Guatemala.

Soft-hair brushes are made mostly from fur-bearing animals of the weasel family. Coarse brushes in this category are made from the hair of the ox and the goat.

The most valuable hair to the brush maker is the red sable, or Siberian mink. Other hairs used are "camel hair" (actually Siberian and Russian squirrel), black sable (civet cat), fitch (tail of the American skunk), American black bear, badger, and genet (dyed hair of the ringtail and other wild cats).

Nylon bristles were developed during World War II to replace Chinese boar bristles. The Chinese bristles had replaced the Russian boar bristles at the time of World War I. The nylon brush is satisfactory in many ways. It lasts much longer than bristle, is uniformly solid, lays a smooth film of paint, and carries paint well. It is resistant to solvents and water, and it can be stored easier without molding. Shellac tends to soften nylon, but the

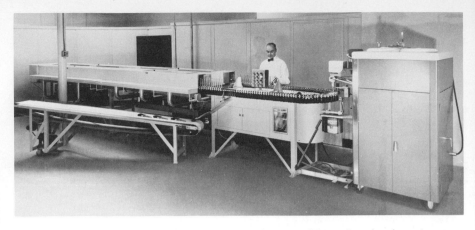

Fig. 122–8   The equipment pictured is that used to manufacture brushes by automation. Brush parts are loaded on a conveyor, which carries them through the various manufacturing operations to the final assembled brush.

nylon bristles will return to their proper condition if the brush is placed in water after it has been cleaned.

Care and use of brushes

Most brushes are discarded because of improper care and use, not because of wear. For longer brush usefulness:

1. Remove loose bristles before using a brush, and dip the brush only part way into the finishing material.

2. Remove excess finish by drawing the flat side of the brush across the lip of the can.

3. Clean brushes immediately after use.

4. Wash completely in the proper solvent. This is usually the thinner for the finishing material used. Wash shellac brushes in alcohol; lacquer brushes in lacquer thinner; varnish, oil-paint, and enamel brushes in turpentine; and water-thinned paintbrushes in water.

5. Squeeze out excess solvent.

6. After the brush is clean, wash it with mild soap or detergent and warm water.

7. Remove excess water, and wrap the brush in clean paper to reshape the bristles as they dry. After drying, wrap the ferrule and bristles in heavy paper and band loosely with a rubber band.

Some painters recommend rubbing a light coat of linseed oil on brushes used in oil-base materials. If the brush is cleaned properly, this is not necessary on nylon bristles. Do not clean nylon-bristle brushes in lacquer thinner or liquids that contain acetone; the nylon would be damaged by the ingredients of these cleaners.

unit 123

Spray finishing

Spray-gun equipment is used to apply many types of finishes. Stain, tones or shades of color finishes, shellac, and varnish are often sprayed on, as is lacquer. Attention must be given to all this equipment, including the spray gun, containers for finishing materials, hose and connections, air transformers and condensers, and the air-compressor units (Fig. 123-1).

For best results, consult spray-equipment manufacturers for answers to particular problems. Only the minimum essentials are discussed here for general spray finishing in small operations.

Safety

Safe practices are absolutely essential in all shops and laboratories, especially in the finishing area. Volatile (vaporizable or explosive) finishing materials are very combustible. When improperly used, these materials can cause a fire, or they can explode. The vapors of most solvents should *never* be inhaled for any extended period of time because they can injure the respiratory system.

Follow these safety practices:

1. Place soiled rags and rags saturated with oil, finishes, and solvents in a special, closed, metal container. Empty the container frequently in some remote area, and see that the rags are disposed of in a safe place.

2. Vapor- and arcproof switches, relays, lights, and other electrical devices should be installed in a finish room.

3. Containers of solvents and finishing materials should be securely covered and stored in a fire-resistant or fireproof cabinet. Safety (fireproof) cans should be secured for those liquids that are most highly flammable.

4. Proper fire extinguishers and fire-fighting facilities should be easily accessible. Water, foam, dry chemical, or the soda-acid extinguishers should be available. Consult your local fire marshal to determine which one is best for local use.

Since many finishes and resinous or plastic materials are being used, *do*

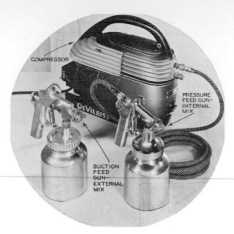

Fig. 123–1 A typical small spray-finishing unit.

not use the carbon tetrachloride (CTC) type of extinguisher. Carbon tet used on certain plastic fires produces a *deadly gas. Never* use water on an electrical fire! Use a soda-acid extinguisher.

5. The finishing area should have proper lighting, ventilation, and exhaust systems.

6. Mechanical, chemical, or combination respirators should be worn for protection against breathing toxic (poisonous) fumes and solid particles (Fig. 123-2).

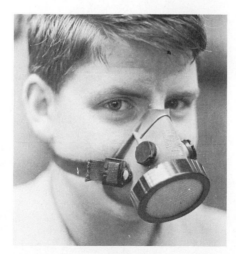

Fig. 123–2 Proper respirators give good protection against breathing toxic fumes when spraying finishes over long periods of time.

7. The face, arms, and hands should be covered with a special protective cream or lotion. Hands should be protected by rubber gloves when handling volatile solvents or toxic liquids such as benzol. Cracked skin and infection result when there is too much natural skin oil lost.

8. Clean the floor and walls, and replace or clean the air filters frequently.

9. Label all cans clearly, and store them in an orderly arrangement. Use older materials first, or discard them. Do not use finishes that have been left standing for several years because these finishes often deteriorate (decline in quality).

10. To pour liquids from a container, turn the can so that the spout or opening is near the top when the can is tilted. Then, air can enter easily, and the liquid will pour smoothly and freely from the can and will not spatter or gurgle. Wipe all excess liquids off the can or other surfaces.

Spray guns and spray finishing

The **airbrush** (Fig. 123-3) is a small spray gun used extensively in sign painting, finishing photographs, and artwork. It operates on compressed air and requires exacting artistic technique to obtain desired results.

Electrostatic spraying is used in many industries. This method, which is airless or which uses air broken into

Fig. 123–3 The airbrush is used extensively in sign painting.

smaller particles, is based on the principle of supplying the material to the dispenser by hydraulic pressure (Fig. 123-4). The airless method delivers the finish to the product by centrifugal force. The air-atomized process is based on the law of physics that states that like charges repel and unlike attract. The air-atomized process can be adapted to nonmetallic products, but it is more successful on metal articles.

The **pressure-feed spray gun** allows air to pass through the gun at all times. This is called a **bleeder gun.** It can be used to spray practically all types of materials from small or large containers. The trigger controls finish flow. This gun is widely used in the automatic-spraying and the air-atomized processes

A **siphon,** or **suction-feed gun** (Fig. 123-5) is probably the most widely used gun in school industrial laboratories, shops, and small operations. This gun is called a **nonbleeder** because the trigger controls both the air and the fluid. It usually has an adjustable external-mix type of nozzle and tip. That is, the air and the finish are mixed just as each comes from the gun. The gun is attached to an air hose, in addition to a quart container that has a special air-vent cap. This vent must be kept open at all times to allow air to create a suction.

The siphon gun operates as a result of the suction created in the cup as air passes through the gun. Only light and thin materials can be sprayed. The principles of feeding and mixing are shown in Fig. 123-6. A variety of sizes of spray heads, nozzles, and fluid needles can be obtained for a general-purpose gun (Fig. 123-7).

Other spraying equipment

The **compressor** takes air from the atmosphere, compresses it, and supplies the air pressure needed to operate a spray gun. Compressors may be large or small (Fig. 123-8). They may be portable (Fig. 123-9) or stationary (Fig. 123-10).

Air from the compressor should go into an **air transformer** (Fig. 123-11), where dust, oil, rust, and moisture are removed. These containers and the compressor should be drained of water frequently, and the filters should be cleaned or replaced as necessary.

The transformer is usually equipped with two gages. One shows compressor-tank pressure. Pressure is greater in the tank than on the spray gun, in order that the spraying pressure may be kept even. The other gage shows the lesser pressure, the pressure at which the spray gun is successfully and accurately operated for the material that is being sprayed.

Fig. 123-4 Finishing material is supplied to the gun through fluid hose lines connected to remote pumps or pressure-feed tanks.

Fig. 123-5 A typical suction-feed spray gun with container.

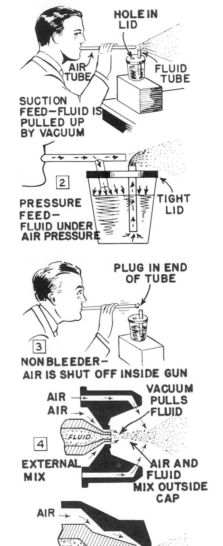

Fig. 123-6 Principles of feeding and mixing finishes in spraying.

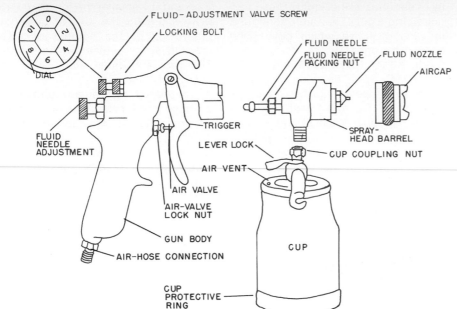

Fig. 123–7 Parts of the common suction spray gun.

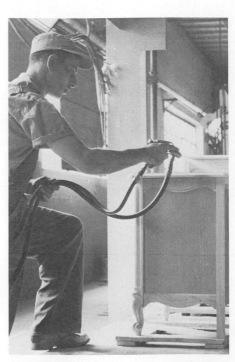

Fig. 123–11 Air transformers have gages to show pressure and filters to clean the air.

Fig. 123–8 A small compressor and spray-gun unit.

Fig. 123–9 A large portable spray finishing unit.

Fig. 123–10 A stationary compressor and tank.

A **hose** is connected from the transformer to the gun. The hose material should be of high quality so that it resists swelling or general disintegration that would clog the air passages in the gun. For production work, one hose may be used for air to the gun, another for finish materials (Fig. 123-12). Both hoses contain pressure.

The **suction cup** is attached to a suction-feed gun. Larger containers come in the **gravity** and the **pressure-feed** types; they force finishes to the gun.

Fig. 123–12 A hose for air and a hose for finish from a large container are connected to the spray gun in continuous spray-finishing operations.

Using a suction-feed spray gun

1. Finishing materials and the clean surface should be sprayed at room temperatures of more than 70°F (21°C). Finishes work best at a specified consistency, called their **viscosity.** A cupful of properly thinned material should flow from a spray gun in a designated number of seconds for best results, according to the manufacturer's specifications.

2. Strain finishes into the container through cheesecloth or fine window screen if there is any possibility of particles in the liquid. These particles clog a gun. They are often found in cans of finish which have been opened for previous use.

3. Attach the cup to the gun.

NOTE: Spray finishing should be done in a special dustfree area. A spray hood (Fig. 123-13) with exhaust makes an ideal location. Air should enter the area through a filter. It should be cleared properly by exhaust fans designed for that purpose.

4. Start the compressor, and let the air pressure increase. Open the air line to the regulator. Check the regulator to see that the pressure is somewhat greater than that needed at the gun. There will be an air loss that must be adjusted. The longer the air hose and the smaller the inside diameter, the greater the loss of pressure, regardless of the volume of compressed air generated by the system. The regulator must allow sufficient passage of air.

5. Adjust the regulator on the gun air-hose line for the pressure needed. Air pressures for spraying are given in Table 123-1.

6. Regulate the fluid-adjustment screw on the rear of the gun. The fluid-adjustment screw controls the amount of finishing material that leaves the gun.

7. Adjust the air cap to the proper externally mixed spray pattern. This could be either a spot or an elongated (elliptical) pattern (Fig. 123-14).

Fig. 123–13 Hoods help concentrate the spray mist to be exhausted from the spraying area.

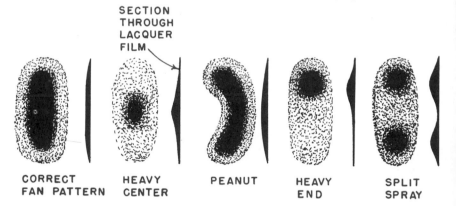

SECTION THROUGH LACQUER FILM

CORRECT FAN PATTERN   HEAVY CENTER   PEANUT   HEAVY END   SPLIT SPRAY

Fig. 123–14 Correct and faulty spray patterns.

Table 123-1 AIR-PRESSURE DROP PER SIZE AND LENGTH OF HOSE

Size of air hose, inside diameter	Air-pressure drop at spray gun					
	5-ft length, lb	10-ft length, lb	15-ft length, lb	20-ft length, lb	25-ft length, lb	50-ft length, lb
1/4 in. @						
40 lb pressure	6	8	$9\frac{1}{2}$	11	$12\frac{3}{4}$	24
50 lb pressure	$7\frac{1}{2}$	10	12	14	16	28
60 lb pressure	9	$12\frac{1}{2}$	$14\frac{1}{2}$	$16\frac{3}{4}$	19	31
70 lb pressure	$10\frac{3}{4}$	$14\frac{1}{2}$	17	$19\frac{1}{2}$	$22\frac{1}{2}$	34
80 lb pressure	$12\frac{1}{4}$	$16\frac{1}{2}$	$19\frac{1}{2}$	$22\frac{1}{2}$	$25\frac{1}{2}$	37
90 lb pressure	14	$18\frac{3}{4}$	22	$25\frac{1}{4}$	29	$39\frac{1}{2}$
5/16 in. @						
40 lb pressure	$2\frac{1}{4}$	$2\frac{3}{4}$	$3\frac{1}{4}$	$3\frac{1}{2}$	4	$8\frac{1}{2}$
50 lb pressure	3	$3\frac{1}{2}$	4	$4\frac{1}{2}$	5	10
60 lb pressure	$3\frac{3}{4}$	$4\frac{1}{2}$	5	$5\frac{1}{2}$	6	$11\frac{1}{2}$
70 lb pressure	$4\frac{1}{2}$	$5\frac{1}{4}$	6	$6\frac{3}{4}$	$7\frac{1}{4}$	13
80 lb pressure	$5\frac{1}{2}$	$6\frac{1}{4}$	7	8	$8\frac{3}{4}$	$14\frac{1}{2}$
90 lb pressure	$6\frac{1}{2}$	$7\frac{1}{2}$	$8\frac{1}{2}$	$9\frac{1}{2}$	$10\frac{1}{2}$	16

8. Test on scrap paper (Fig. 123-15), and perform steps 5, 6, and 7 until the proper spray is obtained.

9. Hold the spray gun 6 to 8 inches (152 to 203 mm) from the surface to be sprayed (Fig. 123-16). Pull the trigger, and make the spray stroke a continuous movement parallel to the surface (Fig. 123-17).

Runs and **sags** result when the gun is held too close, is moved too slowly, or is delivering too much fluid for the operator to control.

When the spray-gun nozzle is held too far from the surface, the material atomizes and too much mist is lost. This results in waste and leaves a cloudy, sandy finish that must be done over.

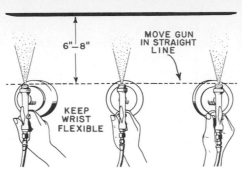

Fig. 123–17 Keep the spray gun parallel to the surface being sprayed. Swinging the gun in an arc gives uneven coating.

A deliberate, steady pass that leaves a full, wet coat is desired. Arching and tilting the gun are the two common faults that result in a streaky effect.

10. Corners of projects should be sprayed first (Fig. 123-18). Turn the project so that the gun is always perpendicular to the surface being sprayed (Fig. 123-19). Tilting allows finish to spill from the air vent and eventually will close it. This stopping up prevents operation until the opening is clear.

11. Move the gun to the corner of the project to be sprayed. As it reaches the leading corner or edge, pull the trigger, and release it near the end. Pull it for the next stroke, and release it at the end. This will prevent fatigue and overspraying. Leave flat surfaces to be done last.

12. Use a round spray pattern for table legs and similar round surfaces. When spraying curved surfaces, hold the gun the same way and at the same distance from the work (Fig. 123-20).

Fig. 123–19 Keep the spray gun perpendicular to the surface being sprayed.

Fig. 123–15 Testing a spray pattern before finishing an object.

Fig. 123–16 Gun must be proper distance from surface for best results.

Fig. 123–18 Corners of objects should be sprayed first.

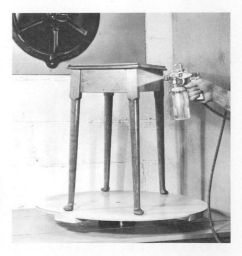

Fig. 123–20 The gun is held in the same way for spraying round work and for finishing other surfaces.

Follow the curvature of the surface (Fig. 123-21).

13. Study each project or object before spraying it. Decide what procedure will be the simplest and easiest, and will require the fewest passes of the gun. Use a round spray pattern on a narrow object or piece, a wide (elliptical) one on larger surfaces.

Cleaning the spray gun and shutting down equipment

The spray gun is a precision tool. It should be carefully handled and maintained. The fluid needle packing, the air-valve stem, and the trigger-bearing screw should have a drop of oil on them daily when the gun is in use. Clean the gun as follows:

1. Loosen the air cap slightly, and remove the cup.

2. Pull the gun trigger and release any material in the gun so that it flows back in the cup (Fig. 123-22).

3. Empty the cup, and clean it thoroughly.

4. Put about a cup of the correct thinner into a container. Spray the thinner to clear out the passageways (Fig. 123-23).

5. Remove the cap and tip. Clean them in the proper thinner as shown in Fig. 123-24.

6. Close the air line to the regulators. Bleed off all pressure on the valves and hose. Release the pressure on the regulator screws. These should read zero (0) pressure, indicating no compressed air in the hose.

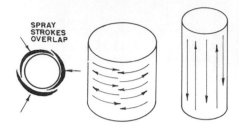

Fig. 123-21 Follow the shape of the object when spray finishing.

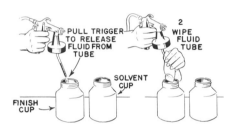

Fig. 123-22 Simple steps in cleaning a spray gun.

Fig.123-23 Spray thinner (cleaner) through the spray-gun passageways to clean out all finish material.

Fig. 123-24 Clean the cap, tip, and cup in thinner but do not put the whole gun in the cleaner.

unit 124

Bleaching, coloring, filling, and sealing woods

There are complete courses of study and a number of books on the many finishing products and procedures. Some of the more popular finishing treatments of wood are presented here.

Bleaching

It is sometimes difficult to remove spots and streaks in wood without causing injury to the wood fibers. Bleaches are often composed of strong chemicals. They require skin protection and utmost safety in use.

Because of their structure and coloring, ash, birch, oak, maple, mahogany, and walnut are easier to bleach than gum, pine, and poplar. Experiment on test strips of the wood (Fig. 124-1).

The use of **oxalic acid** and **sodium hypochlorite** as bleaching agents is widely accepted. **Borax** acts as an alkalizing agent, neutralizing, or counteracting, the acid (Fig. 124-2).

Oxalic acid can be obtained in white crystal form. Approximately 3 ounces (0.085 kg) dissolved in 1 quart (0.95 liters, ℓ) of hot water forms a mild bleaching agent.

The application of the oxalic acid solution is followed by application of sodium hypochlorite (ordinary household laundry bleach). It bleaches most woods several shades lighter. After the bleach has been applied and has dried, it should be neutralized: wash it off with a borax solution of about 1 ounce (0.003 kg) of borax per quart (0.95 ℓ) of water. All solutions are made with hot water, but they are cooled before they are put into use.

Commercial two-solution bleaches are usually the most satisfactory. There are several brands on the market, but only two are discussed briefly here. The manufacturer's instructions should be followed exactly.

A common **two-solution bleach** is **oxalic acid** and **sodium bisulfite.** Each is mixed separately in a 5 to 10 percent solution of water. The acid is applied by spray or brush and allowed to dry. The sodium bisulfite is then applied. Mixture of these two chemicals creates the bleach, **sulfur dioxide.**

Potassium permanganate is the second two-solution bleaching process. It is applied in a 2 to 10 percent solution for one or several coats, depending on the effect desired. A brown color appears and is cleared with a 5 to 10 percent solution of sodium bisulfite. To remove the salts of this chemical reaction, the wood is partially neutralized by sponging with clear water.

Most two-solution bleaches are basically alkaline. They have to be **neutralized** with a 5 to 15 percent **acetic acid** (vinegar) solution and then sponged with clear water. If the caustic salts are left on any part of the proj-ect, they will injure the finish when it is applied.

Allow at least 48 hours for final drying. The grain of the wood has been raised and must be smoothed. Sand it *lightly* to avoid cutting through the thin layer of bleached wood. Woods can be finished by any of the accepted methods after bleaching, neutralizing, drying, and sanding.

Blonding

Blond finishes are obtained by adding white lacquer to clear lacquer. A uniform light coat sprayed on wood as a sealer produces a blond color that does not obscure the wood grain (Fig. 124-3). This technique works very well on light woods, such as maple and birch.

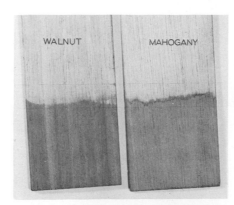

Fig. 124–1 Experiment on test strips of wood for best bleaching results.

Fig. 124–2 Common bleaching materials are available at most drugstores.

Staining

A stain is used to change the color of a surface, and it often emphasizes the beauty and grain of the wood. It is the first step in the finishing operation after finishing in the white.

Stain is used to match lighter woods with the predominant color and to change the color of the entire object. The lighter sap streaks in woods such as walnut can be stained to match the darker heartwood. Inexpensive woods can be stained to resemble walnut or other more expensive woods. Walnut, cedar, and cherry have sufficient natural color so that they do not require stain.

Some furniture (Fig. 124-4) is stained to give the popular colonial maple color. There is no fixed tone for

Fig. 124–3 Blond sealers: add one part white lacquer to five parts clear.

Fig. 124–4 Typical furniture style finished with colonial maple stain.

this maple furniture, however. Necessary materials are shown in Fig. 124-5. The orange-brown antique color is most frequently used. A touch of orange to any medium-brown stain gives the antique maple color.

The object is stained and sealed with a wash coat of orange shellac. A second coat of wiping stain is applied and then wiped, leaving the antique effect. Other finish coats are added to build up the finish.

Many special stains are available in numerous colors. They are divided into four groups: (1) water, (2) oil, (3) spirit, and (4) non-grain-raising (NGR) (see Fig. 124-6).

Water stain comes in concentrated powder form. Water-soluble colors (usually aniline dyes) are dissolved in hot water. Use a glass or enamel container to mix this stain. Water stain penetrates deeply, gives greater transparency, has less tendency to fade, and does not bleed into coats of finish. It does raise the grain, and with a brush or by wiping it is hard to apply without streaking.

Spraying is the best method of application. Raising the grain one or more times and sanding or applying a shellac wash coat before application of the stain help eliminate the necessity for resanding.

These powders can be made into non-grain-raising stains. Use less hot water, and then bring the mixture to proper strength by adding alcohol or special solvents. The usual procedure for water staining is shown by steps in Fig. 124-7.

Oil stains are usually classified as **pigmented,** or **wiping** (ground or mixed in oil), and **penetrating** (soluble in benzol, naphtha, or turpentine). They can be purchased either in powder or ready-mixed forms (Fig. 124-8).

Penetrating oil stains are often used to color wood filler. A thin solution of this filler-stain mixture is sometimes rubbed into the wood to stain and fill simultaneously. For the best quality work, this dual operation is not recommended, especially because oil stain normally penetrates wood less effectively than many other stains.

Oil stains do not raise wood grain, and they are relatively easy to apply to a uniform color. All excess stain should be removed because it bleeds.

Fig. 124–5 Necessary materials for finishing in colonial maple.

Fig. 124–6 Powder stains that are soluble in water, oil, alcohol, and lacquer thinner can be purchased.

Pigmented (wiping) stains are better than the penetrating stains because they fade less.

Apply a coat of boiled linseed oil to all exposed end grain *before* staining. This produces a uniform color when the stain is put on.

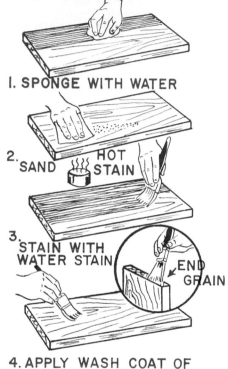

1. SPONGE WITH WATER

2. SAND   HOT STAIN

3. STAIN WITH WATER STAIN   END GRAIN

4. APPLY WASH COAT OF SHELLAC

Fig. 124–7 Steps in the use of water stains.

Fig. 124–8 Applying a ready-mixed penetrating stain.

Spirit stains are mostly aniline dyes that are soluble in alcohol. They are difficult to apply evenly, they fade quickly in sunlight, they bleed, and they cut through most finishes. Because they penetrate easily, they are popular for use in refinishing old furniture.

Staining for refinishing

1. Remove the old finish with a prepared remover and steel wool (Fig. 124-9). A wood file, emery cloth, and steel wool are used to remove finish and clean in close places (Fig. 124-10).

2. Sand all areas with wet-dry sandpaper.

3. Mix a penetrating stain. Test for the desired color on scrap wood (Fig. 124-11) or on the bottom of the project (Fig. 124-12).

4. Apply the stain with a brush to all parts of the object.

5. Remove all excess stain before it dries (Fig. 124-13).

Shading and highlighting

Shading is done by spraying or wiping shading materials on the finished work and wiping it off to give a highlighted or aged (antique) appearance. Wiping or shading stains, tinting colors, and shading lacquers are common materials (Fig. 124-14). Dye is often added to clear lacquer or varnish for use over sealer coats to give a uniform transparent color. Spray shad-

Fig. 124–10 Several items are necessary to remove an old finish or to smooth irregular surfaces.

Fig. 124–13 Remove excess stain before it dries.

Fig. 124–11 Mixing and testing stains on scrap wood.

Fig. 124–12 Matching a stain color on the unexposed surface of the project to be stained.

Fig. 124–14 Common shading materials.

Fig. 124–9 Removing an old finish.

253

ing is used to give a uniform overall tone to make different species of woods look the same (Fig. 124-15).

When pigment instead of dye is added to varnish or lacquer, the finish becomes opaque. Opaque enamels cover the grain, giving a painted effect.

Bone white is a typical **shaded finish** (Fig. 124-16). When the white color is dry, spray on a coat of wiping stain (Fig. 124-17). Wipe off before the stain reaches the tacky (sticky) stage. This leaves **highlights** (Fig. 124-18). Highlighting is also done by sanding spots with steel wool or abrasive paper, blending wiping stain with a brush, or detail shading with a special spray gun (Fig. 124-19).

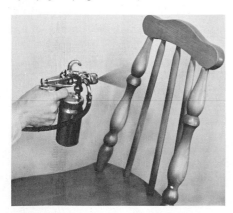

Fig. 124–15 Spray shading to produce a uniform color.

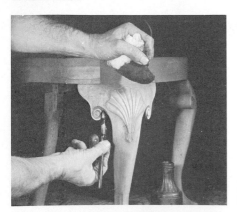

Fig. 124–16 Shading stain applied by brush is used to bring out the beauty of wood. *Kittenger Co.*

Filling

Most of the materials used to fill and seal wood pores are shown in Fig. 124-20. Only two or three, however, are used in one finishing operation.

After thorough sanding, and also after staining when desired, the most

Fig. 124–17 A wiping stain may be sprayed to highlight a bone-white finish.

Fig. 124–18 Wiping off excess stain and leaving a highlight effect.

important operation in obtaining an excellent built-up finish on open-grain woods is the application of a good filler. Filler is *not* a coat of finish; it is a material that fills the pores of the wood.

Wood filler is a product made from **silex,** a ground quartz (flint)

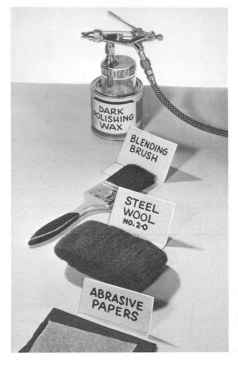

Fig. 124–19 Other materials used for highlighting.

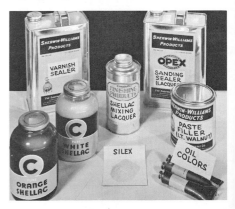

Fig. 124–20 Common filling and sealing materials.

silica mixed with a drier, a solvent (thinner), and a vehicle. Silex and boiled linseed oil were the main ingredients of the older fillers. Small amounts of japan drier and turpentine were added, and wood flour replaced silex, making a different filler.

Two types of filler for wood pores are paste and liquid. **Paste filler** dries slowly because of the linseed oil it contains. It can be thinned as desired with the oil and turpentine, but it requires from 12 to 48 hours of drying time (depending on the oil content) before a sealer should be applied. The oil has a tendency to expand and provides a good lubricant in filler application, and it helps enrich the natural color of the wood.

A shellac sealer coat is the best kind to use over this type of oil-paste filler because lacquer-type sealers tend to check and have an "orange-peel" texture if the filler is not perfectly dry. Some craftsmen prefer to apply a **wash coat** of shellac (1 part shellac to 6 or 7 parts alcohol) *before* filling wood that has very large pores, such as mahogany and ash.

Newer paste fillers are very fast drying because of their synthetic resinbase vehicles. A good general-purpose thinner for most of these fillers is **varnishmakers and painters naphtha** (VM&P naphtha). A minimum drying time of 2 hours is suggested, depending on the driers and reducers (thinners) used to thin the paste or liquid.

Liquid filler is usually made from varnish and a small amount of silex. It is often used on inexpensive work in medium close-grain woods. A thin paste filler is more satisfactory for all work, however.

The following procedure is useful in properly filling the pores for natural colors or toned effects:

1. Apply a wash coat of shellac over stain, or natural-colored woods with large pores (ash, oak, mahogany), before filling.

2. Thin the filler to a workable consistency. Color or tint it as necessary. For example, a white-tinted filler accents the beautiful grains of oak and ash (Fig. 124-21).

3. Apply filler *with* the grain to 1 or 2 square feet (0.093 to 0.186 m²), or to one piece, of a project at a time (Fig. 124-22). Use a cloth or a brush.

4. Let the filler dry until it has a dull appearance. *Do not* allow the filler to dry on top of wood surfaces. It will harden and often require scraping and sanding to remove.

5. Rub the filler across the grain, using burlap, coarse rags, or the palm of your hand (Fig. 124-23). Apply ample pressure to push the filler to the bottom of the pore holes. Filler that catches only in the top portion of the pores may drop or wash out when dry, especially during brush finishing. Air that is trapped in pores that are not completely filled may break through the finish, causing bubbles and blisters in the surface finish coats.

6. Rub flat surfaces across the grain with clean burlap or excelsior (wood wool). This both removes most of the surplus filler and works it more deeply into the pores (Fig. 124-24).

7. Remove surplus filler from all corners, using a cloth, a stick, or a putty knife (Fig. 124-25).

Fig. 124–22   Brush on filler with the wood grain.

Fig. 124–23   Rub, or "pad in," filler across the grain.

Fig. 124–21   White-tinted filler produces an accent on oak and ash grain patterns.

Fig. 124–24   Remove all surplus filler.

8. Use cheesecloth or any other soft fabric to wipe with the grain to remove streaks and all remaining filler on the surface (Fig. 124-26).

9. Allow the filler in the pores to dry thoroughly before completing the remaining finishing operations.

Sealing

Close-grain woods do not require fillers. They do, however, need a sealer coat on which to build a finish. Open-grain woods require a sealer after filler has been rubbed in.

One sealing coat or more are used. They prevent bleeding of the stains or fillers and seal (close) pores and fibers, making a good base for subsequent finish coats. As the first coat of the finish, sealers prevent moisture absorption as well as absorption of other finish coats.

Lacquer sealers and **shellac** are common sealing materials. Both can be brushed or sprayed. Shellac is available in cuts (mixtures) ranging from 2 to 12 pounds (0.907 to 5.443 kg). A common grade is termed **four-pound cut**. This means that 4 pounds (1.814 kg) of lac resin are dissolved in 1 gallon (3.785 ℓ) of alcohol. One part of four-pound cut shellac to three parts alcohol or a mixture of half al-

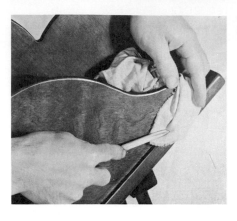

Fig. 124–25 A piece of wood (picking stick) wrapped in a soft cloth will help remove surplus filler from corners.

cohol and half shellac (two-pound cut) can be easily brushed or sprayed.

Because oil-base materials tend to bleed, a *shellac* sealer should be used over all oil-base stains and fillers. This sealer coat should dry at least 2 hours. Varnish sealers should dry overnight before they are sanded.

Fig. 124–26 Use a soft cloth and rub with the wood grain to remove all streaks and remaining filler from surface.

unit 125

Applying oil and wax finishes

Wax that is used as a finish or as a polish to protect other finishes must be renewed periodically to keep a shining surface. It cannot withstand water or excessive heat.

Carnauba (Brazilian) wax is the most important natural polishing agent. It is obtained from a species of palm tree growing in Brazil. It is the hardest of the natural waxes, melting at 185°F (85°C). Carnauba wax is usually mixed with other waxes, such as beeswax (a fairly hard wax produced by honey bees), ceresine (a hard hydrocarbon wax), or paraffin (a soft wax obtained from petroleum), to make it softer and easier to use.

Turpentine is the most common solvent or thinner for waxes.

Raw **linseed oil** is extracted from crushed flax seed. It often takes raw linseed oil a week to dry, but it leaves a tough film on wood. Linseed oil for furniture finishing is kettle-boiled to emulsify (mix smoothly) the film-forming particles. This oil dries in 12 to 24 hours.

Oil or oil-and-wax finishes are used to obtain a beautiful surface on walnut, cedar, and dark-red cherry woods. This attractive finish does not necessarily depend on the amount of oil used; rather it depends on repeated rubbings between coats. This finish is popular on dark-colored antique furniture. It does not offer the protection of other finishes, however, and many days are required to secure a beautiful sheen (gloss). Stains bleed through, so they are not recommended under an oil finish.

Oil finish

1. Remove dust from the wood surfaces.

2. *Very carefully* heat a mixture of one or two parts boiled linseed oil and

one part turpentine. Heat in a double boiler, because both are highly flammable.

3. Apply the heated mixture with a soft cloth tied to a dowel or some other piece of wood. Use only enough oil to soak readily into the wood. Wipe off the surplus.

4. Allow the oil coat to dry about 15 minutes.

5. Rub briskly with a lintfree, rough-textured cloth until the surface shines brightly.

6. Be sure to let the surfaces dry two or more days before repeating steps 3 and 4.

7. Between five and ten applications may be needed before a beautiful sheen glows on the surface. Brisk rubbing and thorough drying of each coat are essential to obtain the proper oil finish.

Oil and beeswax finish

1. Cut about 1 ounce (0.454 kg) of beeswax into fine shavings. Put the shavings into ½ pint (0.4732 ℓ) of turpentine. Let the mixture stand overnight.

2. Heat the mixture. Observe the safety precaution given in step 2 under "Oil Finish."

3. When the mixture is warm, stir in about ½ pint (0.4732 ℓ) of boiled linseed oil. *Heat over hot water* until all the wax is dissolved.

4. Carefully apply a thin coat of the hot beeswax-turpentine mixture to the wood. Use a brush or a soft cloth to apply the mixture. Rub the surface hard with a soft cloth.

5. Let the wood dry 12 hours or more.

6. Reheat the solution. Repeat step 4 several times. The wax and oil tend to fill the pores on open-grain woods. Hard rubbing of each coat and the careful removal of excess wax is the secret of producing a beautiful satin finish when using oil and beeswax.

unit 126

Applying a shellac finish

Lac resins are dissolved in special formulas of denatured alcohol to form shellac in its natural orange color. White shellac is made by bleaching the resins. The cloudy appearance is caused by the natural wax in the shellac. When this wax is taken out, a transparent, or clear, shellac results, which is called **French varnish**. Shellac is actually a **spirit varnish**.

Shellac finish

1. Remove dust from all surfaces. Be sure that the stain or filler is thoroughly dry.

2. Pour some shellac into a container. Mix with an even amount of alcohol to make a thin mixture.

3. Remove drawers and other removable parts of the piece. All removable parts of the work are to be finished separately.

4. Brush (Fig. 126-1) or spray on the first coat of shellac. Begin at the top; work toward the bottom of vertical surfaces. Leave the top horizontal surface to the last. Apply the mixture from one side of a piece to the other. Shellac dries rapidly. Apply the coat evenly and quickly, with as little overlapping as possible.

5. Allow the coat to dry for 2 to 6 hours.

6. When it is dry, rub this coat of finish smooth with No. 2/0 or No. 3/0 steel wool. Rub *with* the grain if possible. Smooth each coat. Do not rub through the shellac on edges and corners.

7. Succeeding coats should dry longer. Dilute the shellac from the container by adding one-fourth alcohol. Very soft woods and those with large pores may require three to six coats to obtain a satisfactory built-up shellac finish.

8. The final coat should dry 8 to 10 hours. Sand it smooth with No. 500 wet-dry paper and rubbing oil. *Do not use water as a rubbing lubricant because it will turn the shellac white.* The final coat may also be rubbed lightly with steel wool.

Apply a coat of good paste wax. Allow the wax to dull, and then rub it briskly to a luster. Use a soft cotton cloth.

Fig. 126–1 Applying shellac with a brush.

unit 127

Applying a varnish finish

Varnish has the excellent qualities of transparent depth, durability, and hardness. It dries slowly and requires a dustfree area both when it is being applied and while it is drying.

Materials in varnish

Materials in varnish include resins or gums, oils, turpentine (for thinning), and drying agents.

Resins or **gums** are the solid portion of varnish, giving the film hardness and luster. They vary in hardness and are blended for each particular kind of varnish. Originally, all good varnishes used imported fossilized gums. Recent developments have produced varnishes based on synthetic (man-made) resins that dry more quickly.

Oils serve as vehicles in varnish. Oil from tung nuts of the Chinawood tree and linseed oil act as binders for the resins, giving the varnish film elasticity (stretch). Larger amounts of oil make the film tougher, more durable, and more water resistant.

Turpentine is the solvent used for thinning varnish (Fig. 127-1) so that it can be sprayed with light equipment or brushed. Turpentine dries by evaporation.

Drying agents are made from oils and from salts of various metals. They speed up the drying process of the vehicle or of the oils. Japan drier, for example, is a compound of lead or manganese salts.

Types of varnish

Varnish formulas are available in three general classifications, according to oil content: long-oil, medium-oil, and short-oil varnishes. There is no all-purpose varnish, but several kinds take care of most requirements (Fig. 127-2). This finish is called **oleoresinous** because it is essentially a mixture of oils and resins.

Long-oil varnishes include spar varnish. As much as 100 pounds (45.36 kg) of oil can be mixed with an equal amount of resins. This varnish is recommended for exterior surfaces that are exposed to water and weather. Spar varnish is slightly darker, it is slow drying, and it gives a moderate gloss. It requires 12 to 24 hours to dry.

Fig. 127–1 Turpentine is the correct thinner for varnish.

Medium-oil varnishes are floor-type finishes. They contain up to 40 pounds (18.14 kg) of oils per 100 pounds (45.36 kg) of resin. They are harder and dry faster than the spar type. Normal drying time is 12 hours.

Short-oil varnishes include rubbing, pale rubbing, and polishing varnishes. They contain up to 10 or 12 pounds (4.5 to 5.4 kg) of oils per 100 pounds (45.36 kg) of resin. Polishing varnish contains hard resins, takes a high polish, and rubs and sands clean without gumming. Drying time is 24 to 48 hours.

Special varnishes are made in several types for specific uses. **Table-top** varnish is very hard; it is heat- and waterproof. The drying time is about 18 hours. Bar-top varnish, often referred to as **bakelite** varnish, is similar to table-top varnish, but it is usually synthetic, drying hard in about 4 hours. Mild acids, water, and alcohol do not affect it. Flat varnish is for interior use, drying to a dull finish in about 12 hours. **Dammar** varnish is a colorless spirit varnish, used in photography. It is quick drying (2 hours), but it is softer and less durable than the others. **Mastic** varnish is made from aromatic resins of a small mediterranean evergreen tree. It is similar to

Fig. 127–2 Several kinds of varnish.

Fig. 127-3 Drawers should be removed before finishing a chest.

Fig. 127-4 Clean out corners carefully with a soft brush before varnishing.

Fig. 127-5 Tack cloths clean the project of dust and other particles.

Fig. 127-6 One method of safely heating varnish.

Fig. 127-7 Extreme care should be used when varnish is heated.

dammar varnish in use and characteristics.

Shellac is the most important and best known of the three spirit varnishes. The others: dammar and mastic.

Tack cloths in varnish finishing

Cleanliness in finishing is an absolute necessity to obtain quality results. A **tack cloth** helps clean the project or piece. This is a chemically treated piece of cheesecloth prepared for this specific use. It picks up particles of steel wool, dirt, lint, and sanding dust that an ordinary dry cloth does not.

If a commercially treated tack cloth is not available, make one from a lintfree soft cotton cloth. Soak the piece in warm water, wring it out lightly, and sprinkle it with turpentine. Pour about 2 teaspoons (10 milliliters, mℓ) of varnish on it; fold, twist, and wring the cloth nearly dry. To keep tack cloths in good condition, sprinkle them lightly with water and turpentine. Store tack cloths in an airtight jar or container.

Varnishing

1. Remove the drawers and separate parts to finish separately (Fig. 127-3). Dust all parts carefully with a soft brush (Fig. 127-4), particularly the corners. Carry the project to a very clean finishing room, where the varnishing is to be done.

2. **Tacking** is the final dusting operation. Use a tack cloth (Fig. 127-5) to pick up all remaining dirt and dust from the project.

3. Varnish can be thinned and sprayed. It is somewhat difficult to spray varnish so that it does not run or ripple. Heating it in a double boiler before spraying will lessen this possibility (Figs. 127-6 and 127-7). The flow is increased, and the mixture sets more quickly. However, sometimes spraying varnish does not allow sufficient time for proper tipping (see step 8).

Varnish can be applied over shellac or lacquer, but do not apply lacquer over varnish. The ingredients in the two finishes do not mix, and the finish will raise and peel.

4. If you brush on varnish, do not use it directly from the can (Fig. 127-8). Use an aluminum saucepan about 4 inches (102 mm) across and 2 inches (51 mm) deep to hold the varnish. Add a wire to the pan on which to strike the brush to remove excess varnish (Fig. 127-9). Cut the handle of this pan, and fold it over to form a loop (Fig. 127-10).

5. Pour a small amount of varnish into the pan. Do not shake the can or stir the contents. Bubbles are formed that will be carried by the brush onto the surfaces being varnished. A brush should be dipped into the varnish only a little over one-third the length of the bristles (Fig. 127-11).

6. The first step in brushing technique is **lining in,** or **cutting in** (Fig. 127-12). Start at the corners of the piece and brush toward the center. Varnish flows best in the temperature range of 70 to 90° F (21 to 32° C).

7. The second step is to apply a full coat by **cross brushing.** Begin at either side and brush toward the middle (Fig. 127-13). Brush from the second side, and lift the brush as soon as the strokes overlap. Cross brushing is usually omitted on top surfaces because the varnish flows together smoothly.

8. The third step is **tipping.** Wipe the brush on the wire, and then use only the tip to finish lightly with the grain (Fig. 127-14).

Fig. 127–12 Line-in, or border, the areas with varnish.

Fig. 127–8 Varnish should not be used directly from the can.

Fig. 127–10 Form the handle to make the container easy to hold.

Fig. 127–13 Cross-brush with a full coat of varnish.

Fig. 127–9 A wire through the container makes an excellent strikeoff bar to remove excess varnish from the brush.

Fig. 127–11 Dip the brush into the varnish about one-third the length of the bristles.

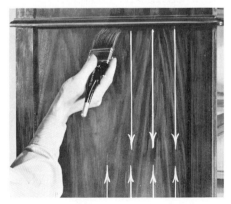

Fig. 127–14 Tipping is smoothing the varnish with the bristle tips.

Use a smaller brush to finish edges. This prevents the bristles from spreading over onto the top surface. Turned parts are brushed around and around to eliminate sagging, especially on sharp parts.

9. As the work progresses, pick out any dust particles that show up on surfaces. Do this with either a sliver of wood or a ball of burnt varnish on the end of a stick (Fig. 127-15). Do not wait until the varnish becomes tacky (sticky). Most bubbles will disappear as the varnish sets (dries).

Pour all unused varnish into another container to store. Never pour unused portions back into the original can because it may have accumulated dust and other particles.

10. Allow each varnish coat to dry completely before the next one is applied. In damp weather more than 2 days may be needed for drying. The usual time is around 36 to 48 hours, but some varnishes dry hard in 4 to 6 hours. When the varnish coat resists the impression of the thumbnail, it is ready to rub or is ready for another coat (Fig. 127-16).

Each coat of varnish should be sanded lightly with very fine wet-dry finishing paper. A milky appearance will remain after rubbing until the next coat is put on. If surfaces have been properly sanded, filled as needed, and sealed carefully, two coats of varnish should give a good surface. Better quality work will need three or four coats.

11. When the final coat has dried hard, complete the finishing according to the procedure in Unit 131, Rubbing and Polishing Finishes.

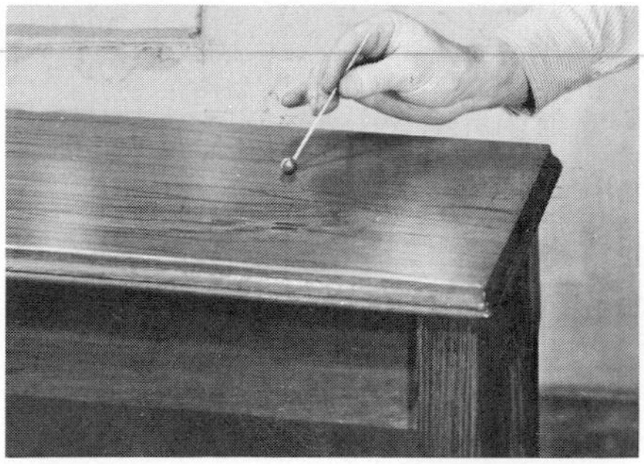

Fig. 127–15 Remove all dust and particles from the surfaces before the varnish dries.

Fig. 127–16 Test the varnish coat with the thumbnail for dryness before applying another coat.

unit 128

Applying a lacquer finish

Most lacquer is synthetic, being made by treating nitrocellulose (cotton and certain wood fibers) with nitric and sulfuric acid. A clear, water-white lacquer is produced when the materials are blended with suitable solvents. Mixtures of various quantities of certain chemicals, gums, and resins make possible synthetic lacquers with any characteristic desired.

Lacquers are relatively low in cost and are durable, transparent, and hard. They can be purchased in acid resistant and waterproof forms. A lacquer coat dries dustfree in a matter of a few minutes and dries hard in 30 minutes to 2 hours.

At least 250 synthetic resins have been developed. Finishes in this classification represent a wide variety of products. Some materials for lacquer finishing are displayed in Fig. 128-1.

Lacquers

A few of the many lacquers are (1) gloss, (2) semigloss, (3) flat, (4) water white, (5) rubbing and polishing bar top, (6) bronzing, (7) shading, and (8) novelty.

Thinners for one brand or type of lacquer may not work with another. Consult the person selling thinner or

Fig. 128–1 Common materials for lacquer finishing.

the manufacturer to get the correct ones.

Basic lacquer finishing differs very little from the varnish schedule. The wood is stained, if desired, and filled as needed; then lacquer is used instead of varnish. The proper lacquers can be secured for brushing or spraying on either wood or metal. Spraying is more common than brushing. See Unit 123, Spray Finishing.

Spraying tips

1. Thin lacquer only when the directions on the can call for thinning.

2. Make a test spray pattern, and adjust the spray gun properly. A heavy, wet center surrounded by globs means orange peel, poor atomizing, and breaking up of lacquer. Correct this by thinning the lacquer, increasing the air pressure, and possibly by cutting the fluid feed.

Peanut-shaped or heavy-end patterns indicate a dirty gun. Clean the air cap, or remove the obstruction from the fluid needle tip.

The split spray is caused by too much air pressure (see Fig. 123-14).

Lacquer finishing

The lacquer finish should be preceded by the basic procedures of sanding, staining, and filling. This depends on the type of wood and the kind of finish desired.

1. Apply a coat of sanding sealer, or use thinned shellac as a sealer. See Unit 124, Bleaching, Coloring, Filling, and Sealing Woods, and Unit 126, Applying a Shellac Finish.

2. Sand with No. 220 dry garnet paper when the sealer has dried.

3. Spray on two to four coats of lacquer. Allow $1\frac{1}{2}$ to 2 hours for each coat to dry. Sand lightly between coats with No. 220 dry garnet paper. See Unit 123. Spray Finishing, for details.

4. Let the final coat dry at least 24 hours before rubbing and polishing.

unit 129

Applying paints, enamels, and decorative finishes

Paints and enamels cover, protect, and beautify woods when natural, clear finishes are not desirable or appropriate. Paint is used on both exterior and interior surfaces. Linseed oil and other ingredients are used as vehicles for paint. Varnish or lacquer and synthetics colored with pigments are the bases for enamel.

Painting and enameling

1. Clean all surfaces thoroughly. Sand if necessary.

2. Read and follow the manufacturer's directions on the can for mixing, thinning, and applying. Numerous color mixtures can be blended at local supply sources (Fig. 129-1). A primer coat may be needed to seal wood pores before other coats are applied.

3. Shake the can vigorously to mix all ingredients thoroughly. If the paint is not completely mixed, pour some of the top solution into another container.

4. Stir the base mixture in the can until it is smooth. Gradually blend in the top solution. A drill press with a stirring device in the chuck is useful in mixing paint (Fig. 129-2).

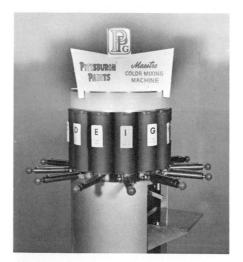

Fig. 129–1 A typical color mixing and blending machine.

Fig. 129–2 A stirring device in the chuck of a drill press makes mixing paint easier.

5. Select a good brush of suitable size. Dip about one-third of the bristle length into the finish. Strike (press) off excess paint.

6. Apply the paint or enamel with long, smooth strokes. Start at the top and work down on vertical surfaces (Fig. 129-3). Paint the inside areas first, and then exterior sides, front, and top (Fig. 129-4).

Start painting across the grain. Finish brushing with the grain. Do not allow the material to run, but keep sufficient paint on the brush to cover smoothly and evenly.

7. Allow the coat to dry according to the directions. Sand lightly between coats, but do not sand the final coat. Use No. 220 garnet or flint paper if more than one coat is applied.

Decorative finishes

Flock is the name of pulverized wool, silk, cotton, rayon, or nylon used to decorate surfaces. Various colored powders and other materials can also be used. Short fibers are used most, but fibers are available in lengths from $1/64$ to $1/2$ inch (0.4 to 13 mm).

Brush or spray varnish or enamel on the surface to be flocked (Fig. 129-5). Apply the flock to the tacky (sticky) surface by blowing through a special container (Fig. 129-6) or sifting (Fig. 129-7).

Stencils are often made and painted, stippled, or flocked to add decoration (Figs. 129-8 and 129-9).

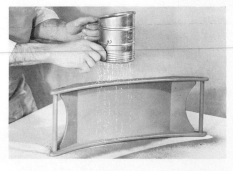

Fig. 129–7 Sifting flock on a surface.

Fig. 129–8 Spraying paint through a stencil to decorate a wall.

Fig. 129–5 Spraying on varnish or enamel in preparation for flocking.

Fig. 129–3 Begin at the top and paint down on vertical surfaces.

Fig. 129–6 Blowing on flock.

Fig. 129–9 Interesting designs can be painted on furniture by using stencils.

Fig. 129–4 Paint the top last and keep sufficient paint on the brush to prevent dragging.

Textured walls are adaptable to many styles of attractive decorative effects. Oil- or water-base paint is brushed on a wall. This heavy-body (thick) paint should be $1/16$ to $1/8$ inch (1.5 to 3 mm) thick. A wood float is applied to the surface and pulled straight back to give a pleasing texture (Fig. 129-10).

Troweling this surface flattens the points to produce a milder effect (Fig. 129-11). Two-tone effects are obtained by going over this same surface with a contrasting color (Fig. 129-12).

Spattering is a technique that uses a special spray-gun nozzle or brush.

Load the brush with paint, and strike the brush sharply against your hand or a stick (Fig. 129-13). Several different spatters of blending colors, applied in successive coats, are attractive on some surfaces.

A spatter variation is obtained by brushing a regular pattern lightly with a brush after the paint has set slightly. Figure 129-14 shows a two-tone spatter being spread.

Fig. 129–13 A spattering technique using a brush.

 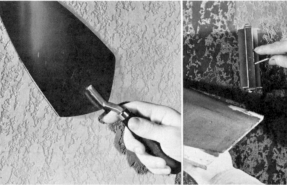 

Fig. 129–10 A float produces a textured finish (left).
Fig. 129–11 A trowel smooths a textured finish to produce another effect (center).
Fig. 129–12 A roller can be used to apply a two-tone color to textured walls (right).

Fig. 129–14 Smoothing a spattered two-tone finish.

unit **130**

Applying a penetrating finish

Penetrating finishes are made thin so that they can be absorbed into the pores of the wood. A wear-resistant, natural appearance is the feature of this type of finish. Several coats build up a satisfactory surface. It is an easy finish to apply because it can be brushed, sprayed, or wiped on.

Wiping on a penetrating finish

1. Prepare the wood as in other finishing operations.

2. Pour a small amount of the finish into an open container.

3. Apply generously with a cloth. Wipe off excess liquid with a dry cloth after the penetrating finish has set 10 or 15 minutes.

4. Allow the first coat to dry overnight; then rub it carefully with fine steel wool.

5. If desired, open-grain wood may be filled before a second coat of finish is put on. Two to four coats make a durable surface. Rub each coat with steel wool; under normal conditions, allow 2 to 4 hours between coats. Finishes dry more slowly in cool, damp air than they do in warm, dry air.

6. Smooth the last coat with fine steel wool.

7. Apply a coat of furniture wax. Polish.

Rubbing and polishing finishes

Smoothing the finish between under-coats makes a uniform surface to

Fig. 131–1 Some of the many materials used for rubbing and polishing.

which the final coat adheres evenly. Rubbing the final coat eliminates imperfections, dust specks, and ripples. A perfectly smooth, glass-like surface is obtained.

Study Fig. 131-1 and Tables 131-1 and 131-2 for rubbing schedules and rubbing and polishing materials.

Rubbing and polishing

1. Rub the first coat with dry abrasive. Use No. 360 or No. 400 **wet-dry silicon carbide** paper. Tear a standard sheet into four pieces. Rub these small pieces together to dull the grit (Fig. 131-2).

2. Rub the second and succeeding coats, up to the final one, with No. 400 or No. 500 wet-dry silicon carbide paper (Fig. 131-3). **Steel wool** (No. 2/0) is excellent for rubbing shellac (Fig. 131-4).

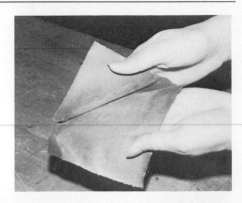

Fig. 131–2 Finishing abrasive papers are rubbed together to dull the grit.

Fig. 131–3 Sand between coats with fine sandpaper or with No. 5/0 or 6/0 garnet paper.

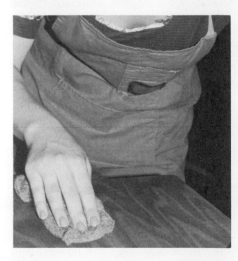

Fig. 131–4 Steel wool is an excellent rubbing material for shellac finishes.

Table 131-1 RUBBING SCHEDULES   *Rockwell International*

Varnish	flat	First coat, 220 garnet finishing paper, dry. Second coat, No. 1/2 or 1 pumice and water. Third coat, No. FF pumice with water or oil.
	satin	Same as above, but third (last) coat No. FF pumice with water, followed by rottenstone and oil or No. 4F pumice and oil.
	polished	Sand filler with No. 180 dry garnet. First varnish coat, No. 220 dry garnet. Second coat, No. 500 wet-dry paper with water. Third coat, same. Final coat rubbed as follows: 1. FF pumice and water 2. Rottenstone and water 3. Clean with benzene; let dry 24 hours 4. Rub with polishing oil 5. Spirit-off with denatured alcohol
Shellac	flat satin polished	Same as above but No. 00 steel wool for all undercoats and oil rub for finish.
	satin	Scuff all undercoats with 220 paper. Sand final coat with 600 waterproof paper with naphtha.
	polished	Follow above with lacquer rubbing compound. Remove compound haze, and polish with lacquer polish.

Table 131-2 RUBBING AND POLISHING MATERIALS

Rockwell International

Rubbing felt	One piece of soft pressed felt, 1/2 by 3 by 5 in. for general rubbing. Several smaller pieces.
Abrasive papers	Grits 400 and finer, waterproof garnet (for varnish), or waterproof silicon carbide (lacquer or varnish).
Pumice	No. 1 for coarse rubbing; Nos. FF and FFF for fine rubbing.
Rottenstone	For fine rubbing.
Rubbing oil	Lubricant for rubbing. Purchased ready mixed. Paraffin oil, crude petroleum, or light motor oil thinned with benzene can be used.
Naphtha	Also sold as benzene. Used for cleaning up rubbing slush.
Polishing oil	For obtaining high polish after rubbing. Purchased ready mixed. Typical formula is half olive oil (sweet oil) and half denatured alcohol. Standard furniture polishes can be used.
Lacquer rubbing compound	For rubbing lacquer. In paste form, ready mixed.
Lacquer polish	For cleaning up compound haze. A large number of ready mixed products are available.
Alcohol	Used to spirit-off polishing oil. Should be denatured (grain) alcohol of average paint-store grade.

Wet-dry silicon carbide paper and a lubricant are used on lacquer and varnish finishes. *Oil* should *always* be used to lubricate shellac, *never water.* Water is the easiest lubricant to use for finishes (except shellac). Back the paper with a felt or cork pad (Fig. 131-5). Using a felt or cork backing pad with the polishing materials helps to obtain a smooth, level surface. Rub the surface with the grain of the wood as much as possible.

3. Clean the rubbed surface with a slightly damp chamois or some other soft cloth. Rub spots that need additional smoothing.

4. Grades No. 2F to 4F pumice are used for the first rubbing of the final coat of varnish. Use a small sifter-top can (such as a saltshaker) to sprinkle generous amounts of pumice powder on the surface. Wet the powder and make a paste mixture. Keep it wet to prevent balls of fresh abrasive from forming and scratching the surface that has been rubbed. Rub the surface with the grain of the wood as much as possible.

5. Lacquer is harder to cut than varnish, and the final coat can be sanded with No. 600 to No. 800 **waterproof paper** backed with heavy felt lubricated generously with water. Naphtha can also be used as the lubricant on lacquer for a beautiful satin finish.

6. Occasionally, wipe a clean place with the side of your hand to inspect the rubbed surface. After all the areas are rubbed, clean with water and a soft cloth or chamois.

Remove the slush from all corners and recesses by using a cloth or a sliver of wood.

7. Repeat the rubbing operation, this time using rottenstone with oil for the lubricant. Rottenstone polishes but does not cut.

Rub the mixture with your fingers, the heel of your hand, a sponge, or a soft cloth. After the final rubbing, clean with water and, finally, with a soft cloth dampened with benzene (naphtha).

8. Apply one coat of a high-grade furniture wax. Let the surface become dull (about 10 minutes). Rub to a high sheen (Fig. 131-6) with a soft cloth. Apply wax only to a small area at a time. Let the polished wax dry several hours. Repeat the operation with one or more coats.

Fig. 131–5 Back rubbing and polishing materials with a felt pad.

Fig. 131–6 Polishing to a high sheen.

266

unit 132

Discussion topics on preparation of wood and application of finishes

1. Name five porous or semiporous hardwoods and five nonporous softwoods; discuss the proper finishes for each.
2. Besides the wood selected for a project, what factors should influence the selection of a finish?
3. What products are used in repairing blemishes?
4. What are some commercial finishing methods that are not practiced in small operations?
5. Compare steel wool and the garnet pad in relation to use, materials, and advantages.
6. Discuss the derivation of the word **varnish.** What is the main ingredient used in its manufacture?
7. Explain how shellac is produced.
8. What are the basic ingredients of lacquer?
9. Explain the development and the differences of water-, casein-, and oil-base paints.

10. When is shellac used specifically as a sealer?
11. What modern product has been developed to replace bristles?
12. Describe precautions that, when observed, will give longer wear to brushes.
13. Explain the different types of spray guns and spray-finishing methods.
14. Be able to explain thoroughly the procedure for using the suction-feed spray gun.
15. What are the important steps in cleaning the spray gun? In shutting down the other equipment?
16. Why is it necessary to bleach some woods?
17. Discuss the advantages and disadvantages of the various types of stains.
18. What are the kinds of wood filler? What are their main ingredients?
19. What is the purpose of wood filler?
20. What makes the bristles of the wild boar especially useful as material for the best brushes?
21. Name the common types of sealing materials.
22. Explain what is meant by **four-pound cut shellac.**
23. What is the most important natural wax?
24. Name three other sources of wax.
25. What is the most common solvent, or thinner, for wax?

26. What woods are successfully finished with oil? Oil and wax?
27. Why is rubbing oil used instead of water to smooth a shellac finish?
28. What special characteristics does varnish have in relation to other finishes?
29. Explain the difference and uses of long-, medium-, and short-oil varnishes.
30. Why is it not advisable to apply lacquer over new varnish?
31. What are the three steps in brushing technique when using varnishing?
32. How is synthetic lacquer made? What raw materials are used?
33. Why is lacquer not recommended as a finish over varnish?
34. What are the special uses of paint and enamel?
35. How are different design effects produced on textured walls?
36. Discuss the advantages and disadvantages of a penetrating finish as related to varnish and lacquer.
37. Explain the purpose of sanding between applications of finish coats.
38. Why is water not used as a lubricant when sanding or working a shellac finish?
39. Why is the first coat dry-rubbed?
40. Discuss the proper procedure and purpose of using pumice, rottenstone, and wax on the final coat of finish.

section **8**

Upholstering

Forms of upholstery

Upholstery is usually classified into three categories: (1) **padded** (or **slip**), (2) **spring,** and (3) **overstuffed** forms of seats and backs. Each of the basic types is designed for specific purposes.

Padded seat and back

There are two types of padded slip seats: the solid base (Fig. 133-1) and the webbed-frame base (Fig. 133-2).

Fig. 133–1 An electric stapler speeds upholstery work on padded solid bases.

Fig. 133–2 Webbed-frame bases are used on better dining room chairs.

Comfort in a padded slip seat depends on the kind and amount of padding or stuffing used. The procedure of upholstering is basically the same.

Spring base and back

The spring base or back may be made of coil springs tied together or of the no-sag zigzag type of wire spring (Fig. 133-3). If properly installed, spring seats make a comfortable, soft base and back on furniture.

Coil springs can be attached to solid bases, sewn or clipped to webbing, or mounted on special steel bars. They are tied together with special spring coils, wire clips, or tying twine. This method of mounting coil springs is sometimes called **tied,** or **tight-spring, construction.**

Overstuffed construction

Overstuffed construction of seats and backs on chairs and divans (Fig. 133-4) is the softest and most comfortable of the three upholstered forms. Special springs are often used under cushions in both the seat and the back. These are filled with cotton, foam rubber, plastic foam sheets, or spring units wrapped in cotton. Overstuffed construction is ideal for living room suites, lounging chairs, and divans.

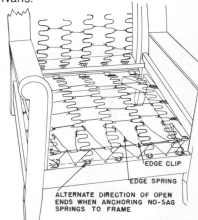

Fig. 133–3 No-sag spring wire can be used in seats and backs.

Fig. 133–4 Overstuffed furniture construction is the softest of the three forms of upholstery.

Upholstering tools and equipment

Throughout this text, metric equivalents are offered alongside customary measurements. In portions of this section on upholstery, however, metric equivalents of sizes of the special tools, materials, and supplies would serve no real purpose in this edition. When the upholstery industry has changed to metric measure, future editions of this text will reflect that change. Metric equivalents of operational sizes and dimensions are continued.

Essential tools

A complete set of tools makes upholstery processes easy and fast. However, all the tools and equipment discussed are not absolutely necessary for most basic jobs.

Basic tools needed for the various forms of upholstery are the upholsterer's tack hammer, a webbing stretcher, a regulator, and upholsterer's shears or scissors (see Fig. 134-1). Additional tools that are very helpful are the steel-webbing stretcher (Fig. 134-2), tack lifter, or tack claw (Fig. 134-3), ripping chisel (Fig. 134-4), needles and skewers (Fig. 134-5), and cushion irons (Fig. 134-6). Most of these tools can be made in the school industrial laboratory or shop.

The **upholsterer's tack hammer** (Fig. 134-1A) is one of the most important tools. The special shape of the head makes it easy to use in many close places. The double-face type,

with one magnetic face, is recommended.

The **webbing stretcher** (Fig. 134-1B) can be purchased or made. This tool, or the **webbing pliers** (Fig. 134-1C), is used to stretch jute webbing on open frames. A **steel-webbing stretcher** (see Fig. 134-2) is useful for stretching steel webbing.

A **regulator** (Fig. 134-1D) is similar to a very large needle. It is used to smooth out irregularities in loose padding or stuffing after the padding has been covered with burlap.

Upholstery shears (Fig. 134-1E) are heavy-duty scissors, serviceable enough to cut coarse fabrics, tying twine, and burlap.

The **tack lifter,** or **tack claw** (Fig. 134-3), has a V notch on the bevel end. This notch makes it easy to get under tacks that have not been driven completely into the frame.

A **ripping chisel** (Fig. 134-4) is similar to the tack lifter, but it has a solid, single-bevel end. It helps to remove tacks that have been driven completely into the wood.

Needles of assorted shapes and sizes (Fig. 134-5) are very useful. The curved needle (Fig. 134-5A) ranges in size from $1^1/_2$ inches to several inches in circumference. The 2- and 3-inch sizes are adequate for sewing corners and for most other purposes.

The straight needle (Fig. 134-5B) is available in numerous sizes with single or double points. An 8-inch double-point needle (Fig. 134-5C) is useful for sewing back and forth through stuffing or other materials without turning it. The bent packing needle (Fig. 134-5D) sews heavier packing materials.

Skewers (Fig. 134-5E) are pins that come in lengths of $2^1/_2$ to 4 inches. Each has a loop for a head. Skewers pin the final fabric cover in place for tacking and sewing.

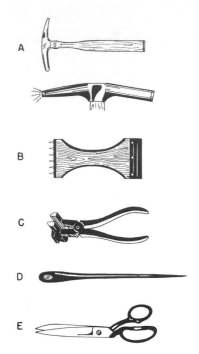

Fig. 134–1 Basic upholstery tools: (A) upholsterer's tack hammer, (B) webbing stretcher, (C) webbing pliers, (D) regulator, and (E) trimmer or upholsterer's shears (scissors).

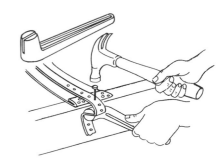

Fig. 134–2 A steel-webbing stretcher.

Fig. 134–3 A tack claw (lifter).

Fig. 134–4 A ripping chisel helps remove tacks that have been driven completely into the wood.

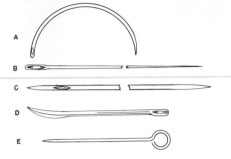

Fig. 134–5 Assorted needles and skewers are useful to sew and pin different types of upholstery work.

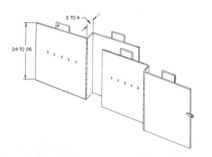

Fig. 134–6 Cushion irons help compress padding in cushions so that the covers can be put on easily.

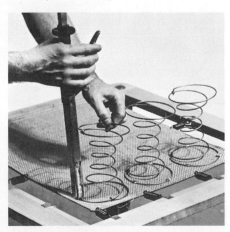

Fig. 134–7 Coil springs are easily attached to webbing with a Klinch-It tool.

Cushion irons, or hand irons (Fig. 134-6), serve in place of a cushion-filling machine. They can be made or purchased. A unit of cushion springs is wrapped in cotton or other filler; it is placed inside the folded iron and compressed. The cushion box (upholstered cover) is fitted around the outside of the irons. The unit of springs with filler is then pushed into the cover.

Miscellaneous tools

The Klinch-It tool (Fig. 134-7), hammer tacker (Fig. 134-8), spring-driven or compressed-air driven staplers, and hog-ring and spring-clip pliers (Fig. 134-9) are special tools. They are used in furniture factories (Figs. 134-9 through 134-12).

Fig. 134–8 A hammer tacker.

Fig. 134–9 Hog-ring and spring-clip pliers.

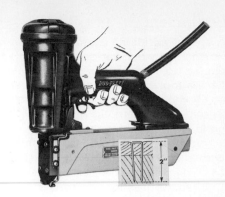

Fig. 134–10 The staple hammer helps speed production.

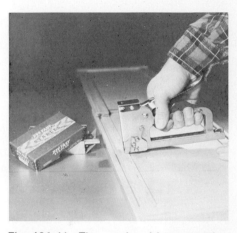

Fig. 134–11 The spring-driven stapler can be used to attach wood strips as well as upholstery material.

Fig. 134–12 Compressed-air driven staples and brads are used to attach corner blocks and trim on this furniture frame.

Equipment

A special **worktable** is useful and convenient to lay out, cut, and handle fabrics up to 54 inches wide. It should have a top approximately 5 by 8 feet, and it should be 30 to 34 inches high. Space underneath the top makes a good material-storage area.

A heavy-duty **sewing machine** and a **cushion-filling machine** (Fig. 134-13) make work easier and faster.

Padded **trestles,** or **horses** (Fig. 134-14), are convenient to set work on.

Fig. 134–13 A cushion-filling machine.

Fig. 134–14 A padded upholstery trestle, or "horse," prevents exposed wood from being scratched.

unit **135**

Upholstery materials and supplies

An immense variety of materials and supplies used for upholstery are available. The finished products vary according to personal needs, ingenuity, and desires.

Tacks

There are three common kinds of tacks: (1) upholstery, (2) webbing, and (3) gimp. Their sizes and lengths are given in Table 135-1.

The **upholstery tack** (Fig. 135-1) has a flat head and a smooth, tapered shank. It is used for tacking most fabrics and for anchoring tying twine. Sizes range from 1 ounce, which is about $3/16$ inch long, to 24 ounce, which is $1^1/8$ inches long. The 4-, 6-, 8-, and 12-ounce sizes are commonly used.

Table 135-1
SIZES AND LENGTHS OF TACKS

No.	Length	No.	Length
1	$3/16$	10	$5/8$
$1^1/2$	$7/32$	12	$11/16$
2	$1/4$	14	$3/4$
$2^1/2$	$5/16$	16	$13/16$
3	$3/8$	18	$7/8$
4	$7/16$	20	$15/16$
6	$1/2$	22	1
8	$9/16$	24	$1^1/8$

Webbing tacks have barbed shanks, which give more holding power to tack webbing. The 12- and 14-ounce sizes are commonly used. The larger (14-ounce) size is about $3/4$ inch long.

Gimp tacks have small, round heads. They range in size from 2 ounces (about $1/4$ inch long) to 8 ounces (about $9/16$ inch long). The 3-, 4-, and 6-ounce sizes are commonly used. They tack decorative gimp (Fig. 135-2).

Decorative nails (Fig. 135-3) are tacks used where the heads will show.

Compressed-air driven **staples** are used by many manufacturers instead of upholstery tacks.

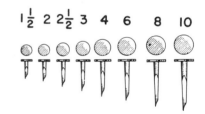

Fig. 135–1 Common upholstery tacks have tapered shanks and very sharp points.

Fig. 135–2 This is one of many designs of decorative gimp used over seams and edges of upholstery material.

Fig. 135–3 Decorative nails are often called tacks. They are used to tack on outer materials where heads are visible.

Webbing

Three basic types of webbing are (1) jute, (2) steel, and (3) decorative.

Jute webbing is the most frequently used, is exceptionally strong, and stretches very little. It is available in rolls that range from 3 to 4 inches wide; the 3½-inch width is the most common.

Steel webbing is about ¾ to 1 inch wide. It is used to support jute webbing. It can also be used in combination with small springs to form a semisolid base support.

Decorative webbing is usually made from plastic or rubber. The plastic type is made in many patterns and colors. It is used on lawn furniture, folding chairs, and other pieces in which the webbing serves as the complete seat or back. Rubber webbing often serves as a base for cushions.

Four representative patterns for arranging and attaching rubber webbing are shown in Figs. 135-4 through 135-7.

Springs

Upholstery springs are manufactured in single coils; zigzag rolls; bars; and in special groups called **marshall units;** base, or **deck, units;** and **back units** (Fig. 135-8). Single coils are purchased by weight; zigzag rolls, by the foot; and bars, by the number of springs per bar.

Springs are classified by their shape, their firmness, and the way the tips of their coils are handled. They are selected according to their intended use, the load they are to carry, and the depth of the frame in which they will be placed.

Coil springs come in three types: (1) seat, (2) back, and (3) cushion. Single-coil **seat springs** (Fig. 135-9A) are loose and smooth at both ends. They are made of soft, medium, and hard firmness. They range from about 4 to 14 inches in height and are usually made of 9-gage (larger) to 11-gage (smaller) wire. If the center of the

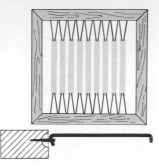

Fig. 135–4   The first of four methods of arranging and fastening rubber webbing.

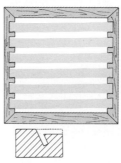

Fig. 135–5   The second method of arranging and fastening rubber webbing.

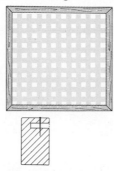

Fig. 135–6   The third method of arranging and fastening rubber webbing.

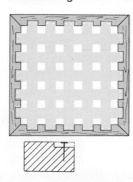

Fig. 135–7   The fourth method of arranging and fastening rubber webbing.

spring coil is smaller than the outside, the spring is harder; if it is larger, the spring is softer. An example of a medium-hard spring is shown in Fig. 135-9A.

Back and **cushion springs** (Figs. 135-9B and 135-9C) in many types of special units are made of small wire (12 to 15 gage). They are tied together by wire or helicals (small springs) to form units for seat decks and backs. Their height ranges from 4 to 8 inches. Cushion springs for marshall units (Fig. 135-8D) are sewn into individual pockets of muslin.

The **bar-spring unit** (Fig. 135-8C) is convenient because no other spring support is necessary. The seat or back spring units are ready to tie; they are already spaced and attached to steel wire or bars. These units are easily mounted on a frame with nails, webbing tacks, or screws.

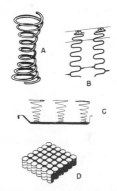

Fig. 135–8   Types of upholstery springs: (A) single coil, (B) zigzag, or no-sag, (C) bar, and (D) marshall unit.

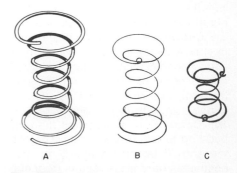

Fig. 135–9   Coil springs: (A) loose seat, (B) back, and (C) marshall unit.

Twine

The best **spring-tying twine** is made from hemp. It has a wax finish. It is commonly purchased in 1- or 5-pound balls. The best twine should be used because it is under great strain. When the springs are correctly tied, the twine lasts indefinitely.

Sewing or **stitching twine** and **thread** are made from nylon or flax, and they may have a wax finish. They are exceptionally strong and are used to sew springs to webbing and to stitch padding materials in place to prevent movement. Another use is to sew edge rolls to spring wire edges. Thread is used to sew the final fabric.

Padding

Padding material is referred to as **stuffing.** It should be clean and strong.

Foam rubber and **plastic foam sheets** are preformed materials. The foam is manufactured in a continuous slab (Fig. 135-10). It can be molded, split, and cut (Fig. 135-11) to provide shapes and sizes of almost any dimension (Fig. 135-12).

Hair is one of the oldest and best stuffing materials. It comes from hogs, cattle, and horses. Hog hair alone is least desirable, so it is mixed with other types. Rubberized curled hair is made in many thicknesses, widths, and lengths of prepared flat strips and rolls (Fig. 135-13).

Moss is a vegetable material obtained from trees in the South. A fine, wirelike hair is obtained after it is heat-treated. It is sold by the pound.

Cotton felt, or **batting,** is prepared in sheets or layers about 1 inch thick and 27 inches wide. It weighs about 1 pound per yard. Batts are made soft, medium, and firm, and they are obtainable in various shapes (Fig. 135-14). Cotton is often used as the only padding for solid-base seats. The cotton should be pulled apart, not cut, because a hard edge results from cutting.

Stuffing materials other than

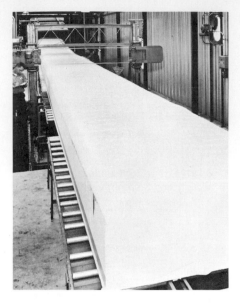

Fig. 135–10 The foam slab resembles a loaf of bread in continuous production. *Nopco Chemical Company.*

Fig. 135–11 A worker is topping a foam bun to provide a block, slab, or sheet of almost any dimension. *Nopco Chemical Company.*

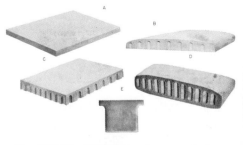

Fig. 135–12 Different shapes of foam padding: (A) slab, (B) crowned, (C) cored, (D) full molded, and (E) reversible "T."

those listed above are **tow** (from flax stalks), **sisal** (from flax leaves), **palm fibers, coco fibers, excelsior, kapok, down** (soft feathers), and **cotton substitutes** (made from wood).

Other upholstery materials

Edge rolls can be purchased by the foot. They require only sewing or tacking into place. Round rolls are used around edges of arms and other places where a soft edge is required. Spring-tied edge rolls are shaped like teardrops. This type of roll is sewn to the burlap that covers the edge wire around the foundation or the deck springs.

Burlap covers the springs after they are tied. It is made from jute yarn. The 8- to 10-ounce weight is very satisfactory; the 40-inch width is useful. Stuffing is placed over a burlap base. It is then covered with muslin or burlap if loose material or rubberized hair is used.

Muslin comes bleached and unbleached. It is from 35 to 54 inches

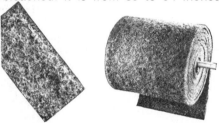

Fig. 135–13 Rubberized curled hair.

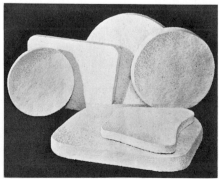

Fig. 135–14 Cotton batts for padding are formed in many shapes and sizes.

wide. It covers cotton and other stuffing material before the outer fabric is put on.

Welt cord can be bought in many sizes. It is made from strong twisted paper or twisted yarn. It is sewn into the final fabric to form a bead around seats, cushions, or other trim areas.

A **tacking strip** is made of stiff cardboard. It is $3/8$ to $1/2$ inch wide. Tacking strips are used in blind tacking of straight welt seams and when the final cover must be blind tacked. In blind tacking, the tack is driven into place so that the material can cover the head of the tack.

Cambric is a starched or stiff glazed cotton fabric. It is usually tacked underneath seats to close the bottom. It prevents stuffing particles from eventually falling to the floor when they work loose.

The **final covering** of upholstered furniture is chosen from an almost unlimited number of materials, designs, and colors. Friezes, tapestries, and velours are easily worked. Leather is a beautiful but expensive covering; however, durable leather substitutes and numerous forms of plastics have been successfully developed.

Some synthetic products, without cloth backing, are more difficult to work than the fabrics. Plastic or vinyl materials are sometimes bonded to specially woven fabric backings. Figure 135-15 shows the suggested amount of final covering to buy for some shapes of furniture.

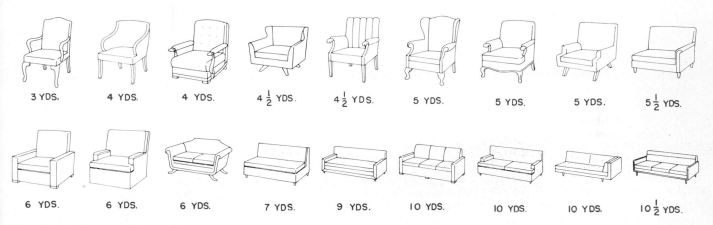

3 YDS.   4 YDS.   4 YDS. $4\frac{1}{2}$ YDS. $4\frac{1}{2}$ YDS.   5 YDS.   5 YDS.   5 YDS. $5\frac{1}{2}$ YDS.

6 YDS.   6 YDS.   6 YDS.   7 YDS.   9 YDS.   10 YDS.   10 YDS.   10 YDS. $10\frac{1}{2}$ YDS.

Fig. 135–15 Suggested amounts of upholstery material for different sizes and shapes of furniture.

unit 136

Upholstering the padded seat

Simple padded construction is often found on the seats and backs of several kinds of chairs in the home, such as kitchen, dining room, and desk chairs. The upholstering is done on a solid base or on an open frame, where it is known as slip seat construction.

Upholstering an open frame

1. Construct or obtain an open frame for a seat. If the frame is made to fit a particular opening, allow $1/8$ inch (3 mm) of space on each side for the thickness of the upholstery materials. If it is to be a chair slip seat, make it from $3/4$-inch (19-mm) stock. The dowel butt joint is a good choice for corner construction. (Note: Follow only steps 8 through 15 when a solid base is used.)

An open frame can be built as shown in Fig. 136-1. This frame can be adapted for either a webbed, padded seat or for coil or no-sag springs.

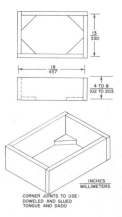

Fig. 136–1 Open frames can also be adapted for use with most kinds of springs.

275

2. Round all corners slightly to help prevent wear on the upholstery material.

3. Determine how many strips of webbing are needed. Space them from $1/2$ to 2 inches (13 to 51 mm) apart. The space between the frame edge and the first webbing strip should be approximately the same as the space between the strips.

Do not cut the webbing into strips until after each is fastened. Tack one end of the $3^1/2$-inch jute webbing roll to one side of the frame (Fig. 136-2). Use No. 12 webbing or upholstery tacks. Space three tacks evenly. Allow about $3/4$ to 1 inch (19 to 25 mm) excess length of webbing for folding back over these tacks. Anchor this fold with two more tacks (Fig. 136-3).

4. Use the webbing stretcher to stretch the webbing tight. Tack it to the opposite side of the frame with three tacks (Fig. 136-4).

5. Release the webbing stretcher. Cut the webbing about $3/4$ to 1 inch (19 to 25 mm) beyond the three tacks. Fold it back over them. Secure the end with two more tacks, as in step 3.

6. Continue fastening other strips of webbing in a basket-weave pattern until the frame is covered (Fig. 136-5).

7. Cover the webbed frame with one thickness of closely woven burlap (Fig. 136-6). Tack snugly in place with No. 6 or No. 8 upholstery tacks. Space

them about $1^1/2$ inches (38 mm) apart. Some seats need an edge roll around the edges.

8. Cut a section of 1-inch foam rubber, plastic foam sheet, or rubberized hair to fit the seat (Fig. 136-7). If loose stuffing is used, tear it apart and cover the seat evenly to a depth of about 2 inches (51 mm). Be sure that all foreign particles are removed.

9. Cover the rubberized hair (or other stuffing) with burlap. Drive the tacks in only about halfway so that they can be easily removed if necessary. Moss or other loose padding is adjusted to a smooth layer with a stuffing regulator.

10. Cut the surplus burlap from the corners to eliminate a bulge under the final cover.

11. Tighten the burlap. Drive in the tacks.

12. Cover the burlap with a layer of cotton felt or batting. Some craftsmen prefer to use only the rubber or plastic foam sheet. This eliminates use of the cotton and rubberized hair.

13. Cover the cotton with a piece of muslin. Tack it to the frame.

14. Cut the final upholstery, and place it over the muslin. Pull it smooth and snug, and tack it underneath the frame.

15. Tack the cambric to the under part of the frame. Attach the legs.

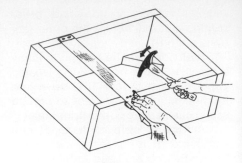

Fig. 136–4   Stretch the webbing and tack it to the opposite side of the frame.

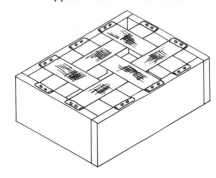

Fig. 136–5   Cover the frame with strips of webbing in a basket-weave pattern.

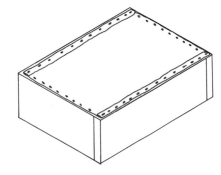

Fig. 136–6   Cover the webbing with burlap.

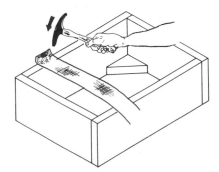

Fig. 136–2   Tack an end of the webbing roll to the frame.

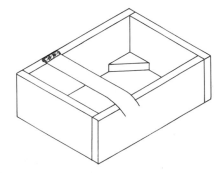

Fig. 136–3   Anchor the fold with two additional tacks.

Fig. 136–7   Rubberized hair or foam sheets make smooth layers of padding.

Spring upholstering

No-sag springs are widely used in upholstering. The 9-ounce weight (size) is used for seats and the 11-ounce for backs.

No-sag spring construction

1. Make or obtain a wood frame for a chair (Fig. 137-1) or an ottoman.

2. Tack clips on opposite sides of the frame so that the lines of no-sag spring stock will be about 4 inches (102 mm) on center. Use barbed webbing tacks for better holding power. On chairs, place the springs from back to front or from top to bottom.

Handle the spring wire carefully. It is steel and will therefore be difficult to handle. It may be necessary to get someone to assist you.

3. Place one end of the spring stock into a metal clip. Roll out the length to the opposite side. The spring contour should rise above the frame from 1 to 2 inches (25 to 51 mm), depending on the softness of the seat desired.

4. Cut the stock to the required length. Make a notch with a file, a hacksaw, or a bolt cutter. The no-sag stock is made of spring steel and will break easily where it is notched. *Hold the ends in a vise,* or with other tools, to prevent the resulting sharp ends from springing loose.

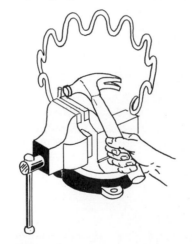

Fig. 137–2 No-sag springs hold in the clips easier when the ends are slightly bent.

5. Check the first piece of spring for proper length. Cut all the others.

6. Grind the ends of the pieces smooth. Place the tip ends of the spring pieces in a machinist's vise. Bend them slightly (Fig. 137-2) to hold better in the metal clips or the hinge links (Fig. 137-3).

7. Place the no-sag springs in the clips. Anchor the clips permanently with webbing tacks (Fig. 137-4).

8. Tie the rows of no-sag springs with connecting wire springs. Clothes-hanger wire is very good for tying the middle rows together. Special helicals (small springs) can be used for all, or part of, the tying on the sides (see Fig. 137-4). Regular upholstery spring-tying twine can also be used for tying the rows crosswise.

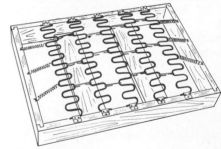

Fig. 137–4 Clips should be firmly anchored to the frame. Note how the wires and springs hold the no-sag rows.

Fig. 137–1 Some chairs are adaptable for upholstering with pad, no-sag spring, or coil-spring construction.

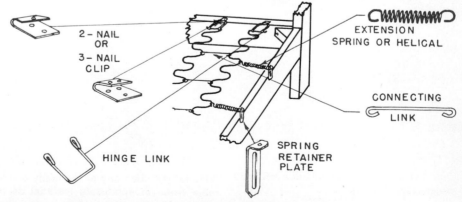

2 – NAIL
OR
3 – NAIL
CLIP

EXTENSION SPRING OR HELICAL

CONNECTING LINK

HINGE LINK

SPRING RETAINER PLATE

Fig. 137–3 Some of the special hardware used with no-sag springs.

9. Cover the no-sag springs with a layer of burlap (Fig. 137-5).

10. Tack and sew an edge roll around the frame edges to build up the seat and to protect the final covering from wear. This roll can be purchased or built up (Fig. 137-6).

11. Continue building the edge roll until the desired height is obtained (Fig. 137-7).

12. Add layers of filler padding (foam rubber, plastic sheeting, or rubberized hair). Cover the entire seat with burlap (Fig. 137-8). Chalk lines show where to sew through the top layer of burlap down to the spring-covering burlap to make filler compact.

13. Add a layer of cotton or foam padding. Cover it with muslin (Fig. 137-9). Tack it underneath firmly.

14. Complete the seat by covering with upholstery material (Fig. 137-10). The corners of the final covering fabric should be shaped as illustrated in Fig. 137-11. A bead, or welt cord, sewn in the fabric gives the final covering a finished appearance. The entire silhouette can be changed by using less depth in the frame and padding and a different style of legs (Fig. 137-12).

Fig. 137–5   Springs covered with burlap.

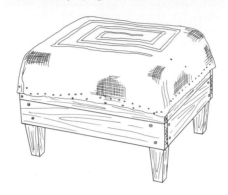

Fig. 137–8   Add filler padding and cover the whole seat with burlap.

Fig. 137–6   A padded roll placed around the edges builds up the seat and reduces wear of the final covering.

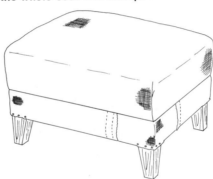

Fig. 137–9   Add a layer of cotton or foam padding and cover with muslin.

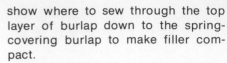

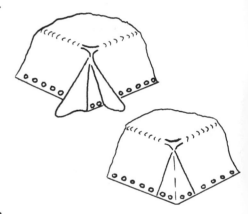

Fig. 137–11   A method of shaping corners.

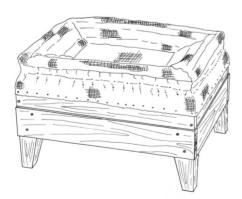

Fig. 137–7   The additional edge roll adds height and comfort.

Fig. 137–10   Use any of the many available types of upholstery material as a final cover.

Fig. 137–12   Different frames, legs, and heights change the appearance of similar upholstered pieces.

Tight-coil spring construction

Coil springs can be mounted with clips to webbing, on wood slats (Fig. 137-13), or on metal bars. Decide how high the seat is to be built and how soft it is to be. Test several sizes of springs. Determine the size and number needed for the frame. Openings between springs should be no greater than the size of a spring coil. This open area will be crossed by wires or hand ties to prevent the padding from sagging.

1. Make a suitable furniture frame to be upholstered with coil-spring construction (see Fig. 137-13).

2. Select the springs. Mount them in the frame. Check the rows for alignment and spacing. Loose springs are attached to a wood base with staples. Burlap is placed underneath the spring to act as a silencer. Springs are attached to a webbed base with sewing twine or wire clips.

3. Drive a No. 8 or a No. 10 upholstery tack about halfway into the frame edges in line with the center of each row of springs.

4. Cut several pieces of tying twine to the correct length. This is about 2½ times the length or width of the frame.

5. Wrap one end of the twine around a tack. Drive it in securely. Leave about 1 inch (25 mm) of surplus twine. Anchor it with a second tack (Fig. 137-14, *right detail*).

6. Hold the first spring in the position for the height of seat desired. Pull the tying twine over the spring edge nearest the tack. Tie the twine to the spring with the spring-tying knot (Fig. 137-14, *left detail*).

7. Tie to the opposite side of the spring. Proceed across the row of springs with the same pattern of tying. Fasten the twine to the opposite frame edge with the same knot.

8. Continue tying rows of springs crosswise (two-way tie) and diagonally (four-way tie) as shown in Fig. 137-14.

A smooth contour will result.

9. Cover the springs with a layer of closely woven burlap. Fold the edges. Tack it to the frame.

10. Follow steps 8 through 15, Unit 136, Upholstering the Padded Seat.

Wire-edge coil-spring construction

1. Make a frame for the kind of springs and mounting desired. The procedure explained is for bar-spring (drop-in) units, but it is virtually the same as other operations after the springs are mounted.

2. Mount bar-spring, or drop-in, units to the frame with screws (Fig. 137-15).

3. Bend a piece of spring-steel edge wire to the shape of the wood frame. It should fit the outer edges of the springs when they are standing straight.

Fig. 137–13 Easy attachment of coil springs.

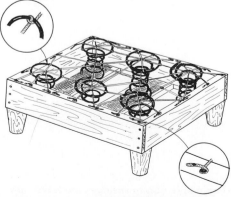

Fig. 137–14 Coil springs properly tied.

4. Tie the edge wire to the outer edges of the coil springs. Follow the procedure shown in Fig. 137-16.

5. Drive a No. 8 or a No. 10 upholstery tack about halfway into the frame edge, aligned with the center of each outer spring. Loop one end of the spring-tying twine around the tack. Drive it in to hold the twine securely.

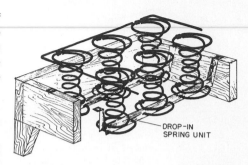

Fig. 137–15 The bar spring, or drop-in, unit is easy to attach to the frame with screws.

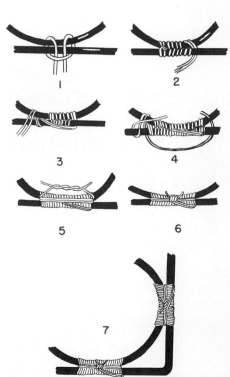

Fig. 137–16 Procedure for tying edge wire to coil springs.

6. Start another tack into the frame near the first one. Wrap the loose end of the twine around it. Drive the tack into place (Fig. 137-17).

7. Tie the surplus end of the twine to the wire edge to obtain the proper height for the springs. The rows are then ready to be tied together. Lengths of the twine should be about 2½ times the length of the frame.

8. Repeat step 7, working around the frame. The wire edge should be level all around.

9. Tie the springs with the long end of the tying twine, as shown in Fig. 137-17. Continue tying the coils with the twine crosswise and diagonally until a smooth, flat seat is obtained.

10. Cover the springs with a layer of closely woven burlap. Tack it to the frame (Fig. 137-18).

11. Sew a hard teardrop edge roll to the burlap around the edge of the wire frame (Fig. 137-19).

12. Pad the seat with rubberized hair and cotton or foam padding. Cover it with muslin.

13. Complete the upholstered seat by covering it with the final upholstery material.

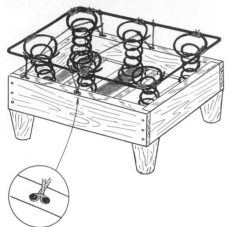

Fig. 137–17   Attaching tying twine to the frame.

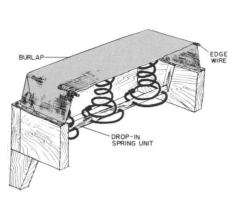

Fig. 137–18   Cover springs with burlap.

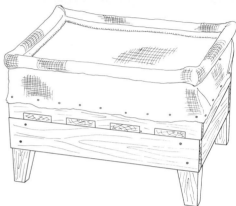

Fig. 137–19   Sew a hard teardrop edge roll over the edge wire to prevent wear and add comfort.

unit 138

Upholstering overstuffed furniture

Many types of springs are used in overstuffed furniture construction. Seats and backs are built up in many ways. Coil springs can be mounted on steel webbing and tied (Fig. 138-1) to form a base. The seat and back can be made with sets of springs as a complete unit (Fig. 138-2) or as separate units with loose cushions.

Cushions are upholstered as

Fig. 138–1   Coil springs mounted on steel webbing would look like this.

Fig. 138–2   Some chairs do not use loose cushions.

separate units for either seats or backs. Marshall-unit springs, or formed-foam units, are also used to form cushions.

Much modern overstuffed furniture has been developed for functional, multipurpose use. Typical examples are (1) the sofa-sleeper unit (Fig. 138-3), (2) the reclining chair (Fig. 138-4), and (3) the two-seat settee (Fig. 138-5). Mechanical hardware action speedily converts the settee into a guest bed (Fig. 138-6).

Constructing overstuffed furniture

Operations are explained for one type of overstuffed furniture. Refer to special books on upholstery for additional information and operations. Cutaway and cross-section views of overstuffed furniture are shown in Figs. 138-7 and 138-8.

1. Make (or obtain) a strong chair frame. The chair should have two arms (Fig. 138-9) or no arms (Fig. 138-10).

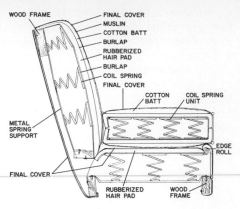

Fig. 138–8 Cross section of an upholstered chair, showing the deck, back, and loose cushion.

Fig. 138–3 Metal frames fold out to support a mattress. *The Seng Company.*

Fig. 138–6 A settee converts to a guest bed. *The Seng Company.*

Fig. 138–4 Special hardware converts a chair into a recliner. *The Seng Company.*

Fig. 138–9 Chair arms and legs that are to be seen on finished upholstered furniture are built into the final frame.

Fig. 138–5 A multipurpose settee. *The Seng Company.*

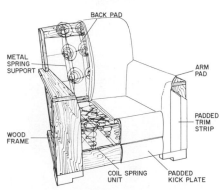

Fig. 138–7 Cutaway section of an upholstered chair with the cushion removed.

Fig. 138–10 Arms are left off some chairs and off the center portions of sectional furniture.

Or you may use two chairs together. Each of these chairs has one arm. They form sectional furniture (Fig. 138-11).

2. Attach and fasten coil springs in the seat and no-sag springs in the back (Fig. 138-12).

3. Add the wire edge to the seat springs. Tie the coil and no-sag springs (Fig. 138-13) as explained in Unit 137.

4. Cover the springs on the seat and back with plain burlap or burlap with interwoven wire (see Fig. 138-14).

5. Interweave and attach webbing to the inside of the chair arm.

6. Sew an edge roll to the open sides of the seat. Tack a smaller roll to the frame around the back and over the chair arm (Fig. 138-14).

7. Place a layer of rubberized hair or other padding on the arm. Cover it with burlap (Fig. 138-15). Repeat this padding on the seat and back. More than one layer of padding is necessary when cushions are not used.

8. Add one layer of cotton or foam on the arm and one or more on the seat and back. Cover each part separately with muslin (Fig. 138-16).

9. Cover the cushion units, and upholster all parts (Fig. 138-17). The order of upholstering is (1) seat, (2) front of back, (3) inside of arm, (4) outside of arm, (5) back, and (6) cambric underneath. Welt cords are sewn into the outer fabric to add a decorative, beadlike appearance.

Fig. 138–15 A chair arm also needs padding.

Fig. 138–11 One arm is built on opposite sides of sectional units.

Fig. 138–13 Loose coil springs in a chair seat need an edge wire and proper tying to hold the seat in place.

Fig. 138–16 Cotton or foam padding is covered with muslin.

Fig. 138–12 Coil and no-sag springs can be mixed on different upholstered parts.

Fig. 138–14 An edge roll gives protection from wear.

Fig. 138–17 Cushions can be loose or covered and attached as a one-piece unit.

10. Cover the fronts of the arms with panels. To make panels, saw ¹/₄-inch (6.35 mm) plywood to the shape desired. Cover it with a thin layer of cotton; then cover this with upholstery material.

11. Nail the panel in place with small finishing nails or wire brads. Use a center punch to set the nails beneath the fabric so that they are out of sight.

12. Cover the outer side of the arm and back with the same upholstery material as other parts. Use tacking strips. Use gimp tacks or decorative nails, or sew with a blind stitch to overlap material to attach this material smoothly to the frame (Fig. 138-18).

13. Tack cambric to the frame underneath the seat.

Fig. 138–18 Furniture has a finished appearance when the back is covered with the same material.

unit 139

Discussion topics on upholstering

1. What are the advantages of each type of upholstery classification?
2. Describe the assorted sizes and shapes of needles.
3. Where are skewers used?
4. List some special tools that would be convenient to use in upholstering furniture.
5. Give the names and purposes for some special machines and equipment used in upholstering.
6. Name and explain the differences between, and the uses of, the kinds of upholstery tacks.
7. What are the three kinds of webbing?
8. In what shapes or quantities can upholstery springs be purchased?
9. Name five stuffing or padding materials.
10. What type of joint is recommended for slip seat frames?
11. Why is a basket-weave pattern used when webbing is attached to a frame?
12. Name the tools used in no-sag spring construction.
13. Why is no-sag spring wire dangerous?
14. What are the minimum and maximum heights this spring wire should rise above the frame?
15. What is an edge roll for?
16. What tools and materials are used in coil-seat construction which are not needed for a padded seat?
17. What advantage does the four-way tie have over the two-way tie?

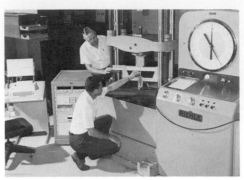

section 9
Technology of Woods

unit 140

American forests

There are over 775 million acres of forest land in the United States. The official SI metric unit for area is the square meter (m²); 1 acre is equal to a little less than 4047 m². To describe large land areas, the square meter may not be a convenient unit. For example, 775 million acres becomes 3 136 313 400 m², or more than 3 billion square meters. The next larger recommended multiple in SI units is 1000 (kilo). Converted to square kilometers (km²), the 775 million acres is a little larger than 3136 km². The forest land is about one-third of the total U.S. land area. Almost 70 percent of these forests are commercial (approximately 535 million acres or more than 2165 km²). National forests cover about 180 million acres (over 728 km²) of the total forest lands; 95 million acres (more than 384 km²) of these forests are considered accessible and profitably usable. These are called **commercial.** The national forests are properly managed for many purposes and are called **multiple-use forests.**

The remaining 240 million acres (over 791 km²) of the total forests, including some national ones, are called **noncommercial.** This acreage includes parks, rough mountains, wilderness areas that are not easily accessible, and swamps.

American continental forests

The 50 states have 10 different forest regions (Fig. 140-1). Climate and elevation partially determine these areas. Continental forests are divided into six general areas: (1) West Coast, (2)

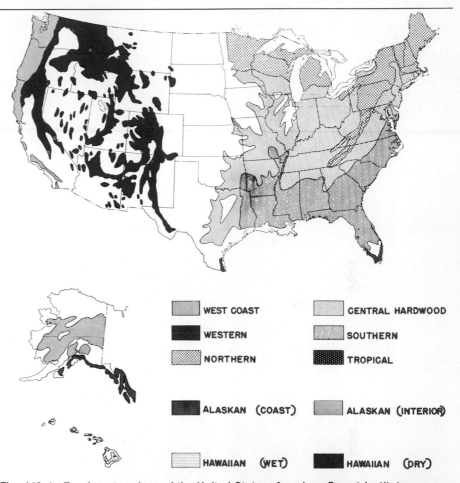

WEST COAST	CENTRAL HARDWOOD
WESTERN	SOUTHERN
NORTHERN	TROPICAL
ALASKAN (COAST)	ALASKAN (INTERIOR)
HAWAIIAN (WET)	HAWAIIAN (DRY)

Fig. 140–1 Ten forest regions of the United States. *American Forest Institute.*

Western, (3) Northern, (4) Central Hardwood, (5) Southern, and (6) Tropical.

The **West Coast Forest** (Fig. 140-2) is on the Pacific Coast and the western slopes of the Cascade Mountains. This area is in the states of Washington and Oregon and in northern California. The most famous trees in this forest are the giant redwoods, which grow in a narrow belt 10 to 30 miles (16.1 to 48.3 km) wide along the northwest coast of California.

The West Coast Forest region contains most of the Douglas fir. It produces almost one-third of the

Fig. 140–2 A stand of ponderosa pine in the West Coast Forest. *Western Wood Products Association.*

285

lumber in the United States, about one-fifth of the pulpwood, and nearly all the fir plywood.

Examples of other woods that are characteristic of the area are sugar and lodgepole pines, incense and Port Orford cedar, true firs, and Sitka spruce. Bigleaf maple and red alder are common hardwoods.

The **Western Forest** (Fig. 140-3) contains 89 million acres (a little more than 360 km²) of timber and produces nearly one-fourth of the United States lumber. It lies in 12 states from Canada to western Texas and in Mexico. The general boundaries are from the eastern slopes of the Rocky Mountains to within 50 miles (80.5 km) of the Pacific Ocean.

The area is known as the **Western Pine Region** because pine species predominate, especially the famous ponderosa, Idaho white, and sugar pines. Some other important timber trees are Douglas fir, Engelmann spruce, and lodgepole pine. Aspen is the predominant hardwood.

The **Northern Forest** (Fig. 140-4) extends from Wisconsin to Maine. This forest follows a long, narrow, mountainous ridge from Maine to parts of North Carolina, Tennessee, and northern Georgia. The area includes about 115 million acres (over 465 km²) and produces about one-tenth of the United States lumber and almost one-fifth of its pulpwood.

Some softwoods (conifers) found in this region are red (or Norway) and jack pine, and they grow in almost pure stands. Others are tamarack and white pine. Some hardwood (broadleaf) species are black, yellow, and paper birch; maple; oak; black cherry; and basswood.

The **Central Hardwood Forest** (Fig. 140-5) has the largest forest area; it contains 131 million acres (more than 530 km²). The thin strip of Northern Forest on the Appalachian Mountain range is excluded.

The Central Hardwood Forest extends from the central prairies to the Atlantic coastal states and almost to the Gulf of Mexico. Parts of it are in northern Arkansas, western Oklahoma, and eastern and central Texas. This area is the source of about one-twentieth of the lumber and almost one-tenth of the pulpwood for the nation.

Among the many hardwood species in this forest are sweet or red gum, tulip or yellow poplar, oak, beech, red maple, hickory, elm, ash, sycamore, cottonwood, and walnut. Conifers are the shortleaf and Virginia pines and the red cedar.

The **Southern Forest** (Fig. 140-6)

Fig. 140-3 Idaho pine region of the Western Forest. *Western Wood Products Association.*

Fig. 140-4 A New Hampshire tree farm located in the Northern Forest region. *American Forest Institute.*

Fig. 140-5 A virgin stand of hardwoods in the Central Hardwood Forest. *American Forest Institute.*

produces about three-fifths of the United States' pulpwood and nearly one-third of its lumber. It covers 12.3 million acres (almost 50 km³) in a belt along the Atlantic and Gulf Coasts from New Jersey to eastern Texas. Shortleaf, longleaf, loblolly, and slash pines, as well as cypress, are predominant conifers. Leading hardwoods are red gum, black gum (tupelo); red, white, water, live, and pin oak; willow; ash; and pecan.

The **Tropical Forest** (Fig. 140-7) is essentially noncommercial. It is the smallest forest region lying in the southern tips of Texas and Florida.

Alaskan forests

The **Alaskan Coast Forest** (Fig. 140-8) furnishes pulpwood and lumber from its 5 million commercial acres (over 200 km²). Most of the production is from four major conifers: western hemlock, Sitka spruce, western red cedar, and Alaska yellow cedar.

The **Alaskan Interior Forest** is not especially useful at the present time because it is so remote. Its 40 million acres (almost 162 km²) of potential commercial forest cover most of the heartland of this state.

Hawaiian forests

Except for fuelwood and fence posts, the **Dry Forest** of Hawaii is relatively noncommercial. Algaroba, koa, haole, wiliwili, and monkeypod grow here.

The **Wet Forest** (Fig. 140-9) contains a million acres (a little more than 4 km²) of commercially valuable trees. Production is mostly for furniture, lumber, and souvenirs. These are made from ohia, koa, tree fern, kukui, mamani, tropical ash, and eucalyptus.

Fig. 140–8 The Alaskan Coast Forest contains timber stands like this. *American Forest Institute.*

Fig. 140–6 A young Southern slash pine forest. *Texas Forest Service.*

Fig. 140–7 A large eucalyptus tree in the Tropical Forest area. *American Forest Institute.*

Fig. 140–9 Stilt roots of an ohia tree in the Hawaiian Wet Forest. *American Forest Institute.*

Classification and characteristics of trees

The classification and characteristics of trees should be understood to appreciate the technology of woodworking. Knowledge of locations and uses is also of major importance.

Classification of trees

Trees are a division of seed plants termed by botanists as **spermatophytes.** Two general designations are (1) **endogens** (monocotyledons) and (2) **exogens** (dicotyledons). Endogenous (inward-growing) trees have no commercial value. Most of their growth takes place inwardly in a hollow trunk, as in bamboo, yucca, and palm trees.

Exogenous trees are outward growing. Layers of growth (annual rings) form the trunk and branches and indicate the age of the tree. In moderate climates, one ring is added each year. When food and water are abundant, the tree grows more and the rings are wide. The rings are narrow when there are adverse conditions of drought and lack of food. The light band of an annual ring is spring growth; the dark one is formed in the summer.

The valuable, lumber-producing exogens are divided into two classes, **angiosperms** and **gymnosperms** (Figs. 141-1 and 141-2). Angiosperms are called **hardwoods,** or **deciduous** (meaning "leaf-losing") **woods.** They

are often fruit and nut bearing, are broad leaved, and have covered seeds. **Hardwood** is a common term, but it is not always precise in relation to softness or texture. For example, basswood, balsa, butternut, and poplar are softer than southern yellow pine and yew, which are classified as softwoods. Although most hardwoods shed their leaves annually, such trees as holly, live oak, and magnolia in tropical and subtropical regions keep theirs.

The more important hardwoods are ash, basswood, beech, birch, cherry, elm, and gum. Also in this category are hickory, mahogany, maple, magnolia, oak, Osage orange, poplar, and walnut.

Gymnosperms are classified as softwoods, evergreens, or conifers (meaning "cone bearing"). They have needlelike or scalelike leaves. The name was derived from the Greek word gymnos meaning "naked," as the seeds are. **Softwood** and **evergreen** are common names for conifers, but they are somewhat misleading. It was mentioned that some softwoods are harder in texture than some hardwoods. Likewise, some evergreens, such as larch and bald cypress, shed their foliage annually.

Most lumber for building construction is cut from the softwoods. Included in this group are cedar, bald cypress, fir, hemlock, larch, pine, spruce, and redwood.

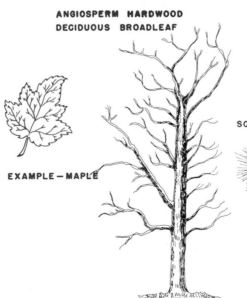

Fig. 141-1 Angiosperm hardwood example and classification. *Paxton Lumber Company.*

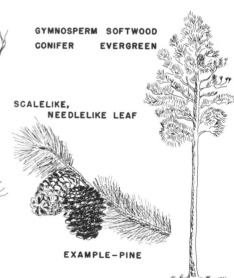

Fig. 141-2 Gymnosperm softwood example and classification. *Paxton Lumber Company.*

Outer tree structure

The three main parts of a tree are the **roots,** the **trunk,** and the **crown.** Figure 141-3 shows clearly the total tree structure.

In the **root structure,** the taproot grows deepest. This growth begins as a seed sprouts. It continues to develop through the seedling and the sapling stages (Fig. 141-4) to maturity. Countless surface roots, containing many root hairs, serve to support and anchor the tree. The root hairs, which are living cells, absorb water from the earth and dissolve the minerals and nitrogen necessary to make food. Roots also help to hold soil against erosion. A layer of growth cells at the root tips makes new root tissue during the growing season.

The **trunk,** or main stem of a tree, is the part that is of greatest commercial value. It supports the crown and produces the most useful wood. Figures 141-5, 141-6, and 141-7 show cross sections of a tree. The outer bark of the trunk protects the tree from injuries. The inner bark **(phloem)** carries food made in the leaves down to the branches, trunk, and roots.

The **crown** of the tree is formed by the branches and leaves. Leaves have been called the most important chemical factories in the world. Millions of green microscopic bodies called **chloroplasts** manufacture sugar inside each leaf. The green pigment in leaves is **chlorophyll.** Power is generated by combining radiant energy from sunlight with water from the earth and roots and carbon dioxide from the air (see Fig. 141-3, crown insert).

Oxygen is a by-product; it is released through the leaves. Water vapor is discharged from living plants through pores **(stomates)** on the undersides of leaves. Air passes in and out. This breathing process is called **transpiration.** The manufacturing process of storing energy and making sugar is termed **photosynthesis.** Each year trees increase in height and spread of branches. New growth comes from young cells in buds at the ends of twigs (see Fig. 141-4, insert).

Every living cell from roots to crown produces new products with the aid of chemical substances called **enzymes.** In general, enzymes break down the sugar that is combined with minerals and nitrogen to form various substances. Some of the sugar is used directly for energy in the growing buds, cambrium layer, and root tips.

Cell-wall substances such as cellulose, lignin, and suberin utilize sugar to make wood and bark. Enzymes change some sugar into the starches, fats, oils, and proteins which help to form seeds, fruits, and nuts. Other sugar is converted into products of special use to industry. These include resin and turpentine from southern pines and syrup from maple trees. Other products are chewing gum, made from chicle gum taken from sapodilla trees and spruces, and tannin, made from oaks, hemlocks, and chestnuts.

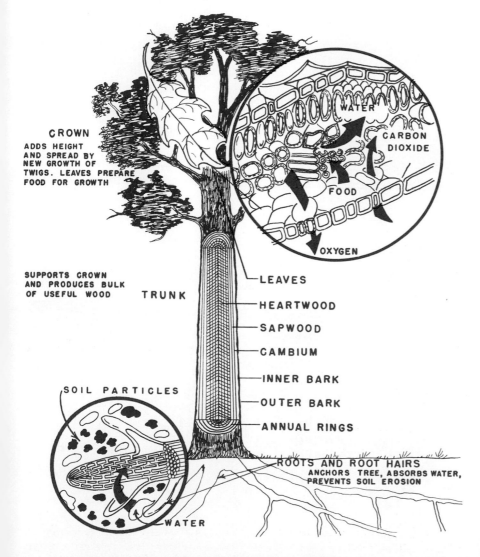

CROWN
ADDS HEIGHT AND SPREAD BY NEW GROWTH OF TWIGS. LEAVES PREPARE FOOD FOR GROWTH

WATER

CARBON DIOXIDE

FOOD

OXYGEN

SUPPORTS CROWN AND PRODUCES BULK OF USEFUL WOOD

TRUNK

LEAVES

HEARTWOOD

SAPWOOD

CAMBIUM

INNER BARK

OUTER BARK

ANNUAL RINGS

SOIL PARTICLES

WATER

ROOTS AND ROOT HAIRS
ANCHORS TREE, ABSORBS WATER, PREVENTS SOIL EROSION

Fig. 141–3 The total tree structure. *American Forest Institute.*

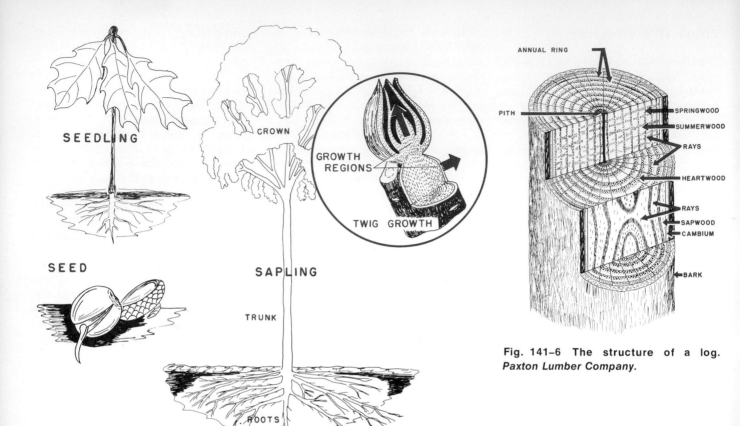

SEEDLING

SEED

CROWN

SAPLING

TRUNK

ROOTS

GROWTH REGIONS

TWIG GROWTH

Fig. 141-4 The growth cycle of a tree from seed to maturity. *American Forest Institute.*

ANNUAL RING

PITH

SPRINGWOOD

SUMMERWOOD

RAYS

HEARTWOOD

RAYS

SAPWOOD

CAMBIUM

BARK

Fig. 141-6 The structure of a log. *Paxton Lumber Company.*

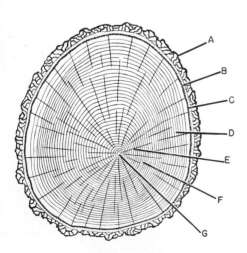

A
B
C
D
E
F
G

Fig. 141-5 Identify the parts of the cross section of a tree trunk. *Paxton Lumber Company.*

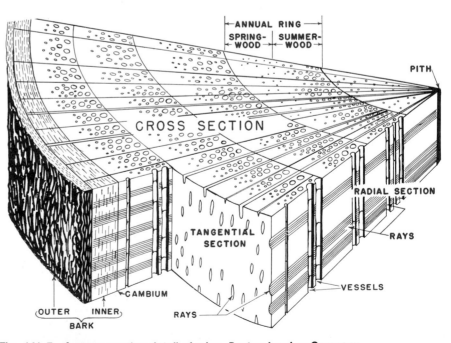

ANNUAL RING
SPRING-WOOD
SUMMER-WOOD

PITH

CROSS SECTION

RADIAL SECTION

TANGENTIAL SECTION

RAYS

VESSELS

CAMBIUM

OUTER INNER
BARK

RAYS

Fig. 141-7 A cross-section detail of a log. *Paxton Lumber Company.*

290

Inner tree structure

The **cambium** is a thin layer of cells between the bark and the wood. This layer is where growth in diameter occurs. The cells are capable of dividing and forming new ones in the part toward the sapwood (xylem), and the bast cells (phloem) in the part toward the inner bark.

Sapwood contains food cells (parenchyma), which store and conduct food vertically. Sap is carried from the roots to the leaves through tiny openings, or cells, called **vessels.** Heartwood was once sapwood; it matured and became inactive. It is composed of strong fibers that give the tree strength. Fiber length, we should mention, is another means of differentiating between hardwoods and softwoods. On an average, softwood fiber length is two to four times greater than that of hardwood. Sap in softwoods is conducted through fibers. They have no open-end cell structure; they are **nonporous** (Fig. 141-8).

Hardwoods are **porous** (Fig. 141-9), having open-end cells. Comparison of cell structure is one of the best methods of wood classification. In relation to porosity, hardwoods are called **open-** and **close-grain** woods.

Walnut, oak, and mahogany, for example, have larger open-end cells than maple or cherry. These cells are "arteries" through which sap travels to all parts of the tree. Hardwood and softwood cells are compared in Fig. 141-10.

Air in the cells of dry wood allows most wood to float when placed in water. The dry weight of different woods varies because of these hollow cells. Balsa is exceptionally light, weighing approximately 7 pounds per cubic foot (112 kilograms per cubic meter). Oak weighs about 40 pounds per cubic foot (640 kg/m³) and lignum vitae, 70 pounds per cubic foot (1120 kg/m³). Lignum vitae, rosewood, and ebony are almost solid woods. They sink in water because there are only a relatively few air-filled cell cavities.

The size, shape, and function of wood cells vary. Cells store food, conduct sap, and give strength to wood. The lines, or rays, running from the **pith** to the bark in all exogenous trees are called **medullary rays** (see Figs. 141-6 and 141-7). These rays store and conduct food horizontally. They are very noticeable in plain oak, beech, and sycamore and are easily seen as flakes in quartersawed lumber. Medullary rays add beauty to some woods and are important when drying

lumber. This accounts for the difficulty in drying many hardwoods, as compared with the softwoods.

The cell structure of some woods makes them more valuable as building materials. Nails and screws hold better in such soft-textured woods as pine, redwood, cypress, mahogany, and basswood. Paint does not usually scale off wood, as it does from metal. A natural insulator, wood protects against heat, cold, and sound. The size and arrangement of cells, along with color pigments, add to the beauty of the wood by enhancing the figure, or grain.

Most of the characteristics mentioned are means of identifying and classifying woods of various kinds and species. Color and additional qualities and properties of many common woods are given in Table 141-1.

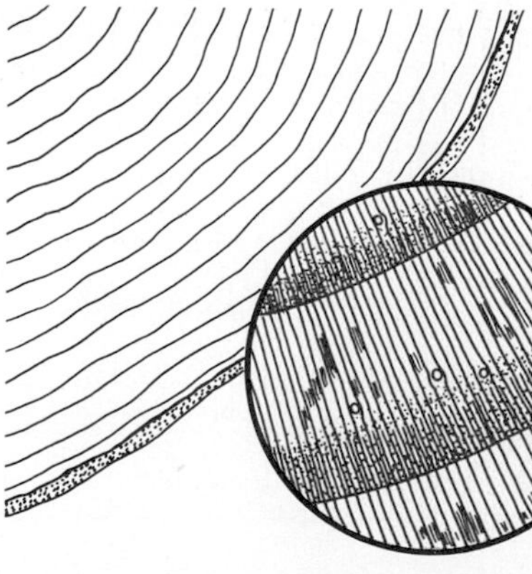

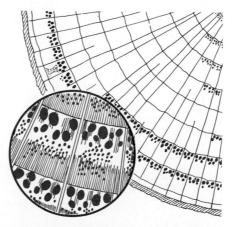

Fig. 141–8 Cross section of nonporous end cells of softwood. *Paxton Lumber Company.*

Fig. 141–9 Cross section of porous end cells in hardwood. *Paxton Lumber Company.*

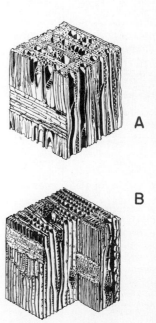

Fig. 141–10 Enlarged cell structures: (A) hardwood, and (B) softwood. *Forest Products Laboratory.*

Table 141-1 CHARACTERISTICS OF MANY COMMON WOODS

Species	Comparative weights[1]	Color[2]	Hand tool working	Nail-ability[3]	Relative density	General strength[4]	Resistance to decay[5]	Wood finishing[6]	Cost[7]
Hardwoods[8]									
Apitong	heavy	reddish brown	hard	poor	medium	good	high	poor	medium high
Ash, brown	medium	light brown	medium	medium	hard	medium	low	medium	medium
Ash, tough white	heavy	off-white	hard	poor	hard	good	low	medium	medium
Ash, soft white	medium	off-white	medium	medium	medium	low	low	medium	medium low
Avodire	medium	golden blond	medium	medium	medium	low	low	medium	high
Balsawood	light	cream white	easy	good	soft	low	low	poor	medium
Basswood	light	cream white	easy	good	soft	low	low	medium	medium
Beech	heavy	light brown	hard	poor	hard	good	low	easy	medium
Birch	heavy	light brown	hard	poor	hard	good	low	easy	high
Butternut	light	light brown	easy	good	soft	low	medium	medium	medium
Cherry, black	medium	medium reddish brown	hard	poor	hard	good	medium	easy	high
Chestnut	light	light brown	medium	medium	medium	medium	high	poor	medium
Cottonwood	light	grayish white	medium	good	soft	low	low	poor	low
Elm, soft, northern	medium	cream tan	hard	good	medium	medium	medium	medium	medium low
Gum, red	medium	reddish brown	medium	medium	medium	medium	medium	medium	medium high
Hickory, true	heavy	reddish tan	hard	poor	hard	good	low	medium	low
Holly	medium	white to gray	medium	medium	hard	medium	low	easy	medium
Limba	medium	pale golden	medium	good	medium	medium	low	medium	high
Magnolia	medium	yellowish brown	medium	medium	medium	medium	low	easy	medium
Mahogany, Honduras	medium	golden brown	easy	good	medium	medium	high	medium	high
Mahogany, Philippine	medium	medium red	easy	good	medium	medium	high	medium	medium high
Maple, hard	heavy	reddish cream	hard	poor	hard	good	low	easy	medium high
Maple, soft	medium	reddish brown	hard	poor	hard	good	low	easy	medium low
Oak, red (average)	heavy	flesh brown	hard	medium	hard	good	low	medium	medium
Oak, white (average)	heavy	grayish brown	hard	medium	hard	good	high	medium	medium high
Poplar, yellow	medium	light to dark yellow	easy	good	soft	low	low	easy	medium
Primavera	medium	straw tan	medium	medium	medium	medium	medium	medium	high
Sycamore	medium	flesh brown	hard	good	medium	medium	low	easy	medium low
Walnut, black	heavy	dark brown	medium	medium	hard	good	high	medium	high
Willow, black	light	medium brown	easy	good	soft	low	low	medium	medium low
Softwoods[9]									
Cedar, Tennessee red	medium	red	medium	poor	medium	medium	high	easy	medium
Cypress	medium	yellow to reddish brown	medium	good	soft	medium	high	poor	medium high
Fir, Douglas	medium	orange brown	medium	poor	soft	medium	medium	poor	medium
Fir, white	light	nearly white	medium	poor	soft	low	low	poor	low
Pine, yellow longleaf	medium	orange to reddish brown	hard	poor	medium	good	medium	medium	medium
Pine, eastern white (Pinus strobus)	light	cream to reddish brown	easy	good	soft	low	medium	medium	medium high
Pine, ponderosa	light	orange to reddish brown	easy	good	soft	low	low	medium	medium
Pine, sugar	light	creamy brown	easy	good	soft	low	medium	poor	medium high
Redwood	light	deep reddish brown	easy	good	soft	medium	high	poor	medium
Spruces (average)	light	nearly white	medium	medium	soft	low	low	medium	medium

[1] Kiln-dried weight.
[2] Heartwood. Sap is whitish.
[3] Comparative splitting tendencies.
[4] Combined bending and compressive strength.
[5] No wood will decay unless exposed to moisture. Resistance-to-decay estimate refers only to heartwood.
[6] Ease of finishing with clear finishes.
[7] Prices for best grade.
[8] Leaf-bearing tree.
[9] Cone- and needle-bearing trees.

Species of wood

Variations in climate and geography influence the development and growth of the many different kinds of trees found in the United States. Over 1000 species have been identified. About 100 are suitable for manufacturing into lumber, paper, and other commercially valuable products. Approximately 60 percent of the commercial species of trees are hardwoods; the remainder are softwoods.

Color and grain patterns

Color plates on pages 306a through 306h show some of the American species most often used in forest-products industries, school industrial laboratories, and retail lumber markets. There are **14** hardwoods and **10** softwoods shown.

Color and grain of surfaces are of help in identifying woods. The manner in which lumber is sawed from the log will show the flat- or edge-grained pattern of annual growth rings.

Flat-grained and **edge-grained** are terms used in reference to softwoods. **Plainsawed** and **quarter-** **sawed** generally refer to hardwoods. In each color illustration a cross section, or end grain, is shown at the top. The middle section shows edge-grained, or quartersawed, lumber. The lower section displays flat-grained, or plainsawed, surfaces.

Common hardwoods (broad leaves)

Oak is probably the most important commercial hardwood. Other valuable species are cherry, walnut, maple, ash, and yellow poplar. In addition, there are red (sweet) gum, black gum (tupelo), beech, birch, cottonwood, basswood, aspen, hickory, sycamore, magnolia, willow, and pecan.

The paragraphs that follow contain descriptions of some of the outstanding species of, first, hardwoods, then softwoods. Listed are the common and Latin names, density, characteristic hardness, properties, uses, and general color and appearance of the wood. Figures 142-1 through 142-19 show a leaf or needle; the fruit, cone, or nut; and the summer and winter silhouette.

American beech *(Fagus grandifolia).* Figure 142-1. Heavy (45 pounds per cubic foot, or 720 kg/m³). Hard. Extensive shrinkage when dried; high strength and shock resistance; readily bent when steamed. Lumber, veneer, cooperage (for example, curved pieces, or staves, for barrels), food containers, boxes, cabinetwork, pulpwood, and novelties. Heartwood white with reddish tinge to reddish brown. Tiny pores not visible; conspicuous rays.

American sycamore *(Platanus occidentalis).* Figure 142-2. Medium heavy (34 pounds per cubic foot, or 544 kg/m³). Medium hard. Close texture; interlocking grain; large shrinkage; difficult to season; warps easily. Inexpensive furniture, boxes, baskets, cooperage, veneer. Heartwood reddish to flesh brown. Very small pores not visible to the naked eye; rays visible on all surfaces.

American elm *(Ulmus americana).* Figure 142-3. Medium heavy (35 pounds per cubic foot, or 560 kg/m³). Medium hard and stiff. Good shock resistance; extensive shrinkage; easily glued. Barrels, kegs, other containers, and bent parts of furniture. Heartwood is from brown to dark brown and shades of red. Summerwood pores not visible; springwood pores large and easily visible.

Black walnut *(Juglans nigra).* Figure 142-4. Heavy (38 pounds per cubic foot, or 608 kg/m³). Hard,

Fig. 142–1 American beech.

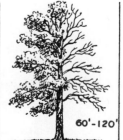

Fig. 142–2 American sycamore.

strong, stiff. Good shock resistance; one of the most durable woods; easily worked: finishes beautifully. Outstanding for solid and veneer furniture, gunstocks, interior woodwork. Chocolate to dark brown and purplish. Easily identified. Pores are hard to see on the end grain; otherwise easily distinguished.

Hickory *(Carya ovata).* Figure 142-5. Very heavy (42–52 pounds per cubic foot, or 672–832 kg/m³). Very hard, strong, stiff. Very high shock resistance; tough (combination of all these not found in any other commercial wood); large shrinkage; good glu-

ing properties. Tool handles mostly, athletic goods, agricultural implements, lawn furniture. Heartwood brown to reddish brown. Pores visible but frequently plugged with **tyloses** (a lump or callus type of growth).

White ash *(Fraxinus americana).* Figure 142-6. Heavy (42 pounds per cubic foot, or 672 kg/m³). Hard, strong, stiff. Shock resistant; excellent bending qualities. Handles, especially those to be bent; furniture, much sports and athletic equipment, particularly long oars and bats. Brown to dark brown with reddish tint. Large pores visible and distinctive.

American basswood *(Tilia americana).* Figure 142-7. Light (26 pounds per cubic foot, or 416 kg/m³). Weak, medium stiff. Low shock resistance; easily worked. Mostly lumber for boxes, crates; veneer for furniture, especially as a core for high-grade veneers. Creamy white to creamy brown or reddish heartwood. Very small pores.

Sweet gum *(Liquidambar styraciflua).* Figure 142-8. Medium heavy (36 pounds per cubic foot, or 576 kg/m³). Hard, medium stiff. Medium shock resistance; above average for turning, boring, and steam bending. Lumber,

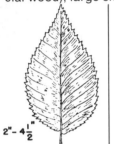  

Fig. 142–3 American elm.

 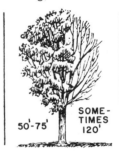 

Fig. 142–6 White ash.

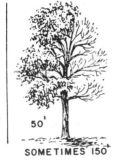

Fig. 142–4 Black walnut.

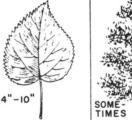  

Fig. 142–7 American basswood.

 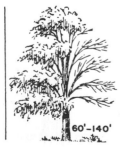 

Fig. 142–5 Hickory.

  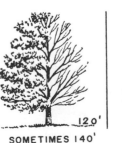 

Fig. 142–8 Sweet gum.

294

veneer, plywood for furniture, interior trim, millwork. Reddish-brown heartwood with streaks of darker color. Pores too small to see; growth rings indistinct.

Black tupelo (*Nyssa sylvatica*). Figure 142-9. Medium heavy (35 pounds per cubic foot, or 560 kg/m³). Hard. Medium in weakness, limberness, shock resistance. Lumber for shipping containers and furniture, veneer, paper pulp. Heartwood pale to medium dark brown or dirty gray. Growth rings inconspicuous.

White oak (*Quercus alba*). Figure 142-10. Heavy (47 pounds per cubic foot, or 752 kg/m³). Hard. High in strength; many species; above average in machining except shaping. Flooring, furniture, cooperage, ships, boats. Heartwood grayish brown. Outline of larger pores usually indistinct; pores usually full of tyloses.

Yellow Birch (*Betula alleghaniensis*). Figure 142-11. Heavy (43 pounds per cubic foot, or 688 kg/m³). Hard, strong, stiff. Very high shock resistance; difficult to work using hand tools but readily shaped by machines. Lumber and veneer for furniture, interior finish, millwork, distillation production of wood alcohol, charcoal, tar,

oils. Light reddish-brown heartwood. Pores barely visible.

Sugar maple (*Acer saccharum*). Figure 142-12. Heavy (44 pounds per cubic foot, or 704 kg/m³). Hard, strong, stiff. High resistance to shock; may occur with curly, wavy, or bird's-eye grain; turns well on lathe. Lumber for flooring, furniture, boxes; distillation industry producing acetic acid, charcoal, wood alcohol. Light reddish-brown heartwood, greenish-black streaks near injuries. Pores extremely small, not visible.

Yellow poplar (*Liriodendron tulipifera*). Figure 142-13. Medium light

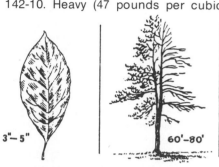

Fig. 142-9 Black tupelo.

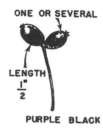

Fig. 142-12 Sugar maple.

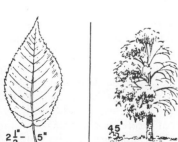

Fig. 142-10 White oak.

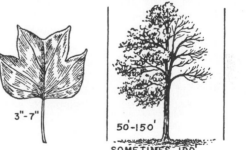

Fig. 142-13 Yellow poplar.

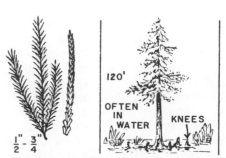

Fig. 142-11 Yellow birch.

Fig. 142-14 Bald cypress.

(35 pounds per cubic foot, or 560 kg/m³). Medium soft, medium low in bending properties, stiffness, shock resistance; intermediate machining properties; glues satisfactorily; exceptional reputation for taking and holding paint, stain, and enamel. Lumber and veneer for furniture, boxes, crates, pulpwood. Heartwood brownish yellow with definite greenish tinge and occasional black streaks.

Black cherry (Prunus serotina). See color plate. Medium heavy (35 pounds per cubic foot, or 560 kg/m³). Medium hard, strong, stiff. High shock resistance; medium-large shrinkage; little warpage after seasoning. High bending strength; glues satisfactorily with care; finishes beautifully. Furniture, backing blocks for electrotype plates in printing, woodenware, patterns and flasks for foundry in metalworking, and interior finish. Distinct light to dark reddish-brown heartwood. End-grain rays just visible; quartersawed, unusual flake pattern.

Red oak (Quercus rubra). See color plate. Heavy (44 pounds per cubic foot, or 704 kg/m³). Hard, stiff. High shock resistance; very similar to white oak except extremely porous and lacking the shellaclike tyloses. Flooring, cross ties and timbers, millwork, crates, agricultural implements. Grayish brown with distinctive reddish tint. Large, distinctive pores.

Common softwoods (needle or scalelike leaves)

Wood for pulp and paper and for most building materials comes from the softwood group. This includes Douglas and white fir, redwood, cypress, larch, hemlock, western red cedar, the spruces, and the pines.

Bald cypress (Taxodium distichum). Figure 142-14. Medium heavy and hard (32 pounds per cubic foot, or 512 kg/m³). Medium strong and stiff; outstanding durability in decaying conditions. All building construction;

containers where decay resistance is required. Heartwood varies from pale to blackish brown with red tinge. No resin canals; abrupt transition from springwood to summerwood, as in redwood.

Sugar pine (Pinus lambertiana). See color plate. Lightweight (25 pounds per cubic foot, or 400 kg/m³). Medium softness and weakness; low shock resistance; easily worked with tools. Used almost entirely for lumber in building, foundry patterns, general millwork. Heartwood from light brown to pale reddish brown. Abundant resin canals; springwood and summerwood have gradual transition.

Western red cedar (Thuja plicata). See color plate. Light (23 pounds per cubic foot, or 368 kg/m³). Medium soft, limber. Low shock resistance. Weak when used as beams. Easy to kiln-dry; little tendency to warp; easily glued; holds paint well; good weather resistance. Shingles, lumber, poles, posts, piling, exterior uses, interior finish, doors, ships, boats. Reddish- or pinkish-brown to dull brown heartwood; cedar odor; no sensation to taste as in incense cedar; confused with redwood except for odor.

White fir (Abies concolor). See color plate. Light (26-28 pounds per cubic foot, or 416–448 kg/m³). Medium soft, stiff; low in shock resistance. Difficult to season; low decay resistance; gluing properties satisfactory. Lumber and pulpwood, building construction, planing-mill work. Nearly white to red-brown heartwood. Lacks normal resin canals; more contrasting rings than eastern balsam fir.

Douglas fir (Pseudotsuga menziesii). See color plate. Medium weight (33 pounds per cubic foot, or 528 kg/m³). Medium strength, hardness, shock resistance. Very stiff. Lumber, timbers, piling; plywood in wide use for sheathing, concrete forms, prefabrication of house panels, millwork, ships and boats, other structural forms. Orange-red to red or yellowish heartwood. Distinctive odor. Resin

canals more abundant than in larch, fewer than in southern pines.

Redwood (Sequoia sempervirens). Figure 142-15. Medium strength, stiffness, and hardness; 28 pounds per cubic foot (448 kg/m³). Outstanding resistance to decay; ranks with cedars and bald cypress as highly resistant to termites. One-half to one-third used for planks, boards, joists, posts, buildings, and similar purposes. Heartwood uniform deep reddish brown. No resin canals.

Ponderosa pine (Pinus ponderosa). Figure 142-16. Medium light (28 pounds per cubic foot, or 448 kg/m³). Variable properties; outer portion of sawtimber has medium weakness, shock resistance, softness. Lumber (principally), piling, posts, mine timbers, veneer, hewn ties, high-grade millwork, boxes, crates, knotty interior finish. Heartwood yellowish to light-reddish brown or orange. Abundant resin canals.

Sitka spruce (Picea sitchensis). Figure 142-17. Medium light (28 pounds per cubic foot, or 448 kg/m³). Medium soft, stiff, shock resistant. Weak in bonding and compression strength. High strength properties on basis of weight; medium-large shrinkage; works easily; not difficult to kiln-dry. Straight grain, few hidden defects; woolly or fuzzy grain under planer knife action; long fibers. Lumber, cooperage, paper pulp, boxes, crates, some furniture, planing-mill products such as sashes and doors. Piano sounding boards. Pinkish-yellow to pale-brown heartwood. Color and more prominent resin canals distinguish it from other spruces.

Western white pine (Pinus monticola). Figure 142-18. Medium light (27 pounds per cubic foot, or 432 kg/m³). Weak, medium softness and stiffness; medium low shock resistance; easily glued and worked. About three-fourths of production used as building construction lumber, matched planks, exterior and interior trim, paneling. Cream-colored to light- or reddish-brown heartwood. Resin canals large and abundant.

Western hemlock *(Tsuga heterophylla)*. Figure 142-19. Medium light (29 pounds per cubic foot, or 464 kg/m³). Medium hard, weak, fairly low shock resistance; satisfactory gluing and working properties; easy to season. Pulp and most construction purposes, plywood core wood, mine timbers. Light reddish-brown heartwood; little color contrast on end-grain surfaces between springwood and summerwood. No normal resin canals.

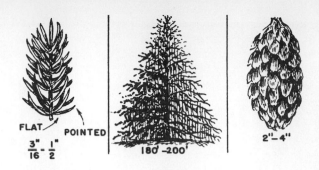

Fig. 142–17   Sitka spruce.

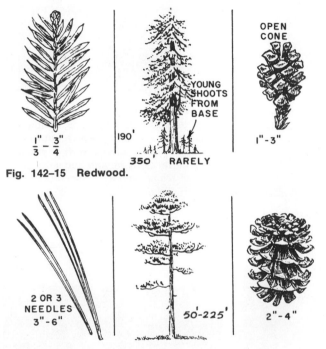

Fig. 142–15   Redwood.

Fig. 142–16   Ponderosa pine.

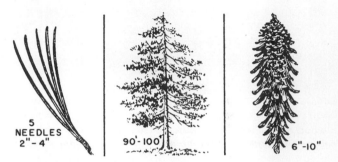

Fig. 142–18   Western white pine.

Fig. 142–19   Western hemlock.

unit 143

Trees from forest to millsite

Technological advancements in mechanical equipment used in the forest and in millwork are helping to develop the industry and speed production of lumber. Some of the numerous methods of harvesting, processing, and grading lumber are explained below.

Logging surveys

A detailed study is first made of a suitable area and source of marketable timber and lumber (Figs. 143-1 through 143-3). Facilities for operations, the method of logging, and timber available for selective harvest-

Fig. 143–1 Commercial stands of redwood are an excellent source of lumber. *Georgia-Pacific Corporation.*

Fig. 143–2 Southern pine forests provide marketable building timber. *Georgia-Pacific Corporation.*

Fig. 143–4 A cruiser marks trees with a spray gun so that loggers will know the trees are to be cut. Selective cutting improves a forest stand, giving younger trees more sunlight and room to grow. *Western Wood Products Association.*

ing must then be determined before an operation is begun.

The approximate volume (amount) of timber is determined from aerial photographs or by persons called **cruisers.** Cruisers go through an area and make careful estimates of the timber by volume, size, and species. After establishing the cutting area, they **blaze** (mark) the trees chosen for cutting: they spray white or yellow marking material on the lower part of the tree trunk, where it can easily be seen (Fig. 143-4). Cruisers may also plan logging and transportation routes. They often suggest camp sites when the logging operation is to extend over a long period of time. (Several industrial cities developed from early logging camps. These include Saginaw, Bay City, and Muskegan, Michigan, and some cities in the South and West.)

Felling trees

Trees are felled by persons called **sawyers,** or **fallers.** They use axes,

Fig. 143–3 The northwest Douglas fir area furnishes construction timber. *Georgia-Pacific Corporation.*

Fig. 143–5 Felling timber with a large power chain saw. *West Coast Lumbermen's Association.*

Fig. 143–6 In former times, trees like this were dramatically topped and then rigged with cables for various kinds of high lead logging to retrieve fallen and bucked logs to a central point. Today, portable steel spar towers have largely replaced the colorful spar tree—and the iron-nerved high topper's job. *Weyerhaeuser Company.*

crosscut saws, power chain saws (Fig. 143-5), and other power units. When the tree is exceptionally tall, it is usually **topped** (Fig. 143-6) before it is felled to prevent damage to itself and other trees.

To fell a tree, a V notch, or **undercut** (Fig. 143-7), is made on one side of the tree. This cut helps control the direction the tree falls and prevents **slabbing** (splitting) and damaging the log. A saw cut is started on the side opposite this notch and slightly above it. On large trees, a wedge is driven into the saw kerf (cut) to prevent binding (sticking) of the saw blade. The wedge also aids in forcing the tree to fall.

After trees are felled (fig. 143-8), the branches are trimmed from the trunks (Fig. 143-9) by workers called **swampers,** or **limbers.** A worker called a **log bucker** (Fig. 143-10) cuts the trunk into standard lengths for logging and transporting.

Logging and transporting

Logs are **skidded** (pulled) from forests to central points of collection (Fig. 143-11). Two-wheeled, wagonlike

Fig. 143–9 A swamper trimming limbs from tree trunk. *Western Wood Products Association.*

Fig. 143–7 Fallers making an undercut on the side of the tree facing the direction it is to fall. Loggers do this with a power saw. *Western Wood Products Association.*

Fig. 143–8 A crew using power equipment fells a large, mature western pine tree. *Western Wood Products Association.*

Fig. 143–10 A log bucker cuts trees into the standard lengths needed for logging and transporting. *Western Wood Products Association.*

trucks, log slides or chutes, or flumes (water skids) may be used. Spar trees and cableways are still used in areas where they are needed (Fig. 143-12). The modern method of logging is to use tractors and special power equipment. Pulpwood is cut to length in the forest and often skidded with slides pulled by a tractor to an area to await further shipment.

Logs are lifted with a wheel loader (Fig. 143-13) and loaded on trucks (see Fig. 143-12) or on railroad cars for shipment.

Logs that have arrived at the mill are placed on land decks (platforms) if they are to be used immediately. At this time they are often scaled (measured) to determine the volume of board feet contained in each (Fig. 143-14). If the logs are to be used later, they are kept wet by sprinklers or in the millpond (Fig. 143-15). Sprinkling or floating in the millpond keeps the reserve logs from drying and cracking. If mixed species of wood are being processed, the logs are sorted and graded before they are sawed. Different species may be sawed for different uses, may require different drying conditions, or may pose different problems in sawing.

Fig. 143–11 Skidding logs from the woods to a landing using a modern machine with a logging arch. *Case.*

Fig. 143–13 Logs are loaded on trucks with a large wheel loader. *Allis-Chalmers.*

Fig. 143–14 A scaler measuring logs to determine the broad-foot volume.

Fig. 143–12 A portable steel spar tower is used in modern logging operations to retrieve felled and bucked logs to a central loading point for delivery to the sawmill. *Weyerhaeuser Company.*

Fig. 143–15 Logs are often kept in a millpond to prevent drying and cracking. *American Forest Institute.*

Automated lumber production

Logs are processed at mills ranging in size from small, open-shed ones (Fig. 144-1) to the newest, most automated kind (Fig. 144-2). The small mill is often portable. It is operated by only a few people. The automated mill features many automatic and high-speed devices.

The processing of logs is similar in all types of mills, but the employment needs and board-foot lumber output are very different. One large automated lumber mill with dry kiln, grading sheds, planning mill, and storage and shipping areas employs only 150 persons. It cuts 10 000 to 12 000 board feet per hour. This is an expenditure of 10 to 12 worker-hours per thousand board feet (MBF). The other mills in that area spend an average of 22 worker-hours per MBF of the same type of lumber.

Modern industrial methods and technology are developing rapidly. Because of this, the operations in an automated plant are described here.

Processing logs for sawing

Logs are unloaded by a railroad crane (Fig. 144-3) onto decks (platforms). They are fed onto a conveyor, which moves them into the scaling shed. A **scaler** can measure and quickly calculate the board feet in each log without moving. The logs continue along the conveyor and enter the **debarker.**

Different types of debarkers handle logs of different sizes. The

mechanical debarker (Fig. 144-4) handles logs from 6 to 26 inches (152 to 660 mm) in diameter at the rate of 47 to 94 linear feet per minute (14 to 29 m/min). Logs over 26 inches (660 mm) across are rejected and are routed by conveyor to a semiautomatic debarker, then conveyed to the mill. The mechanical debarker has metal rollers

Fig. 144–1 A small open-shed sawmill. *Caterpillar Tractor Company.*

Fig. 144–2 This automated lumber mill contains a sawmill, kiln, grading sheds, planing mill, burner, power plant, and shipping area. *Ozan Lumber Company.*

Fig. 144–3 Unloading logs on decks with a crane. *Wood and Wood Products.*

Fig. 144-4 A mechanical debarker for handling logs 6 to 26 inches (152 to 660 mm) in diameter. *Forest Industries.*

Fig. 144-5 Debarking a log under extremely high water pressure. *Weyerhaeuser Company.*

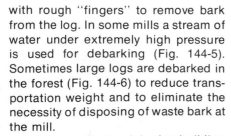

Fig. 144-6 Debarking a large log in the forest. *Caterpillar Tractor Company.*

Fig. 144-7 A pushbutton-controlled lift. *Wood and Wood Products.*

with rough "fingers" to remove bark from the log. In some mills a stream of water under extremely high pressure is used for debarking (Fig. 144-5). Sometimes large logs are debarked in the forest (Fig. 144-6) to reduce transportation weight and to eliminate the necessity of disposing of waste bark at the mill.

Just outside the debarker building

is an automatic metal detector. Logs that have nails, spikes, metal bands and markings, or other metal objects are "kicked" onto a runaround conveyor to an area where the metal is removed. They go back through the detector for another check before proceeding to the saws, which they can no longer damage.

The scale, who can work either

on the ground or on the second-story mill floor, operates a pushbutton-controlled side lift (Fig. 144-7). It takes debarked logs into the mill. The small end of the log is marked to aid the person called a **block setter** in placing the log properly on the carriage to go into the saw. The large end of the log moves into the saw first so that the log can be sawed flat on its sides more

Fig. 144–8 The riderless carriage takes a log to the band mill or headsaw. *Forest Industries.*

Fig. 144–9 The head sawyer is a key figure in the production of quality wood products. This person saws each log into rough slices that are then transported through the mill for further cutting and shaping. The head sawyer must know how to cut each log in order to get the greatest value from it. *Weyerhaeuser Company.*

Fig. 144–10 Slabs and small cants being processed through band resaw. *Forest Industries.*

Fig. 144–11 Pushbutton panels control the operation of 26-inch (660.4-mm) gang saws, set to produce 1-inch (25-mm) lumber. *Wood and Wood Products.*

easily. The large end provides a clear view of the log to the sawyer so that the least waste of log wood results.

Sawing logs into lumber

The block setter works at a pushbutton control panel to position (set) each log on a riderless carriage (Fig. 144-8).

Air-operated setworks (holders) handle the logs.

The carriage takes the log past the **band mill** (band saw) or **headsaw** (Fig. 144-9), which cuts it into a **cant**. A cant is a log that has been slabbed (sawed flat) on two or four sides (Fig. 144-10). The band in this mill travels at 10 500 ft/min (3200 m/min) and can be braked

to a stop in 50 seconds.

The **offbearer**, or **tail sawyer**, operates a series of control buttons and levers. The tail sawyer shunts (turns or pushes) cants toward the horizontal resaws or to one of several gang saws (Fig. 144-11). Pushbutton panels control different sizes of gang saws. A cant is processed in the horizontal

Fig. 144–12 A battery of saws resaw cants into preset thicknesses and widths. *Weyerhaeuser Company.*

Fig. 144–13 A conveyor chain picks up lumber from gang saws, horizontal resaws, and edgers and moves it toward the trimmer. *Wood and Wood Products.*

resaw (Fig. 144-12) as many times as needed to cut all available lumber from it. The waste material remaining is sent automatically to the chipper. The lumber is sent to edger saws.

Edger saws are located on the production line directly behind the resaws. Edger saws cut off rough edges. A special overhead light casts shadows that assist the operator in determining (without measuring) the maximum width which can be cut from each rough board. Waste strips are conveyed to the chipper.

A conveyor chain (Fig. 144-13) picks up lumber from the horizontal resaws, the gang saws, and the edgers. It moves the board to **trimmer saws** located in a hall-like structure between the mill and the sorting building. The trimmers, operated by remote control, square the ends, remove defects, and cut the final lumber to desired lengths. Usable waste is conveyed to the chipper.

Waste utilization is an integral part of any modern mill. Waste wood from each operation in the entire plant is sent to the **chipper** unit to be reduced to uniform chips. These are screened (Fig. 144-14) and conveyed by blower or gravity to waiting boxcars. Several rail carloads per day are sent to paper mills and hardboard or particle board plants. Unsuitable chips,

Fig. 144–14 A screen separates usable ³/₄-inch-long (19-mm-long) chips from sawdust, bark, and unsuitable chips. *Wood and Wood Products.*

sawdust, and bark which cannot be used commercially are consumed as fuel to produce steam power for the sawmill.

After trimming, the boards are carried down troughlike conveyors that run the length of the sorting building. As the lumber travels at high speed, a series of electrical switches operates electronic devices to measure the length of each piece. Gates are activated (opened) to shunt (turn) the lumber to drop into one of 24 bays (sorting compartments, or areas).

The lumber is placed in layers on railroadlike **kiln cars** by a semiautomatic **chain-arm stacker.** Sticks are placed about 2 feet (609 mm) apart between layers to help prevent any type of crooking, such as wind (twisting). As each stack is completed, it is pulled out on rails to the **dry kilns.** After proper drying, the lumber is ready for storage or shipment. It goes to flooring mills, planing mills, construction companies, furniture plants, and other industries that manufacture wood products.

unit 145

Numerically controlled wood-products manufacturing

Fig. 145–1 The router is adaptable for numerical control use. *Woodworking & Furniture Digest.*

Fig. 145–2 Irregular shapes can be cut by using numerical control and the router. *Woodworking & Furniture Digest.*

The automated production concept is not new in the woodworking industry, but its introduction into the total industry has been slow. Some types of controlled production, such as with tapes, have been even slower to find their way into industrial woodworking use. Some manufacturers are using this form of mechanization because of labor shortages in their areas and increasing overall costs of outdated operations. Others are beginning to use the system because of more efficient control of production in time, costs, and product quality for their particular business.

Automated lumber production, as explained in Unit 144, has become common practice in this and similar line production industries. More specialized production in wood is evident and is being initiated through the use of numerically controlled (N/C) machines (Fig. 145-1). **N/C** has become accepted as a standard abbreviation and designation in a number of industries for the term **numerical control.**

The N/C concept originated in 1949 from an Air Force research study. Large purchases of such controlled machine tools came a few years later when plants across the country began using these machines for actual production. The N/C machine has been limited largely to work application in the metals industries but has been adapted for use in some woodworking production operations. The use of N/C production in wood is increasing.

The router (Fig. 145-2), double-end tenoner, shaper, turret drills, and combinations of these machines are examples of those adapted to tape-controlled use. Plans are ready for furniture- and wood-machining systems of the future to be controlled by command sequence units (Fig. 145-3), including control of conveyors and other product-transfer or feed mechanisms.

N/C manufacturing and use

Many machinery manufacturers are producing standard or traditional machines for woodworking by using N/C equipment in their own plants. N/C machines may have a possible output capacity of ten or more times that of old machine models. The improvement in total quality is of equal significance in the use of numerical control.

How N/C works

Numerical or tape control is simply explained as a tape into which holes have been punched and which becomes the means of regulating the motion of a machine through electronic circuits. The holes have been punched to represent coordinate measurements of parts sizes. Photoelectric cells "read" these holes,

Fig. 145–3 The cabinet containing the electronic equipment and programmed tape is a major part of the N/C equipment and operation. *Woodworking & Furniture Digest.*

amplify the reading, and feed the information to automatic or servo-mechanisms through electronic circuits. Combinations of holes and electronic impulses generated in the circuitry tell the machine or machine part to move. For example, the cutter head of the machine is told or caused to move automatically in any direction—up or down, in or out, right or left—or to follow a continuous curved or straight line. Other impulses tell the machine to speed up, slow down, raise or lower a head, or stop. Each bit of information on the tape combines to give these various commands to motors or hydraulic drives to make the machine move or react and cut wood to as small a tolerance as two-thousandths of an inch (0.05 mm) or less.

Sophisticated metalworking operations such as multiple pattern drilling, diesinking, and milling can be repeatedly performed much more accurately with tape controls than could be done with manual controls. Except for the cutting tool shape and spindle speed, vertical milling (Fig. 145-4) is very similar to routing in woodwork (Fig. 145-5). It should be remembered that machining of wood is often done in feet per minute and that metal may cut much slower, in inches per minute or per hour. In either industry, the initial cost may be high, but N/C operations such as routing in woodwork can prove advantageous and valuable.

How N/C tapes are cut

There are companies available that provide tape punching or automatic programmer services. An engineer, technologist, technician, or any other worker can program or cut a tape if she or he understands numerical control systems and has the necessary equipment.

A pattern or sample of a part to be made (Fig. 145-6) can be used, and

Fig. 145–4 The numerically controlled vertical milling machine in metalworking is similar to the router in woodworking. *Woodworking & Furniture Digest.*

Fig. 145–5 This woodworking router is similar to the vertical milling machine in metalworking. *Woodworking & Furniture Digest.*

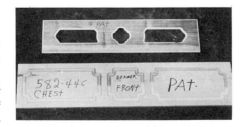

Fig. 145–6 Patterns and sample parts can be used to give specifications for making an N/C tape. *Woodworking & Furniture Digest.*

from it the necessary specifications can be taken to give information to make a tape. An exact pattern can also be used for locating or setting the exact depth of a tool cut (Fig. 145-7).

A drawing is one of the most common references used to make a tape. An accurate, scaled drawing is not an absolute necessity; but the dimensions, radii, finish notes, or any other information related to the part to be made must be very accurately recorded. The speeds and feeds for proper work can be incorporated on a drawing and also worked into the tape.

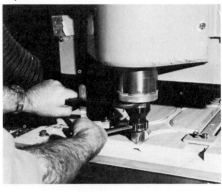

Fig. 145–7 A sample of a part can be used for setting the depth of an N/C cut. *Woodworking & Furniture Digest.*

The programmer or person punching a tape should have basic knowledge of many things. However, some of the knowledge this person should have is basic learning related to the machine—the machining it does and can do. A thorough knowledge of reading everything on a drawing is also necessary. Understanding of the mathematical x, y, and z axes is one of the basic principles of programming. The ability to type would also help speed the operation of cutting a tape. However, a program for making a part can be written by one person and punched into the tape by a second person.

Tapes are punched on a machine similar to a standard typewriter. One such machine is the Flexowriter (Fig.

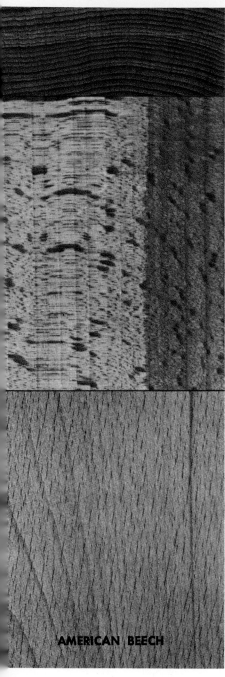

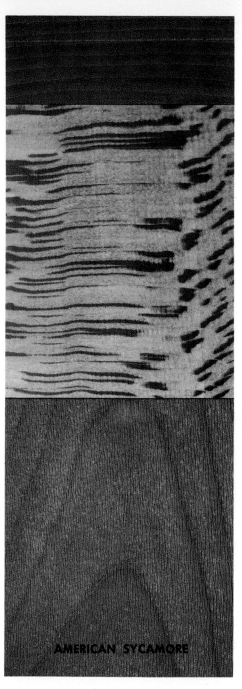

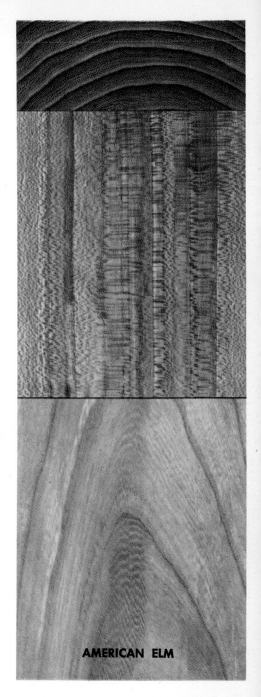

AMERICAN BEECH

AMERICAN SYCAMORE

AMERICAN ELM

rd and heavy, high in nail-withdrawal resist-
:e; spilts easily. Hard to work by hand;
chines smoothly. Heartwood: reddish-white
reddish-brown. Pores invisible without mag-
cation, but wood rays (radial strips of cells)
be see on all surfaces. Average weight
lb to cu ft.

Moderately hard, strong, stiff. Difficult to split.
Not durable when exposed to conditions favor-
able to decay. Reddish-brown or flesh brown in
color; close texture, interlocking grain. Pores
not visible to unaided eye, but rays are
visible on all surfaces. Average weight 34
lb to cu ft.

Moderately heavy, strong. Bends easily; resists
shock; moderate resistance to decay, nail with-
drawal. Heartwood: brown, often with red.
Some single summerwood pores visible, others
in concentric wavy lines; springwood: large
pores in single row. Average weight 35 lb to
cu ft.

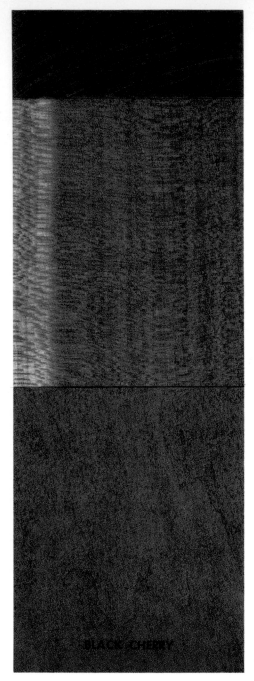

BLACK CHERRY

TRUE HICKORY

Strong, stiff, good shock resistance. Holds shape after seasoning; durable; easy to work. Handsome grain pattern. Light to dark chocolate-brown, often with purplish streaks. Pores faint on end grain, appear on longitudinal surfaces as darker grooves. Average weight 38 lb to cu ft.

Stiff, strong, moderately hard and heavy. Hard to work by hand but machines well. Old sapwood narrow and nearly white. Heartwood: light to dark reddish-brown with distinctive luster. End-grain rays faint; appear as flakes on quarter-sawed surfaces. Average weight 35 lb to cu ft.

Shagbark, shellbark, pignut, mockernut h ories. Very tough, heavy, hard, strong: uni combination in native commercial woo White sapwood; reddish heartwood. Pores sharply outlined. Sapwood and heartw same strength. Average weight 42 to 52 to cu ft.

306b

WHITE ASH

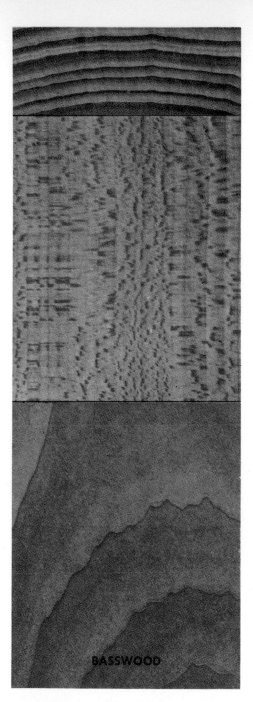

BASSWOOD

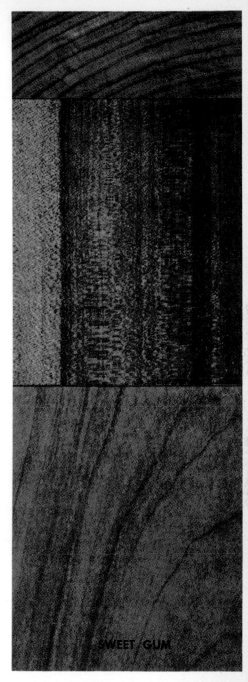

SWEET GUM

ong, stiff. Holds nails well; easily worked, t splits easily. Heartwood: brown to dark wn, sometimes reddish. Sapwood: light, or rly white. Large-pore area usually sharply fined. Small wood rays generally visible only quarter-sawed surfaces. Average weight 42 to cu ft.

Soft, light in weight; fine, even texture. Straight grained; easy to work with tools. Highly resistant to warping; does not split easily. Heartwood: pale, yellowish-brown; occasional darker streaks. Pores are very small; growth rings generaly faint. Average weight 26 lb to cu ft.

Fairly hard, heavy, strong. Holds nails, resists splitting fairly well. Two classes of lumber: sap gum (light colored sapwood), and red gum (reddish-brown heartwood above). Pores invisible; growth rings usually faint; rays visible on quarter-sawed faces. Average weight 36 lb to cu ft.

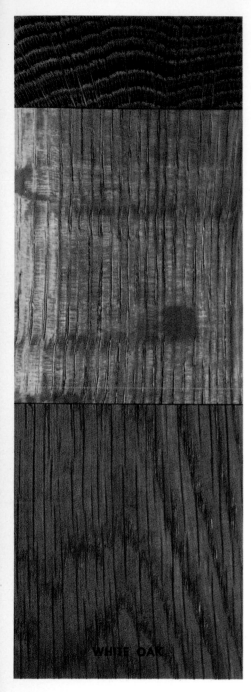

WHITE OAK

RED OAK

YELLOW BIRCH

Heavy, very hard, and strong. Machines very well. Heartwood: grayish-brown; resists decay. Heartwood pores indistinct and plugged with tyloses; wood is thus impervious to liquids. Rays lghter than background on end faces, darker on side faces. Average weight 47 lb to cu ft.

Properties similar to white oak except it is extremely porous. Heartwood: grayish-brown with reddish tint. Larger pores distinct. Wood rays commonly ¼ to 1 in. high along grain. On end-grain surfaces, rays appear as lines crossing growth rings. Average weight 44 lb to cu ft.

Fine, close grained, uniform. Heavy, ha stiff. Hard to work by hand, but machi well. Holds nails well; decays easily. Li reddish-brown; very small pores. Growth ri visible on plain-sawed surfaces; wood ra on quarter-sawed surfaces. Average weight lb to cu ft.

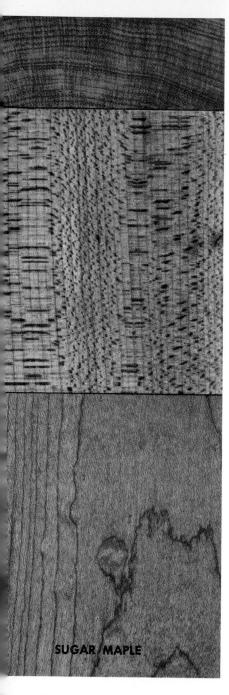

SUGAR MAPLE

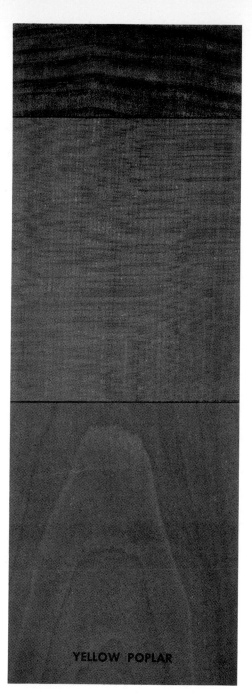

YELLOW POPLAR

BALD CYPRESS

ong, stiff, moderately decay resistant. Holds
s well; markedly resistant to abrasive
. Light reddish-brown, often with green-
black streaks. Very small pores. Wood
faint on end grain, very clear on
rter-sawed faces. Average weight 44 lb to
ft.

Moderately soft, moderately stiff. Intermediate in machining properties. Low nail-withdrawal resistance; little tendency to split when
nailed. Holds paint well. Fairly decay resistant. Heartwood: brownish-yellow, usually with
definité greenish tinge. Average weight 30 lb
to cu ft.

Straight, mild grain; moderately strong, hard,
and heavy. Works easily; resists decay. Certain
wood, called pecky cypress, contains localized
areas of fungus growth; cutting and drying ar-
rests the fungus decay. Heartwood: pale to
blackish-brown, sometimes reddish. Average
weight 32 lb to cu ft.

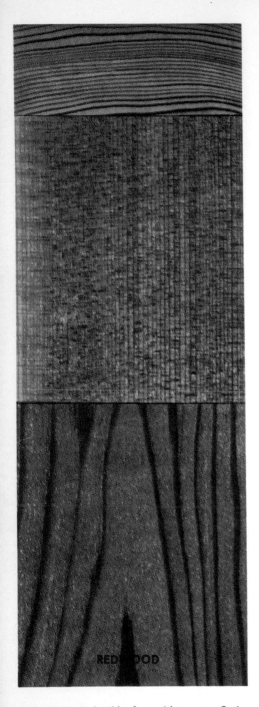

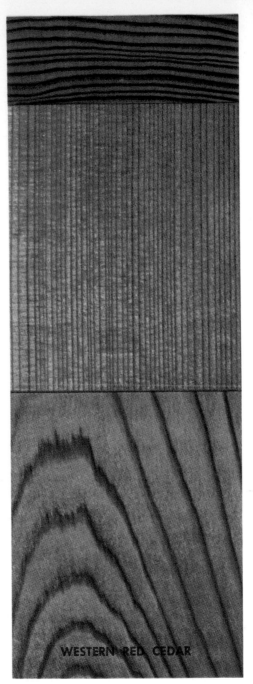

REDWOOD

WESTERN RED CEDAR

PONDEROSA PINE

One of most durable for outdoor use. Grain mild, straight, with smooth, silky sheen and thin, dark lines. Moderately hard, strong, and stiff. Holds nails fairly well, paint well; works easily by hand. Heartwood is usually uniform deep reddish-brown. Average weight 28 lb to cu ft.

Lightweight; shock resistance low; weak as post or beam. Fairly soft; resists decay; holds paint well. Nail-holding poor. Heartwood: pinkish- to dull brown. Cedar odor. Springwood to summerwood change abrupt, making growth rings prominent. Average weight 23 lb to cu ft.

Outer wood fairly lightweight; strength soft, stiff. Texture uniform; straight-grai not easily split. Heartwood: low to mode in decay resistance; light reddish-brown. Sp wood-summerwood change abrupt; sum wood bands narrow. Average weight 28 l cu ft.

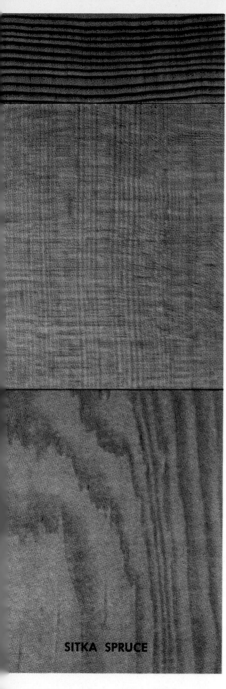

SITKA SPRUCE

SUGAR PINE

WESTERN WHITE PINE

...in straight; fine, uniform texture; fairly ...ong; works easily; holds nails well; decay ...istance low; often produces fuzzy grain under ...er knives. Heartwood: pinkish-yellow to ...e brown. Springwood-summerwood change ...; flat-grain surface rings faint. Average ...ght 28 lb to cu ft.

Straight grain, fairly uniform texture; easy to work; holds nails well. Lightweight; strength moderately low; not stiff. Fairly decay resistant, soft. Heartwood: pale reddish-brown. Resin canals abundant and commonly stain the wood surface. Average weight 25 lb to cu ft.

Straight grained, easy to work; kiln-dries easily and stays in place well after seasoning. Lightweight, moderately soft and stiff. Low to moderate in decay resistance. Heartwood is cream colored to light brown or reddish-brown. Resin canals abundant. Average weight 27 lb to cu ft.

306g

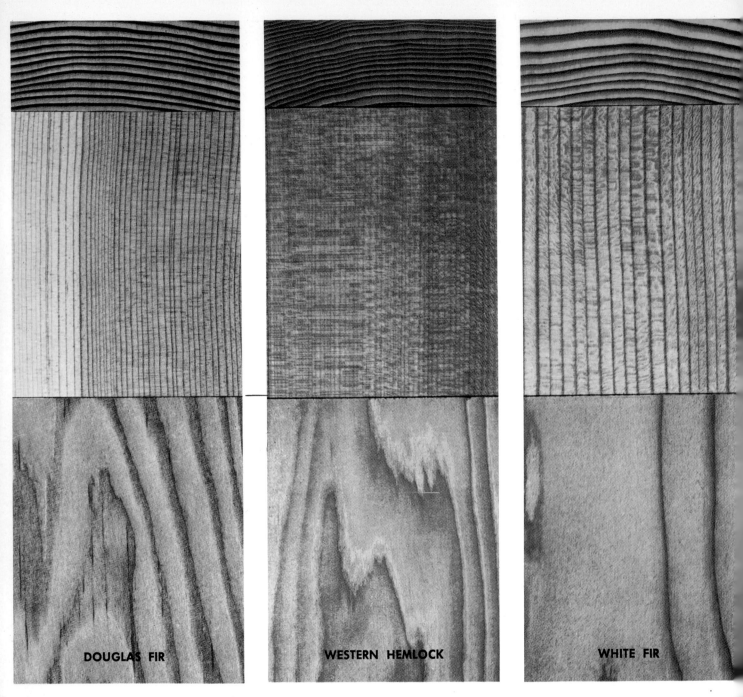

DOUGLAS FIR

WESTERN HEMLOCK

WHITE FIR

Varies widely in weight and strength. Most old-growth wood is moderately heavy, strong, hard, and shock resistant. Very stiff and difficult to work, but holds nails well. Moderate decay resistance. Heartwood: orange-red to red or yellowish. Distinctive odor. Average weight 33 lb to cu ft.

Moderately lightweight, moderately low in strength. Fairly hard, stiff. Heartwood low in decay resistance; easy to work. Heartwood: light reddish-brown, often with purplish cast, especially in summerwood bands. Wood lacks normal resin canals. Average weight 39 lb to cu ft.

Fir species names—white fir, grand fir, Pa silver fir, California red fir, noble fir. Ligh weight, moderately soft and weak, low in holding power and decay resistance. H wood: nearly white to pale reddish-br Wood lacks normal resin canals. Average we 27 lb to cu ft.

306h

145-8). This machine has special attachments and parts to hold blank tape and to punch holes. The tape may be made from such material as paper or Mylar (polyester film).

Fig. 145–8 The Flexowriter shown is used for making N/C tapes. *Woodworking & Furniture Digest.*

In programming a tape for a machine cut, the information is "typed" into this mechanism. Holes are punched in the tape according to what you want the machine to do, such as the sequence of movements or the speed and feed which the cutting head or table is supposed to make until the entire cut or part is completed. Additional programming will tell the machine to hold for another cut or stop. Tapes can be made in an endless roll (Fig. 145-9) to cause the work to be repeated with rapid, exact, and continuous operation. Tapes can be programmed so that cuts will be made in a continuous curved path (Fig. 145-10). Usage of this part is shown on the furniture in Fig. 145-11. Tapes for curved cutting are called **continuous path programming,** and straight line cuts are called **point-to-point programming.**

Using the tape

The tape is removed from the "writer" and placed in a photoelectric "reader" or electronic control cabinet (Fig. 145-12). This mechanism senses numbers and the sequence of operations

Fig. 145–9   The control cabinet may hold an endless tape for repetitive and continuous work operations. *Woodworking & Furniture Digest.*

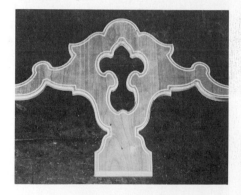

Fig. 145–10   A bed headboard part cut by numerical control. *Woodworking & Furniture Digest.*

Fig. 145–11 The headboard of a bed showing the part in Fig. 145–10. *Woodworking & Furniture Digest.*

from the punched holes in the tape. The control cabinet is connected to the working machine by a cable of wires (Fig. 145-13) through which electric impulses are fed to the machine; these impulses control the final cuts desired.

Fig. 145–12 The programmed tape is placed in the electronic control cabinet after the tape has been punched. *Woodworking & Furniture Digest.*

Fig. 145–13 The electronic control cabinet is connected to the machine by cables of wires that feed impulses to the machine. *Woodworking & Furniture Digest.*

Efficiency of tape control

The efficiency of N/C or tape control is best explained by an example. For one woodworking manufacturer, N/C reduced the time needed to cut a table leg decoration by 75 percent per piece. The time was $22\frac{1}{2}$ seconds by tape control to $1\frac{1}{2}$ minutes with a conventional pattern and single-pin router. The machine could have gone faster but was limited by the number of pieces the operator could handle.

Machinery manufacturers have developed tape-controlled equipment for practically all kinds of woodworking machines. The carving machine (Fig. 145-14) is a router operation automatically making multiple cuts for drawer front decoration (Fig. 145-15).

A great percent of the machines developed in the future years will probably be capable of production through some form of N/C because of the speed, accuracy, and versatility of this form of production.

The versatile double-end tenoner

The woodworking industry may be slower than most industries to use automation, but the double-end tenoner is one of the most versatile machines available. It can now be made to perform automatically the many operations it is capable of doing.

The first tenoner was a single-end model developed by J. A. Fay in 1834 and designed to machine tenons to fit mortises invented by George Page in the same year. The date of the first commercial double-end tenorer is somewhat obscure but is believed to be about 1890.

Over the years, as the tenoner came into universal use, additional saws, cutters, and special tools have been provided as attachments and accessories for unlimited applications. These additions will handle such jobs as double-end cutting off, trimming, squaring, angle cutting, mitering, tenoning, end and edge shaping, multi-

Fig. 145–14 A carving machine for making multiple cuts on drawer decorations. *Woodworking & Furniture Digest.*

Fig. 145–15 Drawer decorations made by using N/C. The carving machine is a router operation. *Woodworking & Furniture Digest.*

ple and angular dadoing, slotting, grooving, rabbeting, dovetailing, sanding, applying glue, cutting other forms of joints, boring for dowels, drilling for screws, edge beveling, corner rounding, and antiquing edges of furniture parts. The operations are almost unlimited, but the speed, accuracy and quality of machining is improved. Millwork plants, such as furniture, door, and window sash manufacturers, use this versatile machine. The machines are easily adapted for cutting plywood, particle boards, or solid wood. It would be easy to forget that the original purpose of a tenoner was to machine tenons to fit mortises for mortise-and tenon joints. The tenoner does not replace all other machines, but it can be adapted to perform many operations other machines perform, and it can also be controlled automatically.

unit 146

Sawing, drying, grading, and purchasing lumber

The exact date the first sawmill was established in America is not known, but sawmills were in operation around the year 1610. One of the earliest methods of sawing lumber during colonial American times was **pit sawing.** Figure 146-1 shows **whipsawing,** which was a modification of this earlier procedure.

Methods of sawing lumber

The two general methods of sawing lumber are **plainsawing,** often also called **common, flat,** or **slash** sawing (see Fig. 146-2), and **quartersawing,** of which there are four methods (see Fig. 146-3).

A slab (Fig. 146-2A) is the first cut in plainsawing. The log is slabbed on either two or four sides to form a cant, from which other plainsawed lumber is cut. Plainsawed lumber has several advantages over quartersawed: (1) more lumber is produced when grain and figure are not considered, (2) it is cheaper to cut, and (3) under similar conditions it dries more rapidly.

Quartersawing can be done by any one of four methods: (1) radial (Fig. 146-3A), (2) tangential (Fig. 146-3B), (3) combined radial and tangential (Fig. 146-3C), and (4) quarter-

tangential (Fig. 146-3D). The log is quartered (thus the name) and then cut radially from the bark to the center. This is perpendicular to the annual rings and parallel to the medullary rays. A few pieces of plainsawed lumber, however, fall in the quartersawed category (Fig. 146-2B).

Quartersawing has the following advantages over plainsawing: (1) the wood does not twist (wind), and it warps less; (2) there is less shrinkage in width (lumber shrinks very little in length); (3) the wood lasts longer and wears more evenly when used for such purposes as flooring; and (4) it does not surface check (crack) as easily during seasoning (drying).

Seasoning, or drying, lumber

Seasoning lumber is the removal of moisture (water) from the wood until a specified dryness is obtained. Correctly seasoned wood has more strength, is more stable in use, and is more resistant to decay than unseasoned stock. In seasoning, the moisture content (MC) is expressed as a percentage. The lower the percentage figure, the drier the wood.

Wood has an equilibrium mois-

Fig. 146–1 Whipsawing is a method of cutting timber which was used by American colonists. *United States Forest Products Laboratory.*

ture content (EMC) when the moisture in the wood equals the humidity (moisture) in the surrounding air so that it neither gains nor loses moisture. When wood is dried to the correct EMC it is more stable (shrinks or swells less).

Damp wood in dry air shrinks; dry wood in damp air swells. The MC is only slightly affected by temperature, but it is considerably influenced by humidity. The EMC varies under differ-

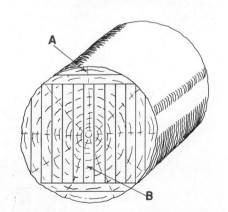

Fig. 146–2 Common, flat, or slash sawing: (A) slab, and (B) plainsawing.

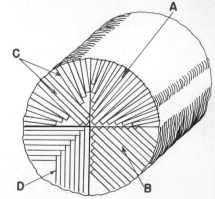

Fig. 146–3 Four methods of quartersawing: (A) radial, (B) tangential, (C) combined radial and tangential, and (D) quarter-tangential.

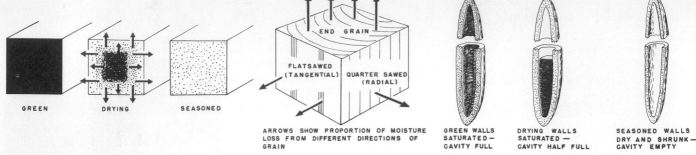

Fig. 146–4 How wood loses moisture. The three illustrations on the right help to explain how moisture is lost in the three stages of seasoning illustrated on the left.

ent weather conditions. As an example, if lumber is too dry, doors and drawers of chests swell and fit too tightly.

Methods of drying

Lumber may be **air-dried** (AD), **kiln-dried** (KD), or both. Several days or weeks of kiln drying equal several years of air drying. The method of drying, the loss of moisture, and the time required for drying affect shrinkage of a particular wood during seasoning (Figs. 146-4 and 146-5). Softwoods can usually be dried faster than hardwoods, by either method.

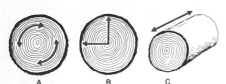

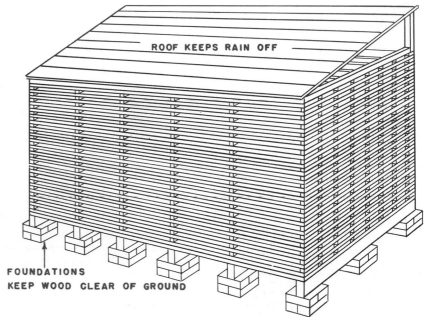

Fig. 146–6 The proper method of stacking lumber for air drying, or seasoning. *Paxton Lumber Company.*

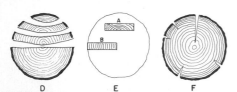

Fig. 146–5 Shrinkage during seasoning: (A) shrinkage is greatest in the direction of the growth rings; (B) shrinkage is about half as much radially; (C) shrinkage is least in length; (D) the effect of shrinkage is seen on outer boards; (E) shrinkage in board B is about half as much as in board A; and (F) splits are caused by excessive shrinkage.

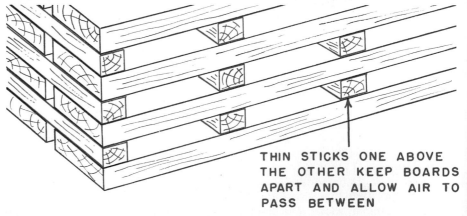

Fig. 146–7 Detail of stacking lumber for air drying. *Paxton Lumber Company.*

310

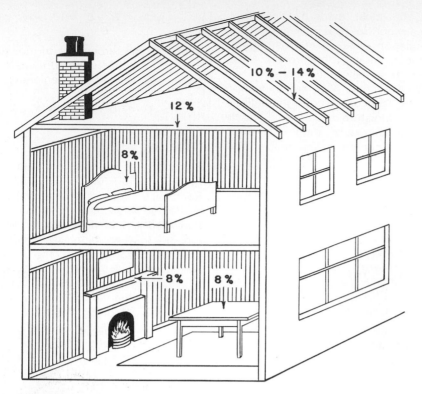

Air drying reduces the moisture content of lumber to a minimum of 12 to 15 percent. Lumber is often stacked for air drying when it is to be used for exterior purposes. It may be air-dried only, or it may be partially dried and then sent to a kiln. In both air and kiln drying, space is left between layers of lumber for proper air circulation (Figs. 146-6 and 146-7).

A good rule to apply is the following: the drier the climate, the drier the wood preferred.

Most lumber is kiln-dried to about 12 percent MC or less for ordinary uses (Figs. 146-8 and 146-9).

Dry kilns are of two types, compartment and progressive. After lumber is sawed, it is usually seasoned (dried) in kilns. It is stacked and enters the **compartment kiln** (Fig. 146-10). In this type of kiln it usually remains in one location until it is dry.

A **progressive kiln** is similar to an assembly line. A carload of lumber enters the kiln and goes through each of several drying compartments, or stages of drying.

Fig. 146–8 The average moisture content of lumber for various uses. *Paxton Lumber Company.*

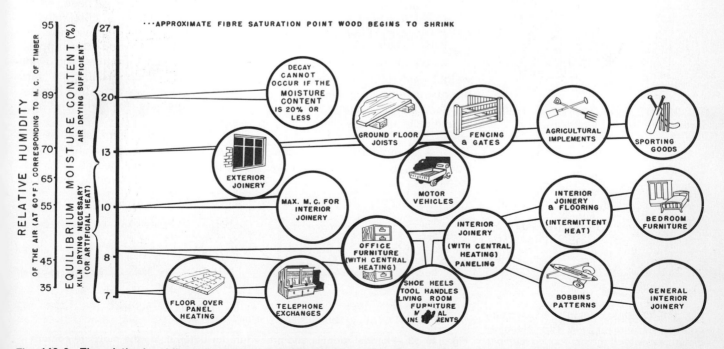

Fig. 146–9 The relative humidity and equilibrium moisture content of some manufactured wood products. *Paxton Lumber Company.*

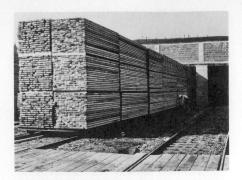

Fig. 146-10 Stacks of lumber entering a dry kiln. *Weyerhaeuser Company.*

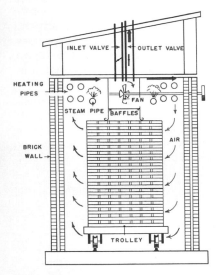

Fig. 146-11 Cross section of a dry kiln. *Paxton Lumber Company.*

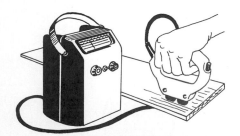

Fig. 146-12 Determining the moisture content of lumber with an electrical moisture-content meter. *Paxton Lumber Company.*

The most modern kilns scientifically control heat, moisture, and air circulation, using special instruments. At the beginning of the process, the air is exceptionally moist and cool (Fig. 146-11). As the drying procedure continues, this condition is gradually reversed. Moisture is decreased and the heat is increased until the correct moisture content of the lumber is secured.

Determining moisture content

Moisture content of lumber can be determined by using an electric moisture-content meter (Fig. 146-12). Perform an MC experiment by observing Fig. 146-13 and following the procedure given below.

1. Select a board from the lumber to be tested. About 2 feet (610 mm) from the end of the board, saw off a piece $1/4$ to $3/4$ inch (6 to 19 mm) long.

2. Weigh the sample as accurately as possible, and record the weight.

3. Place the sample in an electric oven. Set the heat at approximately 215°F (101.7°C). Bake about 30 minutes.

4. Weigh the sample, record its weight, and return it to the oven for approximately 15 minutes.

5. Continue weighing the sample periodically until the weight is constant.

6. The moisture content can be computed by using the following formula:

$$MC = \frac{W - D}{D} \times 100 = \%$$

where MC = percentage of moisture (moisture content)
W = "wet," or beginning, weight
D = "dry" weight

Grading lumber

Grading rules and standards are used by the leading lumber associations. Some of these are the National Hardwood Association, the California Redwood Association, and the Western and Southern Pine Associations. A detailed description of the various grading rules is found in the bulletin *Wood Handbook,* which can be obtained from the U.S. Forest Products Laboratory, Madison, Wisconsin.

Lumber is often graded (Fig. 146-14) both before and after it is taken to the kiln or storage yard. It is moved about the yard by a fork lift or by some other kind of modern carrier.

Softwoods are graded on the basis of the use of the whole board. A uniform standard has been established to simplify the grading rules for common thicknesses, widths, and lengths. Most softwood lumbering associations apply these rules and divide lumber into three groups: (1) **yard lumber,** (2) **factory and shop lumber,** and (3) **timbers** for structural purposes.

Yard lumber in softwoods is graded (1) **select,** or **finish,** A, B, C, and D; (2) **common boards,** Nos. 1, 2, 3, and sometimes 4 and 5; and (3) **di-**

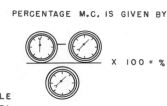

WEIGH SAMPLE ("WET" WEIGHT) DRY IT UNTIL NO FURTHER WEIGHT LOSS WEIGH SAMPLE ("DRY" WEIGHT) PERCENTAGE M.C. IS GIVEN BY ... X 100 = %

Fig. 146-13 Pictorial formula and procedure for determining the moisture content of lumber. *Paxton Lumber Company.*

mension, Nos. 1, 2, and 3. The select, or finish, grades are used in visible construction. Common boards are used for sheathing, general utility, and construction purposes. Dimension grades are used for framing where strength and stiffness are needed. They are usually 2 to 5 inches (51 to 127 mm) thick.

The factory and shop lumber group is for special uses, such as for window sashes and doors. The boards are 1¼ inches (32 mm) or greater in thickness.

Timbers are mostly for structural purposes and are left round or sawed to size and shape. They are graded on the basis of strength, and they are used where working stresses are required. Sawed timbers are either rough or finished. They serve as beams, posts, and joists. Common sizes are 4 inches (102 mm) square or larger, in either thickness or width. Round timbers are sometimes used in framing structures, but they are more frequently employed as poles and piling.

A group of voluntary standards has been accepted by most producers, distributors, and users of softwood lumber. For many years the actual finished size of a two-by-four was 1⅝ inches by 3⅝ inches whether green or dry. The new size will be a minimum of 1½ inches by 3½ inches when dried to an MC of 19 percent, or 1⁹⁄₁₆ inches by 3⁹⁄₁₆ inches when green (undried). Metric sizes have not been officially decided upon.

Hardwood lumber is graded on the basis of the amount of usable lumber cut clear (free) of blemishes from one piece. One face must be **clear** (flawless), the other one **sound** (perhaps knotted but without holes), to rate a high grade. Boards are sawed to standard thicknesses. The widths and lengths are cut so as to obtain the greatest amount of usable lumber.

The two highest grades of hardwood are **firsts and seconds** (FAS), which are usually combined into one category. The third grade is **selects.** Lesser grades are No. 1 common, No. 2 common, No. 3 common, sound wormy, No. 3A common, and No. 3B common.

Grades and grading rules help establish a standard for designating prices according to kind, quality, and use of lumber. The number, type, and condition and location of blemishes or defects (Fig. 146-15) help establish the grade. Defects are classified as heart shake, wind shake, starshake, knots, checks, and splits.

Heart shake is a rot beginning with a hole in the center of the tree from which cracks extend outward. This is common in older trees.

Wind shake is a separation of the fibers or the annual rings.

Starshake is similar to heart shake, but it has solid wood along the cracks with no rot.

Knots are caused as limbs form on a tree. The fibers arrange themselves around this point and form the knot.

Checks and **splits** in logs and timbers result when the outer surfaces of a log shrink faster than the inner portion.

Study the *Wood Handbook* discussion of defects, blemishes, and grades of lumber. The knowledge you will gain will assist you in becoming a wiser purchaser and consumer.

Fig. 146–14 Grading and sorting lumber for thickness, width, and grade. *Weyerhaeuser Company.*

Purchasing lumber

After drying and grading, most softwoods are sent to the planing mill for surfacing and cutting into special or standard sizes. Most softwoods are purchased in standard sizes.

Standard 1-inch pine stock is actually only ²⁵⁄₃₂ inch thick; 2-inch stock is usually 1½ inches thick.

The 4-inch widths are usually 3½ inches wide. The 6-inch widths are 5½ inches wide. The 8-, 10-, and 12-inch-wide boards lose ³⁄₄ inch in width.

Standard lengths range from 8 to 20 feet in 2-foot intervals.

Hardwood lumber is usually left in rough condition. It is purchased in random widths and lengths (RWL) and in thicknesses of ¼-inch intervals. One-inch lumber is called **four-quarter** (4/4); 1¼-inch **five-quarter** (5/4); 1½-inch, **six-quarter** (6/4); and so on.

Lumber is left **rough** (RGH) when it is unplaned, and it is **dressed** when it is surfaced or planed. Common designations of surface lumber are (1) surfaced on one side (S1S), (2) surfaced two sides (S2S), (3) surfaced one side and one edge (S1S1E), and

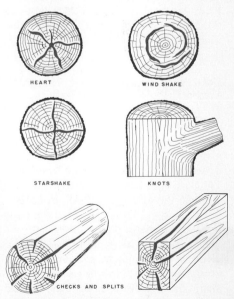

Fig. 146–15 Blemishes and defects of logs and timbers.

(4) surfaced four sides (S4S).

Consider the following points when ordering a bill of lumber: (1) use, (2) species desired, (3) grade, (4) size, (5) quantity, (6) type of drying, and (7) surfacing requirements. An example of a common order would be:

3MBF, 1″ black walnut,
FAS, KD, RGH, RWL

This means: Three (3) thousand (M) board feet (BF) of one inch thick (1″) black walnut, firsts and seconds (FAS), kiln-dried (KD), rough (RGH), random widths and lengths (RWL).

unit **147**

Products of forests and research

Wood was first used for basic necessities, but today over 5000 wood products are used. These are made *of* wood in its natural form or *from* wood that has had its form changed through scientific research and development.

All construction lumber, furniture woods, and plywood are, of course, examples of products composed of wood. This unit discusses things made directly of wood, or coming directly from trees. Unit 152, Miscellaneous Wood Products, deals with items made from wood.

Products of the forests

There are many products made of wood (Figs. 147-1 and 147-2). Gum, turpentine from pines, maple syrup and sugar, fruits, berries, and nuts are a few natural products from trees (Fig. 147-3). Some newer uses of wood are special tanks (Fig. 147-4), duct systems (Fig. 147-5), and chemically treated woods and plywoods.

Wood can be bonded together in layers and pieces to produce exceptional laminated forms used in construction. Resin-impregnated wood will not burn, shrink, swell, warp, or rot.

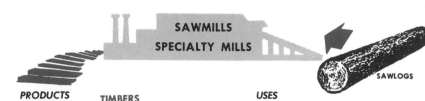

PRODUCTS

TIMBERS

Barges, bridges, building foundations, churches, dams, derricks, docks, factory and warehouse buildings, mine timbers, schools, ships, stringers, trailers, trucks, tugs

CONSTRUCTION LUMBER

Beams, boards, boat hulls and parts, dimensioned lumber, factory flooring, form lumber, heavy framing, joists, light framing, planks, posts, rafters, sheathing, sills, studs, subfloors, walls

FINISHED LUMBER

Baseboard, battens, casing, ceiling, flooring, lath, paneling, pickets, scaffolding, ship decking, siding, stepping

RE-MANUFACTURED LUMBER

Airplane parts, agricultural implements, athletic equipment (baseball bats, skis, tennis racquets, etc.), balusters, bowling alleys and pins, bobbins, boxes, burial boxes, butchers' blocks, cabinets (for radios, television, sewing machines, etc.), car construction and repair, caskets, clothespins, conduits, crates, crossarms, displays, door jambs and frames, doors, dowels, floors, fixtures, furniture, glued laminated structural members, grain doors, gunstocks, gutters, handles, house trailers, ladders, lattice, laundry appliances, machinery, matches, medical supplies, millwork, moldings, musical instruments, novelties, pallets, panels, patterns, pencils, penholders, phonographs, playground equipment, plumbers' woodwork, professional instruments, printing material, pumps, radios, refrigerators, rollers for shades and maps, scientific instruments, ship and boat building (including aircraft carrier flight decks), shiplap, shoe heels and lasts, shuttles, signs, skewers, spools, sporting equipment, stage scenery, surgical supplies, tanks, toothpicks, toys, trim, trunks, valises, vehicles, venetian blinds, wedges, window frames, wood pipe, wooden shoes, woodenware

TIES

Railroad cross ties, mine ties, switch ties

COOPERAGE (STAVES)

Barrels, buckets, cooling towers, kegs, pipes, silos, tanks, tubs

MISCELLANEOUS

Acid washers, benches, corncribs, dunnage, elevators, fence pickets, grain bins, insulator pins, planks, reels, shingles, stakes, trestles, tunnel and mine props, wood chips for making wood pulp, wood turnings (for buttons, jewelry, etc.)

RESIDUES

Fuel, planer shavings for compressed fuel logs and briquettes, poultry litter, raw material for hardboard and particle board, and other bark, pulp, and sawdust products (such as sawdust soil conditioner)

Fig. 147–1 **Products from sawmills and specialty mills.** *American Forest Institute.*

Research in wood

The Forest Products Laboratory (Fig. 147-6) is a public service institution, the world's first devoted to scientific research in wood utilization. Located at Madison, Wisconsin, it was established in 1910 as a part of the Forest Service of the U.S. Department of Agriculture. The research activity yields information that increases the value and usefulness of forests, aids in developing new products and improving old ones, and reduces wood waste. Many of the efficient, economical, long-lasting products that are used today, though seemingly unrelated to wood, have had their origin in the research done at the Forest Products Laboratory.

Over 1 1/2 million tests have been made at the Laboratory to evaluate specifically the mechanical properties of wood and materials derived from it. One test may involve one stroke of a machine and may last only a short time. Another may take years, requiring the specimen to be subjected to millions of repeated stresses. Through scientific research, wood and its by-products are showing unlimited possibilities.

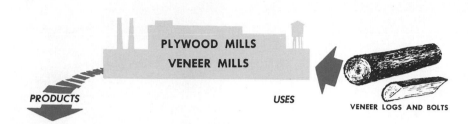

PLYWOOD MILLS
VENEER MILLS

PRODUCTS

USES

VENEER LOGS AND BOLTS

CONSTRUCTION PLYWOOD
Boxcar lining, boxes, cabinets, concrete forms, crates, door panels, finish, prefabricated houses, roofing, sheathing, siding, signboards, subflooring, truck floors and trailer panels, wainscoting, wall panels

MARINE PLYWOOD
Canoes, motorboats, naval craft, racing shells, sailboats

COMPREGNATED PLYWOOD
Airplane propellers, bearings, die stock, table tops, tubing, utensil handles, patterns

PACKAGE VENEER
Baskets, crates, hampers, matchboxes, wirebound boxes

FACE VENEER
Furniture, Pullman car lining, show windows, store fixtures, wainscoting, wall paneling, wallpaper

MISCELLANEOUS VENEERS
Applicators, balloon sticks, book covers, candy and ice cream sticks, cigar boxes and wrappers, floral sticks, ice cream spoons, luggage, mustard paddles, novelties, square stick matches, surgical items, toothpicks, tongue depressors

RESIDUES
Fuel, raw material for other bark and pulp products, paper roll plugs, particle board

Fig. 147–2 Products of plywood and veneer mills. *American Forest Institute.*

Utilizing wood waste

Small pieces, slabs, chips, bark, and sawdust were once discarded or used as fuel. The use of 40 percent of a tree was considered efficient; modern operations utilize over 70 percent. Hardboard and particle board are important products made from wood chips, particles, and flakes.

Logging and milling leftovers once remained in the forest areas or were burned. They now provide about 50 percent of the pulpwood for papermaking.

Bark is used to make insulation, mulch, and fertilizer. Sawdust and shavings are compressed into fuel logs and briquettes and serve as ingredients in sweeping compounds and as bedding for animals. Stumps are made into beautiful veneers and are the material for smoking pipes and other products.

Improvements in mechanical equipment have made it possible to harvest more usable wood. Power saws make it easier to cut trees closer to the ground, leaving less stump. In the mill, thinner-gage (thickness) saws reduce the size of the kerf (saw cut). These thin-gage saws save many board feet and at the same time reduce the amount of sawdust left from the sawmill operation.

MISCELLANEOUS PRODUCTS

PRODUCTS	USES
POLES, POSTS, PILINGS	Antennae, arbors, bridges, channel markers, dams, docks, pole frame buildings, fence posts, flagpoles, foundations, guard rails, jetties, levees, revetments, signposts, tank traps, telephone poles, weirs, wharves
FUEL WOOD	Fireplace, stove, steam boilers
SAP AND GUM	Balsam, birch beer, butternut syrup, gumthus, heptane, larch (Venetian turpentine), maple sugar, mesquite gum, rosin, spruce gum, storax, turpentine
BARK	Adhesives, birch (flavoring) oil, cascara (drug), clothing (wood wool), drilling mud dispersants (oil industry), dye (osage orange and black oak), insulating wool, slippery elm (drug), soil building, tannins (hemlock, chestnut, and tanbark oak)
EDIBLE FRUITS	Butternuts, chinquapins, hickory nuts, pawpaws, pecans, piñon nuts, serviceberries, walnuts, wild plums
NEEDLES	Pine and cedar needle oil
SAWDUST	Absorbent for explosives, artificial leather, artificial wood, body for paint, butcher shops, camouflage, clay products, composition flooring, curing concrete, filler for linoleum, filter for oil and gas, fireworks, glues, hand soaps, ice storage, insulating, insulating brick, livestock bedding, meat smoking, mild abrasives for cleaners, moth deterrent, nursery mulch, packing, plastics, soil conditioners, and wood flour for billiard balls, bowling balls, explosives, molded products
ROOFING FELTS	Roll roofing, shingles
CHRISTMAS TREES	Decorations

Fig. 147–3 Miscellaneous wood products. *American Forest Institute.*

Fig. 147–4 A resin-impregnated acid-drip tank. *Koppers Company, Inc.*

Fig. 147–5 A resin-impregnated plywood duct system. *Koppers Company, Inc.*

Fig. 147–6 Aerial view of the Forest Products Laboratory in Madison, Wisconsin.

unit 148

Veneer and plywood manufacture

Fig. 148–1 Hot-pressing southern pine veneers in plywood experiments. *Forest Products Laboratory.*

The production and use of veneers can be traced back to the earliest days of civilization. The improvement in the appearance and quality of modern veneers has been a result of three developments: (1) machinery for cutting has been improved; (2) new adhesives for bonding have been developed; and (3) more kinds of woods are being used for additional cuts, colors, and decorative designs.

Wood for veneers and plywood

Wood for veneers comes from many places in the world besides the United States. Mahogany and woods that substitute for mahogany veneers come from Mexico, Honduras, South America, Africa, and the Philippines. Rosewood comes from Brazil; zebrawood, from Africa; primavera, from Central America; and satinwood, from India, Ceylon, and the East Indies. Walnut, oak, myrtle burl, red gum, maple, birch, and fir are common United States woods that are used in veneers.

The American southern pine is now being processed into plywood after many years of research and experimentation (Fig. 148-1). The brittleness and other characteristics of the wood formerly made it difficult to find an efficient, economical way of cutting veneer from logs. Flitches (logs) from sycamore, gum, and poplar are also used as center layers of plywood.

Flitches for veneer

A **flitch** is a log or part of a tree that has been prepared for a veneer cutting knife or saw. Flitches come from four parts of a tree (Fig. 148-2): **stumpwood, longwood** (flat, rotary, and quartered), **crotch,** and **burl.** Stumpwood comes from the stump after the tree is cut. Longwood comes from the main trunk. Crotch is obtained from a section just below the point where the crown forks from the trunk. Burl is believed to result from early tree injury.

The finest flitches are sent to **face-veneer mills.** Logs chosen for strength and sturdiness, but not particularly for beauty, are sent to **commercial veneer plants.** The logs are made into boxes and other rough materials.

Some logs at mills are first debarked and placed in the log storage pond and later removed and cut into sections for further processing (Fig.

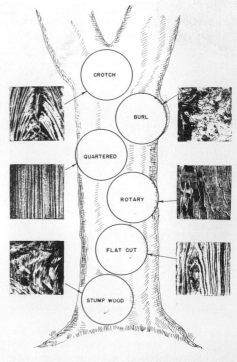

Fig. 148–2 Beautiful veneer figures are made from different parts of the tree.

Fig. 148–3 Some logs are debarked and cut into peeler blocks before they are placed in the storage pond. *Weyerhaeuser Company.*

148-3). Other logs are cut into flitches or lathe-size **peeler logs** and are put into the storage pond before debarking (Fig. 148-4). Peeler logs are removed from the pond and put in steam vats for conditioning (softening). After conditioning, they are placed in a barker machine (Fig. 148-5). Bark is removed by steel claws as the log rotates on a giant turning lathe.

Methods of cutting veneer

Beautiful figures in decorative veneers are determined by six factors: (1) the part of the tree from which the veneer is cut, (2) the pattern of annual rings, (3) the medullary rays, (4) the color distribution, (5) the irregularity of grain structure, and (6) the method of cutting. An expert craftsman decides which one of three methods will be used to cut the log: (1) rotary cutting, (2) sawing, or (3) slicing (Fig. 148-6).

Rotary cutting (Fig. 148-6A) is the most economical. The flitch is prepared and swung into place on a huge lathe or is mounted into position by a chain (Fig. 148-7). The flitch is turned against a sharp steel knife. This produces a continuous sheet of veneer somewhat like unwinding a roll of paper (Fig. 148-8).

Sawing is the oldest method, but it produces only a small percentage of veneer stock. Band saws and special circular saws cut plain- or quarter-sawed veneers. Hard-textured woods are difficult to make into veneer by slicing or by rotary cutting because they split easily.

Slicing is used to obtain special grain effects, particularly for face veneers. There are five ways of slicing: (1) flat, (2) quarter, (3) half round, (4) back, and (5) rift (see Fig. 148-6). Numerous patterns and figure variations are **swirl, fiddleback, stripe, feather, rope, mottle, mixed,** and **patterned grain** (Fig. 148-9).

In slicing, the flitch is mounted in a movable frame and brought straight

Fig. 148–4 Peeler logs (flitches) are often cut to lathe size and placed in the log storage pond with the bark still attached. *Douglas Fir Plywood Association.*

Fig. 148–5 Debarking a peeler log on a giant lathe in preparation for cutting veneer. *American Forest Institute* and *Douglas Fir Plywood Association.*

down or rolled against a stationary knife. This cuts the veneer to the desired thickness, which varies from $1/100$ to $1/20$ inch (0.254 to 1.27 mm). The standard American thickness for face veneer is $1/28$ inch (0.907 mm); for commercial veneer, $1/20$ inch (1.270 mm); and thicker for general use.

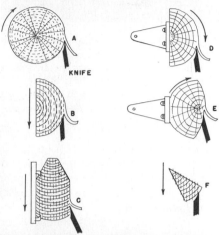

Fig. 148–6 Various methods are used to cut veneer to obtain beautiful grain effects and patterns: (A) rotary cutting, (B) flat slicing, (C) quarter slicing, (D) half-round slicing, (E) back slicing, and (F) rift slicing. *The Seng Company.*

Fig. 148–7 A chain lift moves pine logs into position for rotary veneer cutting. *Georgia-Pacific Corporation.*

Flat slicing (Fig. 148-6B) directly through the heart, or half section, of a log produces a combination of straight grain and heart figures. This method is the most common.

Quarter slicing (Fig. 148-6C) produces a striped effect. Small segments (quarters, sixths, and eighths) are cut at right angles to the annual growth rings.

Half-round slicing (Fig. 148-6D) is accomplished by mounting the heart of a flitch on an eccentric (off-center) holder and cutting off center. Adjacent sheets yield a matching symmetrical veneer pattern with a broader grain pattern than would be obtained by quarter slicing.

Back slicing (Fig. 148-6E) is the opposite of half-round slicing. It produces sheets that come from the center of the log first. The log is mounted to the stay log (holder) on the bark side.

Rift slicing (Fig. 148-6F) is the method used to obtain the combed-grain, rift oak, striped effect. The knife cuts at a 45-degree angle to both the medullary rays and the annual rings.

Fig. 148–8 This huge lathe makes a long, continuous sheet of veneer by "unpeeling" log sections that are specially selected for plywood production. The veneers are then cut to prescribed sizes and are bonded together to produce strong, light plywood. *Weyerhaeuser Company.*

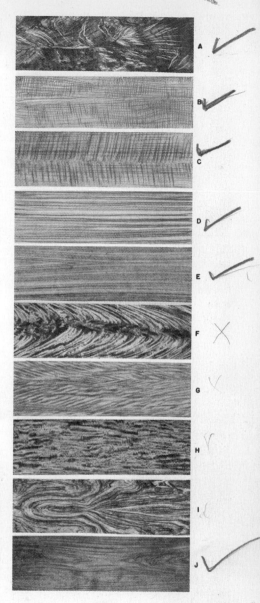

Fig. 148–9 Many beautiful grain patterns in veneer are cut from American and imported woods: (A) swirl figure in mahogany, (B) and (C) fiddleback figure in quartered hardwood and matched teak panels, (D and E) stripes characteristic of quartered tigerwood and zebrawood (zebrano), (F) feather figure in African mahogany crotch wood, (G) rope figure in avondire wood, (H) mottle figure in African mahogany, and (I and J) mixed- and patterned-grain figures in rosewood and walnut. *The Seng Company.*

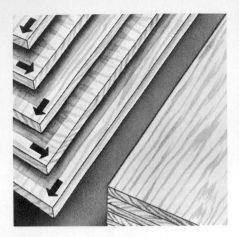

Fig. 148–10 Plywood is made from an odd number of veneer layers with the grain at right angles in adjacent layers. Pound for pound, plywood is stronger than steel. *Douglas Fir Plywood Association.*

Fig. 148–12 Veneer moves from storage trays to the clippers, which cut the veneer into usable widths (up to 54 inches, or 1371 mm) and clip out sections with defects. Clipped veneer then moves by lift truck to the dryers. *American Plywood Association.*

Fig. 148–13 After peeling (cutting) the veneer, some factories clip the sheets to size semiautomatically. At the same time the veneer is graded into three different quality levels as it progresses to the dryers. *United States Plywood Corporation.*

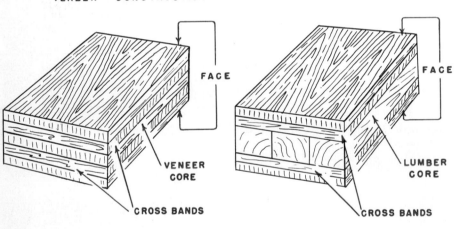

VENEER CONSTRUCTION

LUMBER CORE CONSTRUCTION

FACE

VENEER CORE

CROSS BANDS

FACE

LUMBER CORE

CROSS BANDS

Fig. 148–11 Face veneers and cross bands are glued to a core of veneer or thin lumber. The core may be of a kind of wood different from the face veneers. *Paxton Lumber Company.*

Plywood manufacture from rotary-cut veneer

From the veneers comes plywood. The name is used to designate wood panels of three, five, and seven layers of cross-banded wood (Fig. 148-10). The center layer of plywood is sometimes thicker than other layers; it is called the *core* (Fig. 148-11). Pound for pound, plywood is considered stronger than steel.

After it is peeled (cut), the veneer is clipped (Fig. 148-12). It is cut into sheets and graded (Fig. 148-13) while it is on its way to the dryer. Clipping is done electronically. An inspector marks defective areas with special electrolytic fluid (Fig. 148-14). A few seconds afterward, the fluid sets the clipper knives into motion to remove the defects.

On the semiautomated assembly line, the veneer is fed slowly into the dryer (Fig. 148-15). As sheets come out of the dryer (Fig. 148-16), and before they are graded further, they pass under an electronic **moisture sentry** for a dryness check.

Pieces of the same veneer wood as the face can be tape spliced to form the back (Fig. 148-17). The tape used in the splicing operation is sanded off the back after pressing. Tapeless splicing (Fig. 148-18) is used to form face-veneer panels from several pieces. The backs and faces are glued to the cross bands and the core.

The edges of the core are planed on the jointer. The core stock is edge-glued and cut to panel size by a clipper machine (Fig. 148-19). All the plies are then ready to be glued into a sheet.

Glue is applied to the sheets of veneer as they go through large rollers (Fig. 148-20). The veneer layers are cross-banded as the plies are built up. The use of the giant hot press (Fig. 148-21) is one of the crucial steps in the manufacture of plywood. Extreme pressure and controlled heat are used to cure (set) the adhesive. The bond between the plies becomes stronger then the wood itself. After heating and pressing, skinner and trim saws cut the panel edges and stack the panels automatically (Fig. 148-22).

Fig. 148–14 Electrolytic fluid is applied to defective areas. It activates electronic knives that automatically cut out defects. *United States Plywood Corporation.*

Fig. 148–17 Back pieces of the panel are joined by paper tape. The machine pulls the veneer together and applies thin tape. This tape is sanded off the back of the finished panel after pressing. *United States Plywood Corporation.*

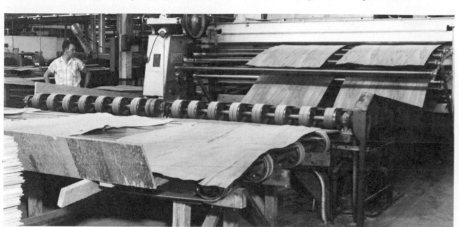

Fig. 148–15 Veneer is fed slowly into the dryer for proper drying before it is used in plywood. *United States Plywood Corporation.*

Fig. 148–18 Pieces of face veneer are spliced without using tape. *United States Plywood Corporation.*

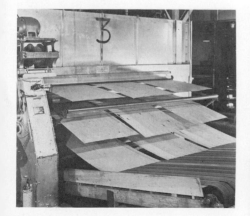

Fig. 148–16 Sheets of veneer emerge from a carefully controlled dryer. *American Plywood Association.*

Fig. 148–19 Edge-glued stock being cut to panel size by clipper machine. *United States Plywood Corporation.*

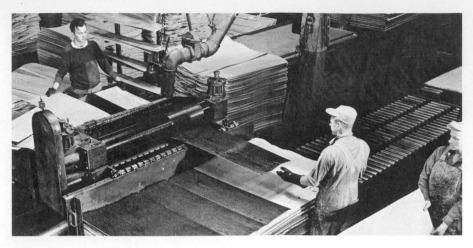

Fig. 148-20   Glue is applied to the veneer by feeding the sheets through large rollers covered with glue. *Douglas Fir Plywood Association.*

Fig. 148-22   A skinner and trim saw trims panel edges and stacks them in one automatic operation after hot-pressing. *United States Plywood Corporation.*

Fig. 148-21   The veneer sandwiches travel through the prepress (center), then on to the hot press (left), where they are pressed together and bonded, under high heat and pressure, to become plywood panels. *American Plywood Association.*

The panels are sanded by a large drum sander (Fig. 148-23) in preparation for further grading.

Types and grades of veneer in plywood

Fir plywood is manufactured in two types: exterior and interior. The type depends upon the bonding agent and the grade of the veneer.

Exterior plywood is manufactured with a completely waterproof glue. No veneer used is less than grade C. **Interior plywood** is made with either waterproof or highly water-resistant glue. The inner plies and back veneers can be of lower grades than the faces. Faces are graded by their appearance, quality, and defects.

The six grades are designated **N, A, B, C, C plugged,** and **D.** Grade N is a grade for special order, a "natural finish" veneer, select, all heartwood, and free of open defects. Grade A is the best standard veneer. It is smooth, with more than one piece joined, and neatly made repairs are permitted. Grade B is a solid-surface veneer, with

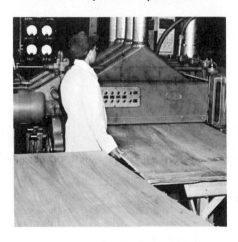

Fig. 148-23   Panels of plywood are sanded in large drum sanders. *United States Plywood Corporation.*

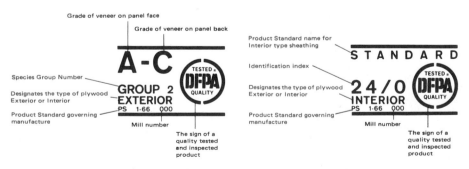

Fig. 148-24   A typical back stamp for designating the grade of plywood. *Douglas Fir Plywood Association.*

Fig. 148–25 Typical exterior edge marks used in grading plywood. *Douglas Fir Plywood Association.*

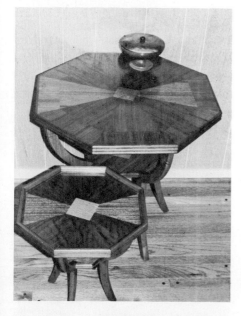

Fig. 148–26 A combination of walnut, rosewood, and bird's-eye maple veneer makes interesting marquetry designs on a plywood base for matched tables.

Fig. 148–27 An example of intarsia decoration.

tight knots and circular repair plugs permitted. Grade C is the lowest-grade veneer permitted in exterior plywoods. Knotholes up to 1 inch (25 mm) in diameter, splits, plugs, and other minor blemishes are accepted. The C-plugged grade is an improved grade C veneer. Grade D is used only in interior-type veneers for inner plies and backs, where specified.

Typical fir plywood stamps (Figs. 148-24 and 148-25) are used to mark the panel grade. Exterior-type edge marks are also used. Some panels are marked on the face, the back, and the edges.

Decorating surfaces with wood and veneers

Decorating the surface of wood is an ancient art which is still practiced.

Five types of surface decoration are **marquetry** (overlaying), **inlaying, intarsia, mosaic,** and **plastic lami-** nates. The first three are discussed briefly.

Marquetry consists of cutting thin wood veneers into desired shapes, taping them together, and gluing them to a plywood surface (Fig. 148-26). The results depend on the difficulty of the design, the amount of time put into the work, and the number of pieces of veneer used. Complicated works of art may contain many hundreds of individual pieces. Approximately the same procedure is used in both simple and complex designs.

Inlaying is the process of inserting a design into a solid surface. See Unit 59, Routing, Inlaying, and Shaping. Common inlay materials are ivory, metal, and wood.

Intarsia, a method of decoration similar to inlaying and marquetry, is of Italian origin. A contrasting color of wood is usually used as a background, and colored segments are sunk into the darker wood (Fig. 148-27). Sometimes entire scenes are created.

Fig. 148–28   An unobstructed floor space is provided when laminated arches and beams are used for a large structure, such as this sports arena. *Forest Products Laboratory.*

Laminating and molding veneers and wood

Using laminated arches and beams, architects and engineers can design as large a structure as a sports arena (Fig. 148-28) with no posts or other obstructions. Beautiful church construction and interior furnishing (Fig. 148-29) and interesting designs for furniture (Fig. 148-30) are made possible by laminated and molded wood.

Laminated wood is stronger and does not expand and contract as much as one piece of solid wood. De-

Fig. 148–30 Unique furniture shapes are made possible by laminating and molding the original forms. *Drexel Furniture Company.*

Fig. 148–31 A shaped, laminated table apron is removed from the press. *Drexel Furniture Company.*

Fig. 148–29   Laminated beams and interior furnishings are used in many modern churches. *Koppers Company, Inc.*

signers have a wide choice in designing pieces that are curved or unusual in shape.

In furniture manufacture, veneers are coated with special adhesives and placed in a mold for laminating. They are held in place as the press moves into position. After 30 seconds in the laminating press, the mold is opened. In Fig. 148-31, a curved table apron has been formed.

Similar manufacturing operations laminate various large and small products. Steps in the manufacture of golf club heads (Fig. 148-32) are excellent examples.

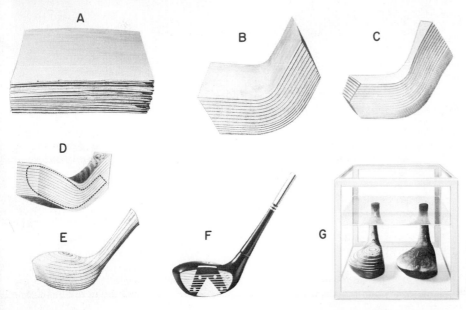

Fig. 148–32 Basic steps in laminating and forming a golf club head: (A) veneer layers stacked in special pattern, (B and C) forming angles for head and neck, (D) pattern mark on a block of bonded layers, (E) shape after turning on a lathe, (F) finished club head, and (G) test for retention of shape. *Wilson Sporting Goods Company.*

Fig. 148–33 Hardwood plywood used for kitchen cabinets and paneling. *Hardwood Plywood Institute.*

Uses of veneers and plywood

Fir and hardwood plywood are used for many products such as house siding, main floors and subfloors, sides and ends of railroad boxcars, shelving, loading and stacking pallets, and beam construction.

Many hardwood plywood products are used in the home and in the office. Some examples are kitchen cabinets and paneling (Fig. 148-33),

Fig. 148–34 Modern furniture and wall panels of hardwood veneers. *Hardwood Plywood Manufacturers Assoc.*

Fig. 148–35 Beautiful veneers are used in the manufacture of musical instruments, such as this electric organ. *Hardwood Plywood Institute.*

Fig. 148–36 Rare and exotic-grained myrtlewood veneer was used to make this breakfront cabinet by coauthor Chris Groneman.

Fig. 148–37 Veneers are also cut and matched by hand by the home craftsman. *National Association of Furniture Manufacturers.*

Fig. 148–38 This bowling pin of laminated white, hard maple demonstrates the versatility of plywood. *Hardwood Plywood Institute.*

Fig. 148–39 The wood for this beautiful bow is laminated maple. Mercury vials are built into rosewood handle to cushion the shock when the bowstring is released. *Ben Pearson, Inc.*

furniture and wall panels (Fig. 148-34), musical instruments (Fig. 148-35), breakfront cabinets (Fig. 148-36), and veneer for use in the home workshop (Fig. 148-37).

Plywood can be impregnated (saturated) with chemicals and compressed to develop **impreg** and **compreg.** Special products from this denser, harder plywood include foundry patterns, knife and tool handles, and propellers.

Veneers and plywood for sports equipment have practically unlimited uses. Tennis rackets, bowling pins (Fig. 148-38), snow and water skis, hockey sticks, boats, and hunting bows (Fig. 148-39) illustrate only a very few of the thousands of sports items which are or can be made from hardwood plywood.

unit 149

Production and uses of hardboard

Hardboard is panel sheet manufactured from tiny wood fibers, whereas timber, lumber, and plywood are wood in its natural state. Hardboard fibers have been rearranged during manufacture to form hard panels. Only hardboard uses natural lignin to hold the fibers together. Other types of wood sheets use various synthetic binders or adhesives to hold the wood chips or the thin wood sheets together to form panels.

Wood from trees has certain defects which are eliminated in hardboard. For example, there are no knots or natural grain structure to allow splitting.

American manufacturers (Fig. 149-1) produce about one-half the world's hardboard supply.

Discovery of hardboard

An unforeseen accident made possible the discovery of hardboard in 1924 at Laurel, Mississippi, by William H. Mason, an early associate of Thomas A. Edison. Mason found that small wood chips could be "exploded," or fiberized. The process was somewhat like that used in papermaking; chips were cooked with high-pressure heat and steam.

Mason was attempting to make a strong, tough paper or an efficient insulating board. He obtained a small press with steam-heated platens, or plates (Fig. 149-2), from a paper mill. He placed a wet lap (layer) of fibers between the platens. As a safety precaution, Mason turned off the steam when he went to lunch. However, one day a faulty valve allowed steam to continue to heat the press. By the time he returned, the lap had been pressed into a sheet of grainless, dry, ironlike board unlike any board previously produced. From this accident the extensive hardboard industry developed. The first plant was established in 1926; the first piece of Masonite **Presdwood** (hardboard) was made.

Raw materials

Practically any form of wood can be the raw material for hardboard.

In the eastern and southern United States, plants chiefly use wood from pine, gum, tupelo, magnolia, cottonwood, willow, aspen, and oak trees. In the West, the major tree species used are Douglas and white fir, redwood, and lodgepole pine.

Manufacture of hardboard

In addition to the use of residue materials, trees are selected, felled, peeled, and cut into 5-foot (1524-mm) lengths. These dry for a brief period and are then delivered to the mill. Figure 149-3 is a diagram of the manufacturing process.

Materials are run through **chippers,** which cut the wood diagonally across the grain into 3/4-inch (19-mm) lengths. The chips are **screened,** and the wood dust is removed for fuel. Large pieces are rechipped and rescreened.

Either of two **defiberizing** processes is used. In the first, chips are sent to fibering machines. These machines tear the chips apart and reduce them to fiber. They are stored in large tanks (Fig. 149-4) for later use. In the second process, the chips are defiberized by steam pressure and are exploded through a large gun. The chips are poured into vertically mounted, thick-steel gun barrels. Valves at the top of the barrels are closed, and extremely hot steam enters at the bottom. This creates great pressure. The chips dissolve and explode with tremendous speed from the guns into catching chambers called **cyclones.** Actually the chips are no longer chips; the explosion leaves a fine, fluffy, brown mass of fibers covered with a film of lignin. This covering, a major component of wood, makes it stick together naturally.

Refiner machines take fiber masses and reduce them to individual fibers. From this machine, fibers are formed into **mats** in one of two ways. In the **water-suspension** method, fibers are mixed in a tank of water and fed to a screen to form a mat. In the **air-suspension** method, they are blown into a large metal cone, where they settle like snowflakes, forming a mat. Depending on the amount of moisture

Fig. 149–1 An aerial view of a hardboard plant that covers 30 acres (121 406 m²) of land, with 4 acres (16 187 m²) of manufacturing area under one roof. *Kroehler Manufacturing Company.*

Fig. 149–2 The steam-heated press that produced hardboard by accident. *Masonite Corporation.*

327

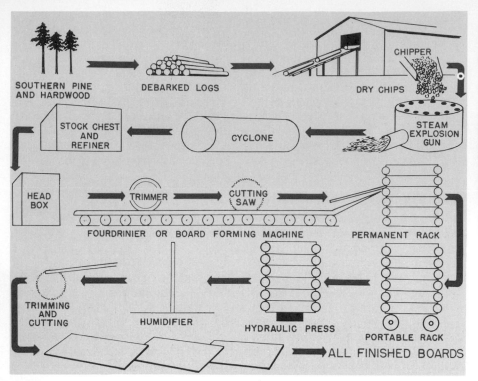

Fig. 149–3 A diagram of the hardboard manufacturing process. *Masonite Corporation.*

Fig. 149–5 Mats of loose fibers being transported on a conveyor to the steam press. *Kroehler Manufacturing Company.*

Fig. 149–6 Hot presses dry the mats under hundreds of pounds of pressure per square inch. *Masonite Corporation.*

used, the various processes are called **air-, dry-, semidry-,** or **wet-suspension** processes.

Mats are thick blankets of loose fibers which are trimmed approximately to size as they travel toward the

Fig. 149–4 Wood fibers stored in gigantic tanks. *Kroehler Manufacturing Company.*

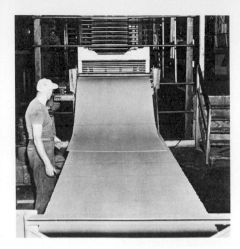

Fig. 149–7 Thin, dry hardboard emerges from the hot press. *Forest Fiber Products Company.*

Fig. 149–8 Hardboard is stacked and transported to storage to await shipment to consumers. *Masonite Corporation.*

press (Fig. 149-5). Up to 20 mats are hauled and placed in a **hot press** (Fig. 149-6) which develops pressure up to 310 pounds per square inch (2 137 375 Pa) on the board surface at a temperature of 330°F (165.6°C). The thin, dry board emerges (Fig. 149-7).

Because the hardboard is so dry, the sheets are placed in a **humidification chamber,** where a small amount of moisture is added.

Boards are then carefully inspected, and samples are tested for defects. Several high-speed saws trim them to one of the standard sizes. They are stacked and transported to storage (Fig. 149-8) for later shipment to consumers.

Classifications, textures, and sizes

Standard, tempered, and **service** are basic commercial classifications of hardboard. All must meet the standards of the hardboard industry.

Standard hardboard can be worked easily with hand tools (Fig. 149-9) as well as with power machines.

Tempered hardboard has certain chemicals added to it; then it is sent through a heat-treating process. It is often prefinished with colored plastic film, which makes it very serviceable.

Service hardboard is suitable for general use, but its properties are moderate in relation to standard hardboard. Its lighter weight is an advantage that makes it a typical board for interior paneling (Fig. 149-10).

Surface patterns include **perforated, striated** (ridged), **grooved, tiled,** and **embossed.** Perforated panels are particularly useful in the kitchen and in the home workshop (Fig. 149-11). It can be obtained prime coated, prefinished, in wood-grain patterns, and in colors ranging from blond to dark brown.

Standard panel dimensions range up to 5 feet (1524 mm) in width and 16 feet (4877 mm) in length. Thicknesses are $1/12$, $1/10$, $1/8$, $3/16$, $1/4$, etc., to $3/4$ inch (2.1, 2.5, 3.2, 4.8, 6.4, etc., to 19.0 mm). Special thicknesses, widths, and lengths are available.

Fig. 149–9 Hardboard is easily worked with ordinary hand tools. *Masonite Corporation.*

Uses

The large size of hardboard panels makes them particularly useful for both exterior and interior construction.

Exterior uses include those for concrete forms, siding, fences, shutters, trailers, signs, and homes (Fig. 149-12). **Interior** sheets are used for storage cabinets and shelves (Fig. 149-13), drawers, ceilings, merchandise racks, wall panels, and cabinetry. (Fig. 149-14).

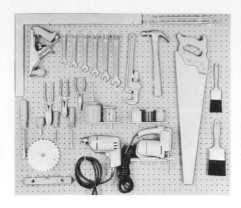

Fig. 149–11 Pegboard panels accommodate home workshop tools. *Masonite Corporation.*

Fig. 149–13 A modern arrangement of hardboard storage cabinets and shelves. *Masonite Corporation.*

Fig. 149–10 Hardboard wall panels with a wood-grain finish produce the effect of any wood grain or color. *Masonite Corporation.*

Fig. 149–12 A home can use hardboard panels for exterior as well as interior construction. *Masonite Corporation.*

Fig. 149–14 Quarter-inch (6.35-mm) hardboard panels make excellent sliding doors in cabinets. *Masonite Corporation.*

unit 150

Manufacture of particle board

Particle board is a manufactured sheet that is made in various shapes and sizes from wood particles. These particles include flakes, splinters (Fig. 150-1), and chips and shavings. Called **furnish,** they are bonded together with various synthetic resins.

Chipboard and **flakeboard** are other common names for particle board. Typical brand names include Cedawood, Chipcore, Customwood, Duraflake, Flakewood, Laneboard, Novoply, Resincore, and Timblend.

Materials

All commercial species of hardwoods and softwoods can be used in making the many types of particle boards. Common softwoods which are used for the manufacture of particle board are hemlock, fir, pine, cedar, and redwood. Hardwoods which are often processed into particle board are willow, aspen, walnut, gum, and oak.

Fig. 150–1 Particle board made from mixed hardwood splinters. *American Forest Institute.*

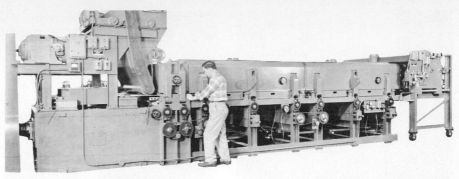

Fig. 150–2 A 50-inch (1270-mm) continuous chipboard extrusion press. *Adamson United Company.*

Production processes

Various characteristics of wood species affect the production and final selection of a panel for a given use. Physical properties and uses are affected by such factors as (1) the process, (2) the type and amount of binder, (3) the kind of particles, (4) the amount of compression, and (5) the type of finish.

There are two types of particle board: **platen pressed** and **extruded.**

In the extrusion process the particles are forced through an opening of specified size and shape. The board can be continuous, and special machines (Fig. 150-2) are designed for making it. Molded items in different shapes are produced by closely related operations of compression and extrusion.

Manufacture

Wood arrives at the particle board plant as waste and residue particles from other wood-products mills or in the form of 5-foot (1524-mm) logs (Fig. 150-3). The logs range in size from 4 to 16 inches (102 to 406 mm) in diameter.

From the storage area, a crane feeds logs to a conveyor belt into the **debarker.** Debarked logs are carried by a conveyor to **slasher saws,** which cut them into **billets** (short logs). Billets, lumber residue, and slabs are

Fig. 150–3 Moving pine logs to an automated particle board plant. *United States Plywood Corporation.*

Fig. 150–4 Wood slabs being fed into a flaker cutting head. *International Paper Company.*

converted into particles in a **flaker machine** (Fig. 150-4).

Particles from the other sources and regular supply stock are stored in bins and sheds (Fig. 150-5) and are sent to **beater mills** (Fig. 150-6). The mills break the wood into flakes of the specified size. The green (unprocessed) flakes are then stored in a green-flake holder, or bunker (Fig. 150-7).

The flakes leave the bunker to go through **dryers,** which reduce the moisture content to the desired level. From the dryers, the particles go to separators, or **sorting screens** (Fig. 150-8). These screens separate the correct sizes from the oversize (overs) and undersize (fines) particles. The overs return to the hammer mill (beater) for reprocessing. Fines can be

Fig. 150–5 Storage of raw materials, including chips and shavings. *Duraflake Company.*

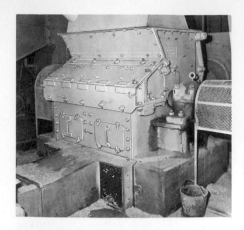

Fig. 150–6 Chips are pulverized in a hammer mill. *Weyerhaeuser Company.*

Fig. 150–8 Sorting screens sort the correct size, from oversize to fine particles. *Weyerhaeuser Company.*

Fig. 150–10 Sawing individual mats and inspecting flakes. *Duraflake Company.*

Fig. 150–7 Green flakes stored in bunkers before transfer to dryers. *International Paper Company.*

Fig. 150–9 The belt-balance and blending machine, where synthetic-resin adhesive and emulsified wax are sprayed on flakes. *Duraflake Company.*

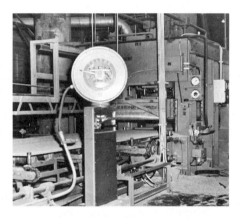

Fig. 150–11 The weight of the mat is checked with a scale before it is sent to the cold prepress. *Duraflake Company.*

used as fuel or as additional wood products, such as wood flour in some glue and in filler used to fill wood pores before finishing.

Acceptable flakes flow to a mixer, or **blending machine** (Fig. 150-9). The flakes are continuously weighed as they pass over a belt balance or scale. Their weight regulates the flow of synthetic-resin adhesive and emulsified (thoroughly mixed) wax.

Forming machines accept the coated flakes and spread an even, continuous mat on moving **cauls** (plates). Cauls are placed end to end and are bridged at their joints. For a ³/₄-inch (19-mm) finished board, the

Fig. 150–12 A steam-heated hot press binds the materials into particle board. *Collins Pine Company.*

Fig. 150–13 Automatic feeders and stackers prepare the panels for the sizing saws. *Weyerhaeuser Company.*

mat is about 4 inches (102 mm) thick. The continuous mat is separated into single ones by sawing (Fig. 150-10).

Each mat proceeds on its caul to a **weight controller** (Fig. 150-11) before it is conveyed to a cold prepress. Mats of incorrect weight are automatically rejected because they do not meet manufacturing specifications. They are returned for reuse as properly made mats. The prepress compresses the mat to about one-half its original thickness. One operator at a pushbutton panel controls all the operations.

The mats pass through **trim saws,** which trim the edges and recover the trim for reuse. Mats are automatically loaded into the steam-heated **hot press** (Fig. 150-12). The time, temperature, and pressure used in pressing vary in accordance with the thickness and grade of particle board required. Automatic **feeders** and **stackers** (Fig. 150-13) prepare the panels for the **sizing saws** (Fig. 150-14).

During the various operations, particle board is constantly tested for quality, durability, and grade. Thickness is checked by **electronic monitors** that automatically signal any variation from required thickness (Fig. 150-15).

Particle boards are stored where they are conditioned (cured) several days before they are cut to final size

and sanded to exact thickness (Fig. 150-16). Forklift trucks move the finished sheets to the main storage areas (Fig. 150-17).

Sizes, types, and uses

Standard panel sizes of particle board range up to 5 feet (1524 mm) in width and 16 feet (4877 mm) in length. Thicknesses range from $1/8$ inch to $1^{1}/2$ inches (3 to 38 mm).

Some panels have a uniform flake, shaving, or particle appearance on all surfaces. These are called **homogeneous** (one-kind) particle boards. Others are manufactured with various sizes of particles to create a type of

Fig. 150–14 Sizing saws automatically cut panels to size. *Weyerhaeuser Company.*

Fig. 150–15 Sensitive electronic monitors check panel thickness. *United States Plywood Corporation.*

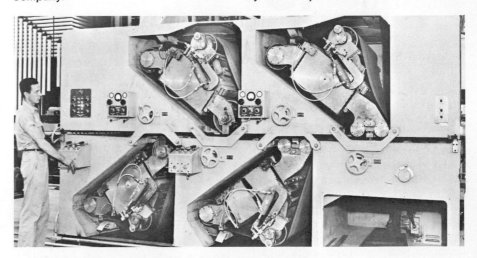

Fig. 150–16 Both faces of panels are sanded simultaneously at speeds up to 150 ft/min (45.7 m/min). *United States Plywood Corporation.*

"plyboard." Coarse particles are sandwiched between faces of fines, which provide smoother surfaces.

Panels can be cut to size and banded with solid wood strips. Glue is applied to these pieces (Fig. 150-18), and hardwood face veneer is attached for use as furniture panels.

Particle board sheets make excellent core stock for plastic laminates (Fig. 150-19), bathroom cabinets, and cabinet parts covered with plastic or wood veneer (Fig. 150-20).

The main uses of particle board are for furniture core stock and subfloors. The largest volume is used in home construction and where smooth surfaces are required.

Some particle board products are counter fronts and display shelves, doors and tables of all kinds, serving trays, and lamp bases.

Fig. 150–19 Placing plastic laminate on a preformed particle board core. *Weyerhaeuser Company.*

Fig. 150–17 Panels in storage ready for shipment. *Duraflake Company.*

Fig. 150–18 Applying glue to banded particle board cores. *Weyerhaeuser Company.*

Fig. 150–20 A wood veneer over particle board cabinet doors, shelves, side, and top. *Weyerhaeuser Company.*

unit 151

The paper industry

Paper was invented by the Chinese about 1000 years ago. Until the nineteenth century, one sheet at a time was generally made, by hand, from straw, rags, or hemp. Paper was scarce and expensive. Chemical methods and the wood pulp, paper, and paperboard industry are about 100 years old.

Approximately 97 percent of the paper consumed annually comes from wood. Almost any tree species can be used. About four-fifths of the pulp for paper mills comes from pine, spruce, hemlock, and fir trees. Most pulp mills use regular pulp logs. Some paper products are made from flax, cotton fiber, and bagasse (sugar cane pulp) instead of wood pulp. However, similar methods are used in the manufacture of all paper.

Wood-pulping methods

Five principal methods are used for making pulp: the **mechanical** process, three **chemical** processes (soda, sulfite, and sulfate), and the neutral **semichemical** process. Study a chemistry book for a full description of the chemicals used in papermaking.

The mechanical process makes ground-wood pulp, and the lignin is not removed. Newsprint paper is a typical low-grade paper product made by the mechanical process.

The chemical processes involving soda, sulfate, and sulfite separate lignin for other uses by cooking the wood chips in chemical solutions and in steam under heat and pressure. Each process produces cellulose fiber, a second major part of wood. The differences are primarily in the types of chemicals used in the cooking and in the wood species being used as pulp.

The soda process makes paper that is noted for its fine texture and printing qualities. Sulfate and sulfite pulps are used in the manufacture of cellophane, explosives, plastics, and rayon.

The sulfate process uses primarily Douglas fir and pine.

The wood fibers are separated from the chemicals and blown into a storage tank to be made eventually into paper. The cooking liquor and other residues (leftovers) are fed into a special furnace which recovers the chemicals for reuse. The sulfate process is especially adaptable for kraft (brown) papers.

Sulfite pulp is made in much the same way as sulfate pulp, but the usual tree species used are hemlock, spruce, alder, and white fir. Magnesium oxide (MgO) is a primary chemical in the sulfite process. This permits recovery of over 85 percent of the pulping chemicals. It is also highly effective in keeping streams, harbors, and air free of pollution.

The neutral semichemical (sulfite) process is a combination of the chemical and the mechanical methods. It is particularly adaptable for making pulp from alder and native western hardwoods. Alder was once regarded as a "weed" tree, or one having little value. Today it is an excellent furniture and cabinet wood. The difference between the regular chemical processes and the semichemical process is in the wood species, chemicals, and fiberizing methods that are used.

Chemical pulp- and papermaking

A pictorial flowchart (Fig. 151-1) tells the story of pulp- and papermaking, from the forest to the finished paper product. Pulp, paper, and board mills are frequently found in one location (Fig. 151-2).

Pulpwood for paper is cut in the

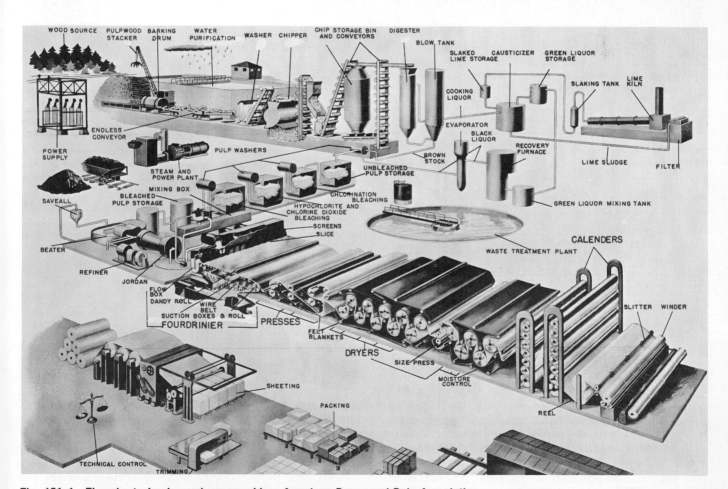

Fig. 151–1 Flowchart of pulp- and papermaking. *American Paper and Pulp Association.*

Fig. 151–2 Kraft pulp, paper, and board mills are often in one location. *American Paper and Pulp Association.*

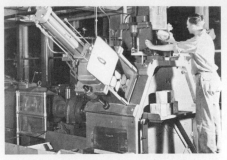

Fig. 151–5 A grinder used in preparing ground-wood and chemiground-wood pulp at the Forest Products Laboratory. *American Paper and Pulp Association.*

Fig. 151–3 Mechanical loading of hardwood pulp. *American Paper and Pulp Association.*

Fig. 151–4 Wood for pulp stored in huge stacks. *Caterpillar Tractor Company.*

Fig. 151–6 Pulpwood chips screened to uniform size are conveyed to large pressure vessels called digesters. *American Paper and Pulp Association.*

Fig. 151–7 Dry pulp folded into laps and hauled to storage for shipment or use in making paper. *American Paper and Pulp Association.*

forest, loaded onto trucks (Fig. 151-3), hauled to the paper mill, and dumped for storage. The 4-foot (1219-mm) lengths of pulpwood are often piled high over many acres (Fig. 151-4).

Removal of the bark is the first step in the manufacturing process.

The sticks (pulpwood logs) are tumbled together in a barking drum. Steel bars running the length of the drum catch the logs and carry them up, then drop them over and over until they are free of bark. In some mills, high-pressure water jets blast away bark.

Fig. 151–8 The hollander, or beater, refines pulp by beating and mixes colors uniformly. *American Paper and Pulp Association.*

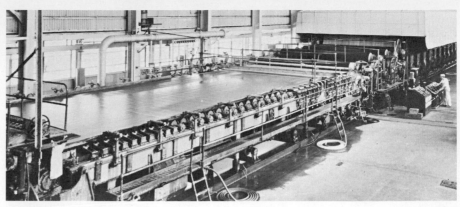

Fig. 151–9 The "wet end" of a Fourdrinier paper machine. *American Paper and Pulp Association.*

Fig. 151–10 Paper wound in huge rolls at the "dry end" of the Fourdrinier machine. *American Paper and Pulp Association.*

The logs are washed and fed into a high-speed **chipper machine.** They are sliced by rotating knives into chips about 1/8 inch (3 mm) thick and 1/2 to 5/8 inch (13 to 16 mm) long. Smaller pieces of logs are cut in a pulpwood **grinder** (Fig. 151-5) to prepare groundwood and chemigroundwood pulp used in research at the Forest Products Laboratory.

Chips pour out of the chipper in a continuous stream and pass across **shaker screens.** They flow on a conveyor belt (Fig. 151-6) to storage silos (bins) and large "pressure cookers," or digesters.

Wood chips and chemicals are cooked under high pressure and steam heat from 3 to 4 hours. This process dissolves the gluelike lignin and frees the long, flexible cellulose fiber pulp from which paper is made. A **lap machine** takes the liquid pulp, spreads it over a wire-mesh cylinder, and draws the water out by suction. The damp pulp is picked up on a felt

blanket, becomes a dry blanket itself, and is stored in **laps,** or folded layers (Fig. 151-7).

If pulp is to be used immediately, it is bleached and goes to a deep tub or bowl with an agitator (beater) in the bottom. For fine papers it is beaten again in the **hollander,** or beater (see Fig. 151-8). It passes under a roller in the bottom of the tub which grinds it into a fiber of the proper length for specialized grades of paper. During

the beating, necessary dye and sizing (stiffener) are added. White pulp is blended with artificially colored pulp to obtain the desired shade.

Pulp then goes to the **jordan.** In this machine two cones with steel bars are nested within each other. The cones rub and cut the fibers still more, providing pulp for the particular grade of paper being made.

As the pulp flows on its journey, it is again washed, and more water is added. The saturated material enters the "wet end" of a **Fourdrinier machine** (Fig. 151-9). It is poured smoothly from a headbox (reservoir) through a slice (slit) onto a moving wire screen to make a uniformly thick layer. Some of these machines are as long as a city block.

Pulp fibers flow on the fast-moving screen like logs moving downstream. They line up with the direction of flow. The screen shakes from side to side, causing the fibers to tangle and cross. This is the secret of papermaking.

On the screen, the continuous sheet is about 90 percent water and 10 percent fiber. The sheet of "paper" moves along the various rolls at a speed of about 30 miles per hour (approximately 2600 f/min, or 792 m/min). Suction boxes at the end of the screen remove some water. Felt sheets pick up the "paper" and carry it through a series of press rolls. Each of the rolls removes more water.

The longest part of the machine is the drying section. Steam-heated rolls turn at different speeds to allow for shrinkage as the sheet dries and to prevent breaking the web of new paper. At the "dry end" of the machine the paper is ironed dry as it passes through **calender stacks** (vertical rolls). As the dry paper comes from the drying stacks, it forms huge rolls (Fig. 151-10).

The large rolls of paper are cut into required lengths. It is rewound (Fig. 151-11) at speeds up to 3000 ft/min (914 m/min) into rolls which may be 60 inches (1524 mm) or more in diameter. Before it is shipped to other paper-product manufacturers, it is given many bursting-strength (Fig. 151-12) and tear-strength (Fig. 151-13) tests to determine that the paper will meet their needs.

Fig. 151–11 Rewinding rolls of specially cut lengths of paper. *American Paper and Pulp Association.*

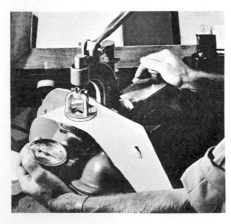

Fig. 151–12 Paper being tested for bursting strength. *American Paper and Pulp Association.*

Fig. 151–13 A technician testing paper for tear strength. *American Paper and Pulp Association.*

Pulp and paper products

Hundreds of pulp and paper products are manufactured (Fig. 151-14). Paper for magazines, books, and catalogs; business and wrapping papers; newsprint; and facial and other personal tissues are just some of the products.

Laminated paper (paper put together in layers) has greater strength and becomes paperboard, boxes, and shipping containers. For moisture-proof containers, wax, asphalt, polyethylene, and starch are used. A large amount of paper is molded into such products as plates, trays, and egg cartons.

High-grade printing papers are further ironed, or calendered, and coated to produce flat, shiny surfaces. Some paper is run through printing presses, where designs (such as for wallpaper) are imprinted (Fig. 151-15).

The chemical industry is producing many new lignin and cellulose chemical products from **spent liquors** left over from the pulping processes.

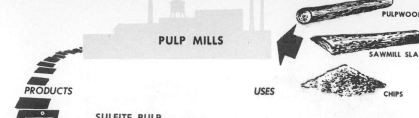

PULPWOOD

SAWMILL SLABS

PULP MILLS

CHIPS

USES

PRODUCTS

SULFITE PULP

Paper and paperboard for bags, blotters, printing papers, boxes, bristol board, envelopes, folding boxboard, fruit wrappers, greaseproof packaging, insulation, labels, paper napkins, patent coated boards, photo processing paper, sanitary tissues, stationery, stencils, tag board, wallpaper, waterproof packaging, wrapping

Dissolving pulps for cellophane, explosives, lacquers, plastics, photo film, rayon

SULFATE PULP

Paper and paperboard for bags, printing papers, bond paper, boxes, bristol board, chart paper, coating raw stock, condenser tissues, corrugated boxboard, envelopes, food containers, folding boxboard, insulation, ledger paper, liner board, offset paper, onionskin, parchment, sheathing paper, stationery, tag stock, towels, twisted cord and rope, waxed paper

SODA PULP

Paper and paperboard for blotters, printing papers, bristol board, corrugated paper, filters, insulating and wallboards, labels, liners for coated boards, stationery, testliners

SEMI

Corrugated paper, egg cartons, insulating board, testliners, wallboard, printing papers, glassine paper

GROUNDWOOD PULP

Absorbent papers, bags, boards, building and insulating papers, newsprint, printing papers, wallboard, wood cement boards and blocks, wrapping paper, writing papers

RESIDUES (Liquor containing leftover cellulose and lignin not used in paper manufacture)

Sulfite liquors used in making adhesives, building briquettes, core binder, cymene, dyes, emulsifiers, ethyl alcohol, fatty acids, feeding yeast, fertilizers, fuel briquettes, linoleum cement, mordants, paint and varnish remover, plastics, road binder, tannins, vanillin

Sulfate liquors used in making acetic acid, acetone, dimethyl-sulfide, fatty acids, furfural, methyl alcohol, oxalic acid, pine oil, rosin soap, rosin acids, tall oil, turpentine, ore flotation, pharmaceutical chemicals

Soda liquors used in making acetic acid, acetone, calcium carbonate, methyl alcohol, oxalic acid, plastics

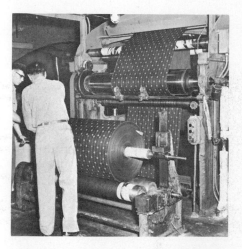

Fig. 151–15 Rolls of paper are run through a printing press, where designs are imprinted. *American Paper and Pulp Association.*

unit 152

Miscellaneous wood products

Many products have been created from wood substances as a result of chemical analysis and experimentation. The form of wood is changed when wood is broken into its basic units of **cellulose** and **lignin.** All parts of the tree contribute raw materials for products made from wood. Some of these are made in distillation and hydrolysis plants (Figs. 152-1 and 152-2).

Cellulose products

Two-thirds of the wood in a tree is cellulose, the woody, tubelike fiber of the wood. It can be treated by chemical and mechanical processes. Cellulose is divided into two product groups: **fiber** and **chemical.**

Fiber products are further divided into two parts: **fiberboard** and **paper.** Fiberboard products include boxboard, hardboard, insulation board (Fig. 152-3), and wallboard.

The cellulose chemical group includes hundreds of items. None of these products has the appearance of wood, but they are made *from* wood. Explosives such as dynamite and gunpowder are in this group. Glycerine, alcohol, and a solid-fuel rocket propellant are products made from wood pulp and nitrocellulose (a chemical nitrate of cellulose). Other products in this category are photographic film, felt, yeast, plastics, adhesives, and phonograph records.

Many other wood products contribute to modern living. Synthetic textiles (Fig. 152-4) and rayon are used in clothing, home furnishings, and carpeting. Carboxymethylcellulose (CMC) acts as a suspension agent in powdered detergents (Fig. 152-5) and as a controlling additive in oil-well drilling needs. Viscose reinforcing cord used in belts (Fig. 152-6) and tires is a product made from wood. An ingredient for water-base latex paints (Fig. 152-7) is hydroxyethylcellulose (HEC). New interior acrylic paints and lacquers used in furniture and automobile finishes are also made from cellulose fibers. Additional products include coatings for welding rods and acetate sheeting (Fig. 152-8).

Lignin products

One-third of wood is composed of lignin and wood sugar. The exact composition of lignin remains a mystery to chemists, but progress is being made

WOOD DISTILLATION PLANTS

BOLTS
LIMBS
STUMPS
EDGINGS

HARDWOOD DISTILLATION PRODUCTS

PRODUCTS	USES

ACETIC ACID
Acetate solvents, cellulose acetate for rayon, photo film, lacquers, and plastics; coagulant for latex, perfumes, and textile dyeing; manufacturing inorganic acetates, white lead pigments

ACETONE
Acetylene, explosives (cordite), solvent

CHARCOAL
Activated carbon, black powder explosives, chemical manufacture, fuel, livestock and poultry foods, manufacturing charcoal iron, medicines, metacase hardening compounds, producer gas, water purification

METHANOL
Antifreeze, dry-cleaning agents, formaldehyde, manufacturing chemical compounds, paints, pyroxylins, shellac, textile finishing agents, varnishes

PITCH
Insulation in electric transformers, rubber filler

TAR OIL
Flotation oils, gasoline (inhibitor oil), paints and stains, preservatives, solvent oils, wood creosote

SOFTWOOD DISTILLATION PRODUCTS

PRODUCTS	USES

CEDAR OILS
Furniture polish

CHARCOAL
Activated carbon, black powder explosives, chemical manufacture, fuel, livestock and poultry foods, manufacturing charcoal iron, medicines, metacase hardening compounds, water filtration

CREOSOTE OILS
Cattle and sheep dips, disinfectants, medicines

DIPENTINE
Solvent for reclaiming old rubber

LACQUER SOLVENT
Lacquers, paints, varnish

PINE OIL
Disinfectants, fabric dyeing, flotation oil, paints

PINE TAR
Coating and binding materials, disinfectants, manufacturing cordage, medicines, oakum, soaps

ROSIN
Paper sizing, varnish, soap, greases, waterproofing, linoleum

TAR OIL SOLVENTS
Disinfectants, flotation oils, paints, soaps, stains

WOOD TURPENTINE
Paint and varnish manufacture, synthetic camphor for celluloid manufacture

Fig. 152–1   Wood products derived from wood distillation plants. *American Forest Institute.*

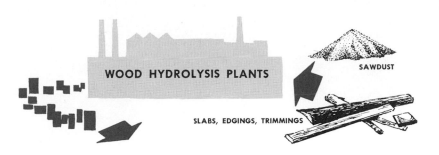

WOOD HYDROLYSIS PLANTS

SAWDUST

SLABS, EDGINGS, TRIMMINGS

PROCESS	PRODUCTS	USES
WOOD HYDROLYSIS	ACETIC ACID	Textile manufacture, white lead pigment, cellulose acetate, perfume
	BAKING YEAST	Bakery products
	BUTADIENE	Synthetic rubber
	CARBONIC ACID	Industrial chemicals
	ETHYL ALCOHOL	Solvents
	ANIMAL FOOD	Cattle feed, chicken feed
	FURFURAL	Resins, plastics
	GLYCERINE	Medicines, industrial chemicals
	LIGNIN POWDER	Plastic and laminates
	SUGARS	Stock feed, ethanol
WOOD CONDENSATION	FURFURAL	Resins, plastics
	SOIL CONDITIONER	To make soils more porous
ALKALINE FUSION	OXALIC ACID	Bleaching, industrial chemicals
	PYROGALLOL	Stains
	RESINS	Plastics

Fig. 152–2 Commercial products from wood hydrolysis plants. *American Forest Institute.*

Fig. 152–3 Insulation board is made from the cellulose-fiber-products group. *Acoustical and Insulating Materials Association.*

Fig. 152–4 Synthetic textiles made from wood cellulose are colorful and serviceable. *Forest Products Laboratory.*

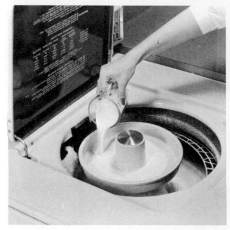

Fig. 152–5 Household detergents include carboxymethylcellulose as a suspension agent. *Rayonier, Inc.*

Fig. 152–6 A conveyer belt made from industrial rayon-rubber reinforcing cord. *Rayonier, Inc.*

Fig. 152–7 An ingredient for water-base latex paints is a product made from wood called hydroxyethylcellulose. *Rayonier, Inc.*

Fig. 152–8 Acetate sheeting for boxes is a product made from wood. *Rayonier, Inc.*

in research efforts to analyze it. Lignin is used in mixing concrete for road-building and for other purposes, in tanning leather, and as a water softener and purifier.

Lignin is also used as a base in fertilizers and as an ingredient in perfumes, cosmetics, food preservatives, drugs, and plastics. These plastics are used in telephones, radio and television cabinets, electrical equipment, combs, toys, dishes, and jewelry.

Vanillin was the first item to be produced successfully from lignin on a commercial basis. From this product comes vanilla food flavoring, vanillic acid, and fibers similar to Dacron.

Women's hose can be derived from wood, since xylose is a wood sugar that can be converted into **furfural,** a base for nylon.

unit **153**

Discussion topics on the technology of woods

1. What were some of the early American methods of transportation which were almost entirely dependent on wood?
2. Other than to supply lumber and wood products, what major functions do the forests fulfill?
3. Approximately how many million acres of forest lands are there in the United States?
4. What are the six general forest areas of continental United States? What are the other United States forest areas?
5. Where is the majority of the pulpwood in the United States produced?
6. Into what two general classifications can all trees be divided?
7. Classify the kinds of trees growing in your state and in your specific locality.
8. Discuss the methods by which we can differentiate between softwoods and hardwoods.
9. Discuss the qualities and characteristics of such woods as walnut, maple, cherry, and oak.
10. What species of woods are especially useful for handles, athletic equipment, and similar uses?
11. What woods have properties which make them adaptable for bending?
12. What is meant by the term **cooperage,** and which woods are used in this industry?
13. Define or explain the terms **flat-grained, edge-grained, plain-sawed,** and **quartersawed.**
14. What is noticeably different about the growth rings of elm and gum compared to most other woods?

15. Approximately how many species of woods have been identified? How many are suitable for manufacturing lumber and other commercial products? What percentage of these are hardwoods?
16. What is meant by the expression **to blaze a tree**?
17. What is the function of an undercut?
18. Name several methods of skidding logs.
19. How do mills prevent stored logs from cracking?
20. Organize the class and plan a group project to locate pictures in newspapers and magazines to make a pictorial flowchart of lumber production from the forest to the consumer.
21. Briefly explain what **tape control** means in relation to a machine.
22. What do the letters **N/C** stand for?
23. Briefly explain the difference between point to point and continuous path programming.
24. Name some woodworking machines that are particularly adapted to tape control use.
25. In what industry was N/C originally used?
26. Discuss the advantages of each method of sawing lumber.
27. Name the two kinds of kilns used for drying lumber.
28. Select several pieces of lumber and perform an experiment to determine the moisture content of the various samples cut from the pieces.

29. Explain the meaning of these lumber abbreviations: (a) S2S, (b) AD, (c) KD, (d) S4S, (e) FAS, and (f) No. 1 common.
30. What are some of the defects and their causes which affect the grade of a particular piece of lumber?
31. Discuss the major functions of the Forest Products Laboratory.
32. What are briquettes?
33. What are some uses of stump wood?
34. What are some natural products obtained from trees?
35. Explain the differences between veneers and plywood.
36. What special parts of a tree are used to produce beautiful grain designs in veneers?
37. From what parts of the world do the various mahoganies and mahogany substitutes come?
38. What are the methods used to cut veneer?
39. Name five patterns, or figures, produced in cutting veneers.
40. What do **G1S** and **A-D** mean in relation to plywood?
41. What are five sports which use hardwood laminated-plywood equipment?
42. Organize, or enter into, a class project to make either a pictorial or a miniature flow chart for plywood manufacturing.
43. What are the differences among marquetry, inlay, and intarsia?
44. What is the major difference between hardboard and particle board?

45. What woods are chiefly used in hardboard?
46. Name several surface patterns available on hardboard.
47. Give six trade, or manufacturing, names of particle board.
48. What are the two types of particle board?
49. Explain or define the words **extrusion, caul, platen, conveyor,** and **billet.**
50. What are the sizes of particle board sheets available?
51. What are the principal methods of making pulpwood for paper?
52. Enter into a class project and make a large flow chart of pictures showing the orderly procedure of making paper.
53. Name three products used for paper besides wood pulp.
54. Why are the high-grade papers calendered, or ironed, more than lower quality grades?
55. What becomes of the liquids left over from the paper-pulping processes?
56. What are the two products or divisions of wood cellulose? Name some products made from each.
57. Name 10 products made from lignin.
58. What is meant by angiosperm and gymnosperm?
59. Name the three main parts of a tree.
60. What is the formula for determining moisture content in wood?
61. Name several products made from the parts of a tree which were once considered waste.

section **10**

The Building Construction Industry

Common building and carpentry terms

The terminology selected for this unit includes words and terms that are frequently used in carpentry and building construction. Examples of many terms are seen in the various drawings and photographs.

General building terms

Batter Boards. Boards nailed to posts at the corners of the proposed building. Strings stretched between them indicate the outline of foundation walls.

Brace. Any piece of wood fastened to two or more pieces. The brace usually forms a triangle with the other pieces to give them greater strength.

Building code. The legal requirements designed to protect the general welfare, health, and safety of those in and around buildings.

Scaffold. A temporary platform built to assist workers in reaching high places.

Sheathing. Narrow boards spaced on rafters to which shingles are attached, also boards, plywood, or other wallboards placed solidly over studding or rafters.

Sheathing paper. Paperlike material placed over subfloors, on walls, or on roofs to help prevent air passage.

Toenailing. Nailing at an angle through one surface into another; usually done when one piece is perpendicular to another.

Foundation terms

Footing. The lower portion of a foundation wall or pier. It is usually made wider than the wall to distribute the load.

Foundation. A footing, wall, or piers which support the remainder of the building.

Ledger strip. The piece nailed to girders or beams. The ends of the floor joists rest on it.

Sill. Usually a horizontal member that rests on the foundation. Supports the uprights of the frame, and may also form the lower part of an opening, as a windowsill does.

Flooring terms

Bridging. Bridging pieces, equal to the width of the joists and fitted between floor joists. Crossed pieces, placed in pairs between joists from the top of one to the bottom of an adjacent joist. Brace to distribute loads.

Joists. Parallel beams, 2 by 6 inches (51 by 152 mm) (or larger), on 16- or 24-inch (406- or 610-mm) center to support floor and ceiling loads; joists are themselves supported by bearing walls, girders, or larger beams.

Subfloor. Straightedge or matched lumber which is placed diagonally across joists and over which the finish floor is laid; plywood or some other sheet-wood product may be used.

Wall terms

Bay window. Any window space projecting outward from the regular wall; in various shapes.

Baseboard. A board placed around the bottom of a wall to finish and decorate between the wall and the floor.

Base shoe. A molding or carpet strip placed next to the floor against the baseboard.

Jamb. A frame that surrounds and contacts the window or sash; supported by framing.

Girder. Often used interchangeably with *beam* to mean a large structural member that supports a heavy load in walls, a roof, or a floor.

Header. Often called a **lintel,** a horizontal beam placed perpendicularly between studding over window and door openings or in framing for a chimney or stairway opening.

Partition. Any wall-dividing unit within a building to support a load is a **bearing** partition; if **nonbearing,** it supports only its own weight.

Siding. Can be beveled or lap, strong drop siding (tongue-and-groove joints), or shiplap (rabbeted or lap joints) for exterior wall covering.

Sole plate. Usually a 2- by 4-inch (51- by 102-mm) wood piece laid flat, on which wall and partition studs rest.

Stud (also studding). The vertical members of walls and partitions, usually placed on 16- or 24-inch (406- or 610-mm) centers.

Wallboard. Plywood, wood pulp and other material made into large, rigid sheets fastened to internal and external walls, partitions, roofs, and the framing of a building.

Roofing terms

Beam. Sometimes called a **girder,** a structural member that supports a load in the roof, walls, or floor.

Gable. An inverted V formed between the slopes of two roof sections.

Pitch. The ratio of the total rise of the roof to the total width. In addition, pitch is the number of inches of vertical rise to each foot of horizontal run.

Trim. Exterior or interior finish materials, such as moldings placed around windows, doors, floors, and ceilings.

Rafters. The framing pieces on which other roofing is placed. **Common** rafters are those that run square from the top of the wall plate to the peak (ridge) of the gable. **Cripple** rafters are pieces cut to fit between valley and hip rafters. **Hip** rafters extend from corners, or the outside angle of the wall plates, to the apex of the roof. **Jack** rafters are those that run square from the wall plate, or ridge board, and intersect hip or valley rafters. **Valley** rafters extend from the inside angle of wall plates to the ridge center line of the building.

Rise. The height of a roof measured vertically from a point on the outside face of the top wall plate to the ridge of the roof.

Roof. Covers the top of a structure.

Run. Half a span; the horizontal distance from the face of one wall to the ridge of a roof.

Shingles. Wood pieces, or other materials, cut and packaged in standard thicknesses, widths, and lengths.

Span. The horizontal distance between any structural supports, such as outside walls, columns, beams, girders, piers, or trusses.

Square. A unit of measure of 100 ft^2 of roofing and sidewall materials, often packaged and sold by the square.

Truss. A structural frame of rafters and other parts, usually in triangular form; laminated or curved units that are used to support roofs or other heavy loads over long spans.

unit 155

Construction lumber

About three-fourths of the lumber produced for interior and exterior construction of homes and buildings comes from the many softwoods, such as fir, pine, redwood, and spruce. Softwood lumber is classified by **manufacture, use, size,** and **grade.**

Manufacture classifications

Rough lumber has not been dressed (planed). It has been sawed, edged, and trimmed and usually shows saw marks.

Surfaced, or **dressed, lumber** has been surfaced or planed to a uniform size on one or two sides (S1S or S2S), one or two edges (S1E or S2E), or a combination of sides and edges (S1S1E, S1S2E, S2S1E, or S4S).

Worked lumber has been dressed and worked for a particular purpose in a matching machine, molder, or other special equipment. Examples of worked lumber are rabbeted edges for

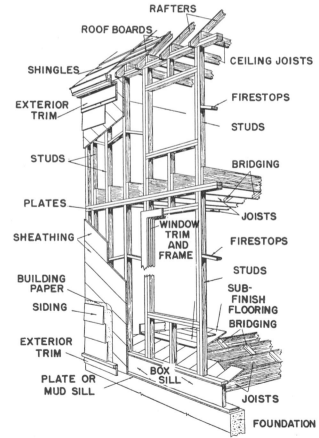

Fig. 155–1 Suggested uses of lumber for standard construction. *Douglas Fir Plywood Association.*

shiplap, tongue-and-groove matching, and molding.

Use classifications

Yard lumber in all sizes and patterns is intended for general-purpose building.

Factory and **shop lumber** is worked into doors, windows, and similar millwork.

Structural lumber is used where stress and heavy loads are supported.

Size classifications

Boards are called **strips** if they are less than 6 inches (152 mm) wide. This grouping includes pieces less than 2 inches (51 mm) thick and 1 inch (25 mm) or more wide, such as fencing, sheathing, and roofing.

Dimension stock is from 2 inches (51 mm) up to, but not including, 5 inches (127 mm) thick and 2 inches (51 mm) or more wide, such as joists, studs, and rafters.

Timbers are pieces with a minimum dimension of 5 inches (127 mm). They include beams, posts, and sills.

Because of seasoning and surfacing, lumber dimensions are smaller than the common sizes by which they are known. Minimum thicknesses and widths for actual sizes are specified for each type of softwood lumber in the *American Lumber Standards.* For example, a standard, dressed 2- by 4-inch piece actually measures less. However, the standard size is used in all lumber sales and in bookkeeping.

Grade classifications

The exact grading rules for all species of lumber, both softwoods and hardwoods, are established by agencies maintained by the lumber industry. These grading rules cover the appearance and the performance of individual species of wood. The agencies maintained by industry also supervise grading and inspection.

Select grades are intended for finish purposes. A and B grades are usually combined and sold as **B and better.** C and D grades are more economical, and they serve many purposes just as well as the higher grades.

Common grades are utilized where knots and other surface characteristics are decorative. These are intended for general construction purposes.

Dimension grades of softwood are classified according to the natural characteristics that affect their stiffness, strength, and other load-bearing qualities. The appearance of joists, studs, and heavy construction parts is usually of secondary importance.

Structural lumber is 2 inches (51 mm) or more in thickness and width. A separate grading system, based on strength characteristics, is used.

General suggestions in the choice of lumber for standard building construction are shown and named in Fig. 155-1.

unit 156

Planning and constructing the foundation of a house

Three main essentials are needed to build a satisfactory house: (1) correct planning, (2) proper materials, and (3) sound construction. These principles apply to a house of any design, size, or cost. Construction details vary in different localities, but the fundamental principles apply anywhere.

Location and excavation of the site

Compare the size of the building plot to the size of the house desired. Check local building codes for minimum setback from streets, side clearance, and back (or alley) requirements. Building permits are usually necessary.

Determine subsoil and drainage conditions and depth of water-table level before beginning any construction. The depth of a basement and the location of sewer pipes may depend on the natural ground water line, or water table.

Small stakes are located at each corner of the proposed house. Batter boards (Fig. 156-1) are placed at the corners outside the planned foundation lines. A common excavation plan is shown in Fig. 156-2.

Footings and foundations

The footings and foundation walls are usually made of poured concrete or some other masonry product. The thickness and type of construction are controlled by local building codes, and the thickness varies. When basements are planned, 6 to 10 feet (1829 to 3048 mm) should be the minimum

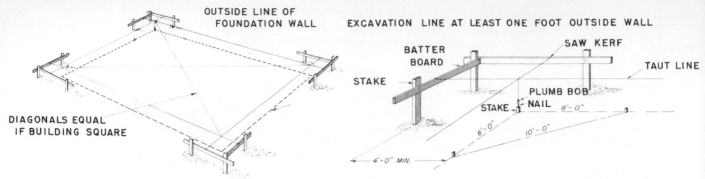

Fig. 156–1 Batter boards are used at the corners of a plot to stake and lay out a house. *USDA booklet 73,* Wood-Frame House Construction.

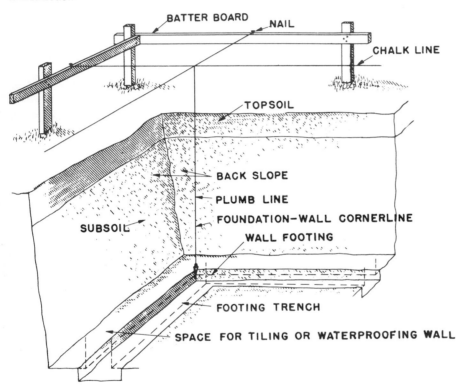

Fig. 156–2 A common excavation plan, showing the use of batter boards and chalk lines for layout. *USDA booklet 73,* Wood-Frame House Construction.

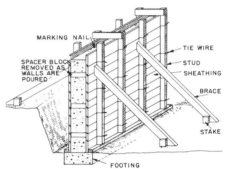

Fig. 156–3 Typical formwork for pouring concrete walls. *USDA booklet 73,* Wood-Frame House Construction.

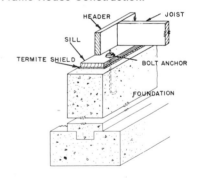

Fig. 156–4 Anchoring joists and floor structure to the foundation. *USDA booklet 73,* Wood-Frame House Construction.

height from the basement floor to the bottom of the joists that form the first floor of the house.

Tight forms must be made, braced, and tied. The concrete is poured into these forms for the footings and foundation walls until it hardens. A typical method of handling forms is shown in Fig. 156–3.

Frames and forms

Frames for basement windows or doors are set in place when the concrete forms are built. Nails are placed in the top of the form to show the level to which the concrete should be poured. Pouring should be a continuous operation.

Forms are removed after the concrete has set (hardened) sufficiently to support loads. Hot tar is used to waterproof the outside walls from above the surface grade line to the footing.

The joists and other floor structures are anchored to the concrete walls (Fig. 156–4). Bolts should be placed in the concrete before it sets.

Floor framing

Floor framing uses posts, beams or girders (Fig. 157-1), sills, joists, bridging, and subfloors. Chemically treated lumber should be used for all floor framing in areas where termites are a problem.

Posts and beams

Steel or **wooden posts** are used to support beams or girders (Fig. 157-2). The beams support the inner ends of the first-floor joists, and they often rest on either masonry pieces or wooden

Fig. 157–3 A design feature of this octagonal home is the exposed pole and beam construction shown outside the cedar-clad walls. *Western Wood Products Association.*

posts. Exposed poles (posts) and beams can add interest to a design (Fig. 157-3).

Beams can be either solid or box (Fig. 157-4) and can be built up (Fig. 157-5) with two or more pieces of 2-inch-thick (51-mm-thick) dimension lumber. The end joints are staggered, but they usually join over a post.

Short beams can be butt-joined by using special metal connectors (Fig. 157-6). At least 4 inches (102 mm) of the beam end should rest (bear) on masonry walls. The top of the beam should be flush (level) with the sill plate unless notched joists are set on ledger strips (Fig. 157-7). Girders are specially spaced to allow for utility lines between them.

Fig. 157–1 Floor joists, beams, and two types of bridging are shown in the house framing. *National Lumber Manufacturers' Association.*

Fig. 157–4 Plywood box beams, solid beams, posts, and other footings are often mixed in one construction job. *Western Wood Products Association.*

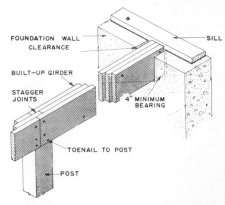

Fig. 157–5 Built-up beams have staggered joints which join over a post. *USDA booklet 73,* Wood-Frame House Construction.

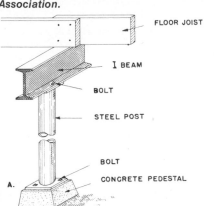

Fig. 157–2 Posts and beams: (A) steel post and I beam, and (B) wood post and built-up wood beam. *USDA booklet 73,* Wood-Frame House Construction.

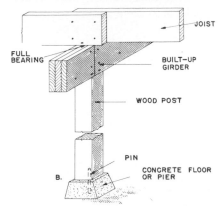

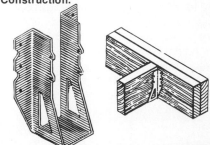

Fig. 157–6 Metal connectors can be used to connect building parts. *Timber Engineering Company.*

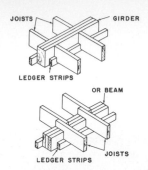

Fig. 157–7 Ledger strips are nailed to beams or girders to support joists. *U.S. Army Technical Manual TM 5-460.*

Sill and floor joists

The two common types of construction used over the foundation wall are platform and balloon. **Platform** construction (Fig. 157-8) uses a single sill anchored to the foundation. In **balloon** construction the joists and studs both rest directly on the double sill or the sill plate (Fig. 157-9).

Studs are nailed to both the joists and the sill. A nailing strip or fire stop must be placed between the studs when diagonal subflooring is used in balloon construction. Balloon framing is preferred when the outer construction is to be stone or a brick veneer because there is less potential shrinkage of exterior walls.

The selection of joists depends on the strength and stiffness required to eliminate annoying vibration. Joists are usually 2 inches (51 mm) thick and 6, 8, 10, or 12 inches (152, 203, 254, or 305 mm) wide. The choice depends on the load to be carried, the length of the span, the spacing between joists of 16 or 24 inches (406 or 610 mm) on center, and the species or grade of lumber used. Joists used under load-bearing partitions and as framing around fireplace openings, stairwells, and other openings should be doubled.

Bridging and subfloors

Bridging is used between joists to stiffen the joists and to help distribute loads. Bridged pieces are used at midspan, but not over 8 feet (2438 mm) apart. Long spans will certainly require several lines of bridging (Fig. 157-10).

Smaller pieces can be cut at an angle to fit diagonally between joists. They are nailed to the top and bottom of the joists. The bottom is frequently not fastened until the house framing is complete. Bridging and other floor framing for platform construction are shown in Fig. 157-10.

Subflooring is made of $3/4$-inch (19-mm) construction plywood or square-edge or tongue-and-groove boards. Boards should be no wider than 8 inches (203 mm) in standard 1-inch (24-mm) surfaced lumber. They should rest on at least two joists and be laid diagonally. The usual angle is 45 degrees. The end joints of adjacent lines of boards should not be together on the same joists.

The finished floor can properly be laid parallel or perpendicular to the joists when subfloor boards are laid diagonally in relation to the joists. If subfloors are laid at right angles (in a perpendicular position) to the joists, the finished floor itself should be laid at right angles to the subfloor. Figure 157-11 shows two kinds of subfloors.

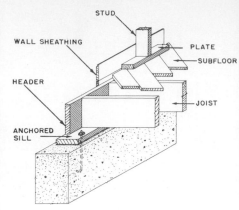

Fig. 157–8 A single sill is anchored to foundation in platform construction. *USDA booklet 73,* **Wood-Frame House Construction.**

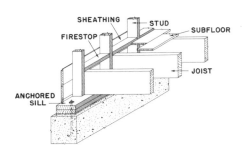

Fig. 157–9 A double sill or sill plate is used in balloon construction. *USDA booklet 73,* **Wood-Frame House Construction.**

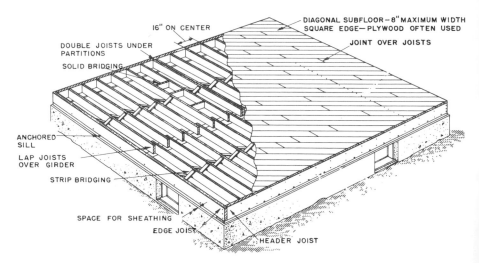

Fig. 157–10 Typical platform floor framing. *USDA booklet 73,* **Wood-Frame House Construction.**

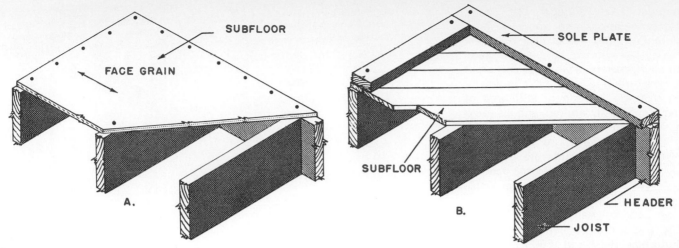

Fig. 157–11 Subfloor material is called *underlayment:* (A) plywood and (B) boards. *Housing & Home Finance Agency booklet,* Technique of House Nailing.

unit 158

Wall framing

Wall framing refers to the use of vertical and horizontal two-by-fours for exterior and interior walls. These serve as a base for nailing on wall-covering

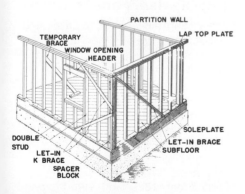

Fig. 158–1 Single-story platform wall framing. *USDA booklet 73,* Wood-Frame House Construction.

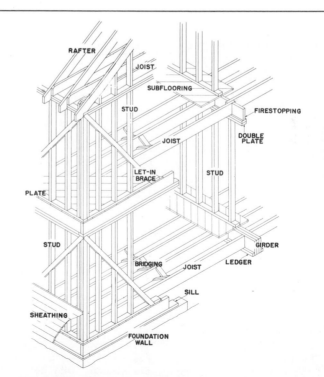

Fig. 158–2 Two-story platform wall framing. *National Lumber Manufacturers' Association.*

materials and support the upper floors, ceilings, and roof. If large plumbing pipes are placed in a wall, two-by-sixes should be used for studs for either the entire wall or a portion of it. Wall-framing lumber should be good grade, seasoned, stiff, free of warp, and easily worked, and it should possess nail-holding power.

Ceiling heights are preferably 8 feet (2438 mm). Studs are generally placed on 16-inch (406-mm) centers, but they are placed on 24-inch (610-mm) centers in some one-story buildings. Different wall framing is used on one- and two-story platform construction (Figs. 158-1 and 158-2).

Framing corners

Posts made of multiple studs should be used at exterior corners and at intersections of walls. These posts provide a nailing base, especially for interior wallboard.

Figure 158-3 shows a common arrangement of studs on an exterior corner. They are arranged to give good nailing surfaces where interior walls cross and where a partition meets a wall or partition (Fig. 158-4).

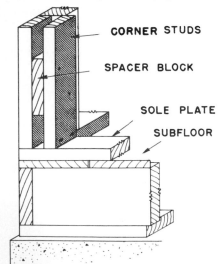

Fig. 158–3 The proper arrangement of studs on corners is very important. *USDA booklet 73,* **Wood-Frame House Construction.**

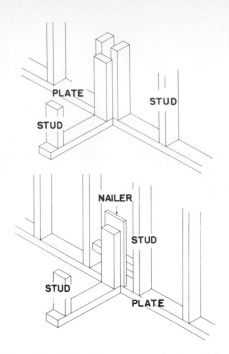

Fig. 158–4 Partitions properly framed to other walls. *USDA booklet 73,* **Wood-Frame House Construction.**

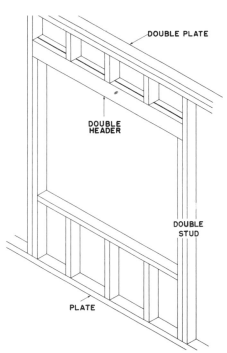

Fig. 158–5 Exterior window openings are stronger with double headers and studs. *National Lumber Manufacturers' Association.*

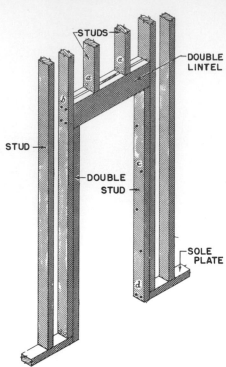

Fig. 158–6 Typical header and studs for doors. *Housing & Home Finance Agency booklet,* **Technique of House Nailing.**

Braces on walls and corners are usually made of one-by-fours set into the studs or two-by-fours cut and placed at an angle between the studs (see Figs. 158-1 and 158-2). If sheathing is placed at an angle on exterior walls, the braces can be eliminated.

Framing doors and windows

Extra strength is needed to carry vertical loads over window and door openings. Double lintels, or headers (usually 2 by 6 inches), should span the opening at the top. These headers rest on studs at each end.

Metal framing anchors are sometimes used without the double stud when an opening is less than 3 feet (914 mm) wide. Triple studs are recommended when the opening exceeds 6 feet (1829 mm), with the ends of the lintel resting on two studs. Typical door and window framing is shown in Figs. 158-5 and 158-6.

unit 159

Ceiling and roof framing

Ceiling joists are nailed to each rafter to act as ties between exterior walls and interior partitions. Joists and rafters are often put together as roof trusses. In two-story structures, joists support the ceilings on the first floor and help to support the second floor. All parts of the roof should be securely tied together to the exterior and interior walls. Roof construction should be exceptionally strong to withstand all types of unfavorable weather conditions.

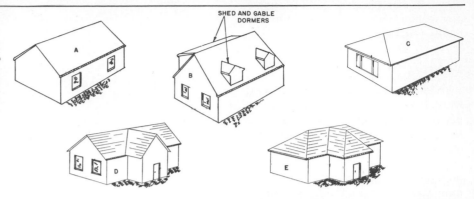

Fig. 159–2 Simple and combined pitched roofs: (A) gable, (B) gable with shed or gable dormers, (C) hip, (D) gable and valley, and (E) hip and valley.

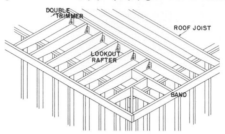

Fig. 159–3 Special construction is necessary on a flat roof when the combination rafter and ceiling joist is used. *National Lumber Manufacturers' Association.*

Types of roofs

There are two general types of roofs: **flat** and **pitched.** Both have variations. Joists of flat roofs serve both as rafters and as ceiling supports. The joists are laid level, or they are laid with a very slight slope to provide better drainage.

The flat roof and the variable flat shed roof are illustrated in Fig. 159-1. A flat roof with overhang requires special construction and arrangement of the combination rafter and ceiling joists (Fig. 159-3).

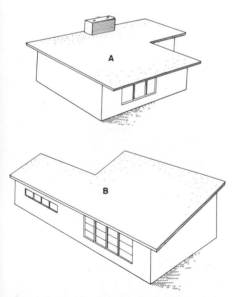

Fig. 159–1 Flat roofs: (A) rafters and ceiling joists are same pieces; and (B) rafters and ceiling joists are separate. *USDA booklet 73,* Wood-Frame House Construction.

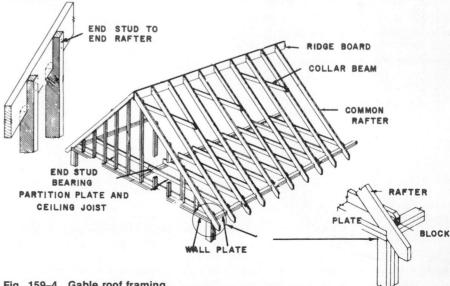

Fig. 159–4 Gable roof framing.

The simplest pitched roof is the **gable** (Fig. 159-2A). Others are the gable with **shed** or **gable dormers** (Fig. 159-2B), **hip** (Fig. 159-2C), **gable and valley** (Fig. 159-2D), and **hip and valley** (Fig. 159-2E).

Valleys in a roof

A **valley** in roof construction is formed when the slopes of two sides of a roof join. The roof part connecting these slopes is the valley rafter. If the two slopes are equal in size, this rafter is doubled to carry the roof load. It is 2 inches (51 mm) wider than the common rafter to permit the full end of the jack rafter to come in contact with it. Framing for the various pitched-roof types, including the valley, is pictured in Figs. 159-4 through 159-7.

Types of rafters

There are three major types of rafters which extend from the wall plate to the ridge board: (1) **common,** (2) **hip,** and (3) **valley.** They are nailed to the wall plate or attached with special fasteners (Fig. 159-8).

The jack rafter is shorter than the common rafter. It does not extend from the ridge board to the plate (Fig. 159-9). The hip jack extends from the ridge to a hip rafter. The cripple jack extends from a hip to a valley rafter and does not touch the ridge. The valley jack is also called a cripple rafter.

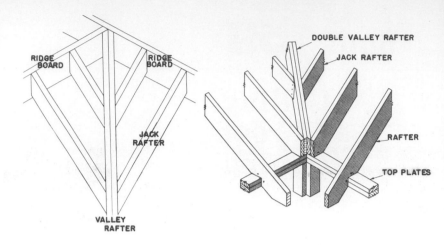

Fig. 159–6 Framing a valley. *USDA booklet 73,* Wood-Frame House Construction.

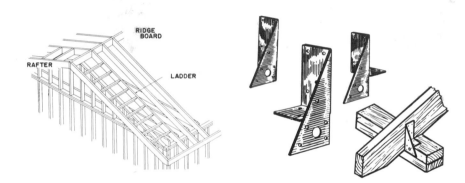

Fig. 159–7 Framing a gable and overhang. *National Lumber Manufacturers' Association.*

Fig. 159–8 Special fasteners are sometimes used to join rafters to wall plates. *Timber Engineering Company.*

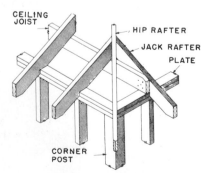

Fig. 159–5 Hip roof framing. *USDA booklet 73,* Wood-Frame House Construction.

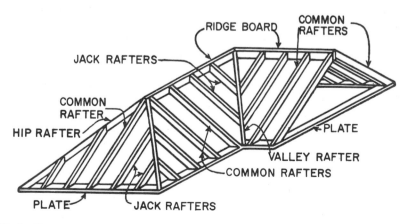

Fig. 159–9 Use of different rafters in hip and valley roof framing. *Stanley Tools Division, The Stanley Works.*

354

The framing square

The framing square is indispensable to the builder and the carpenter. It is made in the form of a right angle. The principles of roof framing are based on the geometric principles of the right triangle.

The framing square

The steel framing square is used to lay out lengths and cuts on various rafters used in framing the roof. Its main parts are the **blade** (body) and the **tongue** (Fig. 160-1). Study the scales, divisions, and tables given on the face and back of this square.

Figure 160-2 shows how the roof-framing terms relate to gable roof members and the framing square. Study these terms in Unit 154.

The framing square is also available in metric dimensions (Fig. 160-3).

Brace length

The length of a brace is quickly measured on the steel framing square by consulting the **brace measure table**. It is measured along the center on the back of the tongue (Fig. 160-4).

Example:

Find the length of a brace when the run on the post (or stud) and beam (or plate) is 48 inches.

Find $\frac{48}{48} 67^{88}$ on the table.

Solution:

The length of the brace, then, is 67.88 inches, or $67^{7}/_{8}$ inches for practical uses.

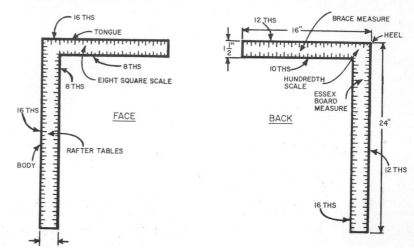

Fig. 160–1   Parts of the steel framing square. *Stanley Tools Division, The Stanley Works.*

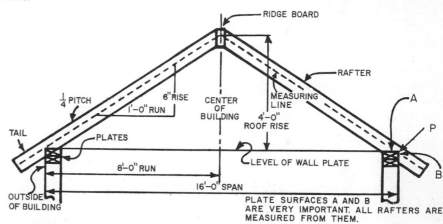

Fig. 160–2   Span, run, rise, and pitch of a gable roof. *Stanley Tools Division, The Stanley Works.*

Board measure

Board-foot (bd ft) measure for most sizes of construction lumber is on the board measure table on the back of the steel square body.

Inch graduations along the outer edge of the square are used in combination with numbers along the seven parallel lines beneath these graduations. *The 12-inch mark is the starting point for all calculations* (Fig. 160-5).

The number 12 represents a board 1 inch thick, 12 inches wide, and 12 feet long, or 12 bd ft. The inch graduation on *each* side of the 12 represents the *width* of the boards. The numbers *beneath* the 12 indicate the *length* of the boards.

The board measure tables are given for boards 1 inch thick. For other thicknesses, multiply the figure

Fig. 160–3 This framing square has been partially converted to metric measure for general-purpose use. Note that the rafter-framing and lumber figures are not shown. *Stanley Tools Division, The Stanley Works.*

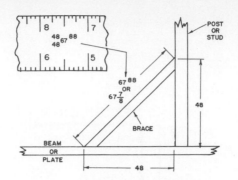

Fig. 160–4 Use of the brace measure on the square saves time in calculating the length of brace needed. *Stanley Tools Division, The Stanley Works.*

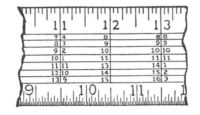

Fig. 160–5 The board measure table on the square is easy to use. *Stanley Tools Division, The Stanley Works.*

given in the table by the thickness of the lumber.

Follow this procedure:

1. Find the *length* of the piece under the number 12.
2. Locate the standard *width* of the piece along the inch graduations.
3. Follow the line on which the length is stamped until it intersects the line of figures under the given width. The figure stamped at this point is the board measure in the piece.

Example:

What is the board measure of a piece of lumber 10 feet long and 11 inches wide?

Solution:

Find the number 10, representing the length, in the vertical column under the 12-inch mark (see Fig. 160-5). Follow the horizontal line to the left until it intersects the column of figures under the 11-inch mark, representing the width. The number at this point is 92 (9-2) or $9^2/_{12}$. The number of board feet in the piece is $9^1/_6$.

unit 161

Roof pitch and rafter layout*

Roofs of the same width can have different pitches, depending upon the heights of the roofs. The principal pitches (Fig. 161-1) show the amount of rise in inches per foot of run, or the ratio of rise to span.

Special acknowledgment is due the Stanley Tools Division, Stanley Works, for the contents of this unit.

Determining pitch, rise, and run

Pitch, rise, and **run** can be determined from a basic formula when two of the quantities are known. For example, if a building is 24 feet wide *(span)* and the *rise* is 8 feet, the *pitch* is $1/_3$.

$$P \text{ (pitch)} = \frac{R \text{ (rise)}}{S \text{ (span)}}$$

$$P = \frac{8}{24}, \text{ or } \frac{1}{3}$$

$$R \text{ (rise)} = P \text{ (pitch)} \times S \text{ (span)}$$

$$R = \frac{1}{3} \times 24, \text{ or } 8 \text{ ft}$$

Using the same 24-foot span, the rise in inches for each foot of run can be determined: the rise is 8 feet, or 96 inches (8 feet × 12 inches per foot). The run is one-half the span, or 12 feet ($1/_2$ × 24). Therefore:

$$\text{Rise per foot of run} = \frac{96}{12} = 8 \text{ in.}$$

The rise in inches per foot of run is always the same for ordinary pitches:
Pitch.................................... $1/_2$ $1/_3$ $1/_4$ $1/_6$
Rise per foot of run........... 12″ 8″ 6″ 4″

Using metric measure the pitch is easily determined by substituting metric dimensions for customary dimensions. For example, a rise of 2.67 meters over a span of 8 meters gives a pitch of $1/_3$. Since there is no convenient equivalent of the foot in the met-

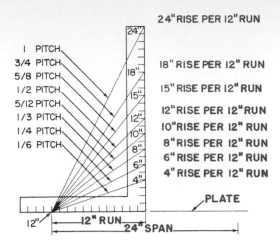

24" RISE PER 12"RUN

1 PITCH
3/4 PITCH
5/8 PITCH
1/2 PITCH
5/12 PITCH
1/3 PITCH
1/4 PITCH
1/6 PITCH

18" RISE PER 12" RUN
15" RISE PER 12" RUN
12"RISE PER 12" RUN
10"RISE PER 12" RUN
8" RISE PER 12" RUN
6" RISE PER 12" RUN
4" RISE PER 12" RUN

PLATE

12" RUN
24" SPAN

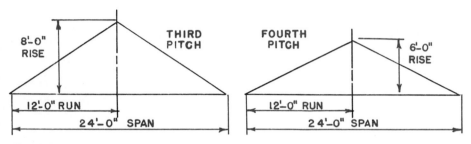

Fig. 161–1 Pitches of roofs. *Stanley Tools* and *Housing & Home Finance Agency booklet,* Technique of House Nailing.

ric system it will be up to the building industry to determine if it will be convenient to use a number of millimeters rise per meter of run. A direct conversion of inches to millimeters for the rise per foot of run would serve no useful purpose.

Rafter length tables

The rafter tables on the steel framing square are based on the rise per foot of run (length). Numbers in the table show length of common rafters for any rise, as indicated in Fig. 161-2.

The roof illustrated has a span of 6 feet. The run (divided into three equal parts of one foot), the rise, and the total rafter length represent a right triangle *ABC.* Vertical lines through each part of the run also divide the rafter into three parts. The length of a rafter per foot of run will be different for each pitch. Therefore, the rise per foot of run must be known before rafter length can be established.

Rafter lengths can be obtained by three ways besides using tables on

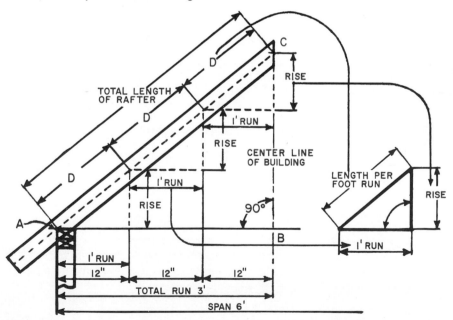

Fig. 161–2 The relationship of rafter length to foot of run. *Stanley Tools Division, The Stanley Works.*

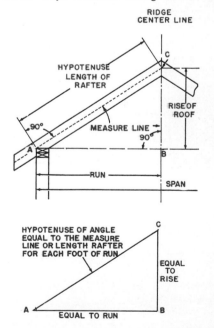

Fig. 161–3 Figuring the true length of a common rafter. *U.S. Army Technical Manual TM 5-460.*

357

the square. They are (1) mathematical calculation, (2) measuring across the square, and (3) stepping off with the square. However, using tables on the framing square requires less time than calculation, and the chances for a mathematical error are lessened.

Determining common rafter length

The length of the common rafter is the shortest distance between the center-line point of the ridge to the outer edge of the plate. This length is taken along the measuring line (Fig. 161-3).

Inches and sixteenths of an inch ($1/16$) are found on the outside face of

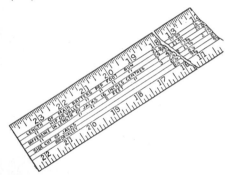

Fig. 161–4 Rafter tables on the face of the framing square. *Stanley Tools Division, The Stanley Works.*

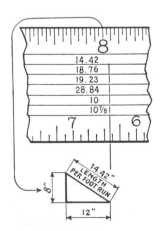

Fig. 161–5 Using the rafter table to determine the length of a common rafter per foot of run. *Stanley Tools Division, The Stanley Works.*

the square on both the body and the tongue. The first line on the body gives the length of common, or main, rafters per foot of run (Fig. 161-4). The 17 main rafter tables begin under the 2 inch mark and continue through 18 inches.

To find the length of a common rafter, multiply the number of feet of run times the length given in the table.

Example:

If rise equals 8 inches per foot of run ($1/3$ pitch) for a building 20 feet wide (span), the run is 10 feet.

Solution:

1. Find the 8-inch mark on the body of the square.

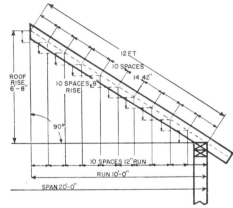

Fig. 161–6 Determining the length of a common rafter. *Stanley Tools Division, The Stanley Works.*

2. On the first line under the 8 will be found the number 14.42 (Fig. 161-5). This is the length of the common rafter in inches per foot of run.

3. Multiply 14.42 times 10 feet of run to secure 144.2 inches of rafter.

4. Divide 144.2 inches by 12 inches per foot; the common rafter length will be 12.01, or 12 feet for practical use (Fig. 161-6).

Top and bottom cuts on common rafters

The top cut on the rafter is the place where the upper end rests against another rafter or the ridge board. This cut is parallel to the center line of the roof. The bottom, or heel, cut is at the lower end of the rafter, horizontal to the plates. This makes the top and bottom cuts at right angles to each other.

The manner in which the cut is made is illustrated in Fig. 161-7 with a large imaginary square placed on the rafter. The tongue coincides with the top, plumb, or ridge cut; the blade coincides with the bottom, heel, or plate cut.

To obtain the layout of the heel and the plumb cuts, use the 12-inch mark on the body and the rise per foot of run on the tongue (Fig. 161-8). The horizontal cut is marked along the

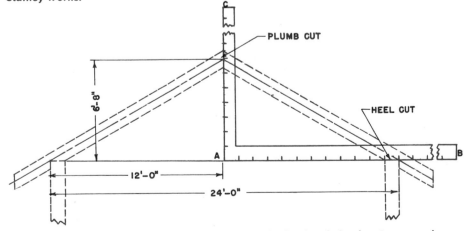

Fig. 161–7 A large imaginary square shows how the heel and plumb cuts are made on a common rafter. *Stanley Tools Division, The Stanley Works.*

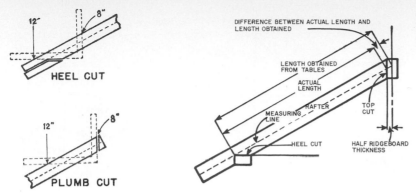

Fig. 161–8 Laying out the heel and plumb cuts. *Stanley Tools Division, The Stanley Works.*

Fig. 161–9 Allowance in length of the rafter must be made when the ridge board is used in construction. *Stanley Tools Division, The Stanley Works.*

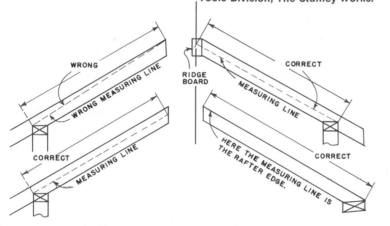

Fig. 161–10 The length of a rafter must be measured accurately. *Stanley Tools Division, The Stanley Works.*

body of the square, and the vertical cut is marked along the tongue.

The lengths of rafters obtained from the tables are actual lengths from the center line of the ridge to the outside edge of the plate when there is no overhang. When a ridge board is used, deduct half the thickness of this board from the total length of the rafter before the top cut is made (Fig. 161-9). The correct and incorrect methods of measuring rafter length are shown in Fig. 161-10.

After the total length of the rafter has been established, both ends should be marked. Add length for the overhang. Subtract half the thickness of the ridge board if this board is used.

Example:

If a rafter is 16 feet 6 inches long and the rise is 9 inches per foot of run, how are the top and the bottom cuts obtained?

Solution:

1. Study Fig. 161-11. Points *A* and *B* are the rafter ends.

2. For the bottom, or seat, cut, lay the square on the rafter so that the 12-inch mark on the body coincides with point *A*, and the 9-inch mark on the tongue coincides with the rafter edge.

3. Mark along the body to obtain the line for the seat cut.

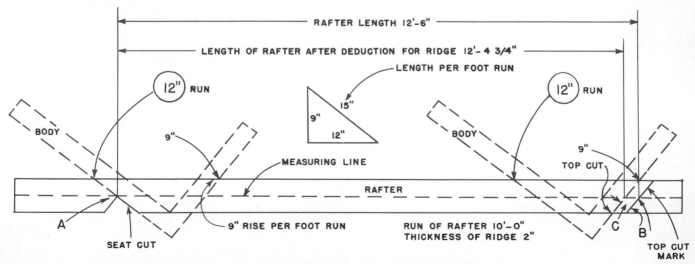

Fig. 161–11 Correct layout is necessary for top and bottom cuts on a rafter. *Stanley Tools Division, The Stanley Works.*

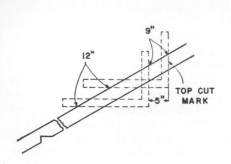

Fig. 161–12 Add odd inches to the lengths of common rafters. *Stanley Tools Division, The Stanley Works.*

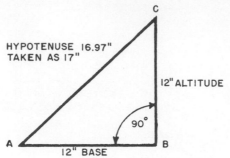

Fig. 161–13 "The square of the hypotenuse is equal to the sum of the squares of the other two sides" is a mathematical principle of the right triangle which also applies to rafter layout. *Stanley Tools Division, The Stanley Works.*

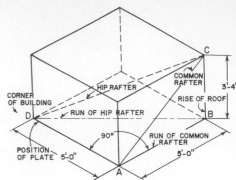

Fig. 161–14 Position of the hip rafter in relation to the common rafter. *Stanley Tools Division, The Stanley Works.*

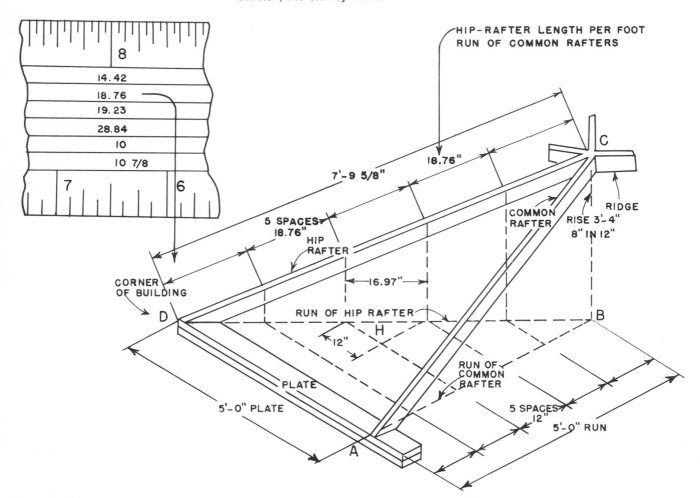

Fig. 161–15 The length of the hip rafter is related to its position. *Stanley Tools Division, The Stanley Works.*

4. Move the square to the top end of the rafter. Place it in the same position coinciding with point *B*.

5. Mark along the tongue to obtain the line for the top cut.

6. Deduct half the ridge board thickness, measuring at right angles to the top cut line. The plumb cut is made parallel to the top cut line, as at *C*.

7. Add tail-overhang length to the bottom end.

8. Cut two rafters. Place them on the building to check their accuracy. Correctly cut rafters can be used to lay out all the others.

If a common rafter must be cut for a roof that has an odd number of inches in the span, such as 24 feet 10 inches, this is done by following the example in Fig. 161-12. The run of such a building would be 12 feet 5 inches. The additional inches can be added as illustrated. They are added at right angles to the last plumb line after the numbers obtained from the square for each foot of the run are measured.

Determining hip and/or valley rafter length

The relation of hip and/or valley rafters to common ones is the same as that of the sides of a right triangle. If the sides forming a right triangle are 12 inches each, the hypotenuse, or side opposite the right angle, is equal to 16.97 inches, usually considered to be 17 inches (Fig. 161-13).

The position of the hip rafter, as related to the common rafter, is illustrated in Figs. 161-14 and 161-15. The prism has a base 5 feet square and a height of 3 feet 4 inches. *D* is the corner of the building; *BC* is the total rise of the roof; *AB* is the run of the common rafter; *AC* is the common rafter; *DB* is the run of the hip rafter; and *DC* is the hip rafter.

Figure *DAB* is a right triangle the sides of which are the portion of the plate *DA*, the run of common rafter *AB*, and the run of the hip rafter *DB*. The run of the hip rafter opposite the

right angle *A* is the hypotenuse, or the longest side of the right triangle.

Assume a 1-foot run of common rafter and a 1-foot plate length, and the right triangle *H* is formed (see Fig. 161-15). The sides are each 12 inches long, and the hypotenuse is 17 inches. The hypotenuse of this small triangle *H* is a portion of the run of the hip rafter *DB*, which corresponds to a 1-foot run of common rafter.

Remember the rule that the run of the hip rafter is always 16.97 inches for every 12 inches of run of the common rafter. The total run of the hip rafter therefore, will be 16.97 inches multiplied by the run, in feet, of the common rafter.

The lengths of hip and/or valley rafters are marked on the *second* line of the rafter table as "Length of hip and valley rafters per foot run." Numbers in this table indicate the length of hip and valley rafters per foot of run of common rafters.

To find the length of a hip or valley rafter, multiply the length given in the table by the number of feet of run of the common rafter.

Example:

Find the length of a hip rafter if the rise of roof is 8 inches per foot of run. This indicates a 1/3 pitch when the building is 10 feet wide (see Fig. 161-15).

Solution:

Proceed in the same way as for common rafters. Find the number along the edge of the square corresponding to the rise of roof, which is 8. On the second line under this figure is

18.76. This is the length of the hip rafter in inches for each foot of run of common rafter for a 1/3 pitch.

The common rafter has a 5-foot run. Therefore, there are five equal lengths for the hip rafter, as seen in Fig. 161-15.

The length of the hip rafter is 18.76 inches per 1-foot run. Its total length will be 18.76 times 5, or 93.80 inches. This is 7.81 feet, or, for practical purposes, 7 feet 9⅝ inches.

Top and bottom cuts on hip and valley rafters

To obtain the top and bottom cuts of hip or valley rafters, use 17 inches on the body and the "rise per foot run" on the tongue. The numeral 17 on the framing square body will give the seat cut, and the figure on the framing square tongue will give the vertical, or top, cut (Fig. 161-16).

Measuring hip and valley rafters

The length of all hip and/or valley rafters is always measured along the center of the top edge or back. Rafters with overhang are treated like common ones except that the measuring line is the center of the top edge.

Deduction from hip or valley rafter for ridge

The deduction for the ridge is measured like that for the common rafter except that half the diagonal (45 degrees) thickness of the ridge must be used.

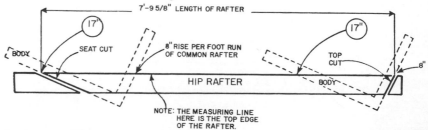

Fig. 161–16 Laying out top and bottom cuts on hip and/or valley rafter. *Stanley Tools Division, The Stanley Works.*

Side cuts

Hip and valley rafters must also have **side,** or **cheek,** cuts at the point where they meet the ridge. These side cuts are found on the *sixth* (bottom) line of the rafter tables, which is marked "Side cut hip or valley—use." The numbers given in this line refer to the graduation marks on the "outside edge of the body."

The numbers on the framing square have been derived by determining the number to be used with 12 on the tongue for the side cuts of the various pitches. From a plumb line, the thickness of the rafter is measured and marked at right angles (Fig. 161-17A). Square a line across the top of the rafter; the diagonal points connect (Fig. 161-17B). Line *B* (side cut) is obtained by marking along the tongue of the square.

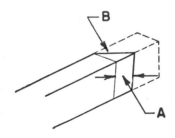

Fig. 161–17 Laying out the side, or cheek, cut on a hip rafter. *Stanley Tools Division, The Stanley Works.*

To obtain the **side cut** for hip or valley rafters, use the number given in the table on the body of the square and 12 inches on the tongue. Mark the side cut along the tongue where it coincides with the point on the measuring line.

Example:

Find the side cut for a hip rafter when the roof has 8 inches rise per foot of run (1/3 pitch).

Solution:

Figure 161-18 represents the position of the hip rafter on the roof. With the rise of roof 8 inches per foot of run, locate number 8 on the outside edge of the body. Under this number in the bottom line is $10^7/_8$. This number is used on the body and 12 inches on the tongue. The square is applied to the edge of the back of the hip rafter. The side cut *CD* is along the tongue.

Deduct for half the thickness of the ridge in the same way as for the common rafter except that half the diagonal (45 degrees) thickness of the ridge must be used.

In making the **seat cut** for the hip rafter, an allowance must be made for the top edges of the rafter. These edges would project above the line of the common and jack rafters if the

corners of the hip rafter were not removed, or backed. The hip rafter must be slightly lowered by cutting parallel to the seat cut. This amount varies with the thickness and pitch of the roof.

The 12-inch mark on the square tongue is used in all angle cuts at the top, bottom, and side. The number taken from the fifth or sixth line in the table is the only other one to remember when laying out side or angle cuts. The side cuts are always on the right hand, or tongue side, of rafters.

Odd inches of hip and valley rafters

Additional inches in the run of hip or valley rafters are added in a way similar to that explained for common ones (Fig. 161-12). The diagonal (45 degrees) is used. Approximately $7^1/_{16}$ inches for 5 inches of run is added.

Determining jack rafter length

Jack rafters are common rafters that have been "cut off" by the intersection of a hip or valley before reaching the full length from plate to ridge. They lie in the same plane as common rafters and are usually spaced the same and have the same pitch. They also have the same length per foot of run as the common rafters.

Jack rafters rest against the hip or valley rafter. When equally spaced, the second jack must be twice as long as the first one; the third is three times as long as the first. This length multiple continues for each additional rafter.

Lengths of jack rafters are given in the third and fourth lines of the rafter tables on the framing square, as follows:

Third line: "Difference in length of jacks—16-inch centers."

Fourth line: "Difference in length of jacks—24-inch centers."

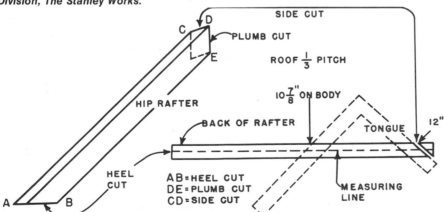

Fig. 161–18 Finding top and bottom cuts on a hip rafter. *Stanley Tools Division, The Stanley Works.*

Numbers in the table indicate the length of the first, or shortest, jack, which is also the difference in length between the first and second, and between the second and third jack, and so on for each rafter.

To find the length of a jack rafter, multiply the value given in the tables by the number indicating the position of the jack. From the obtained length, subtract half the diagonal (45 degrees) thickness of the hip or valley rafter.

Example:

Find the length of the second jack rafter when the roof has a rise of 8 inches to 1 foot of run of the common rafter spaced 16 inches apart.

Solution:

On the outer edge of the body, locate number 8, which corresponds to the rise of the roof. On the *third* line under this number, locate

19.23. This indicates that the first jack rafter will be 19.23 times 2, or 38.46 inches. For practical use, the length is 3 feet $2^1/_2$ inches. From this length, deduct half the diagonal thickness of the hip or valley rafter, as on the hip rafter for the ridge. The same procedure is used when jack rafters are spaced on 24-inch centers.

Top and bottom cuts on jack rafters

Jack rafters have the same rise per foot of run as common rafters. The method of obtaining the top and bottom cuts is the same. Use 12 inches on the body and the rise per foot of run on the tongue. The 12 inches will locate the line for the seat cut; the figure on the tongue will locate the plumb cut.

Side cut on jack rafters

A side cut is required on a jack rafter where the end meets the hip or valley rafter. Side cuts for jacks are found on the *fifth* line of the rafter tables. It is marked "Side cut of jacks—use."

To obtain the side cut, use the number shown in the table on the body of the framing square and the number 12 on the tongue. Mark along the tongue for the side cut.

Example:

Find the side cut on jack rafters for a roof having an 8-inch rise per foot of run ($^1/_3$ pitch) see Figs. 161-19 and 161-20).

Solution:

Under 8 on the edge of the square, locate 10 in the *fifth* line of the

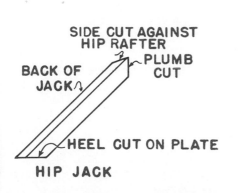

Fig. 161–19 Side cut for hip jack rafter. *Stanley Tools Division, The Stanley Works.*

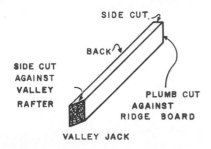

Fig. 161–20 Layout of a side cut for a valley jack rafter. *Stanley Tools Division, The Stanley Works.*

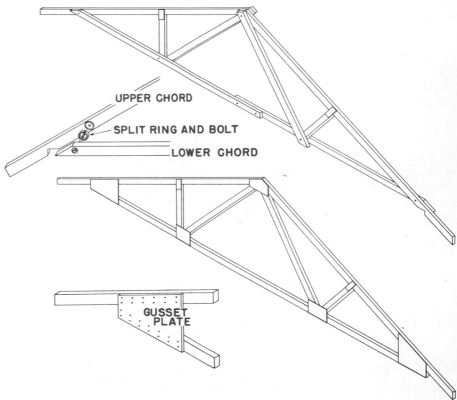

Fig. 161–21 Typical methods of assembling roof trusses. *National Lumber Manufacturers' Association.*

table. Use this 10 on the outside edge of the body and 12 inches on the tongue. The two will give the line for the required side cut.

Fig. 161–22 Roof trusses are assembled on the ground or at the factory. They are easily installed as complete units. *Southern Pine Association.*

Fig. 161–23 A gusset plate is attached with staple nails to parts of a truss. *Stanley Tools Division, The Stanley Works.*

Trusses for pitched roofs

The lightweight roof trusses (Fig. 161-21) are installed as complete units (Fig. 161-22). They save material and time. Trusses are designed according to accepted engineering practices. They are joined with glue, nails, staple nails (Fig. 161-23), bolts, and special connectors (Fig. 161-24).

Trusses eliminate the need for interior load-bearing partitions. In this type of construction, gable ends are usually framed in the conventional manner, using a common rafter to which the gable and the studs are nailed. Overhangs at eaves are provided by extending the upper chords of the trusses beyond the wall (Fig. 161-26) or by nailing the overhand framing to the upper chords.

Where hip and valley construction is necessary, modified trussed rafters or conventional framing is used. Trusses are spaced 16 to 24 inches apart. This depends on the type of truss and roof sheathing and the ceiling covering used.

Ventilation of attic space

Moisture condensation in cold weather, and heat in hot weather, are eliminated or reduced by ventilating the

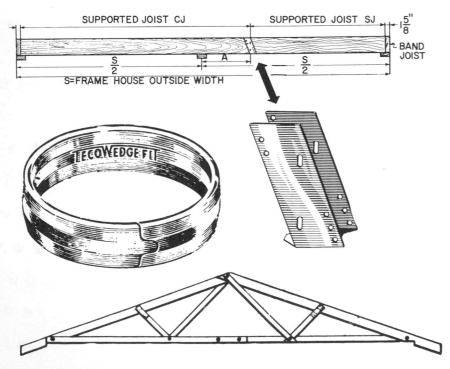

Fig. 161–24 Special connectors can be used to join parts of a truss. *Timber Engineering Company.*

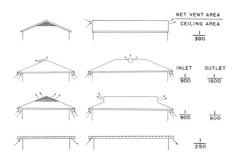

Fig. 161–25 Roofs must have openings for proper ventilation. *National Lumber Manufacturers' Association.*

364

attic space. For gable roofs, screened louvers can be used. The net area of the louver opening should be about $1/300$ of the area of the ceiling below. A sheet-metal ventilator near the peak of the roof and a $3/4$-inch slot beneath the eaves are used on hip roofs. The net area of the inlet should be $1/900$ of the ceiling area below; that of the outlet, $1/1600$ of the area.

For flat roofs, blocking and bridging should be arranged to allow free movement of air. Such roofs can be ventilated along the overhanging eaves. The net opening area should be $1/250$ of the area of the ceiling (Figs. 161-25 and 161-27).

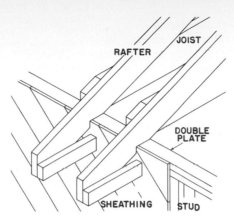

Fig. 161–26 Rafter extensions or upper truss chords are used to form the roof overhang. *National Lumber Manufacturers' Association.*

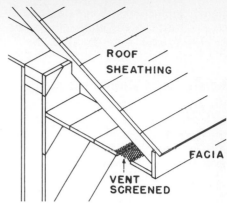

Fig. 161–27 Roofs are frequently ventilated by leaving openings in the overhang. *National Lumber Manufacturers' Association.*

unit 162

Bay windows, dormers, and stairs

Bay windows and dormers are functional. They provide additional space, lighting, beauty, and ventilation (Fig. 162-1). Stairs serve as passages to different levels of a building. They should be designed to afford safe, comfortable passage to the occupants and enough space for moving furniture.

Bay windows and dormers

Bay window projections are arranged so that floor joists extend beyond the foundation wall (Fig. 162-2). The extension should usually not exceed 2 feet (610 mm). Additional support of the roof over this window opening is necessary.

Fig. 162–1 Bay windows add beauty, lighting, and ventilation. *Sumner Rider & Associates.*

Dormers should be framed when a house is first constructed. Extra framing must be added (Fig. 162-3 and 162-4). This framing is similar to that already explained, but it should be planned in advance of construction. Dormers provide lighting and ventilation and make possible future expansion or additional attic rooms. It is also possible to obtain additional light by using skylights (Fig. 162-5).

Laying out steps and stairs

Principal stairs should provide comfort and convenience. Service stairs to attics and basements are usually steeper and often are constructed of less expensive material.

Stairs can be built either in place or as separate units and then set in place. They can be built in a winding pattern; in a straight, continuous run (Fig. 162-6); or with an intermediate platform. The latter two forms are considered safer and are most often used in homes. Safe stair designs and terms used are shown in Fig. 162-7.

The fundamental layout for straight stairs is shown in Fig. 162-7. Dimensions for the riser and the tread (a **tread** and a **riser** make a step) are selected to make stairs easy and comfortable to ascend or descend. Follow these pointers in stairway layout:

1. Determine the height, or rise, from the first-floor level to the next.

2. Figure the run, or distance, measuring horizontally.

3. Lay out the risers and treads on a stair horse, or stringer, for a preliminary plan. Fractions of an inch often result.

Fig. 162–5 Skylights add natural light. *Western Wood Products Association.*

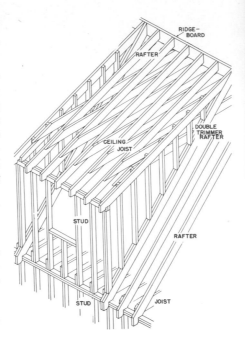

Fig. 162–3 Framing a shed dormer. *National Lumber Manufacturers' Association.*

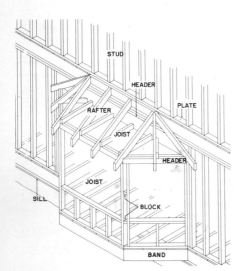

Fig. 162–2 A properly framed bay window. *National Lumber Manufacturers' Association.*

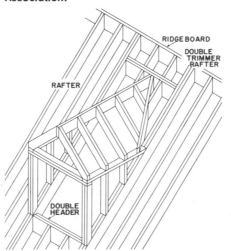

Fig. 162–4 Framing a gable dormer. *National Lumber Manufacturers' Association.*

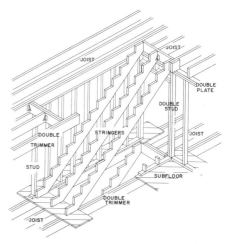

Fig. 162–6 A typical layout and framing for a straight-run stairway. *National Lumber Manufacturers' Association.*

Example:

$$\frac{\text{Total rise}}{\text{number of risers}} = \frac{\text{height of}}{\text{each riser}}$$

$$\frac{8' \ 3^{3}/_{4}'' \ (99.75'')}{14} = 7.125''$$

4. Lay out, or space off, the number of treads wanted in the horizontal distance, or run. There is always one less tread than there are risers. If there are 14 risers, there are only 13 treads.

Figure 162-7 shows a 10-inch-wide tread and a 7-inch-high riser. The stair stringer (stair horse) may be laid out (stepped off) with the framing square, ready for cutting.

Deduct the thickness of the tread from the first riser to make the first step the same height as all the others.

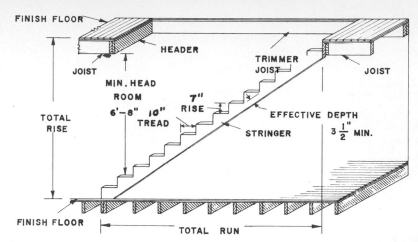

Fig. 162–7 Some of the terms used in stair design. *USDA booklet 73*, Wood-Frame House Construction.

unit 163

Wall, roof, and floor coverings

Coverings for exterior (Fig. 163-1) and interior walls, ceilings, roofs, and floors add beauty, strength, and insulation to various parts of a building. Sheathing serves as the underlayment, or base, for nailing on roofing, siding, and interior coverings. Experiments show that woodframe construction and insulation reduces heating or cooling losses.

Sheathing roofs and walls

Four types of roof and wall sheathing are commonly used in modern construction. These are (1) **lumber** (Fig. 163-2), (2) **plywood** (Fig. 163-3), (3) various **fiberboards** (Fig. 163-6), and (4) **gypsum board.** Lumber is put on walls and roofs either horizontally or diagonally (Fig. 163-4). Plywood, fiberboard, or gypsum board can be

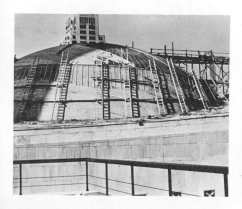

Fig. 163–1 Treated lumber was used to cover the exterior walls of the United Nations General Assembly Building. *Koppers Company, Inc.*

Fig. 163–2 Lumber is used as spaced board sheathing for wood shakes or shingles. *Western Wood Products Association.*

Fig. 163–3 Plywood panels weighing as much as 1300 pounds (590 kg) were used as sheathing on this modern church. *Douglas Fir Plywood Association.*

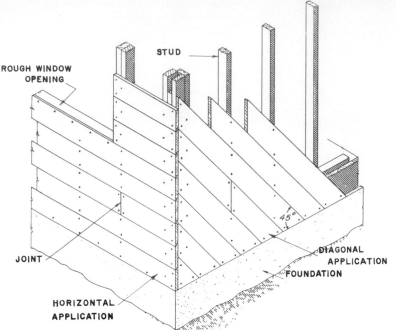

Fig. 163–4 Sheathing lumber is attached horizontally or diagonally. *USDA booklet 73,* Wood-Frame House Construction.

Fig. 163–6 Fiberboards for wall sheathing are strong and help insulate and eliminate noise. *The Sheet Metal Worker.*

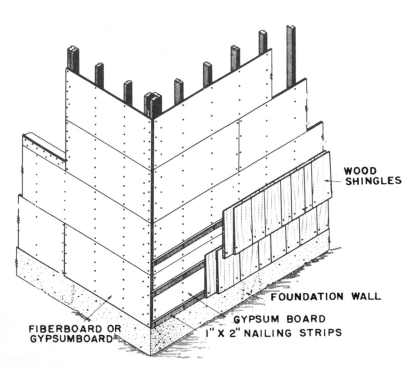

Fig. 163–5 Walls can be sheathed horizontally with 2- or 4- by 8-foot (609- or 1219- by 2438-mm) sheets of plywood, fiberboard, or gypsum board. *USDA booklet 73,* Wood-Frame House Construction.

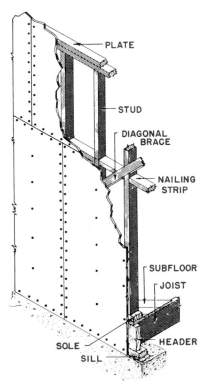

Fig. 163–7 Sheets are also used to sheath walls vertically. *Housing & Home Finance Agency booklet,* Technique of House Nailing.

attached to walls horizontally or vertically (Figs. 163-5 and 163-7) and to roofs as shown in Fig. 163-8.

Sheathing materials are made in numerous thicknesses and widths. Common sheet rock is usually manufactured in 2- and 4-foot (610- and 1219-mm) widths and in lengths of 4, 8, and 12 feet (1219, 2433, and 3658 mm) (Fig. 163-9). These sizes can easily be fitted and nailed to framework placed on centers of 16 and 24 inches (406 and 610 mm).

Siding for walls

Numerous types of exterior siding are available. Several kinds of wood siding, methods of nailing, and application are shown in Figs. 163-10 through 163-14.

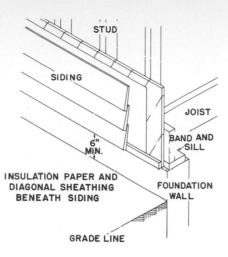

Fig. 163–10 Clearance should be made between the siding and ground level. *National Lumber Manufacturers' Association.*

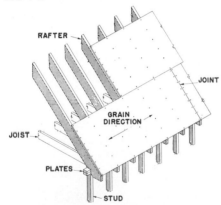

Fig. 163–8 Roofs can be sheathed with plywood. *USDA booklet 73,* Wood-Frame House Construction.

Fig. 163–9 Sheathing materials may be as long as 12 feet (3657 mm). *Insulation Board Institute.*

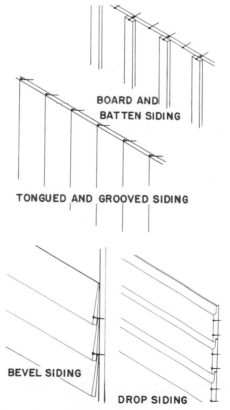

Fig. 163–11 Typical kinds of siding and methods of nailing. *National Lumber Manufacturers' Association.*

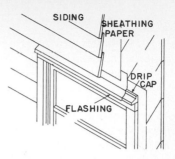

Fig. 163–12 Bevel siding above a window over diagonal lumber sheathing. *National Lumber Manufacturers' Association.*

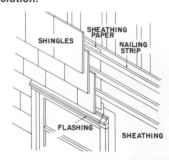

Fig. 163–13 Special strips are nailed to studs when wood shingles are used without sheathing as underlayment. *National Lumber Manufacturers' Association.*

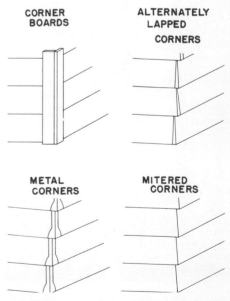

Fig. 163–14 Typical methods of covering corners on siding. *National Lumber Manufacturers' Association.*

Covering the roof

The most common roof coverings are (1) **asphalt shingles** (Fig. 163-15); (2) **wood shingles,** or **shakes** (Fig. 163-16); and (3) **built-up roof coverings.** Some principal shingle woods are western red cedar, redwood, and bald cypress. These are cut from heartwood, they are all edge grain, and they are tapered. They are highly decay-resistant and are low in shrinkage. Asphalt and wood shingles can be attached as shown in Figs. 163-17 and 163-18.

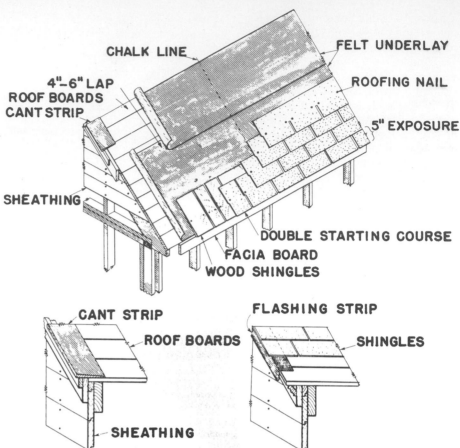

Fig. 163-15 Special staple nails or roofing nails are used to attach asphalt shingles. *Spotnails, Inc.*

Fig. 163-17 Procedure for laying asphalt shingles. *USDA booklet 73,* Wood-Frame House Construction.

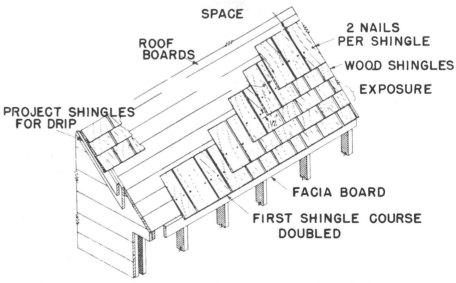

Fig. 163-16 Roof shakes (shingles) make a decorative, long-lasting roof covering. *Red Cedar Shingle & Handsplit Shake Bureau.*

Fig. 163-18 Procedure for laying wood shingles. *USDA booklet 73,* Wood-Frame House Construction.

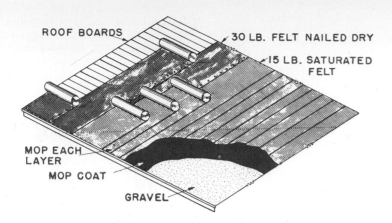

Built-up roofs (Figs. 163-19) are usually installed by specialized roofing companies. Special decks are also used (Figs. 163-20 and 163-21).

Floor covering

Subfloors should be clean and level. They are covered with a sound-deadening felt or with building paper. See Unit 157, Floor Framing.

Many types of materials and designs are available for finish flooring (Fig. 163-22). It is laid after the ceiling and the interior walls are completed.

Strip flooring should be laid crosswise on the floor joists, and it is usually laid lengthwise in a rectangular room.

Fig. 163–19 Procedure for laying a built-up roof. *USDA booklet 73, Wood-Frame House Construction.*

Fig. 163–20 Lumber frames covered with plywood are used to make some roof panels. Insulation can be added inside between the plywood sheets. *Douglas Fir Plywood Association.*

Fig. 163–21 Wood panels are used as decks on some roofs. *Simpson Timber Company.*

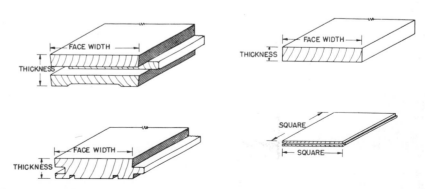

Fig. 163–22 There are many types of finish flooring. *USDA booklet 73, Wood-Frame House Construction.*

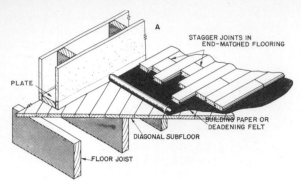

Wood floor tile, linoleum, asphalt tile, and rubber tile floors are popular. Correct installation of these materials is important (Figs. 163-23, 163-24, and 163-25). Most manufacturers of special types of flooring materials provide instructions for doing an efficient, satisfactory job of installation. These directions should be followed.

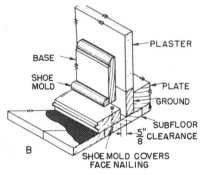

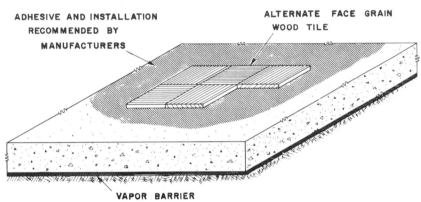

Fig. 163–24 Follow the manufacturer's recommendations in laying special floors. *USDA booklet 73,* Wood-Frame House Construction.

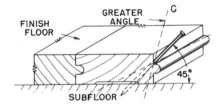

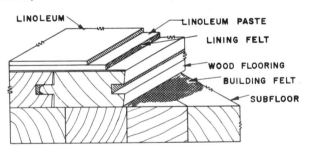

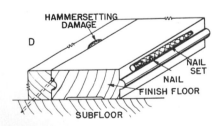

Fig. 163–23 (A) Laying and nailing strip flooring, (B) laying the first strip, (C) method of nailing, and (D) method of setting nails. *USDA booklet 73,* Wood-Frame House Construction.

Fig. 163–25 Various subfloors are used for different types of flooring. *USDA booklet 73,* Wood-Frame House Construction.

Concrete slab construction

Concrete slab construction is used where drainage is not a problem. Improved methods of construction reduce heating or cooling losses, and in addition, they lessen former disadvantages of slab construction, such as floor sweating.

Basic foundation and slab construction

The finished floor level should be above the finished ground grade for complete drainage. Topsoil and all foreign matter should be removed. All loose soil should be thoroughly packed. Sewer, water, and gas lines, as well as any other subsurface work, must be completed before the slab is poured.

Space between the soil level and the slab is filled and packed with at least 4 inches (102 mm) of coarse gravel or rock. This is covered with a solid plastic sheet, which serves as a **vapor barrier** (Fig. 164-1). Succeeding steps for frame construction of plates, studs, walls, and floors are also in this illustration.

The combined slab and foundation, with reinforced footing, is poured as a complete unit. This type of construction is suitable in climates where frost penetration is not a problem.

Independent slabs and foundation walls

In climates where the ground freezes deeply, the foundation is poured separately from the slab. The footing and foundation walls should extend below the frost line to solid, unfilled soil.

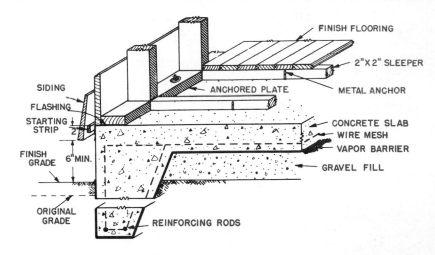

Fig. 164–1 Coarse fills are covered with a special sheet to serve as a vapor barrier between the soil and the combination concrete slab and foundation. *USDA booklet 73,* **Wood-Frame House Construction.**

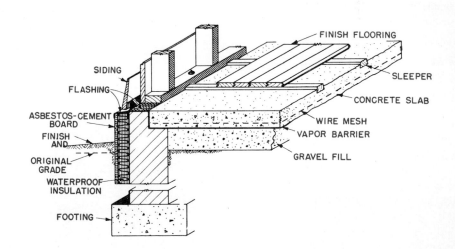

Fig. 164–2 Insulation is added to the outside of the foundation wall when the slab and foundation are separated. *USDA booklet 73,* **Wood-Frame House Construction.**

Insulation is added to the outside of the foundation wall (Fig. 164-2), or it is put inside, and independent of, the slab (Fig. 164-3). The vapor barrier is on the warm side of the insulation and below the slab. Space is left above the insulation, and it is filled with hot tar to the top of the slab. The tar serves as a protection against termites.

Vapor barriers and slab insulation

A vapor barrier should give high resistance to vapor transmission, resist damage by moisture, and withstand rough treatment before the concrete is poured. A polyethylene film four thousandths (0.004) of an inch (0.1016 mm) or more thick is considered to have these properties.

Slab insulation materials must be highly resistant to heat transmission and to crushing by floor loads, slab weight, and expansion forces. They must be durable when exposed to frost, dampness, and fungus or insect attack.

Materials that have these desirable properties are cellular glass, insulation board, and glass fibers with plastic binder. Special insulating concrete is made with specific aggregates (mixes) of mica, pumice, or slag. Some wood or plant fiberboards are used under certain dry-climate conditions.

Forced-air ducts and radiant heating in slabs

Ductwork for cold-air return in some forced-air heating systems is located in a slab around the exterior wall (Fig. 164-4). A vapor barrier is added to both sides of the insulation to stop soil moisture and cold weather condensation.

Different construction is used when a forced hot-water radiant heating system is used (Fig. 164-5). Copper or steel pipes are embedded in the concrete slab floor in a regular pattern.

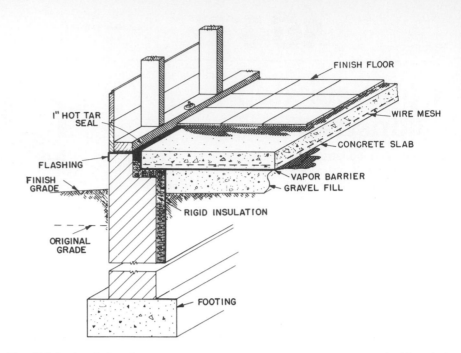

Fig. 164–3 Insulation is also located around exterior walls on the inside of the foundation wall separating the wall and slab. *USDA booklet 73,* **Wood-Frame House Construction.**

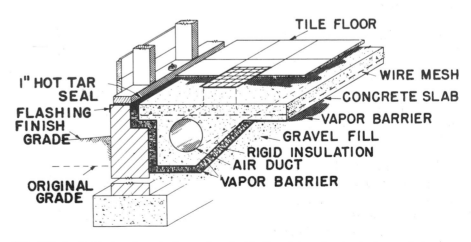

Fig. 164–4 Cold-air return ducts are located in the slab around exterior walls in some forced-air heating systems. *USDA booklet 73,* **Wood-Frame House Construction.**

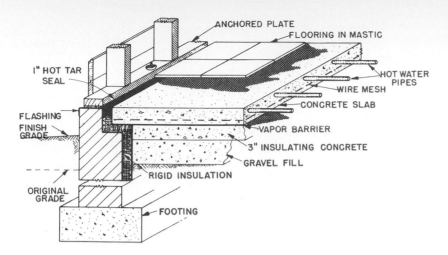

Fig. 164—5 Radiant heating pipes are embedded in the slab for some hot-water radiant heating systems. *USDA booklet 73,* Wood-Frame House Construction.

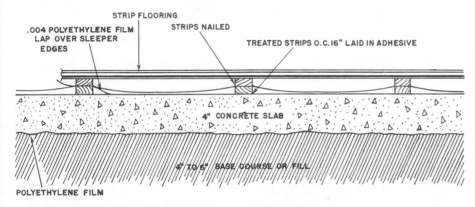

Fig. 164—6   A cross section of an accepted method of installation of strip flooring on a concrete slab. *National Oak Flooring Association.*

Floors in slab construction

A finished concrete floor is sometimes used in slab construction, but it feels cold to the touch. Asphalt or other tiles are often laid in mastic (adhesive), according to the manufacturer's directions.

Strip oak flooring is frequently laid over concrete slabs. Tests show that this method, which does not use wood subfloors, offers substantial savings and superior floor performance. This method is also accepted by the Federal Housing Administration (FHA).

A cross section of the materials used and the construction by this method are shown in Fig. 164-6. Proper installation is shown by five major steps in Figs. 164-7 through 164-10.

Fig. 164—9 A second layer of strips is placed over the sheet. The strips are nailed into the bottom layer. *National Oak Flooring Association.*

Fig. 164—7 Special concrete nails are used to imbed 1- by 2-inch (25- by 51 mm) strips (sleepers) in a special adhesive. *National Oak Flooring Association.*

Fig. 164—8 A four-thousandths–inch (0.004″ = 0.1016mm) polyethylene sheet is laid over the first layer (course) of strips (sleepers). *National Oak Flooring Association.*

Fig. 164—10 Strip flooring is nailed at right angles to each sleeper. One-half-inch (13-mm) expansion space is provided between the flooring and the wall. *National Oak Flooring Association.*

Prefabricated and modular housing

Fabricate means put together. If *pre* is added to the word, it indicates that parts are put together *before* they are sent to the building site.

Prefabrication is not a new idea. Almost everything in our modern economy is mass-produced. Factory-finished components are used in many parts of the prefabricated home (Fig. 165-1).

The time-, motion-, and method-analysis techniques used in factory engineering and production control have been borrowed by home-builders. Automated procedures are now used in the prefabrication of all parts of the home, from foundation to roof.

Centuries of building prefabrication

About 3000 years before the birth of Christ, the Great Pyramid, a monument to Pharaoh Khufu, was built by prefabrication of over 2 million limestone blocks. These were shaped in the quarries and then hauled to the construction site. Other great temples and buildings of biblical times were similarly erected.

Prefabrication in America

Records in the Library of Congress show that the English shipped a wood-paneled house to the Colonies in 1624. It was to be used by their fishing fleet when the men were ashore between trips.

Thousands of prefabricated homes were produced in New York during the California gold rush in the 1850s. They were shipped around Cape Horn to the West Coast to be sold to prospectors.

In 1861, some Boston and New York lumber dealers patented a system of building houses. These houses consisted of a few standardized panels and many interchangeable parts that could be assembled in a few hours.

Thomas A. Edison built panels and other prefabricated parts for two homes that were erected in the nineteenth century. They still stand.

The boyhood home of Mark Twain is a historical landmark that is still standing in Hannibal, Missouri. It was prefabricated in Cincinnati, Ohio, and shipped by boat to Hannibal.

Twentieth-century prefabrication

The use of precut housing has increased during the twentieth century. Until World War II it was a modified "do-it-yourself" concept. Companies gradually ventured into the production of a more complete house package, which included floor panels, walls (Fig. 165-2), and ceilings.

Fig. 165–1 A typical prefabricated home. *National Homes, Inc.*

Fig. 165–2 All components of a house are produced at a prefabrication plant. *National Homes, Inc.*

Fig. 165–3 Doors are attached to the door frames at the plant. *National Homes, Inc.*

Fig. 165–4 Roof trusses are laid in place, and the gable end is placed in position on walls. *National Homes, Inc.*

A better, less expensive window sash could be produced in a millwork plant than could be made by hand on the job. Preassembled components followed. These included medicine and kitchen cabinets, doors and frames (Fig. 165-3), gable ends (Fig. 165-4), roof trusses (Fig. 165-5), and all other parts of the house.

The walls of small units are sometimes preassembled on the subfloor deck. These small unit walls are easily handled by a few workers (Fig. 165-6). Larger sections of precut housing are also assembled and set in place (Figs. 165-7 and 165-8).

The framing is cut, and complete walls are assembled (Fig. 165-9) in some factories before shipment to the building location. Sheathing is at-

Fig. 165–7 Large wall sections are swung into place with overhead cranes. *Andersen Corporation.*

Fig. 165–10 Attaching sheathing with an automatic nailer. This machine can drive 22 nails in a single stroke. *National Homes, Inc.*

Fig. 165–5 Trusses are swung in place and nailed to prefabricated walls. *National Homes, Inc.*

Fig. 165–8 Parts for complete walls are sometimes erected on the subfloor deck and then raised into place. *National Forest Products Association.*

Fig. 165–11 Insulation is glued between studs and layers of sheathing on the inside and the outside of prefabricated walls. *National Homes, Inc.*

Fig. 165–6 Small modular wall units are easily handled by two workers. *National Forest Products Association* and *Hedrich-Blessing.*

Fig. 165–9 Cutting and framing walls at the plant. *National Homes, Inc.*

Fig. 165–12 Outer walls of aluminum sheathing can be attached with an adhesive. *National Homes, Inc.*

tached with automatic nailing machines (Fig. 165-10). The frame is reversed, and insulation is glued between the studs (Fig. 165-11).

External sheathing is attached, and a quick-drying adhesive and aluminum sheets are laid on (Fig. 165-12). The unit is passed through rollers that firmly join (press) the sheathing and the aluminum (Fig. 165-13).

Special routing machines cut window and door openings in the aluminum, gypsum board, and sheathing (Fig. 165-14). Similar operations are used to produce other parts of the home.

The UNICOM method of house construction

The UNICOM method of house construction also permits fast planning and erection. The name **UNICOM** was chosen by the National Lumber Manufacturers' Association because the use of modular coordination and dimensional standards provides a uniform basis for the manufacture of components. This system cuts builders' inventory costs, offers unlimited design flexibility, and conforms to accepted legal requirements in all regions. It can be used efficiently by both the large builder and the custom builder who erects only a few houses per year.

The method is applicable to either on-site or shop fabrication. It is based on standard lumber sizes. It deals with the total house: floors, walls, roof vari-

Fig. 165–13 An aluminum wall is permanently attached to sheathing by passing the wall section through special rollers. *National Homes, Inc.*

Fig. 165–14 Routing window and door openings through sheathing and walls. *National Homes, Inc.*

ations, partitions, and stairways. It is adaptable to one-, one-and-one-half, and two-story houses, as well as split- and multiple-level houses.

Applying the UNICOM method

The concept of **modular coordination and design** is basic to the UNICOM method (Fig. 165-17). A **module** is a standard, or unit, of measurement. Ar-

chitecturally, it is the size of some one part. Emphasis is placed on the importance of the use of a **modular planning grid** as a design control.

The wall, floor, and roof elements are not tied to any fixed panel size. A complete house is divided into basic horizontal and vertical elements at regular modular (unit-of-measurement) intervals (see Fig. 165-15). The elements are shown as planes without thickness, but allowance is made for wall thickness and tolerance variables (Fig. 165-16). These are based on fixed (not imaginary) module lines at the outside faces of the exterior wall studs.

Complete exterior walls and partitions may have overall thickness variables. This depends on load-bearing or non-load-bearing use, and also on the covering materials. Floor and roof construction elements vary in thickness, depending upon their structural requirements and their types of framing and finishing.

Figure 165-18 shows how separations of exterior wall elements are made at natural division points between solid portions and door and window openings. Overall house dimensions are based on the 48-inch major module (unit) and the 24-inch minor module.

Maximum flexibility in location of door and window openings (for good proportion) is achieved by adhering to a 16-inch module. Location of wall openings to this 16-inch unit of measurement eliminates the extra wall framing that is commonly needed in nonmodular planning.

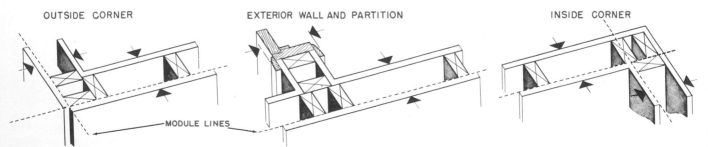

OUTSIDE CORNER   EXTERIOR WALL AND PARTITION   INSIDE CORNER

MODULE LINES

Fig. 165–15 Plane sections with thickness and tolerance variables for a home division. *National Lumber Manufacturers' Association.*

Building materials should have new metric dimensions convenient for building around the metric planning module. That module will probably be 300 mm.

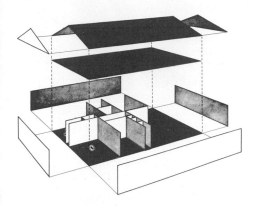

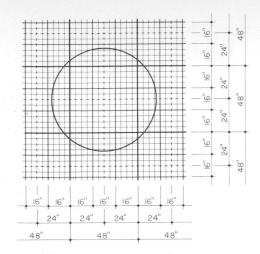

Fig. 165–17 The modular planning grid shows the principle of the UNICOM method. *National Lumber Manufacturers' Association.*

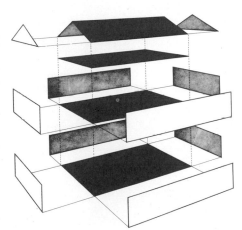

Fig. 165–16 Basic planes for modular (unit-of-measurement) study. *National Lumber Manufacturers' Association.*

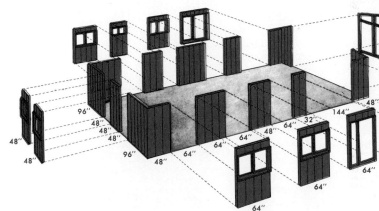

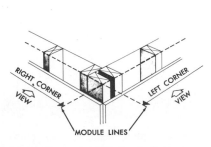

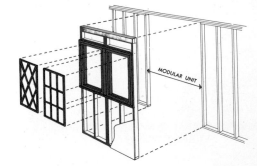

Fig. 165–18 Separations are made at natural division points in modular exterior walls. *National Lumber Manufacturers' Association.*

Mobile homes

Mobile homes (Fig. 166-1) and travel trailers (Fig. 166-2) have become the permanent homes for thousands of persons. The units can be moved on wheels, but they often remain in one location.

Mobile-home construction

The foundation of the mobile home is a steel-frame chassis (Fig. 166-3). Lumber, plywood, and many other wood products go into the completed home on wheels.

Framing is added to the steel foundation in almost the same way as for the conventional house (Fig. 166-4). To the basic frame construction are attached insulation, electrical wiring, heating and cooling ducts (Fig. 166-5), flooring, paneling (Fig. 166-6), cabinets (Fig. 166-7), plumbing, and other utilities and interior finishings.

Some mobile homes have complete living, dining, kitchen, and bedroom facilities (Fig. 166-8). Some have sanitary facilities and fireplaces. All new mobile homes must meet standards for construction, plumbing, heating, and electrical installation.

Fig. 166-1 A typical mobile home. *American Coach Company.*

Fig. 166-2 A typical travel trailer. *Lonergran Corporation.*

Fig. 166-3 A steel chassis is used under mobile homes and travel trailers. *Mobile Homes Manufacturers' Association.*

Fig. 166-4 Framing and siding similar to that of regular house construction is used for mobile homes. *Georgia-Pacific Corporation.*

Fig. 166-5 Heating and cooling ducts are placed between floor joists. *American Coach Company.*

Fig. 166-6 Wood paneling is a typical interior wall covering. *American Coach Company.*

Fig. 166-7 Cabinets are built in the kitchen and other areas of the mobile home. *American Coach Company.*

Fig. 166-8 Most facilities of modern homes are included in many mobile homes. *Liberty Coach Company, Inc.*

unit 167

Discussion topics on the building construction industry

1. Explain the difference between a beam, a joist, and a truss.
2. What is the meaning of the expression **squaring of roofing**?
3. What are the lumber grades?
4. Name five checks that should be made concerning the location and the excavation of a house.
5. How much hardening time should be allowed load-bearing concrete?
6. Discuss the sizes of beams and how they are joined, built up, and placed on foundations.

7. What are the two popular types of house construction over foundation walls?
8. What is the recommended height of ceilings and spacing of studs?
9. Make a sketch to show how studs are put together to form a corner post. What are the main reasons for this construction?
10. When is it possible to eliminate wall braces?
11. Describe the construction of gable dormer, hip, and gable and valley and hip and valley roofs.
12. Name the three major types of rafters that touch both the ridge board and the wall plate.
13. Using the square, find the number of board feet (bd ft) in two pieces of lumber $2'' \times 10'' \times 8'$.
14. What is the proper length of a brace if the run on the plate or stud is 36 inches?
15. If a building is 36 feet wide and the rise of the roof is 6 feet, what is the pitch?

16. What are the standard pitches?
17. What are the heel and the plumb cuts on rafters?
18. Which rafters have sides cut on their ends?
19. Why is construction cost increased by bay windows and dormers?
20. If the total rise is 9 feet, determine the height of each riser. Lay out a set of continuous stairs.
21. If the total rise is 9 feet, lay out a set of stairs using one platform.
22. What are the four common types of wall and roof sheathing?
23. How should strip flooring be laid?
24. Discuss the problems and procedure of building on a concrete slab.
25. Why has the development of pre-cut housing increased so rapidly since World War II?
26. What major house components can be factory assembled?
27. Define **module** and **modular**.

section **11**

Patternmaking

unit 168

The importance of patternmaking

Very early, people discovered that poured molten copper would take the shape of an impression in the sand. They soon realized that many intricate shapes could be obtained by making different impressions. These discoveries led to the development of the important art of patternmaking. This art has helped people to make metal fit their needs better.

The patternmaker

A master patternmaker is one of the most important and skilled woodworkers in industry. Patternmaking requires expertise in the use of woodworking machines and tools. Proficiency in reading drawings is also a must. With this knowledge the patternmaker can make three-dimensional patterns (Fig. 168-1) by following the drawings of the designer.

Fig. 168-2 Pouring metal into core molds after melting by the induction method. *American Foundrymen's Society.*

Fig. 168-3 A wood pattern is needed to make the mold for pouring a permanent aluminum cope and drag pattern. *American Foundrymen's Society.*

A patternmaker must also have enough knowledge of foundry work to make the pattern so that it can be properly extracted from the molding sand. A knowledge of the shrinkage of metals and metal alloys is also necessary. Molten metal is poured into shapes made in the sand by a pattern or core mold (Fig. 168-2). In addition, a patternmaker can help eliminate the waste of time, effort, and money by knowing the problems of the machinist.

Temporary patterns are made both of wood and of other materials, such as plastic. More permanent metal patterns are then made (Fig. 168-3).

Practically all motors and machines used in modern industry are dependent upon patternmaking. For this reason, foundry work and patternmaking are closely related. Before a pattern can be used, the molding sand must be prepared properly. It is prepared either (1) by hand, (2) by portable units (Fig. 168-4), or (3) in larger machines for more extensive foundry work.

Fig. 168-1 Wood patterns are made for numerous machine parts. *American Foundrymen's Society.*

Fig. 168-4 A portable sand aerator used to condition foundry sand. *American Foundrymen's Society.*

Fig. 168-5 A remote-control sand "slinger," continuous turntable, pin-lift machines, and an automatic sand strike-off are used in high-production miscellaneous pattern molding. *American Foundrymen's Society.*

Patterns are placed in a flask in preparation for molding (Fig. 168-5). Sand is rammed (packed) around the pattern. The next step is the careful separation of the mold in order to remove the pattern from it. Necessary cores (Fig. 168-6) are added as needed.

The cavity, or hole, left in the sand is poured full of molten metal to produce the required casting (Fig. 168-7). The final casting would not be possible without the patternmaker's knowledge and ability to make an accurate pattern.

Fig. 168–6 Use of sand slinger to fill huge molds at the rate of 1 ton per minute eliminates hand filling and ramming. *American Foundrymen's Society.*

Fig. 168–7 Thirty to ninety huge molds are poured per hour as they travel along a continuous conveyor. *American Foundrymen's Society.*

unit 169

Patternmaking and foundry terms

The patternmaker works with such materials as wood, plastic, and plaster. The person in the foundry melts various metals and pours (casts) them into molds. The patternmaker must also be familiar with foundry work and its terms. The terminology is directly related to both areas of work.

Definition of terms

Alloy. A combination of two or more metals.

Blow hole. A hole in a casting, caused by air or gases trapped in the mold which prevent a smooth, solid casting.

Bottomboard, or moldboard. A platform or large board on which the flask and molded sand rest.

Casting. A metal shape resulting from pouring molten metal into a mold (Fig. 169-1).

Cheek. The middle part of a flask, if more than the cope (top) or drag (bottom) portions, are used for a mold.

Cope. The top portion of a flask.

Core. The portion, usually made of sand and binder, placed in the mold opening to create various holes or cavities in the finished casting.

Core box. A box, or mold, in which the core is shaped.

Draft. The small taper on patterns which allows them to be removed easily from the sand.

Drag. The bottom portion of a flask.

Drawing. Removing the pattern from the sand.

Flask. A wood or metal frame (sides) with no top or bottom, consisting of the cope, the drag, and possibly the cheek.

Fillet. A concave shape made from wood, leather, wax, or other material to round (shape) sharp internal corners when two pieces intersect.

Gate. The opening, or channel, cut in the sand through which the molten metal runs from the sprue and riser to the casting cavity left by the pattern.

Green sand. Special molding sand

Fig. 169–1 A typical large machine-tool casting.

that has been dampened and conditioned (tempered) for proper foundry use.

Green sand core. An unbaked molding sand core. (See **core**.)

Kiln drying. A process of drying lumber to a specific moisture content under controlled heat and humidity conditions.

Master pattern. An original pattern from which permanent metal patterns are cast (Fig. 169-2).

Match plate. A special plate (Fig. 169-3) to which the pattern is attached at the parting line, or where the mold (flask) parts (separates).

Model. An exact likeness of a finished object.

Mold. The molded sand or other material which contains the cavity left by the pattern to form a casting when poured full of metal.

Molding sand. A special sand that can be conditioned (tempered) uniformly.

Parting line. The line, or joint, where the flask separates to allow removal of the pattern.

Pouring. The actual filling of the mold cavity with molten metal.

Ramming. Packing the sand over and around the pattern in the mold or flask.

Fig. 169–2 Skill is required to produce a master pattern. *Steelways Magazine.*

Fig. 169–3 A pattern match plate is attached where the molding flask parts. *American Foundrymen's Society.*

Rapping. Jarring the pattern so that it loosens from the sand and can be more easily removed.

Riser. An extra hole in the molding sand into which molten metal either can be poured or can rise from the cavity to feed (fill) the casting as it shrinks during solidification.

Shrinkage. The amount of decrease in volume when molten metal cools and solidifies.

Snap flasks. Flasks that have hinged sides and latches that allow (1) flask parts to be removed from around the

molded sand before pouring, and (2) multiple molds to be made with one flask, when necessary.

Split pattern. A pattern made in two, or several, parts for convenience in molding and removing from sand.

Sprue. The hole, or opening, through which the molten metal is poured, entering the mold by way of the gate.

Vent. An opening that is often made in sand before the pattern is removed. It allows air and gases to escape when pouring molten metal into the cavity.

unit 170

Tools and equipment for patternmaking

Patterns are made by using a wide variety of hand tools, portable and

stationary power machinery, and various supplies.

Special hand tools

Some of the particular layout and measuring tools used in patternmaking are the **straight** and **bent-point scribers,** the **center head** for the **combination square,** and various **gages.** Special **hand planes** used are the circular, core, box, round-sole, left-side, right-side, and bullnose rabbet planes.

Shrink rules are needed to make measurements for patterns used in molds into which metal is poured. When molten metal cools, it usually shrinks a uniform amount, according to the kind of metal. Knowledge of this amount of shrinkage for each type of metal permits a decision as to which specific shrink rule to use. To allow for shrinkage, graduation on the shrink rules resemble those on the common rule, but each division is greater.

Inside and outside ground **gouges** with straight and bent shanks and **wood carving tools** of various shapes are necessary to produce delicate pattern designs. Long and short bent **chisels** and V-shape **veining chisels** are included. All these special tools are variations and adaptations of the basic hand tools discussed in SECTION 3, "Measuring, Layout, and Hand Tool Processes."

Special machine accessories

Standard woodworking machines are often used to prepare and work material for patternmaking. **Saws** for fine, smooth cutting; special **grinding wheels; sander spindles;** shaper and router **cutters;** and **bits** of various kinds are required accessories.

Special supplies

In addition to regular woodworking supplies, special materials and supplies are needed. These include pearl, flake, and pulverized glue; fillets made of wax; materials such as leather, paper, wood, metal, and composition; and brass or other metal dowels.

unit 171

Patternmaking materials

Wood is the material that is most often selected for making patterns. Plastic resins, ordinary plaster, and various low-melting-point alloys are used in varying quantities for specific needs.

Wood for patterns

The majority of pattern lumber is obtained from white or sugar pines. Redwood and Alaskan and red cedar are also used when they are easily obtained. White pine from the northern Appalachian region is considered one of the best woods; the dimensions of this species change very little when moisture conditions vary.

Some hardwood lumber is used by patternmakers. The Mexican and Central American species of mahogany are most often used commercially. Maple and hard cherry are often formed into parts of a pattern that may receive severe wear.

Seasoning pattern wood

Most pattern wood can be kiln-dried to a moisture content as low as 6 per-

cent. This shrinks the material and brings out imperfections.

Many pattern craftsmen believe that water curing and then air seasoning is the best method of preparing pattern wood. Logs are cut to length and placed in water, where they remain for as long as 2 years. The soaking extracts various resins and tends to cure the log. Because the resulting lumber is more mellow and has fewer strains, it is easier to work.

Lumber cut from the cured logs is stacked carefully in the woodyard. The average drying time is 1 year per inch (25 mm) of thickness.

From the yard, air-dried lumber is taken to the pattern shop and again carefully stacked. The drying time necessary is from 6 months to 2 years, depending upon the thickness.

About 3 to 5 years would be necessary to prepare top quality 1-inch (25.4-mm) pattern lumber by the water-curing, air-seasoning method. Modern methods, materials, and production costs make the water-curing, air-seasoning operation less desirable than modern drying methods.

Another form of wood and pattern is shown in Fig. 171-1. Veneer core pieces $^1/_{10}$ inch (2.54 mm) thick are impregnated with phenolic resin and bonded into panel form for fabrication into die molds.

Plasters for patterns

Patterns, molds, and models have been made from plaster for hundreds of years. The material commonly used was plaster of paris. In recent years, numerous mixtures of gypsum cements have been formulated to meet specific pattern needs of the aircraft, spacecraft, transportation, and plastics industries.

Gypsum cements, called **hard plasters,** are gray or white natural minerals. They must be ground and processed into the many mixtures they can make.

Hard plasters are very adaptable to irregular and intricate shapes, and they save time because they are simple to use.

Fig. 171–1 Veneer is impregnated with phenolic resin and bonded into panel form to make die molds. *Hardwood Plywood Institute.*

Dental, or casting, plaster is often called **soft plaster.** It is processed and formulated for purposes different from those of hard plaster.

Cast plastic patterns

Organic plastics are generally divided into three groups: (1) thermoplastic, (2) thermosetting, and (3) chemical setting. The **thermoplastic** types are softened by heat and become hard when they cool. These can be reworked by reheating after they have hardened. **Thermosetting** plastics may be soft or in liquid form when they are heated and formed, but then they take a permanent shape when cool and cannot be reworked (Fig. 171-2). These types are used in casting patterns. **Chemical-setting** plastics harden when the correct chemicals are added.

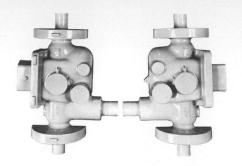

Fig. 171–2 The cope and drag halves of a plastic pattern. *American Foundrymen's Society.*

Plastic production patterns are cheaper, they eliminate finishing and nearly all draft, and they can be made identical to master patterns.

Epoxy resins have excellent properties for laminating, casting, and surface coating. Proper proportions of the hardening agent and the resin are mixed in their liquid forms. A chemical reaction occurs and cures the resin into a hard material. Epoxies are versatile, strong, and very stable when they are stored under correct conditions. They adhere to most surfaces and have the lowest shrinkage of the resin types.

Metal-alloy patterns

Low-melting-point alloys are used in connection with wooden patterns. These alloys are not new, but they are receiving special use in modern production techniques. **Bismuth** is the base for the patternmaking metal alloy. Various alloys are produced by adding cadmium, tin, lead, zinc, and other low-melting-point metals to form a combination that melts at a temperature less than 212°F (100°C).

unit 172

Discussion topics on patternmaking

1. Of what importance is the wood patternmaker to the metalworking industry?
2. Besides being an expert woodworker, what other trades and occupations must the patternmaker know something about?
3. With what craft is the work of the patternmaker most closely associated?
4. Name 10 items cast in metal for which a wooden pattern was needed originally.
5. Describe each of the following: (a) moldboard, (b) cope, (c) drag, (d) cheek, (e) fillet, (f) core box, (g) master pattern.
6. In what industries are patternmakers usually employed?
7. Name several special hand planes used in patternmaking.
8. What is the name and the purpose of the special measuring rule used in patternwork? Why is it necessary?
9. Name five other special patternmaking tools.
10. List some special machine accesories that are useful in patternmaking.
11. What special supplies are needed?
12. What materials are used for patterns? What material is used the most?
13. Name the softwoods and the hardwoods that are especially adaptable for patterns.
14. Why is the northern Appalachian white pine one of the best woods for patterns?
15. Discuss the seasoning of pattern wood as it differs from ordinary lumber seasoning.
16. What benefits are derived from soaking pattern woods over long periods of time?
17. What types of plasters are used for patterns?
18. Explain the differences between the types of plasters.
19. Discuss the importance of the new epoxy resins.

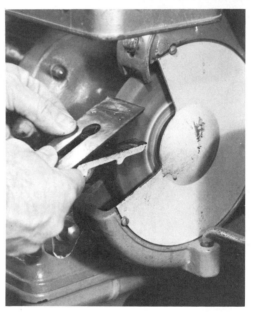

Conditioning and Sharpening Tools

Maintaining basic hand tools

Tools that are dull and improperly maintained cause poor workmanship, require expenditure of more energy in their use, and are unsafe. The safe, careful craftsman sharpens and conditions hand and machine tools when necessary.

Causes of dulling

Some of the causes of dulling tools are improper care and use, improper adjustment, feeding too fast for cutter-head speed, and the binding or sticking of boards in a machine. Dust and grit on lumber also dulls tools.

Dulling results from improper cutting angles on the cutting edges of tools. Cracks and chips appear when cutting edges are ground too thin and when the edges are overheated and burned during grinding or in use.

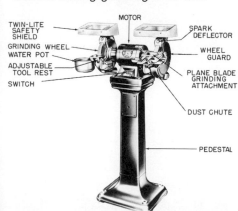

Fig. 173–1 A standard grinder can be used with special grinding attachments to sharpen most hand tools. *Rockwell International.*

Tool grinders

Two common grinders used in limited operations are the standard grinder (Fig. 173-1) and the small tool grinder (Fig. 173-2). Many sizes and shapes of both grinders and grinding wheels are produced. Specific recommendations

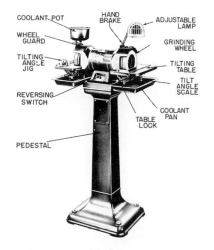

Fig. 173–2 A special tool grinder helps to sharpen tools more accurately. *Rockwell International.*

should be obtained from the manufacturers when special sharpening and conditioning are required. Determine the correct speed for a particular size, shape, and type of wheel before it is mounted.

Safety

Observe the following safety precautions when operating any grinder:

1. Wear safety goggles when doing any grinding.
2. Keep all hoods and guards in place.
3. Keep the work rest adjusted close to the wheel to prevent the work from being caught between the rest and the wheel.
4. Avoid touching the moving wheel or the work being ground.
5. Tuck in all loose clothing so that it cannot be caught in the wheel.
6. Hold all work securely.

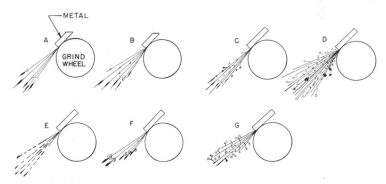

Fig. 173–3 The simple spark test helps determine the kind of metal. (A) Wrought iron: distinct torpedo spark; a few small radial sparks caused by carbon; (B) mild steel: more radial sparks than wrought iron; (C) tool steel: slight torpedo; good shower of radial sparks; (D) high-carbon steel: great number of radial sparks, igniting close to the wheel; (E) high-speed steel: dull, red, broken line; dewdrop at the end of line of sparks; (F) cast iron: torpedo with feathery tail; (G) manganese iron or steel: branching sparks from main line. *Rockwell International.*

7. Occasionally cool the piece being ground. This prevents burning or annealing (softening) the metal. Water and kerosine are sometimes mixed for use as a coolant in tool grinders. This coolant does not rust the parts, and it cools the metal as the grinding operation is performed.

Determine the kind of metal being ground by the spark test. As tiny metal particles are thrown off by the abrasive wheel, they combine with oxygen to form a spark. The sparks from different metals vary (Fig. 173-3). Test known kinds of metal to get a better idea of the spark patterns.

Three things should be observed when testing metals by grinding: (1) the **color** of the spark as it leaves the wheel and as it explodes, (2) the **shape** of the explosion as the metal particle ignites, and (3) the **distance** from the wheel at which the explosion occurs.

Plane irons, spokeshaves, and wood chisels

Plane irons, spokeshaves, and wood chisels should have **hollow-ground** (concave) bevels on their cutting edges. They enter the wood better and last longer. Grinders cut the steel fast and give this type of edge. These tools are sharpened with a 20- to 30-degree bevel, depending upon their use:

1. Push the tool straight into the grinding wheel lightly to remove all nicks (Fig. 173-4).

2. Adjust the tool rest, or chisel-grinding attachment, to the required angle to grind the bevel (Fig. 173-5).

3. Place the tool in the holder, and work it evenly across the wheel (see Fig. 173-1). If the attachment is not available and the tool rest does not adjust to the proper angle, hold the tool as shown in Fig. 173-6.

4. Continue grinding until a complete hollow-ground bevel is produced. Make the bevel twice the thickness of the blade to secure the

30-degree angle that is used for most cutting operations (Fig. 173-7). A 20-degree bevel can be used on softwood, but it crumbles when used on hardwood.

5. Grinding forms burrs on plane blades and chisels (Fig. 173-8), and the burrs must be removed. Place the bevel on an oilstone with the heel of the bevel slightly raised (Fig. 173-9). Stroke it back and forth on the stone, pressing with both hands (Fig. 173-10). Lubricate the sharpening stone with thin oil or kerosine to float metal particles away so that they do not be-

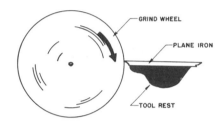

Fig. 173–4 Nicks in a blade should be ground off before sharpening the blade. Push the blade straight into the wheel.

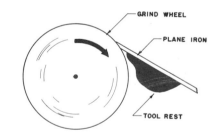

Fig. 173–5 Adjust the tool rest to the proper angle for grinding blades.

Fig. 173–6 A steady hand is needed when a support is not available.

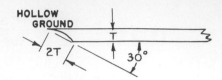

Fig. 173–7 The bevel on plane irons for most cutting operations is twice as long as the plane-blade thickness.

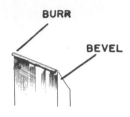

Fig. 173–8 A burr is formed on the cutting edges of plane irons and chisels when grinding. Rockwell International.

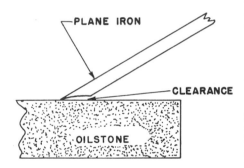

Fig. 173–9 Honing the bevel on an oilstone helps to remove the burr.

Fig. 173–10 Hold the plane iron or chisel in both hands when honing. Rockwell International.

come embedded in the stone. Wipe the stone after using.

6. Turn the tool over and stroke the flat side lightly against the stone (Fig. 173-11). Alternate honing on the bevel and the back until the burr is removed.

Honing produces a small second bevel on the cutting edge and gives a clean edge. As the tool becomes dull through use, additional whetting and honing are necessary. Eventually the second bevel becomes too long; the original one begins to round (Fig. 173-12) and does not cut well. The tool should then be reground.

Scrapers

Scrapers smooth a wood surface after planing. If properly sharpened, they will remove a fine shaving. Scrapers should be tilted away from the worker

and pushed, or tilted toward the worker and pulled. To sharpen an edge:

1. Place the scraper in a vise, and file the edge flat (Fig. 173-13). Draw-filing is also used to square the edge. For fast cutting, file a bevel of about 30 degrees, similar to that on the chisel or plane iron.

2. check the edge against a flat, smooth surface. (A concave edge causes the scraper to leave scratches on the work.)

3. Lay the scraper on an oilstone. Hone the edge, or edges (if filed flat), until the corners are absolutely square.

4. Replace the scraper in a vise. Run a burnisher firmly over the filed edge at an angle of approximately 15 degrees to press the steel out from the edge (Fig. 173-14).

5. Repeat the operations at

about 5 to 8 degrees to bend the hook for the cutting edge or edges (Fig. 173-15).

Auger and wood bits

Auger and wood bits are sharpened with the small, half-round file (Fig. 173-16A), the auger-bit file (Fig. 173-16B), and a specially shaped honing stone. A small, square file or a triangular one can also be used.

Touch-up filing on bits is done through the throat of the bit (Fig. 173-17A). A half-round file is used if the throat is rounded; the auger-bit file is used if the throat is open. The cutting

Fig. 173-15 Turn the burr or hook on both edges of a scraper that has been filed square; turn it on one edge for bevels.

Fig. 173-11 Honing the flat side of blades helps to remove the burr and sharpen to a keen edge. *Rockwell International.*

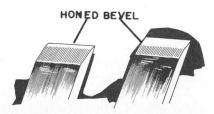

Fig. 173-12 After blades are honed several times, they must be reground to remove the long honed bevel. *Rockwell International.*

Fig. 173-13 File the edges of a hand scraper square.

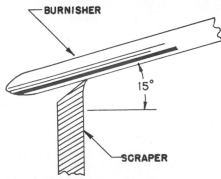

Fig. 173-14 The hook is turned by beginning with the burnisher at an angle of 15 degrees to the bevel.

Fig. 173-16 Files for sharpening bits are (A) the half round, and (B) the auger bit. *Rockwell International.*

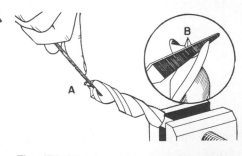

Fig. 173-17 (A) Touch up the cutting edge of a bit by filing through the throat; and (B) spurs on wood bits are always filed on the inside. *Rockwell International.*

lip of the wood bit should be filed from the lower side. Maintain the original bevel.

Spurs on bits are *always* sharpened on the inside (Fig. 173-17B). The top edge of the wood bit is filed as shown in Fig. 173-18. File only the upper edge on wood auger bits (Fig. 173-19).

Twist drills

The main parts of the twist drill are the **point,** the **body,** and the **shank.** Study the diagrams in Figs. 173-20 and 173-21. The angle across the web (center) on the point (Fig. 173-20A) has a close relationship to the lip clearance (Fig. 173-20B and C). The angle of the point and the lengths of the cutting lips must be equal (Fig. 173-20D).

To sharpen a twist drill:

1. Square the surface of the grind wheel with a grindstone dresser. Place the tool rest close to the wheel.

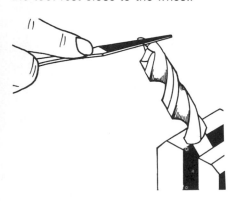

Fig. 173–18 The top edges of twist-drill-pattern wood bits are easily filed when held in a vise. *Rockwell International.*

 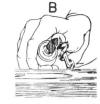

Fig. 173–19 File only the upper edge of auger-bit cutters (A), and insides of spurs (B). *The Irwin Auger Bit Company.*

2. Firmly grasp the end of the twist drill near the point with the tips of the fingers of your right hand. Lay your middle finger on the tool rest to act as a fulcrum, or pivot point.

3. Hold the shank of the drill with your left hand.

4. Move the drill shank until the cutting lip is horizontal with the tool rest and parallel with the face of the grinding wheel. The twist drill will be pointed at an angle toward the wheel.

5. Move the drill slowly toward the wheel until it touches.

6. Use the middle finger of your right hand as a pivot. Push the shank of the drill slightly downward with your left hand. *Do not roll the drill.*

7. Continue grinding each cutting lip and clearance surface until the properly ground point is found.

8. Check the point for accuracy with a drill-grinding gage. If the shank of the drill is pushed downward too much, the opposite cutting-lip clearance will require regrinding.

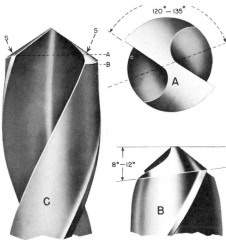

Fig. 173–20 Parts and standard angles of twist drills: (A) proper angle of web line, (B) lip-clearance angle at the circumference of the drill, (C) heel line at B is lower than the cutting-lip line at A, and (D) equal angles and equal lengths of cutting lips. *The Cleveland Twist Drill Company.*

Handsaws

The two types of handsaws are **crosscut** (for sawing across wood grain) and **rip** (for cutting with the grain). In the manufacturing process, hand saws are cut to shape and are toothed, ground, and polished in preparation for proper setting and sharpening.

In small industrial operations, and in some of the larger school shops, the saw is retoothed with a special machine and is filed in an automatic filer (Fig. 173-22). The saw can also be set and filed by hand if desired or necessary.

Handsaw filing should be done with a triangular, tapered file. Saws with 4 1/2 to 6 points per inch should be filed with a 7-inch (178-mm) slim taper file. Those having 7 or 8 points per inch are filed with a 6-inch (152-mm) taper file, and those with 10 points per inch are filed with a 5-inch (127-mm) slim taper file. Use a 5-inch extra-slim taper file on 11- or 12-point saws.

A number showing the points per inch is usually stamped below the handle on the heel (left rear) of the saw. If no number is there, lay a rule along the teeth with an inch mark on one saw point. Begin counting with this point. Continue to a point nearest the next inch mark to find the number of saw points per inch. There is always one less tooth than there are points per inch.

To sharpen a crosscut handsaw:

1. Place the saw in a special saw clamp or between two boards in a vise so that the teeth are slightly exposed.

2. Joint the teeth to make them equal in height by laying a common, fine file (an 8-inch mill file is suggested) flat on the teeth and filing lightly (Fig. 173-23).

3. File straight across the gullets if they are not equal in depth. The height of teeth, depth of gullets, and fronts and backs of teeth must have the same shape and angle to cut accurately.

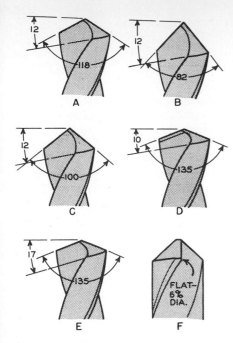

Fig. 173–21 Points of drills vary for drilling different materials. (A) Standard: satisfactory for all materials, specifically for soft to medium steel; (B) sharp: for wood, thermoplastics, high-silicon aluminum; 60-degree angle also used; (C) medium: high-silicon aluminum, hard copper, cast iron, hard rubber, and fiber; (D) blunt: all very hard steels; lips should be ground to zero rake; (E) blunt: all soft-to-medium aluminum alloys; good for drilling in very thin sheets; and (F) zero rake: soft-to-medium brass, copper, most plastics, and very hard steels. *Rockwell International.*

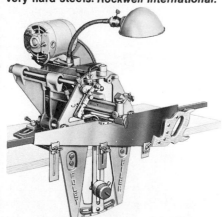

Fig. 173–22 Automatic saw filers sharpen saws very accurately. *Foley Manufacturing Company.*

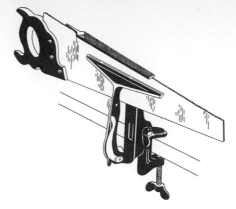

Fig. 173–23 Jointing the teeth of a handsaw with a flat file.

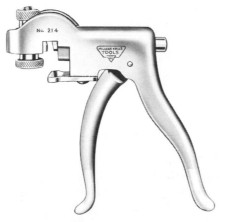

Fig. 173–24 Typical pistol-grip handsaw set. *Millers Falls.*

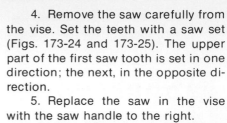

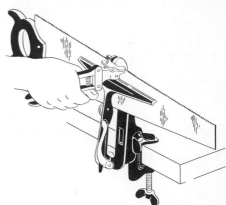

Fig. 173–25 Setting saw teeth.

4. Remove the saw carefully from the vise. Set the teeth with a saw set (Figs. 173-24 and 173-25). The upper part of the first saw tooth is set in one direction; the next, in the opposite direction.

5. Replace the saw in the vise with the saw handle to the right.

6. The teeth should be filed as shown in Fig. 173-26A, B, and C.

Hand ripsaws are filed in the same way except that there is no bevel on the teeth. The gullets are filed straight across (see Fig. 173-26D). File every second gullet and turn the saw around. If it is filed from one side only, the saw will tend to pull to one side when ripping a line.

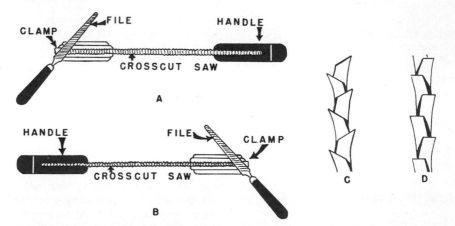

Fig. 173–26 The position of the file for sharpening, and final teeth appearance: (A) file in position, left; (B) file in position, right; (C) crosscut teeth; and (D) ripsaw teeth.

Sharpening circular saw blades

The general classes of circular saw blades are (1) crosscut, (2) rip, and (3) combination (which is used for both purposes). A dado head is a combination set of saws and chippers or cutters.

Crosscut blades

Crosscut saw blades are made for both rough and smooth cutting. Some of the various types of crosscut teeth are shown in Fig. 174-1. True rim travel, proper setting, and taper grinding give the smoothness of cut required and desired.

Side clearance helps produce smooth cuts, and coarse and fine teeth are set before grinding tapers (Fig. 174-2). More efficient cuts are made when every fifth tooth is a **raker** type. This cuts the V left by the other teeth, speeds the cutting, and reduces friction (Fig. 174-3). Some raker-tooth blades for fine, smooth crosscutting are not set.

Large and small saws are conditioned (prepared) by the manufacturer on precision machines (Figs. 174-4 and 174-5). Very accurate work is required to recondition saws by hand.

Ripsaw blades

The teeth of ripsaws are shaped like a group of small wood chisels. The saw is used to cut wood in the direction of the grain. Each ripsaw tooth must be

strong and have an adequate back clearance. The swaged ripsaw tooth has a real chisel shape and cuts a flat kerf (Fig. 174-6A). The set ripsaw tooth leaves a slight V notch in the center of the kerf, or cut (Fig. 174-6B). If a rip tooth is set, it should be set on a setting stake close to the tip as shown in Fig. 174-6C.

Combination saw blades

The combination saw is usually made up of sections of four cutting teeth

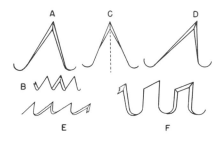

Fig. 174–1 Various angles and shapes are used on crosscut circular saw teeth: (A) rough work; (B) fine, small work where smoothness is not essential; (C) saw drags and dulls quickly, so is used where the material passes under the saw; (D) desirable for most large-tooth saws; (E) desirable for most small-tooth saws; (F) adapted for smooth-cutting saws. *E. C. Atkins and Company.*

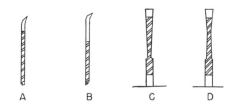

Fig. 174–2 Proper setting and taper grinding give a smooth cutting action: (A) set for coarse teeth, (B) set for fine teeth, (C) even-taper grinding to collar for slow cutting, and (D) abrupt-taper grinding for fast work. *E. C. Atkins and Company.*

and one raker. The raker tooth in each section is filed $1/64$ to $1/32$ inch (0.4 to 0.8 mm) shorter than the cutting teeth to improve cutting and to reduce the chip load in the cut.

The saw filer can be used to sharpen a combination saw (Fig. 174-7). The saw should be checked for proper layout of the shape and angle of the teeth. A layout for one form of combination saw is shown in Fig. 174-8.

Refitting and conditioning circular saws

Proper cutting and accuracy of circular saws is assured only when the original manufactured shape of the teeth is maintained. The saw must be round, and each tooth must be even in length

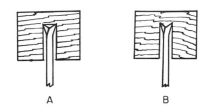

Fig. 174–3 Saws with raker teeth (A) clean the V from the saw kerf. *E. C. Atkins and Company.*

Fig. 174–4 Large circular saws are conditioned by manufacturers on precision machines. *H. K. Porter Company.*

Fig. 174-5 Circular saws are properly conditioned for best operation before they are to leave the manufacturer. *H. K. Porter Company.*

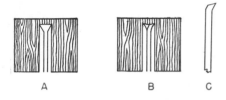

Fig. 174-6 The effect of swaged and set teeth on circular saws: (A) swaged tooth, (B) set tooth, (C) rip tooth set close to the tip. *E. C. Atkins and Company.*

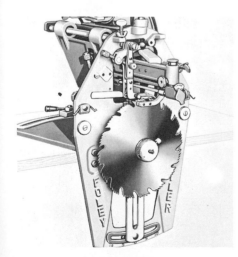

Fig. 174-7 Bench saw filers can be used to file combination saw teeth. *Foley Manufacturing Company.*

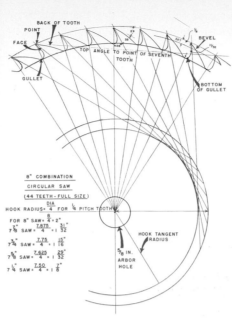

Fig. 174-8 The layout for reconditioning a combination circular saw blade. *Rockwell International.*

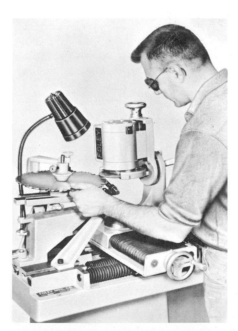

Fig. 174-9 A precision carbide saw grinder is needed to assure accurate conditioning of carbide-tip saw teeth. *Foley Manufacturing Company.*

and sharpness and swaged or set evenly to operate properly. Some of the factors to consider in purchasing, using, and conditioning circular saw blades are (1) size, (2) gage, (3) hole size, (4) speed of use, (5) number of teeth, (6) type of set, (7) flat or hollow grind, and (8) general classification.

An accurate pattern of the original teeth should be made immediately after a saw is purchased. All information about the saw should be added on the pattern, including the degree of set and the filing angles.

Special precision grinders may be needed to **gum**, or **grind**, special saws with carbide-tip teeth (Fig. 174-9). The following general procedure will assist in refitting circular saws by hand:

1. Disconnect the electric power to the table saw. Reverse the saw on the arbor or mandrel. Lower the blade below the saw table.

2. Place an oilstone or a discarded fine grinding wheel flat over the saw. Prepare for jointing by raising the saw until it touches the stone lightly (Fig. 174-10A).

3. Turn the saw by hand in its regular direction to joint (grind) the teeth. Joint them only enough to level them.

4. Hold a pencil to the saw as it is turned by hand to show the bottom of the gullets (Fig. 174-10B). File or grind (gum) to the line, and maintain the original shape of the teeth. This operation is called **gumming** and is necessary only after the saw has had several previous filings.

5. Set alternate teeth right and left with a hand set or with a suitable setting stake (Fig. 174-10C). Do not exceed the amount of set specified for the particular saw. Raker teeth of flat-ground combination saws should not be set. Teeth and rakers of hollow-ground combination saws should not be set.

6. Place the saw in a saw clamp, and use a mill file to file the face of the teeth straight across for the ripsaw (Fig. 174-10D). Bevels on the back of

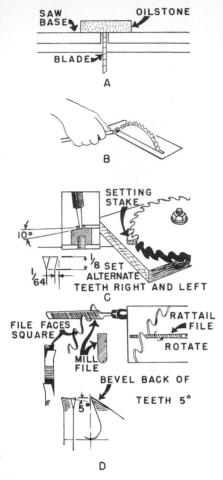

Fig. 174–10 Conditioning saw blades: (A) jointing, (B) mark for gumming (grinding gullets), (C) setting, and (D) filing. *Rockwell International.*

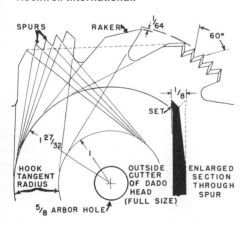

Fig. 174–11 A section of the dado head saw. *Rockwell International.*

some combination saw teeth, crosscut saw teeth, and other types must be filed according to specifications.

7. Clean and smooth the gullets with a rat-tail (round) file (Fig. 174-10D). Sharp corners and nicks in gullets cause cracks to form in the saw.

Reconditioning the dado head

The two saws and several chippers or cutters comprising the dado head are filed several times before refitting or reconditioning is needed. Count the file strokes and use an even pressure on the file for each cutting tooth (spur) or raker. A section of the outside cutter is shown in Fig. 174-11.

Follow this suggested procedure:

1. Reverse the outside cutters on the saw arbor. Joint the cutting teeth or spurs by turning the saw arbor (Fig. 174-12A).

2. Joint rakers 1/64 inch (0.4 mm) less than spurs. Use a crosswise motion of the oilstone. Wrap paper around the stone to protect the saw table. Joint inside cutters at the same setting (Fig. 174-12B).

3. Place an outside cutter on the setting stake and set the spurs only. Set all spurs in one group in one direction (Fig. 174-12C); joint outside cutters lightly on the side to equalize set.

4. Put outside cutter in a saw clamp. File spurs with a square file to original tooth angle (Fig. 174-12D).

5. File the rakers square across the top and face, using a mill file (Fig. 174-12E).

6. Place each inside cutter in the saw clamp. File the top of the teeth (Fig. 174-12F). Do not file the face.

When each cutter has been correctly filed, the dado cut will be smooth and even. Uneven cutters and lack of set will cause the wood edges and the cutters to burn (Fig. 174-12G).

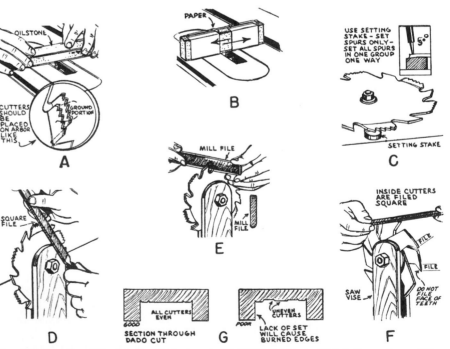

Fig. 174–12 Conditioning the dado head: (A) jointing spurs, (B) jointing rakers, (C) setting spurs, (D) filing spurs, (E) filing rakers, (F) filing inside cutters or chippers, and (G) examples of even and uneven cut of cutters. *Rockwell International.*

unit 175

Sharpening jointer and planer knives

Jointer and planer knives (blades) will cut very smooth surfaces when properly sharpened and installed in the machines. Dull knives cause the jointer to chatter.

Special grinding attachments are available to grind jointer and planer knives without removing them from the machines. The same grinding attachments, or other special accessories, are equipped for honing (whetting) and jointing knives. Detailed instructions are included with each accessory. When such equipment is not available, sharpening can be done by hand honing, jointing and honing, or grinding and honing.

Honing jointer knives

To hone knives:

1. Cover most of a fine oilstone with paper so that it will not mark the table.

2. Place the stone on the front (infeed) jointer table, as shown in Figs. 175-1 and 175-2.

3. Turn the cutter head until the stone is flat on the bevel of the knife. The stone will face each knife.

4. Clamp the head in place.

5. Hone (whet) the knife by stroking the stone lengthwise with the blade. Use the same number of strokes for each knife blade. Uneven honing causes blades to differ in length.

Jointing jointer knives

Knife jointing can be done with a special hand-knife jointer that contains an oilstone or with the stone held in the hand. Special care is needed in hand jointing because the cutter head is revolving. Thorough understanding of the operation and the machine is necessary.

1. Cover most of the oilstone with paper. Place it on the rear (outfeed) table (Figs. 175-3 and 175-4).

2. Lower the rear table until the stone barely touches the knives as the cutter head is turned slowly by hand.

3. Remove the jointer fence, if necessary. Attach a stop block to the front table (see Fig. 175-3). The cutters should not strike the block.

4. Pick up the stone. Start the machine.

5. Hold the stone securely. Slowly place it on the rear table and against the stop block until it barely touches the rotating knives.

6. Move the oilstone along the stop block slowly until the full length of all the knives is completely jointed. All knives should be exactly even and level with the rear table.

7. Stop the machine. Hone the knives.

Grinding jointer and planer knives

Jointer and planer knives are usually ground at an angle of 35 to 36 degrees. The angle can be varied according to the type and size of machine, the blade thickness, and the predominant type of soft- or hardwood to be planed. When a grinding attachment for the machine is not available, the knives can be ground by hand. Grinding jointer and planer knives is always done dry.

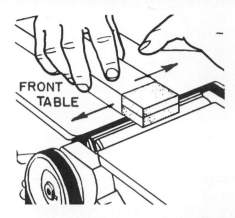

Fig. 175–1 Honing or whetting jointer knives. *Rockwell International.*

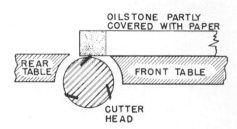

Fig. 175–2 Placement of the oilstone for whetting. *Rockwell International.*

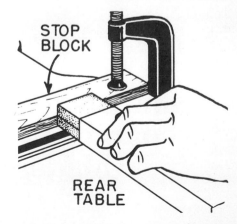

Fig. 175–3 Jointing the knives. *Rockwell International.*

1. Make a knife-holding block. Saw a kerf (cut) through a piece of hardwood to fit the thickness of the blade snugly (Fig. 175-5). Saw with the block in either position shown, depending upon the method used for grinding.

2. Add a flat-head wood screw at the end of the knife to hold the blade securely. The screwhead should be flush (even) with the wood surface.

3. Adjust the tool rest of the grinder to the required angle.

4. Attach a guide block squarely across the grind wheel to ensure a straight cut on the knife (Fig. 175-6).

5. Make a single, *light* cut on each of the knives. Heavy cuts on high-speed steel will burn the knife and ruin it.

6. Paste a strip of paper along the edge of the holding block with rubber cement. The paper sets the next light cut without any change of the guide block.

7. Make several cuts to give each knife the proper cutting edge.

8. Replace the knives in the machine. Hone them.

A cup wheel mounted on a drill press (Fig. 175-7), a grinding wheel on a table saw, or a disk sander can sharpen knives.

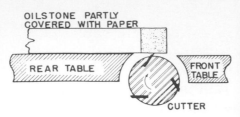

Fig. 175–4   Placing the oilstone for jointing. *Rockwell International.*

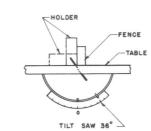

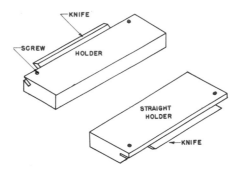

Fig. 175–5   A jig can be made to hold jointer knives for sharpening.

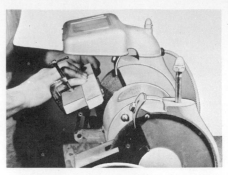

Fig. 175–6   Using a handmade jig to hold jointer knives for sharpening. *Rockwell International.*

Fig. 175–7   A cup wheel can be used on the drill press for sharpening jointer knives. *Rockwell International.*

unit 176

Sharpening band saw blades

The band saw was invented in France and patented in England around 1808. Developments have been continuous, resulting in saws of various lengths, widths, and thicknesses. They are sharpened and set by hand or with special filers (Fig. 176-1).

Types of band saw teeth and sets

There are three kinds of teeth and sets on band saws: (1) regular tooth, (2) skip tooth, and (3) hook tooth. The regular tooth is the oldest and it is used for general cutting. Teeth are set alternately right and left. Other sets are the raker and the wavy (Fig. 176-2).

The **raker set** is common on all three kinds of teeth. Two teeth are set alternately right and left, followed by a straight raker tooth, which reduces the chip load and improves cutting.

Wavy-set saws reduce saw breakage, eliminate teeth stripping, and completely remove chips for faster cutting to close tolerances. Each fourth tooth is straight, and the next three are set alternately to the right and left.

Hook-tooth and skip-tooth blades (Figs. 176-3 and 176-4) are slightly different. The hook tooth has more hook and rake. Skip-tooth saws remain sharp until they are worn out.

Hand sharpening mounted band saws

Light filing and touching up are easier when the blade is reversed on the wheels of the band saw machine, with the teeth pointing upward (Fig. 176-5).

Fig. 176–1 The millwright uses special filers to sharpen large band saws. *Weyerhaeuser Company.*

Fig. 176–2 Regular band saw teeth with a raker and a wavy set. *Paxton Equipment and Supply Company.*

A 6-inch (152-mm) extra-slim taper file is recommended for use on saws having 8 points (seven teeth) per inch or finer; a 7-inch (178-mm) extra-slim taper file for saws with 6 and 7 points per inch; a 7-inch (178-mm) slim taper file for a 5-point saw; and 8- and 10-inch (203- and 254-mm) slim taper files for 4- and 3-point saws.

To hand-sharpen:

1. Use your left index finger as a guide. File every other tooth lightly straight across.

2. Reverse the procedure, and file alternate teeth.

3. Tilt the file slightly to obtain a hook in the teeth (Fig. 176-6).

Fig. 176–3 The hook-tooth band saw blade with a raker set. *Paxton Equipment and Supply Company.*

Fig. 176–4 A raker set on a skip-tooth band saw blade. *Paxton Equipment and Supply Company.*

Fig. 176–5 Light filing of a band saw blade is easily done by reversing the saw on the wheels. *Rockwell International.*

Refitting unmounted band saws by hand

An automatic filing machine (Fig. 176-7) makes band saw sharpening easy. When a machine is not available, the band saw blade may be sharpened by hand:

1. Place the saw on a long bench with the entire length supported on the same level.

2. Use a vise or a clamp to hold about 40 to 50 teeth at once.

3. Joint each section of teeth. Make them of uniform height; run a mill file lightly over the tops (see Fig. 173-23).

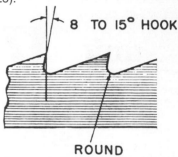

Fig. 176–6 A slight hook is obtained on band saw blades by tilting the file slightly during sharpening. *Rockwell International.*

Fig. 176–7 An automatic filer is valuable in sharpening band and other saws. *Foley Manufacturing Company.*

4. Select the correct file for the particular number of teeth per inch.

5. Hold the file in a horizontal position. File the teeth straight across at right angles to the blade (Fig. 176-8). Use an even pressure, and file each tooth the same. Lift the file on each back stroke.

When setting is necessary, do it before the teeth are filed. Setting can be done with an automatic band saw setter (Fig. 176-9) or with a pistol-grip saw set (see Fig. 173-24). For straight-line cutting, the least set possible is best. In curved cutting, sufficient set is needed to clear the blade in the cut.

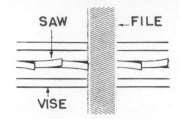

Fig. 176–8 File band saw teeth straight across at right angles to the blade. *Rockwell International.*

Fig. 176–9 Setting a band saw is easily done with an automatic band saw setter. *Foley Manufacturing Company.*

unit 177

Sharpening shaper and router cutters

Two types of shaper cutters can do most work. One is the cutter that consists of two separate knives mounted between two specially grooved collars. The other type, and the safest, is the one-piece, two- or three-winged cutter. The one-piece cutter is available for shapers and routers. Molding heads for the table saw or other machines are occasionally used for shaping.

Cutters can be machined and ground from solid stock, but they are usually obtained from manufacturers. These are already formed and sharpened for use. After cutters become dull, they must be resharpened. Grinding and whetting are most successful when the correct angles and bevels are known.

Rake angle on cutters

The **rake angle** of a cutter determines its shape and cutting action. The length of a cutter working at an angle must be greater than if the cutter is worked straight across the wood (Fig. 177-1).

Rake angles are used on all shaper cutters. They are greatest when mounted in a molding head, as compared with other types of cutters used on the shaper or router (Fig. 177-2). The greater the rake angle, the greater the difference should be between the shape of the knife and the molding it cuts.

Bevels on cutters

Bevels on the edges of shaper cutters vary from 30 to 45 degrees. A bevel that provides clearance at one cutting

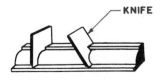

Fig. 177–1 Cutters operating at an angle to the work must be longer and have more clearance on the cutting edge than cutters that operate straight across.

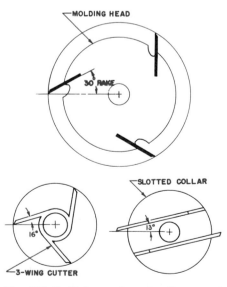

Fig. 177–2 Rake angles of cutters used in a molding head are greater than the three-wing, or loose, cutters used on shapers. *Rockwell International.*

circle may not give clearance on a smaller one (Fig. 177-3).

The factory-sharpened cutter has the most bevel at the inner edges of the knife (Fig. 177-4). This maintains the exact, even amount of clearance. Side bevels require only a minimum angle to provide necessary clearance.

Grinding shaper cutters

A silicon carbide stick or a diamond-wheel dresser is used to form desired shapes on the edges of grinding wheels used to grind cutters. Regular grinders are used, or the cutter can be mounted on a special spindle in the machine. It can then be ground with a shaped wheel on a tool post grinder.

Using either method, the cutter and the grinding wheel are positioned so that the rake angle and the bevel on each wing of the cutter are ground exactly the same. In addition, stops, guides, and indexing pins are used to grind accurately.

Sharpening knives

Factory-ground shaper knives should be sharpened by honing the flat side of the cutting edge (Fig. 177-5). The involute (coiled) bevel retains the same shape regardless of the amount of honing.

Straight bevels can be resharpened in the same manner, and the bevel itself can be honed. No grinding or honing should be done on cutters with involute or curved bevels.

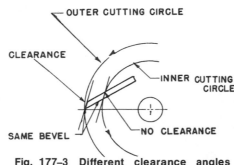

Fig. 177–3 Different clearance angles are required for cutters used on different cutting circles. *Rockwell International.*

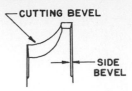

Fig. 177–4 A great amount of bevel is put on inner edges of factory-sharpened cutters. *Rockwell International.*

Fig. 177–5 Hone only the flat side on factory-sharpened shaper cutters.

unit 178

Discussion topics on conditioning and sharpening tools

1. Name several conditions that cause tools to dull.
2. What is the effect on a tool when its cutting edges are too thin?
3. List several personal safety precautions to observe when sharpening tools on a grinder.
4. What effect does honing have on the plane-iron blade?
5. What advantage is there in sharpening a flat hand scraper straight on the edge?
6. Name two kinds of files needed to sharpen wood and auger bits.
7. Describe the differences between filing hand crosscut and ripsaws.
8. What are the purposes of raker teeth on a circular saw blade?
9. Describe the difference between a swaged tooth and a set tooth on a saw blade.
10. What is the probable result when sharp corners are filed in the bottoms of gullets?
11. Why are the chippers placed between saws when using the dado head?
12. What is the purpose of the stop block when jointing jointer knives by hand?
13. At what angle are jointer and planer knives usually ground?
14. What are the three kinds of teeth and sets on band saw blades?
15. How can a band saw blade be filed lightly while on the wheels?
16. At what angle is the file held in relation to the band saw blade when filing?
17. What are the two types of shaper cutters for ordinary use?
18. What is the purpose of the rake angle on a shaper or router cutter?

section 13
Project Ideas

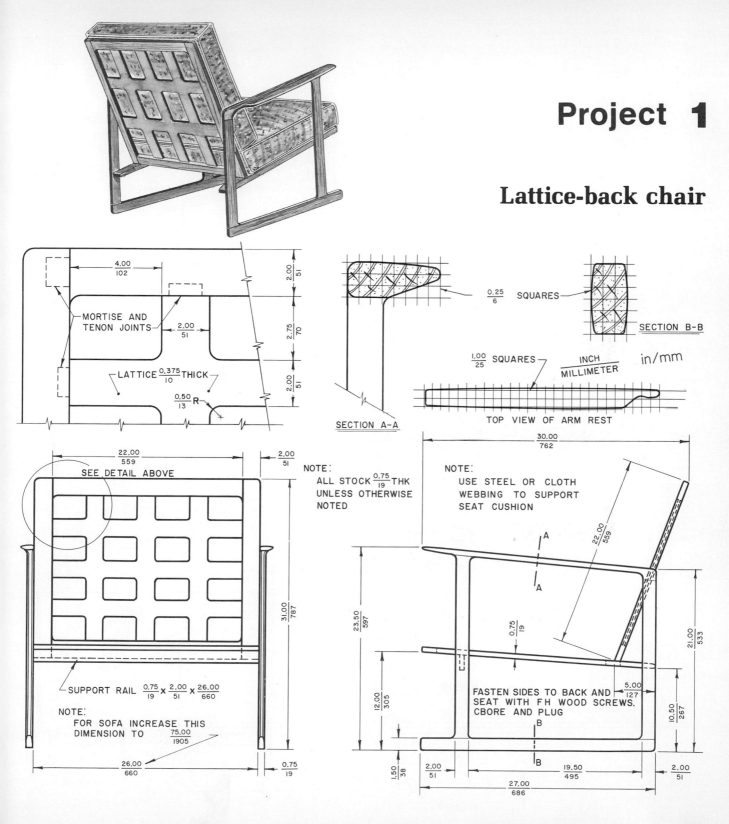

Project 1

Lattice-back chair

MORTISE AND TENON JOINTS

$\frac{4.00}{102}$

$\frac{2.00}{51}$

$\frac{2.00}{51}$

$\frac{2.75}{70}$

$\frac{2.00}{51}$

LATTICE $\frac{0.375}{10}$ THICK

$\frac{0.50}{13}$ R

$\frac{0.25}{6}$ SQUARES

SECTION B-B

$\frac{1.00}{25}$ SQUARES

$\frac{INCH}{MILLIMETER}$ in/mm

SECTION A-A

TOP VIEW OF ARM REST

$\frac{22.00}{559}$

$\frac{2.00}{51}$

SEE DETAIL ABOVE

$\frac{31.00}{787}$

SUPPORT RAIL $\frac{0.75}{19}$ x $\frac{2.00}{51}$ x $\frac{26.00}{660}$

NOTE:
  FOR SOFA INCREASE THIS
  DIMENSION TO $\frac{75.00}{1905}$

$\frac{26.00}{660}$

$\frac{0.75}{19}$

NOTE:
  ALL STOCK $\frac{0.75}{19}$ THK
  UNLESS OTHERWISE
  NOTED

NOTE:
  USE STEEL OR CLOTH
  WEBBING TO SUPPORT
  SEAT CUSHION

$\frac{30.00}{762}$

$\frac{22.00}{559}$

A

A

$\frac{23.50}{597}$

$\frac{0.75}{19}$

$\frac{21.00}{533}$

$\frac{5.00}{127}$

$\frac{10.50}{267}$

$\frac{12.00}{305}$

FASTEN SIDES TO BACK AND
SEAT WITH FH WOOD SCREWS.
CBORE AND PLUG

B

B

$\frac{1.50}{38}$

$\frac{2.00}{51}$

$\frac{19.50}{495}$

$\frac{2.00}{51}$

$\frac{27.00}{686}$

Project 2

Stereo cabinet

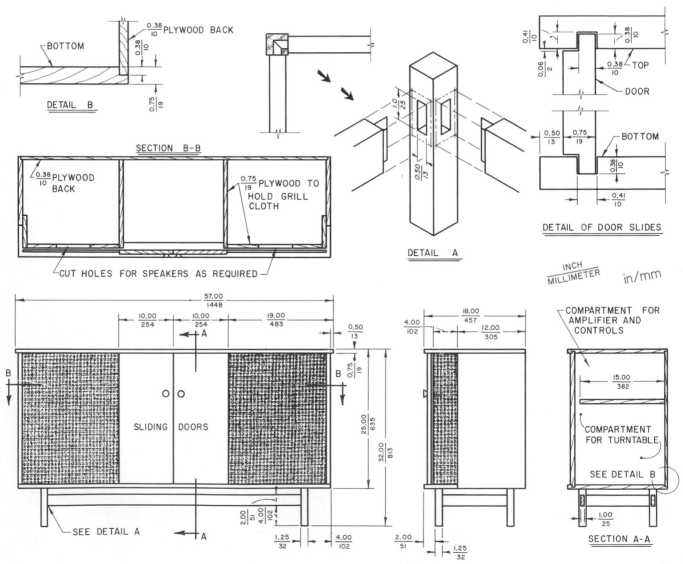

DETAIL B

0.38/10 PLYWOOD BACK

0.38/10

0.75/19

BOTTOM

SECTION B-B

0.38/10 PLYWOOD BACK

0.75/19 PLYWOOD TO HOLD GRILL CLOTH

CUT HOLES FOR SPEAKERS AS REQUIRED

DETAIL A

1.0/25

0.50/13

0.41/10

0.38/10 TOP

0.06/2

0.38/10 DOOR

0.50/13   0.75/19   BOTTOM

0.38/10

0.41/10

DETAIL OF DOOR SLIDES

INCH/MILLIMETER   in/mm

57.00/1448

10.00/254   10.00/254   19.00/483

0.50/13

0.75/19

25.00/635

32.00/813

SLIDING DOORS

B   B

A   A

2.00/51   4.00/102   102

1.25/32   4.00/102

SEE DETAIL A

4.00/102   18.00/457   12.00/305

2.00/51   1.25/32

COMPARTMENT FOR AMPLIFIER AND CONTROLS

15.00/382

COMPARTMENT FOR TURNTABLE

SEE DETAIL B

1.00/25

SECTION A-A

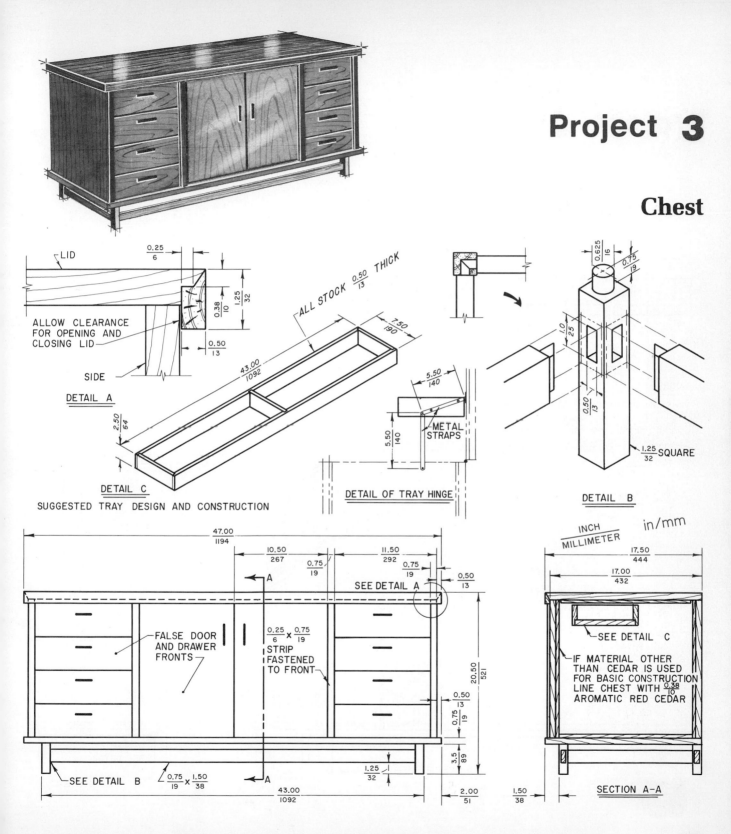

Project 3

Chest

LID

0.25 / 6

1.25 / 32

0.38 / 10

0.50 / 13

ALLOW CLEARANCE FOR OPENING AND CLOSING LID

SIDE

DETAIL A

ALL STOCK 0.50 / 13 THICK

7.50 / 190

43.00 / 1092

2.50 / 64

DETAIL C

SUGGESTED TRAY DESIGN AND CONSTRUCTION

5.50 / 140

5.50 / 140

METAL STRAPS

DETAIL OF TRAY HINGE

0.625 / 16

0.75 / 19

1.0 / 25

0.50 / 13

1.25 / 32 SQUARE

DETAIL B

INCH / MILLIMETER   in/mm

47.00 / 1194

10.50 / 267

0.75 / 19

11.50 / 292

0.75 / 19

0.50 / 13

A

SEE DETAIL A

FALSE DOOR AND DRAWER FRONTS

0.25 / 6 x 0.75 / 19

STRIP FASTENED TO FRONT

20.50 / 521

0.50 / 13

0.75 / 19

3.5 / 89

SEE DETAIL B   0.75 / 19 x 1.50 / 38

1.25 / 32

A

43.00 / 1092

2.00 / 51

17.50 / 444

17.00 / 432

SEE DETAIL C

IF MATERIAL OTHER THAN CEDAR IS USED FOR BASIC CONSTRUCTION LINE CHEST WITH 0.38 / 10 AROMATIC RED CEDAR

1.50 / 38

SECTION A-A

Project 4

Base-unit cabinet

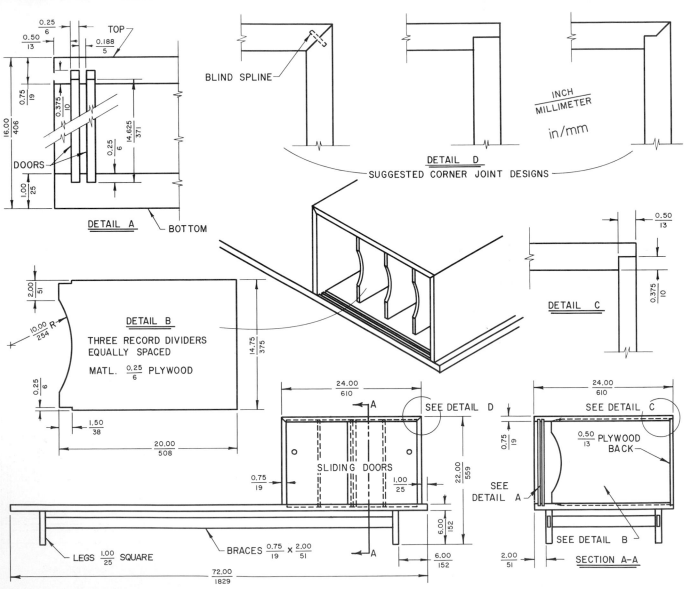

TOP

0.25 / 6

0.50 / 13

0.188 / 5

16.00 / 406

0.75 / 19

0.375 / 10

14.625 / 371

0.25 / 6

DOORS

1.00 / 25

DETAIL A

BOTTOM

BLIND SPLINE

INCH / MILLIMETER

in/mm

DETAIL D

SUGGESTED CORNER JOINT DESIGNS

2.00 / 51

10.00 R / 254

DETAIL B

THREE RECORD DIVIDERS EQUALLY SPACED

MATL. 0.25 / 6 PLYWOOD

14.75 / 375

0.25 / 6

1.50 / 38

20.00 / 508

0.50 / 13

0.375 / 10

DETAIL C

24.00 / 610

SEE DETAIL D

22.00 / 559

0.75 / 19

SLIDING DOORS

1.00 / 25

0.75 / 19

6.00 / 152

24.00 / 610

SEE DETAIL C

0.75 / 19

0.50 / 13 PLYWOOD BACK

SEE DETAIL A

SEE DETAIL B

LEGS 1.00 / 25 SQUARE

BRACES 0.75 / 19 x 2.00 / 51

6.00 / 152

2.00 / 51

SECTION A-A

72.00 / 1829

406

Project 5

Bookcase

DETAIL A
SUGGESTED JOINT DESIGNS

$\frac{0.188}{5} \times \frac{0.50}{13}$ SPLINE

$\frac{\text{INCH}}{\text{MILLIMETER}}$

in/mm

$\frac{0.50}{13}$ PLYWOOD BACK

$\frac{0.38}{10}$

DETAIL B

DRAWER CONSTRUCTION

NOTE:
ALL STOCK $\frac{0.75}{19}$ THICK UNLESS
OTHERWISE NOTED

$\frac{58.00}{1473}$

$\frac{29.00}{737}$

A

SEE DETAIL A

$\frac{10.00}{254}$

SEE DETAIL B

$\frac{1.00}{25}$

$\frac{0.25}{6}$

$\frac{72.00}{1829}$

$\frac{0.75}{19}$

SECTION A-A

SEE DETAIL C

$\frac{10.50}{267}$

$\frac{12.00}{305}$

$\frac{9.00}{229}$

DETAIL C

$\frac{0.38}{10}$ R

DRAWER
SEE DETAIL

$\frac{24.00}{610}$

$\frac{10.00}{254}$

DOOR

B

B

SEE DETAIL A

SIDE OF BASE

$\frac{20.00}{508}$ $\frac{20.00}{508}$ $\frac{2.00}{51}$

A

$\frac{2.00}{51}$

$\frac{60.00}{1524}$

$\frac{10.00}{254}$

$\frac{12.00}{305}$

SECTION B-B

Project 6

Wall components

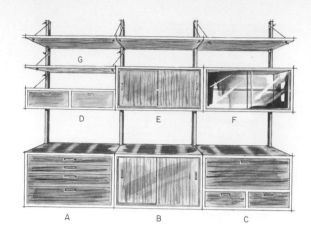

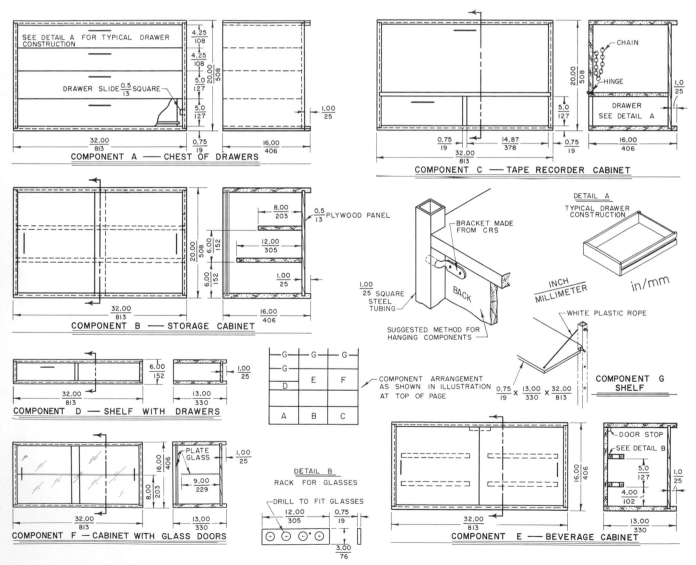

SEE DETAIL A FOR TYPICAL DRAWER CONSTRUCTION

DRAWER SLIDE 0.5/13 SQUARE

4.25/108
4.25/108
5.0/127
5.0/127
20.00/508
0.75/19
32.00/813
16.00/406
1.00/25

COMPONENT A — CHEST OF DRAWERS

CHAIN
HINGE
DRAWER SEE DETAIL A
20.00/508
1.0/25
5.0/127
0.75/19
14.87/378
0.75/19
32.00/813
16.00/406

COMPONENT C — TAPE RECORDER CABINET

8.00/203
12.00/305
1.00/25
0.5/13 PLYWOOD PANEL
6.00/152
6.00/152
20.00/508
32.00/813
16.00/406

COMPONENT B — STORAGE CABINET

DETAIL A
TYPICAL DRAWER CONSTRUCTION
in/mm

BRACKET MADE FROM CRS
BACK
1.00/25 SQUARE STEEL TUBING
SUGGESTED METHOD FOR HANGING COMPONENTS

INCH MILLIMETER

6.00/152
1.00/25
32.00/813
13.00/330

COMPONENT D — SHELF WITH DRAWERS

G	G	G
G		
D	E	F
A	B	C

COMPONENT ARRANGEMENT AS SHOWN IN ILLUSTRATION AT TOP OF PAGE

WHITE PLASTIC ROPE

0.75/19 x 13.00/330 x 32.00/813

COMPONENT G SHELF

PLATE GLASS
1.00/25
16.00/406
8.00/203
9.00/229
32.00/813
13.00/330

COMPONENT F — CABINET WITH GLASS DOORS

DETAIL B
RACK FOR GLASSES
DRILL TO FIT GLASSES
12.00/305
0.75/19
3.00/76

DOOR STOP
SEE DETAIL B
5.0/127
4.00/102
1.0/25
16.00/406
32.00/813
13.00/330

COMPONENT E — BEVERAGE CABINET

Project 7

Wall desk

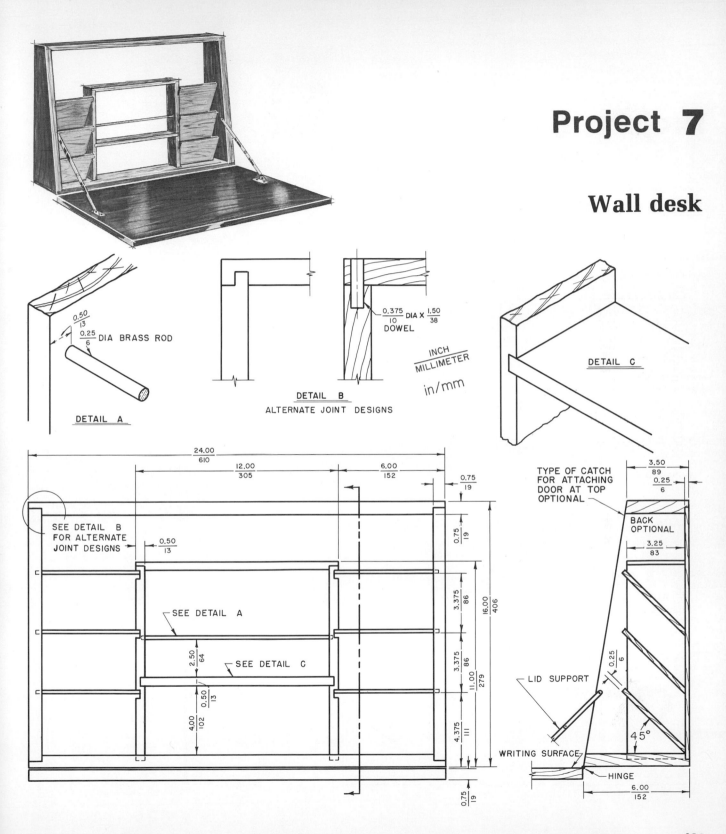

$\dfrac{0.50}{13}$

$\dfrac{0.25}{6}$ DIA BRASS ROD

DETAIL A

$\dfrac{0.375}{10}$ DIA X $\dfrac{1.50}{38}$

DOWEL

$\dfrac{\text{INCH}}{\text{MILLIMETER}}$

in/mm

DETAIL B
ALTERNATE JOINT DESIGNS

DETAIL C

$\dfrac{24.00}{610}$

$\dfrac{12.00}{305}$

$\dfrac{6.00}{152}$

$\dfrac{0.75}{19}$

SEE DETAIL B
FOR ALTERNATE
JOINT DESIGNS

$\dfrac{0.50}{13}$

$\dfrac{0.75}{19}$

SEE DETAIL A

$\dfrac{3.375}{86}$

$\dfrac{16.00}{406}$

$\dfrac{2.50}{64}$

SEE DETAIL C

$\dfrac{3.375}{86}$

$\dfrac{0.50}{13}$

$\dfrac{11.00}{279}$

$\dfrac{4.00}{102}$

$\dfrac{4.375}{111}$

$\dfrac{0.75}{19}$

TYPE OF CATCH
FOR ATTACHING
DOOR AT TOP
OPTIONAL

$\dfrac{3.50}{89}$

$\dfrac{0.25}{6}$

BACK
OPTIONAL

$\dfrac{3.25}{83}$

$\dfrac{0.25}{6}$

LID SUPPORT

45°

WRITING SURFACE

HINGE

$\dfrac{6.00}{152}$

409

Project 8

Kitchen cabinets

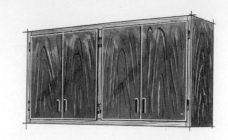

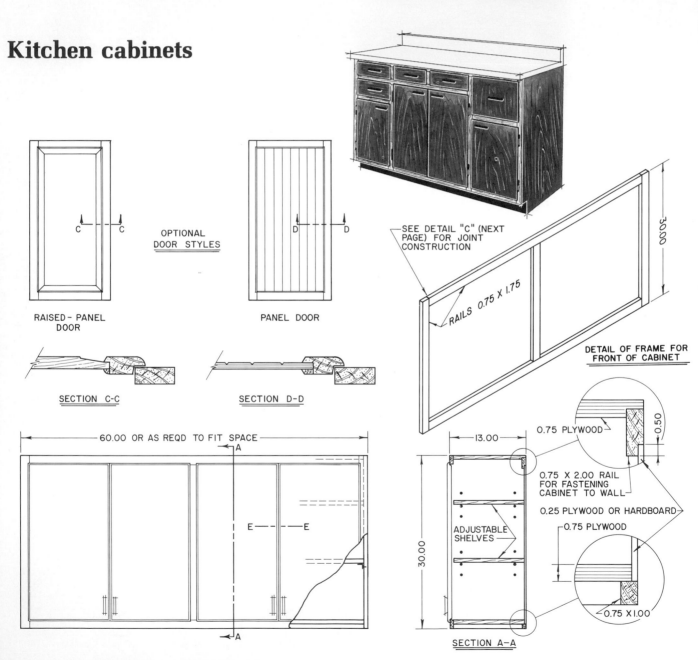

OPTIONAL
DOOR STYLES

RAISED - PANEL
DOOR

PANEL DOOR

SECTION C-C

SECTION D-D

SEE DETAIL "C" (NEXT
PAGE) FOR JOINT
CONSTRUCTION

RAILS 0.75 X 1.75

30.00

DETAIL OF FRAME FOR
FRONT OF CABINET

60.00 OR AS REQD TO FIT SPACE

A

E — — E

A

13.00

30.00

ADJUSTABLE
SHELVES

SECTION A-A

0.75 PLYWOOD

0.50

0.75 X 2.00 RAIL
FOR FASTENING
CABINET TO WALL

0.25 PLYWOOD OR HARDBOARD

0.75 PLYWOOD

0.75 X 1.00

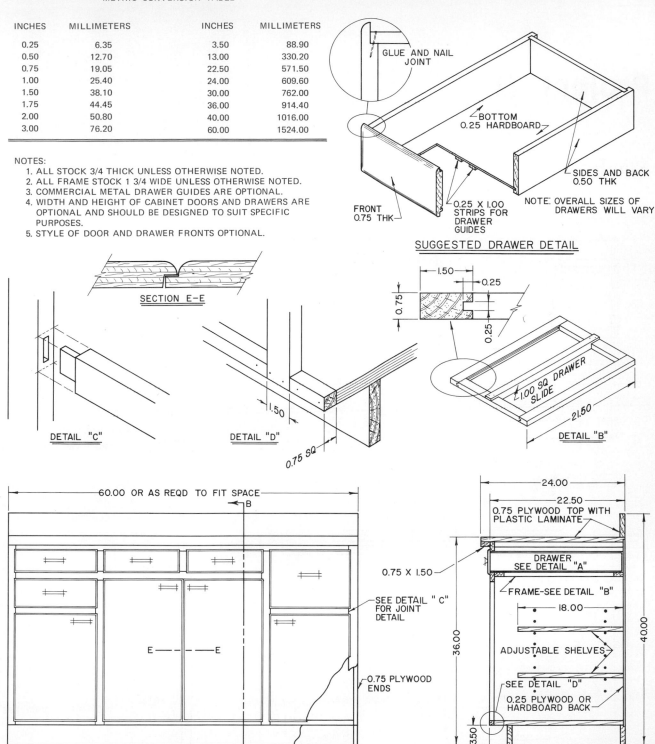

METRIC CONVERSION TABLE

INCHES	MILLIMETERS	INCHES	MILLIMETERS
0.25	6.35	3.50	88.90
0.50	12.70	13.00	330.20
0.75	19.05	22.50	571.50
1.00	25.40	24.00	609.60
1.50	38.10	30.00	762.00
1.75	44.45	36.00	914.40
2.00	50.80	40.00	1016.00
3.00	76.20	60.00	1524.00

NOTES:
1. ALL STOCK 3/4 THICK UNLESS OTHERWISE NOTED.
2. ALL FRAME STOCK 1 3/4 WIDE UNLESS OTHERWISE NOTED.
3. COMMERCIAL METAL DRAWER GUIDES ARE OPTIONAL.
4. WIDTH AND HEIGHT OF CABINET DOORS AND DRAWERS ARE OPTIONAL AND SHOULD BE DESIGNED TO SUIT SPECIFIC PURPOSES.
5. STYLE OF DOOR AND DRAWER FRONTS OPTIONAL.

GLUE AND NAIL JOINT

BOTTOM 0.25 HARDBOARD

SIDES AND BACK 0.50 THK

FRONT 0.75 THK

0.25 X 1.00 STRIPS FOR DRAWER GUIDES

NOTE: OVERALL SIZES OF DRAWERS WILL VARY

SUGGESTED DRAWER DETAIL

SECTION E-E

DETAIL "C"

DETAIL "D"

0.75 SQ

1.50

0.25

0.75

0.25

1.00 SQ DRAWER SLIDE

21.50

DETAIL "B"

60.00 OR AS REQD TO FIT SPACE

B

E — — E

SEE DETAIL " C" FOR JOINT DETAIL

0.75 PLYWOOD ENDS

B

24.00

22.50

0.75 PLYWOOD TOP WITH PLASTIC LAMINATE

0.75 X 1.50

DRAWER SEE DETAIL "A"

FRAME-SEE DETAIL "B"

18.00

ADJUSTABLE SHELVES

SEE DETAIL "D"

0.25 PLYWOOD OR HARDBOARD BACK

36.00

40.00

3.50

3.00

SECTION B-B

Project 9

Desk

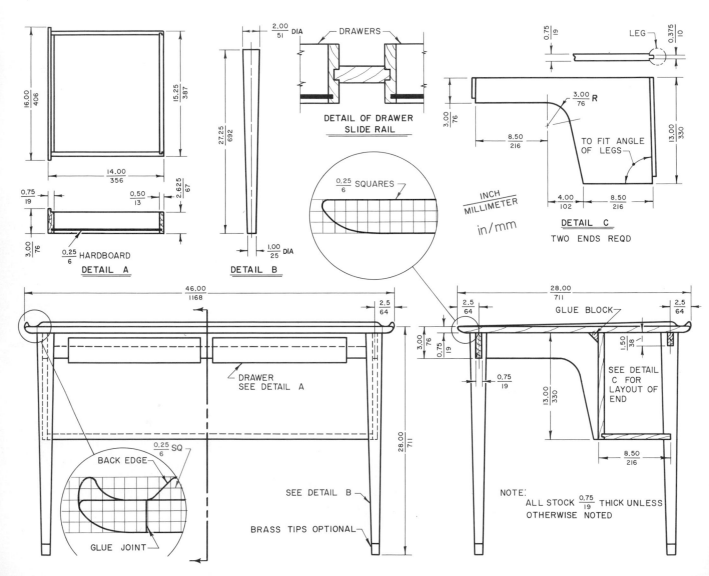

16.00 / 406

15.25 / 387

14.00 / 356

2.625 / 67

0.75 / 19

0.50 / 13

3.00 / 76

0.25 / 6 HARDBOARD

DETAIL A

2.00 / 51 DIA

27.25 / 692

1.00 / 25 DIA

DETAIL B

DRAWERS

DETAIL OF DRAWER SLIDE RAIL

0.25 / 6 SQUARES

INCH / MILLIMETER

in/mm

0.75 / 19

LEG

0.375 / 10

3.00 / 76

8.50 / 216

3.00 / 76 R

TO FIT ANGLE OF LEGS

13.00 / 330

4.00 / 102

8.50 / 216

DETAIL C

TWO ENDS REQD

46.00 / 1168

2.5 / 64

DRAWER SEE DETAIL A

0.25 / 6 SQ

BACK EDGE

GLUE JOINT

SEE DETAIL B

BRASS TIPS OPTIONAL

28.00 / 711

28.00 / 711

2.5 / 64

2.5 / 64

GLUE BLOCK

1.50 / 38

SEE DETAIL C FOR LAYOUT OF END

3.00 / 76

0.75 / 19

0.75 / 19

13.00 / 330

8.50 / 216

NOTE:
ALL STOCK 0.75 / 19 THICK UNLESS OTHERWISE NOTED

Project **10**

Desk with file drawer

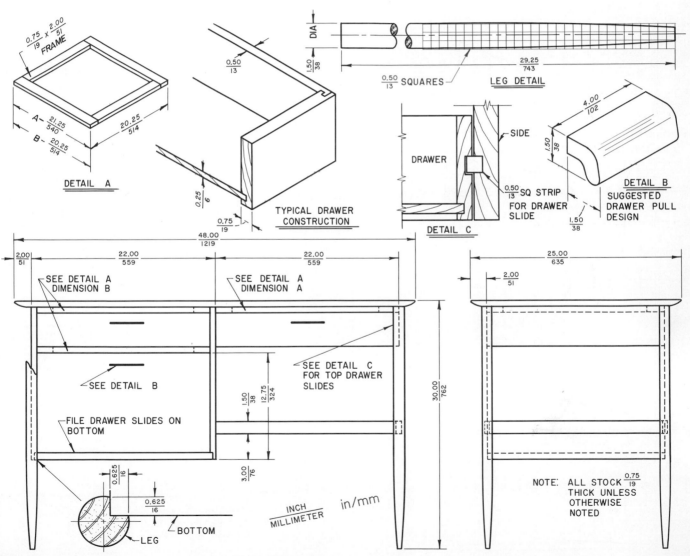

$\frac{0.75}{19} \times \frac{2.00}{51}$ FRAME

A ~ $\frac{21.25}{540}$
B ~ $\frac{20.25}{514}$
$\frac{20.25}{514}$

DETAIL A

$\frac{0.50}{13}$

$\frac{1.50}{38}$

$\frac{0.25}{6}$

$\frac{0.75}{19}$

TYPICAL DRAWER
CONSTRUCTION

DIA

$\frac{29.25}{743}$

$\frac{0.50}{13}$ SQUARES

LEG DETAIL

$\frac{0.50}{13}$

SIDE

DRAWER

$\frac{0.50}{13}$ SQ STRIP
FOR DRAWER
SLIDE

DETAIL C

$\frac{4.00}{102}$

$\frac{1.50}{38}$

$\frac{1.50}{38}$

DETAIL B
SUGGESTED
DRAWER PULL
DESIGN

$\frac{48.00}{1219}$

$\frac{2.00}{51}$

$\frac{22.00}{559}$

$\frac{22.00}{559}$

SEE DETAIL A
DIMENSION B

SEE DETAIL A
DIMENSION A

SEE DETAIL C
FOR TOP DRAWER
SLIDES

SEE DETAIL B

FILE DRAWER SLIDES ON
BOTTOM

$\frac{1.50}{38}$

$\frac{12.75}{324}$

$\frac{3.00}{76}$

$\frac{30.00}{762}$

$\frac{0.625}{16}$

$\frac{0.625}{16}$

BOTTOM

LEG

$\frac{\text{INCH}}{\text{MILLIMETER}}$ in/mm

$\frac{25.00}{635}$

$\frac{2.00}{51}$

NOTE: ALL STOCK $\frac{0.75}{19}$
THICK UNLESS
OTHERWISE
NOTED

Project 11

Tray table

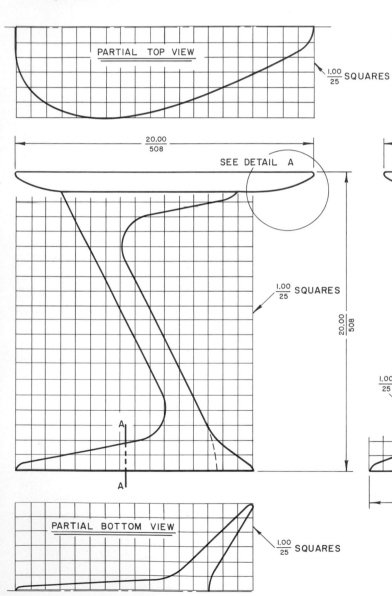

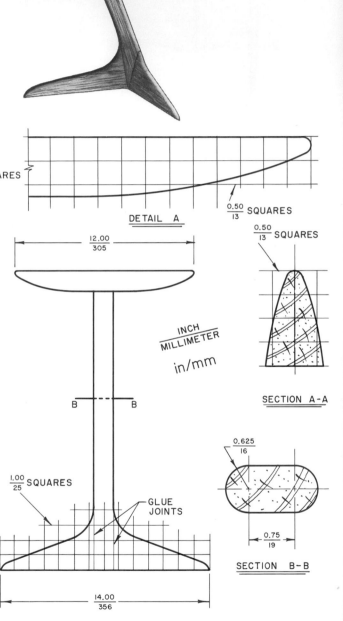

PARTIAL TOP VIEW

$\frac{1.00}{25}$ SQUARES

DETAIL A

$\frac{0.50}{13}$ SQUARES

$\frac{0.50}{13}$ SQUARES

$\frac{20.00}{508}$

SEE DETAIL A

$\frac{12.00}{305}$

$\frac{1.00}{25}$ SQUARES

$\frac{20.00}{508}$

$\frac{INCH}{MILLIMETER}$

in/mm

SECTION A-A

A

A

B   B

$\frac{0.625}{16}$

$\frac{1.00}{25}$ SQUARES

GLUE
JOINTS

$\frac{0.75}{19}$

SECTION B-B

$\frac{14.00}{356}$

PARTIAL BOTTOM VIEW

$\frac{1.00}{25}$ SQUARES

NOTE:

ALL IRREGULAR SHAPES MUST BE
HAND CARVED.

TEMPLATES SHOULD BE USED TO
ENSURE ACCURACY.

414

Project **12**

Coffee table

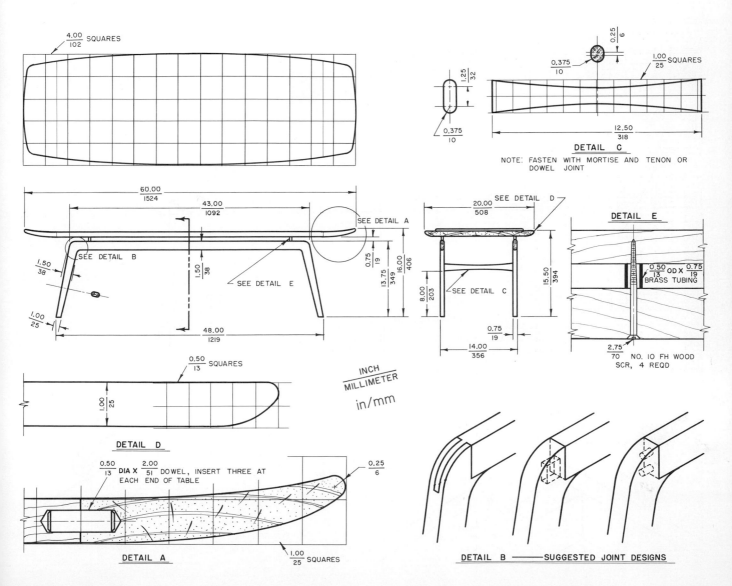

4.00/102 SQUARES

0.25/6

0.375/10

1.00/25 SQUARES

1.25/32

0.375/10

12.50/318

DETAIL C

NOTE: FASTEN WITH MORTISE AND TENON OR
DOWEL JOINT

60.00/1524

43.00/1092

SEE DETAIL A

SEE DETAIL B

1.50/38

SEE DETAIL E

0.75/19

16.00/406

13.75/349

1.50/38

1.00/25

48.00/1219

20.00/508

SEE DETAIL D

DETAIL E

8.00/203

SEE DETAIL C

15.50/394

0.50 OD X/13 0.75/19
BRASS TUBING

0.75/19

14.00/356

2.75/70 NO. 10 FH WOOD
SCR, 4 REQD

0.50/13 SQUARES

1.00/25

DETAIL D

INCH/MILLIMETER

in/mm

0.50/13 DIA X 2.00/51 DOWEL, INSERT THREE AT
EACH END OF TABLE

0.25/6

1.00/25 SQUARES

DETAIL A

DETAIL B ———— SUGGESTED JOINT DESIGNS

Project 13

Table tennis table

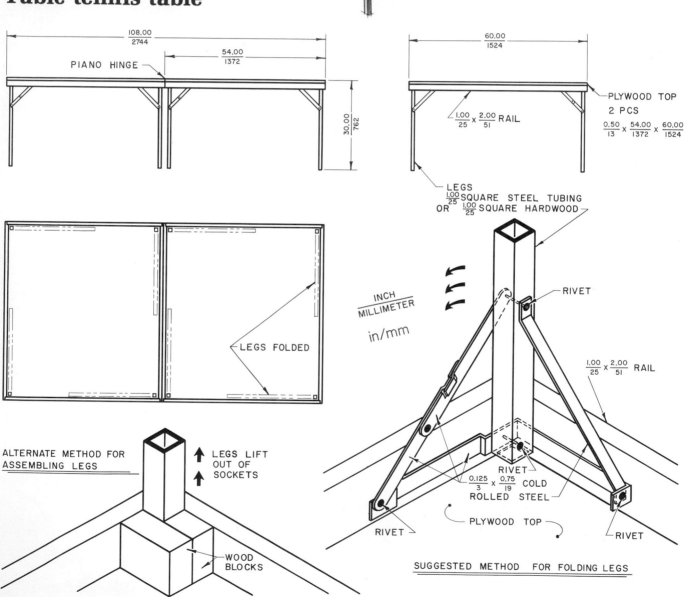

108.00 / 2744

54.00 / 1372

PIANO HINGE

30.00 / 762

60.00 / 1524

$\frac{1.00}{25} \times \frac{2.00}{51}$ RAIL

PLYWOOD TOP
2 PCS
$\frac{0.50}{13} \times \frac{54.00}{1372} \times \frac{60.00}{1524}$

LEGS
$\frac{1.00}{25}$ SQUARE STEEL TUBING
OR $\frac{1.00}{25}$ SQUARE HARDWOOD

LEGS FOLDED

INCH / MILLIMETER

in/mm

RIVET

$\frac{1.00}{25} \times \frac{2.00}{51}$ RAIL

RIVET

$\frac{0.125}{3} \times \frac{0.75}{19}$ COLD
ROLLED STEEL

PLYWOOD TOP

RIVET

RIVET

ALTERNATE METHOD FOR
ASSEMBLING LEGS

LEGS LIFT
OUT OF
SOCKETS

WOOD
BLOCKS

SUGGESTED METHOD FOR FOLDING LEGS

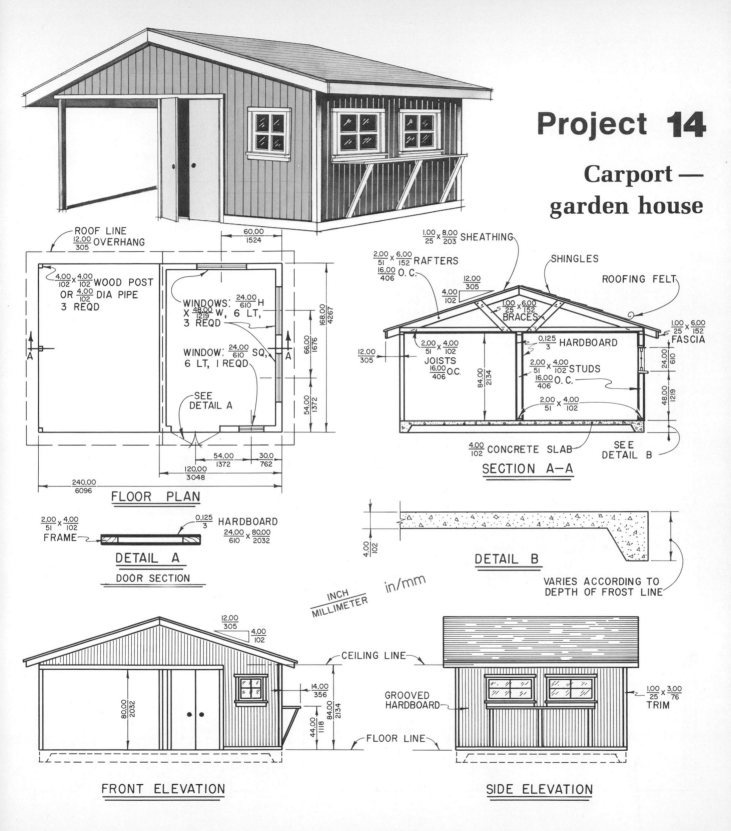

Project **14**

Carport — garden house

FLOOR PLAN

ROOF LINE $\frac{12.00}{305}$ OVERHANG

$\frac{4.00}{102}$ × $\frac{4.00}{102}$ WOOD POST OR $\frac{4.00}{102}$ DIA PIPE 3 REQD

WINDOWS: $\frac{24.00}{610}$ H X $\frac{48.00}{1219}$ W, 6 LT, 3 REQD

WINDOW: $\frac{24.00}{610}$ SQ, 6 LT, 1 REQD

SEE DETAIL A

$\frac{60.00}{1524}$

$\frac{168.00}{4267}$

$\frac{66.00}{1676}$

$\frac{54.00}{1372}$

$\frac{54.00}{1372}$ $\frac{30.0}{762}$

$\frac{120.00}{3048}$

$\frac{240.00}{6096}$

SECTION A—A

$\frac{1.00}{25}$ × $\frac{8.00}{203}$ SHEATHING

$\frac{2.00}{51}$ × $\frac{6.00}{152}$ RAFTERS $\frac{16.00}{406}$ O.C.

SHINGLES

ROOFING FELT

$\frac{12.00}{305}$

$\frac{4.00}{102}$

$\frac{1.00}{25}$ × $\frac{6.00}{152}$ BRACES

$\frac{1.00}{25}$ × $\frac{6.00}{152}$ FASCIA

$\frac{0.125}{3}$ HARDBOARD

$\frac{2.00}{51}$ × $\frac{4.00}{102}$ JOISTS $\frac{16.00}{406}$ O.C.

$\frac{2.00}{51}$ × $\frac{4.00}{102}$ STUDS $\frac{16.00}{406}$ O.C.

$\frac{84.00}{2134}$

$\frac{12.00}{305}$

$\frac{24.00}{610}$

$\frac{48.00}{1219}$

$\frac{2.00}{51}$ × $\frac{4.00}{102}$

$\frac{4.00}{102}$ CONCRETE SLAB

SEE DETAIL B

DETAIL A

DOOR SECTION

$\frac{2.00}{51}$ × $\frac{4.00}{102}$ FRAME

$\frac{0.125}{3}$ HARDBOARD $\frac{24.00}{610}$ × $\frac{80.00}{2032}$

DETAIL B

$\frac{4.00}{102}$

VARIES ACCORDING TO DEPTH OF FROST LINE

$\frac{INCH}{MILLIMETER}$ in/mm

FRONT ELEVATION

$\frac{12.00}{305}$ $\frac{4.00}{102}$

CEILING LINE

$\frac{80.00}{2032}$

$\frac{14.00}{356}$

$\frac{84.00}{2134}$

$\frac{44.00}{1118}$

FLOOR LINE

SIDE ELEVATION

GROOVED HARDBOARD

$\frac{1.00}{25}$ × $\frac{3.00}{76}$ TRIM

Project **15**

Pepper mill and saltshaker

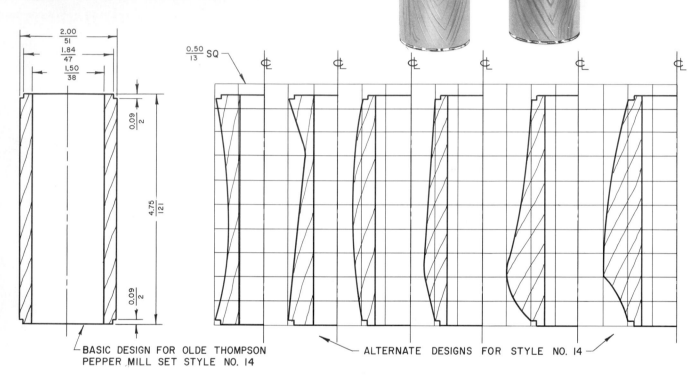

$\frac{2.00}{51}$

$\frac{1.84}{47}$

$\frac{1.50}{38}$

$\frac{0.09}{2}$

$\frac{4.75}{121}$

$\frac{0.09}{2}$

$\frac{0.50}{13}$ SQ

BASIC DESIGN FOR OLDE THOMPSON
PEPPER MILL SET STYLE NO. 14

ALTERNATE DESIGNS FOR STYLE NO. 14

$\frac{\text{INCH}}{\text{MILLIMETER}}$ in/mm

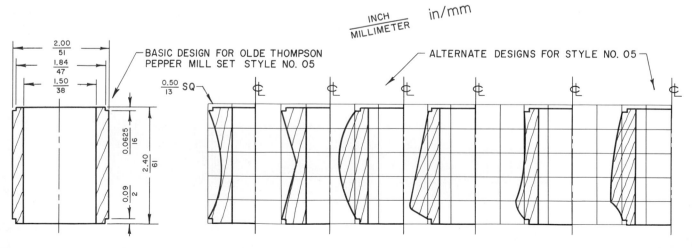

$\frac{2.00}{51}$

$\frac{1.84}{47}$

$\frac{1.50}{38}$

BASIC DESIGN FOR OLDE THOMPSON
PEPPER MILL SET STYLE NO. O5

ALTERNATE DESIGNS FOR STYLE NO. O5

$\frac{0.0625}{16}$

$\frac{2.40}{61}$

$\frac{0.09}{2}$

$\frac{0.50}{13}$ SQ

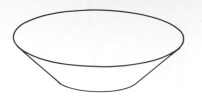

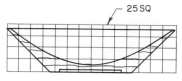

Salad bowl

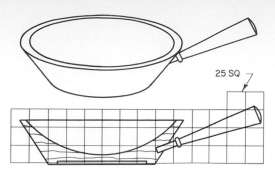

Chip server

CONVERSION	
mm	In.
25	1.00
114	4.50
152	6.00
165	6.50
203	8.00

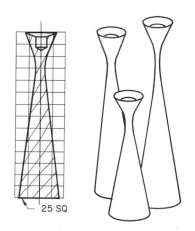

Candlesticks

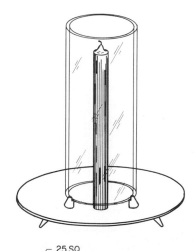

Hurricane lamp

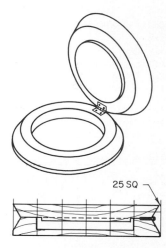

Hamburger press

Bongo drums

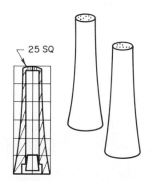

Salt and pepper shakers

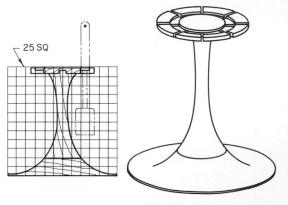

Kitchen utensil caddy

project suggestions
Planters
and containers

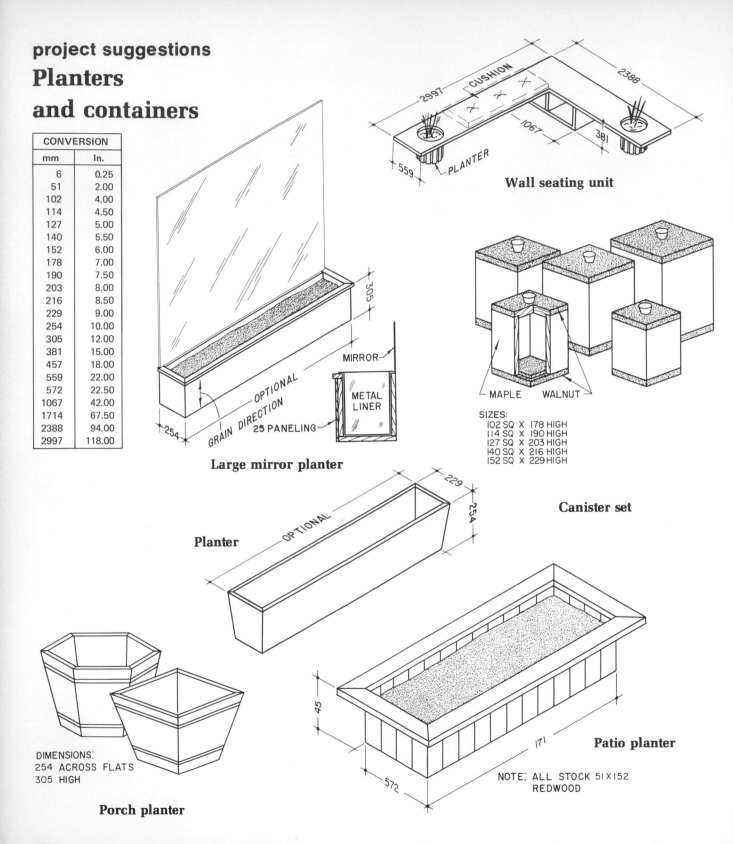

CONVERSION	
mm	In.
6	0.25
51	2.00
102	4.00
114	4.50
127	5.00
140	5.50
152	6.00
178	7.00
190	7.50
203	8.00
216	8.50
229	9.00
254	10.00
305	12.00
381	15.00
457	18.00
559	22.00
572	22.50
1067	42.00
1714	67.50
2388	94.00
2997	118.00

Wall seating unit

CUSHION
PLANTER
2997   2388
1067   381
559

MIRROR
305
254
OPTIONAL
GRAIN DIRECTION
25 PANELING
METAL
LINER

Large mirror planter

MAPLE   WALNUT

SIZES:
102 SQ X 178 HIGH
114 SQ X 190 HIGH
127 SQ X 203 HIGH
140 SQ X 216 HIGH
152 SQ X 229 HIGH

Canister set

OPTIONAL
229
254

Planter

45
171
572
NOTE: ALL STOCK 51×152
REDWOOD

Patio planter

DIMENSIONS:
254 ACROSS FLATS
305 HIGH

Porch planter

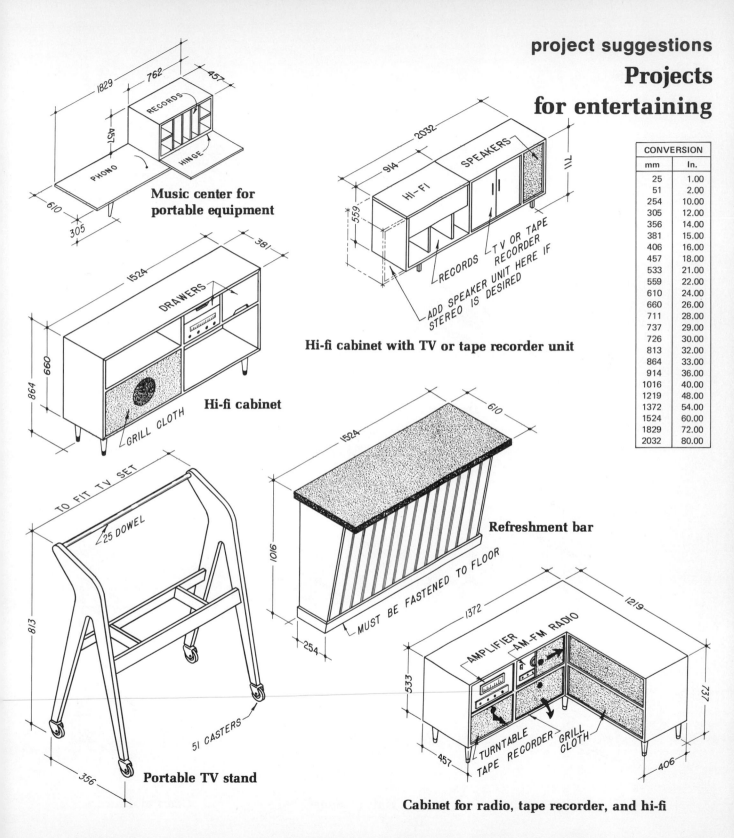

Projects for entertaining

Music center for portable equipment

1829 · 762 · 457 · 457 · 610 · 305

RECORDS · PHONO · HINGE

Hi-fi cabinet with TV or tape recorder unit

2032 · 914 · 711 · 559 · SPEAKERS · HI-FI · RECORDS · TV OR TAPE RECORDER · ADD SPEAKER UNIT HERE IF STEREO IS DESIRED

CONVERSION	
mm	In.
25	1.00
51	2.00
254	10.00
305	12.00
356	14.00
381	15.00
406	16.00
457	18.00
533	21.00
559	22.00
610	24.00
660	26.00
711	28.00
737	29.00
726	30.00
813	32.00
864	33.00
914	36.00
1016	40.00
1219	48.00
1372	54.00
1524	60.00
1829	72.00
2032	80.00

Hi-fi cabinet

381 · 1524 · 660 · 864 · DRAWERS · GRILL CLOTH

Refreshment bar

1524 · 610 · 1016 · 254 · MUST BE FASTENED TO FLOOR

Portable TV stand

TO FIT TV SET · 25 DOWEL · 813 · 51 CASTERS · 356

Cabinet for radio, tape recorder, and hi-fi

1372 · 1219 · 533 · 737 · 457 · 406 · AMPLIFIER · AM-FM RADIO · TURNTABLE · TAPE RECORDER · GRILL CLOTH

project suggestions
Cabinets
and chests

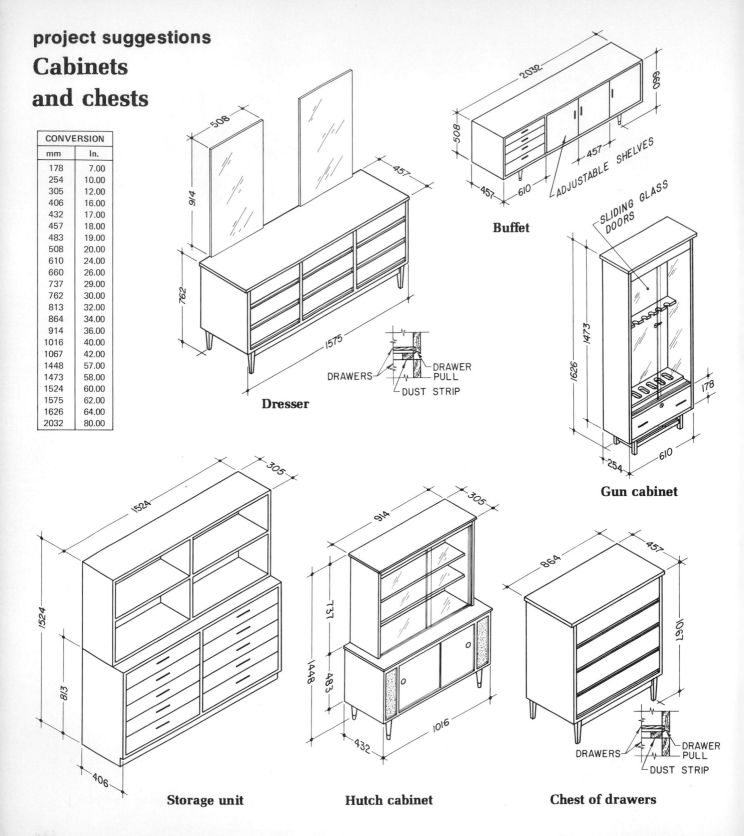

CONVERSION	
mm	In.
178	7.00
254	10.00
305	12.00
406	16.00
432	17.00
457	18.00
483	19.00
508	20.00
610	24.00
660	26.00
737	29.00
762	30.00
813	32.00
864	34.00
914	36.00
1016	40.00
1067	42.00
1448	57.00
1473	58.00
1524	60.00
1575	62.00
1626	64.00
2032	80.00

Buffet

ADJUSTABLE SHELVES

DRAWERS
DRAWER PULL
DUST STRIP

Dresser

SLIDING GLASS DOORS

Gun cabinet

Storage unit

Hutch cabinet

DRAWERS
DRAWER PULL
DUST STRIP

Chest of drawers

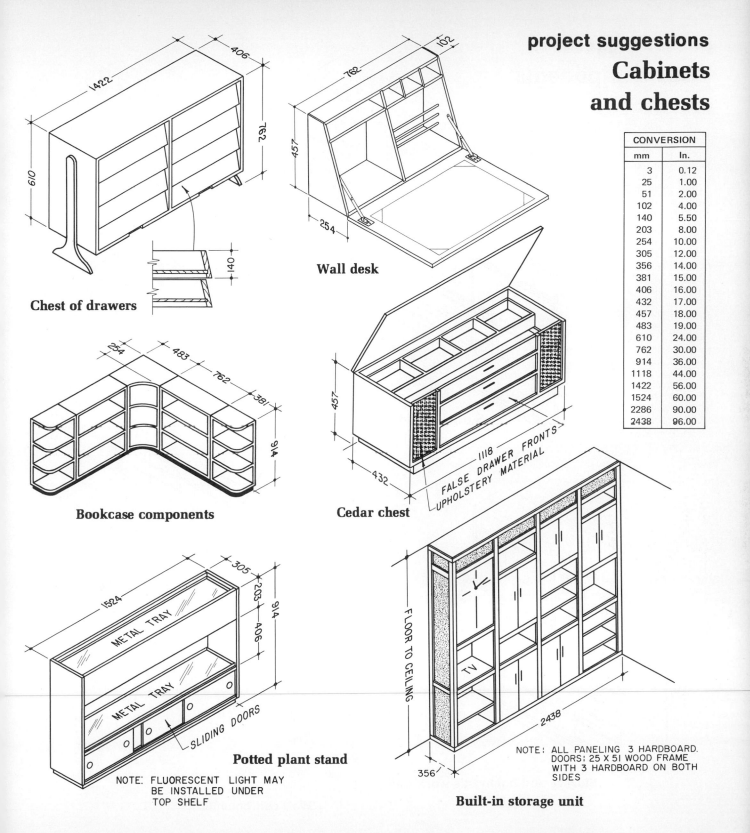

Chest of drawers

Wall desk

Bookcase components

Cedar chest

FALSE DRAWER FRONTS
UPHOLSTERY MATERIAL

Potted plant stand

METAL TRAY

METAL TRAY

SLIDING DOORS

NOTE: FLUORESCENT LIGHT MAY BE INSTALLED UNDER TOP SHELF

Built-in storage unit

FLOOR TO CEILING

TV

NOTE: ALL PANELING 3 HARDBOARD. DOORS: 25 X 51 WOOD FRAME WITH 3 HARDBOARD ON BOTH SIDES

CONVERSION	
mm	In.
3	0.12
25	1.00
51	2.00
102	4.00
140	5.50
203	8.00
254	10.00
305	12.00
356	14.00
381	15.00
406	16.00
432	17.00
457	18.00
483	19.00
610	24.00
762	30.00
914	36.00
1118	44.00
1422	56.00
1524	60.00
2286	90.00
2438	96.00

423

project suggestions
Wall components

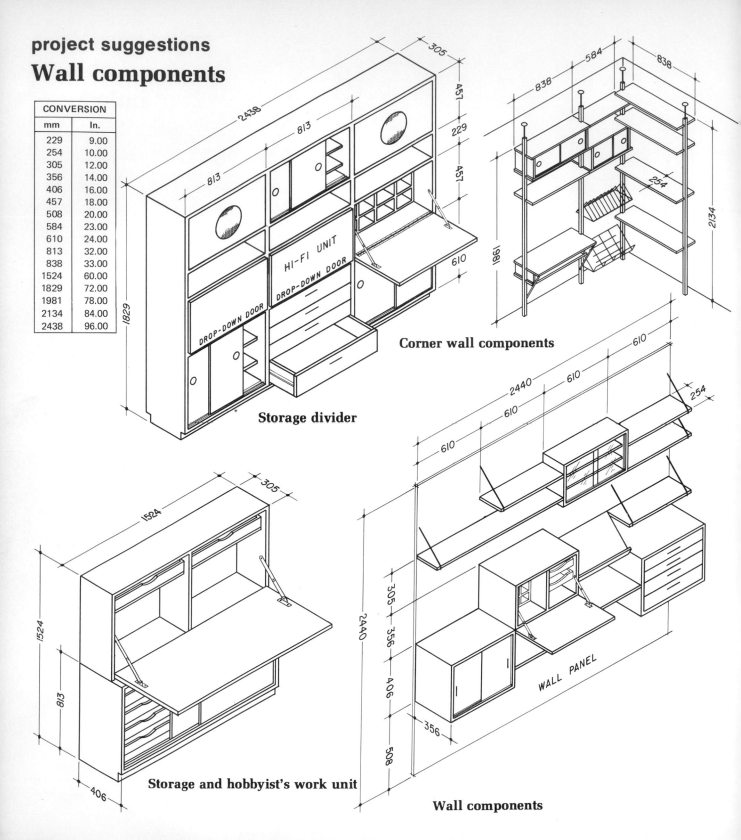

CONVERSION	
mm	In.
229	9.00
254	10.00
305	12.00
356	14.00
406	16.00
457	18.00
508	20.00
584	23.00
610	24.00
813	32.00
838	33.00
1524	60.00
1829	72.00
1981	78.00
2134	84.00
2438	96.00

HI-FI UNIT

DROP-DOWN DOOR

DROP-DOWN DOOR

Storage divider

Corner wall components

Storage and hobbyist's work unit

WALL PANEL

Wall components

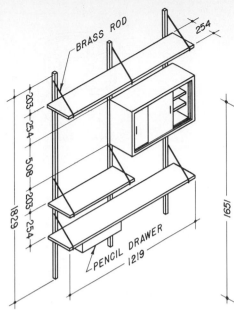

Bookshelf and storage divider

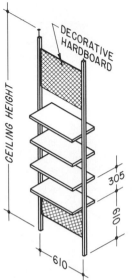

Bookshelf room divider

Shelf divider

CONVERSION	
mm	In.
76	3.00
152	6.00
203	8.00
229	9.00
254	10.00
305	12.00
356	14.00
406	16.00
457	18.00
508	20.00
610	24.00
762	30.00
813	32.00
1067	42.00
1219	48.00
1524	60.00
1651	65.00
1829	72.00

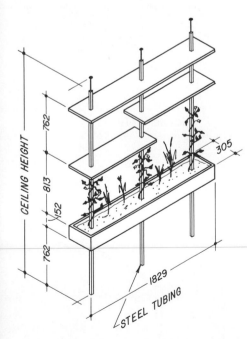

Entrance planter-divider

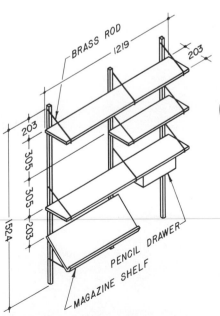

Bookshelf-magazine rack divider

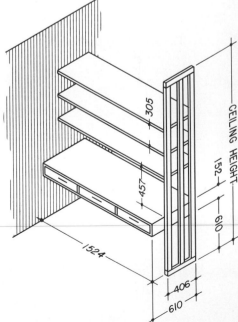

Desk divider

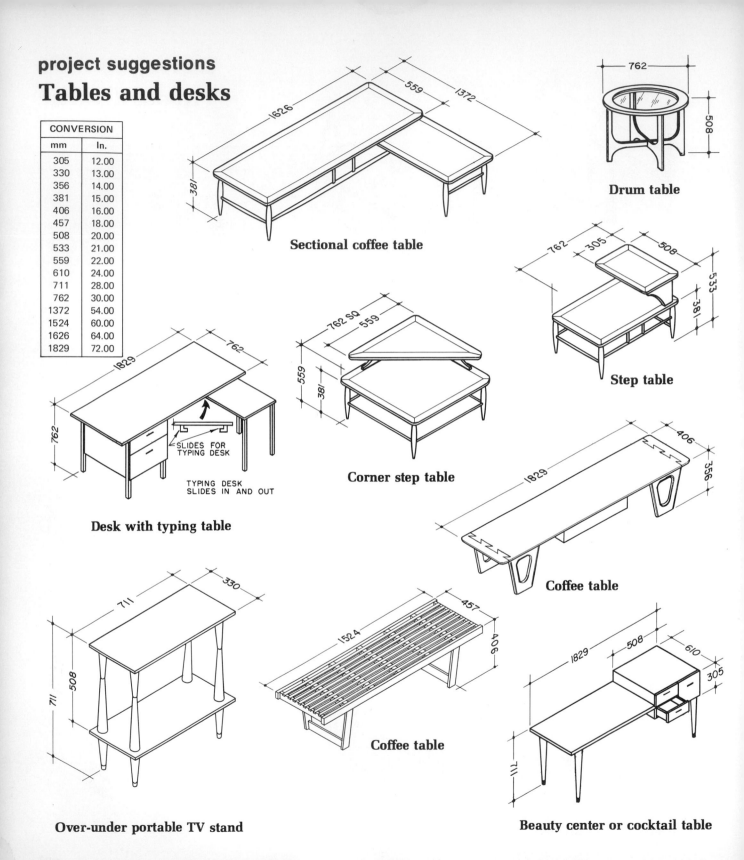

project suggestions
Tables and desks

CONVERSION	
mm	In.
305	12.00
330	13.00
356	14.00
381	15.00
406	16.00
457	18.00
508	20.00
533	21.00
559	22.00
610	24.00
711	28.00
762	30.00
1372	54.00
1524	60.00
1626	64.00
1829	72.00

Sectional coffee table

Drum table

Step table

Desk with typing table

SLIDES FOR TYPING DESK

TYPING DESK SLIDES IN AND OUT

Corner step table

762 SQ

Coffee table

Coffee table

Over-under portable TV stand

Beauty center or cocktail table

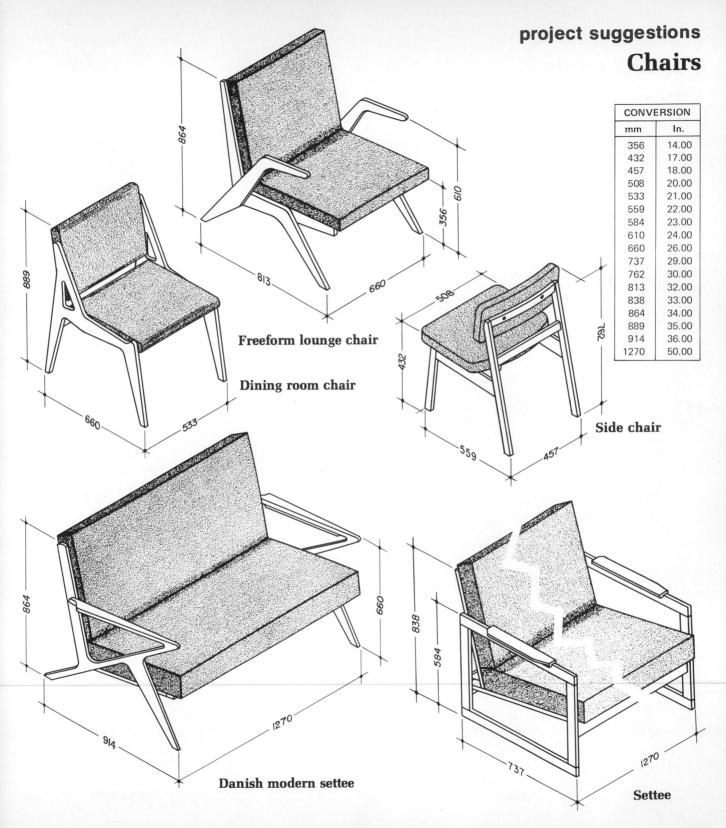

CONVERSION	
mm	In.
356	14.00
432	17.00
457	18.00
508	20.00
533	21.00
559	22.00
584	23.00
610	24.00
660	26.00
737	29.00
762	30.00
813	32.00
838	33.00
864	34.00
889	35.00
914	36.00
1270	50.00

Freeform lounge chair

Dining room chair

Side chair

Danish modern settee

Settee

427

project suggestions
Furniture for outdoor living

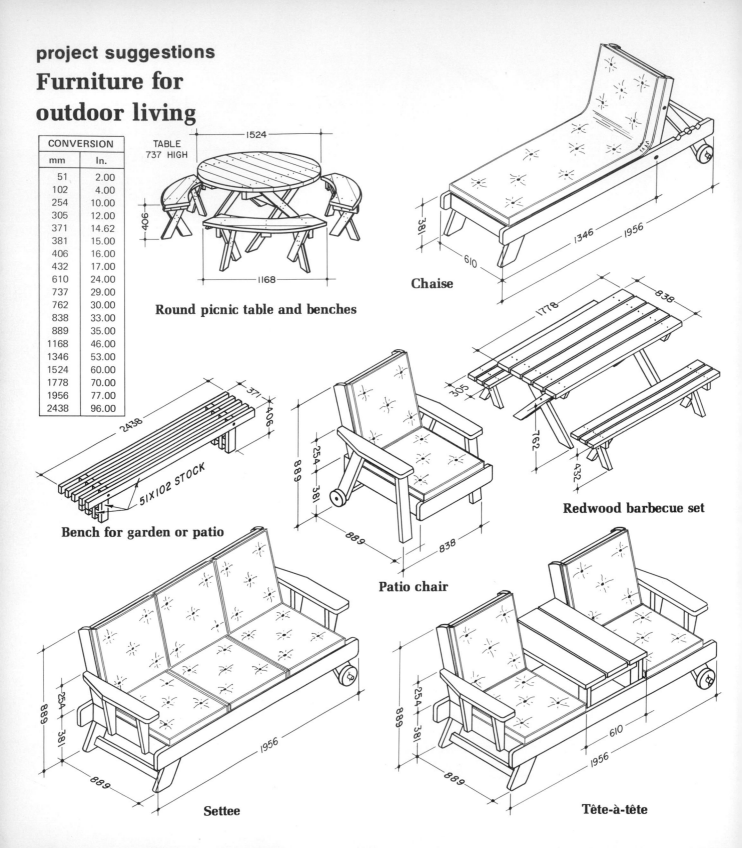

CONVERSION	
mm	In.
51	2.00
102	4.00
254	10.00
305	12.00
371	14.62
381	15.00
406	16.00
432	17.00
610	24.00
737	29.00
762	30.00
838	33.00
889	35.00
1168	46.00
1346	53.00
1524	60.00
1778	70.00
1956	77.00
2438	96.00

TABLE 737 HIGH

Round picnic table and benches

Chaise

Bench for garden or patio

51X102 STOCK

Redwood barbecue set

Patio chair

Settee

Tête-à-tête

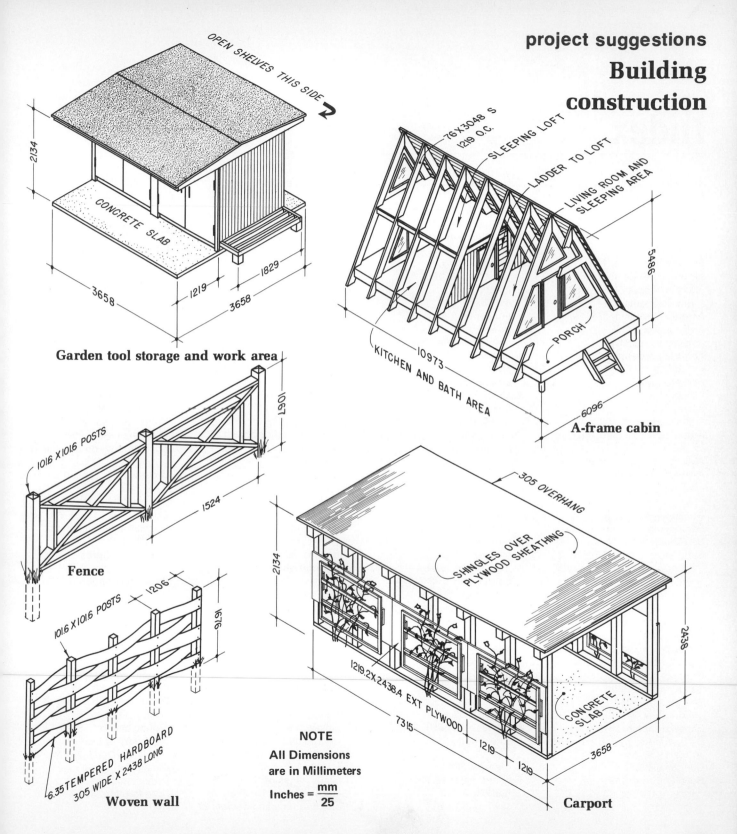

2134

OPEN SHELVES THIS SIDE

CONCRETE SLAB

3658

1219

1829

3658

Garden tool storage and work area

76 X 3048 S 1219 O.C.

SLEEPING LOFT

LADDER TO LOFT

LIVING ROOM AND SLEEPING AREA

5486

KITCHEN AND BATH AREA

10973

PORCH

6096

A-frame cabin

1067

1016 X 1016 POSTS

1524

Fence

1016 X 1016 POSTS

1206

1676

6.35 TEMPERED HARDBOARD 305 WIDE X 2438 LONG

Woven wall

305 OVERHANG

SHINGLES OVER PLYWOOD SHEATHING

2134

1219.2 X 2438.4 EXT PLYWOOD

7315

1219

1219

CONCRETE SLAB

2438

3658

NOTE
All Dimensions are in Millimeters

Inches = $\dfrac{mm}{25}$

Carport

Index

430